Engaging All
by CREATING HIGH SCHOOL LEARNING COMMUNITIES

Engaging All
by CREATING HIGH SCHOOL LEARNING COMMUNITIES

JEANNE GIBBS and **TERI USHIJIMA**, ED.D.

With a special chapter on Resiliency by Bonnie Benard

In collaboration with
Teachers and Administrators Extraordinaire

CENTER SOURCE
SYSTEMS

WINDSOR, CALIFORNIA

Published in the United States of America by
CenterSource Systems, LLC
7975 Cameron Drive, #500
Windsor, California 95492

Library of Congress Cataloging-in-Publication Data
Gibbs, Jeanne
  Engaging all by creating high school learning communities / by Jeanne Gibbs and
Teri Ushijima.—1st ed.
      p. cm.
   ISBN 978-0-932762-60-3 (pbk.)
  1. High school teaching—United States. 2. School improvement programs—United States.
3. Group work in education—United States. I. Ushijima, Teri II. Title.

   LB1737.U6G53 2008
   373.1102—dc22

                                                                    2008017795

Book Design: Lynn Bell, Monroe Street Studios, Santa Rosa, California
Illustrations: Pat Ronzone, Sausalito, California
Printing: Creel Printing, LLC, Las Vegas, Nevada

PRINTED IN THE UNITED STATES OF AMERICA
     10   9   8   7   6   5   4   3   2   1

Contents

Jessica: Yes, I've been getting straight "A's" so far. I get new ideas easily and like to read. I figure you just have to figure out what the teacher wants, do it and turn in work on time. My mom goes to work very early, so before school and at lunch time I usually spend time studying or reading in the library. I'm kind of quiet. I had a friend here last year but she moved. My mom says I should get into some after school activities, but I'd rather go home. What do I want to do when I grow up? I don't know. Go to college, I guess. Sometimes I think I'd like to create films and stories that display my ideals and ideas, the world as it is, and the world as it could be.

Kyle: Yeah, this school's OK I've been in a lot of schools because my dad's in the army and we've moved a lot. I'm trying out here for the school football team so I'm not cutting school anymore. Can't miss a practice. School work? That's what I don't like. Teachers talking at us all day. Back in a middle school one teacher used to have us in teams to do stuff together instead of alone. That was better. I like to be with a lot of people.

What do I want to be when I grow up? In my future I can see many things. Some of those are a family, with kids who can think for themselves—but sure not always win the arguments with me! Maybe I should be a lawyer! But it might be too hard.

* Source of the student statements: interviews, focus groups and written material contributed by high school students, teachers and youth program personnel.

Mike: Mostly I like to hang out at the Oaktree District Park with friends—yeah, we're always the last to leave after nine pm. My dad and I live in the housing complex. He's a taxi driver. School? Hate it. I only passed half the classes last year and had to repeat one course. The teacher said it was my poor attendance and I didn't do assignments. The real reason I didn't like that class was because the teacher always picked on me. So far this year my attendance is pretty good.

College? I don't think so. I hope for a career in which I can have fun and still do something that will provide what I need. I want to be able to live humbly but to still have extravagances— if that would ever work. Mostly, I hope to keep trying to make sense of the world. And somehow make a difference in it!

Angel: I'm new here so I don't know much about this school. My parents sent me to live here this year with my grandmother. They didn't like the friends I was hanging out with in our town. My mom said a teacher wrote that I social-ize with others in the classroom too much. And that it's not OK to take out my compact once or twice during the period to check my make-up when she's giv-ing a class lecture. Yikes! She was always giving a lecture!

What do I want to do when I'm an adult? I don't know. I guess people will judge me by my family background and education, and that's OK But there is more than just all that. I believe a person can shape her own personality and rise above her past and become the person that she, only she, wants to become.

Jeremy: I've always been in special classes because I'm just different. I don't hear well in one ear so always get to sit up front. Once I noticed a report my father had that said I have "ADD", and need extra time on assignments and tests. I have some cool friends. We like to dress in black. People notice us then.

What do I want to do in life? Oh, I already know. I want to paint the sides of buildings with scenes of peo-ple laughing, dancing and working together... the way life ought to be. I have lots of drawings at home. I'm not sure why we don't get to do art anymore at school. That's what I do instead of taking notes in classes.

The Time Is Now . . . Listen to the Voices

Listen…can you hear the sound
Of hearts beating all the world around
Down in the valley, out on the plain
Everywhere around the world
a heartbeat sounds the same
Black or white, red or tan,
It's the heartbeat of the family of man.[1]

It's the quickening heartbeat of millions of high school students each time one thinks about moving out as a young adult into today's 21st century *rapid change world*. Black or white, red or tan, youthful hearts beat more quickly whenever hopes, uneasiness or questions come to mind. "What will I be doing? Can I get a job? Will I be able to go college? Am I ready?" Years of schooling, supposedly, have prepared them well for the future. That has been the promise. Families, teachers, communities, business leaders, legislators and politicians have affirmed that. Yet, now in the midst of the mandate for high stakes testing, millions of students in the United States and in some other countries are hearing that their schools are considered inadequate—and that they are not prepared as well as promised. Somehow the promise has not been kept.

The phrase "All children can learn" has been reassuring. Yet it rings hollow whenever the disheartened reply, "If all can learn, why aren't they?" Unfortunately, the challenge to prepare today's students for a global technological information era, beyond anything even imagined before, largely has become a narrowed-down focus on mathematics, science and literacy. Teachers are directed to do *more of the same only harder*. The wholeness of children in their full humanity as social, emotional, physical, and spiritual beings is being dismissed as irrelevant to their intellectual learning and achievement.

If we could look at a report card giving information on the results of present day "schooling" in the United States it would tell us that:

▶ ⅔ of 14 million adolescents who enter ninth grade graduate with regular diplomas four years later[2]

▶ ⅓ of the 14 million drop out before graduation—and half of are Afro-American, Latino or Native American[3]

▶ 40% of high school graduates are considered inadequately prepared to enter college or qualify for an entry level job[4]

- 45% of students entering universities need to take proficiency courses in language and math[5]

- 64 million working adults between the ages of 18–64, essentially more than 90% of the nation's workforce, are in need of improved language skills, a high school diploma, or enhanced basic skills that will allow them to meet the demands of the modern workplace[6]

- Business organizations in the United States are spending inestimable millions every year to improve young employees' skills in math and writing.[7]

Tom Vander Ark, director of the Melinda and Bill Gates Foundation, refers to the drop out rate as a "civic, social and economic disaster."[8] The dropout epidemic and fragmented quality of education for adolescents entering society effects every community and the nation.

It becomes evident that doing more of the same only harder cannot improve the nation's report card. The traditional 19th century factory model of "doing school" is an *anachronism* in our 21st century world more than a millennium later. It is the major reason that school reforms failed throughout the 1990's. The industrial era factory model no longer fits. It does not reach or connect to the active ways in which youth today learn. The generation has been growing up in a rapid change technological culture of television, computers, I-Pods, electronic games and cellular phones—all of which have conditioned them to learn through *imagery, constructive thinking, meaningful experience and active involvement.* The passive direct instruction, question-response, individual desk work model may have served their parents and grandparents well, but it does not engage adolescents who now perceive and assimilate knowledge in very different ways. One size no longer fits all! The fine report, *Breaking Ranks II,* published by the National Association Secondary School Principals in partnership with the Carnegie Council on Adolescent Development echoes our concern that . . .

> *Many teenagers are disengaged from the hard intellectual work expected by their schools and the larger community, and are unprepared for the harsh world beyond those schools.....Schools good enough for yesterday will not serve as good enough for tomorrow—in every community, rich and poor across the country.*[10]

The same alarm has been sounding for more than two decades, and a myriad of high school reform initiatives have been undertaken. Largely, many schools engaged "outside"

The American high school is obsolete.[9]
—LEON BOTSTEIN
PRESIDENT OF BARD UNIVERSITY

agencies or consultants to work with "inside" planners to make voluminous strategic plans to redefine standards, tests, curriculum, computer programs, facility improvement, personnel positions, budgets and schedules. A prominent national consultant shares: "All of this was then transferred into fat, published documents, replete with columns and boxes for each category."[11] As comprehensive as the plans may have been, they were difficult to implement and monitor. Instructional quality and levels of achievement were typically unaffected by any of the processes.

Something very important has been missing . . .
The majority of planning groups overlooked listening to the voices of students—
their most important customers.

Denise Clark Pope, researcher and author of the fascinating book *Doing School, How We Are Creating a Generation of Stressed Out, Materialistic and Miseducated Students,* tells educators: "Listen to the students and you will hear a different side of their success." Success for many is in figuring out ways just to "do school." One boy tells Pope, "Everybody does the minimum required to get by and everybody focuses on grades instead of learning the material." A girl says, "If you learn how to manipulate the system, then you learn how to survive in high school without going nuts." Another at the end of a long school day sighs, "If only things could be different here."[12]

Respected scholar Michael Fullan poses the significant question: *"What would happen if we treated the student as someone whose opinion mattered in the introduction and implementation of reform in schools?"[13]*

Our disregard of the voices and perspectives of students not only discounts their experience of school but also overlooks the social emotional quest in which all are trying to find themselves in the most formative stage of their lives. Whether we or they realize it or not, all are striving to achieve:

- ▶ Autonomy and independence
- ▶ Social competency
- ▶ A sense of purpose and positive expectations for the future
- ▶ A capacity to problem-solve on their own.

As teachers, parents, school leaders and policy makers we try to control the restless behaviors rather than find ways to support positive development of them. The competencies are essential to living successfully in the adult world. Nor do we understand how to *engage all*—so that they succeed academically, socially and emotionally. Lack of adult awareness drifts into oblivion in the urgency to produce the next "comprehensive school reform plan" intended to transform the high school system.

What would happen if we treated the student as someone whose opinion mattered in the introduction and implementation of reform in schools?

—MICHAEL FULLAN

Something else also has been missing. High school reforms in the1990s failed because they left the *overall nature of teaching and learning unchanged.*[14] Years of research on cognitive learning and environmental factors that affect the whole development of adolescents and their ways of learning largely have been ignored. Consequently, high quality professional development for the teaching staffs within local schools has been dismissed as a non-essential expenditure. "All teachers learned how to teach when they went to college—whenever that was!" So... millions of teachers are limited to doing more of the same 19th century teacher-lecture direct instruction that minimizes their ability to reach, motivate and accelerate learning for 21st century high school youth.

Peter Senge, researcher and author of the fine book, *Schools That Learn*, states:

> *There is an emerging consensus across the nation that high quality professional development is essential to successful education reform. Professional development is the bridge between where educators are now and where they will need to be to meet the new challenges of guiding students in achieving higher standards of learning.*[15]

The very title of the groundbreaking National Association Secondary School Principals (NASSP) report *Breaking Ranks* is clear. Breaking away from the 19th century factory high school model depends on courageous informed leaders gaining knowledge on *why* change is critical, *what* changes are needed and *how* the high school learning community can collaborate to bring about change.

What to do and *how* to do it no longer is a mystery. The place to begin is to look at the evidence that the *most promising strategy* for sustained, substantive school improvement is building the capacity of school personnel, *"the insiders"* to function as a *professional learning community.*[17] The path to student success and achievement for all levels of learners is through collegial learning teams in which teachers collaboratively learn research-based principles and practices, where they tailor curricula to ways in which students of today's world best can learn, where they support each other in implementation, and where they reflect together continuously on their own enhanced learning—as well as that of their students.

Teacher school-based learning communities achieve:

- ▶ higher-quality solutions to instructional problems
- ▶ increased confidence and collegiality among faculty
- ▶ increased ability to support one another's strengths and to accommodate weaknesses
- ▶ more systematic assistance to beginning teachers, and the ability to examine an expanded pool of ideas, research on learning, constructive pedagogy and materials.

> Only the organizations that have a passion for learning will have an enduring influence.[16]
> —STEPHEN COVEY

In combination these elements cannot help but produce "remarkable gains in achievement."[18]

No matter the size of the high school, collaborative teams of knowledgeable teachers— "the insiders" are the ones who try to listen daily to the voices of adolescent learners, who are aware of moment-to-moment interactions, frustrations, hopes and levels of students' learning. They and knowledgeable school leaders are the experts who best can transform their own high schools into *authentic learning communities* that ready today's youth for this 21st century Era of Learning.

We want you as a reader to know that you will not find a nuts-and-bolts plan for the overall reform of a high school, nor a step-by-step packaged program to replicate, nor prescribed curriculum to teach. You will discover a *research-based developmental process* that is student-centered, that creates a caring learning culture, that structures productive learning communities, and that provides sound principles and practices to accelerate learning and development for students within your high school.

Roland S. Barth, renowned educator and author of the fine books, *Improving Schools from Within* and *Learning By Heart,* states from his own wealth of experience and heart...

"I believe that schools are lighthouses. I believe that every school harbors within its walls the capacity for grown-ups and students to become inventers and reformers, to engage in authentic change...The school that becomes a self-renewing enterprise will— shape its own future."[19]

The time is now.

Listen to the Voices

1 Listen to the Voices

IN THIS CHAPTER YOU WILL

▶ Learn what many of today's youth are thinking, feeling and saying about high school

▶ Realize that the perspectives, experiences and developmental needs of high school learners must be the focus of high school reform

▶ Recognize the first step towards improving the high school system

When one has no stake in the way things are, when one's needs or opinions are provided no forum, when one sees oneself as the object of unilateral actions, it takes no particular wisdom to suggest one would rather be elsewhere.[3]
—SEYMOUR SARASON

It seems ironic that we require young people to attend high school, and yet we know relatively little about what they think of the place.[1]
—DENISE CLARK POPE

Do you know of any multi-billion dollar successful business that is capable of serving millions of customers well without being certain of the diversity of their needs, preferences and what they think about the service being provided? Of course not! Such disregard would result in a loss of customers and certain failure of the business. Yet this practice is largely what has been affecting the lives of millions of high school adolescents in the Unites States and untold numbers in other countries despite the cry to reform the high school system.

A search of the literature since the mid-1980s confirms that hardly any research has been done that places the student's experience at the center of attention. The focus is on defining rigorous curriculum, higher standards and tests to measure student achievement. Yet we do not know their interests or known or unknown anxieties. Nor do we know how the school as a system is shaping their attitudes, behavior and hopes for the future. Rarely is the perspective of the student himself explored or valued. It is little wonder that drop-out rates, school failures and youth problems have continued to escalate. The comprehensive document, *Breaking Ranks II*, recently published by the National Association of Secondary School Principals, deplores the failure:

> *More than thirteen million students currently in high school rely on principals and teachers to help them fulfill their dreams, to reach heights never before imagined and to embrace a lifelong love of learning. Failure in these, the most important of life's course, is not acceptable.[2]*

For years the indicators of school failure have largely been regarded and treated as dysfunctional individual problems with little consideration of the disconnect between the needs and ways of learning of 21st century youth and the "one-size-fits-all" factory model. High school teachers may have 150 or more students in and out of their classrooms every crowded day, and to their credit many say that somehow they do try to listen and do know a few. Yet the stream of students moving through crowded halls and 50 minute classroom periods packed with unrelated subjects sustain anonymity and give little or no time to talk to teachers. Too many young people are carrying loneliness, fears of failure, self-doubts, numbing boredom and anxiety about the future in their emotional backpacks. There are those who remain silent—and those who act out or drop out.

Concerned educator Larry Cuban writes:

"Many academically successful students describe high school as a boot camp for college, filled with anxiety, physical exhaustion, cheating and a disregard for learning. They have mastered the game of doing school and pay a steep price for their success. Reformers dead set on making all students academically successful need to hear these student voices."[4]

The good news is that now the public has become aware, and is alarmed. Now additional funding is happening. Now business corporations, foundations, state legislatures, universities, politicians, publishers and consultants are advocating specific organizational changes, strategic planning formats, curricula and high stakes tests. Yet all is with little regard to the critical developmental needs, ways of learning and perspectives of today's high school students. Catherine Pinot, deputy director of urban high school initiatives at the Carnegie Corporation concurs that...

"If we're trying to transform high schools, what better thing to do than to talk to young people? The hard work is to get adults to open up and value the expertise of young people. In the past, we haven't listened to them. We are not going to succeed if we continue to use the old paradigm of adults creating reform efforts for young people."[5]

The voices of students need to be heard at several levels:

▶ First, what are their learning needs, hopes and goals?

▶ Second, what seems to defeat or support learning for them in their school?

▶ Third, what thoughts and suggestions do they have on how to improve the high school?

Turn back now to the five high school students, Jessica, Kyle, Mike, Angel and Jeremy whom you met in the first pages of this book. Listen to them again. This time try to hear what they are saying in response to each of the three questions above.

Throughout the pages of this book we'll be inviting the five students to come back and forth to continue calling our attention to what is happening for them in our (virtual) personalized, active learning and caring high school. Hopefully, you will be able to connect their needs, perceptions and qualities to youth that you know.

Don't just look at students for answers, but look at who we are—who we like, what's hard for us, what's easy for us. If you pay attention, you can see it.[6]

Given that essentially there is no body of research that places the student experience at the center of high school reform, conducting or having students conduct focus groups or action research in your own school is a significant step in the right direction.[7]

A SUMMATION OF WHAT MANY ARE SAYING

Twenty years ago a concerned researcher stated his viewpoint that, "The absence of student experience from educational discourse seems to be a consequence of a systematic silencing of the student voice."[8] Perhaps, this has been true for a long time, but hopefully not any more.

Participants at a Harvard Graduate School conference in 2002 listened to 100 10th graders, present their findings after they had conducted a survey within 10 Boston public schools,. Four requests topped the list. Students wanted:

▶ "active intellectual learning engagement"

▶ personal contact with teachers and administrators

▶ teachers who have high expectations of everyone and challenge them to "understand ideas"

▶ and teachers who focus on important and "substantive issues" rather than simply on low-level information.[9]

Another unusual survey, which was designed and administered by high school students to 6,500 of their peers in five large cities, found that:[10]

▶ 90% of urban high school students said they really wanted to learn but don't believe that adults in their schools are interested in what they have to say.

▶ More than a quarter said there was not one adult in their school they could talk to if they had a problem.

▶ Two-thirds or more said their teachers rarely or never talked one-on-one with them about their schoolwork or other things that matter to them.

▶ 18 percent were thinking about dropping out. Of that number

• 82% said school was boring

• 58% said they did not get along with one or more teachers

• 36% said other students were bullying or harassing them

▶ 87% said that more real-world learning would help them.[11]

It is wonderful to hear how morale soared in the schools where students conducted surveys. One 17 year old said. "Students are more passionate. It made students feel more motivated to realize somebody actually cares for our opinions."

Underlying the voices are messages of high school students who are longing for belonging, social relationships, closer communication with teachers, safe and caring school environments, meaningful curriculum, active real-world learning, team learning, projects, less-authoritarian teachers, democratic classrooms, fairness, social-racial-gender equity, less homework, less stress and someone to talk to about a concern or the future.[12]

Once we begin to listen to the voices and perspectives of high school students it becomes clear why and how today's lock-step system is holding back the development of these emerging adults. In so many ways they have been telling us:

▶ the culture of their schools is impersonal giving few opportunities to work constructively with peers and connect to teachers

▶ instruction is passive and boring rather than active and related to real life issues

▶ the system is undemocratic and at times seemingly unfair

It felt so good to know there was somebody out there who actually heard our voices.

Hearing comments from high school adolescents about "the system" more than likely is interpreted as resistance or "that's just a few saying this." Respected educator, Jacqueline Ancess, writes: "When the faculty can regard student resistance as normative rather than pathological or as willful disobedience or a deeply rooted character flaw, it becomes just one of the variables in the school constellation that factors into how education is organized and delivered for high levels of achievement."[14]

The age group's erratic energy, restlessness, drive for independence, bonding to peers, new capacity to see the needs of others, idealism, curiosity and need for identity are assets for learning.

Too often the teen stage is regarded as an advance stage of "the terrible twos." The reality is they are every bit as wonderful and precious—but less understood! High school adolescents are experiencing the most rapid, self-conscious, physical, emotional and social changes that occur in human life. Certainly there may be increased stress and conflicts with parents who may have little understanding of the normal adolescent developmental issues—especially the need for more autonomy and hanging out with peers more than with family. At the same time moving through the adolescent years successfully depends upon connections to knowledgeable and caring adults. All need one or several adults who

Ignorance about adolescents leads us to trivialize their experience.[13]
—PENELOPE ECKERT

have "an irrational emotional attachment" to them. It is, as Urie Bronfenbrenner states, "the illusion that comes with love."[15]

THE FIRST STEP IS A QUESTION TO ASK

It is understandable how the impersonal culture, procedures and traditional pedagogy of the high school must be changed. Yet, it is easy to conclude, "There's no way to transform all that!" "We'll just do more—only harder!"

The message of this book is that transformation is possible *if* and *when* a school truly becomes a student-centered learning community. One question then will guide all planning and decisions in the high school. Whether about curriculum, personnel, facility changes, policies, style of management, professional development, schedules or evaluation, the first question will be….

> *How does this support the academic, social and emotional learning for all of the students in this school?*

This is what moving to a new responsive paradigm of education means. Throughout our high school we will be creative partners with today's students. We will generate many strategies that engage all in the diversity of their ways of learning, interests, gifts, and hopes for the future.

Yes, that is what this book, "Engaging All by Creating High School Learning Communities" is all about.

2 Learning Who They Are

2 Learning Who They Are

> You have to start where people are, because their growth is going to be from there, not from some abstraction of where you are or someone else is.[1]
> —MYLES HORTON

WHAT REALLY IS THE PURPOSE OF EDUCATION?

Have you ever considered that decades of efforts toward school reform have become controversial due to a lack of consensus on *what **is** the purpose of education?* School planning groups are more likely to leap over the fundamental purpose question to debate or argue about: *What* must all students learn? *What* standards should we set? *What* curriculum? *What* tests?" Many of the business community emphasize that the purpose of education is to prepare students for the work world of consumerism, production, marketing and finance. High tech companies consider the purpose is to prepare every young person for jobs in the informational computerized businesses world. Perhaps it is time for us to consider that the current direction and nature of education primarily is causing students to worry about how to make a living before they know who they are, or even deadening their sense of creativity and wonder. Some parents and educators are certain that the meaning of a good education is simply to be competent in the three Rs—reading, 'riting and 'rithmetic. Others consider that the primary purpose of K–12 schooling is to go to college—and to find a satisfying career while there. It is puzzling that few articulate the purpose as the development of children in all of their wholeness and uniqueness as knowledgeable, competent and caring human beings prepared to live their lives well and contribute to society.

Dismissing the fundamental question of *the true purpose of education* not only is a barrier to transforming high schools but perpetuates the ineffectual one-size-fits-all 19th century factory model of "schooling."

The tragedy for high school students is that the 19th century production line does not address the diversity of their 21st century needs, perspectives and ways of learning. The impersonal traditional system contributes to underachievement, socio-economic-cultural inequities, and failure for one third or more of youth in the United States to graduate.

The good news is that networks of educators, legislators, parents, community groups and the media are questioning whether this is all that education now means for children. Throughout time, respected philosophers and educators from Plato and Aristotle—to

Thomas Jefferson, Albert Einstein, John Dewey, Jean Piaget, Urie Bronfenbrenner, John Goodlad, James Comer, Daniel Goleman, Deborah Meier and Howard Gardner—to name but a few—pursued the discussion at a higher level. Collectively, such thinkers probably would concur with respected educator Lynn Stoddard that:

> *The purpose of education is to develop greatness in human beings—people who have the knowledge, skills and wisdom to make moral and ethical decisions, and live as constructive citizens in community, society and the world.*[2]

This viewpoint was articulated well almost one hundred years ago by John Dewey who asserted that the purpose of education is: *to call forth the intellectual, moral, and emotional growth of the individual—and consequently, the evolution of a democratic society.*[3]

The historic debate is still where education is caught today. On one hand reformers believe that schools will improve through an intense focus on the development of 20% of a student's human capacity—namely, his or her intellect. Pouring facts into kids heads apart from all else they need continues the spiral of failure for kids, schools and nations. Comprehensive studies documented by the respected Collaborative for Academic, Social and Emotional Learning confirm the connection and impact of social and emotional learning to academic learning.[4] Well-being and success for adolescents depends upon supporting the development of their full humanity and it fails without it.

Keith Larick, Superintendent of one of the largest and fastest growing school districts in California, articulates the large challenge for today:

> *"As we look at the 21st century we face great challenges. This will be an exciting time, and we know that our young people are going to be exposed to more information than any generation before. They are going to have more knowledge and possess more insights than any group in our history. And at the same time that is not enough. They've got to have a sense of humanity. They have to balance their lives between what they know and what they do to make this a better world."*[5]

"BUT WE DON'T HAVE TIME!"

True! The lock-step unresponsive impersonal high school system gives no time for teachers to listen or to know students. Many say that they do notice students who are caught in the spiral of failure, but having to deal with a hundred or more young people moving through their classrooms each day locks them into just giving a smile now and then. Understandably, less is expected of the unmotivated ones, who most likely give up, act out or drift into peer groups where belonging and a purpose might be found.

It is easiest to attribute their disinterest in school to difficult backgrounds, lack of parenting or situations in the outside world rather than looking at the mis-match of the high

The purpose of education is to develop greatness in human beings.
—Lynn Stoddard

All of our kids are facing the odds of an education system that is all wrong. The odds are against them because the system works against them instead of with them. If we start by simply paying attention to who kids are and where they are coming from, and then rebuild the system of education around that, we would immeasurably improve the odds that all our kids will succeed.[6]
—Dennis Littky

school system to the needs and ways today's adolescents do learn. High school is their launching pad into the adult world. It is now if not earlier, that all need to discover who they are and discover paths to pursue. For too long too many have been labeled as "youth-at-risk." The imperative is to see all as "youth-at-promise."[7] Indeed, caring dedicated teachers cannot do it all—but the whole school community can do so together once it becomes a personalized and dynamic "system-of-promise."

GETTING TO KNOW ALL AS YOUTH-AT-PROMISE

Our first step in creating a high school that is *responsive* to the developmental learning needs of the young citizens is to move beyond the assumptions, labels, symptomatic behaviors and adjectives of despair or amusement customarily used to describe them. It means taking time to imagine you are walking in their shoes. Being 15 to 18 years old today is not the same as a few decades ago. The impact of technology, the media, the explosion of information, cell-phones, Internet, instantaneous communication, population mobility, economics, a more restless multiethnic society has transformed the ecology that affects the whole scope of their human development. That Psych 101 child development course of some years ago may not have touched at all upon the environmental variables that now affect children and youth development. It certainly did not include, nor could we imagine, the dramatic factors imprinting the lives of today's adolescents.

The path towards developing as healthy and capable human beings is not a neat and predictable one. In fact, it is not a path at all. Research of the last decade recognizes that human development is a life-long *wisdom-based process* occurring over time and in over-lapping stages rather than *age-based* sequential development as earlier concluded by Jean Piaget and Eric Erickson.[7] In other words neuroscientists no longer consider age as the critical issue in the development of thinking, but rather that *sequential stages of thinking* evolve out of stimulation from environmental settings.[8]

Research also recognizes the powerful influences of a child's immediate environment. The graphic that follows illustrates that human development is an ongoing transaction between an individual and many surrounding systems. The nature of each adolescent's growth is affected by...

▶ his or her daily interactions in the settings of life: family, school, community and peer groups;

▶ the cultural norms, languages, beliefs, and mores of the surrounding systems; and

▶ the wider impact of institutions, government, economics, mass media and religion.

Urie Bronfenbrenner, author of *The Ecology of Human Development* gives us this applicable definition: "Healthy human development depends upon one's conception of an ever-widening world and one's interaction with it—as well as a *growing capacity to discover, sustain, or change it.*[9]

It is the last section of the definition that is especially significant for our work with high school adolescents. Recognizing that they are moving into ever-widening worlds, they need to have abundant opportunities in caring and challenging environments to *discover, sustain or change situations and systems* in which they find themselves. As fledgling idealists they have come to believe in democracy—not as represented by political parties but as their right to participate and influence decisions and common goals. As teachers and parents we need to welcome the indicators of the developmental tasks they are determined to achieve. The age group's new strident behaviors, judgments and resistance are emerging out of the very natural quest to develop independence. Decades ago John Dewey asserted that the primary goal of education was...

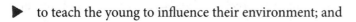

▶ to teach the young to influence their environment; and

▶ to gain the insight to make choices beyond past experiences.

MOVING FROM "ME" TO "WE" TO THE "WORLD"

The ever-widening explorations and interests of young adults signify a growing readiness to move beyond the childhood and younger adolescents' narrow perspective of "ME" as inwardly felt or expressed as "I am the center of the universe." "I am all that matters." It is youth's drive for *social competency and belonging that moves* them into identifying with and considering others, *our* common good and community. Unfortunately, there are those who continue to live within small ego-centered worlds centered on "me and mine," and are more likely to continue on a road to loneliness, intolerance, conflict, alienation, high-risk behaviors, periods of despair or failure throughout life. Mental institutions, alcoholism/drug treatment centers, jails and prisons are filled with "me first—me-only" people. This is not a moral or "lack of character" problem. It is a failure to develop beyond the "me" stage of earlier childhood years. It is a failure to grow socially, emotionally and spiritually as an adolescent and to become a responsible and caring human being.

We must ask, "Is this what limits the futures of so many young people in our country today?" Are they the ones who were never challenged to work collaboratively with others, to discover their innate gifts, to achieve the developmental tasks for adulthood, and to relate in wider worlds of "we" as well as "me?" Development cannot be taught—it must

We have to get past the me first—me only mindset!

Development cannot be taught—it must be lived daily within safe, caring and challenging environments.

be lived daily within safe, caring and challenging environments. That is one of the most important reasons the culture, structures and pedagogy of today's high schools must be transformed. Moreover, there is no mystery how to bring that about. It is essential not only to enhance academic learning but for all students to become considerate, caring, altruistic and fair human beings.

TWO CONFLICTING PARADIGMS

Thomas Armstrong is to be congratulated for highlighting in his fine book, *The Best Schools: How Human Development Research Should Inform Educational Practice*, two paradigms of thought, viewpoints and conflicting discussions in education today—namely, the *"academic achievement discourse"* and the *"human development discourse."* Concerning the prevailing discourse on academic achievement, Armstrong points out that... *"when the dialogue in education becomes limited to the narrow framework of grades, test scores, and scientifically-based research, then a great deal of what education is about gets left behind. Moreover, the excessive concentration on developing uniform standards, implementing a rigorous curriculum, and raising test scores has several negative consequences that are creating more harm to students and teachers than benefits."*[10]

In contrast human development discourse has "a substantially wider perspective" and *"places the greatest emphasis on human beings rather than on academics."*[11] *"Discourse as used in education might be the totality of speech, acts and written communications that view the purpose of education primarily in terms of supporting, encouraging, and facilitating a student's growth as a whole human being, including his or her cognitive, emotional, social, ethical, creative and spiritual enfoldment."*[12]

That is exactly why I became a teacher!

Readers who may be involved in conflicts or discussions about these paradigms, and want to enlighten others, would do well to secure Dr. Armstrong's book, which clearly presents the negative and positive assumptions and consequences of each discourse.

HUMAN DEVELOPMENT IS FUNDAMENTAL TO LEARNING

Embedded in the caring *Learning Community* process for high schools as described in this book are these fundamental research-based tenets of human development and learning:[13]

▶ Human development is a life-long wisdom-based process, occurring over time and in over-lapping *stages*.

▶ Human development is a *resilient process,* motivated by a self-righting, intrinsic human drive and developmental wisdom.

▶ Being student-centered means focusing on the *whole young person's development:* intellectual, social, emotional, physical and spiritual.

▶ Intellectual development and academic achievement are directly supported and enhanced by social, emotional, physical and spiritual development.

▶ The concept of multiple *intelligences* provides a strength-based schema for supporting holistic human development.

The Association for Supervision and Curriculum Development (ASCD) recently has adopted a clear policy that is summarized as follows by Executive Director, Gene Carter.

> *"Students cannot succeed in any subject, including math and science, without attention to all of their learning and developmental needs. ASCD supports challenging goals and accountability that encompass the education of the whole child. In doing so, we advocate a more complete <u>definition of student achievement that supports the development of a child who is healthy, knowledgeable, motivated and engaged.</u>"[14]*

The unfounded assumption that students can learn well intellectually (academically) apart from whatever is going on with their physical, emotional or social concerns contradicts not only common sense but decades of studies that verify the interdependent connection of intellectual, social, emotional, physical and moral/spiritual development.[15] The Yale Study Center's School Development Program (SDP) developed by James Comer has continued since the late sixties to demonstrate that healthy development of the whole child or adolescent is the keystone to academic achievement and life success. Dr. Comer repeatedly states what Comer Schools have more than proven as the clearest message to accomplish school reform: *"We will be able to create successful system of education only when we gauge everything we do on what is known about how children and youths develop and learn."[16]*

Comer adds that "<u>a well-functioning school is a social system in which the developmental needs of students are addressed throughout the school's curriculum, pedagogy, social activities and environment.</u>"[17]

Students cannot succeed in any subject, including math and science, without attention to all of their learning and developmental needs.
—GENE CARTER

We will be able to create a successful system of education only when we gauge everything we do on what is known about how children and youth develop and learn.
—JAMES COMER

Innumerable other research groups such as the Child Development Project (CDP) of the Developmental Studies Center in Oakland, California, consistently have found pro-social and academic outcomes from a "caring community of learners' approach."[18] The American Psychological Association after reviewing research across many fields affirms that "education most likely will improve when educational systems are redesigned with the primary focus on the learner."[19]

The focus on holistic development is discussed in book after book telling stories of schools not only that are succeeding with students given up by others but in engaging all.

RAGING HORMONES AND DUMB DECISIONS

It's difficult to look at the holistic development of adolescents without thinking of a few that cause us either to smile or shake our heads. "Yes," we say, "It's the flood of hormones that makes their behaviors so erratic and exasperating."

It's helpful to look at neurological scanning studies which now provide significant insight into what is going on from the age of teenage puberty up to the adult years of 25 years old. Every parent of a teenager somehow recognizes that: *hormonal puberty and the cognitive controls needed for mature behavior do not develop simultaneously.* Emotional outbursts, reckless risk-taking, rule breaking and the impassioned pursuit of sex, exciting music or alcohol and drugs can be best understood by understanding what is happening in the adolescent brain.[20]

MRI (magnetic resonance imaging) studies can follow developmental changes at different ages. Just prior to puberty in children National Institute of Mental Health (NIMH) scientists have noted a spurt of grey matter, growth that predominates the frontal lobe of the brain, which is the seat of "executive functions"—planning, impulse control and reasoning. Unlike grey matter, the brain's white matter, wire-like fibers that establish neurons' long-distance connections between brain regions and that thicken progressively from birth on in humans, begin to be enveloped in a layer of insulation called myelin—which makes the neural fibers more efficient. As teens grow older temporal "gut reaction" brain activity shifts to the frontal lobe—not only giving them more reasoned perceptions and decision-making but improved performance. UCLA researchers comparing MRI scans of young adults, 20–23, with those of teens,12–16, discovered large increases in myelination in the frontal cortex of the adults signifying the maturation of cognitive processing and other "executive" functions. In the teen brain temporal areas mediating spatial, sensory, auditory and language functions were mature.[22]

First of all, no longer can we consider adolescent development as age-stage-grade related. The new research recognizes that development is a *wisdom-based process* affected by the powerful influences of a child's immediate environment…namely, the family, school, community and peers as well as the cultural and institutional environments. All freshmen are not the same, nor are all sophomores, juniors or seniors. Packaging them as ages or stages imposes unreal and harsh expectations on all. The path to maturity varies

John Dewey began this century with an eloquent plea for the education of the whole child. It would be good for us to get around to it by the end of the century.[21]
—ROBERT SYLWESTER

wherever each teen may be in the process—all of which affects the health of the brain, body and soul.

THE CHARACTERISTICS OF YOUNG ADULTS' WHOLE DEVELOPMENT

There are five human assets (strengths) that we all continue to develop over time as supported by environments in which we live. Looking at adolescents is always more of a challenge due to the rapid changes that they go through in a few years.

As you read through the characteristics taking place at different times in high school students' development, try to identify students you may know who seem to be in a similar place in their intellectual/cognitive, physical, social, emotional/psychological and moral/spiritual development.

What does all this tell us?

The summary profiles that follow were defined from the literature on adolescents and confirmed by groups of experienced (and still jovial) high school teachers.[23]

Intellectual/Cognitive Development

High school adolescents are in a transition from relying primarily on concrete cognitive skills to the development of abstract thinking. They now are acquiring the ability to imagine hypothetical situations, to reconcile contradictions, to predict long-term consequences of immediate behavior, to question the validity of information and to view situations from other people's perspectives. All are not at the same point in their cognitive development. The concrete thinkers may consider the abstract thinkers weird, and the abstract may regard the concrete thinkers slow or dense. The daily difficulty for teachers is to deal with the range of cognitive development levels.

High school students are juggling learning two sets of skills. To become educated adults and to graduate they are learning the content of curriculum, and also the "rules of the game of school." Anxious questions such as the following are asked repeatedly in class: "What if I turn in a paper late?" "How much does this assignment count?" "How many tests this semester?" "How will our team project be graded?" "What choices do we have?" The positive aspect of learning the rules of the system is the development of self-management, the ability to focus, listen, organize information, solve problems and know what to study. The negative aspect is dealing with different rules in different classes, making efforts to please teachers, cramming for tests, memorizing facts, copying from others, being compliant and playing the game known as "doing school."[24]

As any high school teacher knows, the age group enjoys a wide range of options and prefers active learning experiences over passive teacher instruction—most of all, learning in interaction with peers which supports their drive for social competency. Another "plus and minus" is that they are increasingly more intellectually curious about the world, themselves and others, and thus are more likely to challenge facts, concepts and teachers authority.

Physical Development

The rapid irregular growth, bodily changes and varying maturity rates of adolescents often cause many to be anxious, restless and fatigued. All seem to sense an increase in energy, and the need to release energy can lead to sudden meaningless bursts of activity. In spite of new energy many lack physical fitness and have low levels of endurance, strength and flexibility. They may adopt poor health habits (junk food, experimentation with alcohol, drugs and sex) and be physically vulnerable. Some who have little aptitude for physical activities may consider PE a waste of time and get little meaningful exercise. Others consider the best part of being in high school is the opportunity to be involved in athletics and opportunities to strengthen their physical development through aerobics, dance, drama, hiking, outdoor explorations and community service projects. Studies show that regular enjoyable physical activity is a significant factor that contributes to academic achievement. It also connects to teenager's quest for a sense of identity and social competency.

Social Development

All youth have a strong need to belong to a group. Younger high school adolescents still lagging behind in social and emotional maturity may exhibit immature behavior. This group tends to model their behavior after older, esteemed students or adults beyond the family. Though still dependent on parental beliefs and values, most seek to make their own decisions. The age group does want attention and guidance from adults. The drive for independence results in liking attention-getting fads (clothes, hair colors, earrings), new slang and phrases adults do not understand. Their big search is to have social acceptance and recognition in a peer group, especially a group that is well-respected by other students. This desire to have recognition within a peer group and work with peers is one of the reasons the use of small cooperative learning groups enhances academic learning.

Emotional/Psychological Development

Adolescents are psychologically vulnerable because at no other stage of development are they more likely to encounter and be sensitive to so many differences between themselves and others. Believing that their feelings and problems are unique to themselves, they can experience unpredictable and intense mood swings. Highly sensitive to personal criticism, many tend to be self-conscious, are lacking in self-esteem, are easily discouraged, and have a strong need for approval. Peer acceptance and approval become more important as adult approval decreases in importance. Seeking to become increasingly independent as a young adult may provoke parents. It also can be the basis of resistance to teachers and other adults in authority.

Moral/Spiritual Development

Our young adult friends are generally idealistic, wanting to become socially useful and make the world a better place in which to live. Many are in a transition from a focus of "what's in it for me" to considering the feelings and rights of others. At the same time it is easy for them to see flaws in others.

The group increasingly shows compassion for others and interest in community, environmental and political issues. Many begin to assess moral matters in shades of gray instead of the black and white terms of younger youth. When facing a difficult decision, many still rely on parents and significant adults for advice. They seek adult role models who will listen and affirm their actions and goals. Increasingly adolescents are aware of and concerned about the inconsistencies between values exhibited by adults and the conditions they see in society. The age group values direct experience in participatory democracy. They are very capable of offering their opinions and leadership.

Never doubt that the positive is also happening. All experience many small joys whenever positive aspects of their personalities and character qualities are affirmed. As personal value systems develop, societal issues assume more importance. Physical energy, athletics, leadership and new aspects of moral judgment become ways to achieve identity, belonging and approval.

CHANGING OUR PERSPECTIVE

Dealing with adolescents in various stages of their individual development, disruptive behaviors, attitudes and needs at times seems overwhelming enough for some high school teachers to think about giving up teaching, or perhaps to go back to teaching in earlier grades.

The wide range and diversity of adolescents' stages of development, characteristics, needs and assets could seem overwhelming enough for many teachers to go back to teaching first grade! But take heart! We need to see these *wannabe adults* and their behaviors in a developmental way, rather than problems or behaviors to control. It is helpful to reframe our customary perspective from the *needs* of adolescents to the developmental *tasks* they are consciously or unconsciously trying to achieve.

Understanding the *developmental tasks* that high school adolescents are driving to achieve as a stage of their human development gives a perspective on the puzzling characteristics and behaviors of the age group. More than all, it helps educators and parents understand that rather than trying "to fix these kids" we need to understand and help them to achieve the very essential competencies for their lives as adults.

"Need" means something's lacking— something that has to be fixed. "Task" means something I'm working on and achieving.

Now and then I did think about quitting! But crazy as it seems, I'd miss them and the drama!

VOICING A DEVELOPMENTAL QUEST

Underlying the forthright voices, behaviors and attitudes of high school students is a clear message that no longer can we treat or teach them as younger adolescents. They now are "young adults" rapidly moving on roads to manage their own lives. Whether we or they realize it or not, they are trying to achieve a set of personal competencies that are essential for doing well in the adult world. It is a normal human quest—*a vital step* in developing each person's life-long strengths. Somehow they sense that becoming grown up rightfully takes achieving four essential competencies. Their quest is to gain...

> ▶ autonomy and independence
>
> ▶ social competency and identity
>
> ▶ a sense of purpose and positive expectations for the future, and
>
> ▶ a capacity to problem-solve on one's own.

Acquiring these competencies is the developmental task of adolescence. Amazingly enough, the four tasks are identical to the well-researched characteristics of *resiliency* which is the human capacity to survive, to progress through inevitable difficult life situations, and to be able to bounce back and move on positively again and again in life. The resilient strengths are exhibited in life by well-balanced healthy adults who one way or another have internalized the same four competencies. Those who still may be seeking or have failed to develop these essential strengths are likely to face on-going awkward struggles in relationships and work performance. Lacking a sense of social competency and independence limits opportunities in leadership, initiative and self-direction. Those still longing for a sense of purpose or lacking positive expectations may drift without motivation; and those unable to solve own problems may never become self-directed.

We need to understand that many of the behaviors of adolescence, so often annoying for parents and teachers are *indicators* of the growth youth are trying to achieve. What parent has not heard: "Don't tell me what to do." "I'll figure it out." "I'd rather be with my friends."

Since adolescence is the age of the final establishment of a dominant positive ego identity, it is then that a future within reach becomes part of the conscious life plan.[25]
—ERIC ERICKSON

RELATIONSHIP OF INDICATORS TO DEVELOPMENTAL TASKS

BEHAVIORAL INDICATOR	DEVELOPMENTAL TASK
talking back rudely to adults	seeking independence
less compliant or non-cooperative	seeking autonomy
connection to peers	seeking social competency
lack of interest and boredom	seeking sense of purpose
resistence to others' decisions	seeking to do own problem solving

Yeah, I say "don't tell me what to do" a lot!

Our reaction as adults is to try to control youth behaviors with more rules, regulations, admonitions, rewards and punishments. Control responses certainly are appropriate when dealing with unsafe or unhealthy behaviors. However, as Leon Botstein, President of Bard College reminds us: "The very qualities we deem destructive can be the motivation to learn."[26] As caring adults our challenge is to recognize the underlying task, and our responsibility is to become "turnabout people" who transform high schools into "turnabout systems."

HOW THE DEVELOPMENTAL PROCESS KNOWN AS TRIBES LEARNING COMMUNITIES SUPPORTS THE TASKS OF ADOLESCENCE

Now and then the question is asked, "Can you recommend a curriculum we can use to teach resiliency and achievement of the developmental tasks?"

Sorry, it just doesn't happen that way! The developmental tasks and the attributes of resiliency cannot be taught. They develop by being *lived daily* in positive environments, caring relationships and democratic reflective systems. Our responsibility as knowledgeable educators is to create and sustain these elements throughout all classes and structures in our high schools.

The very qualities we deem destructive can be the motivation to learn.[26]
—LEON BOTSTEIN

Creating the conditions to help students succeed

How does the process of Tribes help kids develop?

I'm so glad you asked! That is what this book is all about!

Let's look at the chart on the following page that lists ways in which the process of Tribes TLC® supports the development of the adolescent tasks.

How the Process of Tribes TLC® Supports
the Tasks of Adolescent Development

ADOLESCENT TASKS	THE PROCESS OF TRIBES
AUTONOMY & INDEPENDENCE	
self-actualization	• builds personal identity • identifies skills, talents and gifts • empowers leadership • celebrates diversity
independence	• develops self-responsibility and resilience • teaches independent and democratic decision-making
internal locus of control	• uses reflection on behavior and interpersonal interactions • practices independent thinking within peer groups • affirms "right to pass" in group activity • teaches self-responsibility
self-esteem	• uses appreciation statements within peer learning groups • develops positive self-image • values respect for diversity
SOCIAL COMPETENCY	
pro-social behaviors	• trains adults to model and have students reflect on caring character qualities
communication skills	• teaches twelve communication/social skills
belonging/inclusion	• structures long-term membership groups (tribes) in every classroom • assures inclusion of every student in a social learning group • uses many inclusion strategies
active participation	• trains teachers in use of cooperative and constuctivist active learning methods • engages students actively through strategies that give influence and a sense of being valued
self-control/self-discipline	• involves peer groups to reflect upon and encourage helpful behavior • trains students in supportive peer-to-peer feedback

ADOLESCENT TASKS	THE PROCESS OF TRIBES
SENSE OF PURPOSE identity	• uses strategies for inclusion, presentation of self, and discovering gifts
positive expectations	• centers on high expectations for each and every person
personal goals	• encourages and practices attainment of personal and group goals, and service to others • focuses on sharing, caring and community values
PROBLEM-SOLVING abstract thinking	• develops conceptual and contextual thinking • sets aside time to reflect on learning, group interaction, meaning and synthesis of ideas
open-mindedness and flexibility	• seeks alternatives and builds creativity
emotional intelligence	• promotes conscious choice, social responsibility and resiliency
collaboration	• structures small groups and teaches collaborative skills so that learning groups work well together • teaches and practices democratic values, fairness and equity

The most exciting breakthrough of the 21st century will occur not because of technology, but because of an expanding concept of what it means to be human.[27]

—John Naisbitt

A Teacher's View

Michele Cahall, M.A.

Michele has worked as a
special education teacher
of communicatively
handicapped students
for more than 20 years.
She currently serves as a
Speech-Language Pathologist
with El Dorado County
Schools in California. She
is a Certified Tribes TLC®
Trainer and Professional
Development Consultant
for CenterSource Systems.
Michele has been deeply
involved in the development
of Tribes TLC® training
and materials. In the midst
of meetings, she can be
counted on to remind
everyone of her own
primary purpose—"to
improve the lives of kids and
their families."

Preparing Special Needs Students for the Adult World

I celebrate my opportunities to work with high school educators of special needs students. It is an opportunity for me to share the Tribes process and the many benefits of high school learning communities for their students. Typical special education classes emphasize the academics and basic life skills along with the Individual Educational Plan (IEP). While these areas are important, high school special needs students need an "active learning community" to help foster a happy and successful experience in and beyond high school.

The Developmental Process of Tribes serves as a sequential framework for building all high school learning communities. Focusing on the essential tasks of adolescents—autonomy/independence, social competency, a sense of purpose and problem solving—is important while moving through the Developmental Process of Tribes.

All of the essential tasks of adolescents are equally important and should be addressed through the many strategies outlined in Chapter 17. Social competency is an especially important task for a successful high school experience and beyond. Special needs students typically need to develop a wide variety of social skills depending on their skill level. Some of the social skills that are important for this population to develop are: understanding social conventions, eye contact, initiating peer interaction, learning conversational techniques, resolving conflicts, interacting with authority figures and learning self-advocating skills. It may feel like an enormous task, but implementing the developmental learning process of Tribes process is the most effective way to meet this important challenge. Of course, depending on the cognitive level of the student, additional assistance may need to be considered.

Special needs students need to be taught social skills explicitly through direct instruction, repetition and practice opportunities. Many social skills can be actively learned by selecting appropriate Tribes strategies and using the "Seven Steps in Teaching Collaborative Skills" process described in

Chapter 12. Repetition and role playing especially increase student understanding of the social skills being taught.

More than all, it is especially helpful for teachers to participate in Collegial Learning Communities to address the social and emotional needs of students. I encourage special education teachers to share with all teachers of the high school the techniques that ensure the full range of human development and meaningful learning for the special needs students. Post-secondary transition for students with disabilities is an important and time-consuming task. The Tribes process and social skills increase the ability of special needs students to form connections, to enjoy learning, and to move successfully into higher education and the adult world. Trust the process! It works!

AND WHAT ABOUT THE GIFTED?

And what about the gifted?

It is time to sound an alarm! Faced with national mandates to raise test scores of under-performing students, the gifted with abilities beyond others their age largely are being neglected, underserved and left behind. Bored and underchallenged, some tune out, drop out or simply do not live up to their full potential. It is startling to learn from statistical reports from the Davidson Institute for Talent Development that 20 percent of U.S. school dropouts test in the gifted range. The impact upon their lives and loss to society is sobering especially when one learns that although three to five percent of the general adult population is gifted, 20 percent of the prison population is reported to be.[28]

It is well recognized by most teachers that all young people have gifts that are not limited or demonstrated by IQ tests. The National Association for Gifted Children (NAGC) defines a gifted person as "someone who shows, or has the potential for showing, an exceptional level of performance in one or more areas of expression." Developmental scholar J. S. Renzulli proposes that gifted behavior occurs when there is an interaction among three basic clusters of human traits: above-average general and/or specific abilities, high levels of task commitment (motivation) and high levels of creativity.[29]

Many gifted and talented children are misdiagnosed as having ADHD, depression, obsessive-compulsive, mood or bi-polar disorders. The literature points out that these common mis-diagnoses stem from an ignorance about specific social and emotional characteristics of gifted children.[30]

Fifty years of research shows that moving highly capable students ahead through the academic curriculum at a faster rate is motivational, makes them more ambitious and happy.[31] Challenged academically they earn graduate degrees at higher rates. Forms of acceleration include grade skipping, Advanced Placement (AP) courses and early entrance to higher education. High school teachers may inherit students who have never been recognized as gifted or talented, and especially need to be sensitive to their different ways of learning, unique talents and potential. To provide appropriate learning experiences, the NAGC emphasizes that teachers need to possess:

▶ A knowledge and valuing of the origins and nature of high levels of intelligence, including creative expressions of intelligence

▶ A knowledge and understanding of the cognitive, social and emotional characteristics, needs, and potential problems experienced by gifted and talented students from diverse populations

▶ A knowledge of and access to advanced content and ideas

▶ An ability to develop differentiated curriculum appropriate to meeting the unique intellectual and emotional needs and interests of these students, and

▶ An ability to create an environment in which they can feel challenged and safe to explore their uniqueness and interests.[32]

The challenge can and is being met in Tribes Learning Community schools in which well-prepared teachers are focusing on student development as well as learning, are creating caring cultures and are using responsive "active learning" components of education. Along with others in their own teacher Collegial Learning Communities, they are able to create differentiated learning experiences such as project learning, inquiry, web research, artistry and other motivational challenges to engage the unique gifts and talents of students in their classes. Teachers' renewed learning, competency and enthusiasm in reaching gifted and talented students is a transformative power in any school.

SOCIAL AND EMOTIONAL INTELLIGENCE SUPPORTS ACADEMIC LEARNING

Perhaps as never before, concerned educators, parents and even political leaders are beginning to raise an important question that lifts local and national discussions beyond debates over standards and tests scores. Invite your staff and administrators to talk about this *bigger question:*

What really is most important in preparing today's young people to become knowledgeable, responsible and caring citizens?

Hm-m! Tougher courses in science and math? Computers for every child? Smaller class sizes? Smaller high schools! A longer school day or year? More federal $$$? Strong discipline policies? More awards?

Scattered unrelated topics tend to dominate school meetings and planning rather than the greater question above from which all teaching and student learning should rightfully flow. Unfortunately, school leaders and practitioners are less apt to recognize the critical connection of social and emotional development to significant academic learning. How a young person feels about himself cannot be separated from learning curriculum content. The reality is that high grades and SAT scores do not predict satisfaction and productivity throughout life—nor a good citizen make.

Esteemed research educators and scientists such as Daniel Goleman, Howard Gardner, Maurice Elias, Roger Weissberg, Jonathan Cohen, Ragozzino, et.al. (to name but a few) have been announcing what might still be breakthrough news for some educators and school systems. Namely that *academic performance is enhanced by social and emotional competence.* Jonathan Cohen responds to the "big question" by stating:

> *"The essential foundation for both academic learning and the capacity to become active constructive citizens is having knowledge of ourselves—and others as well—and being able to gain and use meaningful knowledge to solve problems creatively."*[33]

The respected Collaborative for Academic, Social and Emotional Learning (CASEL) defines social emotional learning (SEL) as "the process of developing fundamental social and emotional competencies or skills in children and creating a caring and supportive school climate."[34]

Daniel Goleman uses the term "social intelligence" and defines it as the capacity to:

- ▶ relate well to others
- ▶ conceptualize and manage social relations, interpersonal problems and conflict
- ▶ be empathetic, patient and considerate of cultural, racial and gender diversity
- ▶ collaborate, and
- ▶ enjoy working for the common good.

He further states that the development of social intelligence depends upon the degree of development of a person's:

- ▶ self-awareness
- ▶ the ability to handle emotions
- ▶ self-motivation
- ▶ empathy, and
- ▶ social skills.[35]

All are self-reflective capacities. They give one the ability to recognize what others are thinking and feeling. Moreover, they dramatically affect children's ability to learn and succeed in life.[36] Schools that make a consistent practice not only of having learners reflect on academic learning but also reflect on their inner knowledge of self, nurture students' social and emotional learning.

Yes, for thousands of years we've known that to fly well, one has to .... 'Know thyself.'

3

*The Times Are
A' Changing*

The Times Are A' Changing

IN THIS CHAPTER YOU WILL

▶ Consider how changes in the world require very different knowledge and human strengths

▶ Recognize global trends that affect the world of work and life today

▶ Reflect upon the new competencies, skills and attributes young people need in order to do well in life

▶ Realize how fostering the development of resilient attributes in students matches their quest to achieve the essential tasks of adolescence

We are now at a point where we must educate our children in what no one knew yesterday, and prepare our schools for what no one knows yet.[1]

—MARGARET MEAD

"THE BASICS" FOR THE NEW MILLENNIUM

Time out to think about it all! There have been three other ages in history when humankind moved through massive transitions that totally altered the world—three other times when humankind had to become competent in very different "basic skills" in order to survive. The ancient Age of Hunter-Gatherers gave way to The Age of Agriculture as nomads began to protect choice territories. The Age of Agriculture led to the Age of Industry as populations grew and mass production of goods and services were needed. Now the high-tech Information Age is impacting every aspect of life throughout the world.

HUNTER-GATHERERS

AGRICULTURE

INDUSTRY

INFORMATION

The skills and knowledge developed in each of the Ages through time have been very different and critical to survival in the respective Age. The following chart highlights a few that people living in past Ages had to develop in order to live in their period of time.

Knowledge and Human Strengths for Three Past Ages

HUNTER-GATHERERS	AGRICULTURE	INDUSTRY
Knowledge	*Knowledge*	*Knowledge*
survival in nature	survival from the land	survival in work organizations
making primitive tools	man/animal drawn tools	mechanization
tracking game	raising domestic animals	control of workers
fire building	planting/harvesting	mass production of goods and services
sharing resources	trading/selling products	advertising
		reading, writing +mathematics
Strengths	*Strengths*	*Strengths*
physical	physical	physical, social and emotional
respect for nature	respect for family and land	respect for authority
independence	inter-dependence	co-dependence

Imagine what would have happened to people moving into the next new Age in time if they assumed the "basic skills and knowledge" of the past were sufficient for generations of the future. They would have continued to teach children:

▶ how to read animal tracks rather than literature

▶ how to use hand-plows rather than tractors

▶ how to communicate through oral legend rather than also writing

▶ how to use an abacus but not adding machines and calculators

▶ how to relate and live with one's own kind but not with a diversity of people in cities and workplaces.

It needs to be said again and again—human beings must acquire totally different knowledge, skills and strengths in order to survive and thrive in an increasingly more complex world.

HOW MANY 19TH CENTURY HIGH SCHOOL SYSTEMS ARE STILL IN YOUR TOWN?

The Industrial Age of the last 150 years consisted of centralized workplaces in which people worked on pieces of prescribed tasks that required minimal communication with others, little knowledge or influence over the end product, and little satisfaction beyond their paychecks. Factory model systems had (and still have) rigid prescribed methods and quantitative measures of output from production lines. The industrial authoritarian system, just like DNA in cellular bodies, permeated all systems in American culture—particularly schools which became factory models. Students were taught to be punctual, to follow orders and to do repetitive "seat-work." Question-answer-response pedagogy was the norm throughout teacher-centered classrooms. Tests that assessed memorization of information and facts measured student achievement. Little time was set aside for constructive thinking or creativity. Principles of participatory democracy were preached in schools but seldom modeled as a way of relating, managing or teaching others. If some of this sounds familiar it may be that you know of a school that is somewhat still there.

LOOKING AT TODAY'S VERY DIFFERENT WORLD

Welcome to the 21st century, friends! Welcome to instantaneous information, world-wide communication, satellite positioning systems, global economics, multinationalism, rapid systems' change... and cell phones in our pockets! Many years ago visionary writer Alvin Toffler coined the phrase "high-tech/high-touch," meaning that the coming 21st century era would usher into the world a "fortuitous dichotomy of technology and relatedness."[2] He predicted the 'high-tech/high-touch" Age would need responsive-analytical-creative people at all socio-economic levels—citizens who not only could sort out and synthesize complexities of information but also have relational "people skills" in order to interact collaboratively and well with wide-diversity of humanity. It is evident the gentleman not only was correct but forecast the learning challenge now for humankind's survival.

Research and literature in the area of employment trends show that there are common competencies that employers are seeking when hiring new employees. Although cognitive skill requirements continue to grow, "many studies also suggest that employers place as much or greater weight on non-cognitive factors, such as work effort and cooperative attitudes."[3] Employers are taking a closer look at the affective domain, and it is becoming commonplace for business organizations to administer affective based personality assessments to determine a potential worker's personal qualities, such as emotional stability, conscientiousness, openness to experience, teamwork, ethics and other traits.

CONSIDERING TRENDS THAT AFFECT
THE WORLD OF WORK AND LIFE TODAY[4]

The new Age in which we find ourselves just did not happen suddenly when our calendars moved to January 1, 2000. Recognizable trends forecasted the transformative 21st century for many decades. The majority of organizations and systems implemented changes along the way as they recognized and prepared for new opportunities based on how they perceived how the trends were beginning to affect population needs and services. Regretfully, the business of education, serving 17 million high school adolescents, paid little attention to the monumental trends that would affect learning, development and the futures of its clients.

The purpose of the chart that follows is to give you an opportunity: (1) to consider seven major trends that are changing the nature, culture and structure of the world of work and our lives today; and (2) to jot down in the right-hand column whatever you perceive needs to take place in high schools to better prepare and educate youth today.

Sure, it's OK to write in this book—it's yours.

Global Trends and Recommendations

TRENDS	RECOMMENDATIONS
 **GLOBALIZATION** The boundaries between countries are becoming a blur due to globalization in international trade, finance, business/industry, intercontinental transportation, political/government issues and common concerns over global warming, pollution of the oceans, health and humane issues. Companies are not only outsourcing production of products and parts, but also order fulfillment, banking, credit card and data-base management—all, of course, to lower labor costs. Emerging markets, particularly in the Far East, are making corporate and consumer business relationships interchangeable. Increasingly, more students from less developed countries are seeking education in universities and colleges in professionally advanced countries.	*Kids need to know what is going on in the world around them. Not just the — sphere, but understand the world.* *Languages* *Business* *Politics* *Cultures*
 **DIVERSITY** Today approximately five billion of the six billion people throughout the world are people of color. If we could shrink the earth's current population to a village of precisely 1000 and all of the existing human ratios remain the same the world would look like this:	

Global Trends and Recommendations

TRENDS

There would be:

564 Asians and Oceanians
210 Europeans
86 Africans
80 South Americans
60 North Americans
Moreover,
820 would be people of color
180 would be white
50% of the world's entire
wealth would be in the hands
of only 60 people
700 would be unable to read
500 would suffer from malnutrition
600 would live in sub-standard housing[5]

From generation to generation, a diversity of people while preserving unique aspects of their ethnic heritage have become assimilated into the mainstream of developed countries culture. They, as are people in all developed countries, are confronted either with fair or unequitable practices in the work place. Opportunities particularly for women to move upward in management and to enter medical schools and technological fields has grown as acceptance increasingly is based on merit instead of gender. The same can be said for skilled well-trained workers no matter their ethnicity. *It is their knowledge, experience and competency that counts.* International trade, monetary policies and business relationships now with a wide spectrum of countries, more than ever before makes a deeper understanding and respect of cultural differences critical. Cultural anthropologist Jennifer James emphasizes the need for current and future generations to have *cultural intelligence,* which she describes as the ability to "unpack" one's own stories, and to "unpack" the stories of others so we can go beyond tolerance to appreciation.[6]

RECOMMENDATIONS

We live in a world that is mixed with culture. We need to understand others and their importance

TRENDS

RELATIONSHIPS & TEAMS

Business organizations today constantly are looking at multiple ways to improve employee performance and productivity in order to achieve profit or survive. Yet the element too often overlooked is building and sustaining positive relationships among fellow employees.[7] Fortune 500 recruiters emphasize an employment mantra: "It's all about teams, teams, teams."[8] Working in teams can be particularly difficult for those who traditionally have embraced the "what's in it for me" individualistic creed that has long been part of the business culture. Today's workplace is seeking individuals who have *collaborative skills and the capacity to work well with others* within planning and productive teams, not only to enhance their own careers but continually to strengthen the organization.

ACCOUNTABILITY & ETHICS

More organizations are shifting from top-down hierarchical structures with many levels of middle managers, to flattened, more participatory, horizontal structures where employees not only are accountable for specific responsibilities but are noticed for their contributions. It is no longer enough just to somehow "get the job done." One is expected to "do the job well." Perhaps due to the rash of business and personal scandals highlighted in current media, one's ethical conduct is now held to a higher standard than ever before. Forward looking organizations today are seeking employees who are *ethical, trustworthy and loyal.*

RECOMMENDATIONS

How others affect you and how you affect others.

Need to be a contributing member of a team.

It's not about the grades, it's about the learning.

Character

Morals

SDT

Global Trends and Recommendations

TECHNOLOGY

Technology not only is playing a major role in shrinking our world today, but is revolutionizing how business is being done. From e-mail to cell phones, to PDAs to video conferencing, technology continues to advance exponentially as predicted 40 years ago by Gordon Moore, co-founder of Intel. Employees today are expected to have skills to effortlessly send documents through cyberspace, and simultaneously have the ability to use technology in new and innovative ways to enhance efficiency and productivity.

All now are challenged to keep up with on-going rapid changes. All have to be committed *to learning continuously.*

CREATIVITY & INNOVATION

Youth moving into today's high-tech world will struggle unless they are capable of *thinking critically, constructively and creatively.* They need to be able to examine possibilities for their organizations and lives through multiple lenses. They (and all of us) need to be proficient in accessing information, analyzing and interpreting meaning, synthesizing and linking knowledge to existing needs, planning and applying findings, and reflecting and evaluating results for on-going refinement or change. These constructive thinking skills not only are critical to facilitate collaboration and creativity in business systems, but also throughout *all people systems*—including family, school and community organizations.

Needs to be taught in schools, but make sure the pedagogy is there first.

Need to be able to think critically!

Global Trends and Recommendations

TRENDS

CHANGES-FLEXIBILITY

Change is inevitable, constant and not always easy to face. Organizations that are successful constantly are reflecting on and assessing ways to improve management, production, product marketability and service. More than ever policies, procedures and technology from the past are recognized as ineffective and obsolete. Concurrent with change is the need for organizations continually to prepare, train and educate personnel. Personnel not only need to be able to adjust to and *embrace change as it occurs*—but also to have sufficient *flexibility* to anticipate and consider future changes.

RECOMMENDATIONS

Theory of change model or teleological approach to change

Even the government is catching on!

The future now belongs to societies that organize themselves for learning.[9]

—RAY MARSHALL AND
MARC TUCKER

The U.S. Department of Labor has been publishing a continuing study known as the SCANS Report, the **S**ecretary's **C**ommission on **A**chieving **N**ecessary **S**kills.[10]

The landmark report has emphasized a wider more comprehensive set of skills and competencies that young people entering the adult world of work now need to have.

Notice that the chart, "Skills for the 21st Century," summarizing the findings of the SCAN's report, goes well beyond simply citing the need for competency in the basic skills. Thirteen other skills and personal qualities now are considered very necessary. Updated studies continue to define additional competencies needed to prepare young adults and workers for the 21st century information/service-based economy.[11] Newer competencies are mainly in the affective domain, and are considered important factors for success in today's radically changed environment. Summarily they are: optimism, goal-setting, goal-orientation, self-efficacy, self-regulation, autonomy, ambition, compassion and courage.

Why then in this day and Age has education in America narrowed down to largely an exclusive focus on teaching academic content but ignoring the need for today's youth to attain critical human competencies? High schools may well be fulfilling the shocking prophecy contained within the SCANS Report.[12]

> *More than half of our young people leave school without the knowledge or foundation required to find and hold a good job. These young people will pay a very high price. They face the bleak prospects of dead end work interrupted only by periods of unemployment.*

Moving between ages depends upon whether one is apprehensive and reactionary or knowledgeable and realistic. Clinging resolutely to "what was good enough for me in school" or "we just need more reading, writing and math" limits youth of today to yesterday's world. Perhaps the predicament taking place now in high schools touches upon Albert Einstein's warning:

> *"The world will not evolve past its current state of crisis by using the same thinking that created the situation."*

ACQUIRING HABITS OF MIND

The need to prepare youth to be successful in today's world are emphasized by respected educator, Arthur Costa, co-author of ASCD's four volume series *Habits of Mind*. He emphasizes that...

> *"We must help students think powerfully about ideas, learn to critique as well as support others' thinking, and become thoughtful problem solvers and decision makers. The habits of mind provide a set of behaviors that discipline intellectual processes. They can be an integral component of instruction in every school subject, and they may determine achievement of any worthy goal as one moves out into life."[13]*

Skills for the 21st Century

Basic Skills	Thinking Skills	Personal Qualities
Reads, writes, performs arithmetic and mathematical operations	Thinks critically, makes decisions, solves problems, visualizes, knows how to learn and reason	Displays responsibility, self-esteem, sociability, self-management, integrity, and honesty

Basic Skills

Reads, writes, performs arithmetic and mathematical operations

READING
locates, understands, and interprets written information in prose and in documents

WRITING
communicates thoughts, and messages in writing, and creates documents such as letters, directions, manuals, reports, graphs, and flow charts

ARITHMETIC/MATHEMATICS
performs basic computations and approaches practical problems by choosing appropriately from a variety of mathematical techniques

LISTENING
receives, attends to, interprets, and responds to verbal messages and other cues

SPEAKING
organizes ideas and communicates orally, speaking well

Thinking Skills

Thinks critically, makes decisions, solves problems, visualizes, knows how to learn and reason

CREATIVE THINKING
generates new ideas

DECISION MAKING
specifies goals and constraints, generates alternatives, considers risks, evaluates and chooses best alternative

PROBLEM SOLVING
recognizes problems, devises and implements plans of action

SEEING THINGS IN THE MIND'S EYE
organizes and processes symbols, pictures, graphs, objects, and other information

KNOWING HOW TO LEARN
uses efficient learning techniques to acquire and apply new knowledge and skills

REASONING
discovers a rule or principle underlying the relationship between two or more objects and applies it when solving a problem

Personal Qualities

Displays responsibility, self-esteem, sociability, self-management, integrity, and honesty

RESPONSIBILITY
exerts a high level of effort and perseveres toward goal attainment

SELF-ESTEEM
believes in own self-worth and maintains a positive view of self

SOCIABILITY
demonstrates understanding, friendliness, adaptability, empathy, and politeness in group settings

SELF-MANAGEMENT
assesses self accurately, sets personal goals, monitors progress, and exhibits self-control

INTEGRITY/HONESTY
chooses ethical course of action

Costa and his co-author Bena Kallick define habits of mind as <u>intelligent behaviors that are often evident in successful students and adults</u>. They identify the following sixteen dispositions that can be learned:

▶ Persisting

▶ Managing impulsivity

▶ Listening with understanding and empathy

▶ Thinking flexibly

▶ Thinking about thinking (metacognition)

▶ Striving for accuracy

▶ Questioning and posing problems

▶ Applying past knowledge to new situations

▶ Thinking and communicating with clarity and precision

▶ Gathering data through all senses

▶ Creating, imagining, innovating

▶ Responding with wonderment and awe

▶ Taking responsible risks

▶ Finding humor

▶ Thinking interdependently

▶ Remaining open to continuous learning.

These habits of mind provide another layer to the necessary collaborative skills needed in today's world. They not only can be integrated into curriculum and consciously taught, but developed and assessed. They deepen the richness of classroom and school community interaction.

We recommend that high school teaching staffs examine the **Habits of Mind Developmental Series**, as researched and authored by Arthur Costa and Bena Kallick.

Calling Forth Effective Global Leaders

Imagine a world where nations commit themselves to a set of core values that show regard for the rights, dignity and common good of others; where unselfish concern and empathy are shown; where honesty and integrity are valued; where leaders exhibit caring for the environment; and where leaders commit and adhere to a common set of goals in the promotion of world peace, human rights, and the eradication of hunger and disease. The story I'm about to share took place with a group of high school students at the International School of Dakar (ISD), Dakar, Senegal. It illustrates the power of the Tribes process and the impact it had on our students and their role as future leaders.

After many years as a teacher and administrator in the United States, I moved overseas to continue my career in international education. I quickly came to realize that the youngsters attending international schools were different than those I had worked with at home. Fully bi-lingual, resilient, politically astute young people, they had a level of cross cultural understanding that was astounding. Their knowledge of hot-button issues like poverty, religion, war, disease, and human rights, was not simply an article in *Newsweek* or *National Geographic*, it was real. They were seeing and experiencing these issues first hand, and furthermore, their personal insight placed them in a perfect position to become positive global leaders. Since it was likely that the majority of these kids would work and live overseas as adults, the significance of offering them leadership training seemed vital. With hope and enthusiasm, ISD's teachers and administration committed to a three-day, off-campus retreat to include every high school student and our entire high school faculty.

Because we were a Tribes school, we knew the power of "group process" and we felt strongly that our students must not only learn about leadership, but also experience it. Further, we believed that for the process to work, the participants must feel comfortable, safe, and a sense of belonging before addressing tough issues. We knew that in real-life situations, leaders seldom trusted one another or experienced a sense of belonging before tackling burning issues, and for this reason successful negotiations were rare. We believed that if our kids could experience the power of inclusion and see it as a necessary first-step to managing conflict and reaching consensus, they

—*Continued on page 40*

Judith Fenton, M.Ed.

Judith has taken the process of Tribes to more than seven countries abroad as the director of the International School of Dakar, Senegal, the deputy head of Carol Morgan School, Santo Domingo, Dominican Republic, as a teacher at the American School in Shanghai, China, and as a conference speaker in several South American countries. Judith is a seasoned Certified Tribes TLC Trainer and educator who firmly believes that in our rapidly changing world, the need to feel connected and to be resilient is more critical than ever.

—Continued from page 39

would hopefully carry this principle forward as global leaders. Three goals were established to carry out our on-going mission:

1.   To experience the stage of inclusion and understand the critical first-step it plays in solving real-life problems

2.   To practice leadership skills within the stage of influence and be able to approach conflict in non-aggressive manner (problem solving, decision making, conflict resolution, consensus, collaboration)

3.   To commit to and demonstrate competencies essential to becoming an effective global leader, namely: reflection, introspection, sensitivity to emotions and cultures, and a capacity to see beyond oneself.

Although no formal data was collected, our faculty met daily during the workshop to reflect upon participants' strengths and needs. We also held numerous conversations with our students to hear their reactions to the training.

▶   100% of our students connected on a meaningful, personal level. Students who had been ignored previously were embraced and made to feel welcome. Even our shyest students came out of their shells. In the end, we concluded that the process works for all kinds of students and that they all have the same human need for connection.

▶   Although all learned to approach conflict in a non-aggressive manner, our juniors and seniors made deeper, more lasting connections to the process than their younger peers, perhaps due to maturity. The upper classmen could clearly articulate the importance of inclusion as a precursor to solving problems.

▶   As we neared the end of the training, our seniors began to realize their full potential as honorable, caring citizens and leaders capable of building bridges to global interdependence. Their conversations took on a more serious tone. At the conclusion of the training we asked them to make a life map depicting what they would do, individually, to contribute to the world. Their maps were so sophisticated that we shared them with parents and friends at their graduation ceremony.

> ▶ Gains made on the competencies essential to becoming effective global leaders were noteworthy.

Throughout on-going implementation of the process in our high school we concluded that the Tribes collaborative skills provide a natural bridge to leadership, for not only our students, but for all kids!

Will our students become positive, effective global leaders? Will they make a difference? As an experienced educator who was fortunate enough to work with them, I believe with all my heart many will. Having consistently demonstrated unselfish concern, cultural sensitivity and empathy, they possess the ingredients to be caring, effective leaders. Add maturity and confidence—and the circle is complete.

DEVELOPING FUTURES OF PROMISE[13]

Indeed, even considering how to prepare high school students for futures in today's world is an overwhelming thought. To compound that, consider poverty, unemployment, lack of health care, inadequate childcare, community crime, divorce, alcoholism, drug abuse, and stress that surround many young adults in our classrooms. Today's world is harsh for many young people.

Yet there are those who somehow live through deprivation, adversity and stress more easily than others. Even in the same family one wonders why some children do well while others raised in the same environment fail? Who or what helps them to grow up to "love well, work well, play well and expect well?"[14]

The answer is to be found in human resiliency research—which, simply said, is the universal capacity for healthy human development. Unlike the typical problem focused pathology approach that diagnoses what is wrong with kids (risk factors), resiliency research identifies the positive factors in children's lives that enable them to develop their innate human strengths and to do well in life in spite of inordinate stress and difficulties. Among the most powerful and informative longitudinal studies are those conducted by Emmy Werner and Ruth Smith who followed the lives of 700 children for 40 years from birth to adulthood—all of whom were growing up in the midst of multiple risk factors such as neglect, poverty, war, parental abuse, physical handicaps, depression, criminality and alcoholism. A consistent, yet amazing, finding *was* that most *of the high-risk youth who exhibited serious coping problems in adolescence, had managed to turn around their lives by mid-life. Only one out six of the adults (32–40 years old) were still struggling.*[15] The greater number had developed the capacity to face and overcome life difficulties. Werner described the cohort of children as "vulnerable but invincible."[16]

Resilience is the capacity to meet and handle the difficulties, crises adversity and stress that inevitably we all face in life. It enables one not only to work through difficult situations but to survive, bounce back and move on positively again and again. Resilience is not a quality possessed by some and not by others. Its strengths transcend culture, age, gender and socioeconomic status. Human development scholar Bonnie Benard emphasizes:

> *"From a resilience perspective, the capacity for healthy development and successful learning is innate in all people. It is an inborn developmental wisdom that naturally motivates individuals to meet their human needs for love, belonging, respect, identity, mastery, challenge and meaning."*[17]

A set of four strengths or attributes have been identified in resilient children, youth and adults. The set consists of...

▶ **Autonomy/Independence:** an internal locus of control, a strong sense of , self-efficacy, identity, self-discipline, self-awareness, mindfulness and control of impulses.

▶ **Social Competence:** pro-social behaviors, relatedness, empathy, caring, compassion, altruism, responsiveness, communication skills and a sense of humor.

▶ **A Sense of Purpose and Future:** healthy expectations, goal directedness, belief in a bright and compelling future, optimism, hope, special interests, motivation, persistence, hardiness, a sense of anticipation, a sense of coherence.

▶ **A Capacity to Problem-Solve:** abstract and constructive thinking, a capacity to analyze and reflect on possibilities and creative solutions; flexibility.

Yes, you met the four strengths earlier in Chapter 2 of this book. Amazingly enough, they are the same as the developmental tasks adolescents are determined to achieve, consciously or unconsciously. Moreover, they are identified by two very separate fields of studies: the longitudinal research on individual resilience, and the psychology of adolescent development. The fact that the positive life competencies are the *very same* gives high schools all the more reason to create positive school cultures. All students need to have abundance of developmental learning opportunities during their high school years.

Take a moment now and think of those times in your own life when somehow you were able to move through a difficult situation or period of time, when you were able to face a seemingly insurmountable difficulty and overcome it—due to your own resilient strengths.

Congruence of Human Development Tasks and Attributes to Competencies Needed in the 21st Century World of Work

HUMAN DEVELOPMENT ADOLESCENT TASKS	RESILIENCY ATTRIBUTES	WORKPLACE COMPETENCIES
Autonomy	Autonomy	Self-efficacy Self-management Mindfulness
Social Competence	Social Competence	Caring + Supportive Trustworthy + Ethical Communication Skills Collaborative
Sense of Purpose/Future	Sense of Purpose/Future	Open to experiences Visualizes Goal oriented Motivated Optimistic
Problem Solving	Problem Solving	Constructive thinking Creativity Conflict resolution

The tasks and resiliency attributes certainly are the competencies needed for success in the world of work!

IT TAKES CHANGING THE QUALITY OF THE SYSTEMS

As highlighted earlier in Chapter 2, our process for learning communities has been based on the developmental ecology of respected Professor Urie Bronfenbrenner, meaning that: *Human development is an ongoing transaction between each of us and the systems surrounding our lives.*[18] The quality of the systems in which we find ourselves affect the quality of our lives. Thus, it is the daily environments within high schools, families and community that support or undermine students' social, emotional, intellectual, physical and spiritual development and learning. Positive qualities in systems are known as *protective factors,* in that they not only protect (or buffer) children, youth and all of us from risk, but help to call forth the innate strengths and personal best in all. That's why we also call them *factors for success.*

That's what we'll discover by flying over to the next chapter written by Bonnie Benard! Com'on...

4

*Assuring Futures
of Promise*

4 *Assuring Futures of Promise*

IN THIS CHAPTER YOU WILL

▶ Learn what smart schools do to help students develop the attributes of resiliency

▶ Realize how the resilient strengths support individual achievement, health and life-long well-being

▶ Learn how your high school can assure *futures of promise* for all learners

A Research Perspective

Bonnie Benard, MSW

Bonnie, a Senior Program Associate at the West Ed Regional Educational Laboratory, is an internationally known figure in the field of prevention and youth development theory, policy, and practice. She is credited with introducing resiliency theory and applications in the fields of education and prevention. Her most recent publication, **Resiliency: What We Have Learned** (2004) synthesizes a decade and more of resiliency research. Her work and insights have long served as guiding principles for the caring principles and culture of Tribes Learning Communities.

> Resiliency requires changing hearts and minds.[1]
> —BONNIE BENARD

CREATING RESILIENT HIGH SCHOOL SYSTEMS BY ENGAGING THE DEVELOPMENTAL WISDOM OF ADOLESCENCE

Bonnie Benard

In an age of standards-driven educational reform and get tough on youth social policies, we must ask, where is human development? We see, once again, human development (referred to as youth development during the adolescence years), pushed aside as a "nice" but nonessential concern for education and prevention. Ironically, this is happening at a time when the best of social and behavioral science research is consistently documenting that the most effective, efficient, and joyful approach to meeting standards and preventing health-risk behaviors in young people is by creating environments in our schools that meet adolescents' developmental needs and thereby engage their intrinsic motivation.

Brain science, multiple intelligence research, motivational psychology, effective schools research, child and youth development, and long-term studies of individual resilience in the face of risk and challenge are finding that healthy development and successful learning are the product of critical developmental supports and opportunities. However, it is to resilience research—the long-term studies of positive human development in the face of environmental threat, challenge, stress, risk, and adversity—that educators and preventionists can turn to find the most powerful research-based answer to what these supports and opportunities should look like for all young people in all schools. They consist of three simple and common-sensical principles of effectiveness:

▶ caring relationships

▶ positive expectation messages and beliefs, and

▶ opportunities for participation and contribution.[2]

CARING RELATIONSHIPS

Caring relationships are the supportive connections to others that model and support healthy development and well-being. Ultimately, they weave the fabric of a safe and resilient school. *Caring relationships* have been identified by the human resilience longitudinal studies, program evaluation research, the recent National Longitudinal Study of Adolescent Health,[3] qualitative studies, and personal stories as the most critical factor protecting healthy and successful child and youth development even in the face of multiple risks.

Caring relationships are those of mutual trust in which someone is there for a youth. This is demonstrated by having adults in the school who take an active interest in who the young person is, being respectful, having compassion for a youth's life circumstances, paying attention, actively listening to and talking with the young person. During adolescence the peer group emerges as a critical provider of this essential support.

HIGH EXPECTATION MESSAGES

High expectation messages refer to the consistent communication of direct and indirect messages affirming that the young person can and will succeed. These messages are at the core of caring relationships and reflect a teacher's, other adult's or friend's belief in the youth's innate resilience and ability to learn. Resilience research shows that positive expectation messages are a pivotal protective factor in the family, school, and/or community environments of youth who have overcome the odds.

In addition to this challenging and supportive message, a high expectation approach conveys firm guidance—clear boundaries and the structure necessary for creating a sense of safety and predictability—not to enforce compliance and control but to allow for the freedom and exploration necessary to develop autonomy, identity, and self-control. A high expectation approach is also individually-based and strengths-focused. This means identifying each young person's unique strengths, gifts, and callings and nurturing them as well as using them to work on needs or concerns.

OPPORTUNITIES FOR PARTICIPATION AND CONTRIBUTION

Resilience research has documented the positive developmental outcomes, including reductions in health risk behaviors, and increases in *academic success factors,* that result when youth are given the chance—to belong to a group; to have responsibilities; to be involved in relevant, engaging, and respected activities; to have a voice and choice; to make decisions, to plan; and to have ownership and leadership. Most importantly, resilience research and outcome evaluations of service learning and cooperative learning find positive academic and social outcomes when youth are given the opportunity to give back their gift—to be of service to other people, to nature, to their community and world.

Whenever and wherever you find a school achieving positive academic outcomes for **all youth**—not just the few—you will find this commonsense philosophy driving the mission of the school.[2]

You can make it! You have everything it takes to achieve your dreams. I'll be there to support you.

Providing young people with opportunities for meaningful participation is a natural outcome of schools and classrooms that convey high expectations.

It is no coincidence that resilience and other social and behavioral research continually identify these three characteristics as supporting healthy and successful outcomes. It is precisely through caring relationships, high expectation messages, and opportunities for participation and contribution that high schools can engage students' intrinsic motivation—their drive to meet their developmental needs for safety, love, belonging, respect, mastery, challenge, power and identity—and ultimately, for meaning.

The people and places most often identified in the resilience research as providing these three "protective" or factors for success—thus meeting students' developmental needs—were teachers and schools. In the words of Emmy Werner,

"One of the wonderful things we see now in adulthood is that these children really remember one or two teachers who made the difference. They mourn some of those teachers more than they do their own family members because what went out of their lives was a person who looked beyond outward experience, their behavior, and their often times unkempt appearance, and saw the promise."[4]

Having high expectations assumes that 'one size never fits all.'

Resilience research has also found that schools that not only have these *turnaround teachers* but that have fair and equitably enforced rules, lots of and varied opportunities to succeed, and that give students a decision-making voice and opportunities to work with and be helpful to others, become safe havens for students to develop cognitively, socially, emotionally, physically, and spiritually. In the words of one student, *"School was my church, it was my religion. It was constant, the only thing that I could count on every day... I would not be here if it was not for school."* In other words, they become places where students' developmental needs are honored and placed centrally in the mission of the school. For schools and especially high schools the central mission, culture, structures and pedagogy assures:

- ▶ Safety

- ▶ Love and belonging

- ▶ Respect

- ▶ Mastery and challenge

- ▶ Power and authority, and

- ▶ Meaning

Safety refers to both physical and emotional safety. For healthy development and successful learning to occur adolescents must feel safe in their classrooms and schools. Brain research tells us that when children do NOT feel safe, their brain stays in a vicious fight-flight circuit. In order to engage higher order thinking skills and creativity, a high school student must feel safe.

The gut response measures often taken by politicians and some school administrations to school safety often become barriers to achieving real school safety. The hiring of more police officers and security guards; installing sophisticated weapon detection and student surveillance devices; toughening punishments for children who misbehave; and attempting to identify students at risk often only further marginalize youth that are "different"—making them feel even more unsafe. Investigation indicated that Columbine High School students Eric Harris and Dylan Kliebold did not feel safe in their schools. Real safety only comes through building an inclusive school community in which diversity is honored and all students are welcomed into the circle. A first step in creating a safe classroom and school is inviting students to create and honor their own agreements/ground rules... such as occurs in schools using the process of Tribes Learning Communities.

Love and belonging refers to basic *affiliation and attachment* needs—the need to be connected to people and places that ultimately gives all of our lives meaning and hope. Meeting academic standards requires starting with relationships. No quote has ever stated this more eloquently than the following words of Nel Noddings:

> "At a time when the traditional structures of caring have deteriorated, schools must be places where teachers and students live together, talk with each other, take delight in each other's company. My guess is that when schools focus on what really matters in life, the cognitive ends we now pursue so painfully and artificially will be achieved somewhat more naturally... It is obvious that children will work harder and do things—even odd things like adding fractions—for people they love and trust."[5]

What does this mean for your school? It means we must put *relationships* at the heart of what we do in our classrooms and schools. There are hundreds of ways to do this: *making one-to-one connections* with a student—even for a few seconds is a powerful acknowledgement; shaking hands, actively listening, being available, showing an interest, noticing something they're doing right, and so on. In some high schools, every student has an *available adult friend* who checks in with him or her at least once a week.

In addition to structuring student-teacher connections, we have to create inclusive classroom communities where *all* students feel invited in. Collaborative classroom learning groups, peer-assistance programs, upper-classmen/freshmen orientation groups, artist-to-artists, techies to younger techies—even challenged students relating to younger youth—are critical strategies for building belonging. It means paying special attention to who's not currently included and including them. Healthy development requires that students stay connected; relationships must be maintained and responsibilities honored.

Class size reduction can be an effective support for teacher-student relationship-building. It gives classroom teachers more and more opportunities to get to know and connect with their students. At the high school level, it means breaking up large schools into smaller schools such as schools-within-schools, academies, and career magnets. In classrooms, it means that each student is a member in an on-going tribe. Relationships cannot happen in large anonymous groups.

It is human nature to create our own small groupings because we are all seeking safety and belonging. As educators we need to create small heterogeneous groupings, not only for students but also for teachers, in which everyone has a place and diversity is honored as it is Tribes Learning Communities.

Respect The need or drive to be respected—to be acknowledged and honored for who we are is a powerful motivator. Lack of respect—along with lack of caring and boredom—are usually the top three reasons school dropouts give for leaving school. May I suggest that if we want good outcomes in the traditional three R's: Reading, Riting, Rithmetic, we need an additional three R's: Relationship, Respect, and Responsibility. Debra Meier's turnaround school, Central Park East in Harlem, put both relationships and respect at the heart of her school's mission. She wrote,

> *"Maybe mutual respect is what we're all looking for—which means feeling sure the other person acknowledges us, sees us for who we are—as equal value and importance. When there's enough respect, perhaps we're able to give up tight control over our youngsters, and give them more space to make their own decisions, including their own mistakes."*[6]

There are hundreds of ways school staff can show respect to students. Primarily, however, if we want students to be respectful to us, we must model it first. Attentive listening and speaking nonjudgmentally, shaking hands, using a Namaste greeting which means, "I

If we want good outcomes in the traditional three R's: Reading, Riting, Rithmetic, we need an additional three R's: Relationship, Respect, and Responsibility.

greet the soul within you." Once again, a small group process like Tribes is a powerful structure for promoting a respectful climate in which teasing, harassment, bullying, and other forms of violence are not tolerated.

Mastery and challenge The drive for accomplishment—to be good at something—is inborn in all of us. Where we have our problems in schooling is that we have very narrowly defined what that "something" can be. We have assigned greater value to mathematical and linguistic intelligences and in terms of the physical—to sports participation than dance—than the rest of these intelligences. This is what our culture values and yes, students need to learn. However, what Howard Gardner and his disciples of multiple intelligences tell us is that we need to use the strengths—the intelligences students are especially good in—to address the areas of challenge. To have someone with the power of a teacher acknowledge your gifts is an incredible motivator that facilitates learning in the challenging areas. I would like to point out that the strengths especially found in resilience literature include competencies in all these areas—especially the inter- and intra-personal areas and creativity and outlets for the imagination.

So what does this mean for schools?

It means we have to create opportunities for success in each of these intelligences. We need to do activities in school in which we learn the interests, strengths, gifts, and dreams of each of our students. We need after school clubs *where students* can explore their interests in small groups. What about sports teams open to any student that wanted to play? We need to value each of the gifts our young people bring. Our artists need to have their work displayed and honored as much as the athletes have their trophies displayed. I might mention that in Columbine High School the sports trophies were showcased in the front hall—the artwork down a back corridor. Sports pages in the yearbook were in color, a national debating team and other clubs in black and white. The homecoming king was a football player on probation for burglary.

Challenge is a related drive to mastery but refers more to the idea of taking risks. Adolescents especially need to have opportunities to take *healthy risks*. Do you know *risk-taking* is often on lists of risk factors? It is also one of the characteristics of successful people. We now have a wonderful study of *adventure learning* that illustrates how this approach (also referred to as Outward Bound and outdoor experience programs) not only helps adolescents achieve all of the developmental tasks—autonomy and independence, social competency, a sense of purpose, and problem-solving, but positive academic outcomes as well—even though it is a nonacademic approach.[7] Why is this so powerful? Among many attributes, adventure programs create a restorative environment—especially through group process and support—in which most of adolescent developmental needs are met.

Research also makes the case for experiential learning—hands on, working in groups under adults supervision and facilitation, and time for reflection. Sound familiar? These are also the characteristics of the process of Tribes.

Power and autonomy are the needs not only to find one's *identity* but to discover oneself as an autonomous person. We're talking here about self-efficacy—knowing you can take action and influence your environment. Youth who feel a sense of their own worth and power don't need guns to feel powerful; they don't need to hurt others or themselves to prove they exist and matter.

How do we meet student's need to have some power and control? We give them opportunities to participate and contribute in an ongoing way in our classrooms and schools. Once again, while approaches like cooperative learning, peer helping, and service learning meet this drive, the bottom line is having personal control—chances to make decisions about their own schooling. This means we as teachers and administrators don't impose our ideas of what students need—*we ask them*. This is the simple strategy of asking students their opinions, their needs, their ideas—and acting on them—not tokenizing them. Having your students create the governing rules of the classroom is a key strategy. When a problem develops, we can bring the students in on it, inviting their ideas of how we—as a classroom community—can solve it. In order to develop healthy psychological autonomy, adolescents need safety and the room to grow *within* the structure of a caring community.

Meaning Last—and certainly not least but probably the most important!—is the search for meaning that lies at the heart of every human life. Humans, including the adolescent variety, have the need to find meaning in what they do. Our genetic code makes us meaning-makers, constructors of our own knowledge. We must find purpose and relevance in what we do or we experience a *disconnect*—a sense of alienation from our true *sense of calling*. The loss of meaning is probably one of the major underlying reasons

The search for meaning lies at the heart of every human life.

—BONNIE BENARD

that 40% of our teens have unmet mental health needs—especially depression and stress. Government figures from 1998 show reductions in almost all teen health-risk behaviors: violence and alcohol, tobacco use, and drug abuse. However, depression, suicidality, and suicide are statistics that are *not* going down.

High schools need to be safe places for the exploration of the critical existential questions that drive not only the adolescent search for meaning but all of our quests for a meaningful life.[8]

▶ *Who am I? What is my true nature?*—This is the search for identity.

▶ *What do I love? What are my interests, and dreams?*—This is the search for autonomy and meaning.

▶ *How shall I live? What values do I wish to live by?*—This is the search for morality.

▶ *What is my gift to the family of the earth? What are my strengths and gifts? How can I make a difference?*—This is the search for purpose.

These questions of purpose are not particularly comfortable for schools. In fact, purpose is primarily taught in the curriculum through goal- setting and decision-making, and career exploration—most often with strictly rational techniques. We need to include the spiritual dimension—the above questions—if we are to help students make the deepest connection of all—to see themselves as interconnected to others, to nature, and to life itself.

How do schools do this? Some schools use a council process, a circle or group process that creates a climate of safety, respect, and honor to reflect and share in community these deep yearnings.[9] Tribes Learning Community groups accomplish this by sustaining the caring community culture of connectedness.

Educators can also provide experiences that honor the questions and allow students to give their gifts to the world through creative expression—theater, dance, photography, video production, art, music, storytelling, and creative writing. Research on the arts is documenting the power of creative expression to achieve the developmental tasks of adolescence—as well as positive academic outcomes.[10] Similarly, research on *community service learning,* in which students can connect what they learn in schools to the real world and see themselves as active contributors, also achieves the developmental tasks and promotes academic success.[11]

The common denominator running through the above strategies and approaches that meet adolescent developmental needs and thus help them achieve their developmental tasks is that of small group process. Group process is the vehicle for creating a caring community—for students and for educators. In fact, Thomas Sergiovanni writes, *"The need for community is universal. A sense of belonging, of continuity, of being connected to others and to ideas and values that make ourselves meaningful and significant—these needs are shared by all of us."*[12]

Schools will be transformed only when this community-building process is implemented for teachers as well as for students. The critical challenge for the 21st century does not lie in mastering this piece of information or that technology. It lies in creating connectedness—in building schools across the nation that tap the innate developmental wisdom that is our shared humanity, connecting us to each other and to our shared web of life.

5 Weaving Essential
Principles to
Recreate the System

5 Weaving Essential Principles to Recreate the System

IN THIS CHAPTER YOU WILL

▶ Recognize the limitations of the 19th century high school model

▶ Consider some of the many things that perpetuate resistance to change

▶ Learn about the National Association of Secondary School Principals recommendations for reform of traditional high schools

▶ Gain an understanding of the Tribes Learning Community process to accomplish and sustain positive change

▶ Contrast how a competing issue can affect the priority student-centered focus of the high school learning community

Reflecting on the 186 year old high school model

"Many high schools face the prospect of diminished relevance in a future in which time and space, as traditionally used in education, will exert dwindling influence on the ability to deliver learning. Nevertheless, high schools continue to go about their business in ways that sometimes bear startling resemblance to the flawed practices of the past. Students pursue their education largely in traditional classroom settings, taught by teachers who stand before a row of desks. Mostly these teachers lecture at students, whose main participation in class is limited to terse answers to fact-seeking questions. High schools persist in organizing instruction subject by subject with little effort to integrate knowledge. Learning continues to be dispensed in 50 minute segments, as if anything worth knowing can be transmitted to fit a precise time frame in the manner that Procrustes accommodated weary travelers in his one-size-fits-all guest bed."[2]

—BREAKING RANKS: CHANGING AN AMERICAN INSTITUTION.
NATIONAL ASSOCIATION SECONDARY SCHOOL PRINCIPALS

Back in 1821 the country's first public high school was opened in Boston for boys 12 years old or older who were from wealthy families and who could pass an entrance exam. They studied literature, science, math and history. In the late 1950s, Harvard University President James Bryant Conant, was convinced that large high schools populated by students from a wide variety of backgrounds would best serve students and society. The belief was that the one-size-fits-all high school would provide all students access to a wide array of resources, courses, extracurricular activities, support and opportunities. Over time it became evident that large high schools mostly benefit the most privileged, outgoing or driven students whereas the timid, ambivalent or those lacking in support drift or are among the more than 30 percent of U.S. students who start but never finish high school. It is particularly difficult for minorities.[3]

THE MANTRAS OF RESISTANCE

There now are 27,468 public high schools in the United States—all being pressured not only to drastically improve the education they are providing but to motivate and ready as many students as possible to go on to higher education.

Somewhat amusingly, it has often been said that reforming the 186 year old high school institution arouses as much resistance to change as ordering a teenager to clean up his room.[5]

Following is a partial list of perspectives and things that sabotage many attempts to change the American high school. Feel free also to jot down your or your colleagues observations.

▶ *Adult* nostalgia: memories of the dances, romances, football team or a favorite teacher. "The way I learned math worked for me—that's how kids still ought to learn."

▶ *The mantras of district and local educators:* "They won't let us do it!" "Not enough money, not enough equipment, the buildings are too large, too small, too old." "All kids are not capable of learning. "Parents don't care."

▶ The stress: "Oh no! Another strategic plan, state mandate, new curriculum." "Not enough time, too little professional development, too much teacher turn-over."

▶ The mandates: "We just have to get those test scores up, and show a higher AYP (annual yearly progress) rate... one way or another."

▶ Also...

▶ Also...

This is not a problem you can address by tinkering with the old model![4]
—TOM VANDER ARK

There are risks and costs to a program of action. But they are far less than the long-range risks and costs of comfortable inaction.
—JOHN F. KENNEDY

Hey, are they thinking at all about what we really need?

Carole Freehan, Ph.D.

As a Certified Tribes
TLC® Trainer and former
principal of Pearl Harbor
Kai Elementary School in
Honolulu, Hawaii, Carole
trained in-service and pre-
service teachers, clerical,
and support staff to create
a school community that
supported increased student
learning. She earned her
doctorate in Leadership
Studies and currently teaches
Educational Leadership
courses to doctoral students,
modeling the Tribes process
for future educational
leaders.

Embracing Resistance

If you have been in education for any length of time, you have experienced the following over and over. The principal gets up and starts explaining a new change that will be taking place in the coming months. You glance around the room and can read the reaction as your eyes move from face to face. "Oh, no, not again." "We did that before and it didn't work then, why should it work now?" "Just because it works at that school does not mean it will work here; we are different from them." "Wow, a new way to look at the problem, where do I sign up?" "I'm happy with the way things are, I don't see any need to change anything." "Well, it could help our situation, but aren't we rushing into things? We need to study it more." In fact, the reactions will typically run the gamut from the innovators who are all ready on the train and ready to implement the change (yesterday!) to those who are resolutely digging in their heels in their effort to resist the change to the actual saboteurs who actively work to prevent any change.

As a leader working with young adult/adult learning groups, I learned that by announcing any significant change I doomed the change to failure or at best to lip-service implementation that disappeared when I no longer focused on it. If I really wanted the change to become part of the fabric and culture of the school, I needed to approach resistance as an opportunity for the group to learn together, not as a challenge to be overpowered. Following are some of the lessons I learned about how to work with resistance and resisters:

▶ Change is a journey, not an event. Everyone processes change at his or her own rate and as a leader I had to value that process.

▶ Involve as many stakeholders as you can in the planning process for any change. Be sure to include some who are vocal in their resistance to change. Being part of the planning process can help the resistance fade. Actively seek supporters as well as those who are less enthusiastic.

> ▶ Be flexible. Although you know your ideas are good, they become better as others join in with their thoughts. Accept contributions from all and let the group collaboration process thrive.
>
> ▶ Listen to the resisters. Between their words you can hear the fear of the unknown, but by listening not only to their words but also their hearts you can often help them overcome that fear. Acknowledge their concerns.
>
> ▶ Do not to take others' resistance to change personally; conflict is a part of the change process and being able to resolve conflict constructively always helps the group learn.
>
> ▶ Realize that once you begin on the journey to change that you will have to work at it everyday, building trust within the group. The Tribes agreements are invaluable in forming the foundation for the group process, keep them foremost in mind. Working through resistance can be a bumpy road with set backs, but by working together in a collaborative and trustful manner; you can help ensure an enduring change process.

LOOKING AT RECOMMENDATIONS FOR CHANGE

The national debate on how to reform high schools is bringing an unprecedented number of recommendations for change. Among the most significant came in 1996 and 2004. In 1996 after two years of discussions with educators, researchers, principals, policymakers, teachers and students, the Commission on the Restructuring of the American High School published the outstanding document, *Breaking Ranks: Changing an American Institution*. With support from the National Association of Secondary School Principals (NASSP) and the Carnegie Foundation for the Advancement of Teaching, it listed more than 80 recommendations on changes that are necessary to prepare high school students for life in today's drastically different world of on-going rapid evolution. Then in 2004, the NASSP published *Breaking Ranks II—Strategies for Leading High School Reforms* as a resource for school principals and leaders ready to take on the challenge to "break ranks."

The latter document contains 31 recommendations considered essential for the transformation of a typical high school. The recommendations are clustered into three core areas:[6]

1. Personalization

2. Collaborative leadership and professional learning communities

3. Curriculum, Instruction and Assessment

The themes as summarized from both NASSP documents emphasize that better education depends on:

▶ personalizing the high school experience for students

▶ lending coherency to their education

▶ organizing time differently

▶ using technology at every opportune point

▶ revitalizing the ongoing professional education of teachers and administration, and

▶ enhancing leadership at every level at which it can affect teaching and learning.

AN IMPORTANT NEED EVEN FOR SMALLER SCHOOLS

Increasingly, a bandwagon of large high schools are dividing their student populations into smaller "houses" and/or separate clusters for technology, the arts, sciences, communication and other career interests. The Bill and Melinda Gates Foundation so far has contributed 734 million dollars to support smaller "personalized" high schools that accommodate no more than 600 students. Reportedly, Bill Gates says, "It's a tough sell in part because breaking up big schools really messes up the football team."[7] Our concern and that of many other educators, leaders and researchers is that the efforts need to be as much about changing the culture and learning process for adolescent students as shrinking school size. The important question to consider is: How can a learning community of 600 or even fewer inherently be any more personalized and caring than a school of 2000? A smaller high school population of 600 still means being in the midst of a crowd every day—with all seeking inclusion, recognition, identity, motivation, competency, purpose and support. Challenging curriculum as rigorous as it may be isn't all. We have only to remember what the student voices were saying and their search for belonging. Much more is needed.

Smaller structures make sense, but they also need deliberately to...

▶ focus on the students' development as well as academic learning

▶ create and sustain an inclusive and caring school culture

▶ structure the whole school into an active learning community

A smaller high school population of 600 still means being in the midst of a crowd every day.

- maximize teacher and student interaction, communication and trust

- involve teachers in continuous on-site professional development in learning and implementing sound principles and practices that correspond to and engage the diversity of students' interests and different ways of learning.

THE "WHY," "WHAT" AND "HOW" OF CHANGE

The excellent *Breaking Ranks* reports more than justify **WHY** change is necessary and **WHAT** changes are needed, but not **HOW** to make the changes happen. The NASSP authors point out that the reports are *not* primarily research documents, but are *a set of principles* and recommendations based on the experiences of many high school educators and leaders over two years of discussions. **HOW** to bring about identified changes can best be accomplished by engaging the whole faculty and school leaders, the "insiders," to work together as a Collegial Learning Community to transform their school into a dynamic learning community of educational excellence. It is far less likely that "outsiders" (contract consultants, strategic planning experts or costly management organizations) can achieve significant lasting reforms as effectively as an on-going dedicated learning community can.[8]

Yes! This is what "Engaging All by Creating High School Learning Communities" is all about!

THE CALL FOR LEARNING COMMUNITIES

The abundance of literature on high school reform recommends organizing and sustaining learning communities in which every person is actively involved in various types of action groups. Explicitly, *Breaking Ranks II* calls for a learning community where the spirit of teaching and learning *is driven by inquiry, reflection and passion.*

Dialogue on *"HOW can we"* questions, such as the following, is essential in initiating change.

- HOW can our school build learning communities like that and sustain them?

- HOW can it birth a culture of inclusion, caring, respect and trust?

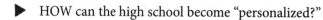

▶ HOW can the high school become "personalized?"

▶ HOW can our teachers learn to use research-based principles and practices to engage and improve student learning?

▶ HOW can reflection and a passion for learning be brought about for all students and teachers?

No longer can a student-centered focus be ignored in favor of just jumping on to one thing after another. Ted Sizer's warning noted at the beginning of this chapter needs to be taken seriously: *"A good school emerges from the creative weaving of distinctive parts into a whole cloth rather than a mindless assemblage of discrete programs, each protecting its independence."*

Our high schools have used a mindless assemblage for decades too long.

AN INTRODUCTION TO THE DEVELOPMENTAL PROCESS OF TRIBES LEARNING COMMUNITIES (TLC)

The process known simply as "Tribes" is being used throughout thousands of schools in many countries.[9] The active learning process was first implemented in elementary, middle schools and youth serving agencies. This document for high schools contains additional research and strategies that pertain specifically to the young adult population, and improvement of the system. Many high school teachers have been using the TLC Learning Community process in their classrooms throughout the years. In fact, as of this writing, more than one-hundred high school teachers and administrators have become Certified Tribes District Trainers in order to train personnel in their own schools and districts and to teach Tribes TLC® courses in universities and colleges. This capacity building approach gives ownership and professional support to the "insiders" themselves to transform their high schools into self-renewing systems.

ABOUT CALLING THE PROCESS "TRIBES!"

At times people wonder why this active learning process is known as "Tribes." It's hard to remember exactly when it happened. It just kept happening. Teachers and school leaders experiencing training kept saying, "Being in this small group is like being in a family." "No," others would add, "it's like we're a team." "Better yet—like being in a *tribe*." Participants talked about the social support, the respect for individual differences, and the sense of belonging that throughout time indigenous populations depended upon for security and their community's well-being. The word "team," denoting competition never seemed to fit as well, although today, the group development process is used widely for "team-building." The word "tribes" symbolized the affection and caring that so many of us in Western society long for today.

We urge high school teachers and university instructors to call student learning groups whatever is most appropriate to the subjects or themes being learned. Many do call their

Hey! I think we better tell our high school friends how the process became known as "Tribes."

learning groups "tribes." Others refer to them as teams, as research, inquiry, project groups—or as learning communities. No matter, it is the collaborative group process and active learning pedagogy that makes the difference so that teachers as well as students gain support and achieve.

Here's why the Tribes learning community process works and what it looks like.

THE DEVELOPMENTAL PROCESS OF TRIBES LEARNING COMMUNITIES

The validity and success of any approach proposing to maximize and support student learning, student development and system improvement depends upon the soundness of the principles and research on which the innovation is founded. The developmental process widely known as Tribes Learning Communities (or Tribes TLC) is based on four principles and beliefs—namely, that:

▶ The goal of education is to develop greatness in young human beings, active constructive citizens who are valuable contributors to society. Therefore, to educate is to call forth all aspects of a student's human development—the whole person's intellectual, social, emotional, physical and spiritual strengths and being.

▶ Intellectual, social and emotional learning is an interdependent growth process. It is influenced daily by the quality of the systems in a student's life.

▶ Schools of excellence are student-centered. They have caring cultures, supportive structures and pedagogy that correspond and respond to the level of development and diversity of students' learning needs.

▶ School reform depends upon the whole system learning and working together as a community—a school community committed to continual reflective practice toward achieving improvement and educational excellence.

These four principles and beliefs are the foundation of the dual mission and goal of Tribes Learning Community schools:

*The **Mission of Tribes Learning Communities** is to assure the healthy development of every young person so that each has the knowledge, competency and resilience to be successful in today's rapidly changing world.*

*The **Goal** is to engage all teachers, administrators, students and families in working together as a learning community that is dedicated to caring and support, active participation and positive expectations for all students.*

THE DESIGN OF THE FRAMEWORK

The design moves the four critical principles and beliefs forward into a clear framework for student development, learning and school renewal. The four-step framework is grounded in a synthesis of literature and research on human development, child and adolescent development, ideal learning cultures, resiliency, cognitive theory, multiple intelligences, cooperative group learning, constructivism, technology, multicultural/gender equity, democratic group process, classroom management, system change, professional development, reflective practice and authentic assessment.

And more can be added as we all keep on learning together!

The graphic that follows illustrates the framework and 18 researched components that pertain to the four sections. Brief discussions on the four sections and the literature on which they are based follow.

The Reasearch-Based Components of Tribes

STUDENT DEVELOPMENT AND LEARNING

- Adolescents as whole persons
- Stages of development
- Resiliency

A CARING CULTURE

- Protective Factors
- Stages of community development
- Community agreements
- Multicultural and gender equity

THE COMMUNITY OF LEARNERS

- Small group structures
- Collaborative skills
- Reflective practice

RESPONSIVE EDUCATION—
STUDENT CENTERED ACTIVE LEARNING

- Group development process
- Cognitive learning
- Multiple intelligences
- Cooperative learning
- Constructivism
- Reflective practice
- Authentic assessment
- Technology

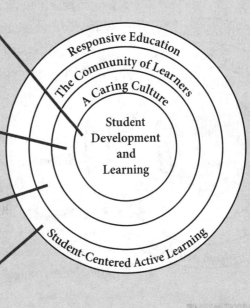

Student Development and Learning—Re-Focusing

Although the goal of the majority of schools today is to have higher student achievement on standardized tests, the promise of that happening depends upon the high school community as a system: (1) becoming student-centered,[11] (2) creating a personalized caring culture, (3) structuring communities of learners, and (4) training and supporting teachers to use active learning pedagogy (effective researched principles and practices) to reach and enable the diversity of students to learn.[12]

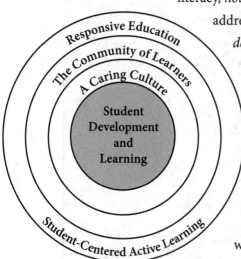

The primary focus of a Tribes Learning Community high school is *not* computer literacy, *not* a new reading program and *not* the year-end tests—although all may be addressed and sequenced into the school's action plan. *The focus is on student development and learning.* All policy, structures, decisions, curriculum and pedagogy depend upon the response to one question: *"How and to what extent will 'this' support the learning and developmental needs of these students?"* Even to begin to know how to respond to that important question, the school staff organizes itself into on-going small inquiry or learning communities. They up-date their knowledge and perspectives on youth and how today's youth learn. Rather than teachers taking courses on their own, the whole staff learns together to better identify and respond effectively to the diversity of students' cultures and needs, and to use multiple ways to accelerate the *inseparable interdependent triad: academic, social and emotional learning.*

A Caring Culture—Re-Culturing

Given that the high school now is committed to being student-centered, the next question becomes, "How do we create an ideal culture to support learning for all of our students?" Comprehensive studies verify that the culture must be safe and caring.[14] The culture in TLC school communities is based on the three well-proven principles that foster human resilience: caring relationships, positive expectations and beliefs, and opportunities for participation and contribution.[15]

The high school culture would be participative, proactive, collaborative, communal and given over to constructive meaning—all of which research considers *an ideal learning culture.*[16] The safe and caring culture is created and sustained by the students, teachers and the whole school community through daily use of four Tribes TLC agreements:

ATTENTIVE LISTENING	APPRECIATION/NO PUT DOWNS
THE RIGHT TO PASS AND PARTICIPATE	MUTUAL RESPECT

The responsibility to honor and to monitor the agreements is transferred from the teacher to the student learning groups. The agreements are posted throughout the school community and soon become norms of the culture. Classroom groups and adult meetings begin with reminders of "how we want to be while we work together." The agreements and the step-by-step community building process of Tribes assure that every student has inclusion (belonging to a small peer group), a sense of identity and value, and a community of supportive peers and adults.

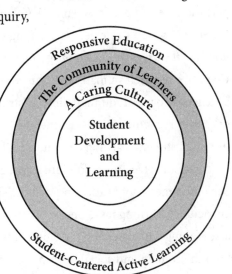

That's cool! I sure would like all that!

The Community of Learners—Re-Structuring

The culture is activated and sustained throughout the many small learning groups in which the students, teachers, administrators, support staff and parents are involved. Teacher teams (collegial learning communities) are allocated time to work on integrating curriculum into active learning strategies (inquiry, research, projects, cooperative learning and constructivism), and assessing student progress. A core leadership team—composed of the principal, several teacher leaders and the high school's or district's Certified TLC on-site trainers help to coordinate overall action planning, implementation and assessments. The leadership team also is an inquiry group, raising questions and learning together. The same inquiry group process moves throughout teacher and parent groups. Training opportunities, courses and events are identified to the leadership team. As much as possible, just as with student learning groups, integration and alignment of curriculum, problem-solving and decision-making is transferred to faculty and parent groups. The school's Certified Trainers participate and facilitate as needed. As learning areas are identified, the core leadership team is informed. Additional courses and new training may be arranged by the TLC trainers. The democratic community-building approach based on the caring culture fosters collegiality, school spirit and achievement for all.

The new model of school reform must seek to develop communities of learning grounded in communities of democratic discourse.[17]

—LINDA DARLING-HAMMOND

Responsive Education—Active Learning

"Responsive Education" is an essential pedagogy for academic achievement. It is a synthesis of artful teaching practices that respond and correspond to the critical developmental needs of age and cultural groups. Its purpose is to enable more students to acquire knowledge in a lasting brain compatible and meaningful way. Crafting a caring culture and trusting small active learning communities throughout a school gives all students opportunities to excel.[19]

CenterSource Systems (CSS) professional development courses and training prepare teachers to be responsive to how the students of the school best can learn and grow socially, emotionally, spiritually (inner development) and intellectually. Teachers learn to teach core academic content through well-proven active learning strategies (cooperative learning strategies, project learning, group inquiry, research, composition projects, debates, team performance and peer assessment). Quality CSS materials provide teachers with approximately 175 group strategies (or learning structures). Reflection on *what was learned and how it was learned* is an on-going practice after every group learning experience. Cognitive research validates that this maximizes the recall of information and concepts.[20] Teachers also use traditional direct instruction as well as active group learning. However, once they recognize and assess the positive results of active group learning, the majority use small student learning communities (SLCs) as much as possible.

A set of twelve group skills are learned so that students can work well together. Separate time is not needed to teach the skills. They are demonstrated and woven into curriculum learning tasks one or two at a time as "social learning objectives" that students assess along with assessing the "content learning objective." The responsibility to achieve both the content and social learning objectives is transferred by the teacher to the SLCs at the beginning of the academic task. The partnership role of students and teacher working consistently together institutionalizes the culture and "responsive education" pedagogy, and moves the collaborative school community toward significant school improvement and higher performance.

> Rather than being powerless and dependent on the institution, learners need to be empowered to think and learn for themselves. Thus, learning needs to be conceived of as something a learner does, not something that is done to a learner.[18]
>
> —CATHERINE FOSNOT

Responsive Education
The Community of Learners
A Caring Culture
Student Development and Learning
Student-Centered Active Learning

Is your school student-centered?   Oh yes! Of course it is!

It is likely that 90% of high school leaders when asked that question also will reply affirmatively. Yet, how can they tell?

A school is *not* student-centered unless the caring *culture*, the personalized *structure* of learning communities and process of *instruction* match learners' needs and ways of learning.

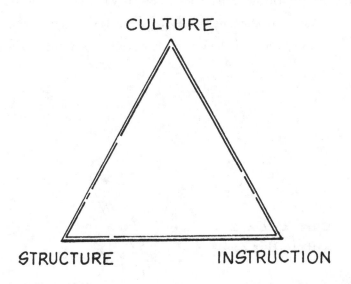

The NASSP *Breaking Ranks* reports emphasize use of this same triad as articulated in the process of Tribes for student success and school improvement:[21]

Michael Fullan, respected school reform scholar concurs that: *"The main reason that change fails to occur... on any scale, and does not get sustained when it does, is that the infrastructure is weak, unhelpful, or working at cross purposes. By the infrastructures I mean the next layers above whatever unit [student learning] we are focusing on. In terms of successive levels, for example, a teacher cannot sustain change if he or she is working in a negative school culture; similarly, a school can initiate and implement successful change, but cannot sustain it if it is operating in a less than helpful district."*[22]

A WARNING TO HEED

Sustaining and protecting the student-centered focus and the "breaking ranks" transition, which the dedicated high school learning community is working on throughout several years, is not always a smooth sailing adventure. In the midst of it all an assortment of other district, local political or funding issues may slip in as "our priority now." It may be new standards and tests, state requirements, computer technology, a union strike, equity issues, etc. Whatever the new issue may be, if it becomes the over-riding focus of the high school it tends to drive and influence everything off the student-centered focus of the system... including the essential triad—the high school culture, structures and instruction.

We would like you to take a few moments to prove something to yourself. Following are two columns, the one on the left labeled "Student Learning." In that column there are a few notes on what the culture, structure and instruction would be like in a truly student-centered high school. The focus in the right side column is "High Stakes Testing." Feel free to write in a different priority issue that your school may now have. Ask yourself, "What would the culture (ways of relating, norms, feelings, spirit) within your high school be like in contrast to the left side column?" Jot down a few descriptive words in the column on the right.

But our school is just about curriculum, homework and tests!

Sure, it's OK to write in this book!

	Focus: Student Learning	Focus: High Stakes Testing
CULTURE	caring and supportive personalized positive expectations mutual respect appreciation inclusion	
STRUCTURE	student peer groups collegial teacher groups collaborative interaction democratic process	
INSTRUCTION	active learning/participatory meaningful peer learning and teaching	

Jot down what you learned in doing this—or conclusions you may have.

Then think about the structures for learning. What would the faculty be doing? Working on? Is there a sense of community, collegiality? Finally, what would the instruction or the teaching process and curriculum be like?

I know which school I'd rather be in.

And not dropping out of!

Oh, yes! I know I
need more than
high test scores
in life!

What if... 21st century high school learning communities defined standards in terms of the knowledge *and* abilities that students could demonstrate or apply?

What if... assessment was about students being able to reflect on the progress they were making throughout four years in becoming competent young adults in many aspects of their individuality? Think back to the SCANS report list of competencies and skills needed for the world of work, and the attributes of resiliency that assure well-being in life.

What if... assessments could reflect on their capacity for abstract/constructive thinking, social competency, leadership, problem-solving and applications of academic knowledge?

Never for a moment think that we do not urge all schools to define *realistic standards* to assess academic learning. The tragedy, however, is that the narrow focus on curriculum, high stake standards and tests dismisses the whole development, well-being, interests and futures of high school young adults. It ignores and disavows the connection of social, emotional, physical and spiritual growth to intellectual competency and achievement. The hundreds of comprehensive research studies assembled by the Collaborative for Academic, Social and Emotional Learning (CASEL) and literature from the educational field repeatedly tell us that *good education is more than achieving higher test scores.*[24]

Of equal importance should be the monitoring and mentoring of youth's *interdependent* essential strengths—social emotional competency and resiliency—that motivate and lead young adults to purposeful and meaningful intellectual learning, school achievement and success in life as competent well-rounded citizens.

We appreciate the clarity that Nel Noddings, respected retired Professor of Child Education from Stanford University, brings to the dilemma. She writes...

"In direct opposition to the current emphasis on academic standards, a national curriculum and national assessment, I have argued that our main educational aim should be to encourage the growth of competent, caring, loving and loveable people. Our society does not need to make its children first in the world in mathematics and science. It needs to care for its children—to reduce violence, to respect honest work of every kind, to reward excellence at every level, to ensure a place for every child and emerging adult in the economic and social world, and to produce people who can care for their own families and contribute effectively to their communities."[25]

None of us can discover new
oceans unless we risk losing
sight of the old shore!

6

*Creating the
Personalized
Caring Culture*

Creating the Personalized Caring Culture

IN THIS CHAPTER YOU WILL

▶ Realize why a caring community culture is the essential first step to accelerate learning and development for high school youth

▶ Learn how the Tribes Learning Community process activates the components of an ideal learning culture

▶ Learn how to personalize classrooms and the high school system by creating and sustaining caring and support, high expectations and meaningful participation for all

▶ Recognize how fairness, equity and social justice affect the personalization of a high school

> It is difficult to think of a reform initiative of significance that can proceed successfully without understanding and attention to the culture of the individual schools.[1]
>
> —JOHN GOODLAD

THE IMPORTANCE OF CREATING A CARING CULTURE

Growing healthy and capable young adults is somewhat like growing geraniums. Whether you have a green thumb or not, plants have little chance to grow unless they are in rich soil and watered well. It just won't do to bring home a bright new geranium and wedge it into the old pot of soil left by a plant that just withered and died.

Getting ready to develop the personal best in high school youth works the same way. For all to bloom and do well, nutrients for growth must be continually available and released all day long. Growing plants in good soil and students in a *nurturing culture* means they do not need one-by-one "fixing." There are too many in the greenhouse to give all individual attention, so in the vernacular of schools, "many will fall through the cracks." Within greenhouses that have rich cultures the whole batch will bloom—each in their own time, radiance and uniqueness.

Look again at the four circle illustration. The shading now is in the **caring culture** circle surrounding the high school's focus on **student development and learning.** A caring culture must be established and activated throughout

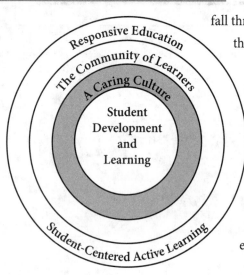

The circles, from outer to inner, read:
Responsive Education
The Community of Learners
A Caring Culture
Student Development and Learning
Student-Centered Active Learning

the whole school. It is the nurturing environment that supports positive relationships in the **community of learners,** and **responsive education** (student-centered active learning) in classrooms. The student-centered trio is the essential *infrastructure to engage all* and to raise the whole high school system to educational and developmental excellence.

I think somehow we realized that but never knew clearly how to make it happen.

It requires that each student be known well. Student "anonymity" has been the most consistent criticism of America's high schools. It must end, whatever it takes.

—TED SIZER

DESIGNING THE HIGH SCHOOL CULTURE

Given that the focus for high schools today needs to be on *each student's learning, abilities and potential,* creating a caring school culture is critical. It is the only way to **personalize** the high school system whether small or large in size.

Highly respected educator, Ted Sizer, asserts:

> *"It requires that each student be known well. Student 'anonymity' has been the most consistent criticism of America's high schools. It must end, whatever it takes."*[2]

In the earlier chapters of this book we listened to the voices of students expressing longings for belonging, social relationships, closer communication with teachers, safe and caring school environments, meaningful curriculum, active real-world learning, team learning, projects, fairness, less homework, less stress and someone to talk to about a concern or the future.

"Standards-based reform" does emphasize the alignment of *curriculum, instruction and assessment,* but disregards two very important factors that affect student learning, and according to the NASSP *Breaking Ranks* study, must be addressed.[3] Namely, the essential factors are...

▶ personalization of the high school system, and

▶ establishing learning communities that rely on collaborative leadership.

Both are essential for school improvement and higher student achievement.[4] Both can be established through on-going implementation of the following three key components of the process of Tribes Learning Communities:

▶ The **group development process** of inclusion (sense of belonging), influence (sense of value and recognition) and community (socialization to work well with others)

▶ The **positive agreements:** listening, appreciation, the right to pass or to participate, and mutual respect, and

▶ The **active learning** of meaningful content in small groups.

This trio of components can be counted on to create the unique and motivational culture that now flows throughout thousands of classrooms and schools in this and many other countries.

RECOGNIZING A SCHOOL'S CULTURE

But how can we figure out what the culture of our school now may be?

Easy! We just have to look at how we all relate—and do things around here!

Walk into several high school classrooms or schools and you will sense that each has a culture of its own. Some are caring and friendly, others harsh and dispassionate. All impact how people in the system live, learn and work together. The main reason that efforts toward school renewal fail is because the nature of the school's culture either is dismissed as unimportant or assumed that somehow it is just fine. Assessment of the existing culture needs to be the initial concern of those committed to transforming the high school into a system that provides adolescents with positive developmental support and success in learning.

Culture is the climate, the environment and spirit that permeates everything that goes on within the high school. It is a complex pattern of norms shaped out of toxic as well as helpful attitudes, beliefs, values, behaviors, ceremonies, traditions, myths and stories. It is the underlying culture that shapes how people in the school behave, think and relate to each other. It's been said by organizational developers that "Culture is to an organization what personality is to an individual."[6] Respected cognitive and developmental psychologist, Jerome Bruner tells us that *all* mental activity and learning itself, is culturally situated. Culture not only shapes the mind, but "it provides us with a toolkit by which we construct not only our world, but our very conceptions of our selves and our powers."[7]

The culture of an organization is seldom recognized or discussed although it affects everything that happens in the system. It is also unbelievably resistant to change. Roland S. Barth, respected Harvard University professor warns that...

> "Unless teachers and administrators act to change the culture of a school, all 'innovations' will have to fit in and around the existing elements of the cultures. That is they will be superficial window dressing, incapable of making much of a difference."[8]

THE INITIAL STEP TOWARD CHANGING THE CULTURE

The initial step toward change is for the high school *learning community* to become aware of "the way we do things around here." That means:

- ▶ observing and identifying unacknowledged beliefs, attitudes, values, traditions and tacit silent agreements that underlie, dictate and affect behaviors and practices in the system

- ▶ discussing the implications of each on student and staff motivation, development and learning.

Have the staff meet in small groups, "learning communities" composed of six to eight people, to gain initial inclusion for honest and productive discussions. Invite them to explore and record both the positive and negative assumptions and beliefs that may exist

Ultimately, a school's culture has far more influence on life and learning in the schoolhouse than the state department of education, the superintendent, the school board, or even the principal can ever have.[5]
—ROLAND S. BARTH

Caroline Wong, M.ED.

Caroline has over 30 years of experience in education as a teacher, principal and Certified Tribes TLC Trainer. As the Principal of Moanalua Middle School in Honolulu, and as a consultant and trainer for the Department of Education of Hawaii, she is striving to assist all schools to develop an integrated and comprehensive system to support the success of all students. Caroline believes that the process of Tribes is an essential key to proactive and preventive support for middle level and high school students.

Why Tribes TLC for High Schools?

A warm Hawaii aloha from a veteran principal of a Tribes school, Moanalua Middle. Seven years ago I contributed a story of our Tribes journey, "Why Tribes for Middle School?," for Jeanne Gibbs' new book, *Discovering Gifts in Middle School.* The powerful incentive to use the Tribes processes in every middle school classroom was truly focused on purposefully creating a school culture. As a former social studies teacher, I refer to *culture* in the broadest sense, i.e., *how we live in this place.* Every school has a culture, which most often is felt by simply walking the campus.

The school culture reflects shared beliefs, sense of purpose, values and practices; common language and vocabulary; how members interact and work together; and what traditions and practices are valued and celebrated. It is not dependent on the principal or a few teachers, but is woven into the fabric of school life, extending into homes and community through partnership with parents and neighborhood groups. For years, research has clearly demonstrated that classroom culture and a supportive learning environment have a direct impact on the learning process and contribute to improved student achievement.

With the pressures for all schools to improve achievement to meet the *No Child Left Behind* (NCLB) mandates, we are compelled to examine the overwhelming challenges facing American high schools. At the *National Education Summit on High Schools* in 2005, Bill Gates addressed educators and government leaders emphatically stating that the *American high school was obsolete* and has one of the highest dropout rates in the industrialized world. A model for changing American high schools was published by the National Association of Secondary School Principals (NASSP) in 1996 as *Breaking Ranks: Changing an American Institution.* However, not enough was done to implement the *Breaking Ranks* model, redesign schools, and significantly change teaching and learning practices in many American high schools. In 2004, a group of top educators, researchers, and high school principals, worked with *The Education Alliance at Brown University,* to provide strategies and manageable implementation tools for high school reform with *Breaking Ranks II.* The Bill and Melinda Gates Foundation supported distribution, including a free copy to each high school principal across the country.

The recommendations of *Breaking Ranks II* focused on three key change areas within the American high school: the culture, the structures, and the instruction. The redesigned high school requires structures that support career academies, internships, entrepreneurial enterprises, apprenticeships, service learning, and mentoring. In *The Best Schools* (2006), Thomas Armstrong advocates for schools that are grounded on human development research. Developmentally appropriate practices in high school must include personalized smaller learning communities that honor and model democracy and equity. Personalization requires authentic relationship building; and we know that organizations do not change, people change. As high schools strive to improve the quantity and quality of interaction between students, teachers, and other members of the learning community, a clear process must be identified and utilized. TRIBES is that process to purposefully create a culture in every classroom, and personalize interactions among and between students and teachers. Tribes will support the change process, which must be personal and developmental. High Schools that venture along the Tribes trail will find that Tribes processes are an integral part of the journey to improve achievement for ALL high school students.

in the current culture of the high school. Suggest that they initiate their inquiry with elemental questions such as:

- ▶ What do we often see, hear and experience?
- ▶ What behaviors are rewarded? What are ignored?
- ▶ What do we hear in the teachers' lunch room?
- ▶ How many students can we greet by name in the hall?
- ▶ How are decisions being made? By whom?
- ▶ How are parents and visitors welcomed when they come to our school?

The inquiry can be expanded by having them brainstorm (list without comment or discussion) statements such as the following that sometimes may be heard around the school:

"Those kids just can't learn."

"As a faculty we don't ask each other for advice."

"All kids can learn—we're just not reaching them."

"But we don't need professional development—we know how to teach!"

"You can't change the bullying here—it's just what those kind of kids do."

"Smart students do as they are told."

"The parents just don't care."

You could use the 'Brainstorm' and 'Exploring the Norms' strategies to facilitate the inquiry. They're in the Strategy section of this book.

Negative perceptions may or may not have factual basis, yet when they permeate a school for a long time they sustain a destructive and impersonal culture throughout a school. If the staff assumes certain teenagers cannot learn, one way or another those students will confirm that in their attitudes, behaviors and self-image. Never doubt that the myths, core beliefs, values, and unspoken relational norms, good or bad, are not an active influence on the school system every day.

We also need to look at some "non-discussables" that our school sustains.

There are also seldom acknowledged traditions and practices in high schools that affect fairness, gender/social equity and democratic equality. Over time they also can become cultural norms, simply written off as... "the way we do things around here." They are the "non-discussables" which are subjects often "so laden with anxiety and taboos that (to quote Roland Barth) "they take place only in the parking lot, the men's room, the playground, the car pool or the dinner table at home."[9]

Non-discussables are like having the proverbial elephant in the living room that no one wants to notice or mention. Are any of the following that affect fairness, equity or democratic equality hiding out in the culture of your school?

▶ Upon entering the high school are cases of athletic trophies and awards displayed prominently, but the works of school artists hung in a back hall or room?

- Are girls' baseball, basketball, soccer and dance teams supported as adequately as boys' teams?

- Do teachers tend to call on boys more than girls—or girls more than boys?

- How are student leaders in classrooms or school selected? By teachers? By students? By election?

- Is fairness in grading practiced by all teachers and departments? How can all be certain?

- What kind of leadership and supervision is taking place? Autocratic? Decentralized? Democratic?

Barth warns that: "the health of a school is inversely proportional to the number of non-discussables; the fewer the non-discussables, the healthier the school; the more the non-discussables, the more pathology in the school culture."[10] In other words the culture can either enhance or hinder learning—both for students and staff.

Threat, intimidation and emotional stress close off cognitive thinking and learning. One freshman told a teacher when asked why he gave up working with a new group, said, "Oh, I just closed down when I got called a name." Whenever threatening negative behaviors become the daily norms of a classroom, most likely the whole class will shut down. Motivation and learning in the high school years (or at any time) is impossible in an unfriendly caustic environment. Discipline policies, curricula, new buildings or an abundance of computers matter little if the school culture centers on institutional mandates and expediency rather than the very human needs of young adults.

Positive school cultures not only correlate strongly with increased student achievement— but also with teacher productivity and satisfaction!

A deliberate *cultural shift* needs to be made whether it is a large or small high school—a shift from the traditional impersonal system to a personalized learning community.

TRADITIONAL IMPERSONAL SYSTEM	PERSONALIZED LEARNING COMMUNITY
Dispassionate	Caring and supportive
Isolation and anonymity	Inclusion and recognition
Focus on weakness	Focus on strengths
Low expectations	High expectations
Limited recognition	Recognition of all
Competitive	Collaborative
Teaching	Learning
Teacher independence	Teacher collegiality
Undemocratic	Democratic
Opinion-based	Research-based

The culture within the personalized high school learning community addresses the interests, abilities and futures of its young adult population. It does so in many ways that provide caring and support, active participation and high expectations. It is a kind, collaborative and challenging culture that all enjoy and daily live together.

THE COMPONENTS OF AN IDEAL LEARNING CULTURE

What then should the culture of an excellent high school be like?

Jerome Bruner writes:[11]

"What is needed in America—as in most countries of the developed world—is not simply a renewal of the skills that make a country a better competitor in the world markets, but a renewal and reconsideration of what is called school culture. On the basis of what we have learned in recent years about human learning—it is best when it is participatory, proactive, communal, collaborative and given over to constructive meanings rather than receiving them. We do even better at teaching science, math, and languages in such schools than in more traditional ones."

Now that's the culture we want for our school!

Those of you who already are familiar with the process of Tribes Learning Communities will recognize how the TLC® process builds upon and activates those components.

Ideal Learning Culture	TLC® Learning Community Process
COMMUNAL	builds inclusion and belonging for all transfers responsibility to peer groups promotes caring and support celebrates community learning
PARTICIPATORY	reaches all students through meaningful participation uses interactive strategies encourages peer leadership

PROACTIVE	uses positive agreements to assure a
	    caring culture
	reaches students of multiple intelligences,
	    abilities and cultures
	trains teachers to use pedagogy responsive
	    to adolescent needs and interests

COLLABORATIVE	uses democratic principles and practices promotes teacher collegiality and leadership facilitates student influence

CONSTRUCTIVE	involves students in research, meaningful
	    content, inquiry and student-led project
	    learning groups

IT IS HARDLY COINCIDENTAL THAT...

The protective factors: *caring and support, high expectations and meaningful participation*, that nurture the development of life-long individual resilient strengths, also serve as a foundation for the implementation of Bruner's ideal learning culture throughout the high school system.

The power and support that the protective factors contribute to individual youth development, you recall, were discussed in Chapter 4, "Assuring Futures of Promise." It follows that these well-proven environmental factors need to be embedded in *the culture* of high school systems in order to support *all students in the school.*

Researcher Bonnie Benard gives a wealth of approaches in her fine book, *Resiliency, What Have We Learned,* on how your school can activate the essential protective factors. We urge readers to secure the book, and especially to read Chapter 6 and Appendix pages 124–126, which list hundreds or more ideas for schools to use. The book is available from CenterSource Systems. See the Resources section.

Here's a brief summary of ways to activate the protective factors into the culture of your school.

CARING AND SUPPORT

"When students are asked to define what they want in their teachers, the answer across studies is unequivocal: They want teachers who are caring and who also accept no excuses—who, in other words care about them enough to refuse to let them fail."[12] Such teachers are referred to as "turnaround people" who tip the scale for a handful of individual students each year from risk to resilience. The same can happen for many students whether in large or small high schools—if and when—their schools deliberately become "turnaround systems."

Research studies point to a number of ways caring classroom and school communities assure caring and support:[14]

> ▶ Every student has a caring relationship with an adult at his or her school.

> ▶ Schools and classrooms feel like communities.

> ▶ Schools and classrooms make use of a number of small group processes.

> ▶ Classes are small, and if possible schools are small.

> ▶ Caring relationships among school staff are encouraged and supported.

Turnaround people help youth see the power they have.[13]
—Bonnie Benard

- ▶ Discipline is designed to keep students feeling connected.

- ▶ Early intervention programs are available.

- ▶ School-based mentoring programs link students with community volunteers.

- ▶ Families and community are invited to partner with the school.

HIGH EXPECTATIONS

Benard tells us that at the heart of caring relationships are high expectations, defined as clear, positive and youth-centered expectations. "Positive and youth-centered messages are those that communicate an adult's deep belief in the young person's innate resilience and self-righting capacities and that challenge the youth to become all he or she can be."[15] Our high expectations, however, must be based on the "strengths, interests, hopes and dreams of youth—not on what we want the young person to do or be."

Research has demonstrated that high expectations with on-going support is an important factor in decreasing the number of students who drop out of school and in increasing the number who go to college. It is also a common characteristic of 'high-performing, high-poverty schools."[16]

Following are a number of strategies that high expectation schools sustain to ensure that students develop a sense of personal competence:[17]

- ▶ Instruction is individualized to accommodate the broad range of students.

- ▶ Learning opportunities are structured so that success is possible.

- ▶ The curriculum is rich with art, music, outdoor experiences and projects.

- ▶ Students have a choice of interest-based clubs and activities.

POSITIVE PARTICIPATION AND CONTRIBUTION

Opportunities for participation and contribution are ensured by the safe and caring culture in Tribes Learning Community schools. Inclusion, respect for diversity and affirmation give students confidence to question, to voice opinions, to make choices, to engage in active learning projects with others, to participate in the arts, athletics, community service or assume leadership. Being involved in a meaningful cause not only can have significant impact, but kindle a career. New motivation and interest in learning is kindled whenever one senses "my idea or contribution" was meaningful and important to others. Such experiences, of being engaged in a joy of learning, hopefully, is what the high school experience will become for all. Positive participation and having opportunities to contribute to others is vital to our goal to "personalize" the high school system and the learning experience for all students.

Schools that commit to giving their "young adult" students many opportunities for positive participation and contribution use many of the following strategies:[18]

She believed in me when I didn't believe in myself.

- ▶ Students experience voice and choice in their daily life at school.

- ▶ Students have many experiential learning experiences.

- ▶ Group process is infused throughout the curriculum and school day.

- ▶ Students have many opportunities to express themselves through the arts.

- ▶ Students have opportunities for service learning.

- ▶ Students have a way to take responsibility for transgressions—replacing retributive discipline practices with restorative practices.

THE CULTURE ASSURES FAIRNESS, EQUITY AND SOCIAL JUSTICE

The responsive high school Learning Community that is focusing on adolescent development, *greatness* in its young human beings, must also sustain a culture of fairness, equity and social justice. Anne Wheelock points out that this culture within a school is the essential "ethos in which young adolescents feel safe enough to be their best selves and 'safe to be smart.'"[19]

It is as though many windows open all at once for high school adolescents—to an awesome wider world that seemingly becomes theirs. They become idealistic and begin to see things from a different perspective... "schooling" being one. The world was more comfortable back in the days of elementary school in which concrete thinking reassured them that "this is how things are." Emerging from the mist of those years into abstract conceptual thinking shakes up just about everything. Now there is a need for a sense of purpose and meaning, questioning systems (particularly school and family values), personal worth, new opportunities, the relevance of school and the four underlying developmental tasks of adolescence. Since the most time is spent in school, sensitivity about social equity and fairness take on major importance. Who has not heard the questions?

"It's not fair."

"People of my race are treated differently by some teachers."

"Why did Sam get suspended just for that?"

"Why aren't the tests about what we've been studying?"

"How come history is all about white people?"

"Why do we only have two Afro-American teachers here?"

"The 'nerds'—those smart kids—get to do special stuff!"

"How come we don't get a choice? Isn't that what democracy means?"

"Why do teachers call upon the boys more than the girls?"

"How come boys are usually the group leaders?"

"How come they cut out some of the art classes?"

"It's not fair..."

In the rush of a high school's busy-ness, statements indicating unfairness are easily ignored simply because they have been heard so much before that they have become lost as unimportant norms in the culture of the school. Seemingly, the protesting voices have little to do with academic achievement, adolescent development or school improvement. This is not so! Indeed, if we are serious about personalizing high school systems, whether large or small, the school culture must be a *culture of fairness and equity*. The fairness that adolescents perceive as a right applies to gender, racial and cultural equity, equal opportunities, school policy, curriculum content, instructional strategies, classroom management, student rights and the extent that students can make decisions about their own learning. Being treated unfairly or treated differently not just by peers but also by teachers, principals or other adults in the school, especially as emerging into adulthood, is likely to lead to paths of failure. High schools may be perpetuating inequity and unfairness whenever...

- ▶ Multiculturalism, gender equity and multiple intelligences are seldom discussed by the faculty, are not emphasized in the school plan, policy. professional development or integrated into curriculum

- ▶ Teachers have never participated in discussions or training about these issues, and unconsciously may be more responsive to some students than others

- ▶ Teachers are not using cooperative learning, democratic class agreements or teaching group skills

- ▶ Generalizations, labels and name-calling are ignored

- ▶ School policy contains biased language and rules

- ▶ Tests are perceived as biased or irrelevant to the curriculum

- ▶ The relationship between a caring community culture, teacher and student morale, and school success is ignored.

It is well recognized that perceived injustice within a school breeds conflict, and destructive conflict in turn may give rise to more injustice. High school learning communities especially need to model inclusion, respect, and a commitment to social justice.

SEEKING A CULTURE OF FAIRNESS FOR GENDER EQUITY

The loss of self begins to encompass girls as they move into high school and are pulled by cultural forces to be attractive to boys while at the same time keeping up grades, being close to mom and dad—and living into their own gifts and dreams. Mary Pipher, author of the groundbreaking book, "Reviving Ophelia... Saving the Lives of Adolescent Girls," asserts that it is not simply new hormones that cause the deep emotional change—it is the culture. By the time girls reach the high school years they have become aware that men manage the world, have more power than women and usually dominate groups and organizations. Women should be attractive and helpful but not too competitive—or too smart. For the first time it begins to seem like an unfair game.

> America today is a girl-destroying place. Everywhere girls are encouraged to sacrifice their true selves.[20]
> —MARY PIPHER

No wonder the football team dominates everything here. No wonder I'm worrying all the time about my looks! No wonder...

It is at this time that girls initiate different strategies to negotiate their school days and find identity. Judy Cohen, author of *Girls in the Middle—Working to Succeed in School*, describes three of the most prominent strategies:[21]

▶ **Speaking Out:** Asserting themselves either positively or negatively; insisting on being heard; assuming positive leadership or becoming highly visible as a maverick leader or troublemaker.

▶ **Doing School:** Conforming to traditional expectations; doing what is asked; outwardly compliant whether to her advantage or disadvantage.

▶ **Crossing Borders:** Moving easily between different sets of norms and expectations; bridging between peers and adults or different racial and ethnic groups.

All adolescent girls desperately need teachers who understand the subtle ways that girls are dis-empowered at this critical time in their lives. All need to be affirmed by caring adults that they are not lesser people meant to be in the background of life.

Boys also are trying to handle the conflicting cultural expectations that engulf them daily. Again, it is not just the hormones! Decades of history have imprinted "the warrior image" upon them. Real men are tough, competitive, aggressive, dominant, unemotional, physical, athletic, in charge and invulnerable. They also, especially at school, are supposed to be respectful, responsible, cooperative, considerate and compliant. Caught in the middle of these conflicting expectations—one set emanating from our Western culture and the other evolving from the school culture—some determine not to show feelings or not to be smart—all in order to appear "cool" in the eyes of their peers while trying to seek their own emerging identities.

And what about the boys?

Ever self-conscious, many previously "high-achieving" boys begin to "dumb down" in order to fit in with a more popular or "macho" crowd. With the conflicting cultural pressure to be future leaders or "in charge," at times adolescent males assume cool, testy, or challenging "leadership" positions which adults may not consider indicators of their search for independence or social competency—the developmental tasks of adolescence.

High school male students begin to form opinions about how important school is to them. Similar to girls, adolescent boys also begin to make choices and develop strategies "to negotiate" school. A few of the most prominent strategies are:

▶ **Speaking Out or Acting Out:** Asserting themselves either positively or negatively; either assuming positive leadership positions, or becoming highly visible by challenging authority and acting out in self-defeating ways.

- ▶ **Doing School:** Compliant, complacent, bored, "getting through by learning the game." Rarely protesting or making their needs known they often become invisible.

- ▶ **Dropping Out:** Giving up; alone, lost or helpless; often socially isolated, shunned or unsupported with a multitude of unaddressed personal or emotional needs.

Boys need a model of manhood that is caring and bold, adventurous and gentle.

—MARY PIPHER

Mary Pipher writes, "Boys need a model of manhood that is caring and bold, adventurous and gentle."[22] They have the same innate human qualities as girls, and need male mentors to assure them that being caring, considerate, cooperative, empathetic, kind and nurturing is tremendously important in the life of men.

More than ever high school personnel need to address the conflicting cultural pressures that students face by continuing to focus on the human development issues that adolescents are struggling to resolve, either consciously or unconsciously. The school culture must support all students by paying attention to inequities, empowering those who long for identity, supporting those who don't feel socially competent, inspiring those who search for purpose and meaning, and helping all to solve problems that come their way.

SEEKING MULTICULTURAL EQUITY

Each person bears a uniqueness that asks to be lived and that is already present before it is lived.[23]

—JAMES HILLMAN

Through the years many have sounded the same wake-up call to the educational community as Spencer Kagan continues to do by saying:

> *"We are facing a severe crisis in education. If we do not change our educational practices, we are headed toward a break-down in race relations, both in our classrooms and in the society as a whole."*[24]

It is predicted that by 2020, 48% of school-age youths will be students of color. Currently it is estimated that the majority of the school-age population in 50 or more major U.S. cities are from language minority backgrounds. Despite gains within the last decade, African American and Latino youths are still significantly behind Anglo mainstream youth on many indices of academic achievement. They also have lower high school graduation rates and higher retention, suspension and dropout rates.[25] Biased conceptions of intellectual ability are reflected in academic tracking, differential access to resources and narrow standardized tests that favor mathematical and linguistic learners.[26] Unfair conceptions about students of color also have led to a focus on individual characteristics and deficiencies of students rather than ways that school systems are failing them.

Whenever you hear or recognize name-calling, teasing, exclusion, meanness, fights or violence—know that the culture of the classroom and school needs rebuilding or treatment—not the kids. Know that when you see a teacher ignore a student of color (perhaps perceived as not having the right answer) or hear chatter in the teacher's lounge that "those kids can't learn," it is time to schedule training and on-going staff discussions on multicultural, racial and gender equity issues. All such bias has direct impact upon academic learning, school culture, and teacher-student and student-student relationships.

REVERSING INEQUITY

Years of research clearly show that cooperative group learning reduces incidents of gender, racial and multicultural bias. The egalitarian social group structures create caring relationships, and a culture of respect in which diversities of people can work collaboratively to achieve common goals. Structuring on-going small learning groups assures inclusion for all students... the positive culture assures mutual respect and appreciation.

In addition to intensifying the use of Tribes TLC® cooperative learning, we strongly recommend that high school staffs participate in a series of meetings to reflect on what may be happening at your high school. The following chart, "Matrix for Achieving Equity in Classrooms," provides a way to structure discussions. It also may be used as an assessment and planning tool.

Schools that are using cooperative learning and the process of Tribes Learning Communities are well on their way to reversing inequity.

If you really want to know what's happening have students design and conduct a survey!

Matrix For Achieving Equity In Classrooms

Use the following matrix to assess six forms of bias in a classroom or a school community. Strategies for reducing bias are included in each component.

	LINGUISTIC BIAS	STEREOTYPING	INVISIBILITY/ EXCLUSION	UNREALITY	IMBALANCE/ SELECTIVITY	FRAGMENTATION/ ISOLATION
WHAT TO LOOK FOR	Language which is dehumanizing or denies the existence of females or males, e.g., "mankind."	Members of a group portrayed in one role or with one characteristic.	The lack of representation of a group.	Misinformation about a group, event or contribution.	Single interpretation of an issue, situation or conditions.	Separating contributions of females and ethnic groups from the mainstream.
POLICY— WHAT TO DO	Review policy for biased language.	Ensure nondiscriminatory discipline policy.	Recognize teaching performance which fosters equity.	Design proactive mission statement to correct past bias.	Earmark money for equity classroom materials and training.	Design staff evaluations inclusive of equity criteria.
INSTRUCTIONAL STRATEGIES	Pluralize subjects to avoid a gender pronoun.	Encourage males and females to express a wide range of feelings, responses and sensibilities.	Encourage contributions from females and ethnic minorities.	Discuss controversial topics of discrimination and prejudice.	Engage students in analyzing and debating an issue.	Call on students equitably. Use cooperative learning.
CURRICULUM CONTENT	Set expectations for students to use non-sexist language.	Select readings that have the females and ethnic minorities in responsible, exciting leadership positions.	Have students count the numbers of male, female and ethnic group members to determine the proportion in relation to a population.	Engage students in conducting research.	Introduce collaborative ways to solve problems and make decisions.	Stress that learning is the result of collaborative efforts and contributions by many.
MANAGEMENT (SCHOOL AND CLASSROOM)	Engage all members in noticing and correcting biased language.	Intervene when slurs or jokes are made at another's expense.	Nurture cooperation among males, females and ethnically diverse students.	Facilitate shared decision making.	Create a supportive climate for differing perspectives to be discussed.	Establish ways of integrating groups during free time.
FAMILY AND COMMUNITY INVOLVEMENT	Attend council meeting and have students present on the use of non-biased language in newspapers, on road signs, etc.	Invite nontraditional role models to teach a lesson on their area of specialization.	Provide students with shadowing opportunities.	Examine the history of discrimination within local laws and history.	Establish Advisory groups that are balanced by sex, ethnicity and disability.	Solicit volunteers from diverse groups to work with students.

Culturally responsive teaching can heal many inequities.[27] It...

- ▶ acknowledges the legitimacy of different ethnic groups

- ▶ builds bridges of meaning between home and school experiences and sociocultural realities

- ▶ uses a wide variety of instructional strategies that are connected to different learning styles

- ▶ teaches students to know and respect their own and each other's cultural heritages and gender strengths, and

- ▶ incorporates multicultural information, resources and materials in all subjects and skills being learned in schools.

Linda Christensen, co-editor of *Rethinking Schools,* emphasizes, *"As teachers we have daily opportunities to affirm that our students' lives and language are unique and important. We do that in the selections of literature we read, in the history we chose to teach, and we do it by giving legitimacy to our students' lives as a content worth of study."*[28]

Every high school is different. For that reason, to a certain extent developing the culture for learning is unique for each one. We appreciate respected scholar Seymour Sarason's wisdom and assurance that, "Creating a setting is one of man's most absorbing experiences, compounded as it is of dreams, hopes, efforts and thoughts."[29]

Each day we need to ask, 'Is the overall climate of our high school caring and supportive? Is it engaging all students in meaningful participation, positive expectations and a culture for success?'

Beyond divisiveness there is that "democracy of the human spirit" that transcends all individuality and binds humankind—somewhere a place for all of us, together.[30] —John Goodlad

Now I get it! The culture of a school is its soul.

Establishing

Community for All

7 Establishing Community for All

IN THIS CHAPTER YOU WILL

▶ Learn the importance and meaning of community to support the development and learning for high school adolescents

▶ Understand how collaborative groups of learners can transform a school system

▶ Realize how four positive agreements activate and sustain the caring culture of the high school

▶ Learn how to use the community building process, the Tribes Trail, to engage and assure learning for students and teachers

Establishing community in our school, meaningful relationships between adults and students was as important as all the changes made in teaching, curriculum and assessment.[1]
—DEBORAH MEIER

In the midst of the nation's search on how to transform factory-like impersonal high schools there is a growing consensus in progressive educational literature (including the NASSP *Breaking Ranks* report, journals, foundation goals, and knowledgeable leaders) that high school systems must become "*learning communities.*" Peter Senge, respected author and M.I.T. university senior lecturer, asserts that the quality of education will not improve until we have "schools that learn." That means not just the students are learning but everyone in the whole system is actively involved in ongoing learning.[2] In the circle illustration for the developmental process of Tribes, the term, "community of learners," is used.

The three circles, caring culture, community of learners and responsive educational pedagogy all support meaningful learning and development for the student in the center. The literature pertaining to high school reform generally refers to the these components as: *culture, structure and instruction.*[3] All three are essential to develop a system into a high performance high school that is dedicated to educational excellence. Should the components be ignored or considered unimportant, *anonymity* will continue to undermine student participation, motivation and learning.

The trio are somewhat like a three-legged stool. Fixing one or two but not all three elements sabotages all improvement efforts.

Ah, now we're in the third circle—the community of learners!

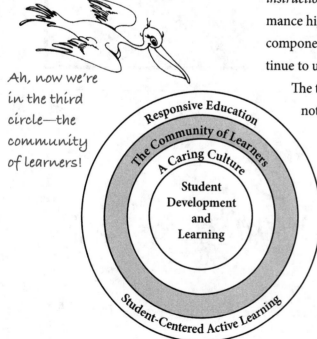

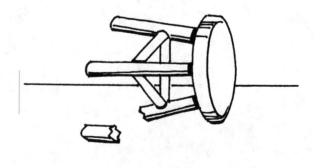

The strengths and quality of the caring culture, the community of learners, and responsive education in classrooms within Tribes Learning Communities in time transform large or small school systems.

WHY HIGH SCHOOL LEARNING COMMUNITIES?

Follow any high school students at lunch time, after school or moments gathering between classes and it is obvious that making connections and belonging to a group or someone is a major quest. There are the computer nerds, jocks, cheerleaders, yardbirds (smokers), cools, wierdos, stars, regulars, and others of more unique nomenclature. Most large high schools have interest clubs that help to fill the underlying very human need to have identity apart from the anonymous crowd. Likes gravitate to likes within good and not-so-good groups, gangs, clubs relationships or organizations. Underlying the very human need is to belong—to be in "a place where everyone knows my name."

High school youth seek connections not only to peers but to teachers who reach out and encourage their emerging gifts of heart and mind. The reality is that it is difficult for most students to make connections with teachers in traditionally organized high schools whether large or small. Largely working alone behind closed doors and dealing with inestimable numbers of students every day, teachers also experience isolation from their peers. Periodic faculty meetings usually are filled with announcements, procedures and instructions but seldom provide opportunities for dialogue and collegiality. The traditional impersonal culture and top-down structure, eliminates the possibility of being able to develop a spirit of community. The very human need for connection is as essential for all teachers and school leaders as it is for all students in the high school.

High school teachers and students in Tribes TLC® schools experience inclusion, belonging, positive identity and recognition within many small "communities of learners." More than one thousand studies on cooperative group learning verify positive academic and non-academic outcomes that result from group learning for children and youth over competitive individualized instruction.[5] Participating in small communities of learners strongly supports high school students' drive to develop the adolescent tasks: independence, social competency, a sense of purpose, and self-responsible problem-solving. In

> Nearly everyone agrees that our schools and our society have a connection problem. And nearly everyone agrees that one way to renew connections is to help schools to become caring communities.[4]
> —THOMAS SERGIOVANNI

the same way, opportunities for teachers to work with colleagues in professional learning groups maximize their learning effective principles and practices—well beyond individual course-taking. This is the reason that the NASSP report, *Breaking Ranks,* recommends establishing teachers' *learning communities!*

COMMUNITY?

The word "community" stirs different memories in everyone. What cherished moments come to mind for you? An inclusive first step for a staff or parent group is to set aside time to share some of those moments when they felt a sense of belonging and value in a group. What made those experiences special? How did people relate to each other? Jot down your sense of what *community* means to you.

Remember, it's OK to write in this book.

Community

Different populations, ages and genders may define the meaning of community in various ways. The nightly news media uses the word to refer to networks of people few of whom know each other: the medical community, the Hispanic community, the gay community, the northside community. Some of us think of farm communities, retirement communities, religious and political communities. Now we want to build *learning communities—communities of learners—*throughout educational systems. How then can the spirit of community be defined?

Alfie Kohn explains the qualities of a learning community as follows:

> A **learning community** is a "place in which students feel cared about and are encouraged to care about each other. They experience a sense of being valued and respected; the children (adolescents) matter to one another and to the teacher. They have come to think in the plural; they feel connected to each other; they are part of an 'us.'"[6]

In a similar way, Thomas Sergiovanni, one of the leading theorists of the school community concept writes:

*"**Communities** are defined by their centers of values, sentiments, and beliefs that provide the needed conditions for creating a sense of 'We' from 'I'."*[7]

And Thomas Likona, respected author on moral development and education, crafted this definition which seems especially relevant for high schools:

*"**To build a sense of community** is to create a group that extends to others the respect one has for oneself, to come to know one another as individuals, to respond and care about one another, to feel a sense of membership and accountability to the group."*[8]

WHAT DO PRODUCTIVE LEARNING COMMUNITIES LOOK LIKE?

Studies by Thomas Sergiovanni show that schools become productive learning communities when they become: [9]

▶ **reflective communities** within which students and teachers develop insight into their own strengths and weaknesses as learners, and use this information to call upon different strategies for learning

▶ **developmental communities** within which it is acknowledged that students (and teachers too) develop at different rates, and at any given time are more ready to learn some things than others

▶ **diverse communities** within which different talents and interests of students (and teachers too) are not only recognized, but acknowledged by decisions that are made about curriculum, teaching, and assessment

▶ **conversational communities** within which high priority is given to creating an active discourse that involves the exchange of values and ideas among students, among teachers, and between teachers and students as they learn together

▶ **caring communities** within which students (and teachers too) learn not only to be kind to each other and to respect each other, but to help each other to grow as learners and as persons

▶ **responsible communities** within which students (and teachers too) come to view themselves as part of a social web of meanings and responsibilities which they feel a moral obligation to embody in their present behavior as students, and future behavior as citizens.[10]

As Tribes practitioners know, Tribes is a process that promotes reflection, development, diversity, conversation, caring and responsibility— and all are promoted in the context of community![11]

—BONNIE BENARD

STRUCTURING COMMUNITY
THROUGHOUT CLASSROOMS AND SCHOOL

Imagine that you are a friendly pelican looking down through the glass roof of a Tribes Learning Community high school. "Reflection," which is her name, would see two kinds of structures in the classrooms.

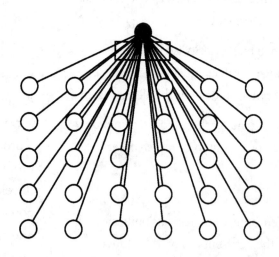

TEACHER-CENTERED INSTRUCTION

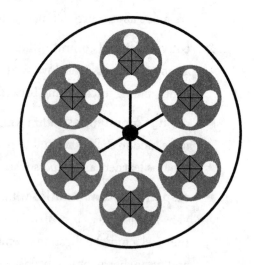

STUDENT-CENTERED ACTIVE LEARNING

She would see many teachers using direct instruction, lecturing facts and concepts. Students are passively taking notes, now and then responding to questions. The teachers are maintaining control and working to keep everyone alert and interested. In the student-centered active learning classes, students are sitting together in small learning communities (teams, project, research, inquiry, dialogue groups—or tribes). Everyone is involved in the learning task chosen or assigned to their group.

Moreover, well-trained teachers are facilitating, guiding and providing assistance as needed. They are using both structures depending upon the nature and depth of learning students are to acquire. The collaborative group learning is compatible with how the human brain constructs and retains knowledge, and maximizes the retention of information[12] and academic achievement.[13] In effect, using small communities of learners in classrooms throughout the high school *engages all*. They provide working and social connection to peers and to the teacher.

Everyone is learning—everyone is teaching!

SAFE ENOUGH TO BE SMART[14]

The culture within all of the high school classes is safe and supportive because the students have made *positive agreements* with each other on how they want to relate and work together. Classrooms are places where it is safe enough to be smart: to ask questions, to speak up in a group, to acknowledge and learn from mistakes, and to ask for help in completing a difficult task. Students know they will not be called names, suffer put-down remarks, or be disrespected for their cultural or individual diversity—all so prevalent in dispassionate impersonal schools. Comprehensive studies have proven that attention, learning, performance, retention and recall diminish when stress and anxiety are high. Eric Jensen, respected author of *Teaching with the Brain in Mind*, confirms that excess stress and threat in schools may be the single greatest contributor to impaired academic learning.[15]

Reflection pelican would also see the teachers, administrators, parents and resource people relating and working in on-going small learning communities—all gaining inclusion, identity and a sense of value as they work together to achieve common goals. The "community of learners" structure decentralizes planning, problem-solving, mentoring, monitoring and assessment. The classroom and whole collaborative school system activates the caring and supportive culture, and transforms dispassionate systems into spirited caring communities. This is what "restructuring schools" should be all about... establishing culture, connections and caring learning communities of trust and respect.

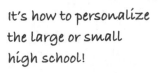

It's how to personalize the large or small high school!

A Perspective from Principals

Sharon Harry
and Paul Currie

Sharon is a Deputy Principal at Southern River College in Perth, Western Australia. With over twenty years in education, she has worked predominantly with "difficult" kids as a classroom teacher, Middle School Coordinator and as an Administrator.

Paul is the Senior School Deputy Principal at Southern River College. As an educator and leader with over 17 years of experience, Paul believes that the Tribes process is the most powerful change agent that he has utilized. Paul and Sharon have implemented the philosophy and process of Tribes to underpin the Values Platform by which the school operates. SRC now is viewed as a "Lighthouse School" and hosts many visitors each year...all seeking to mirror its successes.

The Year of the Phoenix

Re-visioning our moral imperative through the Tribes Process

"The year of the Phoenix" was 2005, consolidating the process of school renewal. Southern River College arose from the ashes of Gosnells Senior High School in 2006.

Situated in an outer suburb of Perth, Western Australia, Gosnells is a low socio economic area experiencing the associated social issues of single parents and melded families, high population transience, unemployment and cultural dislocation. Education was not highly valued, with most parents having left school at age 15 years and the entry level of students being well below state benchmarks for literacy and numeracy. Teaching students by traditional methods was proving extremely problematic.

By 2003 the indicators could not be ignored. Changes needed to be made. Suspension rates were amongst the highest in the state. Abuse of and violent assaults on staff were common place, staff turn over was extreme and morale was low. Yard duty had to be done in pairs using two way radios for support, fighting was a regular occurrence and several staff were seriously assaulted during that year. Struggling to retain good order security officers were often called and the community perception of the school amidst the conflict was extremely poor.

The school had some potentially successful initiatives and programs in place but they were insular and unrelated. What we needed was an all encompassing vision and a mechanism to drive this change. Searching for such a vehicle the school sent two leaders to the Tribes course. This had an almost immediate impact.

Tribes provided a total vision. It showed how a school could create and implement a common values platform. Focussing on quality curriculum delivery and learning in a collaborative manner. The Tribes process was embedded at all levels from day to day operations, to community initiatives to team based curriculum delivery. The leadership team recognised the value of the work being done and arranged for two staff to attain certified trainer qualifications, allowing a whole school vision to be realized.

Our curriculum for years eight to ten has since been completely rewritten to ensure it meets the specific needs of our students. Students are taught by teams of teachers who design thematic programs linking different curriculum areas together. The themes are written to suit the developmental stages of the students and that they support not only academic growth but also the social and emotional development of each student.

In 2008 the College is utilising the Tribes process at all levels. It is a crucial and underpins part of our first four weeks strategy developing the relationships between staff, parents and students. During those weeks the teaching program focuses on:

▶ Who are we? (*Inclusion, Mutual Respect and Appreciation of others)*

▶ What do we want to achieve together? *(Inclusion), a*nd

▶ Under what conditions do I best learn? *(Collaboration skills).*

The Tribes process is used at all meetings in the college. The non-teaching staff have also been trained so that the process is all encompassing.

Parent support for the school is at an all time high. 75% of parents attend portfolio evenings; this is a massive increase from approximately 25%. Our suspensions halved every year for 3 years when Tribes was first implemented. Our year 12 graduation rates have gone from 80% to a perfect 100%. Respect for the environment has increased massively, vandalism and graffiti has virtually been eliminated.

Tribes has had enormous impact on our high school setting. The very nature of the process has drawn us all together. Staff interaction is now positive, supportive and constructive. Acknowledgement that students have different learning styles and needs has seen significant improvement in management of our students overall and in particular of our boys at risk. They now have a valid means of communication as well as a structured support network.

We are viewed as a lighthouse school. We regularly get requests for assistance from across the district, the state and from the East Coast of Australia.

About the Name, Tribes!

Tribes? You smile and wonder when you hear the name. How did the name come about? It's hard to remember exactly when it happened. Throughout the early years teachers who were experiencing our group brand of cooperative learning would remark, "This is like being in a family." "It's like being a team." Inevitably, someone would counter, "No, it's like being a tribe." The feeling of being part of some type of caring small group may be what so many of us in Western society long for today. It also brings to mind the fact that for centuries indigenous people have lived in caring tribal groups for strength and survival.

At times, the question about the name "Tribes" has been raised by Native American and First Nation people. Once they learn about the community culture of Tribes they are appreciative of the value placed upon their beliefs. When their teachers begin to experience the process in training, inevitably some smile and say, "This is our old way of being together... to talk and listen as the old ones still do." It is then that it seems somewhat presumptuous to have titled an earlier book, *Tribes a New Way of Learning and Being Together*. Indeed, it is a valued "old way." It is with great pride that we want readers know that not only are Ojibwe, Navaho and Hopi schools using the process of Tribes, but also schools with native and aborigine populations in Australia, New Zealand, Africa and South America.[16] They have their own educators or leaders trained in order to train their own teachers in the collaborative Tribes Learning Community process. All long to sustain their respective peoples'—"old way of being together."

LEADING THE GROUP AND COMMUNITY BUILDING PROCESS

A process?
What's a process?

OK. If your objective was to drive from San Francisco to Los Angeles for the first time, you would: (1) get a map, (2) study it, (3) plan where to stop, (4) gas up the car, (5) start the trip, (6) check the map along the way, and (7) arrive in L.A. You activated a sequence of events (and probably a few learning experiences) to get to your objective. It was the *process* you used to get to where you wanted to go.

Definition: A *process* is a sequence of events or learning experiences that leads to the achievement of a specific outcome.

Now the journey that you are taking is to transform your high school into a learning community that engages everyone (students, teachers, school leaders and parents) in improving the system.

Using the process of Tribes TLC® requires learning and facilitating a sequence of *three* community building stages and *four* positive agreements that change the culture, structures and ways of learning in the school.

The strange Tribes Trail Map on the following page illustrates *the process* to develop classroom and all working and learning groups throughout the high school system. Schools may have strategic plans with defined goals, objectives, data-collection, rigorous curriculum and evaluations—all WHAT needs to happen, but HOW to have it all happen requires a *democratic people process* that engages everyone in making it happen.

You may think that the map looks more like the cross-section of a gopher-infested garden! It really illustrates the important synchronization that teachers and school leaders gradually facilitate to structure classrooms, staff and other groups into active learning communities. The success of any group's life together and the individual achievements its members can make depends upon the knowledge and ability teachers and leaders have to orchestrate group and community building strategies—as appropriate to the group's particular stage of development.

It strikes us as sad that although all living takes place in groups, we seldom learn how to make groups work well.

Families, labor unions, churches, parent-teacher associations, management staffs, faculties and classrooms... all are in search of positive participation and a reliable democratic process. People leave or drop-out of groups or organizations because they do not feel included and of value to the others. Paid employees (yes, even teachers and administrators) manage to drop out, but in subtle ways, such as not following through on responsibilities, taking leave days, sabotaging a department's plans, caucusing with other disgruntled peers, manipulating meetings, or being apathetic. Students drop out by gradually moving to "flight or fight." Apathy, boredom, lack of participation, shyness, absenteeism,

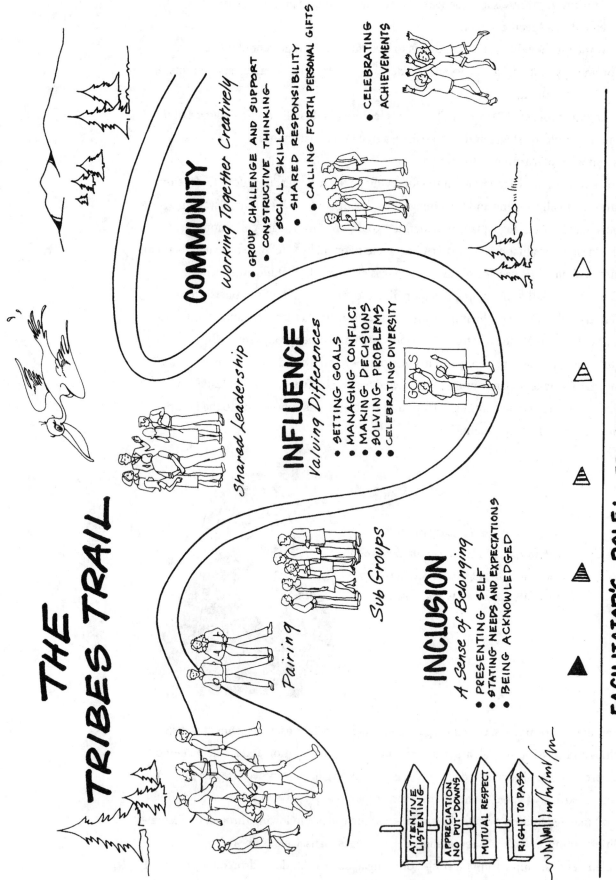

THE TRIBES TRAIL

COMMUNITY
Working Together Creatively
- GROUP CHALLENGE AND SUPPORT
- CONSTRUCTIVE THINKING
- SOCIAL SKILLS
- SHARED RESPONSIBILITY
- CALLING FORTH PERSONAL GIFTS
- CELEBRATING ACHIEVEMENTS

INFLUENCE
Valuing Differences
- SETTING GOALS
- MANAGING CONFLICT
- MAKING DECISIONS
- SOLVING PROBLEMS
- CELEBRATING DIVERSITY

Shared Leadership

GOALS

INCLUSION
A Sense of Belonging
- PRESENTING SELF
- STATING NEEDS AND EXPECTATIONS
- BEING ACKNOWLEDGED

Pairing

Sub Groups

ATTENTIVE LISTENING

APPRECIATION NO PUT-DOWNS

MUTUAL RESPECT

RIGHT TO PASS

FACILITATOR'S ROLE: TRANSFER RESPONSIBILITY TO GROUP

△ ◭ ◭ ◮ ▲

inability to complete tasks are some of the ways of taking flight. Those that fight, or initiate acting out behaviors (such as teasing, hitting, stealing, using foul language, etc.) are delivering the same message: "I don't feel included... nobody cares about me." Few leaders are aware of a basic principle:

> *If a person does not feel included, he/she will create his own inclusion by grabbing influence—attracting attention, creating a controversy, demanding power, or withdrawing into a passive belligerence.*[17]

Yeah!

More than all, we need to get past thinking of individual student behavior problems as hopeless, uncontrollable, or pathological. The majority of youth are in need of inclusion and affection from teachers, family, and peers. If school and family systems can learn how to help all kids feel included and of value to significant others in their lives, one of this country's major concerns, anti-social youth behavior, will be turned around.

THREE STAGES OF GROUP DEVELOPMENT

The process map illustrates three sequential group development stages to facilitate as a class teacher or school leader. Notice the bottom line. It shows a gradual shift in your role from being directive and providing much structure and control, to becoming less directive while transfering leadership to learning groups. Gradually as you lead your class, personnel or others along the stages of inclusion, influence and community people will be pleased to assume leadership in their classroom groups and school meetings. The net effect of this subtle process is that responsibility not only is transferred but calls forth the potential talents, skills and gifts of group members. This engages participation as never before in a classroom or staff, and enables tasks to be accomplished collaboratively (democratically) in satisfying and creative ways.

It is the intentional transfer of leadership in the midst of a positive and caring environment that makes the process of Tribes different from other cooperative learning and management methods. No matter the age level or capacity in learning, this transfer—the calling forth of youth apart from the crowd—gives a loud and clear message—you are capable people who can indeed manage yourselves and help each other!

A SET OF POSITIVE AGREEMENTS— A NEW WAY OF BEING TOGETHER

On the left side of the Tribes Trail Map you will notice a sign posted in the grass. It lists four essential agreements that help people relate and work well in any kind of groups or communities. We might say that these simple agreements help people "travel well" together. The agreements are key in developing and sustaining the caring culture throughout the high school; and they assure having successful social and working relationships in the many learning, task and management groups in the school.

> When one has no stake in the way things are, when one's needs or opinions are provided no forum, when one seems oneself as the object of unilateral actions it takes no particular wisdom to suggest one would rather be elsewhere.[18]
>
> —Seymour Sarason

Building the positive environment for the high school Learning Community begins by replacing negative norms of a school or organization with explicit positive agreements. As discussed before, all groups and organizations have unacknowledged agreements that affect relationships and behavior, and convey "this is how we do things around here"— even though it may not work well for everybody!

In a dispassionate impersonal high school the tacit agreements may be:

Calling people dumb names is OK. It's funny!
Respect? Ha! Not for those people.
Never ask questions.
Stay cool—don't let on how you feel!
Just get through the four years. It's like doin' time.

There is no way to support, let alone reach and teach any age group when negative agreements or norms are operant every hour of every day throughout a school. Admonitions by teachers and attempts to control abusive remarks and behavior consumes the energy of teachers. Tougher rules, regulations and consequences, as Alfie Kohn reminds us, may lead to *compliance* but not to *community,* social learning or change.[19] Inherent in our goal of adolescent development is the encouragement of self-responsibility and the internalization of ethical social principles. Students themselves must identify negative normative behavior and how it affects them daily. It begins by transferring responsibility to students to discuss and define less hurtful ways—of relating and being together. Count on high school students being willing to define agreements on how they want to be treated. Count on them to monitor new agreements with each other. Awakening the empathy within their hearts and constructive problem-solving minds is the most effective way to create safe non-violent schools. The idealism of young adults is a gift waiting to be used.

How to involve high school students in summarizing their ideas into the categories and language of the four essential agreements as posted on the sign is suggested in this book's Active Learning Strategy section. You may want to look at the strategies "The Ideal Classroom" and "Productive Learning Groups," now. What is important to know is that when used consistently the four agreements have been proven to create and sustain positive learning environments throughout thousands of Tribes classrooms and schools or all grade levels. The definitions of those agreements are:

1. **Attentive Listening:** To pay close attention to one another's expression of ideas, opinions and feelings; to check for understanding; and to let others know that they have been heard

The idealism of young adults is a gift waiting to be used.

2. **Appreciation/No Put-Downs:** To treat others kindly; to state appreciation for unique qualities, gifts, skills and contributions; to avoid negative remarks, name-calling, hurtful gestures and behaviors

3. **Right to Pass—Right to Participate:** To have the right to choose when and to what extent one will participate in a group activity; to observe quietly if not participating actively; and to choose whether to offer observations later to a group when invited to do so

4. **Mutual Respect:** To affirm the value and uniqueness of each person; to recognize and appreciate individual and cultural differences; and offer feedback that encourages growth.

Some schools and classes may want to add additional agreements beyond the four. It is important, however, that the list isn't longer than five agreements or students will be more likely to ignore them, and not reinforce them with each other.

The high school agreements need to be posted in prominent places in all classrooms and throughout the school. One of the most unusual but effective poster sites was created by a bus driver at a Navajo reservation school. He designed wooden signs of the school's four agreements and mounted them on the steps going up into his bus. He smiles and says, "Now, we have a peaceful bus!"

Whenever the learning groups begin to work together, it is important to remind everyone of the agreements, or better yet invite group members to review them. One class created an effective "rap" that they laughingly use. Transforming the classroom or school into a positive environment depends upon everyone monitoring and internalizing caring ways of being and learning together.

Another major difference between Tribes Learning Communities and many other classroom group methods is that people maintain membership in the same group for an extended period of time. This is based on research indicating that:[20]

▶ People perform better on learning tasks when they are members of "high cohesion" rather than "low cohesion" groups

▶ Students who feel comfortable with their peers and utilize their academic abilities more fully than those who do not.

The difference between using random groups for tasks and learning communities looks something like this:

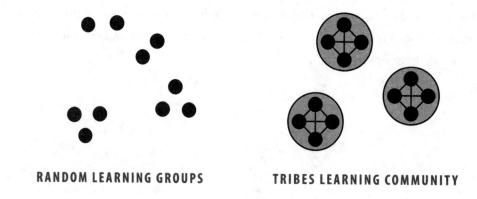

RANDOM LEARNING GROUPS   **TRIBES LEARNING COMMUNITY**

Random groups produce a scattered energy, and since they do not provide ongoing inclusion (truth, safety, and a sense of belonging), it is more difficult for students to work together and harder for teachers to control. The system of long-term membership in learning communities assures support for all within a classroom. This is also true for collegial teacher planning groups. Long-term membership not only supports task achievement and accountability but also individual learning.

STAGES OF GROUP AND COMMUNITY DEVELOPMENT

Jessica, Kyle, Mike, Angel or Jeremy bring their life experiences into all of the high school classes every day. Depending on the class, the teacher, mode of instruction and mix of peers, the many periods throughout the day trigger waves different feelings from interest and exhilaration to boredom and anxiety. Many social and emotional questions such as the following may be affecting learning:

"I wonder if this period will be boring again?"

"Does the teacher by now even know who I am?"

"I like some of the kids here."

"How will they get to know me?"

"I wish I could talk to those who always sit together."

"Why am I nervous?"

"I wish this were the end of the day, not the beginning."

Knowing this, your responsibility is to live up to the name "facilitator," which means "one who makes it easy."

THE STAGE OF INCLUSION

If people stay immersed in initial anxieties, they cannot learn and in time will demonstrate acting-out or dropping-out behaviors. Remember how the brain works? In fear or anxiety, the brain downshifts into a lower state and is not available to reason or learn. Immersed in anxiety, students will take to their own comfort zones... which may not be positive for either themselves or others. A student may simply show restlessness, shuffle papers, get a stomach ache, or in time become regarded as one more learning disability. A teacher who never feels comfortable in her faculty may be inattentive at meetings, irritable with students, and simply suffer through to the end of the year.

In a class it may take several days or weeks for all students to present themselves to the total class or within a small group. In organizational settings (like faculty meetings), initial inclusion means gaining adequate recognition and the same opportunity to present oneself prior to tasks and agendas. It means balancing persons and tasks. This is what makes the big difference in how people finally are able to work and learn together. Moreover, it is one more way to *personalize the high school system!*

Inclusion

In order to have inclusion, three opportunities must be provided:

1. Each person needs to be able to introduce herself, not just by stating a name but offering a short description of her feelings, interests, resources, talents or special qualities.

2. Each person needs to be able to express his hopes or expectations for what will happen during the group's time together.

3. Each person needs to be acknowledged by the group as having been heard, appreciated and welcomed.

It has been said that the first 15 minutes of a meeting defines how a group will relate or work together. As a teacher-facilitator of a new high school class, engage everyone by being inclusive—inviting names, reviewing expectations, and modeling listening and appreciation. Like most good teachers you probably already do this automatically. Hold off talking about the class subject. Allow five or more minutes for people to talk in pairs or triads sharing who they are and a few expectations. Ask them to share the time equally and to give each other *the gift of listening*. The opportunity to talk even briefly with peers not only begins to build inclusion but gives a glimpse of how the class will relate and learn together. After the brief first meeting interaction, ask a *reflection question*:

Invite the pelican that soars over the Tribes Trail map to be your constant companion. Her name is Reflection. She will tell you, rather immodestly that she makes the TLC process work well anywhere. At times, you will want to ignore her calls: "timeout," stop the action, teacher" "time to reflect," or "what's happening now?" Reflection knows that if you watch from the bird's eye view, classroom management goes more smoothly. Refection is a wise bird who can describe just what she sees or hears while people are working together. It is primary method of formative assessment. You will find her questions on the pages of every learning strategy. Reflection clears up confusion and helps everyone soar to greater heights.

"Did any groups discover something you may have in common?"

Observe any organization of more than six people. People very naturally sub-group or arrive at a meeting with one or two others in order to feel less anxious. The intentional use of small temporary groups early as people come together makes it easier for all to feel included at least with a few before relating or speaking in a larger group of people. Using this process, leaders of large conferences sub-group hundreds of people several times early in the gathering just to guarantee that no one is isolated. Agenda items can even be submitted from all of the small groups in order to include everyone's expectations.

Inclusion is a basic human need, and unless it is met people feel vulnerable and defensive. The saying "a camel is a horse designed by a committee" most certainly refers to a committee whose members attempted to undertake a task without first having achieved inclusion together. Time spent up front, building inclusion and trust is the most valuable strategy that a high school teacher (or a school leader with the faculty) can make. Although it takes a bit longer at first, the pay-off in achievement, creativity and morale makes all the difference!

THE STAGE OF INFLUENCE

As mellow as the stage of inclusion can be, in time a very natural restlessness will be seen throughout the class or community. The restlessness is a good sign, because it means people do feel included and are ready to work together. You will begin to notice that:

▶ Members are taking more initiative, are participating and speaking up; they may be making suggestions, asking confronting questions, and even resisting leadership

▶ People are discussing or questioning group goals, ways to work together, and how decisions are made

▶ People are not being as polite or as patient with each other

▶ Different opinions or disagreements are beginning to be expressed.

Rather than panic and decide that groups just don't work, these indicators are positive signals.

The new restlessness means that the time spent in building inclusion, trust, kindness, and a sense of belonging has been achieved. People are now ready to really work on tasks together... the stage of influence has arrived. Congratulations!

The Influence stage centers on the following questions:

"How can each person influence the goals, tasks, and decision-making process of the group?"

"How can members assert their individuality and value in the midst of the group?"

"How can leadership be shared so that the resources and potential of each member is called forth?"

To feel "of influence" is to feel of value (self-worth, power, individual resource to the group). To the extent that each person does not feel important in a classroom or organization, commitment and motivation decrease.

The responsibility of the teacher-leader also is to provide methods for resolving the inevitable differences in issues and concerns. Conflicts and misunderstandings are a natural part, a vital dynamic, of the process and cannot be ignored. They can be resolved through a variety of strategies, such as:

To feel "of influence" is to feel of value.

▶ Reflecting on and discussing the incident or situation that is happening

▶ Helping people to state their feelings clearly

▶ Assisting the group to give constructive feedback

▶ Facilitating problem-solving methods

▶ Role-playing, using role-reversal techniques

▶ Negotiating the priorities of individual members.

If issues are ignored, the energy of the group is deflected away from its capacity to accomplish tasks together!

The sensitive classroom teacher recognizes that continuing to focus on subject matter in the midst of interpersonal or group issues is neither academically nor emotionally helpful. Having people meet in their tribes to resolve a disruptive issue not only transfers responsibility to the class, but promotes a sense of value for the students. Once the conflict has been resolved by students, people will go back to their work on tasks with renewed energy.

Influence

Rather than allowing group members to wrestle for ways to have influence, the skilled teacher-leader introduces a selection of strategies that help people to:

▶ Express diverse attitudes, opinions, positions, and personal feelings

▶ Put forth ideas without others passing judgment; help people to respect individual differences

▶ Use participatory methods for decision making so that all members feel they are influential and of value to the group

▶ Help members share leadership responsibility.

During the influence stage the teacher or leader supports the learning groups to work as much as possible on their own. Contact is maintained with the groups by requesting periodic reports and circulating among them to determine whether assistance is needed. However, you will notice that if you sit down within a group, the dynamic changes immediately. Group members will once again center on you as the leader and cease to participate as much with each other. As the influence stage progresses and issues become resolved, shared leadership begins to emerge from group members. What a delight it is to see a shy young person lead an activity or discussion in his or her tribe! And what a relief it is to see a dominant member sit back as others in the tribe demonstrate their unique skills and talents. Some folks have called TLC Learning Community process magic... but we call it a reality that can be achieved by any committed teacher and school leader.

THE STAGE OF COMMUNITY

Who does not long for a sense of community in the midst of a city, an organization, a staff, a school, the classroom... the impersonal crowd? The deep human longing is our need to be known, to belong, to care and be cared for. Community is the esprit that happens when many minds and hearts come together to work toward a common good. Community happens through inclusion and the appreciation of individual differences. One can tell when community has become a reality. It is the delightful surprise one day that those we are with (no matter what the difference in age, gender, race, culture, intelligence, or talent) are indispensable and beautiful.

The possibility for community, whether in a classroom, school, or any organization, depends upon the belief that interdependence and connection to others is key to human development, learning, and the accomplishment of task.

The caring community we long for doesn't just happen; it can be intentionally developed. It depends upon any group of people deliberately creating *inclusion* for all members, and working through the nitty-gritty issues of *influence*.

You will know that you are in a community if you often hear laughter and singing. You will know you are in a institution or bureaucracy if you hear the silence of long halls and the intonations of formal meetings.[21]

—JOHN McKNIGHT

Community

Creating Community requires:

- ▶ Continuing to using the skills that enable collaboration

- ▶ Sustaining the agreements about how we will relate and work together

- ▶ Dedication to resolving rather than avoiding uncomfortable problems or misunderstandings that may begin to separate members

- ▶ Taking time to reflect on how well we are doing

- ▶ Celebrating individual and group achievements.

Once a class, staff or other type of community has gone through adversity together, its members become filled with confidence that they can handle whatever comes their way. This is the path to resilient relationships, creativity and outstanding results!

At this point in the Learning Community process, the classroom, faculty, or school community can assess itself by asking the following:

"How well do we know the unique strengths and weakness of each of our members?"

"Do we share responsibility for accomplishing goals for the good of the whole community using our diverse talents and skills?"

"Are we freely expressing our caring and consideration for one another?"

"Do we take time to tell stories and reflect on our experiences together?"

"Do we laugh, play, and enjoy each other as we create new approaches or solve old problems together?"

"How well do we recognize contributions and celebrate our community accomplishments and shared traditions?"

THE SPIRAL OF RENEWAL

Each time the members of a learning community or small classroom group come together they need some type of inclusion activity before they begin to focus on task; and influence issues will always need to be addressed. A helpful way of visualizing the continuing growth and evolution of a learning group is to imagine an ascending spiral that moves up through the levels of inclusion, influence, and community as it rises. One full "loop" represents a group meeting so that each time the spiral completes a cycle it goes through the three stages again. But each time a tribe meets, though it still needs to begin with inclusion, it moves on to a slightly higher level of positive interaction. The spiral is continuous and a never-ending process. Graphically, it looks something like this:

The repeated sequence of inclusion, influence, and community enables the group to experience increasingly more profound interaction the longer they are together.

Schools will be transformed only when this community-building process is implemented for teachers as well as for students. The critical challenge for the 21st century does not lie in mastering this piece of information or that technology. It lies in creating connectedness—in building schools across the nation that tap the innate developmental wisdom that is our shared humanity, connecting us to each other and to our shared web of life.

Community

Somewhere, there are people
to whom we *can* speak with passion
without having the words catch in our throats.
Somewhere a circle of hands will open to receive us,
eyes will light up as we enter, voices will celebrate with us
whenever we come into our own power.
Community means strength that joins our strength
to do the work that needs to be done.
Arms to hold us when we falter.
A circle of healing. A circle of friends.
Someplace where
we *can* be free.[23]

—STARHAWK

8

Structuring and Personalizing the Community of Learners

Structuring and Personalizing the Community of Learners

IN THIS CHAPTER YOU WILL

▶ Become familiar with structures that personalize learning communities throughout the high school system

▶ Recognize the systemic nature of schools and importance of structuring learning communities to accomplish change

▶ Learn initial steps in creating the high school learning community

▶ Recognize how structuring classroom active learning communities enhances learning both for students and teachers

▶ Learn how implementing a comprehensive Advisory Program not only supports students' development and career planning, but also maintains a positive motivational culture throughout the whole school

▶ Consider structures beyond the classroom to further personalize the high school for its population of young adults

I see in these kinds of endeavors the concept of the school as a community of learners, a place where all participants—teachers, principals, parents and students—engage in learning and teaching. School is not a place for important people who do not need to learn and unimportant people who do. Instead, it is a place where students discover, and adults re-discover the joys, the difficulties and the satisfactions of learning.[1]

—ROLAND S. BARTH

MOVING THE FOCUS AND CARING CULTURE THROUGHOUT THE COMMUNITY

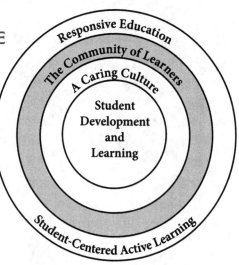

Notice that the four circle framework graphic, first described in Chapter 5, "Weaving Essential Principles," now has the *Community of Learners* circle shaded. *Transformation of the high school system* depends on maintaining the central focus on *student development and learning*—then creating a *caring culture* and spreading the culture in all classes, activities and groups throughout the *community of learners*. The culture of respect, inclusion, appreciation and civility is absolutely critical to maximize learning and development (for teachers as well as students), and to achieve a high performing school.

They say 'it takes a village to raise a child'—but I've observed it takes everyone in a high school to raise the system.

PERSONALIZATION OF THE HIGH SCHOOL COMMUNITY

The need to *personalize* all aspects of high schools is repeatedly emphasized in the NASSP *Breaking Ranks* documents as one of three most important changes. Namely...

▶ Personalization and school environment

▶ Professional learning communities and collaborative leadership

▶ Curriculum, instruction and assessment.

The goal calling for the *personalization of high schools* is quite emphatic:

High schools will create small units in which anonymity is banished.[2]

Banishing anonymity throughout a high school system of hundreds or thousands of people takes more than just creating smaller schools of 500–600 students or houses of 100 within large schools, and expecting that reduced numbers of students assures personalization. The important question is "what would students be experiencing in a high school that is a truly personalized school?"

In our school, now we know that our ticket to doing well in life is the whole big deal. No matter who you are people respect and treat you well. Teachers, administrators, counselors, office staff. And even the bus drivers—greet you—maybe not always by name, but with a wave or "how are ya doin'?" People listen, people care about you. There's a neat feeling here. 'It's the culture', teachers say.

Yeah! And within each class you belong to a group that works together. Our groups have agreements on how to get along to work and learn together. Sometimes it's research, inquiry on topics, experiments, demonstrations—even designing assessments to know what progress we're making. People like how teachers transfer responsibility to our groups instead of lecturing what we're supposed to learn. I'm getting better grades than ever before. It's cool!

THE MEANING OF PERSONALIZATION

Once again we must go back to looking at the needs of the important clients—the adolescents attending our high schools. The teams of researchers from the Education Alliance at Brown University that shadowed students at seven high schools, identified the following six student needs that a *personalized* high school system must to be addressing:[3]

Voice—the need for students to express their personal perspective
Belonging—the need to create individual and group identities
Choice—the need to examine options and choose a path
Freedom—the need to take risks and assess effects
Imagination—the need to create a projected view of self
Success—the need to demonstrate mastery

How well a school is addressing these needs determines the outcomes of its personalization efforts. Breaking Ranks II *contains an excellent chart, "Interactions in Personalized Learning," by J.H. Clarke and E. Frazer that you will find in the Resource Section of this book. It identifies many of the personal needs of students, matching school practices and the resulting benefits the practices may have in meeting the needs of their students.*[4]

The document, *Breaking Ranks II* provides this clear definition as a basis for changing the structures and practices in a high school:

Personalization is a learning process in which schools help students assess their own talents and aspirations, plan a pathway toward their own purposes, work cooperatively with others on challenging tasks, maintain a record of their explorations, and demonstrate their learning against clear standards in a wide variety of media, all with the close support of adult mentors and guides.[5]

The document recommends:

▶ Creating structures so that students cannot remain anonymous for four years

▶ Establishing schedules and priorities that allow teachers to develop an appreciation for each student's abilities

▶ Creating structures in which the aspirations strengths, weaknesses, interests and level of progress of each student are known well by at least one adult

▶ Providing opportunities for students to learn about the values associated with life in a civil and democratic society, their responsibilities within that society and the ability to exercise those values within the school

▶ Offering parents, families, and community members opportunities for involvement in students' education

- ► Ensuring that the physical and mental health needs of students are addressed
- ► Providing students with opportunities to demonstrate their academic, athletic, musical, dramatic, and other accomplishments in a variety of ways.

But how can we assure productive interaction, relationships and learning throughout this complex of structures and practices?

Admittedly, that's a very important question that is not always considered. All of the structures and practices listed above are *what* needs to happen. *How* to do it depends not only on structuring and personalizing the system for students but also for teachers, school leaders, support personnel and parents of the school community. All long to escape from anonymity. All need inclusion, a sense of belonging and value, and recognition. All benefit by being in a caring culture and working with others within democratic relational structures. Everyone's motivation, learning and development is affected by the cultural context of the system, the quality of relationships and the social-emotional learning that is experienced.

LOOKING AT THE WHOLE HIGH SCHOOL AS A LEARNING COMMUNITY

A consensus of current literature is advocating... learning communities, learning communities, learning communities! School learning communities, teacher learning communities and professional development learning communities. It is not a passing fad. It is the logical response after decades of secondary schools tinkering with initiatives that did not (1) truly focus on the whole picture of students' academic, social and emotional development, and (2) take into consideration the interrelated systemic nature of schools, namely, the sub-systems of staff, departments, parents, district committees, and student groups—all of which not only influence each other, but affect student learning and development.

High performing schools use a variety of personalized learning communities for interdisciplinary and departmental inquiry/study, curriculum design, assessment, problem-solving, administrative planning, support staff and community involvement. As we all may have experienced, adult planning groups at times can become divisive, fall into difficult dynamics and fail to achieve task goals. Not so in a Tribes Learning Community school! The same collaborative process that has been used so effectively for years for students' collaborative work in classrooms effectively sustains positive dynamics, communication and relationships in adult groups. In learning how to help students learn, the professional community learns to relate well and be productive.

Typically, schools overlook or dismiss the need not only to develop a positive culture but also collaborative structures. Whether the high school is large or small, the road to educational excellence and learning for *all—staff as well students*—requires all of the sub-systems collaborating—all singing the same song.

RECOGNIZING THE SYSTEMIC NATURE OF SCHOOLS

Underlying the process of Tribes TLC is systems theory, a perspective growing out of the fields of sociology, psychology and biology. It focuses on the inter-related nature of living systems, including individuals, schools, families, organizations and communities. All are living systems which, in the realm of schools, means that individual learning and experiences, both for students and teachers, arise out of the cultural context and interpersonal relationships within the system. It is the reason why "structuring the high school's community of learners" into small learning groups (communities) is essential to developing a positive overall infrastructure that facilitates improvement and system change. Sub-systems never operate in isolation. What happens in one affects all. Improving one improves others. This is why the Tribes TLC theory of change focuses on transforming all of the interrelated systems within a school community into *learning communities*. It is a systemic "inside-out" approach.

CONTRASTING APPROACHES TO SCHOOL IMPROVEMENT

The systemic inside-out approach calls upon everyone to be agents of change, which means building the capacity of "inside" school personnel to transform their own school rather than counting on "outside" professionals (consultants) to lead the way for (so called) "comprehensive school reform." The significant structural differences and relational differences are noted in the two images on the next page.[7]

The inside-out approach for school improvement is systemic. Its cellular structures facilitate overall collaborative interaction, inclusion, communication, personalization and learning among adult teams (communities, tribes or groups) throughout the school. The transfer to "insiders" engages everyone in transforming the whole system. It becomes obvious how impossible this is for any traditional top-down organization to involve all. As soon as a high school is perceived as a "social cultural setting in which every individual is an integral part, and in which every participant is responsible both for the learning and the overall well-being of everyone else" waves of new ideas and energy flow.[8]

The school becomes a community for learning when it is a purposeful place, a communicative place, a just place, a disciplined place, a caring place, and a celebrative place.[6]
—EARNEST BOYER

To succeed, school reform must happen from the inside out.[9]
—RICHARD ELMORE

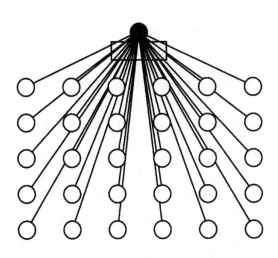 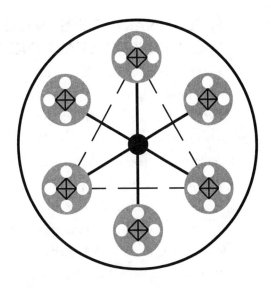

OUTSIDE-IN REFORM

outside consultants

top-down planning

district and agency workshops

less knowledgeable of students

system-centered

passive participation

individual implementation

authoritarian communication

results "wither"

INSIDE-OUT TRANSFORMATION

inside professionals

collegial involvement in planning

capacity-building teachers' learning
communities

knowledgeable

student-centered

active participation

collaborative implementation

network communication

results visible and on-going

How do we get it all going in our high school?

PRELIMINARY STEPS IN CREATING THE HIGH SCHOOL LEARNING COMMUNITY

The transformation of a high school usually begins when a visionary Principal and a few other school leaders believe that students in the school need "something more"—and probably that they and the teachers do too. Perhaps they have heard about other high schools that are "breaking ranks" from the out-dated low performance factory model. Perhaps they have been reading the NASSP documents, *Breaking Ranks*. Their dialogue and energy is what lights the way to change.

It is essential that the Principal shares his/her own personal vision for the high school. It is important not only if the principal is new to the school, but also if he or she has been at the school for awhile. As lead learners, we all need to be continually reflecting on and refining our personal vision as we continually are learning. More than all, we need to keep the whole child, the whole adolescent, in mind—and passionately express what we believe will help both students' development and learning. It is immensely important for a staff to hear a school leader's vision and beliefs. It leads to discussions throughout the whole school community, and helps all to arrive at and carry a common vision.

The first step for the Principal and school leaders is to organize a small Core Leadership Team (six to eight people) to guide, coordinate and reflect on the progress of the change effort. In reality they are the school's first community of learners. McLaughlin and Talbert, authors of the excellent book, "Building School-Based Teacher Learning Communities," point out that the task of the Principal and proactive school leaders is to manage the following three challenges...

▶ Leverage teacher commitment and support

▶ Develop learning resources for teacher communities, and

▶ Support the stages of community development.[10]

Oh, but some people may be resistant!

Some resistance to change... is not unusual. It can be a persistent entrenched pathology in long standing status quo systems. Following is a familiar list of why some staff members may resist change:[11]

- ▶ Administration mandated the change
- ▶ If it ain't broke, don't fix it
- ▶ Fear of rejection or the perception of incompetence
- ▶ Tried it before and it didn't work
- ▶ Don't have time
- ▶ If I need to change, then I must be wrong—I believe what I am doing is right
- ▶ Lack of knowledge and understanding of different methods
- ▶ Basic insecurity.

Folks have to be convinced that the benefits are worth more than the cost of change. At first it is a personal question: "What will I have to give up and what will I get?" Resistance is weakened whenever the critical mass of people in the system begin to express commitment and enthusiasm for the change. The Principal and several school leaders can bring this about by engaging the whole staff in a series of conversations within small groups on core beliefs, such as the following used in the Effective Schools Process.[12]

1. School improvement must be school-by-school and one school at a time.

2. There are only two kinds of schools—improving schools and declining schools.

3. Every adult in a school is important.

4. The capacity to improve a school already resides in the school.

5. You and your colleagues are already doing the best you can, given what you know and the current conditions in which you find yourselves.

6. All children can learn and the school controls enough of the variables to assure that virtually all schools do learn.

The conversations initiate the culture of inclusion and the building of professional collegiality. They give leaders the opportunity to invite all to listen with consideration, to respect the variety of viewpoints and opinions people may have and to express appreciation. The conversations are an introduction to the Tribes Learning Community agreements, the foundation for personalizing the high school system.

> Some resistance to change is not unusual. It can be a persistent entrenched pathology in long standing status quo systems.

As preliminary work, the Principal and Core Leadership Team may choose to assess the current culture and status of the school by looking at hard and soft data gathered through school records, surveys, focus groups and conversations.

STUDENT DATA

▶ Classroom observations

▶ Promotion/retention rates

▶ Absenteeism/drop-out rate

▶ Testing data

▶ Graduation rates/college-bound rate

▶ Student participation in co-curricular activities

▶ Student-led focus groups

▶ Student-led surveys

FACULTY DATA

▶ Classroom observations

▶ Professional development survey

▶ Teacher recognitions/awards

▶ Faculty turnover rate

▶ Informal conversations

▶ Teacher-led focus groups

▶ Informal conversations

It also is a way to establish base-line data to reflect upon and periodically to assess progress.

THE ON-GOING ROLE OF THE PRINCIPAL AND CORE LEADERSHIP TEAM

The collaborative-styled 21st century Principal meets regularly with the Core Leadership Team to:

▶ articulate the vision, philosophy and values of the mission to transform the high school system into an active learning community of educational excellence

▶ gain knowledge on developing the high school system as a learning community

▶ plan how to involve all of the teaching staff in the collaborative change effort

▶ organize and sustain ongoing planning, coordination and dialogue with the Learning Communities, to which all instructional staff members belong

▶ monitor the implementation of change efforts and reflect upon on-going sequence of changes taking place for students, teachers and the school system, and

▶ encourage and oversee celebrations of improvement and success.

We're the cheerleaders and resource folks.

A WORKING FRAMEWORK TO ENGAGE ALL

We suggest that the Core Leadership Team and Principal use the excellent active learning process, the "Five E's" to structure and manage the school learning community project. The Five E's strategy was originally defined by Roger Bybee of the Miami Museum of Science, and now is widely used to design curriculum learning experiences. We'll discuss the curricular use of the "Five E's" in Chapter 15. The strategy, as it could be used by the Core Leadership Team to introduce, coordinate and assess on-going progress moves through the following five sequential phases:[13]

Engage: To awaken the interest of others and involve them in active participation

Explore: To define possible objectives and activities that the high school community might consider or investigate

Explain: To have participants investigate, report back, present information, clarify and define next steps

Elaborate: To articulate learning to the wider community, engaging others in collaborative team action

Evaluate: To assess in a continuous process that involves the community (or learning communities) in defining on-going improvement initiatives.

The five phases can be used continuously in a circular fashion to:

▶ Maintain the flow of information between the many small groups in the high school, the Core Leadership Team and the whole school community

▶ Expand participation to new groups of teachers and/or the parent community

▶ Continually assess progress, revise objectives, improve strategies, activities, learning experiences, etcetera.

Use of the Tribes agreements and community building process by all of the high school learning communities at each phase ensures positive communication, inclusion, a sense of value (influence and recognition), and community for all. It also sustains the culture, democratic decision making and reflective practice throughout use of the process.

As applied to a high school, this is what takes place at each stage.

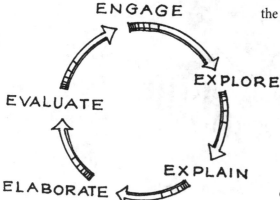

Engage

Choosing how to engage the staff varies inasmuch as every high school is different. School leaders or the Core Leadership Team (CLT) in large high schools initiate cohorts of separate Collegial Learning Communities (CLCs) for teachers one at a time. Each is composed of no more than 30 teachers, and divided into smaller groups (five to six persons) for meaningful dialogue, inclusion, and learning. The Principal and/or CLT leaders share their commitment for school improvement, and steps of the process upon which the whole school is embarking over a period of time. The Tribes TLC agreements and the rational for their use in classroom learning communities as well as staff groups are introduced. Following several inclusion strategies, time-limited discussions are initiated using questions such as the following:

What do you envision as an "ideal" high school? What might it look like, sound like, and feel like?

What beliefs do you have on how to help students become successful learners?

What hopes or best expectations do you have as a teacher for the students in this school?

The purpose of this phase is to engage participation, build inclusion and introduce thoughtful and positive questions. It is important that discussions do not become gripe sessions on what is wrong with the students or the school. Remind people that what was done in the past and continuing to do more of the same does not lead to overall transformation of any organization. Teacher discussions on their own visions, beliefs and learning typically gives the faculty a new sense of motivation. As much as anything this first opportunity to participate with others on how to improve the school begins to change the culture and offer hope.

Explore

The dialogues move the staff towards defining a collective vision and focus on what the school can become. Learning groups within the cohorts are urged to explore and report back what leading educators and the literature have to say about creating high performance high schools. Some groups can examine literature about today's adolescents, how they learn and the natural search that each is on towards moving out into the world. There are many resources to explore... including, of course, the summaries of research and studies in this book, *Engaging All.* Arranging meetings and conversations with other school leaders and teachers using the Tribes Learning Community approach also are very helpful.

Explain

As the staff explores and learns, it is likely that the staff will recognize that the current literature in the field of education carries the common message:

1. It is essential that high schools focus on the whole development of adolescents in all of their potential, skills and interests in order for them to achieve higher academic performance

2. It means creating a caring and supportive school culture, teachers using sound active learning pedagogy that corresponds to how today's adolescents learn

3. It requires "personalization" of the impersonal high school system no matter its size, and

4. Professional or collegial learning communities for teachers are essential to achieve overall transformation of a high school system.

Elaborate

As the "what to do" becomes clear, training in the Tribes TLC active learning classroom process and research-based pedagogy is arranged for the cohorts. Their focus turns to building the caring culture in their classes, designing and implementing active learning curriculum, and assessing student engagement, learning and performance. Connections are also made to state standards, other school initiatives and co-curricular areas. Moving successfully to responsive active learning depends upon the commitment of the instructional staff to engage daily in reflective practice with student groups, and in weekly (or more often) meetings with their CLC teams. Positive change happens through teachers' collaborative reflection on *what is* and *what is not* working well. The practice provides opportunities to tweak, modify, revise and improve curricular learning experiences in small increments. Reflective practice is an on-going transformational process that smart systems use!

Evaluate

Assessment is a continuous process that guides all of the teacher learning groups, provides feedback to their CLCs, the Core Leadership Team and Principal. It is the best way to define on-going improvement initiatives. It plays a crucial role in looking at challenges, possible changes and next steps. Reflective practice and assessment throughout the whole system moves it forward as it faces challenges, opportunities and determines the best route for the school throughout the process. The staff constantly is asking themselves, "what do we need to do, how do we need to do it, and how will we know we are successful."

IT'S ALL ABOUT LEARNING!

Largely, public school districts facing mandates to demonstrate significantly higher student test scores each year dismiss the direct connection between on-going professional development for teachers and student learning—although verified by years of research studies and common sense. Typically, the few days set aside for traditional staff training are used to dispense information on standards, test procedures and data analysis. The message is to "do more only harder." Transformation of the factory model high school system depends upon stakeholders finally realizing that the fundamental purpose of school is *not about teaching... It is about learning!*

You will discover how to develop collegial learning communities in the very next chapter.

THE HEART OF LEARNING AND SCHOOL RENEWAL IS THE CLASSROOM

In a traditional high school where students may have six different classes, sitting passively in rows day after day, listening to teachers lecturing, taking notes and taking tests, personalization is impossible. One teacher, reflecting on the her first year of teaching, was rather shocked when at the end of the school year a student told her she regretted she never had the opportunity to learn the names of others in the class. The following year, this teacher deliberately included strategies for students not only to learn each others' names, but to have inclusion and gain a sense of belonging by working with others. She and others in her school now recognize that a personalized high school classroom has:

The staff constantly is asking themselves, "what do we need to do, how do we need to do it, and how will we know we are successful?"

The fundamental purpose of school is not about teaching... It is about learning!

▶ Clear expectations and agreements

▶ An environment in which students feel emotionally safe, respect among peers and a sense of belonging

▶ Students working in collaborative groups

▶ A caring teacher facilitating active group learning

▶ Students reflecting on their learning and cooperation

▶ Students and teacher in positive rapport, trust and communication.

STRUCTURING CLASSROOM ACTIVE LEARNING COMMUNITIES

Time has proven that moving from the traditional impersonal classroom structure to research-based group learning re-energizes teachers as well as high school students. A teacher in another large school acknowledged that one day she really saw her "standardized self" lecturing to her class of non-standardized restless teenagers, and was startled with the emotion she felt. She was lonely. There seemed to be an impenetrable wall between her and the young adults sitting passively in rows in front of her. She had been noticing the wall ever since she saw this diagram in a Tribes Learning Community course several weeks earlier.[14]

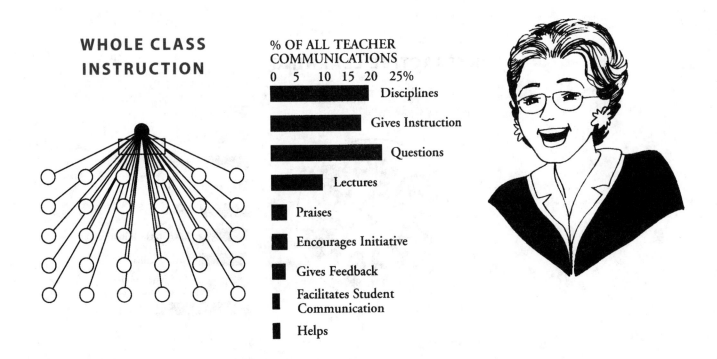

WHOLE CLASS INSTRUCTION

% OF ALL TEACHER COMMUNICATIONS

| 0 | 5 | 10 | 15 | 20 | 25% |

Disciplines

Gives Instruction

Questions

Lectures

Praises

Encourages Initiative

Gives Feedback

Facilitates Student Communication

Helps

Studies verify that when teachers depend upon "whole class instruction" more than 70% of their time is spent lecturing, giving instructions, asking questions and either disciplining or trying to get the attention of restless students. Only 30% of their time can be devoted to doing what the majority long to do... to praise, encourage initiative, give feedback and work supportively with youthful learners. Whole class individualized instruction causes students to be competitive, vying to impress teachers or being quickest to give answers. Good for them, we say, but it sets up a caste system of winners and losers; the non-competitive or shy are seen as low achievers. It is impossible for the traditional individualistic structure to...

▶ actively engage all students

▶ transfer responsibility to students for inquiry, research and discourse on concepts together

▶ engage students in holding each other accountable or reflecting on and celebrating individual or group work done well.

Moreover, the skills needed for the workplace and life in the 21st century are collaborative and relational. If not learned in school, how will they ever be learned?

In contrast to the previous diagram, the same studies show that when classrooms are reorganized into active learning groups, "teacher talk" time lessens from 70% to 25%.

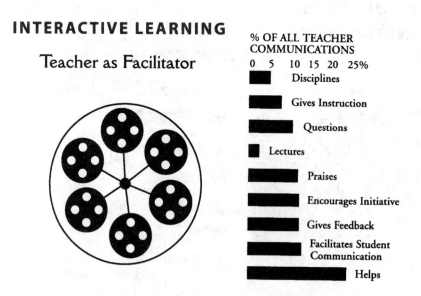

INTERACTIVE LEARNING

Teacher as Facilitator

% OF ALL TEACHER COMMUNICATIONS

0   5   10 15 20 25%

Disciplines

Gives Instruction

Questions

Lectures

Praises

Encourages Initiative

Gives Feedback

Facilitates Student Communication

Helps

Now 75% of the teacher's time can be spent helping and encouraging students, giving feedback, facilitating student communication, praising and celebrating success. The transfer of responsibility to student groups to gather, interpret, and apply information and concepts makes a dramatic difference. When students become responsible to each other, accountability for individual performance and behavior becomes a group concern. Guided by the four agreements for TLC Learning Communities, teachers hardly ever have to intervene but become resource specialists to facilitate group learning.

At best, the old structure gave each student a few minutes to speak, mostly, in response to questions from the teacher. Dialogue with peers in groups minimally provides ten times that amount of discussion time on subject matter. The classroom "breaks ranks" from the impersonal rigid straight rows system. Instead it looks something like this:

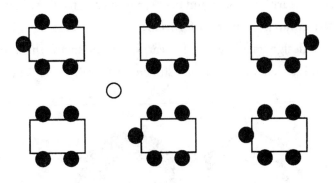

Tables replace desks or desks become centered so that four or five students can face each other and work together. Simply altering the structure of the classroom is the first step in making it student-centered. Personalized interaction in classrooms (and also in faculty meetings) becomes collaborative and looks like this:

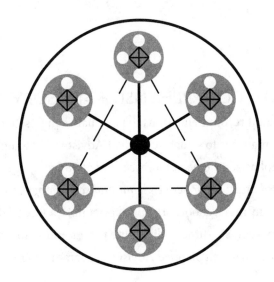

In America's best classrooms, again, the emphasis has shifted. Instead of individual achievement and competition, the focus is on group learning. Students learn to articulate, clarify, and restate for one another how they identify and find answers. They learn how to seek and accept criticism from their peers, solicit help, and give credit to others... This is an ideal preparation for life-times of symbolic analytic work.[15]

—Robert Reich

Thirty-two students of this class now have a sense of inclusion and belonging in learning groups. The eight small student learning communities (SLCs) make classroom management easy for the teacher. It is like having eight departments in a business organization, each of which has the responsibility of managing their "personnel" and quality of work on tasks. Accountability and assessment, as much as possible, takes place within groups. In the same way the students provide support to help each other learn. Management theory has proven that no one person can supervise and support more that six to eight people. Why are teachers expected to do the impossible every day—managing dozens of students many periods throughout every day? One teacher, however, can supervise and give support to five or more small departments. When learning groups, guided by a set positive agreements on how they will work together, are given this responsibility individual motivation and productivity increase immensely.

The connecting lines in the previous diagram indicate that active learning takes place both within the active learning groups and between groups as facilitated by the teacher.

Moving to active group learning transforms the role of teachers. They become facilitators, researchers and designers of meaningful learning experiences. The impenetrable wall between teachers and students vanishes, and student anonymity is banished.

It's true, our role has changed.

And we smile a lot now!

Talk about personalization of this school! It's everywhere!

IMPLEMENTING A COMPREHENSIVE ADVISORY PROGRAM

One of the most important recommendations to personalize high school systems and to improve student performance is to structure student Advisory Programs. The *Breaking Ranks* II document emphasizes the need for *"each student to have frequent and meaningful opportunities to plan and assess his or her academic and social progress with a faculty member."*[16] Unfortunately, many high schools organized brief once a week Advisory classes that were more or less "homerooms"—time to distribute papers and school announcements. Reviews of research show that well planned Advisory programs do much more.[17]

Breaking Ranks II emphasizes that an effective Advisory program has the following five dimensions:[17]

1. **Purpose**: A clearly defined (student-centered) purpose supported by the school community

2. **Organization**: Organized to fulfill the purpose and to ensure personalization

3. **Meaningful Program Content**: Based on the purposes to be achieved for students

4. **Assessment**: Assessment at several levels

5. **Leadership**: Strong leadership by an individual or team charged with designing, implementing, overseeing, and assessing the program.

A review of research identified the results of well-planned programs:

▶ Academic achievement was improved; failing grades were reduced and test scores were increased

▶ More students took college entrance exams

▶ Forty-six percent of teachers believed they influenced several of their advisees to improve their grades

▶ Student attitudes improved significantly (75% by one measure)

▶ Student teacher relations improved

▶ Number of dropouts declined

▶ Transition to high school was eased

▶ Liaison for parents was provided.

What might the Tribes Learning Community Advisory classes look like?

Advisory Programs in Tribes Learning Community (TLC) high schools have additional purposes and benefits:

1. They provide a sense of inclusion and belonging for every student in the school, in that all are members within positive and supportive peer groups. Thereby, they eliminate the persistent anonymity and alienation that undermines large or small high schools.

2. This type of Advisory supports the development of social competency by helping young adults to learn and use positive communication and group skills, and to work well not only in class groups but later in life work, family and community settings.

3. It personalizes the high school experience by assuring that every student has an opportunity to experience a caring and challenging environment that helps to develop the important personal attributes of resiliency. Every student can count on the period as his or her home base community that provides...

▶ **Caring and support**

▶ **High Expectations**

▶ **Meaningful Participation and Contribution.**[18]

4. Of great importance is that the Tribes TLC type of Advisory serves to institutionalize the new culture for learning throughout the whole high school system.

Given that every student needs a *significant adult* who listens, guides, supports and challenges his or her personal best throughout the high school years, it is recommended that the same teacher serves as the consistent adult for four years... encouraging each student to set high expectations, and to persevere towards attaining goals for his/her life beyond high school.

The class meets several periods a week, preferably throughout the whole school at the same time so that every teacher has a class. Students belong to small groups (four to five members) and initially get to know each other through a series of inclusion and group skill strategies. The interactive group learning quickly develops a sense of community conveying that they are there not only to learn and plan for themselves but to support each other. The personal/social development curriculum in which all teachers are trained enables these young adults to define academic and personal goals. Moreover, the meaningful participation with peers fosters resiliency and brings their futures into focus.

The positive culture and active group learning practices learned in the Advisory periods transform the infrastructure as well as the culture of the high school as the group learning process is used in other classes. For example, at the beginning of the school

It's a place where everyone knows your name.

year having these classes focus on learning or reviewing the collaborative group skills and agreements readies all the academic classes in the school to work in groups effectively. Teachers, having been trained in the Tribes TLC active learning process, remind students of the "school wide" agreements and community building process. Anonymity vanishes quickly when new students are welcomed into a small groups in the class. They experience inclusion the very first day, and quickly learn "how this class and the school works." The consistent use of the positive group agreements and caring culture in all classes enables all newcomers to understand "this is how we work and help each other around here."

GETTING THE "BUY-IN" FOR THE COMMUNITY AGREEMENTS

The question that Kyle is asking is bound to be asked at the secondary level. And the importance of students being willing to honor the four positive agreements is critical to establishing a supportive learning culture in the high school. They need to have a voice. Early in the Advisory period, time is set aside for students to discuss how they wish people would treat and help each other to do well. Teachers find it effective to use the strategy, "The Ideal Classroom," that is contained in the Strategy section of this book. It enables students to give their input as to the kind of classroom they feel would be ideal in which to learn. This strategy summarizes their ideas into categories that usually turn out to be closely congruent with the Tribes Learning Community agreements of mutual respect, attentive listening, appreciations/no put-downs, and right to pass/participate. Count on a majority in any one Advisory class to lead the way in urging everyone to honor the clear expectations which in turn make the class, as well as other classes in the school, socially and emotionally safe places.

What's the big difference about having agreements—aren't they just more school rules? I hate rules!

But what about the freshmen?

WHAT ABOUT THE FRESHMEN?

Although students of all grades require a "place to belong" and a significant adult with whom to connect, freshmen in particular will benefit from participation in an Advisory class. Fifty percent of freshmen typically fail at least one of their core academic areas of English, math, social studies, or science.[19] The freshmen class in large high schools has the largest number of students who are not promoted to the next grade. Thus, many high schools are recognizing the need to go one step further for incoming 9th graders as they transition to the high school life.

Having the new ninth graders attend **freshman orientation days** before upper-class students arrive can provide a sense of inclusion in addition to learning about school expectations, classes, schedules etcetera. A helpful option is to preset chairs in groups of 12–14 in a large meeting room, and have a teacher (or the Advisory teacher they will have) and two well-trained upper-class students in each group. Throughout the one or two day orientation have people stay in the same group to participate in getting acquainted (inclusion to present who they are, expectations for the year, interests etc.). Active learning group strategies can be initiated for the freshman class as a whole community. Having upper class students throughout the "welcoming" groups also is very helpful. It is essential to have teachers or trainers who are familiar with the process of Tribes make a detailed timed plan that specifies the objectives to be achieved.

In addition to meeting with upper-class students on orientation days, each freshman may be paired with a carefully selected upper-class "buddy" who meets with them periodically or as needed. Moreover, well-trained "peer assistants" supervised by a school counselor or teacher can help newcomers to discuss interests, concerns and consider goals.

Engaging All to Prevent Dropping Out of High School

An Administrator's Perspective

Terry Doyle

The secret with dealing with students who are dropping out is to get them long before they become school avoiders or poor attenders. While there are many reasons why students do not attend school and perhaps ultimately drop out of high school, we know that the principles and practices of the Developmental Process of Tribes provide a clear framework - a proactive approach to help students to stay and succeed in school.

Understanding the Tasks of Adolescence that are highlighted in this book can provide great insight for teachers and parents. Consider a poor attender deciding whether or not to cut class for the afternoon. His driving need may be to have more *autonomy and independence* or a *sense of purpose* not felt in classes at school. Not motivated and little engaged he or she may conclude, "School just is not for me." Perhaps he is not sharing the other part of the sentence…."At night, I work at my part time job and sleep a lot during the day." Money and work has more immediate purpose than sitting passively in classes.

What if during those early months of transition to high school, as well as teachers and parents, students learned about the normal Tasks of Adolescence that all young people rightfully are trying to achieve? Think how empowering it might be to discuss ways in which they can through *active learning* in their school attain the developmental tasks for life success? Such information could be more readily referenced and understood when a behaviour like cutting class is considered.

As we know, peer relationships become increasingly important during adolescence. All are looking for someone who cares, and someone or something to care about. Creating a *caring culture* throughout the whole school and the many inclusive learning *communities* not only enables adolescents to find positive relationships but also fosters the protective factors of resiliency.

I cannot help but wonder what would happen if our high schools at the start of school changed "Curriculum Night" or "Meet the Teacher Night?" Traditionally these events consist of parents trying to put names with

Before becoming a School Administrator with the Toronto District School Board, Terry was an Itinerant Guidance Counselor for three middle schools where he was responsible for student transition to high school. Terry also worked as an Attendance Counselor at more than eight high schools, addressing needs of students who had poor attendance and who were at risk of dropping out of school. As a Certified Tribes TLC® Trainer, he provides Tribes training for the Toronto District School Board and has facilitated numerous trainings in Canada.

teachers' faces, and teachers handing out lists of the curriculum to be taught that year. What if this forum was spent engaging students, their parents and teachers, together in small groups, to share learners' interests, gifts, prior knowledge and experiences that may connect to topics in the new curriculum?

Let's also have high schools, as part of their transition plans for freshmen, host start-of-the-year barbecues to meet upper-class student buddies, Advisory class teachers and staff mentors. How about having a "Meet the Clubs" invitational where all of the clubs and teams showcase activities and welcome freshman to participate.

When visiting an "alternative program" for preventing students from dropping out, I am always amazed how the skills of caring staff can make a required curriculum *engaging* to a usually jaded class of students. Fundamentally, it comes down to teachers knowing the curriculum in its breath and depth, and facilitating the curriculum *actively* in "response" to students' interests and ways of learning.

It is not surprising that research has shown a correlation between the numbers of courses of study that students successfully complete in their first and second year of high school and their likelihood of staying in school.[20] To this end the secret to addressing students dropping out is to reach them during the transition years long before they become poor attenders or school avoiders. For when students do drop out, we can only hope that our high school somehow has fostered *resiliency and futures of promise* well enough that at some point... they drop back in.

RECOGNIZING THE VALUE AND PURPOSE OF CO-CURRICULAR STRUCTURES

It means reaching the **whole child**... the whole young person's social, emotional, physical, intellectual and moral spiritual being.

Let's get back to the purpose of education again for it will continue to tell us what the full range of the high school experience needs to be for our young adults. Remember back in Chapter Two? We recalled that more than 100 years ago John Dewey believed the purpose is... *to call forth the intellectual, moral, and emotional growth of each individual learner.* Respected others have concurred that it is nothing less than... *developing greatness in human beings.*

That's a big picture for today's high schools to consider. It means going beyond teaching only to the intellect—only to young minds. We'll say it again and again. It means reaching *the whole child*... the whole young person's social, emotional, physical, intellectual and moral spiritual being.

The first things to go when today's high schools are faced with financial crises are the "extra" school activities. Failure to sustain the arts, athletics, interest clubs and service learning denies the need to nurture students' interests, special talents and belonging in a variety of groups. Reaching out and encouraging the emerging wholeness in teenagers cannot merely be considered a lesser or unimportant educational "extra."

Growing research supports the role that the arts, physical activities, social groups and other forms of active experiences contribute to intellectual learning and human development.[21] Not only do co-curricular activities nurture the diversity of student interests, multiple intelligences and gifts, they contribute to the essential adolescent tasks all are trying to develop: autonomy/independence, social competency, problem-solving, a sense of purpose and positive expectations. Co-curricular activities further personalize the high school system.

Physical Activities

High school athletic programs and other school sports appeal to the restless kinesthetic needs of adolescents, and help to develop healthy exercise habits for adulthood. The team sports such as football, basketball, soccer and volleyball not only require team skills and collaboration but put the "we" of the team before the "me"—success for all.

One football coach new to a high school, worked on building a team by focusing on building the "culture" of the program. The coach's philosophy for the players was that they were people first, students second, and athletes third. His emphasis was on high expectations for each player. First be a "good person" making the right choices; then as a student to fulfill classroom responsibilities; and then to focus on becoming the best athlete possible contributing to the success of the team. The coach raised the state grade-point-average playing requirement for his players, and monitored their progress not only during football season, but throughout the school year.[22] An additional expectation in this high school was that all athletic teams did at least two community service projects a season to give back to the larger community. By building the culture of high expectations, providing caring support and putting the "we" before "me," three years later this team made it to the state championships.

Yeah, remember me? I'm not cutting school anymore. I'm getting better grades. I'm on the team!

Although sports such as tennis, golf, swimming, wrestling, judo or gymnastics, appear to be individual sports, they still take a collaborative effort and spirit for the school to have a successful season. Often looked up to by peers, student athletes serve as positive role models. It is more imperative than ever that today's high schools continue to involve students in as many opportunities as possible that promote their resiliency, health and well-being.

The Arts

Historically the arts were woven into a child's whole learning experience. Now reports such as a regretful one from the Royal Conservatory of Music (Toronto) reminds us, "The thickly drawn line between arts and non-arts, so evident in today's schools once did not exist."[23] Yet now we want youth to excel in higher brain functioning, science, math and problem-solving—all of which requires the development of pattern formation and logic. Increasingly, evidence from the brain sciences indicates the arts, especially music, play an important role in pattern formations that correlate with higher brain functioning in logic, math and problem-solving. Research tells us that music and art facilitate constructive thinking and learning. "Kill and drill" teaching does not. The arts whether music, dance, theater, creative writing, storytelling or the visual arts—are forms of active experiential learning that produce both positive academic and youth development outcomes.[24]

Whether it is a marching band of over 200 students, an orchestra of 100, a chorus of 40 students, a jazz band of 25, or a chamber orchestra of eight, it requires each individual to do their part to contribute to the harmony of the performance and their part to the performing community. Skilled music, drama and art instructors know that high school arts are more than teaching students skills.

My art helps me to explain who I am and what I know. I really do know lots!

That we have relieved the arts of their central role in education is a tragedy. The arts represent a natural and experiential way for children to learn.

—Bonnie Benard

Elden Seta, a fine dedicated music director says:

"I believe that education is not just about teaching things in the classroom. It's not just skills. It's not just about test scores. It's not about grades. It's about developing the individual. I always tell every one of my students this before they graduate that before they become a doctor, a policeman, a teacher, they have to be people first... because if you're a great person, people will benefit in many, many ways. But if you're only going to be a great career person, others will only benefit in one way.

I feel that learning should be fun; I don't think everything can be done in classrooms, or a student will think that's all learning is."

"Students need to smile, they need to laugh. Students need to play. They're young and they need to have fun. That enhances learning in the classroom."[25]

Then there is a student, who may barely say a word in regular academic classes, but when given a script to memorize, and a stage with an audience, she transforms brilliantly into different characters. She has discovered her gift and an avenue for self expression and identity. Participation in drama classes or theater also provides opportunities for students to display their various artistic talents in "behind the scenes" tasks such as: designing, building backdrop scenes and stage props; costumes, programs, tickets and publicity; and even writing scripts. Operating as a community with each person doing their part, success is a never-to-be-forgotten learning experience.

The developmental outcomes such as positive self-image, pride, self-discipline, and creativity become visible through involvement in the arts. All kindle a sense of competency. All satisfy adolescents' need for identity, active learning and being in community. Studies show that involvement in the arts not only develops all of the multiple intelligences and prevents depression, but clearly leads to increases in academic achievement and a sense of purpose for the future.[26]

It's no surprise! Keep the arts so all can soar higher!

OTHER PLACES AND FACES

In addition to school athletics and the arts, personalized high schools spawn a wide variety of opportunities in leadership roles, interest and service clubs. Many colleges now ask applicants to list services performed for others in schools and community. Students who provide service to others often acknowledge they experienced a shift in their motive from just "doing something to put on their college application" to realizing the satisfaction of helping others.

I'm not athletic and don't do art things. I really like working on the newspaper and being in the journalism club.

Schools that promote positive identity development are rich in engaging activities in which students can invest their psychic energy. Such schools value the role of relationships at all levels of learning.[27]

—Michael Nakkula

The existence of the kind culture and strutures for personalization throughout a high school not only motivates greater numbers of students to contribute services to others, but nurtures the development of altruism and personal resilience. When a new norm, such as giving service to others, becomes popular in a system, it usually motivates other teens to do the same. Count on this phenomenon to institutionalize not only service learning but also the other positive relational norms.

Would you believe? Chatty me once a week is listening and recording stories that seniors at the Sunset Island Center want to tell. I have them sit in a community circle, like we do in classes, and take three to five minute turns while holding a white feather—then passing it on. That works well so no one gabs on too long. Yeah! We all laugh a lot. And they all really like me to come.

9

Learning in Collegial Learning Communities

9 Learning in Collegial Learning Communities

IN THIS CHAPTER YOU WILL

▶ Realize why developing Collegial Learning Communities is the most effective way to transform today's traditional high schools into high performing school systems

▶ Understand the cultural, structural and professional development changes that need to take place within the high school

▶ Learn how to develop and empower effective teacher learning communities that take collaborative responsibility to help all students succeed

> With dismal regularity, we return to efforts to improve K–12 education. These efforts usually fail because education is conceived narrowly as "schooling."[2]
> —MIHALY CSIKSZENTMIHALYI

> School improvement is most surely and thoroughly achieved when teachers engage in frequent, continuous and increasingly concrete and precise talk about teaching practice.[1]
> —JUDITH WARREN LITTLE

MOVING FROM "SCHOOLING" TO RESPONSIVE PEDAGOGY

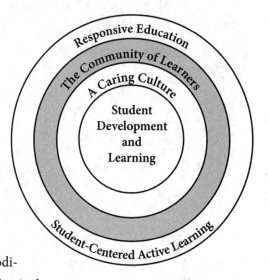

Traditional high school "schooling" has treated knowledge as "a commodity" that is stored in teachers' minds and texts, and that is "delivered" into the heads of students. Like other commodities the assumption has been that it also can be itemized, measured and sold to a wide-variety of customers. At a time when high school students are trying to become socially competent, traditional classrooms minimize peer interaction and collaboration. At a time when these young adults are striving to become self-directed and self-responsible, more controls and restrictions are imposed upon them. At a time when they want to think constructively for themselves, memorization and right answers are rewarded. Compliance is valued over creativity and community.[3] Rarely is historic pedagogy—"schooling"—perceived as dysfunctional—the students are.

LOOKING AT THE CONTEXT FOR CHANGE

The reality is that for more than twenty years schools in the United States and now other countries, increasingly have had to respond to government policies, regulations and "carrot and stick" (rewards and sanctions) accountability measures for an array of student performance standards. The pressure forces teachers to "teach harder rather than smarter."

A wide dimension of stakeholders now are concerned that many teachers have a limited capability to meet the educational needs of today's students. Milbrey McLaughlin and Joan Talbert, authors of *Building School-Based Teacher Learning Communities* insightfully write:[5]

> "They [students] require forms of instruction and pedagogy that are foreign to many teachers, as well as a fundamental reconceptualization of learning. Not enough [teachers] can organize instruction to highlight the cognitive skills that our new knowledge society expects. Not enough can work successfully with students from diverse cultural, ethnic and economic backgrounds. Not enough can relinquish the role of classroom "sage" and knowledge transmitter to assume a new role focused on facilitating problem solving and developing knowledge among students. [edit]. Teachers must make more than technical changes in their practices to provide the learning environments and student outcomes society demands. Their commitment must be to life-long professional learning and collective responsibility for improved student learning."

Richard Elmore, Harvard Graduate School Professor concurs that, "Getting students to learn at higher levels has to entail some change in both the ways students are taught and in the proportion of teachers who are teaching in ways that cause students to master higher-level skills and knowledge."[7]

Elmore's message and those of other prominent researchers and scholars embody the long-standing purpose of *progressive education,* namely, "to change the core of schooling from a teacher-centered, fact-centered, recitation-based pedagogy to a pedagogy based on an understanding of children's thought processes, ways of learning and capacity to use ideas in the context of real-life problems."[8]

The National Association of Secondary School Principals (NASSP) document, *Breaking Ranks—Changing an American Institution,* is emphatic with its message that "high schools need more than tinkering."[9] Piecemeal change has been tried for several decades with little or no lasting improvement of the recalcitrant system. Failure has been inevitable because the complex high school system has many interlocking parts, and when one or a few elements only are altered—all are affected. Like a house of cards, a slight change affects all.

The process of change no longer needs to be hit-or-miss tinkering. As we have been pointing out, *the critical elements of culture, structures and instruction*—all must focus on and support development and learning for the diversity of students in the high school.

Now I get it! Education that isn't progressive is regressive!

INVOLVING EVERYONE IN CHANGING THE HIGH SCHOOL SYSTEM

The document, *Breaking Ranks II* emphasizes that better education depends on personalizing the high school experience, organizing time differently, using technology at every opportune point, and revitalizing the on-going professional education of teachers and administrators.[10]

This is *what* needs to happen. It can be accomplished by involving all teachers and school leaders in collegial learning communities. The smaller structures engender support, respect and trust throughout the learning and working groups. Use of the positive Tribes agreements creates a caring culture throughout the faculty. Of great importance, it makes it safe enough for the "inside" community to look critically at what needs to be changed—and to move ahead in collaboration to do it. Mike Schmoker, author of the book, *Results Now—How We Can Achieve Unprecedented Improvements in Teaching and Learning,* points out that, "Like the medical community after 1910, education must own up collectively to the gap between *what we know and what we do,* between 'what we've always done' and 'what our clients need.'"[11] It takes trust, honesty and courage to change a system.

That's right! How can the young flock learn to fly higher unless we all learn how to fly higher too?

LOOKING AT THE EVIDENCE ON PROFESSIONAL LEARNING COMMUNITIES

A research study conducted by Fred Newmann & Associates among a sample of 24 restructured high schools is considered convincing evidence that teacher learning communities boost student learning. Elaborate survey and field measures of "authentic instruction" grounded in learning theory were used to assess the effects of instruction. Teaching norms and teacher interaction were assessed through measures of "professional community", specifically: shared purpose, collaborative activity in teaching, collective focus on student learning, deprivatized practice and reflective dialogue. The resulting data over several years show strong correlations between measures of how teachers work together and the learning opportunities they provide for their students.[12]

A significant message comes from the prestigious American Institute of Research on studies of high-performing schools. Reports clearly verify the positive impact professional learning communities have for whole school reform models.[13] Among a host of evaluations, Valerie Lee and colleagues conducted three studies that consistently show that *teacher community* has a positive statistical effect on student engagement and achievement gains. The studies further indicate that students do better academically in a school where their teachers assume *collective responsibility for the success of all students.*[14] Additional evidence from studies by Michael Rutter and colleagues conclude that:[15]

1. Students achieved more highly in schools where staff members shared expectations to plan the course of study cooperatively, and encouraged and supported each other in implementation.

2. Students achieved more highly and had fewer behavioral problems in schools where disciplinary rules for the pupils were set by teachers as a group, in contrast to leaving individual teachers to work out the rules of discipline for themselves.

3. Students achieved better in schools where staff norms supported being open and direct with one another. In the less successful schools, faculty members expected one another to be autonomous, private and aloof.

Looking at the effectiveness of *teacher collegiality* on student outcomes, Michael Fullan refers to a study of school restructuring as "providing the most explicit evidence on the relationship between professional community and student performance. Measures of standardized achievement tests as well as 'authentic' performance based measures of learning, indicate significant improvement in studied schools. Specifically, the standard achievement tests in mathematics, science and social science show greater student achievement. The researchers identified the existence of 'high professional community' as the reason for students' better performance."[16] Other reports claim professional learning communities work due to the facts that:[17]

▶ Teachers pursue a **clear purpose** for all students' learning

▶ Teachers engage in **collaborative activity** to achieve the purpose

▶ Teachers take **collaborative responsibility** for student learning

▶ The level of **authentic research-based pedagogy** being learned by teachers directly affects student performance

▶ The schoolwide teacher learning community affects the level of **social support for student learning**—which in turn also affects student performance.

Ann Lieberman, one of the respected scholars of teacher learning communities, advises policy-makers that teachers must have opportunities to discuss, think about, and hone new practices, and she emphasizes, that cannot be done in isolation from colleagues.[18] Teachers learn best though active involvement, thinking about and reflecting with peers what they have learned—*just as high school students do*. The stimulation of mutual support, co-planning, group inquiry, learning and reflective practice in the midst of caring relationships is self and system renewing.[19]

It's time to enlighten policy and decision makers on the results being achieved in schools that are building the professional capacity of teachers through on-site learning communities.

Yes, the worst of times may be the best of times in which to convince weary educators, administrators, school board members and the public to transform high school systems by allocating sufficient time and resources to develop teacher learning communities—and to share this warning from Richard Elmore:

"You can't improve a school's performance or the performance of any teacher or student in it, without increasing the investment in teacher's knowledge, pedagogical skills and understanding of students."[20]

The good news: the money probably is there. The bad news: it's already being spent on something else.[21]

—RICHARD ELMORE

Somewhat encouraging but knowingly Elmore states. "The good news: the money probably is there. The bad news: it's already being spent on something else."

THE "INSIDER" APPROACH TO DEVELOP COLLEGIAL LEARNING COMMUNITIES

OK, let's organize teacher learning communities.

Yes, but not just to have them look at test scores, identify low performing kids—and continue to instruct them in the same way.

The bandwagon of schools initiating "teacher learning teams" or "communities" is grow-ing. Unfortunately, more often than not their focus only is to do what the woman school leader just pointed out. Students cannot achieve more unless their schools prioritize and allocate time and resources to teachers' continuous learning. Recall the admonition made earlier in this chapter by respected educators McLaughlin and Talbert that students today "require forms of instruction and pedagogy that are foreign to many teachers, as well as a fundamental reconceptualization of learning."[22] High school Collegial Learning Communities (CLCs) using the Tribes process have an unprecedented way to continually increase the professional capacity of the whole instructional staff to learn, apply and assess effective forms of instruction and pedagogy that respond to how today's students best can learn. Essentially, it increases their knowledge in three essential practices:[23]

1. Knowledge *of* practice—to analyze information and data on student performance

2. Knowledge *for* practice—to learn research-based principles and best practices to engage and accelerate student learning for the diversity of student learners, and

3. Knowledge *in* practice—to observe and reflect on the effect or response of stu-dents to the curriculum and active learning process.

Teachers learning, implementing and reflecting together on essential practices not only increases their professional capability but engenders support, new motivation and com-mitment to continuous learning. Learning from each other increases their individual and collective expertise to provide high-quality, rigorous instruction, to all students. Their use of the same agreements, group skills and reflection—the same learning process they are using with students—results in a a new sense of self and competency.

Indeed, collaboration can be problematic for any group. In a delightful way, Roland S. Barth, author of the fine book, *Improving Schools from Within*, shares an amusing paral-lel situation. He likens the practice of teachers to work alone to that of two four-year olds playing in opposite ends of a sand-box. This is his description:

We've always worked alone. Collaboration was a challenge.

> *"Jimmy has a shovel and a bucket. Susan has a rake and a hoe. At no time does Jimmy use Susan's rake or hoe, nor does Susan borrow Jimmy's bucket or shovel, let alone do they build a sand castle together. They may inadvertently throw sand in each other's face from time to time, but seldom do they interact. Although in close proximity for long periods of time and having much to offer each other, each works and plays pretty much in isolation."*[24]

Barth suggests that to a certain extent, the developmental stage of three to four year old "parallel play" characterizes teacher behavior in schools. "The price", he says, "of parallel play is that we ward off those who might help us to do things better, and with whom we might do *grander things than we can do alone*. And the price is isolation from other adults."[25]

Collaboration doesn't just happen, even though we may have the intent to collaborate with others. One only has to recall why many teachers gave up using cooperative group learning with students. "It doesn't work!" they said. Of course it did not! The most expert scholars on cooperative group learning repeatedly warned that *"putting students in a learning group and telling them to cooperate obviously will not be successful. Students must be taught the social skills needed for collaboration and be motivated to use them."*[26] This reality also holds true for adult learners.

Collaborative group skills must be learned and used in relationships with others. Having all teachers in the Tribes Learning Community high school participate in an initial training course prepares them to have students learn and use twelve group skills (see Chapter 12). Teachers knowledge and use of the same skills when meeting in their Collegial Learning Communities assures they also can work well together. It becomes safe enough for team members to observe and reflect upon instructional practices in each other's classes. It is safe enough to ask a question, share a problem or ask for help. It is safe enough to offer assistance when needed. Peer-to-peer coaching is more comfortable than having "outside" professionals coaching "inside" teachers who are more knowledgeable about their students and the school.

The democratic community process of Tribes TLC also assures inclusion for all—teachers and school leaders as well as students. The sense of belonging, respect and value sets the stage for collaboration and achieving group success. All of which leads to "collegiality" for teachers—a stage even beyond collaboration. This is why professional learning communities in Tribes schools are known as "Collegial Learning Communities."

Judith Warren Little, a recognized scholar on school-site professional learning communities, defines collegiality as the presence of four specific behaviors:[28]

▶ *"Adults in schools talk about practice. These conversations about teaching and learning are frequent, continuous, concrete and precise.*

▶ *Adults in schools observe each other engaged in the practice of teaching and administration. These observations are reflected upon and discussed. The best become common practice.*

▶ *Adults engage in work on curriculum by planning, designing, researching and evaluating curriculum.*

▶ *Adults teach each other what they know about teaching, learning and leading. Craft knowledge is revealed, articulated and shared."*

Teachers working in isolation, day after day, year after year, no longer is an option.

One teacher wrote, "No longer working in our caves relating all day to streams of students, we're discovering new motivation and commitment after years of working in isolation. Being and working in community with others certainly must be a universal human need."

Collegial Learning Communities in high schools using the research-based process of Tribes...

Collegial learning and implementation is the power that drives "inside-out" school reform.

▶ Commit to life-long professional learning and collective responsibility for student learning

▶ Share their vision and beliefs on student learning, and commit to a focus on student development as well as learning

▶ Define a coherent set of goals that give direction and meaning to student and teacher learning—and teachers' collegiality

▶ Learn evidence research-based principles and practices that maximize learning for all students

▶ Coordinate multiple ways to support the academic, social and emotional development of all student learners

▶ Use active learning pedagogy, reflective practice, technology, constructivism, cooperative learning and authentic assessment to engage students in meaningful learning

▶ Actively engage students themselves in reflecting upon and assessing personal progress

▶ Commit to sustaining professional support, appreciation and respect to each other.

Livia Marlene Perez, M.A

Livia is a Certified Tribes TLC Trainer who is employed at Carol Morgan School, an exemplary Tribes School in the Dominican Republic. She has 24 years of teaching experience at the middle and high school levels. She has worked as a Summer School Director, and is currently completing her Leadership certification. She holds a Masters degree in International Law and Diplomacy, as well as a Masters in Education. As a member of the "trainer tribe" at Carol Morgan School, Livia provides training, leadership, and support to a caring school community that serves an international student population and that has successfully implemented many levels of the Tribes TLC process over many years.

What's Up In an International School?

Seven years ago I sat in yet again another training—this one called "Tribes Learning Community." I had been teaching Social Studies for over 13 years in high school and had my pedagogical automaticity down pat. Wow, as I sat in the course on day one, the trainers were giving names to strategies and practices many of which I had to learn through trial and error. On day two, I was elated, as I felt that all I had been trying to do with my students besides teaching the curriculum needed to be integrated with more. That more was definitely the learning process of Tribes. Two years later, I became a certified Tribes Trainer for the Carol Morgan School in the Dominican Republic. I have been formally living the process of Tribes for seven years, and it just gets better.

I feel so fortunate to have the greatest working scenario. I facilitate the learning of US History to around 80 eighth grade students. After one academic year, most of my students move into my colleague, friend and fellow Tribes Trainer, Brenda Villalona's 9th grade World History class. Sometimes I wish we had recorded our positive conversations about our students. How we now approach our professional endeavor using the process of Tribes is so rewarding. The process is definitely a way of being and living as a community.

The benefits for students' learning in middle and high school are paramount. In my professional opinion after 24 years of teaching, I recognize the endless benefits that the Tribes process yields. It curtails behavior issues, increases retention by using reflection, makes using collaborative learning effective and, most importantly for an international school, assures acceptance and inclusion for others.

As educators of teenagers, Brenda and I also attest that the biggest and most evident gain is that the process truly facilitates classroom management. There are fewer behavior issues, and when they do arise, how we engage students to address them leads to collaborative solutions, student responsibility and community pride. The Tribes community agreements provide a common language and facilitate resolution of behavior issues... because we all listen to each other and own the problem.

As fate would manifest, Brenda and I each had a difficult class one year. We did a lot of internal reflection and had meaningful conversations, particularly about her challenging class, which my son happened to be in. We decided to give both of the classes a massive dose of the process of Tribes. By the end of third quarter an amazing paradigm shift had taken place.

The habit of teaching students to reflect is pivotal, in middle and high school, to increase retention. Reflection is a pillar of the Tribes process. However, as trainers of over 200 teachers we have noticed that this component is not as frequently used by teachers in upper levels. I say to them what I say to my students, "If we don't reflect, the knowledge will eject." This information is scientifically supported by significant brain research. It needs to be emphasized in every Tribes academic learning experience. If you really want all to achieve more.... trust the process!

A VISION OF HOW IT LOOKS

A particular urban high school with a student body of 2000 and a faculty of 130 teachers has been implementing the Tribes Learning Community process for several years. Every teacher belongs to a cross-departmental learning community composed of 13–14 teachers. The CLCs are facilitated by teacher-leaders, a Vice-principal (who also is a Certified Tribes TLC trainer), and often by the Principal who considers and prides himself as a continuous learner. Professional Tribes training courses on active learning pedagogy are led by a team of lead teachers and administrators. Personal Learning Plans are maintained by every teacher. Either individually or in learning communities teachers explore topics pertaining to improving student learning. In any one year a wide spectrum of Inquiries can include learning styles, differentiation, cooperative group learning, constructivism, cognitive coaching, standards based unit planning, formative/authentic assessment and effective use of technology. Teachers apply the principles and practices they have learned; assessments are made, student outcomes are shared, and practices and curriculum are revised by the CLCs as needed. All gain a sense of responsibility for the students within all of their classes. The collegiality developed by the school's professional development approach each year now culminates in the high school hosting an annual conference where teachers share as presenters. They also display projects and distribute copies of a collegial professional journal containing articles they have written to convey their experiences enhancing student learning. The conference now draws people from around the State.

Key to the new learning and spirit in this school is the belief that *everyone is a learner,* and by sharing with others the level of learning is elevated. The proud Principal of the high school has a practice of expressing these high expectations as well as the culture and norms of the school community to new teachers before they are hired.[29] His positive message at times may well be, "It's just how we do things around here!"

The new shy girl is speaking up now when in her learning group.

There's a lot of consideration going on.

Those two difficult kids in my Advisory class no longer are being rude to people.

Yes, I'm beginning to like every hormonal one of them.

10

*Learning How
21st Century Students
Best Can Learn*

10

Learning How 21st Century Students Best Can Learn

IN THIS CHAPTER YOU WILL

▶ Recognize how active group learning promotes social and emotional intelligence

▶ Discover the significance of Responsive Education and the eight components for implementation

▶ Learn how to maximize students' retention of learning

▶ Understand how to engage and motivate students who have different ways of learning

▶ Realize how the principles of student-centered active learning and cooperative group learning benefit adolescent learners

▶ Contrast two very different pedagogical paradigms

Fifty years ago high school students graduated knowing perhaps 75 percent of what they would ever need to know to be successful in the workplace, the family and the community. Today, the estimate is that graduates of our schools leave knowing perhaps two percent of what they will need to know in the years ahead—98 percent is yet to come.[1]

—ROLAND S. BARTH

Yes, now we're flying into the fourth dimension—Responsive Education!

Responsive Education

The Community of Learners

A Caring Culture

Student Development and Learning

Student-Centered Active Learning

The statement above by respected Harvard University professor, Roland S. Barth, is startling. However, he goes on to tell us what needs to happen:

"If the first major purpose of a school is to create and provide a culture hospitable to human learning, the second major purpose of a school is to make it likely that students and educators will become and remain lifelong learners."[2]

But how can we possibly get students to become lifelong learners?

Only by being so ourselves.

THE SIGNIFICANCE OF ACTIVE LEARNING

Active group learning is the heart of Responsive Education. It personalizes learning for high school students and awakens untapped interests, motivation and meaningful purpose toward future careers. It corresponds to how today's 21st century young adults really do learn by having opportunities to be engaged with fellow students in student-managed projects, group inquiry, research, inquiry, technology and assessment.

Based on an international study on active learning in eight countries, David Stern from the University of California-Berkeley states that active learning is the educational practice that "develops the capacity for autonomous lifelong learning," which, he claims, is absolutely essential if humans are to adapt to the rapid economic and social changes in the post-industrial world.[3] "Preparation for lifelong learning at work necessitates a kind of initial education that fosters curiosity and the capacity to manage one's own learning agenda. Employers say they want workers who can take initiative and solve problems, not only in managerial and professional positions, but also in production and clerical jobs."[4] Bonnie Benard points out that active learning helps students develop the critical resilience strengths of autonomy and problem-solving, and that active learning that involves small group collaboration also develops the other resilient strengths, social competence and sense of purpose.[5]

An impressive collection of literature calls for active learning as essential to creating schools that have *intrinsic motivation and powerful learning environments.*[6] Evaluations assembled by the American Youth Policy Forum found active learning a critical ingredient of programs that produce positive academic and behavioral outcomes.[7] Pertinent recommendations for the transformation of high schools come from 12 years of data analysis presented in the document, *High Schools That Work,* which found that students learn more when they are actively and cooperatively engaged with challenging content through planned learning activities that involve them in solving real-world problems.[8]

It becomes obvious that there is no other way for high schools to support adolescents in becoming socially competent and successful apart from learning with peers in meaningful active teams.

ACTIVE GROUP LEARNING PROMOTES SOCIAL AND EMOTIONAL INTELLIGENCE

"Social and emotional learning?" "High schools do not have time for all that!" some say quickly. Unfortunately, educational practice today rarely connects intellectual learning with social and emotional development. Good teachers have always recognized that how a person feels about himself cannot be separated from mastery of a subject. High grades and SAT scores do not predict satisfaction and productivity throughout life—nor a good citizen make. It is well documented that social emotional intelligence is predictive of academic achievement, productive experiences in the world of work and having optimal health.[9] The American Management Association reminds us that more people lose jobs due to their inability to work well with others than for a lack of knowledge or technical skills. Indeed, the essential foundation for both academic learning and the capacity to become an active constructive citizen is having knowledge of ourselves and others, and being able to use this knowledge to solve problems creatively.[10]

The most exciting breakthrough of the 21st century will occur not because of technology, but because of an expanding concept of what it means to be human.[11]

—JOHN NAISBITT

Becoming socially and emotionally competent requires learning in on-going social relationship and community with others. Using active learning curricula within small groups develops *social intelligence* in students. They learn...

▶ to relate well to others

▶ to conceptualize and manage social relations, interpersonal problems and conflict

▶ to be empathetic, patient and considerate of cultural, racial and gender diversity

▶ to collaborate, and to enjoy working for the common good.

Everyone needs Reflection!

Working and learning with others in community also promotes the development of *emotional intelligence*, which Daniel Goleman, renowned Harvard scholar on the brain and behavioral sciences, defines as four essential capacities of self-awareness: social skills, the ability to handle emotions, self-motivation, and empathy.[12]

All are self-reflective capacities. They give one an ability to recognize what others are thinking and feeling, and dramatically affect the ability of children and youth to learn and succeed in life.[13]

Can social and emotional intelligence be taught?

Yes and no! Social skills and character values, indeed, are being taught as *curriculum* throughout many schools today. Acquiring social intelligence, however, depends upon positive environmental factors such as those verified in the resiliency studies and summarized by Benard as: caring relationships, opportunities for participation and positive expectation messages and beliefs.[14]

This is the reason the process of Tribes Learning Communities, unlike other approaches, is effective. Enabling students to live daily within a context of supportive relationships and social learning experiences fosters "habits of the heart"—habits such as empathy, respect, kindness and caring. Self-reflection on newly discovered skills, social competency and personal strengths—is every bit as important to the development of wholeness in youth as intellectual achievement.

It becomes obvious that there is no other way for high schools to support the development of social-emotional competence in students (and thereby intellectual achievement) than by having students work together in on-going cooperative groups. The full range of human development—intellectual, social, emotional, physical and personal/spiritual—from birth to death is an interactive journey made in community with others. Developing "youth at promise" rather than "youth at risk" depends upon our schools building *communities that care.*

BECOMING TEACHERS OF INQUIRY AND CHANGE

It goes without saying that high school teachers and school leaders are deeply committed smart people who want, to the best of their abilities, to make a positive difference in the lives of youth in the most critical years of development before moving out into the world. Renewed energy begins as soon as teachers have the opportunity to explore questions and insights such as:

▶ What determines how much can be remembered?

▶ How can we reach all levels of learners and students who learn in different ways?

▶ What about the gifted kids? What's missing for them?

▶ How do we fit in active learning with standards to be achieved?

▶ Can the use of technology really be helpful? How and why?

The opportunity for high school teachers to pursue questions like these helps them to realize that the most important aspect of being 21st century teachers is to be "teachers of inquiry" and "agents of change."

The document *Breaking Ranks II* urges that: "Every school will be a learning community for the entire community. As such, the school will promote the use of Personal Learning Plans for each educator and provide the resources to ensure that the principal, teachers and other staff members can address their own learning and professional development needs as they relate to improved student learning."[15]

Administrators as well as teachers in high school Tribes Learning Communities maintain personal journals to define their on-going professional learning plans, and to reflect upon results from use of sound researched principles and practices. They catalogue the Collegial Learning Communities on-going conclusions and results of their collaborative learning, planning, assessments of student learning and progress in moving to research-based active learning pedagogy.

Two CenterSource System courses, "Engaging All" and "The Artistry for Learning" provide overall knowledge and experience in implementing the process of Tribes TLC® and the eight components of the Responsive Education process introduced in Chapter 5. The interactive training courses establish the professional development platform for the on-going collaborative work of the Collegial Learning Communities.

WHAT IS RESPONSIVE EDUCATION?

I just looked at Chapter 5 again to recall its description of Responsive Education. Here's the first paragraph.

Responsive Education is an essential pedagogy for academic achievement. It is a synthesis of artful teaching practices that respond (indeed, correspond) to the critical developmental needs of age and cultural groups. Its purpose is to enable more students to acquire knowledge in a lasting and meaningful way. Crafting a caring culture and trusting small active learning communities throughout a school gives all students opportunities to excel.

Responsive Education *responds* to and supports the *whole human development of students*—not only their intellectual learning but also their social, emotional, physical and inner spiritual quests. It also helps students acquire the essential four tasks of adolescence. The chart on the next page shows responsive education practices that contribute to youth development.

Now this is worth knowing about and putting into action!

How Responsive Education Supports the Developmental Tasks of High School Youth

TASK	STAGE OF COGNITIVE DEVELOPMENT	STAGE OF SOCIAL AND EMOTIONAL DEVELOPMENT	RESPONSIVE EDUCATION INITIATIVES
AUTONOMY/ INDEPENDENCE	Capable of cognitive problem solving Can think abstractly and hypothetically Integrates multiple factors to understand concepts	Oriented to peers and family Conflicted on degree of desired family involvement Seeks independence in decision making, although may lack judgment and experience Resists imposed control from adults	Classrooms are student-centered. Well-trained teachers engage students in multiple forms of cooperative and constructive group learning. Didactic teaching is minimized. Teacher teams integrate interdisciplinary thematic curriculum. Focus on relevance to current world, student lives, interests and future. Peer learning groups (tribes) plan, demonstrate and teach.
SOCIAL COMPETENCY		Seeks friends and belonging Attracted to peer leaders and role models Feels awkward with social skills May be motivated by social effects of drug or alcohol use May experiment with initial sexual intimacy	Promote peer leadership, peer helping programs, cooperative learning groups, and discovery of gifts Utilize peer role models for teaching skills Practice democracy and cultural/racial/gender equity Engage in constructivist approach Teach collaborative skills
SENSE OF PURPOSE		Pre-occupied with self-presentation, acceptance by peer group, physical maturity Risk-taking and experimental behavior in order to belong	Encourage acceptance of diversity, respect, and tolerance Nurture/enhance peer involvement and sense of community Involve students in community service activities
PROBLEM SOLVING		Oriented to present rather than future Egocentric Changing emotions, viewpoints, loyalties Differentiates between self and environment	Involve students in affecting immediate environment Teach management of group problems Teach appreciative inquiry

EIGHT RESEARCH-BASED COMPONENTS FOR RESPONSIVE EDUCATION

The well-researched components for Responsive Education are sound principles and practices that "breaking ranks" teachers use to design student-centered active learning. This chapter describes the first four of the eight components, and the next chapter contains the other four. They highlight the importance of the principles to accelerate student learning. We'll focus on using the same principles in Chapters 14 and 15 to design active learning curriculum. Throughout the chapters there are these eight identifying icons for each component:

COMMUNITY BUILDING PROCESS

COGNITIVE LEARNING

MULTIPLE INTELLIGENCES

COOPERATIVE GROUP LEARNING

DISCOVERY LEARNING/ CONSTRUCTIVISM

REFLECTIVE PRACTICE

AUTHENTIC ASSESSMENT

TECHNOLOGY

It is worth acknowledging that there will always be more to learn about each component beyond what can be included in this book. And that's what takes place in those on-going weekly Collegial Learning Communities in your high school.

BUILDING COMMUNITY

COMMUNITY BUILDING PROCESS

The "people process" of Tribes was described In Chapter 7, "Establishing Community for All," along with the "Tribes Trail Map" illustrating the process to develop community in classrooms and other groups throughout the high school system. The fundamental concept is that "community" is created by first building inclusion (a sense of belonging) and influence (a sense of value). The simple concept essentially conditions productive relationships and success in any organization or system. You may have heard teachers say, *"It's the glue that holds it all together."*

COGNITIVE LEARNING

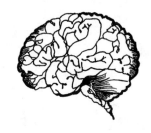

It is time to face a glaring reality! The majority of teachers today continue to teach—teach and instruct—instruct in ways that are incompatible with how the human brain learns. How did we ever imagine that we knew how to reach and teach today's young people without knowing how they best can learn? It's like placing the cart before the horse. *It's like looking up a recipe after taking the fallen cake out of the oven.*

Due to amazing advances in technology and neuroscience more has been learned about the human brain in the last two decades than in all of recorded history.[10] Years of impressive research on cognitive learning affirms that the human brain constructs and weaves all of the incoming data, information, concepts and experiences into its own continuous file system. Like a computer it enters new information quickly into previously created files based on earlier interests, experiences or knowledge. It constructs new knowledge files when information is actively experienced or connections are made to its storehouse of existing knowledge. Symbols and language that is familiar facilitates interpretation and synthesis. In essence the brain is a constructor of knowledge. It is of great importance also is to recognize that the brain's acquisition of knowledge is facilitated by working socially with others in group discourse, collaborative problem-solving and applying information to real-life situations.

Patricia Wolfe, respected scholar on current neuroscience, cognitive science and educational research on teaching and learning, states, "The more we understand the brain, the better we'll be able to design instruction to match how it learns best."[16]

Let's learn why all this is so!

How the Human Brain Learns

Although we all have seen this picture of the brain, we invite you this time to read the description slowly, pausing to consider positive or negative conditions that may affect learning for high school students.

All information comes into the brain from the body's senses (sight, hearing, touch/feeling, smell, taste), and zooms into one of two possible pathways depending upon whether or not a sense of threat or danger is perceived. The body and brain work, one might say, in a co-dependent partnership—so much so that recent researchers are using the term "body/brain."[17]

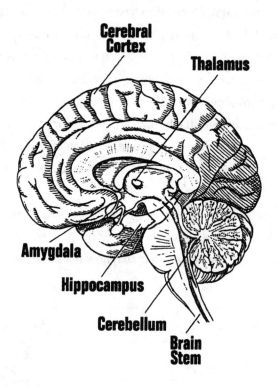

When there is no sense of danger the information travels on a slow pathway to a sensory relay station, called the **thalamus**, onward to the **hippocampus**, the center of learning and memory, and then to the **cerebral cortex**, the center of long term memory and thinking. However, when there is a sense of danger the sensory data **instantaneously activates** mechanisms for survival. The input goes directly to the **thalamus** relay station, which sends it to the **amygdale** which is the center of all fear, threat and passion. There an internal regulator called the **hypothalamus** triggers the pituitary and adrenal glands to release a stress hormone called cortisol. The **cortisol** hormone activates fight or flight behaviors as it races through the body and the brain via the bloodstream. The story doesn't end there! Overwhelmed by the cortisol, the rational **cerebral cortex**, center of long term memory, never has a chance to think things through. With persistent stress, cortisol can be devastating to the learning and memory system and the internal regulator, the **hippocampus**.[18]

Knowing this, gives a better understanding of why the climate of classrooms must be safe and supportive learning environments. Somewhere in the novel "Dune" the frantic hero cries out, "Fear is a mind-killer!" Many kinds of fear kill minds daily in classrooms. There is the fear of asking a question, fear of not giving the right-answer, fear of being teased, called a name or ridiculed for one's culture, gender and diversity. Minds are killed through loneliness, hostility and exclusion by peers. For some it may be intimidation from a teacher, a reprimand that seems unfair, boys being called on more often than girls, or "the smart people" more than others. Whenever the body/mind becomes swamped with the stress hormone cortisol emotional balance is lost and rational thought and memory become unavailable. Repeated incidents inevitably result in a young person seeing him or herself as a loser... and giving up.

It verifies why neuroscience, human development and resiliency research concur that children's academic, social and emotional learning depends upon the existence of a safe and caring threat-free environment. It is the primary reason that the culture, small group structures, student-centered active learning and caring community process of Tribes leads to more lasting learning and greater achievement for students.

Yeah, and lots of us would quit thinking of high school as something just to get through.

The Principles for Student-Centered Active Learning

Understanding how the human brain acquires and best can retain knowledge helps to explain the devastating mis-match and failure of the19th century teacher-centered instruction that is prevalent in 90% of high school classes today.

The chart that follows lists nine well researched principles for student-centered active learning, and that need to be raised for discussion among teachers, administrators, parents, and school board members. They especially need to be understood and embraced by legislators, politicians, public and private funding sources. The principles are especially important for teachers who truly want to reach and help high school adolescents learn in ways that are *responsive—that correspond—*to their ways of learning, interests and meaningful knowledge for their futures. Best of all, hundreds of thousands of uninspired students will no longer view school as "something just to get through."

The Principles for Student-Centered Active Learning[19]

COGNITIVE AND METACOGNITIVE FACTORS

Principle 1. Learning is an active process in which meaning is developed on the basis of experience.

Principle 2. The learner associates and links new information to existing knowledge in memory.

Principle 3. Strategies for "thinking about thinking"—reflection on learning—facilitate learning.

AFFECTIVE FACTORS

Principle 4. Individuals are naturally curious and enjoy learning when in the absence of negative conditions and emotions.

Principle 5. Curiosity, creativity and higher order thinking processes are stimulated by learning tasks of optimal difficulty, relevancy, authenticity, challenge and novelty for each student.

SOCIAL FACTORS

Principle 6. Learning is facilitated by social interaction, discourse and collaboration.

Principle 7. Learning and self-esteem are heightened when individuals are in respectful and caring relationships with others who genuinely appreciate their unique gifts and talents.

INDIVIDUAL DIFFERENCES

Principle 8. Learners differ in their preferences for learning modes and strategies, the pace at which they learn and unique capabilities in particular areas.

Principle 9. Each learner constructs reality and interprets life experiences in a different way depending upon prior learning, beliefs, culture and external experiences.

AN EXAMPLE HOW TO BOOST TEST SCORES

Thousands of comprehensive studies indicate how altering a teaching practice can boost standardized test scores. The following article describes a study that one math teacher read about and that made a huge difference to his students.

Yeah, I may really be smart after all!

U.S. fails math

It was most likely your favorite grade teacher attentively assisted you in solving arithmetic equations—but she probably shouldn't have. New research suggest that American educators don't let students learn to solve problems on the own—causing kids to score lower in math than their Japanese counterparts. In a 1997 study funded by the U.S. Department of Education, James Stigler, Ph.D., of the University of California at Los Angeles, and James Hiebert, Ph.D., from the University of Delaware, analyzed video tapes of 231 eighth grade math classes in Germany, Japan and the United States over one year. As reported in their 1999 book, The Teaching Gap the researchers found that American teachers spent 90% of class time going over procedures, formulas and problem-solving techniques. In Japan, however, students spent over 50% of class time discussing concepts and inventing their own solutions to problems. Although the Japanese students frequently had incorrect answers, Stigler and Hiebert believe they achieved a better understanding of the material than American students who often quickly forgot their memorized facts.[20]

Three years ago, New Jersey based public school teacher, Bill Jackson, adjusted teaching of his math curriculum to reflect this research. That year, his students' standardized test scores increased by 20%; this year, an above-average number entered honors algebra. Jackson says: "To do math, kids must be given a chance to do math."

—Keisha-Gaye Anderson[21]

The opportunity for students in Mr. Jackson's class to discuss concepts, create solutions and problem-solve on their own connects directly to: (1) how the human brain learns through group discourse; and (2) how the different procedure corresponded and appealed to their developmental needs: to *gain autonomy, social interaction with peers, a sense of purpose and problem-solving on their own* (as discussed in Chapter 2). Rather than individually listening to a teacher going over a procedure, a formula and demonstrating problem-solving, they discussed concepts and "invented their own solutions to problems"—all of which increased their standardized test scores.

MULTIPLE INTELLIGENCES

The work of Howard Gardner and other cognitive and behavioral scientists is bringing enlightenment to educators throughout the world. The reality is that human beings have a variety of different intelligences, unique ways, in which we perceive, prefer to learn, relate and meet life situations.[22] We cannot be arbitrarily standardized so that one way of teaching or testing fits all.

Lynn Stoddard, author of the very fine book *Redesigning Education: A Guide for Developing Human Greatness,* deplores the fact that...

> One learns by doing the thing, for though you think you know it, you have no certainty until you try.
>
> —SOPHOCLES

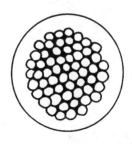

MULTIPLE INTELLIGENCES

> *"Our fixation on curriculum development instead of human development is the enormous dam blocking educational reform. It has caused us to ignore the work of those who reveal the individuality of human nature, how the brain works and how children learn. The result is that the discovery and development of individual learner's intelligences and gifts go unattended."*[23]

A good school for adolescents must engage the attention of every young person.[24]
—LEONARD BOTSTEIN

Gardner summarizes the diversity of intelligences as nine "ways of knowing." The illustrations and brief descriptions in the Nine Intelligences chart on the next page highlight the ways.

Remarkably, it is two of the nine intelligences, verbal/linguistic and logical/mathematical, that are focused upon in the majority of schools in the Western world. Before entering school, children are busy discovering many ways of learning and exploring their environment. By second or third grade in school they discover that their active, physical, rhythmic, imaginative, relational and existential selves have to be set aside—that learning is all about mind stuff. This is especially difficult for children and adolescents coming from other than Western Caucasian cultures, namely: Native American, Asian, Pacific Islanders, Hispanic and Afro-American.

In infancy and early childhood children begin learning through what Gardner calls "raw patterning" to perform simple tasks as the foundation of a given intelligence. Walking, running and jumping are the basics of body/kinesthetic intelligence; just as learning the alphabet is basic to verbal/linguistic intelligence. As children grow they move to greater levels of pattern complexity called "symbol systems," in which they may develop the ability to draw various shapes (visual/spatial intelligence) or make different tones (musical/rhythmic). Each intelligence has its own "notational language" that not only can be taught and learned by others, but also can be recorded in some form, such as a musical composition (musical/rhythmic) or a graphic design (visual/spatial). The years of early adolescent development are especially important—it is at this period that children are becoming aware of their skills and preferences in ways of learning. Finally, in the secondary or college years usually a time is reached when one or more preferred intelligences lead to a career path.

Adolescents especially must have the opportunity to discover the gifts of their own intelligences.

Nine Intelligences

The work of Howard Gardner and other scientists has identified nine intelligences that are common to all human beings and that vary in degree in each person. The multiple intelligences, ways of learning, and knowing, are as follows:

VERBAL/LINGUISTIC

Thinks and learns through written and spoken words; has the ability to memorize facts, fill in workbooks, take written tests, and enjoy reading

MUSICAL/RHYTHMIC

Recognizes tonal patterns and environmental sounds; learns through rhyme, rhythm, and repetition

INTERPERSONAL

Learns and operates one-to-one, through group relationships, and communication; also depends on all of the other intelligences

LOGICAL/MATHEMATICAL

Thinks deductively; deals with numbers and recognizes abstract patterns

INTRAPERSONAL

Enjoys and learns through self-reflection, metacognition, working alone; has an awareness of inner spiritual realities

VISUAL/SPATIAL

Thinks in and visualizes images and pictures; has the ability to create graphic designs and communicate with diagrams and graphics

EXISTENTIAL

Is concerned with ultimate life issues—love, death, philosophy; learns in context with meaning

BODY/KINESTHETIC

Learns through physical movement and body wisdom; has a sense of knowing through body memory

NATURALIST

Loves nature and the out-of-doors; enjoys classifying species of flora and fauna

David Lazear writes: *"If we provide students the opportunity to develop the full range of their intellectual capacities and teach them how to use their multiple ways of knowing in the learning task, they will learn the things we are trying to teach more thoroughly than if we only permit them to learn in the more traditional verbal/linguistic and logical/mathematical ways."*[25]

We will revisit the multiple intelligences in Chapter 14, Designing Cooperative Learning Experiences, and discover hundreds of ways to engage students who learn in the different ways.

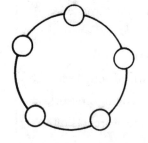

COOPERATIVE GROUP LEARNING

COOPERATIVE GROUP LEARNING

The immense benefits of cooperative group learning not only support the needs of youth but also accelerate academic learning. Drs. Roger and David Johnson of the University of Minnesota worked for many years to assess and document more than 600 studies reporting the benefits of learning through cooperation with others rather than competitive or individualized instruction.[26]

They state on behalf of a host of other leading researchers, "We know more about cooperative learning than we do about lecturing, age grouping, departmentalization, starting reading at age six, or the 50 minute period. We know more about cooperative learning than almost any other aspect of education."[27] Both theoretical and demonstration research, documented in both scientific and professional literature, confirms the effectiveness of cooperative group learning. In the last 102 years, over 550 experimental and 100 correlation studies have been conducted on cooperative, competitive and individualistic learning.[28] Meta-analysis of all of the studies on achievement show that cooperative learning results in significantly higher achievement and retention in contrast to competitive and individualistic learning—teacher-centered whole class instruction.[29] During the last 50 years 106 studies have shown that cooperative learning promotes greater social support—which promotes achievement productivity, physical health, psychological health and the ability to cope with stress and adversity.[30] Over 80 studies indicate the impact that cooperative learning experiences have on self-esteem, intrinsic worth and value of personal attributes to others.[31] The outcomes on achievement, psychological health, and social relationships are overlapping and influence everything else.[32] Moreover, clear evidence shows that *cooperative learning can be used at every grade level, in every subject area and with every task.*

The benefits of cooperation, indeed, are positive factors that not only contribute to well-being and success for students but also school systems, families, workplaces and society. We doubt that the many problems of youth—alienation, violence, drug abuse, gangs, school dropouts, suicide, delinquency and despair—will ever lessen unless school, family and community systems model cooperation and caring.

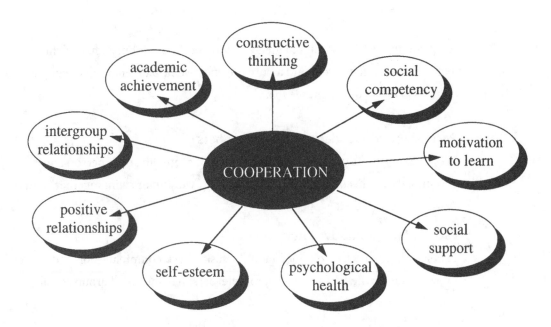

If you are trying to convince your school board, administrators, parents or other teachers that cooperative learning groups are effective, we urge you to lead discussions on the benefits for children and youth. Present and involve them in discussions on the important benefits that evolve from this sound way of teaching and learning.

The proven benefits are:[33]

▶ Greater productivity and academic achievement

▶ Constructive thinking skills: planning, inferring, analyzing, gathering data and strategizing

▶ Social competency: trust in others, perspective taking, sense of personal identity, interdependence, sense of direction and purpose

▶ Motivation: high expectations of success and achievement; high commitment and persistence

▶ Social support: constructive management of stress; high quality relationships that extend life and are helpful to people

▶ Psychological health: the ability to develop, maintain and improve one's relationships and situation in life; success in achieving goals

► Self-esteem: improvement due to positive peer relations and achievement

► Positive interpersonal relationships: supportive friendships; appreciation of peers' skills and contributions

► Intergroup relationships: caring concern; acceptance of multicultural diversity; commitments to the common good.

The years of comprehensive studies made by David and Roger Johnson have defined the five essential elements that occur and assure the effective implementation of cooperative learning. This is what you would see in a classroom:

1. **Positive interdependence among members**

   People undertake a group task with a feeling of mutuality, each person contributing, doing his or her own part, knowing "we sink or swim together" and "together we can do it."

2. **Face-to-face promotive interaction**

   People help each other to understand the task, check comprehension and reflect on what was learned. They use helpful interpersonal and small group social skills.

3. **The use of interactive skills**

   Group members become adept at managing conflict, and developing trust and respect within their group.

4. **Individual accountability**

   Group members take personal responsibility for learning the material, contributing to the group, and assessing both individual and group achievement.

5. **Group processing**

   Members reflect upon and analyze group effectiveness; they define ways to improve group work together.

The reality is that...
cooperative learning is here to stay.

A Best Practice to Create Lifelong Learners

When I participated in my first Tribes training, I thought over and over "I know this" and "I do that." Then a hook was set—brain compatible learning; I wanted to know more. I wanted to be a lifelong learner and was actually willing to take time to read nonfiction. OK, so my first comment was... if I only could read one book about brain-based learning, what one should it be? One led to many!

At Beloit Memorial High School, we work under the "block" system. Classes are 90 minutes long and last for one quarter to earn a ½ credit for graduation. Ninety minutes can and may seem/feel like a long time, but with implementing the process of Tribes the time goes by quickly. It is this process and responsive education that makes a difference. Responsibility, empowerment and engaged learning develop as the students walk through the door to a Tribes classroom. It has been a pleasure to hear the students' surprise as they talk about how quickly the time goes by. They also comment on how they treasure the bonds that they have created with their classmates. Now and then, students will comment on how easy the class was. I have a feeling that it seemed "easy" because the interactive process is a "Best Practice."

One specific example of a Tribes Best Practice is our "reading research" time project in the health classes. On Fridays our students are given 30–40 minutes to read during class about any health/wellness issue. A book and magazine cart that contains a rich collection of materials is brought into the classroom. Students may choose from the collection or bring something of their own if they are able to substantiate how it fits into a wellness area. As the students read, the teacher does too. When it comes time to reflect, the students take notes and meet in small groups to share. We may do milling to music, inside/outside circle, think/pair/share and a few other strategies to enhance the learning process. The teacher is also involved in sharing her reflective piece. It is a great way to show our passion for being lifelong learners. To culminate the quarter, the students then review all that they have gathered during the "reading research" time and create a project of their choice. The project then incorporates a self-evaluation piece that helps students to reflect on their personal journey, creating a sense of value and empowerment.

In the book, *Learning by Heart*, Roland S. Barth says, "If the first major purpose of a school is to create and provide a culture hospitable to human learning, the second major purpose of a school is to make it likely that students and educators will become and remain lifelong learners." Tribes is the way.

A Teacher's View

Shawn Fredricks, M.Ed.

Shawn has been teaching students in the School District of Beloit, Wisconsin for the past 29 years. As a physical education and health teacher at the high school level and as a Certified Tribes TLC Trainer, Shawn enjoys sharing her energy and joy in facilitating implementation of the Tribes process. She has found that Tribes TLC supports and enhances delivery of health, outdoor adventure, and lifetime wellness curricula.

A View from University Instructors

**Lana Daly, M.A.
and Jill Wolfe, M.A.**

Lana and Jill are Certified Tribes TLC® Trainers who work in Teacher Education at California State University in Sacramento, California.
Lana has implemented the Tribes process as a classroom teacher, an innovative program developer, and as an instructor, coordinator, and supervisor.
Jill enthusiastically supports the growth and development of pre-service teachers in the Multiple Subject Credential program by integrating the Tribes process as the basis of classroom leadership. Both have observed how the protective factors foster professional and personal resiliency. They are dedicated to equipping the next generation of teachers with the knowledge, skills, and dispositions to be educational leaders and change makers.

Preparing New Teachers

Throughout our K–12 public school teaching careers in a variety of rural and urban settings the Tribes approach has served as a powerful foundation for fostering the human development of our students. We are grateful for the professional opportunities we were given early in our work with children to discover the Tribes process. Each of us enjoyed delving deep into the research and philosophical underpinnings of Jeanne Gibbs' work. We recognized that the building of a caring community in which all students feel included and encouraged to actively participate in the learning process and in classroom decision-making was the key for us as educators.

Now we are involved in fostering the knowledge, skills and strengths that new teachers need in order to be well-prepared educators and decision-makers, and have learned that this requires a powerful continuity of facilitation, feedback, and reflection throughout their preparation program. We find that immersing them in the Tribes process best allows us to address the huge complexity of what it really means to facilitate effective learning. So what might a snippet of that vision look like in a Teacher Education program?

In Coursework: An introductory pedagogy lesson on differentiated curriculum engages new teachers' participation both in theory and practice. For example, using the Tribes strategy, Milling to Music, each time the music starts they discuss a sequence of posted statements and questions that invite thinking and discourse in three areas to elicit their prior knowledge, "Share a time when you were encouraged to work on a project or assignment that allowed for personal choice." Or talk about the meaning of a pertinent quote, such as "We must take kids on whatever path that is necessary to help them learn," made by Dr. Carol Ann Tomlinson. A third round may focus on a differentiated lesson they designed by asking: "What differences might you predict or notice in student responses regarding motivation, participation or learning outcomes?" Facilitating a thorough reflection through cognitive, social, and personal aspects allows new teachers to make the learning their own.

During Practicum in the Classroom: After a direct experience, student teachers are eager to design lessons using an active learning strategy to accomplish their academic and social objectives. We are equally eager to observe their competency and confidence in using the strategies they have experienced with their students.

In Supervision and Coaching: Our students receive a heavy dose of the research around the reflection piece because of its power to accelerate learning and change—for themselves and their students. During the debriefing conference we use the Tribes process to help students recognize what worked or what may not have worked well. We use and urge teachers to make regular use of "Stop the Action," and "If You Sense They Are Not With You," to help them discover what is happening and what they and their students can to improve learning for all.

We feel strongly that it is both our gift to students and our responsibility to them to model and bring about conscious awareness regarding the impact of the process so that student teachers can use it well. By cultivating their ability to internalize both the theoretical process and active learning strategies of the Tribes book, they are empowered to choose and implement educational practices that will promote meaningful learning for their students, nurture professional relationships with colleagues, and guide their own decision-making in many areas of their lives. By living the Tribes process ourselves, regularly delving into the research, consistently implementing the strategies, and continually attending to the community of our own work together and with colleagues, we are revitalized daily. The process of Tribes is the rewarding thread that brings it all together.

Responsive Education—
The Pedagogy for the 21st Century

Change is never easy! The question usually becomes, "What do I have to give up and what do I have to do? Hopefully by now, you are ready to rephrase the question to... "What do I want to give up and what do I want to do?"

It is important for high school teachers to discuss the contrast between traditional schooling and the well-researched responsive pedagogy for the 21st century. You even may want to add to the lists of contrasts in the chart on the next page.

A Contrast of Paradigms[34]

TRADITIONAL SCHOOLING	RESPONSIVE EDUCATION
Based on ten decades of practice	Based on thousands of research studies
Competitive culture	Cooperative culture
Structure: Teacher-centered	Structure: Student-centered
Focus: academic development	Focus: whole human development
Emphasis: verbal/linguistic and logical/mathematical learning	Emphasis: multiple intelligences
Curriculum relies on texts and workbooks	Curricular learning relies on primary sources of data and manipulative materials
Teacher as information giver	Teacher as interactive facilitator—mediating learning environment
Teacher as expert authority	Teacher as a co-learner
Students viewed as blank slates	Students viewed as creative learners
Students as passive recipients of facts and concepts	Students as active constructors of knowledge
Curriculum presented part to whole with emphasis on basic skills	Curriculum presented whole to part with emphasis on meaning
Criteria and goals given by teacher, not-explicit before instruction	Shared development of goals and criteria for performance
Teachers seek correct answers	Teachers seek viewpoints and conceptions
Learning is decontextualized	Learning is grounded in "real world" contexts, problems and projects
Western bias	Multicultural, global views
Tests that test	Students reflect and assess progress; Tests that teach

The important difference between the two approaches is described simply by research professor, Catherine Fosnot: *"Rather than being powerless and dependent on the institution, learners need to be empowered to think and learn for themselves. Thus, learning needs to be conceived of as something a learner does, not something that is done to a learner."*[35]

Now we're flying over to Chapter 11 to learn about the other four Responsive Ed components. That's right! We're still in flight training!

Learning Through
Discovery
and Technology

Learning Through Discovery and Technology

> All genuine learning is active, not passive. It involves the use of the mind, not just memory. It is the process of discovery, in which the student is the main agent, not the teacher.[1]
> —MORTIMER ADLER

IN THIS CHAPTER YOU WILL

▶ Consider the primary beliefs and assumptions on constructivism

▶ Realize how reflective practice facilitates greater retention of learning

▶ Learn how authentic assessment promotes learning

▶ Learn how technology motivates inquiry and authentic learning for young adults

DISCOVERY IS... "SOMETHING A LEARNER DOES"

Our effort to reach and teach high school adolescents with education that is "responsive" to their developmental needs has progressed from whole class teacher-centered direct instruction to student-centered group learning. In the previous chapter, we became familiar with the *first four of eight* well-researched components, or principles and practices, that are the building blocks of Responsive Education, namely,

COMMUNITY BUILDING PROCESS

COGNITIVE LEARNING

MULTIPLE INTELLIGENCES

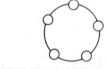

COOPERATIVE GROUP LEARNING

Now we'll consider the other four components that maximize learning and development for high school students. The other four are:

DISCOVERY LEARNING/ CONSTRUCTIVISM

REFLECTIVE PRACTICE

AUTHENTIC ASSESSMENT

TECHNOLOGY

One of our Tribes TLC® courses visualizes and refers to teachers of excellence as "artists for learning." Like all fine artists they have learned to work from a colorful palette of quality colors. They are dedicated to their own learning in order for others to have meaningful experiences. The colors are blended in different ways depending on the artist's knowledge, vision and plan. The eight research-based components are the colors on your palette. They are the principles and practices that enable you to create meaningful active learning for high school learners.

DISCOVERY LEARNING

DISCOVERY LEARNING—CONSTRUCTIVISM

Public education finally is at a point in time where it must cross over to a more promising side of a meandering river. A growing number of educators now are pointing out that we've been clinging so long to the *behaviorist model* of education that too many young people cannot imagine what a love of learning could ever be. The model is so entrenched that it is hardly noticed or ever discussed. Behaviorists see learning as a process of conditioning behavior through reinforcement of a person's response to external stimuli.

> *Example: Show a puppy a cookie (the external stimuli) and tell it to "sit stay." When the puppy performs, he is told,"Good boy!" and receives the cookie—reinforcement of his response to "sit stay." Behaviorism works well for the training of animals. The assumption is the same regarding student learners. Information "delivered" to passive students who "sit stay" and parrot back well are rewarded. The assumption is that the mind is an empty vessel, a tabula rasa, which can be filled with "reliable content". The role of the "transmitter" (educator) is to control, interpret and deliver—or "to cover" the content.*

Recovering A Way of Learning

It is misleading to refer to the process of Tribes as "a new way of learning and being together." The community learning process is a very "old way" that has existed since the beginning of humankind. Communities of people have always survived by working together... to seek, to inquire, to search, to experiment, to observe, and always to search and try again. The path of learning corresponds to how the human brain works... constructing meaning over and over again and building upon previous knowledge and experiences. During the 19th Century Industrial Age this constructive way of learning through discovery disappeared. There was little need for analytical thinking or conceptual problem-solving in the authoritarian workplace. The lives of workers depended upon compliance doing repetitive factory work and not making changes. Rote learning replaced learning through community discourse. It is amazing to realize that the dictates and norms of more than one hundred and fifty years ago perpetuate the predominant model of instruction today—teachers dispensing information, students listening passively, working alone and parroting back "right answers" to teachers and tests. Stroll through the halls of any high school and look into the classrooms. You will recognize that the vast majority not only have not changed but are struggling to engage and challenge students who long to learn in ways that are relevant and meaningful to the world they face today. It is critical that in the midst of the cry to reform public education, especially in high schools, that the pedagogy of 164 years ago is relegated to the past.

Insightful teachers who are crossing the *river* are doing so because they have come to realize that (to quote constructivist authors Bruce Marlowe and Marilyn Page) "a teacher dominated instructional system that delivers information cannot work in an age of information explosion; and that the student who passively receives information has no notion of what it means to be a responsible citizen in a democratic society, or a worker who needs to take initiative and responsibility"[2] Stanford University Professor Linda Darling-Hammond asserts that the culture of this new era requires a new kind of citizen who knows how to "test and apply ideas... look at concepts from many points of view... develop proficient performances... evaluate and defend ideas with careful reasoning and evidence...inquire into a problem using a productive research strategy... produce a high-quality piece of work and understand the standards that indicate good performance... solve problems they have not encountered before."[3]

This kind of learning moves students beyond *memorization* and *recall* into constructive thinking, reflection and creativity. Our only hope of preparing young people for the future is to empower them developmentally as life-long active learners.

Constructivism is a philosophy that describes what 'meaningful knowing is' and how people 'come to know.' And it is not new.

Decades of studies and thought on human development, cognitive learning, neuro-biology, social psychology and anthropology underlie its validity. Centuries of scholars as far back as Socrates, Jean-Jacques Rousseau (1762), Pestalozzi (1830), John Dewey (1896), Jean Piaget (1941), Paolo Freire (1974), Jerome Bruner (1960), Lev Vygotsky (1962) have advocated learning that actively engages learners. John Dewey's description of child-centered learning was greeted as a radical notion in 1899. He and other progressive reformers asserted they were determined "to free students from the shackles of subject-centered schools."[5] They claimed that the rigid, institutional, authoritarian pedagogy left little room for active learning. They believed that children's intellectual, social and emotional needs and interests needed to drive learning and ways of teaching.[6] Now more than 100 years later notable contemporary scholars such as Howard Gardner, Deborah Meier, Nel Noddings, Thomas Likona, John Goodlad, Linda-Darling Hammond, James Comer, Roland S.Barth, Ted Sizer and Pedro Noguera continue to advocate the same.[7]

Although their viewpoints on learning may be expressed in different terms, their theoretical beliefs largely converge into the following principles of constructivism:[8]

1. Knowledge is constructed by the learner.

2. Learning is a self-regulatory process of linking existing knowledge to new insights, constructing new models of reality, thereby enlarging one's perspective and meaning of the world.

3. Each learner creates her own reality- assimilating new information into a living web that already exists in her mind—to understand the world.

4. Conceptual growth and constructive thinking comes from dialogue within a community sharing multiple perspectives, and the reflecting on the simultaneous change of one's personal interpretation in response to the perspectives of others.

5. The role of education is to promote collaboration and group discourse so that learners reach informed self-chosen positions.

6. Such learning can occur in contexts that are reflective of real-world situations.

7. Reflection and authentic assessment are continuous, and are integrated with the task rather than measured later by standardized tests.

Moreover, constructivist classrooms...

▶ Free students from the dreariness of fact-driven instruction and allow them to focus on large ideas

▶ Place in students hands the exhilarating power to follow trails of interest to make connections, reformulate ideas, and reach unique conclusions

▶ Share with students that the world is a complex place in which multiple perspectives exist and where truth is often a matter of interpretation.[9]

> No pedagogy is better suited than constuctivism to the requirements of the information age.[10]
> —OSEAS & WOOD

By allowing students the freedom to lead their own inquiries, the constructivist model enables learners themselves to convert information into meaningful knowledge.

REFLECTIVE PRACTICE

REFLECTIVE PRACTICE

Readers who have followed along this far are well aware that the Tribes Learning Community's intrusive pelican, "Reflection," is our meta-cognitive symbol reminding everyone always to take time *to reflect on what they learned and how their group worked together to achieve a task or goal.* Research studies show that the process of identifying a sequence of events or learning experiences taking place in a group leads to new highs in student achievement. One such study by Yager, Johnson and Johnson examined three different impacts on achievement: (a) cooperative learning in which members discussed how well their group was functioning and how they could improve its effectiveness, (b) cooperative learning without any group reflection, and (c) individualistic learning. The results indicated that high, medium and low-achieving students in the (a) groups achieved higher on daily achievement, post-instructional achievement and retention measures than did the students in the (b) groups using cooperative learning but no reflection and/or the (c) students working alone—individualistically.[11]

I'm a meta-cognitive symbol! Wow!

Other research studies as well as the experience of hundreds of teachers verify that the time taken to ask reflection questions can double the retention of the facts and concepts learned in an academic lesson.[12] Tribes Learning Communities use the word "reflection" rather than "process". It is important to keep in mind that reflection (meta-cognition) is congruent with how the brain learns... how it constructs knowledge by connecting information and experiences to previous knowledge. Reflection is a very necessary skill for living and surviving well in today and tomorrow's complex world of work, information and fast change.

System change, school improvement and assessment... all depend upon this conscious practice becoming a norm throughout the high school community. If in the daily rush no one says, "Stop the action... what's happening?"—academic achievement is minimized.

Howard Gardner warns:

"The push for action is powerful, particularly when it comes from impatient supervisors and parents. But unless one has the opportunity to think about what one is doing and to reflect on what went well, what went poorly, and why, the chances for a long-term improvement curve are slight. Time for individual and joint reflection must be built into the schedule; if it is not, then genuine change is most unlikely to occur."[13]

The regular practice in Tribes of having student groups address "reflection questions" helps them to internalize this critical life-long learning skill.

Reflective practice in the high school classroom is essential to developing a strong active learning community.

On-going reflection on learning experiences transfers knowledge and skills to future interactions and applications. A curriculum activity is only a time-filling activity unless reflection occurs. With reflection, the activity is transformed into meaningful learning.

As pointed out earlier, there are three types of reflections questions to use after a well designed learning experience: content/cognitive, social/collaborative, and personal reflection questions. They ensure the necessary rigor, relationships, and relevance that are recommended in *Breaking Ranks,* the valuable report by the National Association of Secondary School Principals (NASSP).

Content Questions (Cognitive Learning)

Content questions ask students what content or skill they have learned. Carefully chosen questions can stimulate higher level constructive thinking skills such as defined in the levels of Bloom's Taxonomy which all educators are likely to have encountered. The content questions help teachers as they monitor the rigor in their subjects. The chart that follows is an update of the cognitive process dimension, and looks at the levels in relation to the knowledge dimension.[14]

A Revised Chart of Bloom's Taxonomy

KNOWLEDGE DIMENSION	COGNITIVE PROCESS DIMENSION					
	REMEMBER	UNDERSTAND	APPLY	ANALYZE	EVALUATE	CREATE
FACTUAL KNOWLEDGE						
CONCEPTUAL KNOWLEDGE						
PROCEDURAL KNOWLEDGE						
METACOGNITIVE KNOWLEDGE						

Social Questions (Collaborative Learning)

Social/Collaborate questions address how the group worked together, and how a group might make refinements in future work sessions. This is in line with Bloom's Revised Taxonomy of *procedural knowledge* and how the group went through a process to achieve a goal.

Many teachers who initially try cooperative learning claim that students have a hard time getting along and working together. As group members examine the skills they used as a team, and the communication and collaboration that occurred, they begin to deepen relationships and internalize positive group skills. This learning prepares them well for the adult world of work. It also contributes to their quest to gain social competency.

Personal Learning Questions

Personal questions enable students to connect learning and find relevance for their own lives. It helps them to examine and integrate meaning to prior knowledge for deeper and lasting understanding. The metacognitive process contributes to the adolescent quest for a sense of purpose. Over time, the practice of asking oneself awareness questions becomes internalized as a life-long skill—indeed as a life-long gift.

Intensifying Reflective Practice

Learning becomes powerful and teachers grow professionally when they also become aware of their own metacognitive skills. Social scientist, Donald Schoen coined the term "reflective practitioner" and asserts that in order for teachers to improve their pedagogy, it is crucial that they become reflective practitioners. Schoen recommends three stages of reflection to use with students, staffs and meetings. The stages are "Reflecting IN Action", "Reflecting ON Action", and "Reflecting FOR Action.[16]

Reflecting IN Action

Reflection takes place during the time that teachers, leaders or group members are in the midst of instruction, leadership or meeting together as an on-going process. As a teacher you might be asking yourself questions such as:

> *Are the students focusing on the task?*
> *How are they working together?*
> *Is everyone participating?*
> *Are there any noticeable conflicts?*
> *Is the learning strategy appropriate?*
> *Do I need to make adjustments to my initial plans?*

The most powerful form of learning, the most sophisticated form of staff development, comes not from listening to the good words of others, but from sharing what we know with others. Learning comes more from giving than receiving. By reflecting on what we do, by giving it coherence, and by sharing and articulating our craft knowledge, we make meaning, we learn.[15]
—ROLAND S. BARTH

Reflecting ON Action

At the end of the learning experience, it is time to have students reflect on what they learned, how they worked together, and on the personal learning that may have happened. The three types of Tribes questions (Content, Social and Personal) are used to reflect on group action and help teachers gauge the degree to which learners have met objectives or fulfilled the task. Responses to reflection questions may be verbal or written by individual members or the groups.

Reflecting FOR Action

Based on reflecting in action, and on action, teachers and students consider next steps for learning. Teachers participating in Collegial Learning Communities have opportunities to confer with each other, share alternative strategies and/or revise curriculum they are teaching in common.

Once students have learned to reflect in action, on action and for action, they have gained an invaluable life-long personal and workplace skill.

It's like having a compass under your wing all the time!

AUTHENTIC ASSESSMENT

AUTHENTIC ASSESSMENT

Where is the standardized test that truly can measure the development and learning of our five high school kids, Jessica, Kyle, Mike, Angel and Jeremy? Let's imagine that they all are ready to graduate from their Learning Community High School. All "A's" student Jessica isn't socially lost anymore. She joined the Journalism Club and now is the editor of the school newspaper. Kyle, no longer cutting classes, is taking an Advanced Placement physics course, and is determined to become a mechanical engineer. Mike has stayed in school after all. Challenged by his Advisory class teacher, everything turned around for

Mike. He's headed for college. Angel wants to be a teacher. And, special learner Jeremy, discovered he's as great in math as he is in art, and wants to be an architect.

But how did they do on the State tests?

When you put in place a high stakes test that is not applicable to all students, clearly it is a discriminatory act.[19]
—LEONARD ATKINS

Maybe, their scores were not among the highest. The questions on high stake tests primarily are suitable for linguistic and logical-mathematical learners, the predominant intelligences of only 20% of high school learners. Howard Gardner's warning is that: "Poor endowment or learning in one or both of these intelligences is likely to result in poor standardized test scores."[17] The spatial, musical, kinesthetic, interpersonal student learners mentioned above will not do well. In time, they will sense the unfairness that such tests have devalued their intelligences, constructive thinking, problem-solving abilities, social competency, respective gifts... and perhaps their futures. An analysis of the most widely used standardized tests indicated that only three percent of the questions required "high level conceptual knowledge," and only five percent tested higher order thinking skills such as problem-solving and reasoning.[18]

We're caught in the middle—we have to do the State tests!

It is not our purpose to further debate the pros and cons of high stakes tests. Our concern and that of other responsive educators is that assessment needs to look at the *incremental development of the whole student learner.* It is significant that the respected Association of Supervision and Curriculum Development (ASCD) is advocating for American schools to adopt a "New Compact to Educate the Whole Child."

> A recent publication states: *"Current educational practice and policy focus is overwhelmingly on academic achievement. This achievement, however, is but one element of student learning and development and only a part of any complete system of educational accountability."*[20]

The big decision is whether or not your high school community wants to achieve meaningful learning and development for the diversity of youth in the school—and if so, how will you assess the degree that it is happening? Assuming that is your goal, the following is a brief look at *authentic assessment.*

Authentic assessment does not rely on single tests or narrow samples of a student's learning. Teachers and students over time reflect upon and gather evidence on a definable set of academic activities, performances and processes that are considered essential to school and life success. Some examples would be: applying a mathematical theory to a complex problem, designing and conducting an experiment, reading and critically analyzing a text, writing a research paper, conducting and reporting an interview, planning a project, working productively with a team, or presenting a report to the class community. Rather than testing for content facts and information, authentic assessment identifies what students have learned in applying academic concepts to contextual and real life situations.

Authentic assessment:

► is consistent with classroom practices and content; it asks questions about meaningful information, problems that students have solved and the process of doing so

► gathers evidence and reflects on indicators of student learning from multiple learning experiences

► promotes motivation, learning and teaching, and

► reflects local values, standards and control.

What is measured is valued and how it is assessed provides reliable indicators of student performance.[21]

The task of teachers, working together in their Collegial Learning Communities (CLCs) is to make certain that assessments are genuine and fair, that they reflect the valued objectives of their curricula, and that the instructional methods are active, collaborative and engage all learners.

It is helpful and motivational to involve students themselves in defining indicators class members will use to self-assess their own work, abilities and progress. A wide range of assessments, such as the following, can be used:

- ▶ presentations and demonstrations
- ▶ portfolios
- ▶ surveys and inventories
- ▶ journals and letters
- ▶ various forms of conferences.

Portfolios should *not* be collections of teacher-prepared worksheets and inventories, but student collected samples of their work, reflections and documentation of their personal social and group applied skills. The New Tech High School in Sacramento, California, has students build and refine their portfolios for four years, continuing to add samples of work that shows mastery of course content, critical thinking, collaboration and other learning outcomes. Such a portfolio can also include a resume, personal statements, goals and letters of reference. The four year portfolio can be formatted into DVDs to give to potential employers, college-admission counselors or be accessed on-line.[22] This is an ideal project for all students to work on and complete in Advisory classes throughout their four high school years.

Countless studies verify that students are motivated to the degree that they are active participants in their own learning. When provided with choice, control and collaboration in their classes they are intrinsically motivated to learn.[23] This is one of the reasons that students help to define the objectives of their groups' learning experiences, and reflect upon the results of their learning—all of which are clear practices in Tribes TLC®.

Formative and Summative Assessment

Assessment is an integral part of the learning process. As we look to provide opportunities for authentic assessments, we can keep in mind the value that formative assessments can be to know: how students are progressing, how we might provide descriptive feedback to help students reach closer to the targets, and at the same time adjust our instruction for those who are struggling. Summative assessments tell us how closely students have gained the knowledge and skills to meet learning targets at a certain point in time. In recent years, techniques and strategies for classroom and schoolwide assessment has become a study in itself. Readers and Collegial Learning Communities are urged to explore excellent resources such as Rick Stiggins and colleagues' *Classroom Assessment for Student Learning,*[24] and Anne Davies' publication *Making Classroom Assessment Work,* 2nd Edition.[25] In addition, the book, *What's Working in High School,* by Anne Davies and Kathy Busick highlights voices from high school teachers on successful assessment practices.[26]

Standards Based Grading

Standards based grading has become more of a focus and a necessity in recent years. It differs from traditional grading where the mark a student receives on a report card reflects the extent he or she has met the learning standards—as opposed to traditional grading where teachers may favor factoring in a student's effort or class attendance. Teachers using standard-based grading look at the multiple opportunities a student has had to reach the standard, and place greater value on most recent performance. There is much to consider about standards based grading practices. Our intent here is to bring awareness to the grading practice, and to highly recommend teachers learn more through Ken O'Connor's excellent publication, *How to Grade for Learning: Linking Grades to Standards.*[27]

Engaging high school learners in reflection and assessment encourages understanding of what is expected, improves motivation, leads to pride in achievement and offers a realistic appraisal of weaknesses.[28]

The matrix below compares three forms of assessment and the perceived consequences for students.

Forms of Assessment			
ISSUE	REPORT CARDS	TEST SCORES	SELF-ASSESSMENT
What are the outcomes?	Grades	Numbers	Motivation and learning
Who is being compared?	Class	Large populations	Student
Who is in control?	Teacher	Policymaker	Student
What is the student's role?	Passive	Passive	Active

The matrix can be used to help a faculty reflect on the big difference that happens for high school students when self-assessments are used. Staff development that has high expectations, collegial support, and adequate resources to meet its goals is key to moving well into authentic assessment. Training teachers to use authentic assessment not only can balance the high school's obligation to comply with standardized state testing, but to significantly increase student motivation and achievement.

It's time to decide! How should we measure these kids?

Authentically and fairly!

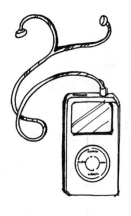

TECHNOLOGY

TECHNOLOGY

In this stimulus rich world where idle time means boredom and a craving for sensory input, we must keep listening to the voices and needs of today's high school learners. Marc Prensky, consultant and game designer in education and learning refers to this generation of students as the "digital natives"—whereas adults may be considered the "digital immigrants."[29] David Gordon, author of the Digital Classroom, refers to today's adolescents as "the screenagers" who use technology as an integral part of their daily communication, information sources, and entertainment. Gordon points out...

> *"New technologies are, in many respects, far more powerful learning tools than books, pencils, paper, and chalk. But in many other ways they're no different, and without high-quality instruction delivered by caring, competent teachers, few students have a chance of succeeding, regardless of whether they have a Pentium 4 processor or a No. 2 pencil... [edit]... The challenge for 21st century educators is to find balance, sensible, and pedagogically sound ways of using these remarkable new tools."[30]*

It seems like common sense that we must begin to connect with students through means they understand. The *Breaking Ranks* NASSP Report concurs that. "Schools will develop a strategic plan to make *technology integral to curriculum, instruction, and assessment, accommodating different learning styles* and helping teachers to individualize and improve the learning process."[32]

We must prepare kids for **their** future rather than **our** past or present.[31]

—David Thornberg

But what does it take to make technology integral to curriculum, instruction, and assessment, accommodating different learning styles?

Technology alone does not change culturally embedded traditional school practices or school systems. It takes changing educational goals, school culture, instructional practices, professional development and ways of working with students. Without these changes, new technology will merely be used to enact traditional practices.[33]

It is, of course, what the principles and practices within this book, *Engaging All,* are all about—that learning is a social interaction process and is fundamental to individual cognitive development. The advent of collaborative groupware technology not only enriches learning environments but engages students interactively and globally.[34]

Howard Gardner reminds us that technology is neither good nor bad in itself, nor should it dictate educational goals. "Before embracing any new technology, we need to declare our educational goals and demonstrate how technology can help us to achieve them."[35] Moreover, in the words of Ian Jukes, educational technology visionary, "It's all about making the move to transcendental teaching... the critical issues we must consider are far less to do with hardware, than they are to do with headware. It's about organizing technology around student learning; not student learning... around technology.[36] More than the hardware or software, knowledgeable teachers working together in a supportive educational context can significantly enhance teaching and learning.

The literature shows that despite the availability of more computers on campuses, teachers use of technology appears to be the exception rather than common practice.[37] Chris Moersch, a school technology consultant, created an on-line survey instrument called the "LoTI"—Levels of Technology Implementation. The survey assesses the extent and levels of teachers' use of technology. It helps to determine next steps to incorporate wider use in the school, and appropriate professional development. Following are the levels of implementation that can be identified from the LoTI data:

Level 0: Nonuse	Level 4A: Integration (Mechanical)
Level 1: Awareness	Level 4B: Integration (Routine)
Level 2: Exploration	Level 5: Expansion
Level 3: Infusion	Level 6: Refinement

> It's about organizing technology around student learning; not student learning... around technology.
> —IAN JUKES

To what extent are teachers using technology in our high schools today?

Moving ahead into effective use of technology has been limited by funding and time for teachers to meet with their colleagues, participate in training, share ways to integrate curriculum and assess progress. A national survey by Education Week found that districts only spend 5% of their instructional technology budgets on professional development.[38] The National Education Association (NEA) recommends 40%.[39]

The chart that follows identifies some of the numerous uses happening in high schools.

Uses of Technology in High Schools

INFORMATION SOURCE	Internet Simulations Gaming Electronic Textbooks Virtual Libraries Other:
COMMUNICATION	Word-processing Email Weblogs Chat networks Publishing Video conferences Video productions Electronic portfolios School News—Closed Circuit Programs Other:
INFORMATION CREATION/ GENERATION	Publishing Video productions Web-pages WiKis Weblogs Broadcast Journalism Podcasting Art—Computer Graphics Music—Composition and production Other:

Welcome to Media Central—
An On-Line Learning Community

The Moanalua High School media communications learning community went online in the fall of 2001, under the name "Media Central" as part of the school website. Since then Media Central has provided a supportive space for students and their families, which would both reflect and extend community building.

The website is organized by subject area and includes highlights of learning center achievements and activities. Student online portfolios are linked here, as are resource materials for their various projects, Word documents for assignments, access to the listserv, email, and online forums.

Besides the website, the two most basic tools of this online community are student email accounts and listservs. Although students prefer their instant messaging and MySpace "comment" format, they eventually realize that such access means, "school on call." Soon, I am getting requests like this one from Krystal: *"This is Krystal and I'm just emailing you because I'm having a little trouble finding an article for civics... I don't know why I guess I just don't know how to search for stuff."*

Student emails include requests for help with technology, assignment directions, and feedback on works in progress. I once got a query about a lost cell phone! This email correspondence provides students with an authentic context in which to develop their skills in written communication. They learn that the most effective queries include precise wording and information about their problem and their progress. And like Krystal, they preserve their identity and voice even in these remote exchanges.

"Hey, Mrs. S, how is your weekend going so far? I was wondering what the poetry analysis was. Do we just write about how we felt about the poem? Or do we include the other four steps in our analysis? Um, if I don't reply right away, I might be at a party or cleaning my room. Just to give you a heads up... Thanks, Mel"

Students also use their email accounts to participate in the class listserv, thus enlarging their community of "trusted friends" who will respond to their ideas and learning. Our MeneMAC listservs[40] **allow** students to learn to teach each other, as in Lorraine's posting in which she gives advice to Alisa about

A Teacher's View

Lynne Sueoka, M.Ed.

Lynne teaches English and Broadcast Journalism in the Moanalua High School Media Communications and Technology Learning Center. She believes in the idea of "reading and writing the world," and welcomes the opportunity to learn with her students how to harness the myriad tools of technology to do just that. Together with her students, she works to build and nurture online learning communities through e-mail, discussion boards, web portfolios, and digital storytelling.

her upcoming video on cooking, "...*you could talk about how cooking helps teenagers bond with their family and you could talk about how this is good because it is at this age where the teen drifts. This is where family recipes and the idea of soul food come in.*"

These exchanges allow everyone in the community to take part in thinking and problem solving. They allow the teacher to cite common successes and common problems, and also provide immediate models for the students to follow in order to exceed the standards on any particular assignment. Margaret Riel, technology author, calls this "shared minds, made visible."[41]

The online discussion forum or message board is another feature of our online learning community—one that also enables parents to share their ideas. It is especially great to have family involvement and sharing in the development of this culture of learning.

Larry Rosenstock, the founding Principal of the California Technical High School in San Diego, California, describes technology as a catalyst, a tool for active hands-on learning; and that working with an energized staff and students in a professional adult-like respectful environment supports project based learning.[42] It brings relevance daily to student learning experiences. Connecting students with adults is key in promoting collaboration, use of technology as a tool, communication, giving ideas form and shape, emphasizing ethics and responsibility—all while developing habits of mind for critical thinking.[43]

It is important to keep in mind three basic principles for the effective use of technology.[44]

1. Technology should not drive learning, learning goals should determine the use of technology. Technology with ineffective teaching will lead to ineffective learning. Incorporating *responsive pedagogy* is essential to the effective use of technology.

2. Technology should promote higher level thinking such as application of information, analysis of data, synthesis of ideas, and evaluation of one's own work as well as collaborative work with others.

3. Technology is a part of who our high school students are. We need to embrace it and use it to engage and maximize learning wisely.

Teachers today can access a wide range of on-line resources for their own learning and that of their students. As an initial step we suggest that your high school Collegial

Learning Community secure copies of David Gordon's book, *The Digital Classroom*, and research Internet sites that may pertain to you, your colleagues and student learners. The international sites are especially engaging and benefit students by:

- ▶ Building connections with students worldwide
- ▶ Discovering commonalities and gaining appreciation for diversity and differing perspectives
- ▶ Engaging in collaborative endeavors, and
- ▶ Nurturing reciprocal respect to work towards global harmony.

Sophie, a girl from Ireland, made the following entry on KidLink, a cyberspace used by youth from 172 countries around the world. Following is her message:

Sophie from Ireland: "We should recognize that the whole world is a community in which interdependence is the world's foundation. If we don't understand the humanity of our fellow human beings, we can never love them properly, without discriminating. We need to be able to ensure that each person receives an equal right to life and that all of the opportunities that this entails will be freely available to all."[45]

This is powerful learning that does not happen through a textbook. Indeed, the Web makes the world a classroom and connects all to Global Communities. It offers mentoring and tutoring for both teachers and students. It creates immediacy, linking lessons to day-to-day events. It makes every person a publisher. Yet, we need to keep in mind the words of Louis Gerstner, CEO of the IBM corporation, that:

"Computers are magnificent tools for the realization of our dreams, but no machine can replace the human spark of spirit, compassion, love, and understanding."

CONCLUSION

Now as we look at the fourth circle, Responsive Education, and design meaningful learning experiences for high school students, we have the tools to engage and address the diversity of student learners in our high school. We have gained initial knowledge and motivation to plan together in Collegial Learning Communities, and to continuously augment our own professional development. Over time, as we integrate curriculum content with the eight essential active learning principles and practices, we can be confident that all learners, students and teachers, will develop and achieve as never before.

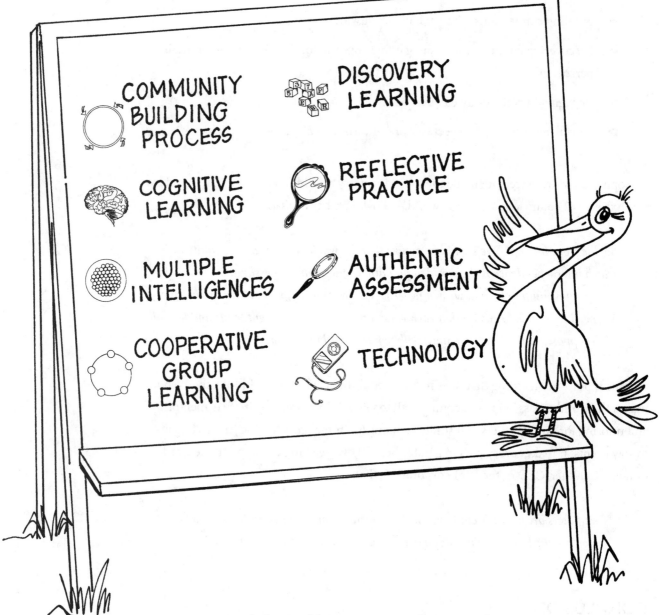

Yes, this is the flight plan to achievement for all!

12

Initiating the Active
Learning Process

12

Initiating the Active Learning Process

IN THIS CHAPTER YOU WILL

▶ Understand how a shift in teaching practices leads to educational excellence

▶ Explore how to facilitate the Community Circle and help students acquire collaborative skills and internalize positive agreements

▶ Learn how to use reflection questions to enhance academic, social and personal learning

The familiar life horizon has been outgrown, the old concepts, ideals and emotional patterns no longer fit— the time for the passing of a threshold is at hand.[1]
—JOSEPH CAMPBELL

THE JOURNEY WE ARE TAKING

Moving from the obsolete 19th century model of didactic instruction to 21st century research-based practice assures futures of promise for 21st century kids. Educators who are committed to high school reform acknowledge that no longer can the wealth of research on adolescent development, academic social-emotional learning, resiliency, multiple intelligences, ideal learning cultures, cooperative group education, constructivism, reflective practice and the use of professional learning communities be ignored. Respected educator Pat Burke Guild emphasizes that these theories offer a comprehensive approach to learning and teaching.[2] "Together they catalyze positive student learning. They force us to learn, to examine our values, and to put our beliefs and learning into practice for the many daily decisions we make."[3] Moreover, each of the theories is *learner-centered*. The time is overdue for high school leaders and teachers to learn what is known about learning and synthesize it into practice.

I'm looking forward to using all we've been learning now with students.

And using active group learning with students.

I'm beginning to realize what I never knew before.

Smart schools synthesize the best of learning principles and practices by:

▶ making adolescent development in all of its aspects, the focus of the school community

▶ establishing and sustaining a culture of caring throughout the school

▶ structuring the whole school community into supportive learning groups (communities), and

▶ supporting well-trained teachers to use educational pedagogy that is responsive to the learning and developmental needs of high school adolescents.

MOVING TOWARDS EXCELLENCE

The journey we are taking—moving from the old 19th century model of didactic instruction to research-based practice assures greater success and futures of promise for 21st century youth. The illustration and chart that follows shows the shift in teaching practice that responsive teachers are making from whole class instruction (lectures and seat work) to student-centered active group learning.

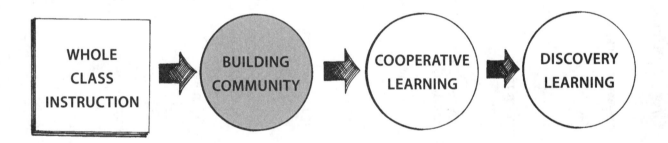

The last three group learning approaches, all grounded in extensive research and the literature of over-lapping fields, clearly support the developmental needs of adolescent students. The progression represents a growing consensus about what needs to happen *more* and what needs to happen *less* in instruction. The shift does not mean that teachers need to completely abandon using whole class instruction. It means that the more that active group learning is used, not only will high school students be more engaged and motivated, but will attain higher levels of development, constructive thinking, intellectual knowledge and individual skills.

The illustration shows the continuum of change in teaching practices that thousands of Tribes teachers and other progressive educators are making to reach and teach students more effectively. And to improve test scores! The "stages towards excellence" are initiated as teachers moderate their use of whole class instruction and move to class community building, cooperative group learning and discovery learning

Stages Toward Excellence Through Active Group Learning

WHOLE CLASS INSTRUCTION	BUILDING COMMUNITY	COOPERATIVE LEARNING	DISCOVERY LEARNING
TEACHER: directs lectures facts and concepts	**TEACHER:** directs initiates activity	**TEACHER:** plans initiates strategy	**TEACHER:** selects topic/problem engages students through inclusion makes connections to past and present learning experiences lays ground work for group task
asks questions	asks questions	**STUDENT TRIBES:** discuss and work on task or problem	**STUDENT TRIBES:** 1. *engage* define inquiry questions and process select question to explore (teacher acts as resource facilitator)
seeks correct answers assigns desk work	affirms multiple answers	seek ideas and report solutions to class	2. *explore* implement activities to explore inquiry manage and assess group interaction
manages behavior	manages behavior builds inclusion	manage task and interaction build inclusion and influence	3. *explain* articulate observations and ideas share and clarify terms/language with facilitator (facilitator determines misconceptions and levels of understanding) present learning/project to whole class or parents justify conclusion based on academic knowledge
tests for facts	**STUDENTS:** use agreements learn collaborative skills work in collaboration reflect on interaction	monitor agreements use appeciation reflect on learning and group interaction assess for knowledge and learning	4. *elaborate* expand on concepts and make connections to real world
STUDENTS: learn alone	learn together	learn together	5. *evaluate* reflect on performance outcomes share appreciation students (and teacher) assess learning

(constructivism) pedagogy. Wherever you and your faculty are now on the continuum is truly OK. What is important is that teachers in your school support each other, coach each other and reflect upon the progress you all are making along the way. Change takes time, but once the direction is clear, it builds a spirit of community, collegiality and excellence in learning throughout a school.

Shifts in Practice	
LESS	**MORE**
Whole class, teacher directed	Experiential, hands-on
Worksheets, seatwork	Active learning
Transmission of information	Demonstration, coaching, and mentoring
Coverage of curriculum	Deep study of a few topics
Textbooks	Primary sources + inquiry
Memorization of facts	Constructive thinking
Tracking and leveling	Heterogeneous groups + classes
Reliance on standardized measures	Reliance on performance + authentic assessment

Active learning is given nearly universal support from researchers and progressive policy makers as the best, and perhaps only way for students to develop capacities in critical thinking, problem-solving and decision-making. The recommended practices of cooperative group learning and constructivism engage students in real time discussion, thoughtful dialogue, open-ended inquiry, research, group projects, presentations, meaningful topics, problem-solving, brainstorming, role-play, virtual simulations, debate, mock-trials, off-site exploration, case studies, town meetings, and interaction with resource persons, and community service projects.

ABOUT THE FOUR STAGES

As soon as teacher groups of the school have become trained in the basic Tribes Learning Community course, either by a Certified District Trainer or a CenterSource staff trainer, they are ready to implement the process by engaging students in a class Community Circle. The objective of this first stage is to build inclusion, to learn to use the four Tribes agreements and to teach students to assess their participation and learning through group reflection. The community circle is, however, teacher-centered—all eyes and ears on the teacher while he or she introduces topics, asks questions and controls behavior. The community circle stage, used consistently, develops inclusion, a community climate and

We'll refer to the stages of the illustration as we move through these "how-to-do-it" chapters.

Lynne Block, M.Ed.

Lynne is an experienced educator having taught at the elementary, secondary and post-secondary levels. She currently teaches at Burnaby Central Secondary School in British Columbia, Canada. As a consultant and Certified Tribes TLC Trainer, Lynne shares the Tribes process with educators, parents and students. She is committed to providing research-based learning to ensure that young people become socially responsible, confident, resilient, lifelong learners.

Actively Learning English Curriculum Content

When I began teaching, I only knew the traditional, fill-them-up-with-massive-amounts-of-content approach. By changing my teaching style from a teacher-directed one to a student-focused one, I could not believe the profound changes, not only in my students, but also, in myself. I rediscovered my joy in teaching. But what happened with my students? Initially, it was a paradigm shift for them. "What do you mean I won't get an A unless I learn to cooperate?" "But if I help my group members, then they might get the good marks, and I may not!" "Why should I learn all these other things when they have nothing to do with English?" These were only a few of the milder responses that greeted my classroom and teaching changes. Colleagues, parents and administration also had concerns. And upon reflecting back to ten years ago, I had similar questions.

So what happened? Was it all smooth sailing? Is the Tribes process perfectly integrated all the time in all my classes? Of course not. Like any class, there are impediments and setbacks. But the wonderful research-based results speak for themselves. Besides learning English curriculum content, students learn social/interpersonal skills as well as learning styles, multiple intelligences, higher level and divergent thinking skills, social responsibility and so much more. So what does this look like in the classroom? Students eagerly come to class on time. They begin to read their respective novels. They are responsible for their learning and for their behavior. While working in groups, facilitators lead the learning task, timekeepers keep their groups on time, encouragers ensure everyone is included and is participating. Active learning strategies such as Jigsaw, a character walkabout, a mind/concept map, or brainstorming a new assessment/evaluation tool for an upcoming project engage all. So with all this focus on active learning, do I manage to teach all the prescribed course content and curriculum? The answer is a resounding, "yes"—and then some!

It has been a pleasure to realize that the depth and breadth of my students' learning of the English prescribed outcomes are far greater because of the Tribes process. If students have been taught how to brainstorm, how to work together, how to be accountable, how to access support, they move much faster, more comprehensively and more happily in learning content. Do they do well on government exams and formal testing? Unequivocally, yes. Valuable time is not spent on behavior management issues, or convincing students to learn the course content and material. They want to learn! Often students say they cannot believe how fast the time passes in their English class. Students who previously, had not great success in English do so much better and feel good about themselves. Learning through their personal learning styles and multiple intelligences, they realize what they *can* do in English.

With the Tribes process fully integrated into my English classes, not only am I able to teach all the prescribed content, but know that students are meaningfully engaged; are excited about learning, and are acquiring social and group skills to interact well with others the rest of their lives.

learning to use social group skills and positive agreements. The community circle provides the foundation for the next stage, Cooperative Group Learning—small communities, teams or tribes.

Once students are familiar with the class community process, the Tribes TLC® agreements and some of the collaborative skills the teacher and students organize small groups for Cooperative Learning. The classroom takes on new energy and motivation among students as the teacher's style changes from whole class direct instruction to facilitating active group learning. Gradually increased responsibility is transferred to students to learn academic material, to monitor the agreements and to manage the interaction of their groups. The transfer from teacher to students not only is motivational, but especially meets the developmental needs of adolescents. No longer do teachers spend 70% of their time lecturing, asking questions, giving instructions and disciplining. As facilitators of cooperative learning, they then have that much time to give support and encouragement to students and guide their use of resources. Best of all, they have time to know their students and tailor learning experiences to their interests and needs.

Many teachers in the past decided that group learning did not work, and based on their limited use, they were right. Simply placing students in groups—students who are socially unskilled—and expecting them to work well together without having learned essential group skills and positive agreements not only can be frustrating but unproductive for all. Unfortunately, teachers who do not realize this and give up group learning, sacrifice the proven benefits their students and they could have.

The process of Tribes is the glue that holds it all together—and makes group learning successful.

And that's what happens in adult groups too.

The move to Discovery Learning—Constructivism adds even a more significant dimension and promise for high school students. The process is based on decades of literature about learning and teaching by such eminent scholars as John Dewey, John Piaget, Jerome Bruner, Howard Gardner and Lev Vygotsky, to name but a few. Even back to the 18th century a Neapolitan philosopher, Gambattista Vico, asserted that humans can only understand what they themselves have "constructed." Today the concept has become known as *constructivism,* and is gaining ever-increasing validity from recent evidence in the brain and biological sciences. The approach engages students in social dialogue to define questions for inquiry and problem-solving, to challenge hypotheses, test/defend solutions, design projects and evaluate their collaborative team results. It transforms academic concepts for learners into meaningful real-world possibilities.

Tribes TLC® Discovery Learning is an integration of two frameworks:

1. the Tribes group development process of inclusion/influence/community, the collaborative group skills and agreements, and

2. a constructivist instructional model, known as the "Five E's" and developed by Roger Bybee, of the Miami Museum of Science.[4] We learned about the significance of using contructivism in Chapter 11, and you will be designing curriculum with the "Five E's" model when we move into Chapters 15.

The complementary frameworks make planning easy for teachers who are committed to being responsive to the learning needs of young adolescents.

INITIATING THE FIRST STAGE—THE COMMUNITY CIRCLE

The special spirit of community doesn't just happen in a class or meeting by using a few "ice-breakers" or cheery activities. Building community is a deliberate process that needs to be facilitated over a period of time. The daily class community circle is step one in actualizing the culture of Tribes and resiliency environment of caring relationships, positive expectations, and opportunities for participation and contribution.

Personalization is assured by creating inclusion for every person within the learning community, and using the set of positive Tribes Learning Community (TLC) agreements:

▶ Attentive listening

▶ Appreciation/No put-downs

▶ Right to pass/Right to participate

▶ Mutual respect

According to the 'Breaking Ranks' documents, it's recommended that all high schools build community.

Yes, the class community circle provides inclusion for every student. They engage all in creating the high school learning community!

Ah! And coincidentally, that's the name of this book!

No matter the subject or type of class, all students within the class need to have inclusion—to become known and to know everyone else. Students are given many opportunities to present themselves as the teacher introduces various inclusion strategies that can be found in this book. As you will learn later in designing learning experiences, curricula subjects can be integrated into the strategies at the same time. During this time, teachers engage students in using the positive agreements and collaborative group skills, and they themselves also make an effort to model the skills and agreements. It is also helpful to have the class meet in a community circle at the beginning of a period for on-going inclusion, continuity in moving to new topics, reflecting on skills, group work and giving statements of appreciation.

At the same time that a teacher begins to help students become familiar with the community circle process, he also begins to have people meet in pairs, triads, and groups of four or five, as an additional way to promote inclusion and to begin working together on academic topics.

Inclusion example: *"Find two people you still do not know very well and for five minutes share why you enjoy a favorite outdoor activity."*

Academic example: *"Turn to a neighbor and for a few minutes talk about what you would do if you ever became the President of the United Nations."*

This use of temporary small groups helps to make the transition to long-term membership groups. It also gives the teacher an opportunity to see how different combinations of students work together.

Getting Started

Remember the Tribes Trail Map In Chapter 7? Notice that in the beginning the teacher needs to be directive to help everyone become comfortable and feel included. The quality of the classroom environment is strongly influenced by a teacher's personal style, the behavior that he or she models and expects from the students. What is talked about during a community circle session may be less important than how the class interacts together. The circle in which people are sitting needs to be large enough so that everyone can see each other. Begin by saying something like, "This year our class will be working together in some new ways—in small groups, so that people can help each other learn and learn from each other. We also will meet often as a whole class in a community circle like this."

During this first introduction, raise your hand and tell the class that this is how you will ask for attention. It is a non-verbal signal for everyone also to raise his or her hand and to stop talking. You might state that using the signal means they will never have to hear you shout.

"Now how many people would like that? (Ask for a show of hands.) It is also a great test of our awareness, or consciousness.

Giving Instructions

Describe the activity or task that the community will be doing, and give the purpose for doing. Use initial Tribes strategies that promote inclusion. Some that may be appropriate are: Community Circle Topics, Something Good, or Wishful Thinking. The Index grid at the beginning of the Active Learning Strategy section helps you to make selections. The primary purpose of active learning strategies is to serve as structures (formats) in which academic content can be learned.

Initiating Sharing

Initiate sharing by being the first to speak on the selected topic, and then invite others to do so by going around the circle. Remind everyone they have the right-to-pass. When someone does pass, openly acknowledge the person with a nod or smile to convey that passing is OK. After going around the circle once, facilitate a second go-around to give those who hesitated to speak the first time a second opportunity.

Keeping Things Moving

It is best to refrain from repeating, paraphrasing or commenting on anyone's contribution. Make mental notes on what you may want to bring up later. However, if someone does get put down (derisive laughter, groans, etc.), deal with the incident in a direct but matter-of-fact way. "People, remember the agreement that we made about not wanting to put anyone down." Or ask the group "Which agreement do we seem to be forgetting?" Let the class identify it rather than you doing so.

Learning and Practicing the Tribes Agreements

The second purpose of the community circle is to teach and practice the Tribes agreements and other collaborative group skills. At the same time that you introduce a discussion topic or an active learning strategy, also announce the skill to be practiced at the same time: "Class, we also will also be practicing attentive listening during our ten minute discussion." Begin transferring responsibility to the class by asking one or two people to keep track of the time, and later reporting their observations on how well people listened to each other.

Encouraging Follow-up

After everyone has had a turn, allow time for questions and comments. Ask people to speak directly to one another and to use first names. Model this by saying something like—"Lisa, It would be exciting to hear more about the set design for the play."

Follow-up by referring to some of those mental notes you were keeping. Invite others to do the same. Do not dominate the discussion yourself. Just facilitate and clarify as needed.

DEFINING COMMUNITY AGREEMENTS

It is important for high school youth to enter into a discussion of what they need in order to feel safe, or trusting in a group. Set aside time to do this even though you may have shared the Tribes agreements earlier or students may have defined or learned them in Advisory period. Students will own them once they have brainstormed what they want the class to be like. This can be done as a brainstorm in small groups or as a community circle discussion. Typically, people will say things like:

> *"I don't like it when people put each other down."*
> *"I don't want to get pushed around."*
> *"I don't want to do something just because everyone else does."*

"I don't want our group to argue a lot."
"I want people to get along together."

After the brainstorm have the class or small groups synthesize and summarize the statements as closely as possible to support:

▶ Attentive listening

▶ Appreciation/No put-downs

▶ Right to participate/Right to pass

▶ Mutual respect

Discuss any statements that do not seem to fit. It's OK if the class feels it needs one more agreement. However, since the purpose of these agreements is to build a positive learning environment, and to have students become responsible for sustaining them, the list should be no more than five. Agreements must not be seen as school or teacher rules. Tribe agreements are positive and relational, defining how people want to relate to and treat each other. Your own modeling is absolutely the most essential factor in altering the learning culture. Modeling is effective when it is authentic, congruent and heartfelt. Owning and living the agreements yourself also means:

▶ Setting aside a lesson plan long enough to tune into a student's concern or pain

▶ Being non-judgmental, patient, and caring even with the more difficult ones

▶ Avoiding subtle put-downs in the midst of frustration or stress

▶ Standing on your own rights...to pass, to state your feelings, to say, "No, I choose not to do that. It would not be good for me."

▶ Affirming through warm eye contact or a gentle touch on the shoulder

▶ Laughing at your own mistakes; conveying your own fallibility and commitment to lifelong growth and learning.

ATTENTIVE LISTENING

Attentive listening is probably the most important social skill to be taught and practiced by everyone in the learning community. Unfortunately, for many young adolescents (as well as adults) the experience of being listened to in a caring way rarely happens.

Attentive listening is a gift to be given. It depends upon...

▶ Acknowledging the person who is speaking- giving him full attention and eye contact

- Withholding one's own comments, opinions, and need to talk at the time

- Paraphrasing key words to encourage the speaker and to let them know they have been heard

- Affirming through body language that the speaker is being heard

- Paying attention not only to the words but also to the feelings behind the words.

Being there means speaking and listening with head and heart.

Too often we half-listen to each other, running the words through our heads that we want to say as soon as it is our turn. Most teachers assume that kids have learned at home how to listen. Most adults assume we all do it well—though we may never have been taught the principles.

The skill of attentive listening needs to be considered a priority within every class because it affects the ability to learn academic material. This is especially important as classrooms move toward group learning, Inquiry, collaborative projects and group discourse.

Begin by teaching students three essential listening strategies to be found in Active Learning Strategy section of this book. Namely, the strategies are:

- Teaching listening
- Teaching paraphrasing
- Reflecting feelings.

you

eyes

undivided attention

heart

ear

APPRECIATION/NO PUT-DOWNS

Since one of our main objectives is to develop a sense of self-worth and self-esteem in adolescents, the scores of derogatory remarks that bombard young people each day must be eliminated. Unfortunately, put-down remarks can be a basic form of communication among teenagers and adults themselves. At times they are used in families to convey affection: "you goof-off, you jerk, you crazy." Though off-hand or flippant, they not only damage self-esteem but undermine the level of trust within a group. A positive climate cannot develop unless we...

▶ Challenge students themselves to point out and object to put-down remarks, and

▶ Encourage students instead to exchange statements of appreciation.

One way to encourage your class to confront put-down statements is to teach them to respond with "I-Messages."

Example: *"I feel angry when I'm called 'stupid'. It's a put-down and hurts!"*

Use the strategy "Teaching I-Messages" from the Active Learning Strategy section.

Statements of Appreciation

Minimizing put-down statements is half of the step toward creating a caring community. Put-downs need to be replaced with statements of appreciation. Helping people of any age to express appreciation often can be like swimming against a strong current. It is a sad commentary on our society that in the course of a day we make five times as many negative comments as statements that affirm the value of others.

Statements of appreciation are invited at the conclusion of every group learning experience, and are modeled frequently by the teacher. It is very important that you search for truths to say. Teens know when something doesn't ring true—is not sincere and honest. To help people begin making statements of appreciation, use such sentence starters as these:

"I liked it when...(describe the situation)."

"I felt good when you..."

"I admire you for...(describe the quality)."

After completing a group activity, write the sentence starter on the chalk board and invite people to make statements. Your own modeling encourages the sharing of positive statements perhaps more than anything. It is important that you model being both a good giver and a good receiver.

Examples:

"I appreciate your help, Joel."

"The ideas that you came up with, Sandy, made our project special."

"I felt honored when you gave me a copy of your own poem."

THE RIGHT-TO-PASS

The right-to-pass means that each person has the right to choose the extent to which she or he will share in a group activity. It is the essence of our democratic system not to be coerced, to have a right to one's privacy, and to be able to take a stand apart from the majority. Without such guarantees, individual freedom within a group is not protected. Choosing the right-to-pass means that the community member prefers not to share personal information or feelings, or to actively participate in the group at the moment. It is his or her choice to remain quiet and to be an observer for a short period of time. This right must be affirmed repeatedly by teachers and peers: "OK, you do have the right to pass. It's just fine to do so." Being a silent observer is still a form of participation. It also gives support to a student who at the time may be concerned with a social or emotional issue.

This protective agreement is essential within all organizational and group settings. It provides control to participants. It encourages adolescents to be self-determining and responsible among peers. It gives youth the practice and courage to stand back from situations that are uncomfortable or contrary to their own values. They need to have repeated opportunities to assert their right-to-pass in the midst of working with peers. It is part of becoming independent and autonomous whether in good or bad groups. It is an essential developmental task and resiliency strength.

Many teachers are anxious that if this agreement is used in classrooms, students will pass on learning subject matter. First of all, the agreement does not apply when individual accountability is required on learning tasks. Students do not have the right to pass on homework, taking tests, responding to the teacher, etc. They do, however, have the right to pass in peer-led interaction. It is important to keep in mind that...

▶ Temporarily withdrawing from activity does not mean a student is not learning

▶ You can count on the tribe, or peer group, to draw the person who usually passes back into an active working role

▶ Healthy human development and resiliency depend upon young people becoming inner-directed rather than remaining dependent upon outer control from others.

MUTUAL RESPECT

The purpose of the mutual respect agreement is to assure everyone that their individual cultural values, beliefs, and needs will be considered and properly honored. It also means that adults demonstrate respect for student's rights, needs, and differences. The rich multicultural diversity of our population is an invaluable resource for this country's future. Where better to learn to live it than within the school community? The agreement means respect for...

▶ Others—no matter what their race, gender, age, color, or learning ability

▶ Newcomers from other neighborhood, cities, states, or countries

I've been to a lot of other schools where I felt like a real loser. This school is different! I'm respected here for who I really am!

▶ Teachers, parents, and other caring adults

▶ Personal property and individual privacy

▶ Individual skills, talents, and contributions.

TEACHING COMMUNITY AGREEMENTS

Invite students to sit together in a community circle. Pre-sketch or draw the following grid on the blackboard and have the class fill in the specific examples:

Agreement: Listening		
LOOKS LIKE	**SOUNDS LIKE**	**FEELS LIKE**
heads together	talking one at a time	great
eyes looking	encouragement	I'm important
people nodding	good idea	people care
leaning forward	uh-huh	I'm smart
smiling	yes!	we're friends

1. Invite discussion on the need for the skill or agreement. Remember the cooperative learning way: Meet them where they are. Don't lecture or talk at them. Invite students to share what they already know and then add to it.

2. Ask people to call out words for the grid: "What does listening look like?" "What does it sound like?" "What does it feel like?"

The four agreements should be posted in a prominent place and reviewed whenever the class community or tribes meet. Consider having a school-wide competition for students to design posters of the four agreements. The award poster then is printed and distributed to all classes.

Support learning of the agreements by affirming the behaviors whenever you see them happening, and in time ask students to do the same.

Example: "I can tell your team is listening well to each other... people are talking one at a time."

Now and then you may inadvertently overlook one of the agreements yourself. Do encourage the class to bring this to your attention. Accept such reminders graciously and without defensiveness. Teenagers can be great agreement and social skills reinforcers. Count on them to monitor and help sustain the positive community environment for the class.

ASKING REFLECTION QUESTIONS

The other key not only to have group learning be successful, but to have students move to new highs in performance and achievement is to follow every learning experience with "reflection questions." Research studies as well as the experience of hundreds of teachers verify that the time taken to ask reflection questions can double the retention of the facts and concepts learned in an academic lesson.[6] In Tribes TLC® we prefer to use the word "reflection" rather than "process" in order to distinguish the learning experience questions from the Tribes group development process. We also want to teach and emphasize that reflection (meta-cognition) is a very necessary skill for living and surviving well in today and tomorrow's complex world of information and change.

As discussed in the previous chapter, now you will be defining three types of reflection questions.

Content (cognitive learning): Questions that are focused on the academic concepts, ideas and knowledge gained from the learning experience; also the constructive thinking skills that were used. The content questions help teachers as they monitor the rigor in their subjects.

Collaborative (social learning): Questions that focus on the interaction and participation of members in the learning group; also the collaborative skills that were used. The collaborative questions deepen relationships and build interpersonal skills.

Personal (individual learning): Questions that help to identify individual learning or skills that helped group complete the task; recognition of one's special interests, gifts, talents or new goals; personal consideration how to use or apply what was learned. The personal questions help students to make relevant connections to their own worlds and discover their strengths and assets.

Here is an example of reflection questions I used with my English class. The class had been reading the book, "The Alchemist," by Paulo Coelho.

Content: *What does your team believe is the main message of the story? How did you go about analyzing the several messages?*

Collaborative: *How did you go about getting everyone's opinion? Is there a particular collaborative skill your team needs to practice next time?*

Personal: *What did you learn from the story? How did you help your group? Is this a skill you have noticed before about yourself? Write your own comments in your journal.*

You do not need to ask all three types of reflection questions after a learning experience, but do use at least two of the different types. Base your choice on what you believe will make the content meaningful and the social or personal learning significant for the majority of students in the class.

Time out for reflection also develops the capacity to learn from experience and understand the working dynamics of groups and systems. It supports the definition of human development: to discover, sustain, and alter "situations"—to move into ever-widening realms of knowledge and experience.

The questions suggested for each strategy in this book may not be the best ones to ask your own class. There simply are no sure-fire questions that are appropriate for all cultural populations and age levels. Your own intuition, creativity, and judgment are needed to draw out meaningful learning for your students.

ENCOURAGING APPRECIATION

The power of the Tribes process on adolescent development also comes from the practice of giving students opportunities to express appreciation to each other after working together. To be able to hear one's peers acknowledge special qualities, skills, and contributions to the group is much more meaningful to most students than periodic affirmation from a teacher. Moreover, how many times a day can any teacher affirm each and every student in the class!

USING TEMPORARY SMALL GROUPS TO BUILD COMMUNITY

If you look again at the Tribes Trail Map in Chapter 7, you will notice that pairs, triads, and temporary groups are also used to build inclusion in the community before people become members in long-term tribes. While your students are working together in these "trial tribes" you can observe how people get along with others. This serves as valuable information when you are ready to have students move into long-term small learning communities.

BUILDING COLLABORATIVE SKILLS THROUGH STAGES OF GROUP DEVELOPMENT

The Tribes process with its sequential stages of group development—inclusion, influence and community—is a pathway for the development of the essential collaborative skills that students (and all of us) need in order to live, love, play, and work well together. Collaborative skills don't just happen, even though we may use learning groups in classes, or have the intent to collaborate with others on a work project. The skills must be taught and practiced over and over in relation to others who share a common purpose, task or goal. This could be a class, faculty, a work team, a board of directors, a neighborhood group, or city council. Collaborative skills are the constructive thinking and social skills set forth in the U.S. Secretary of Labor's report as necessary skills for the 21st century.[5] Whenever human systems do not work well or fall apart, one can be certain that essential people skills are missing.

The graphic on the next page illustrates the twelve skills taught and strengthened during the sequential stages of group development in a Tribes classroom. Inclusion skills prepare the class to handle the influence stage. The essential collaborative skills learned in the influence stage become the foundation for a vital community... working together with others from diverse backgrounds, solving problems, assessing for improvement, and celebrating their achievements. The ongoing practice of these key collaborative skills creates a classroom with high levels of participation on the part of all students and establishes a positive climate for teaching and learning.

Seven Steps in Teaching Collaborative Skills

1. Engage students in identifying the need for the skill (using discussion, role-play, story, or situation).

2. Teach the skill (using the Looks/Sounds/Feels Like structure or other strategy).

3. Practice the skill regularly, and have students give feedback on how well it was used.

4. Transfer the responsibility to the tribes to remind each other to use the skill.

5. Ask reflection questions about the use of the skill in tribes, the class, the playground, at home, etc.

6. Point out times when you notice people using the skill well.

7. Notice and celebrate when the skill is "owned" as a natural behavior in the classroom or school.

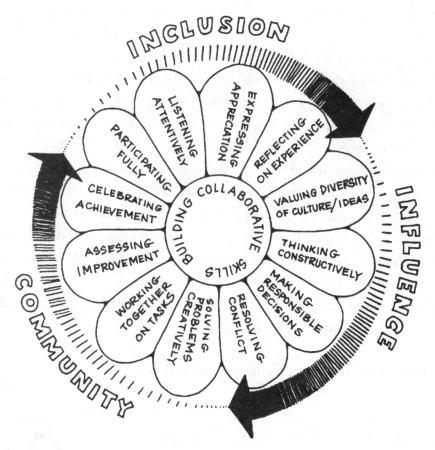

BUILDING COMMUNITY CREATIVELY

Please do not feel limited to the active learning strategies contained in this book in order to develop a sense of community among all your students. An abundance of initial inclusion activities exists in many other books. Use your teacher ingenuity to create whatever will best engage your students. Good community building strategies . . .

► have win-win rather than win-lose outcomes—cooperation rather than competition

► provide inclusion for everyone—all can participate

► draw upon and highlight the contributions that people make in the course of the activity.

"The best kind of learning is learning all together, in little groups or big groups; it's a really good way to teach kids. Learn with each other, not just alone. Kids who don't learn this way are really missing out. I think it's a privilege for us to be able to have this kind of education. People who just learn the traditional way, just by themselves, who don't get help—it's scary."[7]

—JULIA LEWIS, STUDENT, CAMBRIDGE, MASSACHUSETTS

13

Building Classroom
Learning Communities

13 Building Classroom Learning Communities

One learns by doing the thing, for though you think
you know it, you have no certainty until you try.

—SOPHOCLES

IN THIS CHAPTER YOU WILL

▶ Introduce students to the concept of group learning

▶ Facilitate inclusion and a sense of belonging within tribes

▶ Begin to use the process of Tribes for active learning

▶ Transfer responsibility and accountability to student groups

▶ Teach students how to manage group tasks and issues

▶ Learn how to resolve group issues

▶ Help students learn ways to make decisions and resolve problems

Welcome to this chapter!
It shows us how to build
active class learning
communities, and ways
for students to learn
social skills in Advisory
and other classes.

We are convinced, as are many progressive educators today, that "restructuring schools" is about structuring connections by creating small learning communities (LCs, teams, tribes) throughout the whole school system—rather than switching roles, tinkering with policy, inviting in more experts or continually shuffling curriculum. Structuring learning groups in all classes and the staff *personalizes the high school* system into a community of trust, respect and productivity. The connection to peers in small groups, gives every person a sense of belonging (inclusion), a sense of recognition and value (influence) and on-going social support (community). Bonnie Benard writes,

"It is what school reform as well as professional development literature has advocated for over two decades. Furthermore, the best educational research has found this concept to be associated with successful schools that promote student development and learning, teacher empowerment and well-being... and retention."[1]

But how do I know when my students are
ready to work in on-going small groups?

READINESS TO WORK IN ON-GOING GROUPS

Your class is ready to be in small learning groups when you can say "yes" to the following questions:

1. Do students understand and respect the agreements?

2. Do they know one another from having met in a community circle and worked in pairs, triads or other temporary groups?

3. Have students had successful learning experiences working in practice groups?

Introduce the concept by having the class meet in a community circle and discuss their experience of working together, not only in the class circle but in many small groups. Invite them to discuss...

▶ the value of belonging to groups (such as teams, families, clubs, departments, etc)

▶ what makes groups work well

▶ how could on-going groups in this class be helpful for learning subjects?

Tell the class that they will be working together in groups (teams, tribes, etc.) on special projects, research, curricula and to help each other be successful. It may be helpful to share some of the proven benefits realized through cooperation. As discussed in Chapter 10. Do what you can to help the class become invested in the idea of belonging to a learning group rather than working solely on their own. Of course, all will wonder how the groups will be formed and who will be in their group. State that each person will write the names of several people they would like to have in their learning community, and assure your students that one or more of those named, or that someone who has asked for them, will be in their group.

> Learners must come to understand that as they transcend the self and become part of the whole, they will not lose their individuality, only their egocentricity.[2]
>
> Art Costa

SOCIOMETRY MADE EASY—HOW TO BUILD TRIBES

Groups of four, five or six are appropriate. More than six people in a learning group whether high school adolescents or adults can lead to more problematical dynamics and difficulties working in collaboration.

Following is a step-by-step process that you can use to achieve a sociometric balance in your classroom groups, without using any cumbersome instruments. The "Seven Friends" method of building teams enables you to achieve the best mix of skills, cultures, and relationships. It has the added advantage of allowing your students some influence in determining who will be in their group. Be sure to give yourself enough time to do this thoughtfully.

Seven Friends

1. Give each person a 5" x 8" index card. Have people print their names in the center of the card.

2. Ask each person to print the names of seven other people they would like to have in a group, and to put both boys and girls on their lists.

3. Collect all the cards. Remind your students that they will each be in a group with at least one identified friend, but not with all of those listed.

4. Assuming that you will have five groups, select the cards belonging to five leader types, those who have been named the most by others and who also enjoy learning. Spread these cards out on a table.

5. Select the cards of five students who exhibit quiet or less positive behavior. Place one of their cards next to each of the leader's cards.

6. Add the remaining cards to each group, making sure that each card has a name requested by someone in the group.

7. Make any adjustments necessary to achieve a balance of boys and girls.

8. Check once more to be sure that each card is still matched with a friend.

Forming Groups

Once you have determined the composition of the groups, set a date when everyone will move into the groups. Advance notice builds great anticipation.

Choose an interesting or exciting way for people to discover who is in their tribe.

People Puzzles

1. Begin with sheets of poster board, one for each group.

2. Sketch a design on each sheet so that you can cut as many puzzle pieces as the number of students in a particular group.

3. Print a student's name on each piece. Make sure that all the members of a tribe are included in the same puzzle.

4. Distribute puzzle pieces to the students named on the puzzle pieces. Then have students find people with matching pieces.

When everyone has found their team, have them sit together at desks or tables arranged so that tribe members face one another. When all have settled down, ask reflection questions, such as:

Content: *What made this a good way for people to form groups?*

Personal: *What did you learn about yourself in finding members and meeting members of your group?*

After the groups have participated in some initial inclusion strategies, tell the class that people will remain in these groups for at least one month or a specific time. The class then will evaluate how their groups are working and whether any changes need to be made. This defuses the inevitable remark, "I wanted to have someone else in my group!"

Surveys of Tribes teachers at various times show that when students stay in the same group for at least three weeks, teachers did not have to make any membership changes. The secret is that after that much time, the inclusion strategies, group process, and positive agreements have created a sense of belonging, caring, and trust. People have forgotten about wanting particular friends, having made new friends whom they enjoy and do not want to leave.

You may have noticed that we are referring to groups as teams, clubs and learning communities as well as tribes. Do call them whatever seems appropriate in the culture of the school, the subject of a class, or the purpose of a group. At the adult level there may be Collegial Learning Communities, a Core Leadership Group and various other planning, administrative and departmental groups. They all have much in common in the high school that is becoming an integrated whole school Learning Community. All are learning, all are teaching and all are productive in using the same well-proven personalized TLC group process.

BUILDING GROUP INCLUSION

Remember that "Tribes Trail Map" and discussion back in Chapter 7? Now your understanding of it moves into daily application with your class. Although you implemented many inclusion strategies with the class to build community before forming tribes, the need for inclusion continues. Each time a new group forms, people sense the same "stranger anxiety." Moreover, if this issue is not addressed, it limits the ability of a group to work well together. Inclusion must happen again with the newly configured tribes. It is on-going process whenever people come together..

Select a series of inclusion strategies that will help people present *who they are, what they do well, and what their expectations, hopes, and needs* might be. The strategies need to be geared to the interests, age level, and culture of your particular class. Read the preface of Chapter 17: Active Learning Strategies before leaping into using them. Hopefully, you are involved in an in-service training conducted by one of CenterSource Systems' certified Tribes TLC® District Trainers or Associates. If so, you will experience many inclusion strategies appropriate for high school learners that can be easily adapted to your class. Some of the favorites are "Campaign Manager" and "Interview Circle."

A way to feel included is to grab influence.

Taking the time to do this during the initial days in teams makes all the difference in managing the class and having cooperative group learning work well. People are not ready to work together on curricula unless inclusion and trust have been developed within their learning groups. Disruptive behavior happens whenever students do not feel included.

That's what plagues teachers throughout a class period and school year. Anti-social behavior gains attention—"someone notices me" and now cares. It is a way to feel important in the midst of many others. The Tribes TLC® process decreases disruptive behaviors in schools simply because everyone is included, recognized and valued. On the day before the new groups are to be announced, invite people to bring something meaningful to share at the first meeting of their new team. A symbolic item could be a token, article, gadget, sketch or something written and carried within pocket or wallet. Sharing something symbolic helps each person to talk about self and initiates the identification of individual interests, skills or goals. More than all it develops a sense of belonging, personalization and positive energy in the group.

Facilitating Small Group Communities

1. Begin the period by having everyone briefly meet in a community circle.

2. Invite someone to review the class agreements previously discussed in the class community circle.

3. Use an inclusion strategy that engages all. Ask reflection questions.

4. Give, or invite groups to give overviews of the day or period's work.

5. Have people move to their customary group areas.

6. Explain the learning experience or task and the collaborative skills or agreements that people will later assess.

7. Give the directions one step at a time, using as few words as possible. Write steps on the board if there are several.

8. If clarification is needed on instructions, ask that the group confer among themselves before asking you.

9. State how much time there will be to complete the task or strategy. Ask each tribe to make sure that every member participates.

10. While the tribes are working together, observe their progress. Intervene only if absolutely necessary.

11. Signal when time is up, and have each tribe report progress by responding to appropriate reflection questions. Reflection questions can be handled either in community circle or in tribes.

12. Invite statements of appreciation.

TRANSFERRING RESPONSIBILITY

One of the major objectives in using learning groups with these *emerging young adults* is to call forth positive leadership qualities and self-responsibility. This means that an intentional transfer of control needs to be made from the teacher to the group and from the group to its members. As a sensitive teacher you can look for opportunities to have the tribes increase their capacity to function independently. Here are some of the ways in which responsibility can be transferred:

▶ Intervene only as necessary while the teams are working together

▶ Encourage members to remind one another about the agreements

▶ When students ask you a question, refrain from answering immediately; turn it back to the class or tribe, asking "Who can help to clarify the instructions?" "What ideas do other people have?"

▶ Ask members to assume helpful tasks and roles

▶ Invite people to make contact with team members who are absent, and help returning members to catch up with the learning group or the class

▶ Have the learning groups plan events, presentations, parent or community involvement

▶ Invite teams to give feedback to you and to other learning groups following presentations or sharing group work

▶ Ask teams for suggestions to improve lesson plans, academic projects and/or the learning environment.

The process of transferring responsibility to students increases participation—and, if you recall, participation, caring, and high expectations contribute to the development of individual resilience. In addition, on-going development of the adolescent tasks—independence, social competency, sense of purpose and problem-solving—is supported.

OBSERVING THE PROCESS

Admittedly, it can feel strange to be in the background while class learning groups are working on a challenging, engrossing task or strategy. This, however, is not a time to sit idly by, or to catch up on grading papers! During these periods when your busy teams cease to need you, you become the process observer, looking for the new skills, gifts and behaviors to be affirmed. It also gives you time to notice the dynamics within the tribes. Following is a list of some of the dynamics that you can observe and reflect upon while your teams are working together.

Observation Checklist

1. How are people sitting?

   Are they in a close working configuration, or are some people sitting back?

   Are they leaning forward attentively, or are they slouching, sprawling, or lying back?

2. How are people participating?

   Are a few doing all the talking or work? Is participation balanced?

   Are people lively and animated, or lethargic and tentative?

   Is everyone focused on what is happening, or are side conversations taking place?

   Are some people passing a lot?

3. How are people taking care of one another?

   Are they listening to one another?

   Are put-downs happening? (If so, are they being confronted by group members?)

   Are disagreements being resolved in satisfying (win-win) ways?

   Are kindness and cooperation being demonstrated?

   Is appreciation being expressed?

   Is the group drawing in the quieter people?

4. How are people feeling and behaving?

   Are they smiling and/or laughing?

   Is your intuitive response one of warmth and relaxation, or anxiety and tension?

5. Are they working on task well?

   Who has assumed leadership?

   Are the less social or shy learners being included?

   Do they seem mindful of the goal to complete the task on time?

6. What is happening for you?

7. Other

FACILITATING THE PROCESS

What happens when you observe breakdowns in the process? Let's use an example. You are introducing the strategy, "Brainstorming," to your history class teams to learn the non-judgmental process, and then use it to generate alternatives a historical character could have considered. One recorder in each team is furiously attempting to write down all the ideas being voiced by tribe members. While observing the behaviors in each tribe, you notice that Angel, one of the recorders, is having a hard time getting all the information down on paper. People are saying things like, "Hey, you left out my idea!" "Slow poke!" Your impulse is to stride over to the group and take charge. Instead, you take a deep breath and reflect on all that is going on. You observe that only two students, Angel and Jamal, are really "into" the strategy. They're leaning forward and putting forth many ideas. The other team members are sitting back rather apathetically, waiting for the time to run out.

What are your alternatives, other than intervening?

You could do nothing, in which case the situation would either:

1. Stay the same

2. Get better—someone might remind others of the agreements, or volunteer to help Angel

3. Get worse—an argument might erupt.

A better alternative is to raise your hand and stop the action.

USING THE "TIME OUT REFLECTION CYCLE"

Simply call out, "Time out," or "Stop the action!" Wait patiently until order and silence fill the room. Then ask "What's happening?" Ask everyone to look and listen back to what was going on in the classroom or tribes. Give people time to reflect—don't start diagnosing the situation yourself. Suggest that everyone "runs the movie backwards" in their heads, to recall what people were doing. Invite everyone to recall what they saw themselves doing, and to share that in their group using the sentence starter, "I saw myself . . ." Then without using names to describe other specific actions they noticed.

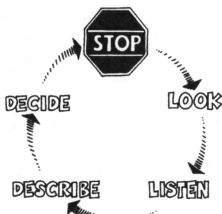

Next invite groups to share how their group time or task may have been affected. Follow the steps of the "Time Out Reflection Cycle," and engage the class in deciding what everyone can do to improve things. It's a good idea to draw a picture of the "Time Out Reflection Cycle" so that everyone becomes familiar enough with the process to use it whenever necessary in their class groups or elsewhere.

Of course, if a team does not report a noticeable behavior that you observed, do comment on it. Not to do so would be interpreted as an indication that you were not paying attention, or that you did not think it was important.

The repeated practice of reflecting on group and community interaction helps people to become aware of the impact their behavior has on others. Reflection is essential to support academic learning and youth development.

KEEPING YOUR PURPOSE AND ROLE IN MIND

Keep in mind that the overall purpose of using the process of Tribes TLC® is nothing less than *"to assure the growth and human development of youth in your school community so that each has the knowledge, skills, and resilient strengths to be successful in a world of rapid change."* The interactive approach when used in every class and every day in a high school is a "here and now" laboratory that enables learners to move from a singular focus on "me" to "we"—and to a concern for others—our community, our nation, and the future of our world.

Teachers need to learn how to sustain caring learning environments and teach responsively to support the developmental tasks that all adolescents are struggling to achieve. Doing just that enables high schools to call forth the best within each and every young person.

LEARNING HOW TO PREVENT AND MANAGE DISAGREEMENTS

One of the most important collaborative skills for today's students and teachers to learn is how to manage disagreements—a dynamic that inevitably arises within any group of people working, playing or living together. Denial or avoidance of a disagreement ultimately undermines relationships, the group environment, and its ability to work well together. Remember the saying, "There is no way around—only the way through."

Disagreements are a natural part of life because as individuals we differ in what we want, need, and think. Within each disagreement or conflict there is an opportunity to gain new knowledge. If our intent is to learn, we will seek to understand how and why the conflict happened. In the process, we discover more about own perceptions and assumptions, as well as those of other people. The result is that relationships become more satisfying, and a few more steps toward *peace in the world* are achieved.

When a group has the commitment and skill to resolve rather than ignore conflict, individuals feel free to raise questions, explore different viewpoints and contribute ideas. This is essential in the process of becoming a learning community of any kind. Understanding and resolving a situation begins with the belief that a "win-win" solution is possible. Strong feelings often make defining the problem difficult, and what appears to be the problem may be just a superficial issue. Once the real problem is identified and agreed upon, it becomes possible for people who have been in opposition to work out a solution that will be fair to all.

A specific sequence of steps is suggested for use whenever two students become involved in a disagreement or conflict:

Step 1: Both students agree to the ground rules.

"*I agree not to interrupt, not to call a name, and I agree to work to solve the conflict.*"

Step 2: One person tells his/her side of the story using I-Messages, saying how she or he feels about what happened, and what s/he wants. The other person listens attentively and restates the problem.

Step 3: The second person restates what the problem is for the first person. Suggestion: begin with "*So the problem for you is...*"

Step 4: Steps 2 and 3 are repeated, with the second student speaking.

Step 5: Both people suggest possible solutions.

Step 6: Both work to agree on a resolution that is:

- specific
- balanced—both people will be responsible for making it work
- realistic—and will solve the problem.

Some high schools have Peer Assistance Programs in which well-trained students are available to counsel, mediate and resolve differences peaceably. They work closely with the high school counselors and teachers. An added feature is that students who have been trained as peer assistants also can be linked into Advisory periods to help students learn communication and group skills.

TEACHING I-MESSAGES

It is also very important to teach high school students (as well as adults!) how to express themselves in heated moments by using I-messages. This skill as well as the skill of *listening* can be learned in high school Advisory classes. The two skills are essential in the workplace and all other roles in life.

An I-Message is a statement of the speaker's feelings in response to the behavior of others. An I-message does not convey judgment, nor is it a put-down as is a blaming "You-message" that fuels dispute. Notice the difference between the following examples:

You-message:

"*Mike, you dummy, you ruined my chance to be the pitcher. You make me angry.*"

I-message:

"*Mike, I feel angry whenever a catcher isn't paying attention.*"

Yeah, it must have been those You-messages I used that got me into all those fights!

In the first example, Mike was rudely put down and blamed for the situation. In the second example, the speaker took responsibility for his feelings, stated them in strong terms... but did not put the blame on Mike. He defined the behavior that he perceived.

The purpose of an I-Message is to communicate feelings in such a way that the other person is not forced to defend himself or avoid the situation. The impact of the You-message blames, shames, or intimidates the other person. It causes the other person to become resistant. The recipient of a You-message hears the message as "you are bad or wrong," and is less likely to consider resolution of the difficulty. Worst of all, You-messages escalate conflict.

I-Messages	You-Messages
State and own the speaker's feelings	Hold another person responsible for the speaker's feelings
Describe the perceived behavior or situation, not a personal judgment	Blame others; judge and put people down

You-Messages can also masquerade as I-messages: "I feel that you are always a nuisance" is a disguised You-message because:

1.   No feelings are stated or owned, even though the speaker says "I feel", he really means "I think" or "I believe".

2.   The phrase "You are always a nuisance" is a judgment, implying that the person is bad or incapable of being different.

In teaching people how to use I-Messages, it is helpful to write this formula on the board:

I feel _____ (name the feeling)

when _____ (describe the situation or behavior).

Give examples:

"I feel confused when people shout at me."

"I feel scared when anyone threatens me."

I-Messages are also a good way to communicate positive feelings:

"I feel happy when I receive a compliment."

"I feel great when everyone participates."

Use the strategy "Teaching I-messages" from Chapter 17, "Active Learning Strategies," to help your students learn this important life skill.

The I-Message is a tricky concept to master, even though it seems quite simple at first. This is another instance in which you need to be an appropriate role model. It may take some time, but with daily practice your students will begin to use them.

KNOWING WHEN TO TAKE CHARGE—YOUR CRITERIA

Yes, there are those crisis times when I-messages just won't work—for instance, when you encounter one student hurting another.

"Stop that this instant!" is much more appropriate for the moment than "I feel upset when people hit each other."

Handling antisocial or inappropriate behavior depends upon thinking through your intervention options in advance:

▶ When to use additional inclusion activities

▶ When to encourage students to use I-Messages with one another

▶ When to use an I-Message yourself

▶ When to use group problem solving

▶ When to be directive and take charge.

RESOLVING GROUP ISSUES

The social climate in your class and your success with the Tribes process will be greatly influenced by the way in which disagreements, conflicts and angry feelings are routinely expressed and resolved. As a responsive teacher, your willingness to acknowledge, discuss, and resolve group issues in a caring, process-based manner will result in growth and learning for you and your students. All groups of people living, playing, or working together experience many interpersonal issues. The chart on the following page gives an overview of typical issues that come up in a group's development, and it gives suggestions on how to resolve many situations.

In the beginning you may hear statements like these that indicate group issues:

"I pass!"
"I don't like my group."
"What about the new kid?"
"Hey, that's a put-down!"
"Let's form new tribes."

1. "I Pass!"

Early in the team-building process, some people may be passing all the time, and others may not be participating. This type of behavior is usually an indication that some people feel unsafe with their groups. Suggestions:

- ▶ Discuss the reasons why some people are not participating, and then have the small groups discuss what to do.

- ▶ Have people work in pairs. Match a shy person with a more confident, outgoing one. (Try the strategy "Interview Circle" in the groups.)

- ▶ Spend some time with the habitual passer. Learn his special interests and talents; encourage him to share them with the tribe.

- ▶ Assign the passer a role or task in the tribe.

- ▶ Make sure that the agreements are being honored so that the environment is safe.

2. "I don't like my group."

A person who feels uncomfortable in his group may say things like:

"I don't like the people in my group."
"I get bored in my tribe."
"People in my tribe are dumb."
"I want to be in Sarah's tribe."

Rather than trying to talk a student out of a complaint, use your listening skills to find out what is really going on. Suggestions:

- ▶ Enlist the help of the tribe to give the person more inclusion

- ▶ Gear some activities to her learning style and interests

- ▶ Ask the person to "hang in" with the tribe for two or three weeks; by this time things usually work themselves out.

In some extreme cases, it may be advisable to transfer a student to another tribe, or to provide her with something to do alone while tribes are meeting. These are last-resort measures, only to be considered if all else fails.

3. "What about the new kid?"

When a new person enters your class after groups have been formed, it is important to give her a special welcome. One way is to have an adoption ceremony.

GROUP ISSUE CHART

	Issues	Questions/Feelings	You, the facilitator, need to
Inclusion	**PRESENTATION OF SELF**	*Will I like this group?* *How will they get to know me?*	Be directive and provide structure; use many inclusion activities that permit each person to share who they are, what feelings, skills, qualities, and resources they have.
		I feel nervous with these new people. *Will they listen to me?* *Will they put me down?*	Have people work in pairs and triads; it feels less threatening. Teach listening skills. Make sure that people respect the Tribes agreements, especially "No put-downs" and "mutual respect."
	EXPECTATIONS AND NEEDS	*Will we finish by 3 o'clock?* *Can you help me with a problem?*	Provide opportunities for each member to state wants, needs and expectations for the time the group is together.
	ACKNOWLEDGMENT	*Will they like me?* *Do I dare tell someone I think she is a nice person?* *Does anyone else feel the way I feel?*	Be a good role model by giving and receiving appreciation easily. Provide opportunities for people to exchange statements of appreciation and good feelings. Ask reflection questions that encourage people to share thoughts and feelings about coming together as a group.
Influence	**ME VS. THE GROUP**	*Will my opinions be respected?*	Provide activities that help people share individual differences and cultural strengths.
	GOALS	*What are we to accomplish together?*	Introduce techniques that elicit input from each member in defining group goals. Model and encourage acceptance of all ideas before choosing group goals.
	DECISION MAKING	*How can we reach agreement?*	Introduce techniques for consensus decision making.
	CONFLICT	*How can we work this out?*	Introduce conflict resolution techniques (active learning, I-Messages, role reversal). Assist group members in reaching win-win solutions. Teach collaborative skills.
	LEADERSHIP AND AUTHORITY	*Do we need a leader?*	Encourage rotation of roles. Urge natural leaders to draw out more passive members.
		I resent it when someone tries to tell us what to do.	Ask reflection questions that help members discuss and resolve leadership problems. Use conflict resolution techniques as needed.
Community	**CREATIVITY**	*I feel good about my abilities.*	Recognize individuals for unique achievements and gifts; encourage group members to do so with one another.
	COOPERATION	*Our group really works well together.*	Assign group tasks that require innovation, cooperation, and creativity.
	ACHIEVEMENT	*We did a great job!*	Assign projects: All group members contribute.
		What shall we tackle next?	Use groups for peer teaching, problem solving, planning and fun! Be alert for inclusion/influence issues; support groups in resolving them.
	CELEBRATION	*I really like our tribe and community.*	Take the time to celebrate—for whatever big or small reason!

During this activity, build inclusion with Angel by interviewing her, letting her know a bit about community learning groups, and that it will be her choice as to which tribe she'll join. The choice may be limited to those groups having fewer people. If you prefer to assign the newcomer to a group, you can still ask all of the groups to come up with creative ideas for helping the person feel welcome and included. Hundreds of parents have expressed their great appreciation to TLC schools that use this ceremony. In a very transient society, it is wonderful to have your student come home the first day and say, "I belong to a group already, and the kids made me real welcome!"

Adoption Ceremony

1. Introduce the new person and then ask the class how many people have ever moved to a new school like our new person, Angel, is doing..

2. In tribes, ask people to share their newcomer experiences. Transfer the time for sharing; five minutes is enough. Meanwhile, visit with Angel.

3. Then ask the question, "What ideas does your tribe have to help Angel, feel welcome and included in our class?"

4. Ask each tribe to brainstorm lists of some helpful things its members could do. Allow five minutes.

5. Have the tribes take turns reading their lists to Angel.

6. After all the tribes have done so, invite Angel to choose which tribe she would like to join.

---

4. "Hey, that's a put-down!"

If you find that in spite of your most heroic efforts, people are still using many put-down statements, you may need to take remedial action. Suggestions:

Have each student write on a card something someone said to them that really hurt. Put all cards in the center and have each draw one and read it without comment. Then discuss how it would feel to receive them.

Initiate an "anti-put-down" campaign.

Challenge the put-down experts to create statements of appreciation that they would like to receive.

Provide lots of opportunities for statements of appreciation

Be a good role model, both in giving and accepting statements of appreciation. Just make sure you are honest at all times.

5. "Let's form new teams!"

If your students begin agitating to change tribes, it is probably an indication that you need to do more full-group community inclusion and intergroup strategies. Suggestions:

▶ Remind everyone that they agreed to remain in the same groups for the period of time you specified before any changes are made.

▶ Combine two teams for a strategy like "Interview Circle." Membership in teams needs to remain as constant as possible. The long-term membership factor develops cooperation, trust and peer support for individual achievement.

Need for Influence

Your students had been in learning groups for a period of time and things are going great. No more agitating to change tribes. Almost no put-downs. And talk about working independently! Then your smooth-running class began to get a little out of hand. Some of the people you counted on as positive role models are restless. You notice subtle and not-so-subtle indicators that disagreements were happening. I-messages and attentive listening are being forgotten. It seems like a terrible setback and you say to yourself, "Forget group learning!"

Congratulations! Your class is now ready to really go to work! The inclusion, or "honeymoon," stage of the community building process has run its course, and the stage of influence has arrived! The new restlessness is a sign that your students are comfortable with the group process—they feel included and safe enough to speak out, even those shy ones.

STAGE OF INFLUENCE

The stage of influence is not about fighting for control or power over others. It is an organizational stage in which people want to contribute value to their group or community. Take a few minutes before moving further into this chapter and review "The Stage of Influence" in Chapter 7.

You thought you had it made?

It's important to remember that if groups ignore the underlying issues of the stage of influence rather than working through them, their capacity to work well together will suffer, and they will never come to appreciate the diversity of group members. There is no way around—only through! Your job as a process facilitator is to recognize the restlessness as a sign of progress, and use strategies that help people express their individuality. A sense of value and positive power then becomes a reality. As soon as that happens, your class (or staff or organization) will be a strong learning community in which everyone participates, shares leadership, leaps ahead in learning—and discovers individual talents, skills and gifts.

It is time to empower the high school learners at this stage of group development. Remember, they all long to grow into their rightful autonomy, social competency, positive expectations/purpose and independent problem-solving. To squelch them now back into whole class instruction and competitive individualistic learning is to dismiss their social and emotional developmental needs—that can only be supported well through interactive group learning supports. Your objectives for this stage are to...

▶ Provide many opportunities for people to state their differing opinions, values, and beliefs openly

▶ Make respect for diversity (culture, gender and multiple intelligences) a focus in the class or whole school

▶ Teach strategies for individual and group decision making

▶ Teach strategies for individual and group problem solving

▶ Allow time for students to define individual and group goals.

Learning to State Opinions

It takes courage and trust to take a stand in the midst of peers and say, "I feel differently about this than the rest of you do." The more that students are given opportunities to state diverse beliefs, the more able they will be when pressured by peers to go along with the crowd. Advising teens to simply "just say no" is inadequate.

Let's say you have a 9th grade history/civics class this year in which you've been using a theme such as "Self and Society." You've been building class community and have five class teams, each composed of five students. Throughout the inclusion stage you also started to use some of the Tribes TLC strategies as formats for academic content.

Today you have decided to tackle the first steps of the stage of influence. To do so begin with the four influence strategies listed below. Tailor the language and topics to fit the sophistication level and cultures of your students. The strategies are:

Thumbs Up/Thumbs Down

Where Do I Stand

One, Two, Three

Put Yourself on the Line

Follow the directions as written in Chapter 17, "Active Learning Strategies," and remember: the strategy alone is not enough! Allow sufficient time for reflection questions so that in-depth learning happens. Use the strategies several times. Ues topics of personal interest or controversial questions from material the class may have been discussing or studying.

To create a classroom where students feel safe enough to challenge each other—and us—is to give then an enormous gift.[3]

—ALFIE KOHN

Examples using the strategy "Put Yourself on the Line:"

> *"The only way to have a safe school is to have more rules, monitors and metal detectors. Where do you stand?"*

> *"The age that teenagers can vote and drive should be substantially lowered. Where do you stand?"*

Ask several types of reflection questions. Although example questions are noted for all of the strategies in this book, craft your own special questions for the content of the experience.

The "Put Yourself on the Line" strategy can be followed up with many other learning opportunities such as the following:

1. People who agree on a position can form temporary new study groups to research and prepare a defense for their position.

2. The people on the extreme ends, who differ the most, can get together in debate and dialogue groups.

3. Students who learn through rhythm/music, visual/spatial, or body/kinesthetic intelligences may want to illustrate the various positions through role play, music, diagrams, or drawings. As you recall, Chapter 10 discussed the Multiple Intelligences and Chapter 14, "Designing Cooperative Learning Experiences" contains hundreds of ways to involve students of multiple learning styles.

The creative controversy that can evolve out of influence strategies not only can produce a wealth of learning in lesson content, but also challenges students' critical thinking and collaborative skills. Best of all, different opinions are affirmed and valued.

DECISION MAKING AND PROBLEM SOLVING

Have you ever wondered why schools limit student choices to the extent that they do? Everything is so predictable for kids for twelve years—the classes one must take, the way the system works, the competition, the tests, the workbooks year after year. The opportunity to make choices is next to zero in traditional schools. If we truly want students to become self-directed and gain a sense of autonomy, learning how to make responsible decisions and solve their own problems is essential. Again, we recognize that this is one of the key developmental tasks high school students are trying to achieve—to gradually gain a sense of power over their lives. The are in the midst of having to make many decisions and solve a new level of personal problems concerning peer relationships, future careers, preparation for college, handling part-time jobs, financing cars and balancing time for school, friends, family and personal interests.

The distinction between decisions and problems is important:

▶ Decisions are judgments made concerning information as perceived by an individual or a group.

▶ Problems are dilemmas, intricate issues, and predicaments that need to be analyzed in order to reach resolution.

The difference between the two defines the preferred sequence to teach decision making and problem solving.

Making Individual Decisions

The strategies used to help students express different opinions also can help them practice making individual decisions

Example strategy: Where Do I Stand?

"Our class will be working on four issues about the Civil War during the next three weeks. Stand by the sign of the topic you want to work on.

1. *Roles of European countries*

2. *The Emancipation Proclamation*

3. *Lincoln's personal and political dilemmas*

4. *Economics in the South and North."*

Individual decision making can be practiced throughout the teaching day by using many influence strategies and reflection questions. Reflection can happen in tribes or through writing in personal journals.

Individual decisions can also be made with the help of trusted group members, teachers, and parents through the Tribes strategy "Let's Talk."

The circle diagram contains four quadrants:
- Individual problem solving
- Making individual decisions (1.)
- Group problem solving (4.)
- Making group decisions (2., 3.)

Man ultimately decides for himself! And in the end, education must be education toward the ability to decide.[4]

—Viktor Frankl

Let's Talk

1. **Define the problem, situation, or concern**

   Example problem: "Whenever I go over to my friend's house after school, his mother is not home and he wants me to drink beer. I don't want to say 'No' because he won't like me if I do."

2. **Repeat the problem back (if in a discussion)**

   "You mean that you think you have to drink with your friend or he won't be a friend anymore? Repeating back the problem usually brings elaboration."

3. **Think it through**

   "Would anybody lose respect for you if you did drink with your friend?"
   "Have you thought about the risks involved?"
   "Are you certain your friend will not see you anymore?"
   "Have you considered some alternatives?"

4. **Look at both sides**

   "What is the best thing that could happen if you said 'No'?"
   "What is the worst?"

5. **Decide and act**

   "Having thought through the consequences, what is the most responsible choice you can make?"
   "Are you willing to accept the possible consequences by acting on your decision?"
   "If so, do it!"

6. **Evaluate the outcome**

   "What happened? What did you learn?"
   "Were you proud of your choice?"
   "Would you make the same one again?"

I learned that making my own decision meant I couldn't blame anyone else when it didn't work out.

Making Group Decisions and Action Plans

The stage of influence calls into question how tribes can make decisions together. Reaching an agreement even on something as simple as, "Who will report for our team?" often proves to be difficult.

First, teach the tribes how to use the strategies of *Brainstorming, Consensus Building* and *Goal Storming.* Keep in mind that once your students are familiar with the strategies, they can be used as active learning formats for academic topics and real-time decision-making.

I'm good at barnstorming— must be the same as brainstorming!

Practicing group decision making prepares young people to live in a democracy— to work responsibly with others. The more that we give students the opportunity to reflect upon and analyze the dynamics that take place in their tribes, the better prepared they will be able to "discover, sustain, and alter" systems, environments and situations in which they find themselves. This contributes to the development of resiliency and responsible autonomy.

Learning communities that make group decisions to work on long term tasks or projects find it helpful to create "action plans" that designate tasks to be done, persons responsible for each task, and expected times for completion. The action plan can be posted, reviewed daily, and revised if necessary. Action plans are "group contracts," which remind people of their accountability to one another.

Action Plan	Tribe Name:	
WHAT	**WHO**	**BY WHEN**

GROUP PROBLEM SOLVING

The maxim is so simple, yet so difficult for adults to put into practice. Our immediate reaction is to suggest solutions, and then become aggravated when students care little about carrying them out. Our basic goal of preparing this generation to do well in today's world depends upon helping kids become responsible citizens. For this reason Tribes trains teachers to transfer responsibility to student groups as much as possible. Having tribes rather than adult personnel solve classroom or school problems is also the key to sustaining a mellow environment. Let's look at two problems in need of student solutions.

Problem #1

Gossip has been a problem that seems to have become more prevalent. During a recent week it led to a fight on campus. Some of the offenders may be in your class or Advisory period, and you would like to have students solve the problem in a safe and caring way. A good strategy is to tell the class about the problem and lead the class learning community through the step-by-step process for group problem solving found on the next page.

What is remarkable in this example is that the identity of the students causing the problem is never discussed. They may, in fact, have participated (somewhat silently) in the problem solving.

Behavior problems can easily be handled whenever peers are given the opportunity to express how they feel about an annoying behavior. Have class teams brainstorm "behavior that bugs me." Count on the power of peer feedback! Just going through the process of identifying conduct that is not appreciated by peers usually results in a behavior disappearing quickly.

Step-by-Step Process for Group Problem Solving

1. Ask the class teams to discuss how they feel about people gossiping and fighting in school. Allow three to five minutes.

2. Distribute large sheets of paper, and ask the teams to brainstorm some ways that they could help solve the problem. Remind them of the rules for Brainstorming.

3. Ask each team to select their three best ideas or solutions to the problem. This can be done by consensus or by having each person write "1, 2, or 3" after three items of their choice. Stickers of three different colors may also be used. In this case, each student selects his/her top choices by placing a blue sticker on the first choice, red on the second choice, and yellow on the third choice. The totals on each suggested solution are counted (blue stickers 15 points, red stickers 10 points, yellow stickers 5 points).

4. Invite two people to record the three ideas from each tribe on the board as they are read to the class.

5. Combine any duplicate or similar solutions.

6. Have all of the students approach the board, team by team, and vote for one solution.

7. Ask for two volunteers to add up the sticker points for each item. The solution receiving the most votes will be the one that the class will carry out.

Problem #2:

You notice that some learning groups are having various interaction problems. You want them to learn how to resolve group problems or issues.

Strategy: Ask the class if they have noticed that people are having difficulties in working together. After hearing their replies, tell them that you also have observed some interaction problems, and that you would like them to figure out how to resolve them.

Then lead them through the active learning process on the next page.

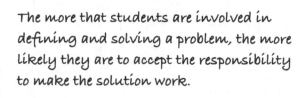

The more that students are involved in defining and solving a problem, the more likely they are to accept the responsibility to make the solution work.

Teams Resolving Group Issues

1. Ask each person to reflect upon the group's interaction in recent work together. Then using a 3" x 5" card jot down any difficulties that seemed to keep them from working well together.

2. Have each group place its cards face down in a pile.

3. Collect the stacks and exchange them among all of the groups so that no group has its own.

4. Give the groups 10 minutes to identify one issue from the cards and make suggestions on what the learning group might do to resolve the problem.

5. Have each group share their suggestions with the whole class.

6. The tribe being discussed remains anonymous.

INDIVIDUAL PROBLEM SOLVING

There is an understandable concern about students sharing personal problems within groups in educational settings. We have always taken the position in Tribes TLC® that it is inappropriate for educational groups to deal with any personal problems that border on the psychological, and that only qualified professionals should do so. Tribe Learning Communities are educational, not therapy, groups!

It is inevitable, however, that personal psychological problems become more evident during stressful adolescent years. We concur with the majority of school district policies that adults are legally required to share information that may endanger a student or others. It is the teacher's responsibility to refer the student to the professional services designated to handle such problems for the school.

Help your students understand that it is not the purpose of their teams to deal with personal or family problems. Class or Advisory Period teams may, however, help people think through concerns related to their school work, career questions, future goals, skill development, roles among peers, and friendships.

Two strategies in particular are helpful in supporting students to solve individual problems.

1. The "Client Consultant" strategy works well for educational, career, or personal interest concerns.

2. Personal journals can provide on-going reflection and assessment. Peers can choose to share or not with a trusted friend, teacher or parents—but only what they believe would be helpful in thinking through a problem.

SETTING GOALS AND MAKING INDIVIDUAL CONTRACTS

Schools and teachers who are committed to supporting the developmental tasks of adolescents also provide time for students to learn how to define purposeful positive goals—a key attribute of resiliency.

One way to start working towards this is to invite students to use the "Goal Storming" strategy independently. Ask people to choose something about themselves that they would like to pursue or improve (social or academic skills, attitudes, or behaviors) during the next weeks. Short time durations are better than long ones. Students may wish to share their goals with other tribe members and write personal contracts, which can be signed by peers who agree to give encouragement and support. There is a form for the personal contract in Chapter 17, "Active Learning Strategies." Positive peer support can work wonders!

Goals also can be recorded in Advisory class personal journals, so that students can continue to reflect upon their experiences, document progress, and record changes. Personal journals are respected as private documents that are shared only if a student chooses to do so.

14 Designing Cooperative
Learning Experiences

14 Designing Cooperative Learning Experiences

IN THIS CHAPTER YOU WILL

▶ Recognize the essential elements of active cooperative learning

▶ Understand how to use a six step format to design group learning experiences

▶ Discover dozens of ideas to reach students through their multiple ways of learning

▶ Gain an overview of differentiated instruction to support learning for all

This is actually astonishing and bears repeating. When classrooms and schools use practices that support holistic development—which does not include didactic teaching to the test—students actually not only achieve more positive developmental outcomes but improve their standardized test scores![1]

—BONNIE BENARD

How to build a student for the 21st century

Our schools today haven't changed much from the time our grandparents attended school. In today's world, success depends on individuals who: are global citizens who understand foreign cultures and speak other languages; who can think outside the box using an interdisciplinary approach to new ideas; who access and use information as a discriminating consumer; and communicate and work in teams with different people.[2]

—TIME MAGAZINE, DECEMBER 18, 2006

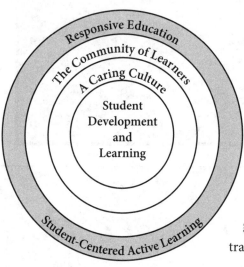

Previous Chapters 10 and 11 discussed the eight essential Responsive Educational components that not only engage adolescent learners but that also maximize achievement. Coupled with Chapter 13, "Building Classroom Learning Commmunities," prepares us to design academic group learning experiences. We're moving along this previously illustrated continuum for educational excellence.

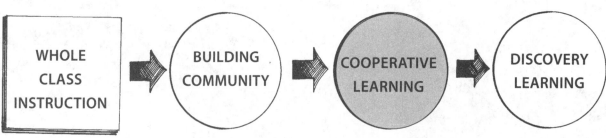

ACTIVATING THE ELEMENTS OF COOPERATIVE LEARNING

Packaging kids into small groups of four, giving them work to do together, and telling them they need to cooperate is *not* cooperative learning. Too many teachers who try just that become convinced that "kids just can't work in groups!" "Forget cooperative learning—it doesn't work." They are right. It won't work at all that way.

Students first must learn how to communicate and relate well by learning and using the four important community agreements: listening, appreciation/no put-downs, right-to-pass and mutual respect. They need to have experienced inclusion, safety and trust in a *class community circle*. Given that experience, students can work well together in small groups. They will be demonstrating five essential elements for productive cooperative group learning:[4]

Your task in designing cooperative group learning experiences is to make certain that the five productive elements (previously discussed in Chapter 10) are taking place in student groups. Following are some sample questions to help you observe how well students are working together and also to have group members assess how they are working.

1. **Positive interdependence among members**

   "Are all of the people in the group contributing to doing the task, and doing their best for group success?"

2. **Face-to-face promotive interaction**

   "Are people helping each other work together, to understand the task, to reflect on progress and what was learned?"

3. **The use of interactive skills**

   "To what extent are group members able to manage any disagreements? Is the group developing trust and respect?"

4. **Individual accountability**

   "Are all group members taking personal responsibility for contributing to the task, learning the material and assessing their own as well as group achievement?"

5. **Group processing**

   "Are members reflecting upon and analyzing group effectiveness, and defining ways to improve how they work together?"

The five elements of active cooperative learning are WHAT happens in productive groups. The community building group process of Tribes TLC is HOW to make it happen. Again, it is the saying heard from many teachers: "Tribes is the glue that holds cooperative learning all together."

> Placing socially unskilled students in a learning group and telling them to cooperate obviously will not be successful. Students must be taught the social skills needed for collaboration and be motivated to use them.[3]
>
> —DAVID AND ROGER JOHNSON

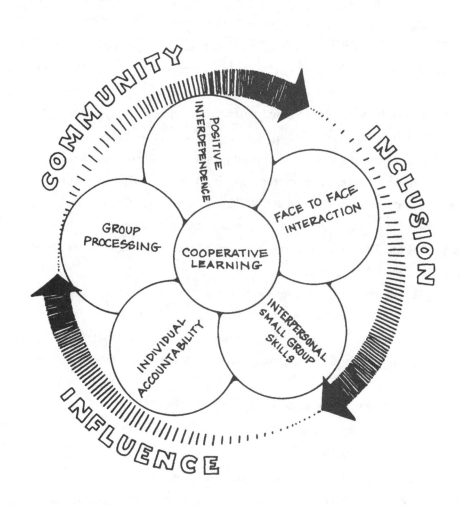

DESIGNING ACTIVE COOPERATIVE LEARNING

You may have noticed that instead of talking about lesson plans, we're talking about designing active *learning experiences* to achieve meaningful learning for students.

The example form that follows, entitled "A Tribes TLC® Learning Experience," gives teachers an easy format to plan and conduct active learning experiences. The form can be used either to teach academic content by using a single Tribes strategy or to organize a sequence of strategies and group structures. It may be used as you plan on your own—or in collaborative group planning with other teachers.

Prior to implementation of a learning experience, teachers...

> ▶ Identify the curriculum content—topic or theme

> ▶ Define the learning objectives and ways to authentically assess student learning or performance

> ▶ And identify appropriate learning strategies and reflection questions.

Define all of the sections of the form clearly. In class first introduce the content and learning objectives (tasks to be accomplished). Then facilitate the other steps of the learning experience:

▶ Provide for inclusion

▶ Identify and facilitate the active learning strategy(ies)

▶ Ask reflection questions based on the objectives

▶ Provide an opportunity for appreciation

▶ Assess learning.

The form can be used to plan each segment of learning—whether lesson content for a single period, over several days, or part of an even larger unit plan. In the case of a unit plan, the format can be used as an umbrella for broader sets of objectives and strategies.

The Resource Section contains a blank Tribes TLC Learning Experience Form to copy for your own use.

IDENTIFY THE CURRICULUM, INSTRUCTION AND ASSESSMENT

The *Breaking Ranks II* document for high school reform makes a series of recommendations relating to *curriculum, instruction* and *assessment.* The following important recommendations are supported well by the Tribes TLC® process.

Now we focus on how all students will be able to learn... what is to be learned.

▶ The content of the curriculum, where practical, should connect to real-life applications of knowledge and skills to help students link their education to the future.

▶ The high school will reorganize the traditional department structure in order to integrate the school's curriculum to the extent possible and emphasize depth over breadth of coverage.

▶ Teachers will be able to use a variety of strategies and settings that identify and accommodate individual learning styles and engage students.

▶ Teachers will integrate assessment into instruction so that assessment is accomplished using a variety of methods and becomes part of the learning process.

Determine what the curriculum, topic, theme, or content will be. It may be from a specific subject area, or it may be interdisciplinary or project based that draws content from different subject areas. The content and objectives, of course, depend upon the curriculum to be learned.

A Tribes TLC® Learning Experience

1. CURRICULUM TOPIC, THEME, OR CONTENT:

2. IDENTIFY THE OBJECTIVES:

Content Objective:

Collaborative Objective:

Personal Objective:

3. AUTHENTIC ASSESSMENT: Determine what and how the objectives or benchmarks will be achieved by the group and/or by the individual students.

4. PROVIDE FOR INCLUSION:
A You Question, Energizer, or Linking Strategy

5. IDENTIFY THE STRATEGY(IES):

6. ASK REFLECTION QUESTIONS BASED ON THE OBJECTIVES:

Content:

Collaborative:

Personal:

7. PROVIDE AN OPPORTUNITY FOR APPRECIATION:

LEARNING COMPONENTS:
(check)

❑ Group Development Process

❑ Cognitive Theory

❑ Multiple Intelligences

❑ Cooperative Learning

❑ Constructivism

❑ Reflective Practice

❑ Authentic Assessment

❑ Technology

Curriculum Content and Objectives

Keep in mind that raising curricula to the level of "big ideas" or "meaningful themes" is especially important for high school students who have moved or are moving from concrete to complex thinking, and who are anxiously seeking *meaning and purpose*—one of the four essential tasks of adolescents. In recognition of this, an ever-increasing number of schools are training teachers to integrate and elevate content to higher universal *concepts*. Marion Brady suggests four content learning areas, which are based on their "probable contribution to human survival."[5]

- ► Learning about our physical environment
- ► Learning about humans who occupy the environment
- ► Understanding states of mind that underlie human action
- ► Understanding how assumptions and beliefs manifest themselves in human behavior.

> Learning is not something you can split up into 45-minute blocks or confined subjects.[6]
>
> —Dennis Liittky

"Big idea" study areas such as these can be synthesized into meaningful themes on national and global issues affecting humankind, and they can be carried over into interdisciplinary learning and student inquiry for an extended period of time.

For example: A literature class studying Shakespeare plays could do so under the larger concept of *understanding how assumptions and beliefs manifest in human behavior*. First the learning communities (LCs) would be engaged by using *inclusion questions* such as:

> *Think of a time when something you had done many times before just didn't work out as well. Why did you believe it would work well again? What had been your assumption?*

Students would think and share (or write and share) the incidents. Or, have the learning communities (LCs) list three behavioral events that happened in their school this or last year.

"*What assumptions, positive or negative, may have led to the events happening?*" Invite each group to summarize their discussion, share it with the class community, or lead a class discussion on how assumptions and beliefs manifest behavior. Each of the LCs could then analyze how characters in a Shakespeare play behaved based on various assumptions they may have had.

The concept could repeatedly be linked to real-life concerns or considerations students may have, and time set aside to write in personal journals. Shakespeare could become very real, perhaps a life-long, admired advisor and friend for many in the class.

That's why I can count on my inner map to take me to wherever I'm going!

I've been wondering a lot about this too!

Active conceptual learning is compatible with how the human brain retains concepts and information, learns and remembers. Teaching this way does not mean that basic academic curriculum is overlooked or ignored. It is woven into a richer more meaningful tapestry never to be forgotten.

The *content objective* needs to be more than just listed concepts or facts to be "taught." The objective needs to cause learners to *think constructively,* to analyze, apply or present what they have learned.

Youth moving into the high-tech information world of the 21st century will be lost unless they are capable of thinking critically and constructively. Two reasons more than justify modifying or giving up lecturing, whole class instruction and memorization. First, the concepts and information that they may memorize today for the test tomorrow are quickly forgotten. Second, the unprecedented amount of rapid ever-changing information driving today's world in every domain makes bits of information memorized for tests irrelevant.

Our emerging adults (and all of us) need to become proficient in...

- ▶ Accessing information from a wide array of resources: computers, libraries, newspapers, books, on-line data banks, public records and face-to-face people interviews

- ▶ Analyzing and interpreting meaning through discussion, writing, graphics, music, drama or dance

- ▶ Synthesizing and linking existing knowledge by comparing, integrating and summarizing concepts and information

- ▶ Planning and applying acquired knowledge to real life issues, opportunities and problems, and

- ▶ Reflecting and evaluating applied knowledge for on-going refinement, change and conclusions.

The constructive thinking skills noted above are supportive of the direction in which our high school young adults are going one way or another anyway... with or without school systems becoming more responsive!

We need only to be responsive to the direction in which these kids and the world is moving... to know how to make learning meaningful.

Collaborative Objectives

The thinking skills needed by young people in today's world may also be considered as *collaborative skills* in every sense of the word. The ability to contribute to a learning group, a work group, or a project team, not only depends upon clear thinking and expression, but also social skills and resilient attributes to interact with relationship and organizational issues.

Having collaborative objectives in the Tribes Learning Experience plan is extremely important to support the social and emotional development of high school learners, and their need to be socially competent. The twelve collaborative skills are embedded and learned through Tribes TLC® strategies and the group process. The skills are social in nature for individuals, and collaborative within groups and organizations. The SCANS and other business reports verify that when critical social skills are undeveloped adult workers face on-going loss of jobs, interpersonal conflict, personal stress and economic problems throughout their lives.[8] The illustration below shows twelve collaborative/social skills that are learned within the Tribes TLC® process. In time, these collaborative "people skills" become part of the culture within a classroom, school, district or other organization. They are the foundation of productive and caring communities.

> Active cooperative group learning promotes a greater use of higher level reasoning and critical thinking than individualistic learning.[7]
> —David and Roger Johnson

COLLABORATIVE SKILLS

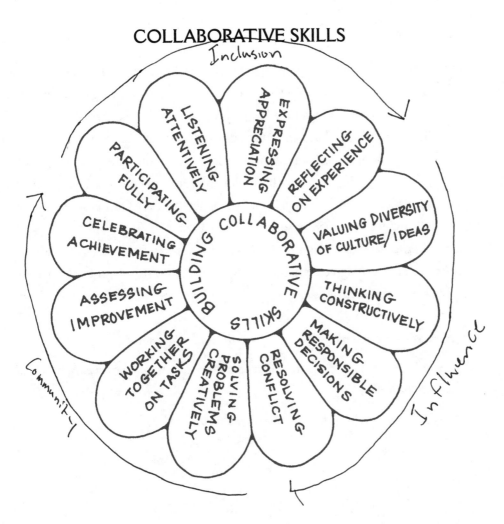

Each time you design a collaborative objective consider highlighting a skill that is timely and appropriate. The learning contributes directly to time on task and enhancing academic learning.

Personal Objectives

Giving students time also to reflect on personal objectives is very important. Define questions that help learners consider valuable learning about self in relationship to the learning group, new perspectives, feelings, identification with a literary or historical character or interests that lead to pursuing additional learning.

Be certain that you always tell students the objectives on which they will be working, reflecting upon, assessing or evaluating. All three types of objectives (content, collaborative and personal) do not necessarily need to be used in every every learning experience. It always is, however, your wise judgment that counts.

PROVIDE FOR INCLUSION

This is brain compatible!

Each time the learning groups come together to work on a task, interest and participation is gained by introducing an inclusive question, strategy or active group activity. At the beginning of the Strategy Section there is a matrix that lists many inclusion strategies. They can be used as written or tailored to respond to the culture, language and special needs of your students. Knowing that learning is accelerated whenever the human brain can link new information to previous knowledge and experiences, an inclusion question personalized as a "YOU question" can be used to connect students' experiences to an academic theme.

For example: The content is an episode about Ulysses journey. After reminding everyone of the four agreements, or having the teams do so, ask group members to respond to a question such as...

*"Have **you** ever dreamed of taking off on an endless journey?"*

*"If **you** knew you were going to explore a remote place for a long time, what would help you to survive?"*

*"If **you** found a priceless treasure what would you do?"*

The *you* question needs to be relevant to students' possible experiences or interests and be introduced before sharing the objectives for the Ulysses team task. The process helps learners identify with the character and content. Responses to YOU questions can be shared in pairs, triads or the whole group. They can be used in a writing activity (such as an imaginary letter to a friend), or recorded in personal journals. It is very important to give sufficient time for students to share prior to introducing the content task.

Start with what they know and build with what they have.
—Lau Tau, 100 B.C.

SELECTING STRATEGIES AND STRUCTURES

Knowing that we want subject matter to be learned in an active and meaningful way, one or several group interaction strategies (process frameworks) are selected to carry the content. The content is WHAT is to be learned... and the strategy is HOW it is learned. For example: Content for a political science class may be "peaceful citizen protest in democracy." The teacher introduces the content by speaking to the class. Peaceful protest is the content, the strategy is "direct instruction." If the teacher had asked groups of students to research forms of peaceful citizen protest, the strategy would be "group inquiry." Dr. Spencer Kagan who uses the term "structure" rather than "strategy" writes:

> *"As educators, we are faced with a range of educational objectives. Teaching is much more than simply imparting knowledge to our students. Students need to learn to be critical thinkers, how to share information, make decisions, reach consensus and get along with each other... [edit]... Using many different structures makes teaching and learning more fun. Teaching and learning are then more characterized by novelty and exhilaration rather than be monotony and tediousness."*[9]

The introduction to the Active Learning Strategy section in this book gives suggestions on making appropriate selections. Your plan may include several sequential Tribes group strategies to help students achieve the content objectives. The group learning strategies or structures that you may discover from other resources to activate the content, need to support the observed stage of the groups' development. For instance, you would not want to use "Where Do I Stand," a strategy for the stage of influence, if the tribes still needed inclusion, a sense of belonging and trust. Moreover, if they are to work on a task involving controversial issues, they should already have practiced a number of influence strategies.

The exciting thing about the Tribes strategies is that they can be used over and over again. They are formats in which just about any academic content can be actively learned.

Shannon Bennett-Pratt
B.Ed.

Shannon is a teacher at
Percy Page High School in
Edmonton, Alberta. She
teaches English and special
education classes and is a
resource person for many
teachers in the school.
Shannon, a Certified Tribes
TLC Trainer, uses the Tribes
process in all her classes.

A Great Way to Learn and to Teach

Where do I fit in? Where do I belong? Who am I? These questions, asked by students of all ages, become more important when they reach high school. High school students are seeking their identity and want to belong somewhere. The Tribes process in my high school English and special education classes gives students a sense of belonging by building inclusion. Indeed, people of all ages and cultures seek a sense of belonging and knowledge of how to develop it for themselves and others. This is what the community building process of Tribes with its active learning strategies and positive agreements provides in high school classes and whole school. It is a learning environment where students demonstrate respect for self and others. Opportunities to learn about each other in turn helps me to gain an awareness of their interests, lives and how they learn. Getting to know and understand each other not only creates a class that requires less management but a class that accomplishes more.

Use of the Tribes active learning strategies, which incorporate the multiple intelligences—the diversity of ways in which high school students learn—engages all learners. Among the many inclusion strategies I have found to be effective in building a safe and caring classroom at the beginning of a school year, semester or quarter are: Bubble Name, Life Map, Slip Game and All in the Family. Other student favorites are listed below, including:

> Dream Quilt—(dream, set goals and use as action plan). I put this behind where I sit so that the students see it every time they come to class. They are reminded of their goals and that I am here to help them achieve them.

Paraphrase Passport	Two Truths and a Lie
Put Yourself on the Line	Slip Game
Something Good	Perception and Transmission
Where Do I Stand	of Information
Fold the Line Reading	Extended Nametags
Personal Contract	Novel in an Hour

As a quick assessment, I use Five Tribles, using a question like: "How well do you understand the concept?" I also can give them an opportunity to share their understanding with others in their tribe or learning group. Then on the back of the Tribles illustration sheet students are asked to write what they believe is their strength and what do they still need to learn. This helps me as the teacher reflect on "What do I need to teach or re-teach?"

Students retain concepts and information because they are experiencing the curriculum and are not just having to endure lectures and sheet work as in typical high school classes where they only are passive recipients of information. Moreover, the reflection questions asked at the end of each learning experience (or strategy) help them to become meta-cognitive learners—students who think about how they learn. Students not only gain a sense that each person is important, they also find my classes interesting and fun, Tribes, what a great way to learn and to teach!

> A different way to learn is what kids are calling for... All of them are talking about how our one-size-fits-all delivery system—which mandates that everyone learns the same thing in the same way all the time, no matter what their individual needs—has failed them.[10]
>
> —SEYMOUR SARASON

DIFFERENT WAYS TO LEARN AND TEACH

Hey, wait a minute! You also need these valuable keys!

The ambitious and somewhat audacious title of this book is "Engaging All!" As emphasized from the first pages onward, engaging all takes incorporating the needs, interests and multiple ways in which *all* learners learn. The cooperative group structures do give teachers a way to observe, relate to and get to know all, far better than when too many remain anonymous in the crowd. But we hear you say, "Analyzing how each learns is impossible! Yes, but all can be reached by using the stunning research of Howard Gardner on Multiple Intelligences and Carol Ann Tomlinson's strategies for Differentiation.

But I don't have time to take all those courses somewhere!

No, we can learn it together in our weekly Collegial Learning Communities.

It is not possible with the space of this book to incorporate all that is known about the eight research-based components of the process of Tribes and the inherent sound principles and practices they represent to transform traditional teaching to active learning pedagogy. After initiating the first Tribes TLC training course in your school, several lead teachers of your school can become Certified trainers, to facilitate on-going on-site quality TLC courses for your school's Learning Communities. The inside-out capacity building approach to school improvement involves everyone in on-going learning, everyone teaching and everyone sharing, assessing and creating authentic change.

Now let's highlight those two keys that Reflection pelican was shouting about!

Reaching All Multiple Intelligences

Picture nine students sitting in a semicircle in front of you. They all have different ways of learning and intelligences. Yet traditional one-size-fits-all teaching reaches only two out of the nine—the 20 percent that learn through verbal/linguistic and logical/mathematical methods. National statistics tell us that at least three out of the other seven will become dropouts if not reached and engaged academically in the secondary years. One thing is for certain—all cannot be written off as "learning disabilities" or "stupid." They simply have different ways of knowing and learning than the students who primarily learn through verbal/linguistic and logical/mathematical intelligences. The others are not failing—their schools are failing to reach and engage them.

I certainly can't create nine different lesson plans everyday.

Of course not!

No, you do not have to create nine different plans. You need to become familiar with the descriptions of the nine multiple intelligences as defined over years through the remarkable research of Howard Gardner.[11] The various ways of knowing are also special gifts for students to discover! Most students have recognized in their younger years that they have a preference or natural ability that is satisfying to use, and that perhaps it is very different from abilities of their siblings or friends. It is not the teacher's task to analyze or diagnose the specific intelligences of each student. Teachers simply need to scatter the many ways of learning throughout academic learning experiences. To help you do so, the Resource Section contains a graphic organizer, "Reaching All with a Circular Curriculum" to keep track of the ways you are weaving the multiple intelligences into learning experiences.

The multiple intelligence chart that follows contains a wide range of ways to engage the diversity of high school students. Many of the ideas evolved out of the work, books and presentations of respected educator Thomas Armstrong, and many were defined by innovative teachers.[12] The graphic icons of the intelligences can be noted on your TLC Learning Experience plans to help you keep track of your efforts each day.

MULTIPLE INTELLIGENCES IDEA CHART

VERBAL LINGUISTIC

Write story problems

Create TV advertisements

Compile a notebook of jokes

Debate current/historical
issues

Play "Trivial Pursuit"

Explain a situation/problem

Create poems

Impromptu speaking/writing

Create crossword puzzles

Teach "concept mapping"

Learn a foreign language

Write instructions

Read stories to others

Describe an object for another to draw

Make up a story about a piece of music

Describe the steps to a dance

Write a role play/drama

Keep a personal journal

LOGICAL MATHEMATICAL

Create a time line

Compare/contrast ideas

Predict the next events in a story

Define patterns in history

Follow a recipe/instructions

Rank-order factors

Analyze causes and effects

Learn patterns

Analyze similarities/differences

Classify biological specimens

Create outlines of stories

Create computer programs

Use a story grid/creative writing

Create a "paint-by-number" picture

Read/design maps

Solve math problems

Teach calculator/computer use

Decipher codes

Compose music from a matrix

VISUAL SPATIAL

Make visual diagrams/flow charts

Illustrate a story/historical event

Design/paint murals

Imagine the future/go back in time

Play "Pictionary"

Teach "mind mapping" for note taking

Write/decipher codes

Graph results of a survey

Create posters/flyers

Create collages on topics

Draw maps

Study the arts of a culture

Make clay maps/buildings/figures

Create visual diagrams/machines

Illustrate dance steps/physical games

Use Tribes energizers

Learn spatial games

Draw from different perspectives

Draw to music

INTERPERSONAL

Role play a historical/literary
or class situation

Analyze a story

Tell stories

Read poetry using different moods

Teach arithmetic, math, computer skills

Review a book orally

Act out a different cultural perspective

Design and act out dramas/role plays

Help tribe come to a consensus or resolve
a problem

Facilitate participation in a group

Use cooperative games

Help people deliver appreciation statements

Solve complex story problems

Discuss/debate controversial issues

Analyze group dynamics/relationships

Learn to sing and lead rounds

Plan and arrange social events

Find relationships between objects

EXISTENTIAL

Engage in reflection and
self-study

Read books on the
meaning of life

Attend some form of worship

Watch films on big life
questions

Record thoughts in a journal

Listen to inspirational music

Study literature, art, philosophy

Discuss life/human issues in a group

Record dreams and mystical events

Paint while listening to music

Create a private "centering" space

NATURALIST

Keep a journal of
observations

Collect and categorize data

Make a taxonomy of plants
or animals

Explain similarities among species

Study means of survival

Examine cellular structures
with a microscope

Illustrate cellular material

Take out-of-door field trips

Visit an aquarium

Camp outside to identify stars

BODY KINESTHETIC

Lead Tribes energizers and
   cooperative games

Practice physical exercises

Lead students in stretching
   to music, deep breathing,
   tai chi, and yoga poses

Learn dances of different cultures and periods
   of history

Practice aerobic routines to fast music

Measure items or distances with thumbs, feet,
   or hands

Illustrate geometrical figures (parallel lines,
   triangles, rectangles, circles) with arms,
   legs and/or fingers

Coach peers and/or younger children

Conduct hands-on experiments

Act out scenes from stories or plays

Design role plays

Invent a new household tool

Prepare food or snacks

Simulate various situations

Learn alphabet through physical movement

Learn/teach sign language

Make up a cooperative playground game

MUSICAL RHYTHMIC

Create "raps" (key dates,
   math, poems)

Teach songs from different
   cultures and eras

Play musical instruments

Make simple musical instruments

Learn via songs and jingles

Learn through drum beats/rhythm

Make up sounds and sound effects

Practice impromptu music

Create interpretive dance to music

Lead singing (songs from different cultures)

Write to music

Reduce stress with music

Teach rhythm patterns/different cultures

Compose music for a dramatic production

Teach dance steps

Identify social issues through lyrics

Illustrate different moods through dance steps

Lead physical exercise to music

Clap a rhythm for the class to repeat

INTRAPERSONAL

Keep a personal journal or feelings diary

Analyze historical personalities

Write on personal learning experiences

Evaluate personal and group strengths/
   weaknesses

Analyze thinking patterns

Understand group dynamics

Use, design, or lead guided imagery

Write an autobiography

Analyze literary characters and historical
   personalities

Define personal reflection questions

Imagine and write about the future

Dance different stages in life

Lead Tribes personal inclusion
   activities

Practice relaxation techniques

Imagine self as character in history or story

Illustrate feelings/moods

Listen attentively

Draw self at different periods in life

Share how music affects feelings

Observe self (metacognition perspective)

REACHING ALL THROUGH DIFFERENTIATION

One of the most important concepts now in education is "differentiation." Along with active learning, it is also a way to engage and reach the needs of all learners. We all are very cognizant that learner needs should be at the center of our curriculum, instruction, and assessment practices. Differentiation is simply meeting the needs of diverse learners, at points in their learning where the differentiation will positively impact student learning outcomes. Although some educators may quickly say that they already differentiate learning for their students, many may not fully understand the principles and practices that underlie the important approach sufficiently enough to make it routine. Carol Ann Tomlinson, author and a leading authority on Differentiation, gives us this definition:

> "*Differentiated instruction is* responsive instruction. *It occurs as teachers become increasingly proficient in understanding their students as individuals, increasingly comfortable with the meaning and structure of the disciplines they teach, and increasingly expert at teaching flexibly in order to match instruction to student need with the goal of maximizing the potential of each learner in a given area.*"[13]

Tomlinson believes that differentiated instruction is the means by which teachers ensure that good curriculum not only is a good fit for each learner, but that it connects students and teachers and content and students. She defines four guiding principles for connecting:[14]

▶ **Connect** through student driven activities, opportunities to share or build on personal interests, journaling and positive humor

▶ **Respect** by learning about and honoring students' cultures, communicating high expectations and making time

▶ **Challenge** by providing meaningful work that extends the known and challenges the unknown

▶ **Support** by giving second chances and deferring grades, clarifying expectations, teaching needed skills, accepting responsibility for student success, and learning students' strengths and weaknesses.

All four are inherent in and activated through the components and on-going use of the process of Tribes TLC.

Instruction should be differentiated in a class whenever a teacher senses it will increase student attainment of understandings and skills. Tomlinson highlights the following four student traits that teachers need to address in order to maximize effective learning and to differentiate instruction:

▶ **Readiness** is the entry point for new learning. It is the prior learning, life experiences, interest and skills that a student brings into the class. Readiness is different than ability. It may vary over time but is noticed by a student's inclination to work at a more difficult or challenging task or level.

▶ **Interest** pertains to topics or subjects that kindle curiousity or purpose to become involved in new learning. Interest includes areas students find intriguing and connect to a passion or skill waiting to be discovered.

▶ **Learning profile** includes learning styles, modalities (visual, auditory, kinesthetic), intelligence preference (multiple intelligences), culture and gender.

▶ **Affect** refers to students' emotions and feelings about themselves, identity, relationships, sense of purpose and opportunities to make a contribution. It also includes how they see themselves as learners, and view their school overall. Tomlinson asserts that "student affect" is the "gateway to helping each student become more fully engaged and successful in learning."

The quality of differentiated instruction depends upon reflection and assessment as an on-going process, teachers' increasing skillfulness in using effective instructional strategies, and instruction that is grounded in sound, meaningful curriculum. Carol Ann Tomlinson wisely points out that:

> "All students must have quality curriculum... I find it impossible, in fact find it unacceptable to talk about differentiation without talking about quality of curriculum because we're asking teachers to spend additional effort and time and focus in attending to individuals and a whole group—and if what we're starting with, our baseline curriculum is not the best curriculum we can get, then we're differentiating fog, or differentiating trivia, differentiating confusion and it's really not very labor effective or efficient to do that."[15]

Readers and Collegial Learning Communities are encouraged to secure and study the excellent Tomlinson books that are listed in the Bibliography of this book.

The 2006 book, *Integrating Differentiated Instruction and Understanding by Design* by Tomlinson and McTighe, addresses creating interdisciplinary units to better mirror real life problems and learning beyond compartmentalized subject areas. The authors recommend using backward mapping design to articulate goals, authentic tasks, relevant learning experiences, and deeper understanding. Having students work in group settings to achieve common goals also is emphasized. The approach fits well with two important *Breaking Ranks II* recommendations for high schools to consider. Namely, that:

- The high school will reorganize the traditional structure in order to integrate the school's curriculum to the extent possible and emphasize depth over breadth of coverage.

- The content of the curriculum, where practical, should connect to real-life applications of knowledge and skills to help students link their education to the future.[16]

OK. Now we know about those two important keys... Multiple Intelligences and Differentiation. Let's go on to the next section of that TLC Form.

Asking Reflection Questions

The most important part of any TLC® learning experience may be the reflection questions that you ask students. As emphasized before, asking good reflection questions within cooperative learning groups can double the rate of the retention of knowledge made by students.[17] In other words, if we want students to achieve higher test scores reflection questions need to be asked after every learning experience. Students begin to understand that they are moving beyond just memorizing information to cultivate higher-order thinking, social, and personal skills—and competencies critical to their futures.

Well-chosen reflection questions are an immediate way to assess how well the content, collaborative and personal level objectives were achieved.

Now you'll see why I am so prominent in this book and Tribes Learning Community schools!

Content (cognitive learning) questions focus on academic knowledge gained from the learning experience

Collaborative (social learning) questions focus on the interaction and participation of members and the collaborative skills that were used

Personal (individual learning) are questions that help identify skills and ways a student contributed to a group to complete the task; also talents, interests and feeling noticed in working with group members or individually.

You'll find examples of each type in the Learning Strategies section of this book.

Plan the questions you will use, and jot them down on the TLC Learning Experience Form. There will be times when you will want to change them due to events that happen during the class experience. Ask questions that will be most relevant and meaningful to the learning experiences.

Appreciation

Last but hardly least, opportunities need to be provided for people to express appreciation to those with whom they have worked. Never let a group finish work together without allowing time for statements of appreciation. The more that appreciation happens, the more cohesive the learning groups will be—the more comfortable and cooperative they will become working together, the better they will accomplish learning tasks, and the greater will be every student's sense of self-worth.

Here's my bird's eye view.

Implementing A Tribes Learning Experience In Six Steps

1. **Inclusion**

   Introduce the learning experience, as people sit either in the community circle or in tribes, with an inclusion strategy (content linked to lesson topic) or a *You* question.

2. **Objectives**

   Tell the students the content and collaborative skill objectives that are to be learned or practiced.

3. **Implementation of Strategies**

   Explain the task, group roles, and time available.
   Ask, "What questions do you have?"
   Observe and monitor the dynamics of the tribes working together, intervening only if they cannot resolve a situation or problem.

4. **Reflection/Accountability**

   Ask reflection questions. Use group and/or individual assessment for accountability.

5. **Appreciation**

   Invite statements of appreciation.

6. **Assessment**

   Use methods of authentic assessment to determine degree of individual or group progress in the achievement of objectives.

ASSESSING STUDENT LEARNING

Tribes TLC® teachers use a variety of ways to determine the degree to which learning objectives are being achieved by individual and group members. Authentic or summative assessments are used for students to *show what they have learned and can do*—whereas standardized tests do not indicate the in-depth more meaningful learning that your students are acquiring through active group learning. The purpose of traditional—"what-is-the-right-answer"—tests is to determine grades. The purpose of authentic assessments is *to learn* how to increase student learning and performance.

The fact that reflection questions are being asked after every learning experience makes it more likely that more information and concepts will be retained. In addition, throughout the year do help your students to see their own progress. Involve the LCs in viewing assessment not as ominous, but as snapshots of where they are on their journey of learning. Look at Chapter 11 again where the results upon student learning of various types of assessment are discussed. Developmental growth and learning especially for high school students is better supported by involving them in...

Tests to learn? Hey, that makes more sense!

- ▶ Generating their own reflection questions for a learning experience or long term project

- ▶ Developing check lists with indicators of learning and giving them to the class or parents when giving presentations, speeches, group reports, role-plays, video productions, etc.

- ▶ Personal appraisal—using portfolios, writing in journals and sharing in tribes or with a buddy.

Teacher interviews with each team or learning community are also helpful. Don't quiz but elicit (draw out) what was learned or not yet clear. After a few times they will trust the discourse process with you, and be proud to share what they are learning. The purpose is not to jot down grades, but to take snapshots of where they are, and to involve them in determining next steps to learn even more.

Assessing Collaborative skills

Form A	Form B	Form C
STUDENT ASSESSMENT	**STUDENT ASSESSMENT**	**STUDENT ASSESSMENT**
Our Group's Work Together	*Participation in My Group*	*My Thinking Skills*

There are three assessment forms in the Resource section that can be used by students to assess their individual participation and thinking skills, and to determine how well their group is working together.

Form A "Our Group's Work Together" can be used either by individual group members or by the whole tribe to reflect on how well they work together. If completed by individual members, the tribe can total and average all of the ratings for a group score.

Form B "Participation in My Group" is used by students individually to reflect on their own participation in their tribe. They can monitor how well they are using certain skills, based on their own reflections over a period of time.

Form C "My Thinking Skills" also is used individually to reflect on the extent to which they feel capable of using various constructive thinking skills.

What if now and then you may sense they are not with you?

There are those inevitable times when you realize your students have tuned you out. They are no longer listening, have a glaze in their eyes, and are drifting— beyond caring about what is going on in the class. You may have been working hard to have a more participatory classroom and are baffled whenever things seem to slip back. Not to worry... it is a signal to take time out, reflect on what is happening and take positive action. This checklist may help you to determine why attention is waning.

1. Are you connecting the topic or lesson to their personal experience and previous learning?

2. Are you talking too long or getting off the topic?

3. How long have your students been sitting or working without physical movement?

4. Have you identified their stage of development and group issues so that you select appropriate strategies?

5. Are you using enough cooperative group strategies to maximize participation?

6. Are you hovering over the tribes, rather than giving them responsibility to work on tasks together, helping each other?

7. After an activity have you tried asking constructive/social reflection questions before asking content questions?

8. Is there a disturbing event that needs to be aired or resolved before learning can be resumed?

9. Are you sensitive to the loss-of-energy dynamic when it begins to happen?

10. Do you "stop the action" and ask students what is going on?

APPRECIATIVE INQUIRY[18]

Because adolescents thrive on acquiring on-going independence and opportunities to solve problems, they are more than ready to assess how well their tribes are working and the extent of their own participation. In some of the Tribes Strategies you will notice collaborative questions that suggest having students look at their tribe's performance. "Appreciative inquiry" questions are based on "What did we, as a group, do well?" rather than "What did we do wrong?" The latter is the traditional organizational management approach—look for a problem, diagnose it and find a solution. Even though a solution may be found the assumption will continue—that we need to keep looking for problems because "we are a problem group." Appreciative inquiry looks for what works in an organization, based on the high moments of where we have been together. Participants, grounded in success, know how to repeat their success. The approach generates positive energy and increases group success.

You can use appreciative inquiry not only to define meaningful reflection questions but also to transfer the responsibility to the LCs to maintain positive management for their team. The lists below show the contrasting scenarios.

PROBLEM SOLVING	APPRECIATIVE INQUIRY
"Felt need"	Appreciating and Valuing
Identification of Problem	The Best of "What Is"
Analysis of Causes	Envisioning "What Might Be"
Analysis of Possible Solutions	Dialoguing "What Should Be"
Action Planning (Treatment)	Innovating "What Will Be"

Appreciative inquiry touches something important and positive and people respond.[18]
—SUE ANNIS HAMMOND

YEARS LATER—AN OUTCOME REPORT

Sometimes it takes years to discover the extent to which learning how to manage group process can influence the future of a young person. Melissa, the director of a city youth project, by chance met a former student whom she hadn't seen in more than twelve years. Later she received this note:

"...You know, after we talked, I remembered that I really wanted to tell you how much you taught me when I was involved in the Topeka Youth Project. You may not recall, but one of the things we really worked on was facilitating the group "process" in our meetings. As a kid, I was always jumping in head first in moving things forward, and not always giving the group a chance to "catch up." Well, as it turns out, I use the group facilitation skills I learned back then everyday in my job at Sprint PCS. As a business analyst, I facilitate groups to gather information and help them understand their work process so we can develop better software. There are times when the group skips over important issues or moves too quickly, and I think back and ask myself, "Now, hang on here. How would Melissa do this?" I really meant to tell you about this the other day, and we just got to talking about so many other things. Anyway, if I haven't said it before, I am saying it now—THANK YOU VERY MUCH for all you taught me... and for the experience."

I hear, I forget
I see, I remember
I do, and I understand!

15

Designing Discovery Learning Experiences

15 Designing Discovery Learning Experiences

IN THIS CHAPTER YOU WILL

▶ Learn how the group process of Tribes TLC® supports constructivism

▶ Consider the primary beliefs and assumptions on constructivism

▶ Learn how to plan, engage and guide students to conduct active Discovery Learning experiences and projects

▶ Learn ways to assess and evaluate Discovery Learning

> Stop choosing between chaos and order and live at the boundary between them where rest and action move together.[1]
> —Rainer Maria Rilke

Human survival always has been based on discovery... the discovery of self and meaningful knowledge.

Right! That's why learning must be something a learner does... not something done to a learner!

DISCOVERY IS... "SOMETHING A LEARNER DOES"

Our effort to reach and teach young adolescents with education that is "responsive" to their developmental needs has progressed from whole class instruction, to building community, to cooperative learning and now to Discovery Learning—Constructivism.

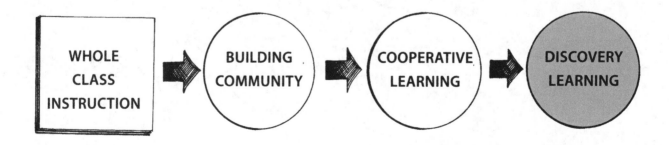

WHOLE CLASS INSTRUCTION ➤ BUILDING COMMUNITY ➤ COOPERATIVE LEARNING ➤ DISCOVERY LEARNING

A transfer of responsibility from teacher to students gradually has occurred, and the role of the teacher has changed from being the source of all information to being a facilitator of learning. Most teachers use all of the approaches in the course of a day or period of time... convening community circles, facilitating cooperative learning experiences, and guiding student groups in learning through discovery and investigation.

ACADEMIC ENGAGEMENT FOR ALL STUDENTS

The question, "What does it take 'to engage all' learners?" causes many just to shake their heads as though the question is far beyond answering. Hopefully, this book is reassuring readers that there are many ways to engage all—if, indeed, we are ready to let go of what has not been working. A very helpful document, *"A Call to Action—Transforming Action for All Youth"* from the National High School Alliance, points out that[2]...

> *"It is vital, particularly for students who are most at risk for disengagement and dropping out, that curriculum and instruction value and connect learning to students cultural and linguistic contexts. Low level courses and general or non-academic tracks-which are common in traditional, comprehensive high schools foster and deepen student disengagement... Students should be engaged in disciplined inquiry, which requires problem-solving, higher-order thinking and the capacity to construct, rather than merely reproducing knowledge."*

"Call to Action" recommends a number of constructivist strategies:

▶ Emphasize project-based learning and other engaging, inquiry-base teaching methods that provide opportunities for students to master academic content, learn workforce skills, and develop personal strengths

▶ Differentiate instruction and provide supports that meet the varied learning needs of multiple student populations

▶ Connect curriculum to real-world contexts that build upon student and community resources

▶ Structure schedules for extended/flexible instructional time blocks

▶ Use multiple measures to assess student outcomes, including performance-based assessments.

The principles change the task of the educator from being the dispenser of knowledge to a provider of opportunities for learners to access and to build knowledge that is meaningful to their lives, communities and the world.

MAKING A MIND SHIFT

"If there is a key to reinventing our educational system, it lies in what our teachers believe about the nature of knowing. Without a reexamination and change in beliefs about the nature of knowing, there will be no substantial change in the enterprise of education; we will stay in a vicious cycle."[3] —Dewey Dykstra

Moving into Discovery Learning constructivism calls for teachers who believe high school youth are capable well beyond the passive pedagogy of "yesterday schools". Many have been listening to high school learners and have come to a new set of beliefs. Check the ones that you believe and those you may need more time to consider.

High school "young adults"...

▶ Can think critically and constructively

▶ Need to believe in their own abilities

▶ Are capable of questioning, investigating, analyzing information and discovering for themselves

▶ Cannot develop their own meaningful knowledge or learn to make decisions simply by listening and remembering information given by the teacher

▶ Have the ability to take responsibility for their own learning.

Yes, we can do all that—just give us a chance!

Collegial Learning Communities are an ideal place for teachers to discuss these beliefs and the implications they have concerning the change needed in teaching methods in order to enhance student learning. If the common philosophy and culture of constructivism is not addressed by teachers moving into the richness of Discovery Learning their efforts will not be well grounded—especially when asked, "Why do you teach that way?" No matter the instructional approach, as professional educators, we must be sufficiently knowledgeable to articulate our craft well.[4]

KEEP THE RESULTS IN MIND

As you begin to change your approach to working with high school adolescents and some days are tempted just to do 50 minutes of chalk-in-hand talking again, keep four well-proven results in mind: When students are actively engaged in their own learning within inquiry (discovery) groups...

▶ they are motivated and they learn more

▶ they are building meaningful and lasting knowledge structures

▶ they are acquiring the ability to think constructively and to solve problems, and

▶ they are engaged in achieving the four developmental tasks of adolescence... gaining independence/autonomy, social competency, a sense of purpose/meaning and the capacity to problem-solve on their own. It all comes together.

Now I ask myself every day... "Is my role just to dispense information or to develop independent thinkers?"

CHANGING THE CLASSROOM LANGUAGE

The language that most teachers use is the language they experienced when they were in school—however many years ago. It is a language of the traditional system that equates learning simply as the passive acquisition of facts and information. The entrenched language makes it difficult for teachers not only to think in terms of creating student-centered classrooms, but to focus on the learner and learning rather than the teacher and teaching. Here are some differences in language:

Traditional	Constructivist
Today I will be teaching about...	*Today you will be learning about...*
This week I have to cover...	*This week you will be discovering...*
Did you do the lesson assignment?	*Did you complete the learning experience?*
Many students just can't learn.	*I need to change my way of teaching.*
Are your reports ready?	*Are your learning experiences ready?*

Our own on-going learning with our colleagues and our students is the key to success.

WHAT IS DISCOVERY LEARNING WITH TRIBES?

The literature and studies on constructivism, just as with cooperative learning, repeatedly emphasize that group learning has but limited success unless students have learned how to relate, monitor agreements, make collaborative decisions, manage group interaction and reflect on their progress. Otherwise, just admonishing students to work "cooperatively" can be a nightmare. It is understandable why some frustrated teachers give up and go back to direct instruction and seat work. The tragedy is that active group learning, the most promising researched based technology capable of transforming traditional education, is written off. More often than not, it is the students who are blamed rather than the lack of an active learning process and responsive pedagogy.

Tribes TLC® Discovery Learning is an integration of two frameworks:

▶ the Tribes group development process of inclusion, influence and community, with its collaborative group skills and agreements, and

▶ a constructivist instructional model, known as the "Five E's" and developed by Roger Bybee of the Miami Museum of Science.[6]

The integration of the process of Tribes with the Five E's model gives teachers and students a clear way to plan and conduct constructivist group learning experiences and projects. The "Five E's" model was highlighted earlier in Chapter 8 as a framework for developing and managing the high school learning community project. You may recall the circular diagram illustrating the five steps: Engage, Explore, Explain, Elaborate and Evaluate. Now we'll use the same sequence to design and implement constructivist curriculum experiences and projects. The collaborative process and positive culture is motivational for all learners whether students, teachers or other adult groups.

THE FIVE E'S GROUP LEARNING FORMAT

Five sequential steps define the Five E approach: Engage, Explore, Explain, Elaborate and Evaluate.

The first step is to engage student interest in the *content* of the learning experience. This is the *inclusion* step that the teacher plans—personalizing to capture student interest—before introducing the instructional task, academic content and objectives.

Content: Whole-to-parts rather than parts-to-whole

The way that a learning issue, content or problem is defined influences the depth of understanding that students will achieve. In traditional schooling, curriculum is presented *parts-to-whole,* whereas in constructivist classrooms the emphasis is on the larger concept or

> What students can do together today, they can do alone tomorrow.[5]
> —Lev Vygotsky

issue—The Big Idea—presenting the whole concept first and then transferring responsibility to student learning groups (LCs) to work on parts.

Here is an example of a traditional parts-to-whole class lesson:

A freshman biology class is studying a unit on fresh water fish. The instructor lectures about the parts of fish, students take notes, dissect fish, and take a test about the fish. A week later the instructor lectures about the pollutants that endanger fish in rivers, and assigns chapters in the science book to read in preparation for an upcoming test. The next day in a teacher-led question/answer period two students point out that the river "right here in River City" no longer has fish. Now the class is interested. People raise questions spontaneously. They want to learn what kind of fish once were there, what caused the pollution and whether something can be done to bring back the fish. After a few minutes the teacher interrupts the flurry of interest on saving the river, announcing there is no more time to spend on the subject. The class had to move on to the next unit. This exemplifies parts-to-whole teaching—and the need to "cover" the curriculum.

The Discovery Learning experience would start with the real-time big idea—*benefits of rivers.* Following interest arousing inclusion questions about fishing, swimming or enjoying boating on rivers or lakes, the teacher initiates a class discussion about the river here in town. Working in their LC groups students talk about the river and list questions they may want to investigate: the river's source, history, traffic, rainfall, currents, the fish, industrial pollution and ways to save the river and fish. Each LC selects a key question on which to conduct an *inquiry* over a specific period of time. Each LC plans how to present their discoveries back to the whole class. Possibly the whole class investigation is presented to community groups or becomes a local project involving town people and authorities. This is meaningful active learning, never to be forgotten.

The contrasting examples illustrate two important constructivist beliefs:

1. Learning is meaningful to students when it incorporates a real-time concern, topic or theme—and moves from whole-to-parts.

2. It is better to go deeper on one topic—rather than "covering" or dumping information for many topics.

Expecting students to build concepts from parts-to-wholes is like asking them to assemble a model airplane part by part without being able to view the big picture on the box. The human brain arranges (constructs) knowledge into pre-existing larger contexts rather than stacking piece by piece into unrelated boxes. This is why many students finally just focus on a few parts of a lesson without ever getting the big picture. The overall concept, its significance and meaning to them is lost.

CONCEPTUAL CLUSTERS AND POLAR CONFLICTS

An excellent way to initiate *whole-to-parts* learning experiences is to present subject matter through conceptual clusters and polar conflicts. The themes that follow were generated by people at the National Center for Improving Science Education as the "big ideas" of science:[7]

I get this stuff now. I can do this! Maybe I really could be a lawyer.

cause and effect
change and conservation
diversity and variation
energy and matter
evolution and equilibrium
models and theories
probability and prediction
structure and function
systems and interaction
time and scale

Polar conflicts that challenge students to reflect on the relationship of opposites also lift curricula to *whole-to-parts* learning. Here is a suggested list you can add to as you discover appropriate others for classes you are teaching:

objective/subjective
static/dynamic
individual/group
inhumanity/sensitivity
fantasy/realism
active/passive
independence/interdependence
impulsivity/reflection
freedom/responsibility
reactive/proactive

A wealth of curriculum topics in all subject areas can be actively investigated, analyzed and reflected upon by beginning with polar concepts and learning from whole-to-parts. High school teachers' Collegial Learning Communities enjoy generating their own rich themes for whatever the curriculum content may be. Many have come to recognize that as soon as students become engaged in reflection and inquiry on a BIG concept, learning becomes relevant, meaningful and fun.

Use a Big Idea that connects to the real world.

Here's the 'how' to do it.

"ENGAGE"

THE INCLUSION QUESTION

Student interest is engaged in the instructional task by first setting the stage with an inclusion question that *contains* the *Big Idea*. In the example that follows the big idea is conflict/recovery. *Example:* The academic task for a history class is to compare the similarities and differences of the American Civil War and World War II. Before presenting the task, the teacher or students remind everyone to honor the four Tribes agreements. The teacher poses the inclusion question.

During the next two weeks, we're going to be learning about conflict and recovery from conflict. Is there anyone who has never been in some sort of conflict?

People laugh when one humorist raises a hand. The teacher continues, "Let's begin by sharing in your Learning Communities—if you so choose—a conflict you know or read about and what people did to resolve it. Give everyone in your group equal time to share in the 10 minute discussion." Next the groups are asked to discuss and make lists of issues that can lead to conflicts, that even could start a war. The teacher has made connection to students' experiences, introduced the theme and promoted inclusion. The class could also be asked to connect the idea of conflict to previous learning, students could be invited to act out situations or the teacher could use an appropriate cooperative learning strategy to elicit opinions and interest.

DEFINING THE OBJECTIVES AND QUESTIONS

Once the students are "engaged," the groundwork for the Discovery Learning task is explained. The teacher details the content and collaborative objectives: to compare similarities and differences of the American Civil War and World War II. After writing the task objectives on the board or a chart, she clarifies the time for completion of the task, reviews requirements (reports, presentations, articles, assessment), and gives students the opportunity to ask questions. If this is an initial Discovery Learning experience for the class, the teacher also should describe her role as that of a *guide*... to consult on group plans, identify resources (materials, search sites, people to interview etc.) and provide support as needed. The proven benefits for students to learn actively in this way could also be highlighted.

Next the LCs discuss topics and/or subtopics to be explored. They list specific *how or why* questions that they consider critical to investigate. Each tribe, after consulting with the teacher, selects a different manageable question to explore. The student inquiry process on various group questions (on subtopics) drives the exploration and completion of task.

All of the LCs (tribes, teams) then *brainstorm* activities that they consider will give them information about their group inquiry. They make a written plan by listing the various activities, check with their teacher-guide on which ones are appropriate and feasible. This gives the teacher an opportunity to suggest learning activities and resources that also include required curriculum information and concepts. The plan needs to be detailed specifying the activities that each student *will do* and *when*.

Here is an example:

The Satellite Learning Community's Action Plan to Explore Racial Tension in the Two Wars[10]

1. Mike will meet with the school librarian on Tuesday at 2:30 p.m. to search for video tapes that highlight racial tension in the two big wars.

2. Jennifer will search the Internet to find speeches that Abraham Lincoln and Franklin Delano Roosevelt gave at the end of the wars.

3. Kevin and Angel are going to research racial issues on the Internet and Monday afternoon at the newspaper archives—probably Tuesday too.

4. Kelly and Alexa are conducting a public citizen poll—interviewing at least 50 people at the Wal-Mart store on Saturday afternoon—on what people think causes prejudice and racial tension in our country today. Also on Monday at lunchtime they are meeting with Dr. Heathcliff, the psychologist at the Piney Road Stress Reduction Clinic, which conducts conflict management classes.

5. Everyone in the LC will search for information in the book suggested by our *teacher guide*.

Activities are implemented and members' discoveries are brought back for discussion in their groups. The teacher-guide checks with all of the groups to assess levels of understanding, clarify information and/or

Once you have learned to ask questions—relevant and appropriate and substantial questions—you have learned how to learn and no one can keep you from learning what ever you want or need to know.[9]

—Neil Postman and Charles Weingartner

recommend additional material that may be needed to meet the learning objective well. The LC groups plan how to report or present their learning experience to the class community. Conclusions must be justified by factual information, and academic concepts

presented to the class community in various active learning ways that they checked with their *guide*. A class familiar with multiple intelligence ideas and cooperative learning strategies will be able to enliven their presentation... possibly even to present it to younger students.

As part of their presentation they also may choose to involve the whole class community in expanding on the concepts they have learned, and make connections to current world real-world issues. The connections can lead to further inquiry and on-going learning for the class community.

The fifth "E," Evaluate, is an on-going diagnostic process that allows the teacher and students to determine how well the learners have attained understanding of concepts and knowledge, and how well they are working together in their learning group. Assessment occurs at all points along the continuum of the discovery process through a variety of ways beginning

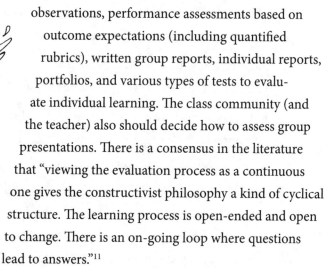

with the *teacher-guide* discussions with the tribes, teacher observations, performance assessments based on outcome expectations (including quantified rubrics), written group reports, individual reports, portfolios, and various types of tests to evaluate individual learning. The class community (and the teacher) also should decide how to assess group presentations. There is a consensus in the literature that "viewing the evaluation process as a continuous one gives the constructivist philosophy a kind of cyclical structure. The learning process is open-ended and open to change. There is an on-going loop where questions lead to answers."[11]

The assessment of the on-going relational and learning process within the small groups has always been the *Tribes way of learning and being together*. The fact that the learning objectives (content/academic and constructive/social) are described for students at the beginning of every learning experience, and at the same time they are given the expectation that they will assess how well their groups attained the objectives... is in itself motivational. The time set aside at the close of every Tribes TLC learning experience to express appreciation and to recognize peers for their contributions and gifts also is empowering. It sustains the culture of achievement and caring.

Summary of The Discovery Learning Steps

1. Engage

The teacher:

- selects topic/problem
- engages students through inclusion
- defines the objectives and tasks of the learning experience
- makes connections to past learning
- lays groundwork for group tasks
- describes role as a "a guide"

2. Explore

Student groups:

- review the four Tribes agreements
- define inquiry questions
- select question(s) to explore
- discuss and list activities for questions
- check with guide
- make an action plan
- conduct exploration
- manage group interaction

3. Explain

Student groups:

- discuss their discoveries
- plan presentations
- clarify with guide
- present learning to class
- justify conclusions from information and academic concepts

4. Elaborate

Student groups:

- involve class to expand on concepts and connect to real-world issues
- discuss how connection can lead to future exploration

5. Evaluate

Student groups:

- ask class prepared reflection questions
- reflect on and assess achievement of objectives
- complete individual and/or group reports
- give statements of appreciation
- acknowledge members' gifts and contributions

Here's what it looks like,
sounds like and feels like in a
Discovery Learning class.

IN A CONSTRUCTIVIST CLASSROOM[12]

Student autonomy and initiative are accepted and encouraged. Teachers help students attain their own intellectual identity. Students frame questions and issues and then go about analyzing and answering them. They take responsibility for their own learning and become problem solvers.

The teacher asks open-ended questions and allows wait time for responses. Higher level thinking is encouraged. The constructivist teacher challenges students to reach beyond the simple factual response, and encourages them to connect and summarize concepts by analyzing, predicting, justifying and defending their ideas.

Students are engaged in dialogue with the teacher and with each other. Social discourse in groups helps students to change or reinforce their ideas, and build a personal knowledge base they understand. Only when they feel comfortable enough in a safe and caring environment to express their ideas will meaningful dialogue occur.

Students are engaged in experiences that challenge hypotheses and encourage discussion. The constructivist teacher provides opportunities for students to generate hypotheses and to test them, through group discussion of concrete experiences.

The class uses raw data, primary sources, manipulatives, physical and interactive materials. The constructivist approach involves students in real-world possibilities and then helps them generate meaningful and lasting concepts.

Bob Perlman, director of strategic planning for the New Technology Foundation emphasizes "For kids to master 21st century skills, you need a system which embeds the skills in the projects they do, and they need to be assessed on them. Collaboration is important, so you've got to work in teams. You don't get critical thinking unless you have complex projects that go in a lot of directions and have very serious content and rigor."[13]

ASSESSMENT OF THE SCHOOL IMPROVEMENT PROCESS AND LONG-TERM OUTCOMES

Did you know? 150 years ago the first large scale standardized testing in the United States was initiated under the Secretary of the State Board of Education of Massachusetts, a renowned gentleman named Horace Mann. The goals were very much the same as standardized testing goals today:

▶ Accountability—to determine the effectiveness of systems and programs

▶ Feedback—to improve instruction by teachers

▶ Classification—to put students into categories, and

▶ Reform—to increase student learning.

Learning this way is great for me. I've learned how working on projects with my team is more meaningful and productive than just doing it alone.

Before that, evaluation was not standardized. In the little red schoolhouse it was individualized and left up to the teacher... who cared, observed, knew how her students were doing day by day, and helped them accordingly. The emergence of testing outside of the classroom changed the nature of educational assessment. Assessment no longer was a tool for the teacher to learn how students were doing, but became an instrument of public policy and politics.[14]

This is the dilemma that exists today in the field of education. On one hand are the not-to-be disputed state mandates for high stakes testing (*"criterion-referenced tests for specific content standards"*), and on the other hand are dedicated classroom teachers who know and care about their students, and cannot bear to short-change them by narrowing down learning to the memorization of information for the test... "to teach to the test." In ever-growing numbers, teachers want learning to be meaningful to empower students to handle complex problems and situations within real-life context. Specific content tests are irrelevant to this purpose. Unfortunately the dichotomy is difficult to overcome because the "outside" public and the "inside" educational community have different purposes and views of learning.

At the school site level all school communities want to know the degree to which various long-term outcomes (such as increases in academic achievement, decreased discipline problems, increased parent involvement, improved school climate, improved attendance, teacher collegiality, etc.) are achieved due to the use of the process of active learning over a period of time. Prior to evaluating long-term outcomes, it is of great importance to conduct periodic *process assessments* to indicate the extent that key components of the research-based process of Tribes are being implemented in classrooms.

> *"Focusing only on outcome data, without simultaneously gathering data on the nature of students' school experiences, provides very little leverage for improvement... Without evidence on processes, evaluation efforts are reduced to 'black box' inquiries with little potential to explain outcomes, whether good or bad."*[15] —Walt Haney

Process assessments are timely snapshots that point to areas to intensify for improvement. *For example:* A desired outcome for a school is to decrease conflict and racial tension among students. If a process assessment indicates that the agreement *mutual respect* is not being practiced or demonstrated significantly in classrooms, teachers can focus on that Tribes agreement by implementing many strategies throughout the school and classrooms that highlight mutual respect. They also can have students identify examples of mutual respect when found in curriculum content.

Tribes school communities can assess their school's progress by obtaining the Assessment Kit: "Reflecting on the Tribes TLC® Process" from CenterSource Systems.

Assessments need to become performance based, reflective and take into consideration the full range of student intelligences and competencies.

Nevertheless... .

It consists of a reliable set of action research instruments designed and piloted by the Northwest Regional Educational Laboratory just for our use. It's purpose is to give teachers and students snapshots of the extent to which the components of Tribes are happening in classrooms, and then to plan together how to strengthen their use.[16] Periodic "reflection" along the trail results in goal attainment on any journey.

"I Confess...

I started out as a creationist. The first days of every school year I created; for the next thirty-six weeks I maintained my creation. My curriculum. From behind my big desk I set it in motion, managed and maintained it all year, lectured—systematic, purposeful, in control. I wanted great truths from my great practices. And I wanted to convince other teachers that this creation was superior stuff. So I studied my curriculum, conducting research to show its wonders. I didn't learn in my classroom. I tended and taught my creation.

These days, I learn in my classroom. What happens there has changed; it continually changes. I've become an evolutionist, and the curriculum unfolds now as my kids and I learn together. My aims stay constant—I want us to go deep inside language, using it to know and shape and play with our worlds. My practices evolve as we go deeper. This going deeper is research, and these days my research shows me the wonders of my kids, not my methods. But it has also brought me full circle. What I learn with these students, collaborating with them as a writer and reader who wonders about writing and reading, makes me a better teacher- not great maybe, but at least grounded in the logic of learning and growing."[17] —Nancy Atwell

The inquiry method is not designed to do what older environments try to do. It works you over in entirely different ways. It activates different senses, attitudes, and perceptions. It generates a different, bolder, and more potent kind of intelligence... It will cause everything about education... to change.[18]
—Neil Postman and Charles Weingartner

16

Embracing the Future

16 Embracing the Future

IN THIS CHAPTER YOU WILL

▶ Look into the kinds of minds, humanity and wholeness youth need as citizens of the future

▶ Recognize the new capacities and multifaceted skills that are inherent in today's young adults

▶ Realize that "engaging all" requires collaborative democratic leadership

▶ Discover how capacity building with a focus on professional development can transform the high school system

We as educators must find that balance between the world of the mind and that of the heart and soul. It is the mind that preoccupies our time and takes us into the information age. But it is the heart and soul that will allow us to remain connected to our own humanity—that will build that bridge between us... and create a good society.[1]

—PAUL D. HOUSTON

CITIZENS OF THE FUTURE

The time is now... to remind ourselves, our school communities, national leaders, standard setters, curriculum developers and hierarchies of funding sources that more than all the fundamental purpose of education is: *to develop meaningful knowledge, humanity and wholeness in youth to enable all to be active constructive citizens and valuable contributors to society.* Howard Gardner takes the purpose further saying, *"I crave human beings who understand the world, who gain sustenance from such understanding, and who want—ardently, perennially—to alter it [the world] for the better."[2]*

Unfortunately, the majority of public high schools today in the United States (as well as in some other countries) are caught in unprecedented national mandates to achieve a narrow set of basic academic standards and high stake test scores... quite apart from supporting the development of youth in all dimensions of their wholeness so that they are prepared to move into and live the future well.

The respected Association of Supervision and Curriculum Development (ASCD) in the United States has been sounding this alarm to Congress, the media and the public:

> *The intense focus on annual testing in selected subject areas has put a huge amount of pressure on schools to focus on a few academic subjects (literacy and numeracy), often eliminating other areas of instruction. While a rigorous academic curriculum is certainly important, we must not forget the curriculum must be a well-rounded curriculum and that schools also have an obligation to help children develop skills to lead engaged and productive lives as adults. This requires adopting comprehensive programs that support all of students' core needs, from physical health to safety to intellectual development. In other words, we must put our focus on educating the Whole Child.[3]*

Readers, of course by now, recognize that educating the whole young person has long been and continues to be the Tribes Learning Community (TLC®) stated mission... *to*

The fundamental purpose of education is to develop meaningful knowledge, humanity and wholeness in youth.

assure the healthy development of every child so that each has the knowledge, competency and resilience to be successful in a rapidly changing world.

The Critical Challenge...

for today's high schools is to recognize that not only do their students have "core needs" beyond learning basics subjects, but that their "wiring" calls for them to learn in ways very different than what is taking place in their schools. This is one of the primary reasons too many young people are struggling, failing or dropping out of high schools today. Neuroscience research tells us that every type of experience alters the chemistry and structures within the human brain. Consider how the minds of today's students have been dramatically altered by the imprint of television, computer games, the Internet, communication technology, visual imagery and rapid access to meaningful information. Marc Prensky, internationally known visionary and author of the timely book, *"Don't Bother Me Mom, I'm Learning,"* believes that computer game playing attracts kids because they are engaged in learning a wide range of new skills from collaboration, risk-taking, strategy formulation and execution to complex and moral ethical decisions—all of which are essential skills for the future. "They thrive on meaningful involvement, using information, networking and multitasking." Prensky refers to this generation as "Digital Natives" and the rest of us as "Digital Immigrants." He emphasizes that, "No matter how much we immigrants want Digital students to learn in our old ways, they cannot go backwards."[4]

> Today's students are no longer the people our educational system was designed to teach.[5]
>
> —Marc Prensky

> For the first time in history students are no longer limited by their teachers' ability and knowledge.[7]
>
> —Mark Anderson

Memories for Digital Immigrants[6]

Do you remember when…

A mouse was a rodent?

A keyboard came attached to a piano?

A cursor used profanity?

A virus was the flu?

A hard drive was a long trip in a car?

A web was a spider's home?

A net caught fish?

A program was a TV show?

A CD was a bank account?

A backup was plugged up plumbing?

An application was for employment?

Log on was adding wood to the fire?

Memory was something that got worse with age?

A menu was something you ordered food from?

A window was something you gazed out of?

THE FUTURE IS NOW

In a synchronistic way, just as nature and history throughout the ages somehow get human-kind ready for wherever we next are going in time, the digital generation is prepared to live into this 21st century world of unprecedented global change. You may recall that many of the changes they face were highlighted in Chapter 3 entitled, *The Times are A'Changing.* Knowing this, our challenge and responsibility as educators is to re-learn, re-think, re-create, model and allign education to fit and support youth moving into the future—*the 21st century future that is already here.*

A timely article, *Becoming Citizens of the World,* in an edition of the Educational Leadership journal, emphasizes the obvious that the new knowledge and skills that students will need go well beyond the current focus on the basic subjects and technology. Graduates now not only need to be knowledgeable about multiethnic, multicultural, multilingual populations, but also socio-economic, political. technological information and issues of the world. All of which implies that they need to be able to communicate in languages other than English.[8] Our concern for the development of the Whole Child, prompts us to add that all high school young adults need to have developed the four developmental tasks of adolescence: a sense of autonomy, social competency, the ability to problem solve, and a positive sense of purpose. Moreover, all need to have internalized the valuable attributes of resiliency to carry them through life well.

WHAT KIND OF MINDS DO WE NEED?

Howard Gardner, renowned scholar on multiple intelligences, deals very thoroughly and beautifully with that question in his 2007 book, *Five Kinds of Minds.* He asks, *"What kind of minds do we need if we are to create a world in which we would like to live?"* In summary, he believes that graduates today have to cultivate:[9]

Mind? What kind of a mind do I really need?

> ▶ a synthesizing mind—the ability to interpret and integrate disparate concepts, ideas and images

> ▶ a creating mind—the capacity to envision, organize and create new form

> ▶ a respectful mind—to revere uniqueness, appreciate diversity and respect the rights of others

> ▶ an ethical mind—a willingness to take on justice, action and responsibility as a world citizen

> ▶ a disciplinary mind—mastery of a major school of thought and at least one professional craft.

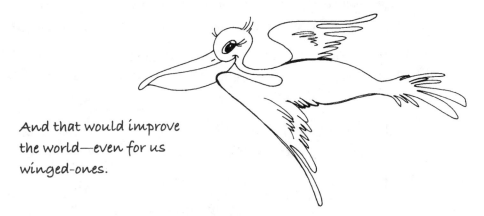

And that would improve the world—even for us winged-ones.

GET ME SOME POETS FOR MANAGERS[10]

Enlightenment on the future also comes from Daniel H. Pink, author of the profound book, *A Whole NEW Mind: Moving from the Information Age to the Conceptual Age.*[11] Pink has been shaking up the business world stating that the future belongs to a different kind of person with a different kind of mind than that of the predominant left-brain (L-Directed) linear thinkers (mathematicians, software engineers, lawyers, accountants, technology experts etc.) who to their credit as "knowledge workers" have master-minded the Industrial-Technological Age. Citing research on the dual hemisphere of the human brain, Pink writes that much now is needed from right-brain (R-Directed) contextual thinkers in order to bring about balance and holistic perception throughout systems of the world.

Briefly, research on the brain hemispheres tells us that:

▶ The left hemisphere is sequential and logical; it analyzes details and *what* is said.

▶ The right hemisphere is simultaneous, sees the big picture, synthesizes elements, recognizes patterns and emotions, and focuses on *how* it is said.

Both hemispheres are essential to human thinking.

Daniel Pink states: "In short we've progressed from a society of farmers to a society of factory workers to a society of knowledge workers. And now we're progressing yet again—to a society of creators and empathizers, of pattern recognizers and meaning makers."[13] He raises the question, "How can we prepare ourselves for the Conceptual Age?" "In the Conceptual Age we will need to complement our L-Directed reasoning by mastering six essential R-Directed aptitudes that can help us develop the *whole new mind* this new era demands.[14]

▶ Not just function but also DESIGN—the ability to create something that is beautiful, whimsical or emotionally engaging

> Business people don't need to understand designers better. They need to be designers.[12]
> —ROGER MARTIN
> DEAN OF THE ROTMAN
> SCHOOL OF MANAGEMENT

- ▶ Not just argument but also STORY—the essence of persuasion, communication, and self-understanding and ability to fashion a compelling narrative

- ▶ Not just focus but also SYMPHONY—to synthesize, to see the big picture, crossing boundaries, and to combine disparate pieces into an arresting new whole

- ▶ Not just logic but also EMPATHY—to understand what makes people tick, to forge relationships and to care for others

- ▶ Not just seriousness but also PLAY—to stimulate the health and professional benefits of laughter, light heartedness, games and humor

- ▶ Not just accumulation but also MEANING—to pursue purpose, transcendence and spiritual fulfillment.

"These six senses increasingly will guide our lives and shape our world... [edit]... The high-concept, high-touch abilities that now matter most are fundamentally human attributes. After all, back on the savannah, our cave-person ancestors weren't taking SAT's or plugging in numbers on spreadsheets. But they were telling stories, demonstrating empathy, and designing innovations. These abilities have always comprised part of what it means to be human. But after a few generations in the Information Age these muscles have atrophied. The challenge is to work them back into shape."[15]

Neuroscientist Robert Ornstein, author of the *Right Mind,* writes:

Many popular writers have written that the right hemisphere is the key to expanding human thought, surviving trauma, healing autism, and more. It's going to save us. It's the seat of creativity, of the soul, and... even good casserole ideas![16]

But can we really transform our high school into a high performance Learning Community?

We're doing it well already. We're implementing this student-centered capacity-building comprehensive process.

ENGAGING ALL TAKES DEMOCRATIC LEADERSHIP

"Schools will be transformed only when a community-building process is implemented for teachers as well as for students. The critical challenge for the 21st century does not lie in mastering this piece of information or that technology. It lies in creating connectedness—in building schools across the nation that tap the innate developmental wisdom that is our shared humanity, connecting us to each other and to our shared web of life."[17]   —National High School Alliance

Thomas Sergiovanni, author of the fine book *Rethinking Leadership,* tells us that engaging parents, community leaders, resource persons, teachers and students themselves to support the transformation of their school into a high-performance system requires the development of democracy throughout the school. Moreover, it is next to impossible to progress to responsive education for students if school leaders perceive the school as an organization to be controlled rather than a community to be inspired and led in a common cause. The majority of schools have been defined as business management systems based on turning out standardized products with employees adhering to regulations and being monitored for compliance. Control driven business management practices may be effective in producing market products but they undermine the diametrically different purpose of schools—"to develop competent human beings to take constructive action in society." The values and cultures are completely incompatible one to the other.[18]

Leading a school community requires leadership that empowers all of the structured groups (teams, departments, and small learning communities) throughout the school to reflect, problem-solve, plan, initiate action, reflect on and assess progress again and again. The millennium school leader is a *transformative leader—a reflective practitioner* who affirms the gifts of others and empowers many in the mission of the high school. James Burns, Pulitzer prize author, states that "transformative leadership occurs when one or more persons engage with others in such a way that leaders and followers raise one another to high levels of motivation and morality. Their purposes, which might have started out as separate but related... become fused. Transformative leadership raises the level of human conduct and ethical aspiration of both leaders and followers, and thus, has a transforming effect on both."[19]

Roland S. Barth, Director of the Principals Center at Harvard University, points out that no longer a remote authority primarily juggling finances, personnel issues and problems, the effective leader frees up time by distributing many traditional activities to a core group, lead teachers, teacher learning communities and support staff.[20] The change in role parallels the one that teachers are making in transferring responsibility to students in classroom learning groups. The same principle applies—no one person can supervise and support more than five or six other people at any one time—but one person can empower and support collaborative teams of people. A growing number of "seasoned"

> Transformative leaders know the difference between power-over and power-to.
> —THOMAS SERGIOVANNI

administrators recognize the truth of organizational studies which indicate that "the only thing of real importance that leaders do is to create and manage the culture."[21]

The 21st century administrator, according to Roland Barth, must be a transformational leader who not only is a reflective practitioner but a learner. He states, "To be a learner is to be able to admit, 'I do not know it all.' To be a learner is to admit imperfection. Who inspires more confidence? Who is the better leader? The principal who is learned and wise or the principal who is an insatiable life-long learner?"[23] Think of a school leader that you consider outstanding. Ten to one you'll say he or she does not govern with dominance and control but by a desire to bring out the best in the people. The effective leader is able to stand back and be reflective in the moment of success or failure. He or she asks, "What am I learning that will help to lead the school community now?" This is especially important for high school principals. Studies verify that the link between principal learning and the quality of teaching, in turn affects the quality of student learning.[24]

BREAKING RANKS

Let's say that having given much study and thought to "breaking ranks" from the out-of-date high school system, you and other school leaders decide it is time to transform your high school into a dynamic Learning Community in which all students and teachers can excel. For some time you have been learning that the best way to achieve school-wide improvement is to include and build the capacity of the whole teaching staff ("the insiders") to focus on the development as well as learning for today's students, and to personalize the culture, class and relational structures and pedagogy. You are convinced that now it is time for your school to base instruction on well-researched principles and practices known to support and accelerate student learning. You and others recognize that in order to create a 21st century high school learning community of educational excellence, time and funds have to be re-allocated. You also realize that both are available—if not traditionally allocated to something else.

Respected scholar, Michael Fullan, has long advised that, "The only way to accomplish the changes we need is through an intense focus on improving classroom practices."[25] Linda Darling-Hammond's studies of reform efforts arrived at a similar conclusion that accountability-only strategies that primarily relied on testing, rather than investment in improving classroom teachers' knowledge and practices, showed little success in raising student achievement.[26] Successful change begins in the classroom—not with accountability and testing, or the shuffling of positions, procedures and requirements again and again.

"I like school now—now that it likes me.

An Inspiring Vision to Engage All

For decades, high school leaders in Hawaii have been guided by an intuitive and instinctive leadership approach that success was attained not merely through state test scores but through the hard work required to create and sustain a nurturing school culture that engages all. Recent research on high school redesign affirms that leadership approach. "Personalizing" a high school—whether large or small—is now a research-based best practice.

The evolution of the "new" three Rs for high schools emphasizes this. First, the framework of "Rigor and Relevance" expanded to become "Rigor, Relevance, and Relationships." Next, the emphasis on personalization led to a change in the priorities—in order of importance, the framework for high schools is "Relationships, Relevance, and Rigor."

Robert Fulgum's wisdom that "everything we had to learn, we learned in kindergarten" is a reminder that high schools can learn so much from the practices of elementary school educators and middle school educators, who excel in providing an inclusive school environment that engages all.

Receiving a 4.0 grade point average, scoring 1600 on the SAT, or attaining the status of valedictorian are student achievements that are meaningless if those students cannot demonstrate a compassion for others. The journey to become a high performing high school is a journey to engage all students through a personalized learning environment. It is more than just a single destination. It is really a continuous journey on the path through inclusion, influence, and community.

At Moanalua High School, our mascot, the legendary Menehune of ancient Hawaii, epitomizes the idea of compassion for others, collaboration, and humility. Our shared vision is for *"a learning community where, in the spirit of the Menehune, everyone works in partnership to strive for excellence."* A learning community that engages all... this is the most powerful and inspiring vision that can personalize and transform our high schools into quality systems of "rigor, relevance, and relationships." The time has come to initiate a kinder culture and ways of learning together. The spirit of the legendary Menehune is calling.

A Principal's Perspective

Darrel Galera, M.Ed.

Darrel has been an elementary and middle school principal, Advanced Technology Research Specialist, and a Deputy District Superintendent for the Hawaii Department of Education before becoming the fifth principal of Moanalua High School where he was once a teacher, Student Activities Coordinator, and a vice principal. Through Darrel's leadership, Moanalua High School has one of the most comprehensive professional development programs in the state where teachers share their learning as presenters at their Annual Professional Development Conference, through technology exhibits, or their annual **Reflections** professional journal publication.

Lynne A. McMahan, Ed.D.

As a teacher and administrator, Lynne introduced the process of Tribes in three public schools in the Albuquerque School District. Her recent dissertation is a fine study of successfully developing a brand new school "from the ground-up." As a Certified Tribes TLC Trainer, now Lynne's intent is to demonstrate on a wider scale that the process of Tribes and responsive leadership can move schools, districts and states well beyond "leaving no child behind" to "bringing the whole child ahead."

Spiritually Responsive Leadership

In these turbulent times of educational reform where top-down mandates and negativity seem to be permeating the learning climate, how does a leader renew and sustain a community for learning? I believe it is through the leader's courage of conviction that schools must prepare students to become healthy, critical thinking citizens who will help to shape a more humane and inclusive future. At the deepest level, schools create a community and family where students can become caring, purposeful, "soul-filled" individuals able to heal this wounded world. In order for students to bring their soul to the classroom we must create a space and a family for nurturing this aspect of the individual child.[27]

The process of Tribes, as I have facilitated it in my classroom and in schools as an educational leader, is a spiritual process that nurtures this caring aspect. It creates a place and space where individuals can be more than statistical test data. The process, for me, has created much healing in the wounded world of education as I have experienced it over the past 15 years. At its highest and best, Tribes helps both teacher and student to co-create an enlightened learning community where healthy interactions and meaningful relationships are the norm; and where individuals realize their potential by participating in a caring environment where mutual respect, collaborative learning and commitment to the whole matter most.

As a spiritual process, Tribes facilitation demands a leader or leaders who are responsive to the needs and cultures of the members within the learning community. I consider this to be "spiritually responsive leadership." It is a leadership that is sensitive to what is held especially dear and sacred—a leadership that responds and adjusts to the concerns in our hearts and minds , that makes the most difference to us as human beings, and that gives meaning and purpose to our lives. This style requires a shift of thinking from improvement to renewal, and from what is the matter with schools, to what really matters in schools. The shift in thinking moves from a single reform approach to a holistic approach: from "no child left behind," to "bringing the whole child ahead."

Leaders need to work from not only their mind but from the heart as well. The heart is what renews and sustains us in times of challenge or celebration. Tribes learning communities transfer the ultimate qualities of leadership—spiritually responsive qualities—to all members of the community. Responsiveness and care are the tenets, the agreements each individual commits to in this culture of realized potential, blurring the lines of "who" is the leader. All members of the community, students and their families, teachers and administrators, share in leadership roles, transforming the process of learning to creativity and renewal.

With a shift in thinking and a different perspective, schools, districts and their leaders can take an alternate, more responsive approach beyond dispassionate reform mandates by creating Tribes Learning Community schools, guided by your own spiritually responsive leadership. Respected educator Parker Palmer tells us, "When we find our place in the movement, we will discover that there is no essential conflict between loving to teach and working to reform education... We need only be in the world as our true selves, with open hearts and minds." [28]

May you find the balance of heart, mind and soul on your continuing educational journey.

CAPACITY BUILDING FOR CHANGE

Engaging all of the "insiders" to collaborate in bringing about change in contrast to having "outside experts" come in to plan and lead "comprehensive school reform"—being less traditional, may initially arouse resistance. We suggest that you take time to turn back to Chapter 5 to Carole Freehan's article, "Embracing Resistance." It not only defines change as an on-going journey, not a top-down formula, but also how to turn around resistance.

Describing change as "innovativeness" rather than an "innovation" also eases the way. Michael Fullan makes the distinction that "innovation" means introducing the *content* of a new program, whereas "innovativeness" is the *capacity* of an organization to engage in continuous improvement.[29] It is the latter that best describes why the process of Tribes Learning Community (TLC®) has always been called a "process" rather than a program. The process of Tribes is a contextual sequence of researched principles and practices that are implemented throughout a system for continuous improvement. Unlike training a few people or department in the high school to innovate a new program (or curriculum), the capacity of everyone in the high school community is developed to activate the learning

Capacity building, at its heart, is a system of guiding and directing people's work, which is carried out in a high professional learning setting. All else is clutter.[31]

—ROLAND S. BARTH

process and bring about improvement. Such an approach over many years has come to be known as a *capacity building strategy with a focus on results.*[30]

Building the capacity of the high school Learning Community consists of initiating and maintaining six organizational strategies, which have been described throughout this book:

► **A Core Leadership Group** to guide the high school learning and improvement process

► **Professional development** for the instructional staff to learn and utilize effective principles and practices for student learning

► **Collegial Learning Communities** to collaborate on learning, implementation and assessing active learning pedagogy

► **Reflective practice and authentic assessment**—on-going use throughout all learning communities to give continual insight on progress and results

► **Visionary democratic leadership** to guide innovativeness and capacity building with a focus on enhancing learning for all students.

THE CAPACITY BUILDING DEVELOPMENT MODEL

A professional development course and coaching for a segment (or cohort) of the high school instructional staff is available from CenterSource Systems the initial year. Future year professional development can be facilitated by several of the high school's own teachers who are selected by the Principal and Core Leadership group to participate in a five day experiential training to become Certified Tribes Learning Community trainers. They are prepared well and receive high quality training materials to conduct on-site courses and on-going coaching for new teachers and the Collegial Learning Communities. They also can design parent and community presentations and programs. The Resource Section of this book describes the Professional Development courses available to Certified TLC trainers in schools of various grade levels. This CenterSource "capacity building system" is being and has been used with much success throughout many countries initiating Tribes Learning Communities. It transfers support and expertise to school "insiders" for continuous learning and use of the process.

LEVELS OF CONCERN

Perhaps you have observed that as welcome or exciting the implementation of a new approach may be, in time there may be a lessening or a "a dip" in implementation and expressions of concern. Letting go of familiar old ways of teaching is hard. You may hear something like the following conversation.

I'm concerned about what we're doing.
How about trying something else?

Oh no. My students are much more
involved. I know I just need to learn more.

The teachers talking are expressing different levels of concern, a natural and inevitable phenomenon that occurs during stages of implementation. G. Hall and S. Hord, authors of the book, *Implementation Change Patterns, Principles and Potholes*, have defined seven levels of concern that take place when teachers are learning to use a new pedagogy. It is important to make teachers aware of the levels that if not addressed, not only can lead to a dip in implementation but weaken the overall school improvement effort. Giving teachers knowledge of the natural Levels of Concern enables them to voice and discuss their concerns with other teachers and in their Collegial Learning Communities.

The levels from the most serious concern ("6") to the least concern ("0") are:[32]

6—Refocusing: I like how I've always been teaching. I have some better ideas.

5—Collaboration: I'm concerned about sharing what I'm doing—whether it's what everyone else is doing.

4—Consequences: I wonder how this really will help the students.

3—Management: It takes a lot more preparation time for me to do this.

2—Personal: I think teaching in this way is helping me too.

1—Information: I want to read and learn more about it.

0—Awareness: I'm enjoying doing it. I'm not concerned.

Now look back at the illustration of the two teachers talking and analyze their different levels of concern.

One of the most important reasons to establish small on-going Collegial Learning Communities to which all teachers belong, is the support they give to all in the midst of learning and implementing. CLCs are an essential structure for curriculum planning, problem-solving, reflection, assessment and innovativeness to achieve school improvement. Michael Fullan reminds us:

"The more that you develop active professional (collegial) learning communities in schools in which teachers observe one another's teaching and work with the school leadership to make on-going improvements, the greater the consistency and the greater quality of teaching across the whole school, at which point all students in the school benefit and keep on benefiting. And the more you do this the more shared meanings and commitments, and related capacities get generated."[33]

THE TIME HAS COME

The respected Association for Supervision of Curriculum and Development (ASCD) is taking leadership at the national level in the United States to promote the adoption of the following five essential elements for high school redesign and reform:

▶ Multiple measures of assessment

▶ Personalized learning strategies

▶ Flexible use of time and structure

▶ New professional development for teachers and school leadership

▶ Business and community engagement.

For favorable transformation to occur, all high students must be taught in a manner that values and nurtures their individuality. The academic progress of these young

people must be expressed not solely by standardized, multiple choice tests but also by a variety of other highly personalized criteria. All teachers must be intellectually and professionally equipped to instruct students with expertise appropriate to the demands of a diverse rapidly evolving and increasingly complex society... The time has come for these measures to be adopted broadly. —ASCD[34]

We offer this book, *Engaging All by Creating High School Learning Communities*, as a foundation process upon which teachers, administrators and others in high school communities, who are committed to advancing development and learning for youth, can successfully do so. To read, to discuss and to synthesize with colleagues this as well as other publications on youth development and learning is the only way high performing personalized high schools will be developed. The time is now—not another frustrated lost generation from now!

> Education is everybody's business. You now may begin to change the world.[35]
> —DENNIS LITTKY

Be sure to check the Bibliography for some of the fine books we've mentioned in Engaging All.
Try 'em—you'll like 'em!

This is the value of the teacher, who looks at a face and says

there's something behind that face—and I want to reach that person.

I want to influence that person. I want to encourage that person.

I want to enrich. I want to call out that person who is behind that face, behind

that color, behind that language, behind that tradition, behind that culture.

I believe *you can do it*.

I know what was done for me. [36]

—Maya Angelou

*A*ctive Learning
Strategies

Active Learning Strategies

An Overview

Carol Rankin, M.Ed., MFCC

Carol oversees program development for Center-Source Systems. As a former school counselor and marriage, family and child counselor, Carol has worked with families and children of all ages. Her strong commitment to quality education stems from years of involvement in her own children's schools. She is appreciative of the skills, expertise and dedication of exceptional teachers and administrators who enrich children's lives everyday.

Many learning strategies in this section have been adapted from other sources, some familiar to you. We are indebted to innumerable creative teachers who have contributed learning strategies over the years, and we invite contributions of your favorite strategies and energizers for future printings of this book.

Strategies are ways to achieve learning objectives, whereas "activities" too often are considered time-fillers. The majority of Tribes strategies provide formats to incorporate academic subject content. See Chapter 14, "Designing Cooperative Learning Experiences," for discussion of designing learning experiences through Tribes. Strategies can be used again and again, and in combination with many other cooperative learning structures from other sources. All strategies can also be effectively used with adults—teachers, staff and parents—to build a collegial learning community, enhance collaborative skills, and develop leadership.

The Learning Strategy Matrix that follows these introductory pages is alphabetized and coded so that you can select appropriate strategies and energizers. Each strategy contains the following notations:

- ▶ Approximate time required
- ▶ Grouping: community circle, tribes, sub groups
- ▶ Materials needed
- ▶ Relevant developmental tasks of early adolescence
- ▶ Objectives
- ▶ Instructions
- ▶ Suggested reflection questions
- ▶ Appreciation
- ▶ Options

Each learning strategy contains a notation of the developmental task it will support. The selected strategies assist students by nuturing the adolescent developmental competencies they are seeking to achieve. See Chapter 2, "Learning Who They Are," for a full discussion of the tasks of adolescence.

Following the objectives and instructions are three kinds of suggested reflection questions:

▶ Content (cognitive learning)

▶ Collaborative (social learning)

▶ Personal learning

You do not need to ask all three types of reflection questions after a learning experience, but do use at least two of the different types. The questions link to the recommendations made by the National Association of Secondary School Principals in the *Breaking Ranks* documents that urge a focus on rigor, relationships, and relevance. The content questions help teachers as they monitor the rigor in their subjects. The collaborative questions deepen relationships and build interpersonal skills. The personal questions help students to make relevant connections to their own worlds and discover their strengths and assets. Base your choice on what you believe will make the content meaningful and the social or personal learning significant for the majority of students in your class.

Many of the collaborative reflection questions are based on the concept of "appreciative inquiry," a process that elicits reflection on what the group did well together to make their learning successful. The personal reflection questions are designed to help students discover their strengths, skills, gifts, and preferred ways of learning and knowing (including multiple intelligences)—all so crucial for achieving the developmental competencies to assure futures of promise. Last, but every bit as important, are invitations for appreciation and recognition of skills and gifts in others. For a full discussion of reflection, appreciative inquiry, and appreciation, see Chapter 14, "Designing Cooperative Learning Experiences."

The follow-up reflection questions and statements of appreciation serve several important purposes. They...

▶ enhance learning and the retention of concepts for academic achievement,

▶ encourage the community to reflect upon and develop collaborative skills,

▶ allow students the opportunity to discover personal strengths and gifts, and

▶ help sustain the positive learning environment.

In the margin on each strategy page, you will see "Options," which are suggestions or examples for using the strategy with academic content material. Remember, if your students liked "Milling to Music" as an opportunity to move and talk about themselves, why not use the strategy as a curriculum learning experience? Your students will become more engaged in the subject matter and will demonstrate better retention of academic material.

Strategies need to be selected carefully and intentionally to follow the stages of group development. As outlined in Chapter 7, "Establishing Community for All," inclusion activities should be used initially to create the caring learning environment. Later, the Tribes will indicate when they are ready to move into the influence stage and, finally, they will be ready to undertake more complex projects during the stage of community. The Learning Strategy Matrix that follows will help you to select strategies that are appropriate to the stage that your classroom is experiencing.

Strategies also need to be carefully tailored to fit the ethnicity, culture, age level, interests, language, and socio-economic status of the students in your class. A strategy that is not sensitive to the community culture undermines the teaching process. Following are some possible examples of this:

▶ Using the names of Christian holidays but not those of other religions;

▶ Urging Native Americans, Latinos, and indigenous populations to make personal statements during the inclusion stage. The opportunity to share first about their culture, family, or group is traditional for them, and therefore more comfortable and inclusive;

▶ Ignoring the economic realities of a community (i.e., using examples of luxury items in a low-income area);

▶ Urging Cambodian, Thai and some of the other Asian students to demonstrate eye contact during attentive listening (when in their own culture averting one's eyes denotes respect).

It is very important to plan and implement strategies well. The following chart will give you a quick summary for implementing Tribes strategies.

Summary: Facilitating Tribes Strategies

REMIND STUDENTS ABOUT THE TRIBES AGREEMENTS:

▶ Whenever appropriate, ask the class or tribe to review the agreements.

▶ Have the agreements posted at all times.

▶ Respect and model the agreements congruently yourself.

GIVE THE INSTRUCTIONS:

▶ Select and tailor an appropriate strategy or series of them to achieve your learning objectives.

▶ Tell your students what the objectives are (what they will learn).

▶ Give instructions simply and concisely; do not get off the track or use too many words.

▶ Tell students how much time they will have to complete the task.

IF STUDENTS ARE IN A COMMUNITY CIRCLE:

▶ Initiate the sharing yourself.

▶ Let the students know who will be next—which way you'll go around the circle.

▶ Ask people to speak directly to one another.

▶ Withhold your own comments on what students share.

▶ Encourage people to use first names.

▶ Make it okay to pass.

▶ Deal with put-downs or a lack of attentive listening.

▶ Give people a second opportunity to share if they pass the first time.

▶ Ask appropriate cognitive, collaborative, and/or personal reflection questions.

▶ Wind things up when people feel bored or restless.

IF STUDENTS ARE WORKING IN TRIBES OR SMALL GROUPS:

▶ Follow suggestions noted above.

▶ If using roles, discuss them, assign them, or have students choose them.

▶ Describe the task to be accomplished (materials, resources, and time for completion).

▶ Ask students to clarify the task to you or each other.

▶ Observe their interaction and assist only as needed.

▶ Ask reflection questions.

▶ Assess (or have students assess) and evaluate outcomes.

INVITE STATEMENTS OF APPRECIATION AND RECOGNITION OF GIFTS:

▶ Suggest sentence starters.

▶ Be a good role model.

Celebrate class, tribe, or individual contributions and achievements!

ENERGIZERS

In the midst of any time together groups of people periodically will experience lower energy within an environment. Concentration becomes more difficult; boredom and sleepiness can set in and will be counterproductive to accomplishing the task at hand. Adolescent students, especially, become restless. They are likely to withdraw or even create a disturbance. The remedy? A quick five-minute physical activity to revitalize the group with an "energizer."

Energizers are satisfying because they engage many of the multiple intelligences, primarily: body/kinesthetic, musical/rhythmic, interpersonal and visual/spatial.

Six outcomes can be achieved through the use of energizers:

▶ The energy of the classroom or group is revitalized.

▶ People's attention can be drawn back to the classroom after a time away (lunch break or some other interruption).

▶ Different types of academic learning activities can be bridged, renewing energy and concentration.

▶ People can feel connected again with one another and the whole community.

▶ Multiple intelligences can be reached and are engaged.

▶ They add to the fun of learning and being together!

At the end of the Learning Strategy section you will find a sampling of some favorite Tribes energizers. Some are more physical than others and, as with other activities in this book, it is up to you to select the most appropriate ones for your students. Much depends upon the level of trust within the class at any one time. A larger collection of 101 tried and true energizers contained in a desktop card file or "Energizer Box" is also available from CenterSource Systems.

STRATEGY TITLE	Page	INCLUSION	Presenting Self	Social Skills	Agreements	INFLUENCE	Decisions/Problem Solving	Resolving Conflict	Goal Setting	COMMUNITY	Energizer	Celebration	ACADEMICS
Active Ignoring	318	●		●		●		●					●
All In the Family	319	●	●	●									●
"Am I Napoleon?"	320	●	●			●				●			●
A Poem by Our Tribe	321	●	●			●	●			●		●	●
Appreciating Others	323	●		●						●		●	●
Architects and Builders	325	●				●	●						●
A Special Friend I Know	326	●	●	●									●
Boasters	327	●	●	●	●								●
Brainstorming	329	●	●			●	●	●		●		●	●
Building a Time Machine	330	●		●		●	●	●					●
Bumper Sticker	331	●	●	●						●		●	●
Bumpety-Bump-Bump	472									●	●		
Campaign Manager	332	●	●							●		●	●
Career Choices	333	●	●			●	●						●
Cares—Concerns—Compliments	334	●	●	●		●				●			●
Celebrity Sign-In	335		●			●	●						●
Chain Reaction	336	●	●	●						●		●	●
Changes	472									●	●		
Clap-Slap	472									●	●		
Client-Consultants	337	●		●		●	●						●
Community Circle	338	●	●	●	●					●		●	●
Community Circle Metaphor	340	●	●	●						●		●	●
Confrontation	341	●		●		●		●	●				●

STRATEGY TITLE	Page	INCLUSION	Presenting Self	Social Skills	Agreements	INFLUENCE	Decisions/Problem Solving	Resolving Conflict	Goal Setting	COMMUNITY	Energizer	Celebration	ACADEMICS
Consensus-Building	342	●		●		●	●	●	●				●
Cooperation Squares	343	●		●		●	●	●					●
Cruising Careers/Finding Tribes	345	●								●			●
Current Events Debate Circle	346	●			●	●	●						●
Dear Abby	347	●	●			●	●	●					●
Do After Me	472									●	●		
Dream Quilt	348	●	●	●		●	●		●	●			●
Electricity	472									●	●		
Extended Nametags	349	●	●	●									●
Final Countdown	350									●		●	●
Find the Word	351	●		●		●							●
Finding All We Have In Common	352	●	●	●									●
Five E's for Discovery Learning	353	●	●	●	●	●	●		●	●			●
Flies on the Ceiling	354	●		●		●		●	●	●			●
Focusing on Our Strengths	355	●	●	●	●					●		●	●
Fold the Line Reading	356	●		●		●		●					●
Fork and Spoon	473									●	●		
Gallery Walks	357	●	●	●		●				●		●	●
Give Me a Clue	358	●		●		●	●						●
Goal-Storming	360	●		●		●	●						●
Graphing Who We Are	361	●		●		●	●						●
Great Graffiti	362	●		●									●
Group Inquiry	363	●		●			●	●		●			●

STRATEGY TITLE	Page	INCLUSION	Presenting Self	Social Skills	Agreements	INFLUENCE	Decisions/Problem Solving	Resolving Conflict	Goal Setting	COMMUNITY	Energizer	Celebration	ACADEMICS
Group Problem-Solving	366	●		●		●	●						●
Hagoo	473									●	●		
I Like My Neighbors	473									●	●		
"I'm Proud" Appreciation Circle	367	●	●	●									●
In the Bag	368	●	●	●									●
Interview Circle	369	●	●	●		●	●						●
I Used to Be; We Used to Be	370	●	●	●	●	●							●
Jigsaw	371	●		●		●	●						●
Joy	372	●	●	●									●
Kitchen Kapers	373	●	●			●	●	●					●
Life Map	374	●	●	●									●
Lineup	474									●	●		
Live Wire	375	●	●	●									●
Making a Choice	376			●		●	●						●
Meet Someone Special	378	●	●	●									●
Milling to Music	379	●	●	●									●
Multiple Intelligence Exploration	380	●	●						●				●
Name Wave	474									●	●		
Newspaper Scavenger Hunt	387	●		●		●	●						●
Novel in an Hour	389	●	●	●	●	●	●		●	●			●
Now I Am	390	●		●									●
Observe the Put-Downs	391	●		●	●	●	●						●
On My Back	392	●	●										●

Learning Strategies Matrix

STRATEGY TITLE	Page	INCLUSION	Presenting Self	Social Skills	Agreements	INFLUENCE	Decisions/Problem Solving	Resolving Conflict	Goal Setting	COMMUNITY	Energizer	Celebration	ACADEMICS
One-Minute History	393	●	●	●									●
One Special Thing About Me	394	●	●	●									●
One, Two, Three	395	●		●		●	●						●
Open Forum	396	●	●	●		●	●						●
Our Treasury	397	●		●		●	●						●
Our World Is Changing	398	●		●		●			●				●
Outlines	399	●	●	●									●
Pantomime	401	●	●										●
Paraphrase Passport	402	●		●	●								●
Paraphrasing	403	●		●	●								●
Partner Introduction	404	●	●	●									●
Path-Maze	405					●	●			●			●
Peer-Response Huddle	407	●		●		●	●						●
Peer-Response Tic-Tac-Toe	408			●		●	●						●
Pen Pals	474									●	●		●
People Hunt	409	●	●	●									●
People Patterns	474									●	●		
People Puzzles	413	●		●									●
Perception and Transmission...Information	414	●		●		●		●					●
Personal Contract	416	●		●		●	●	●	●				●
Personal Journal	417	●	●										●
Problem Solving...Appreciative Inquiry	418					●	●						●
Productive Learning Groups	420	●	●	●		●	●	●	●				●

STRATEGY TITLE	Page	INCLUSION	Presenting Self	Social Skills	Agreements	INFLUENCE	Decisions/Problem Solving	Resolving Conflict	Goal Setting	COMMUNITY	Energizer	Celebration	ACADEMICS
Put Down the Put-Downs	421	●	●		●	●		●					●
Put Yourself on the Line	422	●		●		●	●						●
Rain	474									●	●		
Reason to Roam	423	●		●	●	●	●						●
Reasons and Alternatives	425	●		●									●
Reflecting Feelings	426	●		●		●		●					●
Reporting Information...Intelligences	428					●	●		●				●
Roles People Play	429	●		●		●		●					●
Self-Esteem Cards	432	●	●	●									●
Shred the Put-Downs	433		●			●	●	●					●
Shuffle Your Buns	475									●	●		
Singing the Blues	434	●	●	●									●
Slip Game	435	●	●	●									●
Snowball	475									●	●		
Snowball I-Messages	437	●		●									●
Something Good	438	●	●	●									●
Something I Cherish	439	●	●	●									●
Space Pioneers	440	●		●		●	●						●
Spider Web	442	●	●	●						●		●	●
Student-Developed Lesson Plans	443	●		●		●	●						●
Study Buddies	444					●	●						●
Suggestion Circle	445	●		●		●	●	●					●
Taking a Closer Look	446	●		●		●	●						●

STRATEGY TITLE	Page	INCLUSION	Presenting Self	Social Skills	Agreements	INFLUENCE	Decisions/Problem Solving	Resolving Conflict	Goal Setting	COMMUNITY	Energizer	Celebration	ACADEMICS
Teaching Agreements	448	●		●	●	●	●						●
Teaching I-Messages	449	●		●		●		●					●
Teaching Listening	450	●		●									●
Teaching Paraphras'g/Reflect'g Feelings	451	●		●									●
That's Me—That's Us!	452	●	●							●		●	●
The Ideal Classroom	453	●	●	●		●	●	●	●				●
The Week in Perspective	454	●	●	●									●
Third-Party Mediation	455	●		●		●	●	●					●
Three Ball Pass	475									●	●		
Three for Me!	456	●	●	●	●	●	●		●	●			●
Thumbs Up, Thumbs Down	457					●	●						●
Tower Building	458	●		●		●	●						●
Tribal Peer Coaching	459	●		●		●	●						●
Tribe Mimes/Role-Play	460	●	●			●		●					●
Tribe Portrait	461	●	●	●									●
Tribes Team Together	462	●	●	●						●			●
Two for Tuesday	463	●	●	●	●					●		●	●
Two Truths and a Lie	476									●	●		
Urgent!	464	●		●		●	●						●
What We Need from Each Other	465	●			●	●			●	●			●
What's In Your Wallet?	466	●	●	●									●
What's On Your Mind?	467	●	●	●		●	●	●		●			●
What's the Tint of Your Glasses?	468	●		●		●		●					●

STRATEGY TITLE	Page	INCLUSION	Presenting Self	Social Skills	Agreements	INFLUENCE	Decisions/Problem Solving	Resolving Conflict	Goal Setting	COMMUNITY	Energizer	Celebration	ACADEMICS
When I Really Want to Learn Something!	469	●	●	●	●	●	●		●	●			●
Where Do I Stand?	470	●	●	●		●	●						●
Wishful Thinking	471	●	●	●									●
Zap	476									●	●		
Zoom, Zoom, Brake!	476									●	●		

Active Ignoring

▶ TIME   30 minutes

▶ GROUPING   tribes

▶ MATERIALS none

▶ DEVELOPMENTAL TASKS
    Independence/Autonomy
    Social Competency
    Sense of Purpose
    Problem Solving

OPTIONS

This may be a useful strategy to improve attentive listening skills while discussing content.

Choose an event in literature or history (or a current event) and discuss the active ignoring that took place and its effects and consequences.

Objectives

1. To realize the importance of attentive listening in relationships
2. To be aware of nonverbal behavior as part of communication
3. To promote awareness of the pain experienced by one who is excluded from a group
4. To experience influence

Instructions

1. Have the community sit in tribes.
2. Discuss the importance of inclusion within groups, families, communities, and the class. Tell the students they will conduct a little experiment to learn how people feel when they are excluded.
3. Ask for one volunteer from each tribe. Have the volunteers step out of the room, and wait to be asked to return.
4. Tell the remaining students that they are to talk among themselves in their tribes, and when the volunteers return, to go on talking but to ignore, turn their positions away from, and not listen to the volunteers.
5. While the tribes are choosing what to talk about, tell the volunteers that they are to go back to their tribes and attempt to tell their tribes something special.
6. Allow one minute only for the "ignoring" experience, then stop the activity, and begin with personal reflection questions.
7. If other tribe members want to volunteer, repeat the activity.

Suggested Reflection Questions

PERSONAL REFLECTION
▶ How did you feel when everyone ignored you and went on talking?
▶ How did your feelings change by the end of the minute?

CONTENT (COGNITIVE LEARNING)
▶ How were the other students sitting as they ignored you?
▶ What kinds of gestures did they use while they were talking?
▶ Why is it important to learn what it feels like to be ignored?
▶ What do you think happens to people who are ignored all the time?

COLLABORATIVE (SOCIAL LEARNING)
▶ What social skills were you not using when you were ignoring?
▶ How did you feel ignoring another member?
▶ What can your tribe do to make sure that everyone feels included?

PERSONAL LEARNING
▶ How did you help your group during this activity?
▶ What special strengths did you discover about yourself?

Appreciation

Invite statements of appreciation:
▶ "I appreciated…"
▶ "I liked it when…"

All in the Family

Objectives
1. To build inclusion
2. To promote awareness of how other family members feel

Instructions
1. Ask the students to form groups in different parts of the room according to their birth positions in their families (eldest, youngest, in-betweens, only child).
2. Have each student share with the other members of his or her group:
   - How does it feel to be (firstborn, etc.)?
   - What are the responsibilities he or she has?
   - What are the advantages he or she has?
3. Merge the groups so that the eldest are with the in-betweens, and the only children are with youngest (or mix the groups together whichever way you want).
4. Now ask these groups to share:
   - Who do you think has the most power in your family?
   - How do you feel toward other siblings?
5. Who gets attention in your family and how do they get it?

Suggested Reflection Questions

CONTENT (COGNITIVE LEARNING)
- ▶ What did you learn about birth order and power in a family?
- ▶ What generalizations can you make about birth order?

COLLABORATIVE (SOCIAL LEARNING)
- ▶ What skills did your group use to make this activity successful?
- ▶ How did your group make sure that everyone had a chance to participate fully?

PERSONAL LEARNING
- ▶ How did you feel when you were with others in the same birth position as you?
- ▶ What did you feel about others in the same birth position/different birth position?
- ▶ What did you learn about yourself?
- ▶ How do you contribute to your family in a special way?
- ▶ How can knowing this help you to get along with your sisters and brothers?

Appreciation
Invite statements of appreciation:
- ▶ "I'm a lot like you when…"
- ▶ "I felt good when…"

▶ **TIME** 20 minutes

▶ **GROUPING** subgroups

▶ **MATERIALS** none

▶ **DEVELOPMENTAL TASKS**
Independence/Autonomy
Social Competency
Sense of Purpose

OPTIONS

Students can take on the persona of a literary character or historical figure and infer character responses.

Have students research facts about historical figures including the birth order of those people. Make a graph of the class results of birth orders researched (or the birth orders of students in the class, or the responses to reflection questions).

"Am I Napoleon?"

TIME   20 minutes

GROUPING   community

MATERIALS self-adhesive name tags, colored pencils or felt pens

DEVELOPMENTAL TASKS
Social Competency
Problem Solving

OPTIONS

Use vocabulary words (for example, practice definitions: Am I the word that means "talkative"?)

Use numbers (for example, practice simple equations or order of operations).

Literature: mythology

Social Studies: presidents and historical events

Guidance: careers

Science: Periodic Table elements

Objectives

1. To build inclusion
2. To identify and learn about famous people in history, politics, science, or some other academic content

Instructions

1. Give each person a self-adhesive name tag (an index card and tape can also work) and a pen.
2. Ask each student to print on the card in large block letters the name of some famous person, living or dead.
3. Ask each student to stick his or her "famous person" card onto the back of another student, without letting that student know the name on the tag.
4. Tell the students to find out who they are by milling around and asking other students questions that can be answered "yes" or "no." Students may ask only one question each time they talk to another student. Continue the process until everyone has identified his or her famous name. Simple hints from other students or the teacher may be given to help those having a difficult time.

Suggested Reflection Questions

CONTENT (COGNITIVE LEARNING)
▶ Who were some of the famous people?
▶ What kinds of questions did you ask?
▶ What do you know about the person whose name was placed onto your back?

COLLABORATIVE (SOCIAL LEARNING)
▶ How did you help each other successfully identify your famous people?
▶ What effect did this activity have on the community?

PERSONAL LEARNING
▶ In what ways do you identity with your famous person?
▶ What special qualities do you have in common with any of the famous people?
▶ What skills did you use to discover who your famous person was?

Appreciation

Invite statements of appreciation:
▶ "I liked it when…"
▶ "I'm a lot like you when…"

A Poem by Our Tribe

Objectives

1. To write a tribe poem using individual member contributions
2. To demonstrate synergism and inclusion within the tribe
3. To develop an appreciation of individual contributions to a tribe effort and to experience influence

Instructions

1. Have the community meet in tribes. Tell the students they will be writing a tribe poem.
2. Assign roles for each tribe member:
   - Taskmaster: gets materials and monitors the time
   - Recorder: makes a final copy of the poem
   - Facilitator: ensures that each tribe member's ideas are heard and respected
   - Reader: reads the final version of the poem to the community
3. Have the taskmasters obtain three cards for each tribe member and a different colored felt pen for each.
4. Write on the chalkboard the following sentence starters for use in the tribal poem:
   - I wish…I dreamed…
   - I used to be…but now I am…
   - I seem to be…but really I am…
5. Tell your students: "Here are a number of ways to start a tribe poem. Put your heads together in your tribes. Choose the sentence starter you like best or make up your own."
6. Ask each tribe member to take a piece of scratch paper and write as many versions of the completed sentence as possible during the time available (five to ten minutes).
7. Ask each tribe member to choose his or her two best lines and write one line on each of two cards.
8. Explain that each tribe will put together its poem as follows (steps may be written on the board):
   - each tribe member reads his or her two cards to the tribe
   - the tribe gives positive feedback (feelings, words, etc. that they liked) after each tribe member shares

   When all the tribe members have shared, the tribe cooperates to:
   - pick at least one card from each tribe member
   - decide in what order the lines should go in the tribe poem (the tribe may decide to modify lines only with the consent of the author)
   - decide on a one- or two-word title
9. When the tribe members have agreed on the order of the lines and the title, have the Recorder make a final copy and have all the tribe members sign the poem.
10. Ask the tribes to post their poems, and have each tribe's Reader take turns reading their poem to the class.

▶ **TIME**   50 minutes

▶ **GROUPING** tribes

▶ **MATERIALS** scratch paper, 3 x 5-inch cards, felt pens

▶ **DEVELOPMENTAL TASKS**
   Independence/Autonomy
   Sense of Purpose

OPTIONS

Use this strategy at the end of the quarter, semester, year, or some substantial period of time.

Have students write a poem about an object (personal or classroom), their teacher, classmate, or friend. Suggest certain qualifications, such as physical changes, improvements, insights, etc.

Math: use concepts or topic, e.g., "Congruent seems to be... but it really is..."

Social Studies: "Democracy seems to be... but it really is..."

Health: "Smoking used to be... but now..."

Suggested Reflection Questions

CONTENT (COGNITIVE LEARNING)
▶ What did you learn about writing poetry?
▶ Why would you like to express your feelings using poetry?

COLLABORATIVE (SOCIAL LEARNING)
▶ How were your ideas encouraged and honored by your tribe?
▶ Which agreement is the most important for your tribe to honor in a strategy like this?

PERSONAL LEARNING
▶ How did you help your tribe? What special strengths or talents did you use?
▶ How did you encourage other tribe members to contribute?

Appreciation
Invite statements of appreciation:
▶ "Thank you, (name), for…"
▶ "It was great when…"

Adapted from "Writing a Group Poem," by Nan & Ted Graves, Cooperative Learning, Vol. 11, No. 4, July, 1991

Appreciating Others

Objectives

1. To increase awareness of the importance of stating appreciation
2. To practice the Tribes agreements
3. To provide for initial inclusion
4. To discover personal gifts

Instructions

1. Pass out the "Appreciating Others" worksheet to all class members.
2. In the front of the room post a large visual of the worksheet from which you can use as a model.
3. Ask each student to fill in the boxes with positive statements—one to self, best friend, family member, and a classmate.
4. Ask the students to meet in tribes to share their positive statements.
5. Have one member of each tribe record all the core ideas that are included on the tribe members' worksheets.
6. Ask the recorder from each tribe to report the summaries to the community.
7. Suggest that students tell one of their statements to the person to whom it was written.

Suggested Reflection Questions

CONTENT (COGNITIVE LEARNING)

▶ Why did you learn to give statements of appreciation?
▶ What were three statements shared by your tribe members?

COLLABORATIVE (SOCIAL LEARNING)

▶ How can making statements of appreciation help a tribe work together better?
▶ Why is it important to make statements of appreciation to friends, family, and to others?
▶ What do you appreciate about the community or your tribe?

PERSONAL LEARNING

▶ How do you feel when you receive a statement of appreciation from someone else?
▶ What special qualities do you appreciate about yourself?
▶ What did you learn about yourself from this activity?

Appreciation

Invite statements of appreciation:

▶ "I liked it when…"
▶ "Thank you for…"

▶ **TIME** 45 minutes

▶ **GROUPING** community, tribes

▶ **MATERIALS** "Appreciating Others" worksheets, pencils, large paper, felt pens

▶ **DEVELOPMENTAL TASKS** Independence/Autonomy Social Competency

OPTIONS

Ask how many students would commit to using at least one appreciation statement every day. Have tribes write contracts to do so. Post the contracts and review them regularly.

APPRECIATING OTHERS

Self	Best Friend
Family Member	**Classmate**

Suggested positive statement forms:

_____, I liked it when you…

_____, I appreciate it when…

_____, I'm glad you…

_____, thanks for…

Architects and Builders

Objectives

1. To promote inclusion and influence
2. To work cooperatively on tasks
3. To practice subject-related vocabulary

Instructions

1. Prepare a drawing, picture or collage of items that are familiar to the students. (*Note:* You may include subject-related material in the collage such as geometric shapes, representations of concepts, vocabulary, geographical locations, etc.)
2. Have the tribes designate one person from each tribe to be the "architect." All others are "builders." (*Note:* The method for choosing the "architect" can be a strategy all by itself.)
3. Have the architects leave the room or move to a separate area of the room to study the "plans" (collage).
4. Ask the architects to return to their tribes. Architects must direct the builders to construct a duplicate of the prepared collage using verbal directions *only*. Architects may study the plans as often as they wish during the building process. (*Note:* It is helpful to have architects clasp hands behind their backs to avoid gestures while giving instructions. No pointing allowed!)
5. Allow 15–20 minutes for construction.
6. Call time, and allow 5 minutes for the community to circulate and admire each tribe's creation. If you chose, have an impartial judge choose the most accurate/most creative/most unusual replica.

Suggested Reflection Questions

CONTENT (COGNITIVE LEARNING)
▶ What did you discover about a community member during this activity?
▶ What do you think about the roles and rules in this activity?
▶ What improvements could you make for future "architects and builders?"

COLLABORATIVE (SOCIAL LEARNING)
▶ What was easy/difficult for your tribe about this task?
▶ How were the agreements honored and practiced by your tribe?

PERSONAL LEARNING
▶ How much did you participate?
▶ What strengths or skills did you contribute?
▶ What did you enjoy most about this activity?
▶ Would you rather be an "architect" or a "builder?" Why?

Appreciation

Invite statements of appreciation:
▶ "I appreciated it when…"
▶ "(Name), you were really helpful when…"
▶ "(Name), thank you for…"

▶ **TIME**   40 minutes

▶ **GROUPING** tribes

▶ **MATERIALS** pre-cut shapes, scissors, glue, colored paper

▶ **DEVELOPMENTAL TASKS**
Independence/Autonomy
Social Competency
Problem Solving

OPTIONS

Use geometric shapes for a math review. Assign challenges to group members: one person can't speak, one person may only use one hand, one person speaks a totally foreign (possibly made-up) language.

A Special Friend I Know

▶ **TIME** 30 minutes

▶ **GROUPING** community, tribes

▶ **MATERIALS** none

▶ **DEVELOPMENTAL TASKS**
Independence/Autonomy
Sense of Purpose

Objectives

1. To build community inclusion
2. To share feelings about an aspect of school
3. To experience the "Think—Pair—Share" structure*
4. To discover gifts

Instructions

1. Have the community meet in tribes. Ask the students to think silently for a moment about the following questions:
   - When were you a special friend to someone?
   - What made you a special friend?
   - What did you do or say?
2. Invite each student to turn to a tribe member and share his or her special qualities by speaking in the present tense. Example:
   - "Marie, I would like you as my special friend because (two or three of her special qualities)."

Suggested Reflection Questions

CONTENT (COGNITIVE LEARNING)
▶ What qualities did you share that were similar?
▶ Why is friendship important?

COLLABORATIVE (SOCIAL LEARNING)
▶ Why is being a good listener important in being a good friend?
▶ How did this strategy help you as a tribe/community?
▶ How did the community or your tribe make this activity successful?

PERSONAL LEARNING
▶ How did you help your tribe during this strategy?
▶ What special qualities do you have that make you a good friend to others?
▶ What qualities would you like to develop more of?

Appreciation

Invite statements of appreciation:
▶ "I liked it when…"
▶ "It helped me when…"
▶ "I admired you when…"

OPTIONS

Use the question, "When could I have been a (special) friend?" This can be particularly effective when discussing bullying issues (i.e., bystanders who do nothing vs. bystanders who do something).

This is a structure from Cooperative Learning Resources, *by Spencer Kagan.*

Boasters

Objectives
1. To make statements of appreciation to self and others
2. To build self-esteem
3. To build inclusion
4. To discover gifts

Instructions
1. Duplicate cell phone on the next page (one for each student), or have each student prepare one for him or herself.
2. Ask the community to meet in tribes.
3. Have each student write his or her name on the top of the phone.
4. Instruct the tribe members to pass the paper around the tribe so that each tribe member can write a positive statement or text message on each other tribe member's phone.
5. Have a discussion about complimenting yourself and how it is different than bragging. Then ask each student to write a positive statement or text message about him or herself on his or her own phone.

Suggested Reflection Questions

CONTENT (COGNITIVE LEARNING)
▶ Why is it important to be able to make positive statements about others?
▶ What are two positive statements that you made to others/they made to you?

COLLABORATIVE (SOCIAL LEARNING)
▶ How can making positive statements to each other help us work together better?
▶ What did you appreciate about your group or tribe during this activity?

PERSONAL LEARNING
▶ How did you feel when you knew someone else was writing on your phone?
▶ How did you feel when you read the comments on your phone?
▶ What special gifts do you appreciate about yourself?
▶ Do you ever compliment yourself?
▶ Make a plan for complimenting yourself at least once every day.

Appreciation
Invite statements of appreciation:
▶ "I'm glad you notice that I…"
▶ "I felt good when…"

▶ **TIME**   30–45 minutes

▶ **GROUPING**   tribes, subgroups

▶ **MATERIALS**   12-inch-high cutouts of cell phones

▶ **DEVELOPMENTAL TASKS**
   Independence/Autonomy
   Social Competency
   Sense of Purpose

OPTIONS

Write a text message that summarizes a given reading assignment.

BOASTERS

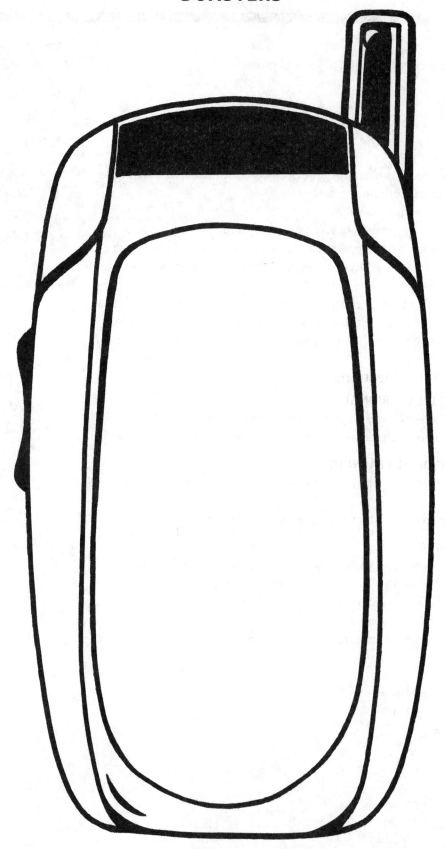

This page may be duplicated for classroom use.

Brainstorming

Objectives

1. To energize a tribe
2. To promote inclusion and influence
3. To experience the fun and creative power of brainstorming as a decision-making or problem-solving technique

Instructions

1. Ask each tribe to appoint a recorder to jot down all the ideas on paper, chalkboard, or newsprint as fast as ideas are called out.
2. Instruct the tribes on the "DOVE" rules that they need to follow in order to "brainstorm."

   D defer judgment

   O off beat, original

   V vast number

   E expand, elaborate

3. Have the community meet in tribes. Explain that each tribe will have five minutes to call out and write down as many ideas as possible on a subject. Examples:
   - "How could we design a better bicycle—one for more enjoyment, efficiency, and comfort than ordinary bikes?"
   - Other possible subjects: better bedroom, car, school cafeteria, school
4. Stop the brainstorming after five minutes. Ask each recorder to read his or her tribe's list. Lead applause after each tribe's creative ideas.
5. If time allows, have the tribes draw their creations. Find a way to include everyone in the tribe.
6. Use sticker voting (Group Problem Solving, p. 366) for decision making.

Suggested Reflection Questions

CONTENT (COGNITIVE LEARNING)

▶ Why is brainstorming fun?

▶ How do the "DOVE" rules help you to brainstorm?

COLLABORATIVE (SOCIAL LEARNING)

▶ What would have happened if we had judged, commented, or discussed ideas as they were offered?

▶ How could you tell that your tribe members were enjoying themselves?

▶ What did your tribe members do well as they followed the "DOVE" rules?

PERSONAL LEARNING

▶ How much did you participate?

▶ How did you contribute to your tribe?

▶ What special qualities did you bring to this activity?

Appreciation

Invite statements of appreciation:

▶ "I liked it when you said…"

▶ "Your suggestions helped me to…"

▶ **TIME**   20 minutes

▶ **GROUPING** tribes

▶ **MATERIALS** markers, large paper

▶ **DEVELOPMENTAL TASKS**
   Independence/Autonomy
   Social Competency
   Problem Solving

OPTIONS

Use for classroom issues or decisions.

Brainstorm possible endings to a story, a list of "meaningful sentences," or multiple examples of a theme.

Government: Use to plan a community service project, or brainstorm ways to improve school spirit.

Any subject: Brainstorm possible culminating projects

Building a Time Machine

- ▶ **TIME** 45 minutes
- ▶ **GROUPING** tribes
- ▶ **MATERIALS** assorted junk
- ▶ **DEVELOPMENTAL TASKS**
  Independence/Autonomy
  Problem Solving

OPTIONS

Use this experience as a writing prompt, for example, have students write answers to reflection questions, the pros and cons of time travel, or a time they would like to travel to and why.

For science, use as a team building activity prior to a project like robotics.

For history, create the time machine from the perspective of a historical figure.

Objectives

1. To encourage tribe members to create something together
2. To have tribes present their creations to the community
3. To experience influence

Instructions

1. Ask the students if they have ever read any books or seen any movies about time machines.
2. Call on a few students to share what they know about time machines.
3. Let the students know that their tribes will have an opportunity to build a time machine.
4. Have the community meet in tribes. Give each group equal amounts of "junk" to build their time machines.
5. Give the tribes the next twenty minutes to construct their time machines.
6. Have the tribes take turns presenting their time machines to the class.
7. Have each student write a letter to someone in another time that could be delivered by his or her tribe's time machine.

Suggested Reflection Questions

CONTENT (COGNITIVE LEARNING)
- ▶ What decisions did your tribe have to make?
- ▶ Why is it important to use your imagination?
- ▶ What did you learn by doing this strategy?

COLLABORATIVE (SOCIAL LEARNING)
- ▶ How did your tribe make its machine?
- ▶ What really helped your tribe to be creative and innovative?
- ▶ What special strengths do you want to continue to develop as a tribe?

PERSONAL LEARNING
- ▶ How did you help your tribe build the time machine?
- ▶ How did you feel while you were working?
- ▶ What special talents did you use/discover about yourself?

Appreciation

Invite statements of appreciation:
- ▶ "(Name), you helped when…"
- ▶ "I liked it when…"

Bumper Sticker

Objectives
1. To present something special about oneself
2. To build inclusion
3. To encourage attentive listening

Instructions
1. Review agreements.
2. Give each student a long strip of paper and a marker or colored pencil with which to create a "bumper sticker" that he or she would enjoy displaying on his or her automobile bumper.
3. Have each student in turn share his or her bumper sticker with the community. Remind everyone to give his or her full attention to the speaker.
4. Tell the students they may ask questions, and express mutual feelings and concerns after everyone has shared.

Suggested Reflection Questions

CONTENT (COGNITIVE LEARNING)
▶ What similar kinds of things did you put on your bumper stickers?
▶ What is one special thing you learned about another student?

COLLABORATIVE (SOCIAL LEARNING)
▶ How well did everyone listen when you shared your bumper sticker?
▶ What did the group do to help others feel more comfortable when they shared?

PERSONAL LEARNING
▶ How did you feel as you shared?
▶ How does your bumper sticker express your unique qualities as a person in this community?
▶ Would you want to put your bumper sticker on your car or your bicycle? Why or why not?

Appreciation
Invite statements of appreciation:
▶ "I liked it when…"
▶ "I admired you for…"

▶ **TIME**   30 minutes

▶ **GROUPING**   community, tribes

▶ **MATERIALS** colored paper strips, colored pencils or markers

▶ **DEVELOPMENTAL TASKS**
   Independence/Autonomy
   Social Competency
   Sense of Purpose

OPTIONS

Use subject area topics, such as "Why study Social Studies?"

Design a bumper sticker pedicting the theme of a book, social studies issue, or math equation.

Campaign Manager

► TIME 60 minutes

► GROUPING tribes

► MATERIALS small circles
with 6-inch diameter,
3 x 5-inch cards, pencils,
small bags

► DEVELOPMENTAL TASKS
Independence/Autonomy
Social Competency
Sense of Purpose

OPTIONS

Use characters from literature, history or current events; or study candidates in a current election.

Variation: Teacher prepares slips of paper for students to draw from a bag. Name may be a literature character, historical figure, scientist, etc.

Slips may be duplicated for student groups to form a campaign committee.

Objectives

1. To build inclusion
2. To foster positive feelings in the community
3. To build self-esteem

Instructions

1. Have students meet in their tribes.
2. Pass out paper circles, cards, and a small bag to each tribe.
3. Instruct each tribe member to write his or her name on a slip of paper and drop it into a bag. Then have each member draw a name out of the bag (making sure he or she doesn't draw his or her own).
4. Tell the students that each is to be the "campaign manager" for the person whose name he or she drew, a person who has been nominated for "Wonderful Person of the Year."
5. Explain that each student will design a campaign button on the circle of paper, and list three good campaign statements on the card to promote his or her nominee. The campaign managers may interview their candidates if they need more information on special qualities.
6. Have the campaign managers deliver the campaign speeches (using the cards) and present their nominees with their campaign buttons. Lead applause and cheering.

Suggested Reflection Questions

CONTENT (COGNITIVE LEARNING)
► What similarities did you notice between the campaign buttons and the presentations?
► Why is it important to make a good campaign speech?

COLLABORATIVE (SOCIAL LEARNING)
► What social skills did your tribe need to make this activity successful?
► What do you value most about being a member of your tribe?

PERSONAL LEARNING
► What special qualities did your campaign manager present about you? How did you feel?
► What skills did you use to present your candidate's campaign?
► What strengths would you bring to the job if you were a campaign manager?

Appreciation
Invite statements of appreciation:
► "I liked it when…"
► "I felt good when…"

Career Choices

Objectives

1. To help the students make choices and honor each other's choices
2. To give the students an opportunity to share some of their career views
3. To experience influence

Instructions

1. Make two signs with a career choice such as "chemist" and "marine biologist" (or use two other occupations) written on each of them and put them up on different sides of the room.
2. Tell your students that they are going to be asked to make a choice about occupations related to the field of science or health.
3. They will make their choice by moving to one side of the room or the other, to stand under the sign of the occupation of their choice. Example: Point out the sign "chemist" on one side of the room and "marine biologist" on the other side of the room.
4. Have students discuss in groups of 3 or 4 why they chose the occupation.
5. Repeat 2 or 3 times with other occupations. See examples under "Options."

Suggested Reflection Questions

CONTENT (COGNITIVE LEARNING)

▶ Why is it important to make choices?
▶ What other occupations did you consider?

COLLABORATIVE (SOCIAL LEARNING)

▶ In what ways did the community honor the agreements?
▶ Which agreement might be the most important in a strategy like this?
▶ What do you appreciate the most about this community?

PERSONAL LEARNING

▶ Why did you make the choice you did?
▶ How did you feel about making your choice public?
▶ How do your special talents or strengths relate to the choice you made?

Appreciation

Invite statements of appreciation:

▶ "I appreciated it when…"
▶ "It was great when…"

▶ **TIME**   40 minutes

▶ **GROUPING**   community

▶ **MATERIALS**   career signs

▶ **DEVELOPMENTAL TASKS**
Independence/Autonomy
Sense of Purpose

OPTIONS

Use current social issues (in school, society, the world). Use scientific hypotheses.

Use as reflective practice (for example, choose a mathematical concept you can explain thoroughly and correctly).

Variation: Choose multiple intelligences or career paths. Examples: high school teacher, elementary school teacher, dentist, surgeon, carpenter, electrician, potter, painter, bus driver, taxi driver, accountant, architect.

Cares–Concerns–Compliments

▶ **TIME**   20 minutes

▶ **GROUPING**   community, tribes

▶ **MATERIALS**   none

▶ **DEVELOPMENTAL TASKS**
Independence/Autonomy
Social Competency
Sense of Purpose

OPTIONS

This activity can also be used on Monday mornings to review the weekend or to share "something interesting, positive, or exciting."

Objectives

1. To build inclusion and influence
2. To gather and appreciate different points of view

Instructions

1. Have the students sit in a community circle, or in their tribes.
2. Review the tribes agreements.
3. Ask the students, "Before we begin our day, who has a care, concern, or compliment to share?"
4. Allow the students to share briefly one at a time with the community or in their tribes.
5. After all students who want to have shared, allow the students to open topics for extended discussion.

Suggested Reflection Questions

CONTENT (COGNITIVE LEARNING)

▶ What did you find out about your community/tribe members?
▶ What thoughts or feelings do you share in common with others?

COLLABORATIVE (SOCIAL LEARNING)

▶ How were the agreements honored and practiced?
▶ In what way(s) did this activity help the community or your tribe?
▶ What makes you proud to be a member of this community/your tribe?

PERSONAL LEARNING

▶ How do you usually express your cares, concerns and compliments?
▶ How much did you participate?
▶ How did you help the community or your tribe in a special way?

Appreciation

Invite statements of appreciation:

▶ "I appreciate…"
▶ "(Name), thank you for…"
▶ "(Name), you were really helpful when…"

Celebrity Sign-In

Objectives

1. To structure a cooperative learning experience for a history topic
2. To enhance communication skills
3. To experience influence

Instructions

1. Give each tribe the name of a celebrity or historical character, and allow time for each tribe to learn as much as they can about the person.
2. Set up a row of chairs in front of the room facing the class.
3. Ask each tribe to select a tribe member to "be" their celebrity.
4. Have each celebrity sign in on the chalkboard and then take a seat in the row of chairs ("interview panel").
5. Ask each character to tell the other panel members about his or her prominence in history. After they have all done so, call time out and let tribe members huddle with their character to remind them of more data to present. After several huddles, invite the audience to ask questions of the "celebrity." Allow tribe members to help answer.
6. Lead rounds of applause after each character's performance.

Suggested Reflection Questions

CONTENT (COGNITIVE LEARNING)
- ▶ What did you learn about the different celebrities?
- ▶ Why is this an interesting way to learn new information?
- ▶ What values were reflected by the characters?
- ▶ In what other ways can you use this activity?

COLLABORATIVE (SOCIAL LEARNING)
- ▶ What did tribe members do to support their celebrity?
- ▶ In what ways did your tribe work well together to make this activity successful?

PERSONAL LEARNING
- ▶ How did you feel while you were portraying your character?
- ▶ What strengths or skills did you use while you were portraying your character?
- ▶ How did you help your tribe or the community in a special way?

Appreciation

Invite statements of appreciation:
- ▶ "(Name), I respect you for…"
- ▶ "(Name), I liked the way you portrayed…"

- ▶ **TIME** varies
- ▶ **GROUPING** community, tribes
- ▶ **MATERIALS** row of chairs in front of room
- ▶ **DEVELOPMENTAL TASKS** Independence/Autonomy Social Competency

OPTIONS

Use people in the news, history, and literature.

Use content standard topics, inviting students to choose a tribe member to explain the topic.

Chain Reaction

▶ **TIME**   15–30 minutes

▶ **GROUPING** community, tribes

▶ **MATERIALS** none

▶ **DEVELOPMENTAL TASKS**
Independence/Autonomy
Social Competency
Sense of Purpose

OPTIONS

Practice vocabulary words, story sequence (retelling), how to construct a persuasive essay, steps in solving quadratic equations.

Objectives

1. To build inclusion and influence
2. To increase communication skills
3. To share personal interests, opinions and ideas
4. To ask each other questions about subject matter

Instructions

Note: This is a good activity for students to help each other prepare for a test.

1. Have the community meet in tribes.
2. Remind the students of their right to pass and to honor the other agreements. Remind tribe members to give full, caring attention.
3. Have one tribe member begin by asking a question of a second tribe member. Have the second tribe member answer the question and then ask another question of a third tribe member. Instruct the tribes to continue the chain until each tribe member has answered and then asked a question. In large tribes have students ask the persons directly across from them. This helps the students to speak loudly enough.
4. Explain that questions may be autobiographical or deal with curriculum or a number of issues (politics, hobbies, education, friendship, family interests).

Option: Have students perpare or brainstorm 3–5 individual questions prior to the activity.

Suggested Reflection Questions

CONTENT (COGNITIVE LEARNING)

▶ What did you learn about your tribe members?
▶ Why is this a good way to find out information about each other?

COLLABORATIVE (SOCIAL LEARNING)

▶ In what ways did your tribe honor the tribal agreements?
▶ How do the agreements protect you?
▶ How well did the group give full, caring attention?
▶ What do you feel about your tribe members now?

PERSONAL LEARNING

▶ How did you feel when it was your turn?
▶ What skills did you use to help your tribe make this activity successful?
▶ What unique qualities did you discover about yourself?

Appreciation

Invite statements of appreciation:

▶ "I liked it when…"
▶ "I admired your honesty when…"

Client-Consultants

Objectives

1. To encourage active listening
2. To experience group support for a concern
3. To assist a peer, colleague, or friend to resolve a problem
4. To promote influence

Instructions

1. Have the class sit in their tribes.
2. Tell the students that each will have a turn expressing a concern or a problem that he or she may be experiencing at school. Each person will have a turn at being a "client" while the other tribe members are listening as "consultants." Explain that the consultants:
   - are to be non-judgmental
   - are not to tell the client what to do
   - are to offer alternative suggestions to the client for solving the problem
   - and may ask for additional information if it seems helpful or necessary.
3. Review or remind the students about their caring listening skills (especially paraphrasing).
4. Allow approximately 10 minutes for each client's turn.

Suggested Reflection Questions

CONTENT (COGNITIVE LEARNING)

▶ What solutions did the consultants suggest for your problem?
▶ Why is having a consultant helpful to you sometimes?

COLLABORATIVE (SOCIAL LEARNING)

▶ What social skills did your tribe members need to be good consultants?
▶ How could you tell when the consultants were really listening well?
▶ How does this activity affect the feeling tone in your tribe?

PERSONAL LEARNING

▶ How does it feel to share your own concern with others?
▶ What did you learn about yourself that you can be proud of?
▶ How did you help others in your group during this activity?

Appreciation

Invite statements of appreciation:
▶ "I felt (feeling) when you..."
▶ "I cared a lot when you said..."
▶ "I feel I would like to help you..."
▶ "I admired you for..."

▶ **TIME** 30 minutes

▶ **GROUPING** tribes

▶ **MATERIALS** none

▶ **DEVELOPMENTAL TASKS**
Independence/Autonomy
Social Competency
Sense of Purpose
Problem Solving

OPTIONS

Use for problems such as current events, general school issues, or social issues that are relevant to students (i.e., dating, peer pressure).

Community Circle

▶ TIME   20 minutes

▶ GROUPING community

▶ MATERIALS none

▶ DEVELOPMENTAL TASKS
  Social Competency
  Sense of Purpose

1. To build inclusion and community
2. To teach social skills

Instructions

1. Have the community sit in a large circle.
2. Review the Tribes agreements.
3. Ask a "Question-of-the-Day."
   Example: "I feel excited when…"
   (*Note:* The best questions are those most relevant to the participants' experiences, interests and cultures. See more suggested questions below.)
4. Have everyone respond in turn to the question. Allow time at the end for those who passed to respond if they desire.

Suggested Reflection Questions

CONTENT (COGNITIVE LEARNING)
▶ What is one new thing you learned in the community?
▶ Why is it sometimes difficult to find something to say in a large group?

COLLABORATIVE (SOCIAL LEARNING)
▶ In what ways did the community listen to what you shared?
▶ How does sharing this way help our class or community?

PERSONAL LEARNING
▶ What new things did you notice about yourself during this activity?
▶ How did you contribute to the community today?

Appreciation

Invite statements of appreciation:
▶ "I liked it when…"
▶ "I feel like you when…"

OPTIONS

Use questions to review material before a test, to practice answering in complete sentences, or to practice using vocabulary words in context.

Suggested Questions-of-the-Day

1. I feel happy when…
2. I feel sad when…
3. I feel angry when…
4. I feel scared when…
5. I feel excited when…
6. I feel annoyed when…
7. I feel stressed when…
8. I feel alone when…
9. The scariest thing is…
10. My favorite hobby is…
11. My favorite pet is…
12. My favorite food/junk food is…

13. My favorite T.V. show is…

14. My favorite weekend activity is…

15. My favorite song is…

16. My favorite type of music is…

17. My favorite book is…

18. My favorite sport is…

19. My favorite color is…

20. My favorite weather is…

21. Rain makes me feel…

22. Wind makes me feel…

23. Sunshine makes me feel…

24. Snow makes me feel…

25. Fog makes me feel…

26. Today I feel…

27. When I think of blue, I think of…

28. When I think of red, I think of…

29. When I think of green, I think of…

30. When I think of yellow, I think of…

31. When I think of orange, I think of…

32. When I think of black, I think of…

33. When I think of brown, I think of…

34. If I were an animal, I would be…

35. If I were a building, I would be…

36. If I were a famous actor/actress, I would be…

37. If I were a famous athlete, I would be…

38. When I think of starting high school, I…

39. When I graduate from high school, I want to…

40. When I become an adult, I want to…

41. When I start my career, I want to…

42. When I daydream, I usually think about…

43. Someday I want to…

44. I can't wait until…

45. Friends are…

46. Families are…

47. Put downs make me feel…

48. Appreciations make me feel…

49. When I am doing math, I am most like what animal?

50. Relate to the curriculum:

   The best/worst thing about this science project is…

   The main character in the book we are reading is like/not like me when…

   These math problems make me feel…

Community Circle Metaphor

TIME 40 minutes

GROUPING community, pairs

MATERIALS none

DEVELOPMENTAL TASKS
Independence/Autonomy
Sense of Purpose

OPTIONS

Use for conflict resolution (bullying).

Use with content topics, such as "During the Renaissance, (person) was like (animal) because..."

Instead of animals, use geographical features, natural disasters, or inanimate objects.

Objectives
1. To build community inclusion
2. To share feelings about an aspect of school

Instructions
1. Begin with everyone in a community circle. Explain that the students will be completing the following sentence:
   "When I am working on (name a subject such as math, writing, reading, art, music) I am most like a (name an animal) because I (name a behavior or quality)."
2. After brief thinking time, have the students form pairs. Ask the partners to face each other and discuss their answers to the question. Give the partners two to five minutes to share.
3. Ask several pairs to share their answers with the community.

Suggested Reflection Questions

CONTENT (COGNITIVE LEARNING)
▶ What did your answers have in common?

COLLABORATIVE (SOCIAL LEARNING)
▶ Why is sharing with a partner easier than sharing with the community?
▶ What did the community do to make this activity successful?

PERSONAL LEARNING
▶ Did you share as fully as you could? Why or why not?
▶ How did you feel about sharing with your partner?
▶ How did you help your partner?

Appreciation
Invite statements of appreciation:
▶ "It felt good when..."
▶ "One thing I liked about what you said was..."

Confrontation

Objectives
1. To provide a way to work out problems
2. To enhance self-awareness
3. To teach communication skills
4. To encourage influence

Instructions
1. One day when a problem between two students comes to your attention, invite the community to sit in one community circle. Ask the two students for permission to share the problem with the community.
2. State the problem or have the two students involved describe it. Example:
   Tanya: "Dawn keeps spreading rumors about me."
   Dawn: "No, I don't. Tanya is the one who thinks she's better than everyone else."
3. Review the agreements carefully, and ask everyone to listen attentively without comment.
4. Have the two students involved sit facing each other in the center of the circle.
5. Ask each to tell the other what he or she is feeling about the problem by using "I-Messages;" help them phrase the "I-Messages" if you need to.
6. Ask each to repeat exactly what the other has stated.
7. Then ask each what he or she could do to help solve the problem.
8. If they have difficulty, turn to the rest of the community for suggestions. Tell the students not to judge who is right or wrong.
9. If the discussion wanders, ask questions to redirect the students to the problem. If the problem cannot be solved, set a time to work with the pair privately.
10. When a solution is reached, have the students write a contract with each other.

Suggested Reflection Questions

CONTENT (COGNITIVE LEARNING)
▶ Why is it important to tell someone that you are upset with him or her?
▶ What do you think will happen now?

COLLABORATIVE (SOCIAL LEARNING)
▶ What kind of listeners were you?
▶ Why is listening important when you're involved in a conflict?
▶ How did the community help the students work out the problem?

PERSONAL LEARNING
▶ How do you feel right now?
▶ What feelings did you have as the discussion was going on?
▶ How did you help the two students or the community in a special way?

Appreciation
Invite statements of appreciation:
▶ "I admire you for..."
▶ "I learned that..."

▶ **TIME**   15–40 min.

▶ **GROUPING** full group

▶ **MATERIALS** none

▶ **DEVELOPMENTAL TASKS**
   Independence/Autonomy
   Social Competency
   Problem Solving

OPTIONS

Use school or social issues pertinent to students' lives.

Use to determine persuasive writing topics, or have students actually write about the decision-making process to practice different genres (persuasive, narrative, and expository).

Consensus-Building

TIME 25–40 minutes

GROUPING tribes, pairs

MATERIALS 5 x 7-inch file cards

DEVELOPMENTAL TASKS
Independence/Autonomy
Problem Solving

OPTIONS

Have tribes research an important event in history and then build consensus on a question related to the topic.

Have tribes use this strategy to decide how to research or present a curriculum topic to the class.

Variation: Student clubs can decide on activities and events, selecting fundraiser projects or community service activities.

Objectives

1. To reach a consensus or agreement on shared concerns, ideas, or priorities
2. To build tribe cohesiveness
3. To experience influence

Instructions

1. Have the students meet in tribes, and distribute 5 x 7-inch cards to each person.
2. Discuss the importance of groups having a way to make decisions together in a way that gives every member a way to contribute his or her ideas.
3. State a question that students will try to come to an agreement on through discussion. Example: Which guest speaker would be most interesting for our class?
4. Ask each student to write down five answers to the question.
5. Have two tribe members get together, compare lists and agree on four ideas eliminating all others.
6. Have two pairs get together, compare lists, agree on 4 out of their 8 combined ideas and eliminate the others.
7. Have the tribes report their four final ideas to the class. Keep a list on the board of all ideas. Have the class discuss all of the ideas and eliminate those that seem unworkable or less possible. Then use "sticker voting" to give each student an opportunity to choose his or her three preferred ideas. (See "Group Problem Solving.")
8. Add up the value of the stickers to determine the final choice of the class. The value of the stickers are: Blue=15 points, Red=10 points and Yellow=5 points.

Suggested Reflection Questions

CONTENT (COGNITIVE LEARNING)
▶ What four ideas did your group come up with?

COLLABORATIVE (SOCIAL LEARNING)
▶ Why might making decisions this way be easier/difficult sometimes?
▶ How did your group come to a consensus?
▶ In what ways did your group work together really well?

PERSONAL LEARNING
▶ How did you feel when your tribe made their final choices?
▶ How did you influence your tribe's decision?
▶ What special strengths or skills did you bring to your tribe?

Appreciation
Invite statements of appreciation:
▶ "I like our choices because..."
▶ "I appreciated it when..."
▶ "Our tribe is cool because..."

Cooperation Squares

Objectives

1. To encourage cooperation
2. To help students become aware of their own behaviors that may help or hinder community effort
3. To build inclusion and influence

Instructions

1. Begin the strategy with a community circle discussion of the meaning of cooperation. List on the board the requirements for cooperation as generated by the community.
2. Ask the community to meet in tribes. Describe the activity as a puzzle that only can be solved through cooperation.
3. Hand out one puzzle set (see next page for instructions) to each tribe.
4. Read or state the following instructions aloud:

   "Each tribe should have an envelope containing pieces for forming five squares of equal size. Each square contains three puzzle pieces. Each tribe needs to select five students who each get three puzzle pieces; the other tribe members can be observers. The strategy is complete when each of the five tribe members has formed a perfect square. While doing this, the five tribe members may not speak or signal for puzzle pieces, but they may give puzzle parts to others in the tribe if they think they might help them complete their squares."

5. Now ask each tribe to distribute the puzzle pieces equally among its five chosen members.
6. Have the observers share their observations after the puzzles are completed.

Suggested Reflection Questions

CONTENT (COGNITIVE LEARNING)

▶ What did you learn about nonverbal cooperation?
▶ Why did you do this strategy without talking?

COLLABORATIVE (SOCIAL LEARNING)

▶ What social skills did your tribe need to make this activity successful?
▶ Why is "giving" a social skill?

PERSONAL LEARNING

▶ How did you feel when someone helped your tribe in a special way? When someone did not notice how to help?
▶ In what ways did you help your tribe during this activity?
▶ What special strengths or gifts did you discover about yourself?

Appreciation

Invite statements of appreciation:

▶ "I liked it when..."
▶ "I felt good when..."

▶ **TIME** 30 minutes

▶ **GROUPING** tribes

▶ **MATERIALS** none

▶ **DEVELOPMENTAL TASKS**
  Independence/Autonomy
  Social Competency
  Sense of Purpose
  Problem Solving

OPTIONS

Use only one set of shapes (duplicate one square per tribe), but use words or phrases that determine a complete square (for example, attributes of a character in literature or history, numbers to form an equation that equals 10, synonyms for vocabulary words). For a real challenge, have the students design the shapes and what is written on each piece.

Variation: Student government (develops cooperation skills amongst officers)

Directions For Making A Puzzle Set

A puzzle set consists of one envelope containing fifteen cardboard pieces that are cut in the design below. When properly arranged they form five separate squares of equal size. Each square contains three pieces. Prepare one puzzle set for each group of five persons.

TO PREPARE A PUZZLE SET:

1. Cut out five six by six-inch cardboard squares.
2. Line them up in a row and mark them as illustrated below, penciling the letters a, b, c, etc. lightly, so that they can be easily erased later.
3. Cut each square as marked.

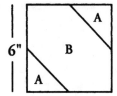 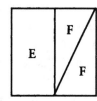 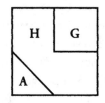 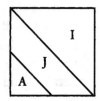

4. Mark 5 envelopes A, B, C, D and E.
5. Place the 15 cardboard pieces, a-j on top of five envelopes as follows:

   A: pieces i, h, e
   B: pieces a, a, a, c
   C: pieces a, j
   D: pieces d, f
   E: pieces g, b, f, c

6. Before inserting the pieces into the envelopes, erase penciled letters and write the appropriate envelope letter on each piece. This will make it easy to return the pieces to the envelopes so that the activity may be used again.

Cruising Careers/Finding Tribes

Objectives

1. To build community inclusion
2. To explore career options
3. To divide people into tribes or learning groups

Instructions

1. Prepare a small slip of paper for each student. Depending on the number of tribes that the community will divide into, select names of different types of jobs or careers. Examples: professional athletes, artists, politicians, engineers, scientists, lawyers, cowboys/girls, teachers, doctors, carpenters, construction workers.
2. Write the name of a career (or use a picture) on each slip so that the students who will be in the "athletes" tribe all have slips marked "athletes," and so on.
3. If you are assigning students to specific tribes, write the name of the student on one side of the slip and the name of the career on the other side.
4. Before distributing the slips, tell the students that they are not to let anyone else know what career names are on their slips.
5. Ask the students to circulate silently while acting out typical activities of the careers named on their slips. Tell them that they need to find the other students who are acting out the same career as themselves.
6. When all the students with the same career names find each other, have the "career tribes" sit together and discuss and reflect.

Suggested Reflection Questions

CONTENT (COGNITIVE LEARNING)

▶ What do you think about this way of finding tribe members?
▶ What made this a fun way to divide into tribes?

COLLABORATIVE (SOCIAL LEARNING)

▶ How did you identify who was in your tribe?
▶ How did your tribe respond when you found each other?
▶ What did the community members do to make this activity successful?

PERSONAL LEARNING

▶ What senses or skills were most helpful to you as you tried to find your tribe members?
▶ Did you discover anything new about yourself while doing this activity?

Appreciation

Invite statements of appreciation:
▶ "I was (feeling) when..."
▶ "Thank you, (name), for..."
▶ "I liked it when..."

▶ **TIME**   15 minutes
▶ **GROUPING** community
▶ **MATERIALS** name slips
▶ **DEVELOPMENTAL TASKS**
    Social Competency

OPTIONS

Have the community divide into tribes by humming or singing familiar tunes.

Multi-cultural and adult groups (teachers and parents) may enjoy using different dance steps.

Reinforce curriculum by using historical or literary characters.

Variations:
1. Tribal dances (ballet, tap, waltz, moonwalk, twist)

2. Barnyard Babble (cow, dog, pig, cat, rooster, horse)

3. Sing-A-Song (current songs)

Current Events Debate Circle

▶ **TIME**   30 minutes

▶ **GROUPING** community

▶ **MATERIALS** none

▶ **SUBJECT**   history, social studies, politics, science

▶ **DEVELOPMENTAL TASKS**
   Independence/Autonomy
   Sense of Purpose

OPTIONS

Use "historical" rather than "current" events, or create "future" events and debate with facts and opinions, acknowledging which is which.

Variations: Should students be given off-campus privileges for lunch?

Science: Should cloning of human organs be allowed?

History: Should the U.S. have used the atomic bomb in the Hiroshima and Nagasaki attacks?

Guidance: Is it important for students to go to college?

Objectives

1. To enable students to express their views
2. To encourage discussion of current events
3. To enhance the student's ability to see different sides of an issue
4. To provide a structure for learning or reviewing the curriculum
5. To experience influence

Instructions

1. Have the class sit in a community circle. Arrange six chairs in a circle in the middle.
2. Tell the community that you would like to have five volunteers sit in the circle to express their views on (topic). Explain that the extra chair is for anyone who wants to come in briefly and add information to the debate (facts, dates, etc.), after which he or she must go back to his or her seat. Examples:
   • Should cell phones be allowed at school?
   • How important is it for people to learn to speak a second language?
   • How can people resist peer pressure to use cigarettes, alcohol, or other drugs?
3. Say that the remaining community members are to be silent until all the students in the circle have been heard.
4. After the circle members have debated the topic, invite the community to direct questions to the circle members.

Suggested Reflection Questions

CONTENT (COGNITIVE LEARNING)
▶ What did you learn about the topic?
▶ Why is the debate circle a good way to learn about a topic?

COLLABORATIVE (SOCIAL LEARNING)
▶ What social skills did the community members need to be good debaters?
▶ How did it help to have the "open" chair in the circle?
▶ How did the group members show that they were listening to each other?

PERSONAL LEARNING
▶ How did you feel being inside/outside the circle?
▶ What part of this activity did you enjoy the most? What does this say about your special strengths or skills?
▶ How did you contribute to the community in a special way?

Appreciation
Invite statements of appreciation:
   ▶ "I liked it when..."
   ▶ "I am glad you said..."
   ▶ "I appreciated you for..."

Dear Abby

Objectives

1. To encourage active decision-making
2. To build appreciation for another's point of view
3. To share a concern or problem anonymously, and have peers suggest solutions
4. To promote influence

Instructions

1. Have the community meet in tribes, and give each tribe a pile of cards on which you have previously written a concern or problem (real issues) appropriate to your students' age level.
2. Ask tribe members to each take a turn at reading a problem out loud from a card to the rest of the tribe. Then have them say, "If I were Dear Abby I would suggest that this person (advice)."
3. Later (that day or a different one), distribute blank cards to the tribes and ask each tribe member to write one real concern or problem on the card, addressing it to the fictitious new columnist, "Dear Abby."
4. Collect the cards and redistribute the cards back to tribe members to suggest what they, as Dear Abby," would advise the person to do.

Suggested Reflection Questions

CONTENT (COGNITIVE LEARNING)

▶ What type of problems seemed to be the most frequent?
▶ Why is being able to solve problems an important skill?

COLLABORATIVE (SOCIAL LEARNING)

▶ How could you tell when your tribe members were listening well?
▶ What is the link between good listening and good solutions to problems?

PERSONAL LEARNING

▶ What did you feel when you listened to other students' concerns?
▶ How did you feel when you were giving a solution?
▶ What expertise did you discover about yourself?
▶ How did you contribute to your group in a special way?

Appreciation

Invite statements of appreciation:

▶ "(Name), you were a good listener..."
▶ "(Name), I liked it when you said..."

▶ **TIME** 30–45 min.

▶ **GROUPING** tribes

▶ **MATERIALS** 5 x 8-inch cards

▶ **DEVELOPMENTAL TASKS**
  Independence/Autonomy
  Social Competency
  Sense of Purpose
  Problem Solving

OPTIONS

Write about historical issues or events in literature, or practice as a letter-writing lesson (content standard).

Dream Quilt

▶ TIME   40 minutes

▶ GROUPING community, pairs

▶ MATERIALS squares of paper: a size that works for your room

▶ DEVELOPMENTAL TASKS
Independence/Autonomy
Sense of Purpose

OPTIONS

Make a dream quilt of "what we learned" in any subject (i.e., for Math, each square is a different math problem that is designed and solved by a student).

Objectives

1. To build community inclusion
2. To share a personal goal for the year

Instructions

Note: This is an excellent strategy to start the year or the semester.

1. Have the community sit in a circle.
2. Ask each student to think of a goal for the year, something he or she wants to accomplish.
3. Ask students to choose a partner and take turns sharing their goals.
4. Now pass out squares of paper to the students and ask them to write or illustrate their goals.
5. In a community circle, ask the students to share their goals with the class.
6. After all the students have shared their goals, have them decorate their square, sign their name, and post all the squares together on a bulletin board in the form of a quilt.

Suggested Reflection Questions

CONTENT (COGNITIVE LEARNING)
▶ What did you learn?
▶ What type of goals did most of you have?
▶ Why are goals important?

COLLABORATIVE (SOCIAL LEARNING)
▶ What skills did the community use to make this strategy successful?
▶ What could the community do to improve this strategy?

PERSONAL LEARNING
▶ How did you feel about putting your goals down on paper?
▶ What other goals didn't you put down that you might want to share?
▶ What personal strengths will you use to reach your goals?

Appreciation

Invite statements of appreciation:
▶ "Thanks, (name), for..."
▶ "I appreciated your sharing..."

Extended Nametags

Objectives

1. To promote inclusion by sharing personal history, interests, beliefs, etc.
2. To enhance communication skills

Instructions

1. Distribute 5 x 8-inch cards.
2. Ask each student to print his or her first name or nickname in the center of the card, and directly under it the quality he or she most values in people.
3. Then have each student write the following in the corners:
   - upper left—his or her favorite place on earth
   - lower left—the name of a person who taught him or her something important
   - lower right—the year he or she went on a big trip
   - upper right—a goal that he or she has for the future
4. Have the students meet in triads. Explain that the triad will talk about the upper left corner of their cards for three minutes, which means each person has one minute to talk. Ask them to keep track of their time and to share equally.
5. After three minutes, have the triads give statements of appreciation. Allow two minutes for the statements. Examples:
   - "I liked it when…"
   - "You're a lot like me when…"
6. Have the students form new triads three more times, sharing the other three corners and giving statements of appreciation after each round.
7. Form a community circle and invite each student to share something special he or she learned about a class member.

Suggested Reflection Questions

CONTENT (COGNITIVE LEARNING)
- Why is it important for the members of a community to have opportunities to share information about themselves?
- Are there other good questions we could ask?

COLLABORATIVE (SOCIAL LEARNING)
- How did you know that others were listening well when you spoke?
- How did this activity help our class community get better acquainted?

PERSONAL LEARNING
- What were you feeling when you were speaking/listening?
- What unique qualities did you discover about yourself?

Appreciation

Invite statements of appreciation:
- "I liked hearing..."
- "I admire your..."

▶ **TIME** 15–25 min.

▶ **GROUPING** community, tribes

▶ **MATERIALS** 5 x 8-inch cards, pencils, clock

▶ **DEVELOPMENTAL TASKS**
Independence/Autonomy
Social Competency
Sense of Purpose

OPTIONS

Variation: Use to introduce a topic. Replace corner topics with content questions.

Use as a review for a test, with students asking questions of each other, or using teacher-designed questions.

Use as a reflective practice after introducing new material. Collect and review, or have students share.

Use milling to music, inside outside circle, or tribe groups as sharing options.

Final Countdown

- ▶ **TIME**　5 minutes
- ▶ **GROUPING**　full group
- ▶ **MATERIALS**　none
- ▶ **DEVELOPMENTAL TASKS**
  Independence/Autonomy
  Social Competency
  Sense of Purpose

OPTIONS

Use the strategy as a "ticket out the door," after a class or lesson. Have students respond to the following prompts: Something I learned... Someone who facilitated or helped the group... How this (learning or lesson) will affect me later in life... Something I liked about class today...

It is even more effective if the students know that they will be accountable for this information before or during class, rather than as a last minute activity.

Objectives

1. To bring closure to a class or a day
2. To provide opportunities for sharing and recognition

Instructions

1. Just before the last five minutes of class, have students prepare to leave and then sit in a community circle for the "Final Countdown."
2. Say, "I need to hear four things before we say goodbye for today." "I need to hear…
   - a statement of appreciation for someone here,
   - something or someone you are thankful for,
   - something good about your day, and
   - a clean, funny joke."
3. Choose volunteers until the "Final Countdown" is completed. Make sure the same people are not chosen each time.

Suggested Reflection Questions

Note: Keep reflection questions very brief, as this is a closure activity.

CONTENT (COGNITIVE LEARNING)
- ▶ Who heard something you know or agree with?

COLLABORATIVE (SOCIAL LEARNING)
- ▶ Who will share tomorrow?

PERSONAL LEARNING
- ▶ Who discovered something new about yourself today?

Appreciation

Invite statements of appreciation:
- ▶ "Thank you, (name), for sharing!"

Find the Word

Objectives

1. To introduce a unit's vocabulary words and their meanings
2. To build inclusion and influence

Instructions

1. Give each student a card with a word printed on it from the social studies, history, science, or language unit. (If the words have been only recently introduced, write a word list on the board.)
2. Have each student pin his or her card on the back of another student without that student seeing it.
3. Tell the students to move around the room and ask each other questions that can be answered "yes" or "no" until each student determines what is written on the card on his or her back. Explain that they may ask each student only one question and then must move along to the next student.

Suggested Reflection Questions

CONTENT (COGNITIVE LEARNING)

▶ What kind of questions did you ask?
▶ Why might this be a fun way to learn new vocabulary words?

COLLABORATIVE (SOCIAL LEARNING)

▶ What social skills did the community need to make this activity work well?
▶ In what ways did you, as a community, help to make this activity successful?

PERSONAL LEARNING

▶ How did you feel when you found out what or who you were?
▶ What did you enjoy most about this activity?
▶ Did you find any hidden gifts or talents about yourself that you were not aware of?

Appreciation

Invite statements of appreciation:
▶ "I enjoyed it when..."
▶ "I liked it when..."
▶ "I'm similar to (name) because..."

▶ **TIME**　　20–30 min.

▶ **GROUPING**　community

▶ **MATERIALS** 3 x 5-inch index cards, safety pins, markers

▶ **SUBJECT**　　social studies, history, reading or vocabulary

▶ **DEVELOPMENTAL TASKS**
Independence/Autonomy
Social Competency
Sense of Purpose
Problem Solving

OPTIONS

Use vocabulary words, review key concepts (people, places, events), demonstrate feeling words; act out or role play.

Finding All We Have in Common

▶ **TIME** 35–45 minutes

▶ **GROUPING** community, pairs

▶ **MATERIALS** none

▶ **DEVELOPMENTAL TASKS**
Independence/Autonomy
Social Competency
Sense of Purpose

OPTIONS

Have students share common facts from the day's lesson. Compare attributes or characteristics. Review what "I know," or share what "I hope to learn…"

Variation: Students take on the persona of a literary, historical, political, or famous person and find commonalities.

Social Studies: Countries and cultures

Objectives

1. To give students an opportunity to introduce themselves
2. To give students an opportunity to work in pairs and find commonalties
3. To build inclusion

Instructions

1. State that we are a unique group about to start an exciting journey together, and that, like any people coming together, we need to learn about each other.
2. Have each student find a partner he or she does not know at all or does not know very well. Say, "In the next five minutes find out all the things that you have in common with your partner (likes, dislikes, qualities, skills, goals or whatever)."
3. Have the community sit in a circle. Have each partner introduce him or herself and tell what he or she discovered.

Suggested Reflection Questions

CONTENT (COGNITIVE LEARNING)
▶ What are things many of you have in common?
▶ Why is finding out what you have in common a good way to get to know somebody?

COLLABORATIVE (SOCIAL LEARNING)
▶ Why is attentive listening so important for this strategy?
▶ How did you and your partner make this activity successful?
▶ What do you appreciate about this community?

PERSONAL LEARNING
▶ How did you feel about finding out/sharing what you and your partner have in common?
▶ What strengths or personal qualities do you and your partner have in common?

Appreciation

Invite statements of appreciation:
▶ "I really liked…"
▶ "It was great when…"

Five E's for Discovery Learning

Objectives
1. To enhance the abilities of students to think constructively by developing the capacity to investigate, analyze, solve-problems and construct knowledge
2. To enable students to take responsibility for their own learning
3. To practice the collaborative skills of team planning, management and assessment

Instructions
Pre-class preparation: Select an academic theme or topic for group exploration and assemble a list of resources applicable to the investigation or project to be carried out by student groups. Define the objectives and outcome tasks for the learning groups.

1. Engage (teacher leadership): Define an inclusion question or strategy that links the topic to students' interests or personal experiences. Connect the topic to past learning. State the objectives, task and the time for the tribes to accomplish their explorations or projects. Describe your role as a "guide on the side" who is available to suggest resources, to clarify the process and to review the tribes' progress.
2. Explore (student leadership): Ask the tribes to review the four Tribes agreements, and then to discuss and list several questions about the topic that they would like to explore. Each tribe selects one question and informs the class what they will research. Each group decides how they will research their selected question (interviews, Internet, videos, books, conduct experiment, etc.). Each tribe makes an action plan (who will do what) and initiates their investigation.
3. Explain (student leadership): The tribes discuss their discoveries, plan presentations (how they will teach the class); they confer with the teacher-guide and present their discovery to the class community, sharing their action steps and justifying conclusions from researched information.
4. Elaborate (student leadership): The tribes involve the class (other tribes) to expand on concepts, create questions, and connect to real-world issues.
5. Evaluate (student leadership): Each tribe asks reflection questions they have prepared. They complete assigned individual or group reports.

Suggested Reflection Questions

CONTENT (COGNITIVE LEARNING)
▶ What was the most important thing that your tribe learned?
▶ How can your tribe's discovery be applied elsewhere?

COLLABORATIVE (SOCIAL LEARNING)
▶ What was difficult for your group to do?
▶ What was most interesting?

PERSONAL LEARNING
▶ What feelings did you have during your tribe's presentation?
▶ What makes this a good way to learn about a topic?

Appreciation
Invite statements of appreciation:
▶ "I appreciated the way our group..."

▶ **TIME** depends upon material

▶ **GROUPING** tribes

▶ **MATERIALS** academic theme or information

▶ **DEVELOPMENTAL TASKS**
Independence/Autonomy
Social Competency
Sense of Purpose
Problem Solving

OPTIONS

Role play this process, and reflect or discuss to help students refine and monitor for success.

Introduce content standards, such as including a business letter in the "explore" stage of discovery learning.

Flies On the Ceiling

▶ **TIME**   35 minutes

▶ **GROUPING** tribes

▶ **MATERIALS** paper, pencils

▶ **DEVELOPMENTAL TASKS**
    Independence/Autonomy
    Social Competency
    Sense of Purpose
    Problem Solving

OPTIONS

Use the strategy as a written reflection or assessment.

Have students summarize (in writing or orally) a sequence of events in history or literature, or even steps in an equation.

Objectives

1. To identify the dynamics of group interaction
2. To process a sequence of learning activities and behaviors
3. To practice reflecting on systems and situations
4. To experience influence

Instructions

1. After students have been working together on a task, have them set aside their books and papers.
2. Ask the students to close their eyes and pretend they had been flies on the ceiling watching their tribe work together during the last few minutes or hours. Tell them to "run the movie backwards now" and think what the flies saw happening.

    Who did what to get you started?
    What did you do while your tribe was working together?
    What did other tribe members do?
    What helpful things happened?
    Who did them?
    Did everyone participate?
    How did you help each other?

3. After a few minutes, have the tribe members share what they as flies saw happening. It is helpful to have each tribe choose a recorder to make a list of behaviors, positions, acts, interactions, etc.
4. Have the tribes give their report to the community.
5. Then ask each tribe to make a list of "things what we could do to have our tribe work better next time."

Suggested Reflection Questions:

CONTENT/THINKING

▶ These questions were handled in #2 above.

SOCIAL

▶ Why is it important to look at how groups are working together?

PERSONAL

▶ How could you use this strategy in other groups and relationships?
▶ How can you help your tribe to work together better?

Appreciation

Invite statements of appreciation:
    ▶ "Thanks for..."
    ▶ "It helped me when..."

Focusing on Our Strengths

Objectives

1. To identify three individual strengths (personal or school related)
2. To build self awareness
3. To build inclusion
4. To discover gifts

Instructions

1. Review the agreements.
2. Ask students to write down three individual strengths.
3. Have each student find a partner he or she does not know at all or does not know very well. Say, "In the next ten minutes take turns sharing your strengths with your partner. Discuss how it became a strength for you. Share how identifying your strengths can be helpful to you in school and beyond."
4. Have the community sit in a circle. Have each person introduce his/her partner to the community and share a strength(s) and how it could be helpful in school and beyond. (Make sure that each partner knows and agrees with what their partner will share.)

▶ TIME   30–45 min.

▶ GROUPING   pairs, community

▶ MATERIALS   paper, pen

▶ DEVELOPMENTAL TASKS
   Independence/Autonomy
   Sense of Purpose

Suggested Reflection Questions

CONTENT (COGNITIVE LEARNING)

▶ Why is it important to focus on your strengths?
▶ How easy/difficult was it for you to identify how a particular strength could be helpful to you in school and beyond?

COLLABORATIVE (SOCIAL LEARNING)

▶ How did you and your partner make this activity successful?
▶ What social skills did you and your partner need to make this activity successful?
▶ How did it feel to hear your strengths and their applications being shared by your partner to the community.

PERSONAL LEARNING

▶ What did you discover about yourself?
▶ What strengths or personal qualities do you and your partner have in common?
▶ Think about a characteristic you have that you might not initially think of as a strength. How can it turn into a strength for you? (i.e., "You are a quiet, shy person... perhaps that means you are an attentive listener.")

Appreciation

Invite statements of appreciation:

▶ "I appreciated it when..."
▶ "You helped when..."

OPTIONS

Have students identify their strengths in a particular subject area.

Fold the Line Reading

▶ TIME   30 minutes

▶ GROUPING tribes

▶ MATERIALS none

▶ DEVELOPMENTAL TASKS
   Independence/Autonomy
   Social Competency
   Sense of Purpose
   Problem Solving

Objectives

1. To build interdependence
2. To practice reading with a partner
3. To experience influence

Instructions

1. Have the students get some identical reading (history, social studies, or other).
2. Ask the students to line up (without talking) across the room according to their birth dates, beginning with January on one side of the room.
3. Starting on one side, have each student in turn state his or her birth month and date.
4. Create two lines by leading the last person, so that each student is facing a partner. Have the partners stand an arm's length apart.
5. Have one partner read the first paragraph of the text. The other partner paraphrases what was read.
6. Next have the other partner read the next paragraph. Partners alternate reading and paraphrasing until they finish reading the selection you assigned.

OPTIONS

Choose an event in literature or history (or a current event), and discuss the active ignoring that took place and its effects and consequences.

Suggested Reflection Questions

CONTENT (COGNITIVE LEARNING)

▶ What did you learn from the material you just read?

COLLABORATIVE (SOCIAL LEARNING)

▶ Why is reading together helpful?
▶ Why is a choosing partner using a lineup fun?
▶ What did you and your partner do to make this activity successful?

PERSONAL LEARNING

▶ How do you feel reading to another person?
▶ How did you help make this strategy successful?
▶ What special strengths or skills did you discover about yourself?

Appreciation

Invite statements of appreciation:

▶ "I liked your reading because..."
▶ "Thanks for helping me..."

Gallery Walks

Objectives
1. To build communication skills
2. To build self-esteem and pride in work
3. To build inclusion and influence

Instructions
1. Invite several students to stand next to projects on which they have been working. Refer to them as "Artists of the Day."
2. Have the remaining students form triads.
3. Invite the triads to take a "gallery walk" around the room to view articles on display, projects-in-making, etc.
4. Have each student artist stand by his or her work and share the origin of his or her ideas, materials used, personal objectives, feelings about finished work, etc.

Suggested Reflection Questions

CONTENT (COGNITIVE LEARNING)
▶ What kind of things did the artists mention?
▶ What different talents do people have?
▶ How did the artists seem to feel about their work?

COLLABORATIVE (SOCIAL LEARNING)
▶ What social skills did "gallery walkers" and artists need to use to make this activity successful?
▶ In what ways could the community make this activity even more successful?

PERSONAL LEARNING
▶ What did you do best when you presented your work?
▶ How did you help to keep the focus on the other artists?
▶ What special talents do you feel proud of?

Appreciation
Invite statements of appreciation:
▶ "I liked it when you said..."
▶ "Some of your talents are..."
▶ "I like your masterpiece because..."

▶ **TIME** 30 minutes

▶ **GROUPING** community, triads

▶ **MATERIALS** student art work or lesson topic

▶ **DEVELOPMENTAL TASKS**
Independence/Autonomy
Social Competency
Sense of Purpose

OPTIONS

Use this strategy for a "work in progress," to help students reflect on their own work for improvement or achievement.

Give Me a Clue

▶ **TIME**   20–30 minutes

▶ **GROUPING** tribes, subgroups

▶ **MATERIALS** clue cards, colored cubes, colored pencils

▶ **DEVELOPMENTAL TASKS**
Independence/Autonomy
Problem Solving

OPTIONS

Have students make clue cards for solving equations, identifying historical figures, or determining scientific classifications. Then have tribes exchange clue cards and solve.

Objectives

1. To demonstrate understanding of geometric vocabulary terms
2. To use spatial reasoning to think in three dimensions
3. To learn that accomplishing a group task depends upon each member contributing skills and knowledge

Instructions

1. Have students meet in tribes or small groups of four to six members.
2. State the objectives and the task: to build a three-dimensional figure with colored cubes, using the information on the "Build It" clue cards.
3. Distribute eight colored cubes (two blue, two green, two red, and two yellow) to each tribe. Have each tribe member draw one clue card.
4. State the rules:
   • the clue card is his or hers alone and no one else may touch it
   • the blocks may be touched only when it is a member's turn
   • students share their clue by reading its information aloud
   • help may be asked in reading the information
   • if a question arises, ask tribe members before asking the teacher
5. Tell students to:
   • read the clues on their cards to their tribe
   • share their thinking to help the tribe come to an understanding of each vocabulary term
   • analyze the clues until a solution seems to have been found
6. Tell the students that they will recognize the correct solution when everyone agrees that the three-dimensional figure matches with the clues.
7. Have the tribes record their solution by drawing it.

Suggested Reflection Questions

CONTENT (COGNITIVE LEARNING)
▶ Which vocabulary words needed to be clarified by your tribe? What do they mean?

COLLABORATIVE (SOCIAL LEARNING)
▶ What did tribe members do to help your tribe be successful?
▶ What did tribe members say or do that opened up your thinking?
▶ Describe the benefits of working as a tribe rather than alone.

PERSONAL LEARNING
▶ What did you do that was helpful?
▶ Did you discover any clues about hidden strengths or abilities you may have? What are they?

Appreciation

Invite statements of appreciation:
▶ "It was helpful when..."
▶ "I liked it when..."

BUILD IT #1

There are six blocks in all.
One of the blocks is yellow.

BUILD IT #1

The green block shares
one face with each of the
other five blocks.

BUILD IT #1

The two red blocks do not
touch each other.

BUILD IT #1

The two blue blocks do not touch
each other.

BUILD IT #1

Each red block shares
an edge with the
yellow block.

BUILD IT #1

Each blue block shares
one edge with each of
the red blocks.

Goal-Storming

▶ **TIME** 60 minutes

▶ **GROUPING** community, tribes

▶ **MATERIALS** large paper, markers, tape

▶ **DEVELOPMENTAL TASKS**
Independence/Autonomy
Sense of Purpose
Problem Solving

OPTIONS

This strategy can be used in combination with the "Five E's" to help students refine goals for each "E" stage.

Use the strategy to solicit student input on classroom procedures or expectations, both social and academic.

Objectives

1. To enable a large group to identify shared goals and concerns
2. To structure interest-related work groups
3. To experience influence

Instructions

Note: "Goal-Storming" is a variation of "Brainstorming." The group should be familiar with the Brainstorming process.

1. Decide upon a relevant question for the full community to address:
   Example: "Where would we like to go on a field trip?"
2. Ask the community to form small groups or meet in tribes.
3. Review the rules for "Brainstorming:"
   D defer judgment
   O offbeat, original
   V vast number
   E expand, elaborate
4. Ask each tribe to choose a recorder and then brainstorm for five minutes, listing all ideas.
5. Ask the recorders to read all the ideas to the community. Discuss consensus and how to form a consensus. (See "Consensus-Building.")
6. Instruct each tribe to form a consensus on three ideas.
7. Record the three ideas from each tribe on the board.
8. Discuss the ideas as a full community. Combine ideas that are repetitive.
9. At this point choose one of these options:
   • Form task or interest groups around listed concerns.
   • Sticker vote as individuals to determine highest priority.

Suggested Reflection Questions

CONTENT (COGNITIVE LEARNING)
▶ Why is this a good way to find out what a group wants?
▶ What makes goal-storming difficult?
▶ Why are the DOVE brainstorming guidelines important?

COLLABORATIVE (SOCIAL LEARNING)
▶ What social skills did the community use to make brainstorming successful?
▶ What skills and strengths did your tribe use that helped you work well together?

PERSONAL LEARNING
▶ How do you feel about the group's priority?
▶ How did you contribute to your group in a special way?

Appreciation

Invite statements of appreciation:
▶ "I liked it when you..."
▶ "I felt good when..."

Graphing Who We Are

Objectives

1. To graph and review information gathered by tribes
2. To develop an appreciation of differences
3. To develop a sense of community
4. To experience influence

Instructions

1. Prior to initiating this strategy, select some different types of graphs (Venn diagram, bar graph, line graph and/or picture graphs) to teach the recording of statistical information. Sketch the graph models on newsprint or the blackboard. Set aside large sheets of paper, one for each tribe.
2. Have the students meet in their tribes, and explain that each tribe will graph information on the large sheets of paper about the members of their tribes (heights, eye colors, numbers of siblings, distance from school, shoe sizes, head circumferences, etc.).
3. Have tribe members choose roles: recorder, reader, measurer, taskmaster. Review the responsibilities of each role. (optional)
4. Ask each tribe to discuss and choose which graph model they will use.
5. Invite a tribe to use you as an example, measuring your height and recording the information. (optional)
6. Have the tribes present their graphs when completed to the community.

Suggested Reflection Questions

CONTENT (COGNITIVE LEARNING)

▶ Why is it important to be able to read graphs?
▶ What did you learn about graphing in this strategy?

COLLABORATIVE (SOCIAL LEARNING)

▶ What social skills did you need, as a tribe, to be successful in this strategy?
▶ What cooperative skills do you think your tribe needs to practice?

PERSONAL LEARNING

▶ How did you help your tribe?
▶ What did you discover that you appreciate about yourself?
▶ What did your tribe appreciate about you?

Appreciation

Invite statements of appreciation:
▶ "I appreciated..."
▶ "It was great when..."

▶ **TIME** 30–60 min.

▶ **GROUPING** tribes

▶ **MATERIALS** wall graph formats, large paper, tape measures, rulers, maps

▶ **DEVELOPMENTAL TASKS**
Independence/Autonomy
Sense of Purpose
Problem Solving

OPTIONS

Once students are successful with various graphs, invite students to graph (any content) information and then assess one another's graphs.

Adapted from All About Us, *by Nan and Ted Graves, Cooperative Learning, Vol. 11, No. 2, December, 1990*

Great Graffiti

▶ **TIME**   60 minutes

▶ **GROUPING**   tribes

▶ **MATERIALS** large paper, colored pencils or felt pens

▶ **DEVELOPMENTAL TASKS**
Independence/Autonomy
Social Competency
Sense of Purpose

OPTIONS

Use content topics such as:

What I know…

What I would like to know…

I wonder….

Be sure that students understand the agreements so that the "graffiti" is productive, appropriate, and content-rich.

Objectives

1. To encourage the sharing of feelings and beliefs
2. To gather and appreciate many points of view
3. To review subject matter in cooperative learning groups
4. To build inclusion and promote influence

Instructions

1. Ask the community to meet in tribes.
2. To each tribe, distribute pens and a large piece of paper (at least 2 x 6-feet long) labeled with one of the following subjects (or an academic topic) on each:

   • pet peeves   • favorite moments
   • what I wonder about   • things that scare me a lot
   • ambitions   • things that are fun

3. Invite the tribes to write "graffiti" on their paper for three to five minutes, all tribe members writing at once.
4. At the end of three to five minutes, ask the tribes to stop writing and exchange papers. Have the tribes now write on their new graffiti papers for the next three to five minutes. Repeat this procedure until all the tribes have had a chance to write graffiti on all the papers.
5. Return original papers to tribes and allow the members time to read the graffiti and discuss similarities in what people wrote.
6. Have each tribe report its findings back to the community.

Suggested Reflection Questions

CONTENT (COGNITIVE LEARNING)
▶ What general things did the community write?
▶ Why did you exchange papers?

COLLABORATIVE (SOCIAL LEARNING)
▶ How did your tribe members cooperate?
▶ In what special ways did your tribe members help each other?

PERSONAL LEARNING
▶ What did you write that told something about yourself?
▶ Which graffiti topic meant the most to you?
▶ What unique qualities did you bring to this activity?

Appreciation
Invite statements of appreciation:
▶ "It was helpful when you..."
▶ "I liked it when you wrote..."

Group Inquiry

Objectives

1. To practice constructive thinking skills (accessing information, interpreting, synthesizing and applying)
2. To practice collaborative team skills
3. To transfer responsibility to students

Instructions

1. Inclusion: Build inclusion within the tribes by using the structure, write/pair/share. Ask people to take 5–10 minutes to write down the skills, talents and abilities that they bring to the group. You may want to list and discuss the various collaborative skills. (See chapter 12 for Tribes collaborative skills.) Have people share their lists first in pairs. Then share with the tribe.
2. Content and Objectives: Discuss the general subject content and sub-content areas to be researched by the tribes. It is optional whether the class or teacher defines the content standards. List the objectives to be learned from the experience. Have the tribes choose or randomly draw slips of content areas. (See option.)
3. Resources: Detail resources they can use for their inquiry or research (books, articles, internet info, library, interviews, films, etc.).
4. Task: Describe the task to be accomplished (group report, presentation, role play, article, etc.) within a specific time; inquiry projects can run from one hour to several weeks or months.
5. Roles: You may want to use roles within the tribes (facilitator, encourager, materials manager, recorder, etc.). If so, have people choose their roles according to the skills and resources they believe they bring to the group.
6. Accountability:
   - For presentations to the whole class, a peer evaluation sheet may be used for feedback. (See "Peer Evaluation of Group Presentation" on the page following this strategy.)
   - Your own observations of individual performance can be made by taking notes.
   - Group and individual reports can be made and graded.

Suggested Reflection Questions

CONTENT (COGNITIVE LEARNING)

▶ What was the most important content (theory, information, etc.) that can be applied to the topic today? (Discuss, share or write about this question.)
▶ Help people to understand the topic.
▶ What would you like to know more about?

COLLABORATIVE (SOCIAL LEARNING)

▶ What was the value for our community in using this teaching method?
▶ What collaborative skills were demonstrated by your tribe?

▶ **TIME** varies

▶ **GROUPING** tribes

▶ **MATERIALS** dependent upon content resources and extent of research

▶ **DEVELOPMENTAL TASKS**
Independence/Autonomy
Sense of Purpose
Problem Solving

OPTIONS

Instead of using sub-topics within tribes, use the "Jigsaw" method and have individual tribe members research the subject in expert groups and then return to teach content to their tribe.

PERSONAL LEARNING
- ▶ What skills did you use to contribute to your tribe in a special way?
- ▶ What skills did you notice in others that you would also like to learn?
- ▶ What skills, talents and abilities are you particularly proud of?

Appreciation

Invite oral or written statements of appreciation to individuals or whole tribes:
- ▶ "Thank you for..."
- ▶ "I liked it when..."

Peer Evaluation of Group Presentation

GROUP NAME:

EVALUATION CRITERIA	EXCEEDS	MEETS	APPROACHING	NOT MET
1. Content				
2. Organization				
3. Cooperation of tribe members				
4. Use of aids: handouts, video, etc.				
5. Involvement/Interest for class				

Specific Suggestions for Improvement:

I Appreciated Learning:

This chart is an adaptation of one in the article "Using Jigsaw Groups for Research and Writing in High School," by Glory-Ann Drazinakis, Cooperative Learning, Vol. 13, No. 2. Winter 1993.

This page may be duplicated for classroom use.

Group Problem-Solving

▶ **TIME** 40 minutes

▶ **GROUPING** tribes

▶ **MATERIALS** large paper, markers, colored stickers

▶ **DEVELOPMENTAL TASKS**
Independence/Autonomy
Sense of Purpose
Problem Solving

OPTIONS

Use in literature study (character, plot line).

Use with complex equations, word problems, and in science labs.

Health: What are three typical problems a person with poor eating habits may have?

Objectives

1. To teach a group problem-solving process
2. To analyze alternatives
3. To experience influence

Instructions

1. Have the class community meet in tribes.
2. Give each tribe five minutes to come up with three typical problems that a student might have with another student—or that a student might have with someone else at the school.
3. Have each tribe read their problem to the class. Make sure that the problems are well defined.
4. Explain that each tribe will have ten minutes to brainstorm and list possible solutions. Review the "Brainstorming" strategy and post the brainstorming rules. Give each tribe a large sheet of paper, a felt pen and three colored stickers (red, blue and yellow).
5. Write the "Group Problem-Solving" process on the board.
   • Brainstorm for ten minutes. Have one person record all ideas.
   • Each person selects three top choices with colored stickers (1st choice blue=25 points; 2nd choice red=15 points; 3rd choice yellow=5 points).
   • Add up the total points for each idea.
   • Present your top solutions to the community.
   Note: If this strategy is used for real-time problems, you may want to teach the tribes how to make a "Tribe Action Plan" as described in chapter 13.

Suggested Reflection Questions

CONTENT (COGNITIVE LEARNING)
▶ What is the value of this process?
▶ What other ways can decisions be made in the tribe?

COLLABORATIVE (SOCIAL LEARNING)
▶ In what ways did your tribe honor our tribe agreements?
▶ What social skills did your tribe use when doing this strategy?
▶ What did you like best about how your tribe worked together?

PERSONAL LEARNING
▶ How do you feel about your action plan?
▶ How do you feel about your participation?
▶ What did you do to help your tribe be successful?
▶ What new strengths or skills did you discover in yourself?

Appreciation
Invite statements of appreciation:
▶ "Thanks for your help..."
▶ "You made a positive difference when..."

"I'm Proud" Appreciation Circle

Objectives

1. To encourage sharing good feelings about oneself
2. To encourage acceptance and appreciation of others
3. To build inclusion

Instructions

1. Discuss the difference between stating appreciation of oneself and bragging.
2. Invite one person in each tribe to sit in the middle of their tribe as the focus person.
3. Have the focus person make an "I'm proud" statement. Examples:
   - "I'm proud that I am…"
   - "I'm proud that I am able to…"
   - "I'm proud that I…"
4. Have the other tribe members give positive feedback or make statements of appreciation to the focus person.
5. Continue the process until each person takes a turn being the focus person.

▶ **TIME** 30 minutes

▶ **GROUPING** community, tribes

▶ **MATERIALS** none

▶ **DEVELOPMENTAL TASKS**
Independence/Autonomy
Social Competency
Sense of Purpose

Suggested Reflection Questions

CONTENT (COGNITIVE LEARNING)

▶ How did you choose your "I'm proud" statement?
▶ What did you learn about your tribe members?

COLLABORATIVE (SOCIAL LEARNING)

▶ Why is it important to be able to acknowledge what we are proud of?
▶ What did your tribe do to show their support when you made your "I'm proud" statements?
▶ What about your tribe makes you feel proud?

PERSONAL LEARNING

▶ How did you feel when you made your "I'm proud statements?"
▶ How did you feel when you gave/received statements of appreciation?
▶ What skills did you use to help the group?
▶ What strengths did the group recognize in you?

OPTIONS

Use the strategy in a community circle. Share or reflect on academic achievements.

Appreciation

Invite statements of appreciation:
▶ Is there anyone who would like to make a statement to anyone else in the class?

In the Bag

▶ **TIME**   50 minutes

▶ **GROUPING** community, tribes

▶ **MATERIALS** each student brings an item in a paper sack

▶ **DEVELOPMENTAL TASKS**
   Social Competency
   Sense of Purpose

OPTIONS

Bring an object in a bag that stands as a metaphor for a literary character or historical figure.

Art: In addition to bringing an object significant to the student, bring one that can be sketched as a three dimensional object or analyzed for color quality.

Objectives

1. To build inclusion
2. To practice active listening
3. To have fun

Instructions

1. Ask each student to bring a an object that is significant and that reflects "something about you" from home in a paper sack. (Allow a few days.)
2. Have the full group (or tribes) sit in a circle(s).
3. Explain that sharing from the sack could take on any of these forms:
   • how these shoes help me to do things that I like to do
   • sharing from the point of view of the shoe (what it's like being the shoe that belongs to the person sharing)
   • sharing from the point of view of the shoe (how I'd like to be taken care of if I could have it my way).

Suggested Reflection Questions

CONTENT (COGNITIVE LEARNING)
▶ How did the item tell you about the students who shared?
▶ How did you go about choosing the item you shared?

COLLABORATIVE (SOCIAL LEARNING)
▶ How did tribe members show they were interested?
▶ How does your tribe show appreciation for each other's uniqueness?

PERSONAL LEARNING
▶ How did you feel sharing your item?
▶ What unique qualities do you bring to the group?
▶ What do others appreciate about you?

Appreciation

Invite statements of appreciation:
▶ Going around the circle, ask each student to give a statement of appreciation to the student on the left.
▶ "(Name), I liked it when..."

Interview Circle

Objectives
1. To build inclusion and influence
2. To enhance communication skills
3. To share personal beliefs, feelings, and interests

Instructions
1. Ask the community to sit in a large circle.
2. Explain that we will interview one student who will sit in the center of the circle and answer three questions. The person will choose the questions from people who raise their hands. He or she has the right to "pass" on any questions that she or he chooses not to answer.
3. Model the activity first by being in the center and responding to three questions yourself.
4. Suggest that questions may be autobiographical or may relate to issues, curriculum, politics, hobbies, friendship, sports, etc.
5. Have the community interview a few students each day until everyone has had a turn.

Suggested Reflection Questions

CONTENT (COGNITIVE LEARNING)
▶ What did you discover about a community member?
▶ Why is it difficult to answer some of the questions?

COLLABORATIVE (SOCIAL LEARNING)
▶ Which social skills did you, as a community, use to make this activity successful?
▶ How could you tell when the community was using good listening skills?

PERSONAL LEARNING
▶ How did you feel about being interviewed?
▶ What did you learn about yourself from this activity?
▶ What unique qualities are you proud of as a result of this activity?*

Appreciation
Invite statements of appreciation:
▶ "I liked it when..."
▶ "I admired your honesty when..."

▶ **TIME** 15–30 min.

▶ **GROUPING** community, tribes

▶ **MATERIALS** none

▶ **DEVELOPMENTAL TASKS**
Independence/Autonomy
Social Competency
Sense of Purpose

OPTIONS

*Suggest that students record their discovered qualities in a journal.

Use in tribes to review subject matter or as an actual assessment.

Encourage substitute teachers to introduce themselves to your class with this strategy.

I Used to Be; We Used to Be

▶ **TIME** 45 minutes

▶ **GROUPING** tribes

▶ **MATERIALS** paper, pencils

▶ **DEVELOPMENTAL TASKS**
    Independence/Autonomy
    Sense of Purpose

OPTIONS

*Suggest that students record their discovered qualities in a journal.

Use as a reflective practice in assessing group or project development after a period of time.

Assess development in a scientific, historical, or social context (for example, geology, countries in Africa, civil rights).

Objectives

1. To give the students an opportunity to look at personal changes
2. To give tribes an opportunity to look at how they have changed
3. To share personal and tribal changes
4. To experience influence

Instructions

1. Have the community meet in tribes.
2. Ask each student to (silently) compare the following things about himself or herself today, and his or her old self in the past: physical appearance, favorite things to do, behavior, hobbies, beliefs, fears, friends, etc.
3. Have each tribe member write a poem, using the following format:
    I used to be…
    But now I am…
    I used to be…
    But now I am…
4. Ask the tribe members to share their finished poems.
5. While students are still in their tribes ask each tribe member to create a poem about his or her tribe, using the following format:
    We used to be…
    But now we are…
    We used to be…
    But now we are…
6. Ask the tribe members to share their finished poems.
7. Ask each tribe to share one or two of its "we" poems with the community.

Suggested Reflection Questions

CONTENT (COGNITIVE LEARNING)
▶ What did you find out about your tribe members?
▶ What changes have your tribe members made?

COLLABORATIVE (SOCIAL LEARNING)
▶ How well did your tribe honor the agreements during this strategy?
▶ How do your tribe members feel about each other now?
▶ What do you appreciate about your tribe?

PERSONAL LEARNING*
▶ How do you feel about how you have changed?
▶ What other changes do you want to make?
▶ What changes or special qualities make you feel especially proud?

Appreciation

Invite statements of appreciation:
▶ "I appreciated it when…"
▶ "Thank you, (name), for…"

Jigsaw

Objectives

1. To structure team learning/team teaching in tribes
2. To build the academic self-image of students
3. To develop tribe spirit and pride
4. To help each student feel valuable to others
5. To experience inclusion and influence

Instructions

1. Select a lesson that you consider appropriate for the following process.
2. Divide it into equal parts (or the number of members per tribe) and define study questions. Prepare sufficient materials for the study groups.
3. Explain the Jigsaw process to your class. Then ask the students to meet in tribes.
4. If you have not already done so, engage them with an activity on the personal feeling level to awaken interest about a topic.
5. Give each tribe one set of lesson materials. Ask each tribe to decide who will become an "expert" for each part of the lesson.
6. Ask people responsible for Part I to move to a jigsaw study group; do the same for the other parts.
7. Tell the groups what their specific task is and the amount of time that will be allowed. Move from group to group, helping only as needed.
8. When all have finished, ask people to return to their own tribes.
9. Beginning with Part I, ask the "experts" to share the materials that they prepared in their Jigsaw group; prepare a format for sharing if you think it will help them.
10. After each segment has been shared, take time for a full group discussion, and then meet in tribes to reflect on the experience.

Suggested Reflection Questions

CONTENT (COGNITIVE LEARNING)

▶ What did you learn?
▶ Why is this a good way to learn a lot in a short time?

COLLABORATIVE (SOCIAL LEARNING)

▶ What skills did you, as a tribe, use to make this activity successful?
▶ What strengths do you see your tribe using more of in the future?

PERSONAL LEARNING

▶ How did you feel to have other students teaching you?
▶ How did you feel teaching others what you had learned? Why?
▶ What special gifts or talents did you discover about yourself?

Appreciation

Invite statements of appreciation:

▶ "I liked it when..."
▶ "I want to thank, (name), for..."

Acknowledgement is made to Elliot Aronson's work. (See Bibliography.)

▶ **TIME** varies depending on lesson task

▶ **GROUPING** tribes

▶ **MATERIALS** vary

▶ **SUBJECT** any lesson topic

▶ **DEVELOPMENTAL TASKS**
Independence/Autonomy
Social Competency
Sense of Purpose

OPTIONS

Use with any content material. Expert groups need not have great amounts of information or text to be successful.

Combine this strategy with a reflective practice (such as, Group Inquiry, Flies On The Ceiling, Two Truths and A Lie).

Joy

▶ **TIME** 20 minutes

▶ **GROUPING** community, tribes

▶ **MATERIALS** none

▶ **DEVELOPMENTAL TASKS**
Social Competency
Sense of Purpose

OPTIONS

Choose any two or three letter word and use the letters to invite purposeful responses, both personal and academic (for example, NOW: something New you learned, One question you have, Write a 10 word sentence summarizing...).

Variations: HOPE: a Happy moment, an Opportunity I wish for, a Personal quality, something I Enjoy for recreation

Create your own with the abbreviation of your school: MHS: Memorable moment, a Happy moment, a Skill I possess

Objectives

1. To give each person an opportunity to share something special with others
2. To practice listening skills
3. To build inclusion

Instructions

1. Ask each student to think of three things that he or she would like to share. Use the letters of the word "joy" to structure what is to be shared:

   J: something in your life that just happened
   O: one thing you would like to do for yourself
   Y: a part of you that makes you a very special person

   Point out that the key letters stand for, "**Just One You!**"

2. Urge the students to listen attentively as each student takes a turn sharing.

Suggested Reflection Questions

CONTENT (COGNITIVE LEARNING)
▶ Why is it helpful to share information about yourself?

COLLABORATIVE (SOCIAL LEARNING)
▶ How could you tell when people were really listening well?
▶ What can we do to help each other to be good listeners?
▶ What did the community or your tribe do to make this activity successful?

PERSONAL LEARNING
▶ What did you discover about yourself?
▶ How often do you give yourself a pat on the back for your special qualities?

Appreciation

Invite statements of appreciation:
▶ "It helped me when..."
▶ "I appreciated..."
▶ "Thank you for..."

Kitchen Kapers

Objectives

1. To build inclusion and influence
2. To experience the creative power of brainstorming as a problem-solving technique
3. To promote creativity and fun

Instructions

1. Prepare packets containing two 3 x 5-inch cards, two paper clips, four tooth-picks, and one pencil in a sealed business-sized envelope.
2. Have the community meet in tribes or form subgroups. Review the agreements.
3. Give each tribe a packet. State that they will have twelve minutes to invent and build "one kitchen utensil every household simply must have." Encourage bizarre, zany, and unique ideas. State that all tribe members need to participate.
4. Stop the "inventors" at twelve minutes.
5. Ask each tribe to then prepare a short, three minute commercial advertising its product. All members need to take part in the commercial.
6. Have each tribe present their commercial to the community.

Suggested Reflection Questions

CONTENT (COGNITIVE LEARNING)
- ▶ What inventions did the tribes create?
- ▶ How did the purpose of the utensil change as you built it?
- ▶ What did you learn from this activity?

COLLABORATIVE (SOCIAL LEARNING)
- ▶ How did leadership in your tribe evolve?
- ▶ How can a building project like this help build tribe spirit?
- ▶ What allowed your tribe to be creative and innovative?

PERSONAL LEARNING
- ▶ How did you feel before your tribe knew what it would build?
- ▶ How did you feel when you completed the invention?
- ▶ How did you help your tribe in a special way?
- ▶ What personal skills or strengths did you discover about yourself?

Appreciation

Invite statements of appreciation:
- ▶ "I felt good when..."
- ▶ "I liked it when..."

- ▶ **TIME** 25–30 min.
- ▶ **GROUPING** tribes , subgroups
- ▶ **MATERIALS** 3 x 5-inch cards, paper clips, tooth picks, pencils, envelopes
- ▶ **DEVELOPMENTAL TASKS** Independence/Autonomy Problem Solving

OPTIONS

Use the "invention" theme and have students develop an invention to accompany a unit of study (for example, a way to move a heavy stone using materials common in Ancient Egypt). Have students write an expository description of the finished product.

Variations: a household cleaning item

an office instrument

a garden tool

a laboratory device

Life Map

TIME 30 minutes

GROUPING tribes

MATERIALS large paper, colored pencils or markers

DEVELOPMENTAL TASKS
Independence/Autonomy
Social Competency
Sense of Purpose

OPTIONS

Make a plot map, story map, unit map, historical timeline, or scientific life map (for example, at age two I had an ear infection, at age ten I broke my finger...).

World language: Use a world language that is being learned to make a map of own life.

Objectives

1. To build inclusion
2. To create a visual illustration of one's life
3. To encourage attentive listening

Instructions

1. Ask the community to meet in tribes.
2. Give each student a piece of paper and crayons or markers and have him or her draw a visual illustration of "my life to date," the significant trends and patterns in the form of a map.
3. Invite each student to share his or her "Life Map" with his or her tribe members, explaining the rationale for "road signs," "place names," ups and downs, and so on.
4. Ask the students to give their full, undivided, caring attention to the speakers; after each student's presentation ask his or her tribe members to draw out more details, ask questions, and express their mutual feelings or concerns.

Suggested Reflection Questions

CONTENT (COGNITIVE LEARNING)
▶ Why is it important to be able to draw a "Life Map?"
▶ How were the maps in your tribe the same?

COLLABORATIVE (SOCIAL LEARNING)
▶ How could you tell that your tribe members were being good listeners when others shared their "Life Maps?"
▶ How did tribe members help each other during this activity?

PERSONAL LEARNING
▶ How did you feel as you made your life map/as you shared with your tribe?
▶ What did you learn about yourself?
▶ How are you a unique and special individual?

Appreciation
Invite statements of appreciation:
▶ "I felt good when..."
▶ "I like it when..."

Live Wire

Objectives
1. To create a visual illustration of one's life
2. To encourage attentive listening
3. To promote inclusion

Instructions
1. Have the community form tribes or triads.
2. Give each student a 30 inch long piece of light, bendable wire with which to construct a visual illustration of his or her "life to date:" the significant trends, patterns, and events of his or her years thus far.
3. Invite each student to share his or her "Live Wire" with other tribe members, explaining the rationale for its design.
4. Review the agreements. After one student shares, the others may ask questions, and express their mutual feelings or concerns.

Suggested Reflection Questions

CONTENT (COGNITIVE LEARNING)
▶ What did you learn in this activity?
▶ What similarities/differences were there among your experiences?

COLLABORATIVE (SOCIAL LEARNING)
▶ Why is the right to pass important for this activity?
▶ In what ways did your group members listen to or help each other?
▶ How can you, as a group, continue to improve your listening skills?

PERSONAL LEARNING
▶ How did you feel as you made/shared your lifeline?
▶ What did you learn about yourself from making or sharing your lifeline?
▶ What special qualities did others appreciate about you?

Appreciation
Invite statements of appreciation:
▶ "I felt good when..."
▶ "(Name), thank you for..."

▶ **TIME** 15 minutes
▶ **GROUPING** community, tribes, triads
▶ **MATERIALS** wire
▶ **DEVELOPMENTAL TASKS**
Independence/Autonomy
Social Competency
Sense of Purpose

OPTIONS

Use as a plot line in literature. Review what was read, and exchange "live wires." Write or create a plot that matches the "live wire."

Social Studies: Events of a war

Making a Choice

TIME 45 minutes

GROUPING tribes

MATERIALS "Making a Choice" handouts

DEVELOPMENTAL TASKS
Independence/Autonomy
Problem Solving

Objectives

1. To learn how to use a point system for evaluating choices
2. To involve students in evaluating choices
3. To create a positive decision-making process
4. To experience influence

Instructions

1. Have the students meet in tribes, and give each tribe the handout "Making A Choice."
2. Have tribe members read the problem aloud, discuss the advantages and disadvantages of the alternatives and make a choice.
3. Tell them to rate the criteria for each alternative by writing one, two or three in the appropriate boxes. Then add up the totals in each column. The tribe choice is the alternative with the highest rating.
4. After the tribes have made their choices, have them present their choice to the class. Point out how often people can have the same information and come up with different solutions.

OPTIONS

Use a historical event, a school issue, or a current event.

Suggested Reflection Questions

CONTENT (COGNITIVE LEARNING)
▶ What have you learned about making choices?
▶ How could a "weighted" point system help you or your tribe make a choice?

COLLABORATIVE (SOCIAL LEARNING)
▶ How did your tribe members help each other?
▶ What social skills did you, as a tribe, need to make a choice this way?

PERSONAL LEARNING
▶ How did you feel when your tribe came up with your solution?
▶ How did you help your tribe?
▶ What new skills or strengths did you discover about yourself?

Appreciation

Invite statements of appreciation:
▶ "I appreciated it when..."
▶ "You helped when..."

MAKING A CHOICE HANDOUT

INTRODUCTION

When we have a problem, we have a choice between alternative ways to solve it. One aspect of making a choice is to identify and compare the advantages and disadvantages of the alternatives. A systematic approach can be used to make the comparison. Study and complete the model chart below so that you can learn to use it to make good choices.

PROBLEM

You are a technology committee for a brand new high school. You have been given the task of deciding what technology you will install first. Your total budget for this year is $32,500 received from a technology grant. The money must be spent within the next three months. You want up-to-date good quality equipment that will have the widest possible use. You want students to be able to use it as soon as possible. There is no chance of more money this year.

ALTERNATIVES	ADVANTAGES	DISADVANTAGES
Interactive smart or white boards	Cost would be within budget	Company can't provide them for seven weeks
Computer Lab with instructional podcasts and online courses	Many students can use at a time	It might cost a bit more than budget
Multimedia center for film and photography	Some students have been asking for it	Uncertain if all students would use it
Computerized diagnostic equipment for autoshop	Important to have, and contractor could install within two weeks	Only some students would use it

Rate the criteria for each: 3=good or high, 2=medium, 1=low or poor

CRITERIA	SMART BOARDS	LAB W/ PODCAST	MULTIMEDIA	AUTO DIAGNOSIS
Installation cost				
Maintenance cost				
Current technology				
Appeals to all students				
TOTAL				

Meet Someone Special

OPTIONS

Use as a class appreciation by introducing "someone special" at the beginning or end of each day.

Have tribes write questions to ask characters from literature or history.

Objectives

1. To introduce individuals to a community
2. To build community inclusion
3. To build self-esteem and appreciation for uniqueness

Instructions

Note: This is a good activity to help new students introduce themselves to each other.

1. Have the community sit in a circle while you give directions.
2. Review the Tribes agreements.
3. Ask each student to stand up, look about for someone he or she does not know well, invite that person to be his or her partner.
4. Have one partner interview the other one for five to ten minutes, listening attentively so he or she will remember important unique qualities and details about the person; at the end of five to ten minutes, have the partners switch roles.
5. After the stated time, call the pairs back to the community circle and ask each student to introduce his or her partner and share the special things he or she learned.

Suggested Reflection Questions

CONTENT (COGNITIVE LEARNING)
▶ What new things did you learn from your partner?
▶ Why did you do this activity?

COLLABORATIVE (SOCIAL LEARNING)
▶ Why don't people take this type of time to get to know each other in other settings? In business and social organizations? In community meetings?
▶ What important social skills were used in this activity?
▶ What did community members do to make this activity successful?

PERSONAL LEARNING
▶ How well did you listen to your partner?
▶ How did you feel to have this much time to share about yourself?
▶ What did you learn about yourself that surprised you?
▶ What important social skills did you use during this activity?

Appreciation

Invite statements of appreciation:
▶ "I appreciated it when..."
▶ "I liked it when..."

Milling to Music

Objectives
1. To build community inclusion
2. To review curriculum topic

Instructions
1. Prepare for each student a slip on which there are four numbered questions. Example:
   - Describe three cities, towns or houses in which you have lived.
   - Share your favorite way to relax or spend vacation time.
   - Describe what your house, apartment, or living space is like.
   - If you were given $100,000 tomorrow, what would you do with it?
2. Give the students their slips with the four topics and ask them to stand up.
3. Explain that when the music starts they are to begin milling around silently but greeting each other as they pass by.
4. Explain that when the music stops (or when you give the hand signal), each student is to stop and discuss question #1 with a student standing close by for 1 minute. Explain that when the music begins again, they are to repeat the process until they have discussed all four questions.

Suggested Reflection Questions

CONTENT (COGNITIVE LEARNING)
- What kind of greetings did you use?
- What similar things did you share?

COLLABORATIVE (SOCIAL LEARNING)
- What skills did you, as community members, use to make this activity successful? (Suggest some: listening, speaking clearly, sharing time, respecting differences.)
- How has the atmosphere changed in the room?
- How do you feel about the community now?

PERSONAL LEARNING
- What did you learn about yourself?
- How are you a unique individual in the community?
- What special strengths are you proud of?

Appreciation
Invite statements of appreciation:
- "I liked it when..."
- "I appreciated the sharing that (name) did."

▶ **TIME** 15–25 min.

▶ **GROUPING** community

▶ **MATERIALS** slips with numbered topics, cassette tape player and lively music

▶ **DEVELOPMENTAL TASKS**
Social Competency
Sense of Purpose

OPTIONS

Use content information to create sharing groups.

Variation: Use with Extended Name Tag or any sharing activities.

Use academic questions instead or a mixture of academic and personal questions.

Multiple Intelligence Exploration

▶ **TIME** varies

▶ **GROUPING** tribes

▶ **MATERIALS** multiple intelligence checklist, pencils

▶ **DEVELOPMENTAL TASKS**
Independence/Autonomy
Social Competency
Sense of Purpose

OPTIONS

Once students are familiar with the Multiple Intelligences, as well as their own multiple intelligence "profile," use the inventory to create a character poem (one line for each intelligence strength or challenge).

Have students assume a character from literature or history or a general career or profession and complete the form "as if…"

Objectives

1. To explore the concept of multiple intelligence as it relates to one's personal experiences and preferences
2. To identify one's learning preferences and ways of knowing (i.e., multiple intelligences)
3. To appreciate others' learning preferences, natural abilities, and differences

Instructions

1. Have the students meet in their tribes.
2. Ask, "Do you notice how you are each special in certain ways? Take a moment to think about how you are different from each other, different from your sisters or brothers, different from your friends in special ways."
3. Say, "See if you can identify and write down three unique qualities that you appreciate about yourself or that others appreciate about you."
4. Say, "Now share one of those qualities with your tribe members."
5. State, "Learning about your natural abilities and valuing your unique gifts can be very helpful. Today we will begin to explore your preferences—your special ways of learning and knowing."
6. Pass out the Multiple Intelligence Checklists and read the directions at the top. (*Note:* It is important to give students unlimited time to complete the checklist. You may want to divide the checklist up and allow time during several different days.)
7. After students have completed the checklists, review the characteristics of each of the nine multiple intelligences (see chapter 10). (*Note:* As recommended by Dr. Thomas Armstrong, this checklist does not contain elements from the Existential intelligence, as it is an area that is best identified through personal reflection.)
8. Have students tally their checklists according to the directions on the Multiple Intelligences Tally Sheet that follows the checklist.
9. Give the students an opportunity to share their preferred ways of learning and knowing with their tribe members.
10. State, "The results of this checklist are 'not cast in concrete.' Your preferred ways of learning may change with time as you develop new interests and experience new things. Share with your tribe members which area(s) you might be interested in developing a bit more." (*Note:* The checklist may be given at other times during the school year. Students may want to develop personal goals about exploring new MI areas through a variety of classroom projects.)

Suggested Reflection Questions

CONTENT (COGNITIVE LEARNING)

▶ What did you learn from this activity?

▶ Which multiple intelligence is the easiest to understand? The hardest to understand?

COLLABORATIVE (SOCIAL LEARNING)

▶ How did you help each other during this activity?

▶ What different abilities did tribe members demonstrate to help make this activity successful?

▶ What special abilities do you appreciate about your tribe members?

PERSONAL LEARNING

▶ What did you discover about yourself?

▶ Did the results of your checklist "fit" or make sense for you?

▶ Which multiple intelligences are the most fun/most comfortable for you?

▶ Through which multiple intelligence(s) do you prefer to learn new material?

Appreciation

Invite statements of appreciation:

▶ "You really helped out with..."

▶ "You are really good at..."

▶ "Thank you for..."

Reference:

"Multiple Intelligences Checklist," adapted from 7 Kinds of Smart *by Thomas Armstrong, ©1993 by Thomas Armstrong. Used by permission of Plume, a division of Penguin Putnam Inc. Educators and human development professionals worldwide appreciate the work that Dr. Armstrong has done to bring the concepts of multiple intelligence to life through enjoyable and meaningful application.*

MULTIPLE INTELLIGENCES CHECKLIST

Instructions:

It is hoped that this checklist will be fun to do and will help you discover your many gifts. This is not a test—it's just for your own information—but it is based on wonderful studies done by many wise people about how we learn and why it is really great to know our own preferences; each one of us is unique and our preferences help us understand our special ways of learning and knowing.

Check any items that seem to apply to you. You may check as many as you like.
Please have a good time and enjoy yourself!

1. _____ I enjoy reading books.

2. _____ I have always liked math and science classes best and I do well in them.

3. _____ I enjoy drawing, painting and doodling.

4. _____ I love being outdoors and enjoy spending my free time outside.

5. _____ I have a pleasant singing voice and I like to sing.

6. _____ I'm the kind of person others come to for advice.

7. _____ I have some important goals for my life that I think about often.

8. _____ I love animals and I spend a lot of time with them.

9. _____ I like English, social studies and history better than math and science.

10. _____ I try to look for patterns and regularities in things, such as every third stair on the staircase has a notch in it.

11. _____ I like to figure out how to take apart and put back together things like toys and puzzles.

12. _____ I am an active person and if I can't move around I get bored.

13. _____ I frequently listen to music because I enjoy it so much.

14. _____ I like going to parties and social events.

15. _____ I think I am a very independent person.

16. _____ I enjoy watching nature shows on television like the Discovery Channel, National Geographic and Nova.

17. _____ I am good at using words to get others to change their mind.

18. _____ I enjoy playing around with a chemistry set and am interested in new discoveries in science.

19. _____ When I watch a movie or video, I am more interested in what I see than what I hear.

20. _____ I think I am well coordinated.

21. _____ I can play a musical instrument.

22. _____ I don't like to argue with people.

23. _____ Sometimes I talk to myself.

24. _____ It's fun to watch birds or other animals, to watch their habits, and to learn more about them.

25. _____ I'm good at Scrabble and other word games.

26. _____ I believe that almost everything has a logical explanation.

27. _____ When I close my eyes, sometimes I can see clear images in my head that seem real.

28. _____ I have good skills in one or more sports and learn new sports quickly.

29. _____ I can easily keep time to a piece of music.

30. _____ I enjoy getting other people to work together.

31. _____ I like to spend time alone thinking about things that are important to me.

32. _____ I'm very good at telling the difference between different kinds of birds, dogs, trees and stuff like that.

33. _____ I like to learn new words and know their meanings.

34. _____ I like to play games and solve brainteasers that require tactics and strategy.

35. _____ I am good at reading maps and finding my way around unfamiliar places.

36. _____ I don't like organized team sports as much as individual sports activities, such as tennis, swimming, skiing, golf or ballet.

37. _____ I know the tunes and titles of many songs and musical pieces.

38. _____ I consider myself a leader (and others call me that).

39. _____ I would rather spend a vacation in a cabin in the woods than at a fancy resort.

40. _____ I enjoy visiting zoos, natural history museums or other places where the world is studied.

41. _____ It's easy for me to memorize things at school.

42. _____ It is fun for me to work with numbers and data.

43. _____ I like some colors better than others.

44. _____ I don't mind getting my hands dirty from activities like painting, clay, or fixing and building things.

45. _____ Sometimes I catch myself walking along with a television jingle or song in my mind.

46. _____ When I have a problem, I'll probably ask a friend for help.

47. _____ I think I know what I am good at and what I'm not so good at doing.

48. _____ I like being outside whenever possible; I feel confident and comfortable there.

49. _____ I like to look things up in the dictionary or an encyclopedia.

50. _____ I like to ask people questions about how things work or why nature is the way it is.

51. _____ I sketch or draw when I think.

52. _____ Sometimes when I talk with people, I gesture with my hands.

53. _____ I like to make up my own tunes and melodies.

54. _____ I have at least three close friends.

55. _____ I have hobbies and interests that I prefer to do on my own.

56. _____ I like camping and hiking.

57. _____ I like to talk to friends and family better than watching TV.

58. _____ I have an easy time understanding new math concepts in school.

59. _____ I enjoy reading things more when they have lots of pictures and drawings.

60. _____ I would rather play a sport than watch it.

61. _____ Often I keep time to music by tapping to the beat or humming the tune when I am studying or talking on the phone.

62. _____ I am easy to get to know.

63. _____ I want to be self-employed or maybe start my own business.

64. _____ I want to become a volunteer in an ecological organization (such as Greenpeace or Sierra Club) to help save nature from further destruction.

65. _____ I like to write things like stories, poems and reports.

66. _____ I like things better when they are organized, categorized or measured.

67. _____ I am good at playing Pictionary, doing jigsaw puzzles, and solving mazes.

68. _____ I like to "ham it up" in skits, plays, speeches, sports or other types of activities.

69. _____ I can tell when notes are off-key.

70. _____ I feel comfortable most of the time, even in the midst of a crowd.

71. _____ I like to spend time by myself thinking about things that I value.

72. _____ When I was younger I used to dislodge big rocks from the ground to discover the living things underneath.

73. _____ I'm really good at describing things in words.

74. _____ I think I am good at working with numbers and data.

75. _____ I am better at remembering faces than names.

76. _____ I like working with my hands in activities such as sewing, carving, or model-building.

77. _____ I know what I like and don't like in music.

78. _____ I am good at making new friends.

79. _____ I like to think about things before I take any action.

80. _____ I have a green thumb and I am really good at keeping plants alive and healthy.

Note: As recommended by Dr. Armstrong, this checklist does not contain elements from the Existential intelligence, as it is an area that is best identified through personal reflection.

Reference:
"Multiple Intelligences Checklist," adapted from *7 Kinds of Smart,* by Thomas Armstrong, copyright ©1993 by Thomas Armstrong. Used by permission of Plume a division of Penguin Putnam Inc. The adaptation was done by Jeanne Mancour, who oversees Training Services for CenterSource Systems and who is a former high school teacher.

MULTIPLE INTELLIGENCES TALLY SHEET

Circle the numbers below that you checked on your Multiple Intelligence checklist.

Then count how many **circles** you have in each **column,** and write that number at the bottom of each column.

	1	2	3	4	5	6	7	8
	9	10	11	12	13	14	15	16
	17	18	19	20	21	22	23	24
	25	26	27	28	29	30	31	32
	33	34	35	36	37	38	39	40
	41	42	43	44	45	46	47	48
	49	50	51	52	53	54	55	56
	57	58	59	60	61	62	63	64
	65	66	67	68	69	70	71	72
	73	74	75	76	77	78	79	80
How many *circles* in each column?								
	LIN	L-M	SP	B-K	MU	NTER	NTRA	NAT

Look at the columns where you counted the most circles. You may have one, two or three areas that stand out. It doesn't really matter how many, but rather what "fits" and seems right for you. See the key below to discover your natural preferences!

LIN = Linguistic

L-M = Logical-Mathematical

SP = Spatial

B-K = Bodily-Kinesthetic

MU = Musical

NTER = Interpersonal

NTRA = Intrapersonal

NAT = Naturalist

Congratulations! You are a unique and special individual with many wonderful abilities, gifts and talents!

Newspaper Scavenger Hunt

Objectives

1. To learn how to find information in a newspaper
2. To work together to find the needed information
3. To experience influence

Instructions

1. Explain to the students that they will have ten to twenty minutes to find all the items in the paper described on the "Newspaper Scavenger Hunt" sheet, circle them in the newspaper with their colored pencil, and write the page numbers next to the items on the sheet. Say that everybody in the tribe is expected to participate and locate items.
2. Have the community meet in tribes. Assign roles in each tribe:
   - Taskmaster: gets the materials and monitors the time
   - Facilitator: ensures that each tribe member works his or her section of the paper
   - Spokesperson: reads the page numbers to the community when called upon
3. Have each taskmaster pick up one copy of the newspaper, one worksheet for his or her tribe, and a different colored pencil or pen for each tribe member.
4. Have each tribe divide the newspaper up between tribe members.
5. When time is up, ask the spokesperson from each tribe to share how many items his or her tribe was able to find. Randomly ask tribes to share what they found for various items on the worksheet.

Suggested Reflection Questions

CONTENT (COGNITIVE LEARNING)

▶ What did you learn about using a newspaper?
▶ What are the sections of a newspaper?

COLLABORATIVE (SOCIAL LEARNING)

▶ Which agreement is the most important in a strategy like this?
▶ How did your tribe help each other to participate in this activity?

PERSONAL LEARNING

▶ How did you feel when you found your items in the newspaper?
▶ What special strengths or skills did you use in your role to help your tribe members?
▶ Which role suits you the best?

Appreciation

Invite statements of appreciation:
▶ "I liked it when..."
▶ "Thanks, (name), for..."

Adapted from Lesson Plan: Scavenger Hunts, *by John Myers, Cooperative Learning, Spring, 1992*

▶ **TIME**   45 minutes

▶ **GROUPING** tribes

▶ **MATERIALS** one complete newspaper for each tribe, "Newspaper Scavenger Hunt" work sheets, colored pencils

▶ **DEVELOPMENTAL TASKS**
   Independence/Autonomy
   Problem Solving

OPTIONS

Use appropriate curriculum topics or themes.

NEWSPAPER SCAVENGER HUNT WORKSHEET

Look through your newspaper and locate the information asked for below. Circle the item in the paper with a colored pencil. Write in the page number where you found the information. When you are finished, fold the newspaper back into its original condition.

1. a comic where two people are arguing_____
2. an ad for a job in local or state government_____
3. a map_____
4. a picture of a famous person_____
5. the word "business"_____
6. an editorial article criticizing local, state, or federal government_____
7. an article about an environmental problem_____
8. the word "conflict"_____
9. an article about conflict in sports_____
10. an advertisement for a used car made five years ago_____
11. news about some aspect of education_____
12. a cartoon making a political statement_____
13. a letter to the editor about local government_____
14. an ad for a movie related to law enforcement_____
15. an article about a foreign country_____
16. a story which has to do with children_____
17. the word "defense"_____
18. an article relating to healthy living_____
19. a birth or death notice_____
20. the circulation (number of papers sold daily)_____

What strategy did your tribe use?

_____

_____

Make up four more questions:

_____

Adapted from Lesson Plan: Scavenger Hunts, *by John Myers, Cooperative Learning, Spring, 1992*

This page may be duplicated for classroom use.

Novel in an Hour

Objectives

1. To comprehend a novel, story or chapter of a book
2. To work cooperatively in small groups to retell the story by using drama, pictures, storytelling or other multiple intelligences
3. To practice listening, respecting and working together creatively

Instructions

1. Divide the chapters of a novel or short story into 5–10 sections, numbering each section.
2. Divide the class into the same number of groups.
3. Introduce the novel with an appropriate personal inclusion question for discussion.
4. Create interest in the novel by sharing something about the characters, theme or dilemma.
5. Describe the structure and process of Novel in an Hour:
   - the novel has been divided into sections (same number as groups)
   - everyone is actively involved
   - everyone takes turns reading the material aloud in their group
   - the group plans multiple ways to share their part of the material with the whole community by using their multiple intelligences (drama, music, illustration, etc.).
6. Have each group appoint a time keeper (example: planning: 20 minutes, and presentation: 30 minutes)
7. Have the groups make their presentations to the community in the order of the sections of the novel.

Suggested Reflection Questions

CONTENT (COGNITIVE LEARNING)
- ▶ Which character was most important in how the story ended?
- ▶ What do you think the author's message is?

COLLABORATIVE (SOCIAL LEARNING)
- ▶ What was difficult for your group in planning your presentation?
- ▶ What was most helpful?

PERSONAL LEARNING
- ▶ What feelings did you have during your group's presentation?
- ▶ What makes this a good way to learn about a novel or story?

Appreciation

Invite statements of appreciation:
- ▶ "I liked it when..."
- ▶ "I appreciated the way that our group..."

- ▶ **TIME** approx. 60 minutes, depending upon material
- ▶ **GROUPING** tribes
- ▶ **MATERIALS** short story or novel
- ▶ **DEVELOPMENTAL TASKS**
  Independence/Autonomy
  Social Competency
  Sense of Purpose
  Problem Solving

OPTIONS

Use science or social studies curriculum or text.

Now I Am

▶ **TIME** 20 minutes

▶ **GROUPING** community

▶ **MATERIALS** none

▶ **DEVELOPMENTAL TASKS**
Social Competency

Objectives

1. To recognize and identify feelings
2. To develop observation skills
3. To build inclusion

Instructions

1. Prepare slips for each person with a different emotion and put in a bag.
2. Have the community sit in a circle; review the agreements.
3. Have students select a slip with a different feeling or emotion.
   Examples:

fear	frustration	surprise	rage
nervousness	hope	soreness	love
dreaminess	anger	uncomfortable	wild
unhappiness	tired	embarrassed	weird
itchiness	stubborn	excitement	sleepy

4. Ask the students to act out their words nonverbally.
5. Have the community guess what each student is acting out.

Suggested Reflection Questions

CONTENT (COGNITIVE LEARNING)
- ▶ Which feelings were the easiest/most difficult to act out?
- ▶ How did you figure out what feeling was being represented?

COLLABORATIVE (SOCIAL LEARNING)
- ▶ How can you help each other discover the feelings you have at different times?
- ▶ Why is it sometimes difficult to act or speak in front of a group? What did the community do to help make it easier and fun?

PERSONAL LEARNING
- ▶ What did you enjoy about this activity?
- ▶ What did you learn about yourself by participating in this activity?

Appreciation

Invite statements of appreciation:
- ▶ "I liked the way you acted it out because..."
- ▶ "I feel a lot like you when..."

OPTIONS

Have students write a story about a person who always acts the same.

Print feeling words on cards, and have people act them out.

Have tribes write a story and act out the feelings associated with a historical, social event, or career.

Observe the Put Downs

Objectives
1. To promote awareness of put-downs and their effects
2. To practice reflecting on systems and situations

Instructions
1. Have a half hour, age appropriate sitcom videotaped and ready to view.
2. Ask the students to predict how many put-downs are present in a typical half hour comedy.
3. Tell the students to watch closely, and write down a tally mark each time they hear a put-down.
4. After five minutes, stop the tape and have the students share what statements from the show they marked as put-downs.
5. Continue watching/tallying until the end of the show. (Note: Do not be surprised if the totals for a half hour show are over 50!)

▶ TIME   40 minutes

▶ GROUPING   community

▶ MATERIALS   taped half hour sitcom, age appropriate

▶ DEVELOPMENTAL TASKS
   Independence/Autonomy
   Social Competency
   Sense of Purpose

Suggested Reflection Questions

CONTENT (COGNITIVE LEARNING)
▶ Why do people laugh at put-downs on TV?
▶ Who is never laughing at the put-downs?
▶ How many of this type of shows do people watch per week?

COLLABORATIVE (SOCIAL LEARNING)
▶ Why is the tribes agreement of "no put-downs" so important?
▶ How can you tell the difference between humor and put-downs?
▶ How can you help others to see the difference between humor and put-downs?

PERSONAL LEARNING
▶ What did you feel as your tally grew larger?
▶ How can you effect a change in put-downs/humor in your own life?
▶ What personal strengths will help you to help others not put people down?

OPTIONS

Have students watch the same sit-com at home and tally positive statements.

Have students record a number of the put-downs verbatim and change to positive statements.

Appreciation
Invite statements of appreciation:
▶ "I appreciate..."
▶ "You were really good at..."
▶ "Thanks for..."

On My Back

▶ TIME   20 minutes

▶ GROUPING community, tribes

▶ MATERIALS large paper, tape, markers

▶ DEVELOPMENTAL TASKS
  Independence/Autonomy
  Social Competency
  Sense of Purpose

OPTIONS

Use as a learning strategy for well-known characters in history, politics, current events, or literature.

Objectives
1. To build self-esteem
2. To encourage giving statements of appreciation
3. To build inclusion

Instructions
1. Give each student a large piece of paper, a felt marker, and two pieces of masking tape.
2. Ask each student to print his or her name at the top of the paper.
3. Have the students attach the papers to each other's shoulders so that they hang down like capes on their backs.
4. Have the students stand and circulate so that each person in the group can write statements of appreciation on other people's paper capes. Emphasize that the statements need to be positive.
5. When each student has several written statements on his or her cape, ask the community to sit in a circle or have them form tribes. Have the students read their statements aloud, have them exchange papers and read to each other, or privately.
6. Encourage people to save their papers, perhaps to use as posters for their bedroom walls.

Suggested Reflection Questions
CONTENT (COGNITIVE LEARNING)
▶ What were some of the neat things people wrote?
▶ What similarities did you see in what people wrote?
▶ How did the fact that this activity was anonymous help you to be honest?

COLLABORATIVE (SOCIAL LEARNING)
▶ How did you take care of each other?
▶ How did you take turns?
▶ What can you do to offer positive statements to others more often?

PERSONAL LEARNING
▶ What feelings did you have while people were writing on your back?
▶ What feelings did you have while your statements were being read aloud or while you were reading your statements?
▶ What statements felt very special to you?
▶ What new gifts did you discover after hearing the statements that were written about you?

Appreciation
Invite statements of appreciation:
▶ "I like it when..."
▶ "I felt good when..."

One-Minute History

Objectives

1. To give each student an opportunity to share his or her background
2. To build inclusion

Instructions

1. Have the community sit in a circle or meet in tribes or triads.
2. Instruct the students that each student will have one minute in turn to tell his or her personal history. Remind the listeners to give full attention without interrupting.

Suggested Reflection Questions

CONTENT (COGNITIVE LEARNING)

▶ What did you learn about someone else?
▶ Why is it important to be able to summarize your life?

COLLABORATIVE (SOCIAL LEARNING)

▶ How could you tell that others were using good listening skills?
▶ Why was a minute enough/not enough time to share?
▶ Did the students who shared later in the activity share more or less? Why?
▶ How did you help each other during this activity?

PERSONAL LEARNING

▶ How did you feel about sharing?
▶ What special skills did you use to help your group during this activity?
▶ How are you a unique individual in the group?

Appreciation

Invite statements of appreciation:
▶ "I liked it when you said..."
▶ "I felt good when..."
▶ "I was particularly interested when you..."

▶ **TIME** 20–30 min.

▶ **GROUPING** community, tribes, triads

▶ **MATERIALS** none

▶ **DEVELOPMENTAL TASKS**
Independence/Autonomy
Social Competency
Sense of Purpose

OPTIONS

Variation: One-minute sharing on a given academic topic.

Review a historical topic and invite students to summarize the content in one minute.

Use as a pre-writing strategy.

One Special Thing About Me

TIME 35–45 minutes

GROUPING community, pairs

MATERIALS none

DEVELOPMENTAL TASKS
Independence/Autonomy
Social Competency
Sense of Purpose

OPTIONS

Share: One thing I learned; one question I would ask of a historical figure or a character from literature; one thing I don't understand.

Objectives

1. To give students an opportunity to introduce themselves
2. To give students an opportunity to work in pairs before sharing
3. To promote inclusion

Instructions

1. Have the community sit in a circle. Say that we are a unique group about to start an exciting journey together and, like any people coming together, we need to learn about each other.
2. Say: "Think about yourself and something about you that people would remember. Think about something that makes you special. It doesn't have to be something big, but it needs to say something about you. It can be silly, fun, sentimental, or kind."
3. State that there will be one minute of quiet time before sharing with a partner.
4. After the minute, ask each student to share with a partner for two to three minutes.
5. After the students have shared with their partners, ask them to re-form the community circle.
6. Then go around the circle, inviting each student to state his or her name and what makes him or her special. Start with yourself to provide good modeling.

Suggested Reflection Questions

CONTENT (COGNITIVE LEARNING)
▶ Why is it difficult to think of something that makes you special?
▶ What types of things make you feel special?

COLLABORATIVE (SOCIAL LEARNING)
▶ Why is it easier to share with a partner?
▶ What social skills did community members use to make this activity successful?

PERSONAL LEARNING
▶ How did you feel sharing with one other person?
▶ How did you feel sharing in the community circle?
▶ What did you discover about yourself?
▶ What is something special that you are proud of?

Appreciation

Invite statements of appreciation:
▶ "I liked it when you said..."
▶ "Thank you for sharing..."

One, Two, Three

Objectives

1. To make choices between competing alternatives
2. To allow students to affirm and explain their choices
3. To practice decision-making
4. To promote influence

Instructions

1. Ask the students to meet in tribes, form groups of four to six, or meet as a community.
2. State that you will ask a question and then offer three alternative answers. Tell the students that you will be asking them to make some choices by ranking the three alternatives in the order of their importance or preference. Tell each student to write down the three alternatives and then put a number 1, number 2 or number 3 after each item according to his or her first, second and third choice. Examples:
   - Where would you rather be on a Saturday afternoon? At the beach? In the woods? Window shopping downtown?
   - Which do you consider most important in a friendship? Honesty? Loyalty? Generosity?
3. Have the students share their choices with each other and explain why they made the selections.

Suggested Reflection Questions

CONTENT (COGNITIVE LEARNING)
▶ How did your choices compare to choices made by others?
▶ Why are some choices harder to make than others?
▶ What choices might be more difficult/easier to make?

COLLABORATIVE (SOCIAL LEARNING)
▶ Why is being able to make a choice an important skill?
▶ What did you, as a community, do to make this activity successful?

PERSONAL LEARNING
▶ What feelings did you have when you had difficulty choosing?
▶ What have you learned about yourself?
▶ What personal strengths or skills helped you make your choices?
▶ In what special way did you contribute to the group?

Appreciation

Invite statements of appreciation:
▶ "I liked it when..."
▶ "I appreciated your dilemma when..."

▶ **TIME** 10–15 min.

▶ **GROUPING** community, tribes , subgroups

▶ **MATERIALS** pencils, paper

▶ **DEVELOPMENTAL TASKS**
Independence/Autonomy
Social Competency
Sense of Purpose

OPTIONS

Use classroom or social issues.

Introduce possible study or assignment topics.

Use the "multiple choice" format to reflect or assess the "best answer."

Prediction for literature, e.g., Do you think the character will face the problem? Avoid the problem? Add to the problem?

Open Forum

OPTIONS

Use questions about current events or social issues.

Use the strategy for questions related to academic content.

Government: What can be done to increase voter turnout?

Guidance: Is honesty always the best policy?

P.E./Health: Should medical marijuana be legal?

Objectives

1. To encourage acceptance of diverse feelings, beliefs, and cultures
2. To build inclusion

Instructions

1. Have the community meet in tribes or subgroups.
2. Tell the students that you will write a discussion question on the board, and each tribe member is to take a turn responding to the question. Discussion is not allowed until each tribe member has had an opportunity to respond to the question. After all tribe members have had a chance to speak, students may ask one another follow-up questions and ask for clarification of what was said.
3. Remind the groups about the tribe agreements, especially "attentive listening."
4. Examples of inclusion questions:
   • What is the best book you ever read? Why did you like it?
   • How did you select your friends?
   • What guides your life?
   • What makes a good hero?
   • What goal do you have for your future?

Suggested Reflection Questions

CONTENT (COGNITIVE LEARNING)
▶ What was something you learned from your discussion?

COLLABORATIVE (SOCIAL LEARNING)
▶ What social skills did your group use to make this activity successful?
▶ How could you tell that your tribe members were being good listeners when you shared?

PERSONAL LEARNING
▶ How did you feel answering the questions?
▶ How did you participate? Are you happy with the way you participated? Why?
▶ How did you help the group in a special way?
▶ What did you learn about yourself from participating in this activity?

Appreciation

Invite statements of appreciation:
▶ "I liked it when..."
▶ "I'm a lot like you when..."
▶ "You're a lot like me when..."

Our Treasury

Objectives
1. To allow for individual influence
2. To practice group decision-making

Instructions
1. Ask the community to meet in tribes.
2. Give each group a fictitious sum of money (or paper money), which is to be its tribe treasury.
3. Tell each tribe to brainstorm about the best uses of this money. (Review the brainstorming process if necessary.) Have the tribes make a list of their ideas.
4. Have each tribe decide what four things on its list it would spend its treasury on.
5. Ask each tribe to report its decision to the community.

Suggested Reflection Questions

CONTENT (COGNITIVE LEARNING)
- ▶ What were some of the things you listed?
- ▶ What did you learn about making choices?
- ▶ Why is deciding how to spend money often difficult?

COLLABORATIVE (SOCIAL LEARNING)
- ▶ How did you resolve differences of opinion among tribe members?
- ▶ What are the most important social skills you need when making decisions as a tribe?

PERSONAL LEARNING
- ▶ How do you feel about the decisions you made?
- ▶ What have you learned about yourself?
- ▶ How did you contribute to your tribe in a positive way?

Appreciation
Invite statements of appreciation:
- ▶ "I appreciated it when..."
- ▶ "I knew what you meant when you said..."
- ▶ "I liked it when..."

- ▶ TIME   60 minutes
- ▶ GROUPING   tribes
- ▶ MATERIALS none
- ▶ DEVELOPMENTAL TASKS
  Independence/Autonomy
  Problem Solving

OPTIONS

Use the fictitious money to "spend" on charity or public service.

Make a personal budget in order to teach life skills.

Our World is Changing

TIME   45 minutes

GROUPING   community, tribes

MATERIALS   paper, pencils

DEVELOPMENTAL TASKS
Independence/Autonomy
Problem Solving

OPTIONS

Have the tribes conduct research, interviews, or make graphs, drawings or collages that show how the world has changed since their parents were born. Expand and elaborate on a single issue, such as how the world has changed. Follow-up with a writing experience, Venn diagram, graph or research project.

History: Compare time periods.

P.E.: Game rules and equipment have changed; how has it impacted the players?

Objectives

1. To create a tribe list of changes in the world
2. To give individuals an appreciation of change
3. To practice brainstorming

Instructions

1. Have the community meet in tribes and have the tribe members greet each other.
2. Review the rules for brainstorming (see "Brainstorming" strategy).
3. Have each tribe select a recorder. Have the recorders raise their hands so you can be certain each recorder is ready.
4. Have the tribes brainstorm and write lists of how the world has changed since their parents (or grandparents) were born. Give the tribes five minutes to brainstorm.
5. Have the community meet. Have tribes report one or two changes that have made an impact on their lives. (*Suggestion:* Ask the student with the shortest hair in each tribe, or some other characteristic, to report.)

Suggested Reflection Questions

CONTENT (COGNITIVE LEARNING)
▶ What do you feel are the most important changes that have happened?
▶ Why is it important to know how the world has changed?

COLLABORATIVE (SOCIAL LEARNING)
▶ Why is brainstorming a good strategy to use?
▶ What social skills did your group need or use to be successful at this strategy?

PERSONAL LEARNING
▶ How did you feel sharing the changes you recognized?
▶ What did you do to help your tribe?
▶ What special strengths or skills do you bring to your tribe??

Appreciation

Invite statements of appreciation:
▶ "I liked it when you said..."
▶ "Thank you for..."

Outlines

Objectives

1. To build inclusion
2. To practice communication and listening skills
3. To discuss academic topics

Instructions

1. Have the students meet either in their tribes or the community circle.
2. Explain the objectives, and pass out "T-Shirt Outline" worksheets.
3. Tell students how to fill in the outline:
   - in area #1 write an alliterative adjective that goes with your first name. Example: "Vivacious Vicki"
   - in area #2 write or draw two to three things you enjoy doing
   - in area #3 name a real or pretend place you would like to visit
   - in area #4 write a word you'd like people to say when they describe you
   - in area #5 write a wish you have for yourself
4. Sharing: First review the Tribes agreements, and ask the students to share the time equally so that each student has an opportunity to speak during each round.
   - Round 1: each student shares his or her name and alliterative adjective with another student, telling why he or she chose the adjective (three minutes).
   - Round 2: each student finds two other people and shares the information he or she wrote in area #2 (four minutes).
   - Round 3: each student finds two other people and shares the information of area #3 (four minutes).
   - Round 4: each finds three to four others and shares area #4 (four minutes).
   - Round 5: each Round 4 group combines with another Round 4 group. Names and alliterative adjectives are shared again with students telling why they chose their particular adjectives.

Suggested Reflection Questions

CONTENT (COGNITIVE LEARNING)
- ▶ What did you learn about your tribe members?
- ▶ What were the similarities among your tribe members' wishes?

COLLABORATIVE (SOCIAL LEARNING)
- ▶ How could you tell when people were listening well to each other?
- ▶ How many students do you feel you know better now?

PERSONAL LEARNING
- ▶ What did you learn about yourself from this activity?
- ▶ What unique qualities do you bring to your group?

Appreciation

Invite statements of appreciation:
- ▶ "I like it when..."
- ▶ "I'm glad you're..."

- ▶ **TIME** 30–40 min.
- ▶ **GROUPING** community, tribes
- ▶ **MATERIALS** "T-Shirt Outline" worksheet, colored pens or pencils
- ▶ **DEVELOPMENTAL TASKS**
  Independence/Autonomy
  Social Competency
  Sense of Purpose

OPTIONS

There are endless other fine questions for this activity: someone you admire, a quality you like in a friend, something you want to learn, favorite subject or book, academic material. Select those most appropriate for the group's age and culture.

Use the outline for a fictitious character or a well-known person.

Have students design other outlines to use for subject content.

T-SHIRT OUTLINE

This page may be duplicated for classroom use.

Pantomime

Objectives

1. To build self-esteem
2. To build inclusion
3. To experience communication without words

Instructions

1. Have the students form two groups. Have each group take a turn doing expressions and movements.
2. There is no discussion until both groups have finished.
3. The following are suggestions of expressions and movement:
   - facial expressions: funny, scared, sad
   - feeling walks: walk angrily, walk sadly
   - weather walks: walk in the rain
   - people walks: robber, clown
   - animal walks: dog, cat, duck
   - characters and situations: an acrobat on a tightrope
   - exploring senses: taste a lemon, smell a skunk
   - handling imaginary objects: play with a yo-yo
   - experiencing different environments: you are on the moon

Suggested Reflection Questions

CONTENT (COGNITIVE LEARNING)

▶ Why was it easy/difficult to demonstrate your feelings?
▶ What did you find out about others in your group?

COLLABORATIVE (SOCIAL LEARNING)

▶ What did we have to do to make this activity successful?
▶ How could you tell that others were being good watchers and listeners?

PERSONAL LEARNING

▶ What did you find out about yourself? How are you a unique individual?
▶ What special skills did you use during this activity?

Appreciation

Invite statements of appreciation:

▶ "I liked it when..."
▶ "I'm like you when..."
▶ "I felt good when..."

▶ **TIME**   20 minutes

▶ **GROUPING**   community

▶ **MATERIALS** none

▶ **DEVELOPMENTAL TASKS**
   Independence/Autonomy
   Social Competency

OPTIONS

Use the strategy to act out or draw vocabulary words or concepts relevant to content.

Drama class: Work on key character's emotional scenes.

Paraphrase Passport

▶ **TIME** 20 minutes

▶ **GROUPING** community, tribes, triads

▶ **MATERIALS** none

▶ **DEVELOPMENTAL TASKS**
Independence/Autonomy
Social Competency

OPTIONS

Use to check for understanding, review content, state opinions (perhaps as a pre-write for a persuasive paragraph or essay).

Role play historical or social issues.

Math: Explain the steps used to solve the problem.

Objectives

1. To follow up on the "Reflective Feeling" strategy
2. To practice listening
3. To practice paraphrasing while discussing a topic

Instructions

1. Review the strategy "Reflecting Feelings" with the community. Have the students discuss how they felt when they played the roles of speaker, feeling reflector, and observer.

2. Tell students they will be discussing topics by using "paraphrasing passports," which is a way to learn how to be a good listener. In "Paraphrase Passport" no one has permission to speak until he or she correctly restates (paraphrases) the idea of the previous speaker. Example:

> John: "I am concerned that violence is increasing in many cities, and believe that unemployment is a major cause."
>
> Sarah: "John, you are concerned about the increase in violence and attribute it to unemployment."

3. Have students again form the triads they were in for "Reflecting Feelings" and choose who will be the first speaker. Explain that the first student contributes an idea and the second student must restate it correctly before contributing his or her idea.

> Topic to discuss:
> "How does good listening help to develop caring and learning in a community?"

Suggested Reflection Questions

CONTENT (COGNITIVE LEARNING)
▶ What did you learn from your discussion about listening?
▶ Why is listening an important social skill?

COLLABORATIVE (SOCIAL LEARNING)
▶ How well did you paraphrase what the person before you said?
▶ How did your group help each other during this activity?

PERSONAL LEARNING
▶ How might "Paraphrase Passport" help you to listen to others?
▶ How could good listening help you to be a better friend?
▶ What communication skills do you feel particularly good at?

Appreciation

Invite statements of appreciation:
▶ "I liked it when you said..."
▶ "It felt good when..."

This structure is from Cooperative Learning, Resources for Teachers, *by Spencer Kagan*

Paraphrasing

Objectives

1. To build inclusion and influence
2. To teach and practice paraphrasing

Instructions

VERSION A:

1. Have the community stand or sit in a large circle.
2. Turn to the student on your left and ask a question. Examples:
   - "What is your favorite holiday?"
   - "What is your favorite fruit?"
3. The next student answers and the first student who asked the question repeats back the answer. Example:
   Student #1: "What's your favorite color?"
   Student #2: "Red."
   Student #1: "Shawn's favorite color is red."
4. Have students continue the sequence around the circle.

VERSION B:

1. Give all the students colored paper strips prepared as follows:
   "_____'s favorite _____ is _____."
2. Have tribe members pair up and decide who is #1 and who is #2.
3. Have partner #1 ask a question and partner #2 give the answer.
4. Then have partner #1 fill in the blanks on his or her strip.
5. Have partners switch so that partner #2 now asks the question.
6. After all the students fill in the blanks on their colored strips have the tribes staple the strips together and display them.

Suggested Reflection Questions

CONTENT (COGNITIVE LEARNING)

- What similarities did you notice in people's answers?
- Why are we learning about paraphrasing?

COLLABORATIVE (SOCIAL LEARNING)

- Why is it important to take turns in this strategy?
- How could you tell people were cooperating during this activity?

PERSONAL LEARNING

- How did you like working with a partner?
- What did you contribute during this activity?
- What "people skills" do you feel most comfortable using?

Appreciation

Invite statements of appreciation:

- "I liked working with you, (name), because..."
- "Thank you for..."

▶ **TIME** 30–45 min.

▶ **GROUPING** community, tribes

▶ **MATERIALS** colored paper strips

▶ **DEVELOPMENTAL TASKS**
Independence/Autonomy
Social Competency
Sense of Purpose

OPTIONS

The strategy can be used for various combinations of curriculum material.

A variation on Version A is to have students ask each other across the circle or to integrate the strategy with the "Spider Web" strategy.

In Version B, students can work in groups of three or four, asking and recording things that they have learned about a lesson or topic.

World Languages: Use the world language being studied and vary the prompts.

Partner Introduction

- **TIME** 35–45 minutes
- **GROUPING** community, pairs
- **MATERIALS** none
- **DEVELOPMENTAL TASKS**
  Independence/Autonomy
  Social Competency
  Sense of Purpose

OPTIONS

Use this strategy to preview or review a unit of study, or apply to actual content standards (for example, have students share everything they know about writing conventions).

Objectives

1. To give students an opportunity to introduce themselves
2. To give students an opportunity to work in pairs before sharing
3. To experience inclusion

Instructions

1. State that we are a unique group about to start an exciting journey together, and, like any people coming together, we need to learn about each other.
2. Have each student find a partner he or she does not know very well. Have the partners decide who will be the interviewer and who will be the interviewed. For one minute the interviewer will tell his partner all the things that he does not know about him. The interviewee is only to listen and not respond. For example, an interviewer might say, "I don't know your name," "I don't know how many people are in your family," etc.
3. The partner being interviewed then responds for two minutes giving information that they would be willing to have shared with the whole community.
4. Have the partners switch roles and repeat the strategy.
5. Have the community form a circle and have each student introduce his or her partner to the community, and share one thing they learned about their partner.

Suggested Reflection Questions

CONTENT (COGNITIVE LEARNING)
- What did you learn about your partner?
- What are the most common things you shared?

COLLABORATIVE (SOCIAL LEARNING)
- Why might interviewing be a good way to get to know somebody?
- Why is attentive listening so important for this strategy?
- What special strengths or skills did community members use to make this activity successful?

PERSONAL LEARNING
- How did you feel to interview your partner?
- How did you feel to have your partner share what you said?
- What communication or "people skills" do you feel particularly good using?

Appreciation

Invite statements of appreciation:
- "One thing I liked was..."
- "Thank you for..."

Path-Maze

Objectives

1. To help pairs begin to experience the stage of influence
2. To develop non-verbal problem solving skills
3. To energize students and build community
4. To reinforce subject related content material

Instructions

1. Use masking tape to draw a giant grid on the floor. Make the grid approximately 10 feet wide by 12½ feet long. Use the tape to make 4 squares across and 5 squares long. Each square is approximately 2½ feet by 2½ feet in size.
2. On a piece of scratch paper, draw the grid and trace an imaginary path through the grid.
3. Have the students line up on one side of the grid and tell them that you have traced an imaginary pathway through the grid from one end to the other. However, let them know that you are the only one who knows the secret pathway. It is their job to find out for themselves the secret path. The students can work individually (intrapersonally) or with a partner (interpersonally) to see if they can find the secret path, however, they cannot talk to each other. If they step on a square that is on the secret path, they will hear (teacher will say) a "ding," which means they are correct. If they step in a square that is not on the secret path, they will hear an "errrrr," which means they are incorrect. If they hear the ding, they can proceed on. If they hear the "errrr," they must go to the end of the line and start over.
4. The next pair in the line must remember the path from the previous pairs' trials and errors as they attempt to find the path through the maze.
5. When an individual or team has found the secret path, the group may talk about the experience.

Suggested Reflection Questions

CONTENT (COGNITIVE LEARNING)
▶ How is this grid like being a new student in a classroom or school?
▶ What multiple intelligences might be useful to solve this puzzle?
▶ How is this activity like "life?"

COLLABORATIVE (SOCIAL LEARNING)
▶ How did you learn to negotiate with your partner when you weren't allowed to use words?
▶ How did you and your partner help each other?

PERSONAL LEARNING
▶ How would you change your approach to solving the puzzle?
▶ What skills did you use to solve the puzzle?
▶ What new gifts did you discover about yourself?

▶ **TIME** 30 minutes

▶ **GROUPING** pairs, community

▶ **MATERIALS** masking tape

▶ **DEVELOPMENTAL TASKS** Social Competency Problem Solving

OPTIONS

This activity may be used to reinforce subject related content material.

Students enjoy making the path more difficult by having "language of the discipline" vocabulary words written in the grid squares. The students must define the words in order to proceed.

With subject related material, allow team members to discuss the answers before they make a decision.

Use a tarp that can be folded and re-used throughout the year. (Perhaps facilitate as an outdoor activity?)

Appreciation

Invite statements of appreciation:

- ▶ "I appreciated…"
- ▶ "I liked it when…"
- ▶ "You were really good at…"

Peer-Response Huddle

Objectives

1. To structure a cooperative learning experience
2. To develop energy and interest in curricula
3. To build pride
4. To promote influence

Instructions

1. Have the community meet in tribes.
2. Have the tribe members count off, beginning with the number one, or pass out numbered cards so that each tribe member has a number.
3. Tell the students that you will call out a question, and that each tribe has thirty seconds to huddle and decide upon one answer. Say you will then call out a number, and that each tribe member with that number will quickly stand up. Say you will ask one of the students standing to give the answer.
4. Keep the questions, huddle time, and responses going as rapidly as possible so that the energy takes on a "popcorn" effect. Don't call on the first person that pops up unless you intend to promote competition. After an answer is given, lead the applause.

Suggested Reflection Questions

CONTENT (COGNITIVE LEARNING)
- What did you learn that you didn't know before?
- Why is this a good way to review information?

COLLABORATIVE (SOCIAL LEARNING)
- What social skills did your tribe need to be successful?
- How can your tribe improve the way it worked together?

PERSONAL LEARNING
- How did you feel when your number was called?
- How did you help your tribe in a special way?
- What personal strengths did you discover about yourself?
- How do you feel about your tribe now?

Appreciation

Invite statements of appreciation:
- "I liked it when..."
- "I want to thank you, (name), for..."

▶ **TIME**   15 minutes

▶ **GROUPING** tribes

▶ **MATERIALS** none, or 5 x 7-inch cards

▶ **DEVELOPMENTAL TASKS**
   Independence/Autonomy
   Sense of Purpose
   Problem Solving

OPTIONS

This strategy is easily used for a spur-of-the-moment check for understanding or reflection on learning.

It can also be used to review an entire unit of study by inviting students to write or define questions.

Acknowledgement to Spencer Kagan's structure, "Numbered Heads Together"

Peer-Response Tic-Tac-Toe

TIME 20–30 minutes

GROUPING community, tribes

MATERIALS paper, pencils

DEVELOPMENTAL TASKS
Independence/Autonomy
Problem Solving

OPTIONS

Use vocabulary taught over time to review previous knowledge.

Use a very general variety of terms from multiple subjects, like political or historical figures; periodic table; concepts in any subject area

Even better, have the students develop the clues for the ten terms used for each game!

Objectives

1. To promote decision-making
2. To review content-related vocabulary

Instructions

Note: This is played similar to "bingo" but on a Tic-Tac-Toe format.

1. Write a list of ten vocabulary words on the board, numbered 1–10. (*Note:* You may also use ten words relating to subject material, such as a historical figure.)
2. Have students meet in tribes or groups of 4–5.
3. Have each student draw his/her own Tic-Tac-Toe board and randomly write down one number in each square, using nine out of ten numbers from 1-10.
4. Say the definition or clue related to a word on the list. Example: This person was an inventor and artist.
5. Have the students, in tribes, discuss which numbered answer is correct, and have them mark an "X" on the numbered square on their individual tic-tac-toe boards.
6. When a winner is declared in each tribe, simply start a new game.
7. After 5–10 minutes, ask various students to come up with the definitions or clues for each word.

Suggested Reflection Questions

CONTENT (COGNITIVE LEARNING)
- What did you learn?
- How did you improve your knowledge of this subject?

COLLABORATIVE (SOCIAL LEARNING)
- How did you know that your group members were listening well to each other?
- What were some things that your group members did to help each other?
- Why is learning in a group more valuable than learning individually?

PERSONAL LEARNING
- How did you contribute to your tribe?
- What personal strengths or skills helped you during this activity?
- How do you usually prefer to learn information like this?

Appreciation

Invite statements of appreciation:
- "I liked how..."
- "One thing I like about this group is..."
- "Thank you for..."

People Hunt

Objectives

1. To promote community inclusion
2. To introduce oneself to others
3. To encourage sharing information

Instructions

1. Give one-third of the students worksheet I, one-third worksheet II, and one-third worksheet III.
2. Have the students circulate around the room, stopping to introduce him or herself, and asking different students the questions listed on his or her worksheet. Tell them to write down the names of those who fit the descriptions.
3. After ten to fifteen minutes, ask the community to meet in tribes or form groups of five for reflection questions.

Suggested Reflection Questions

CONTENT (COGNITIVE LEARNING)

▶ What did you learn that impressed or surprised you?

COLLABORATIVE (SOCIAL LEARNING)

▶ How could you tell when group members were participating fully in this task?
▶ What social skills were used to be successful with this task?

PERSONAL LEARNING

▶ How did you approach this task, did you go to people or did you wait for people to come to you?
▶ What strengths or skills did you use?
▶ What did you learn about yourself from this activity?
▶ Do you feel any different now than when you first walked into the room?

Appreciation

Invite statements of appreciation:
▶ "I liked it when you..."
▶ "I felt good when..."
▶ "I'm like you when..."

▶ **TIME** 40 minutes

▶ **GROUPING** community

▶ **MATERIALS** "People Hunt" worksheets, pencils

▶ **DEVELOPMENTAL TASKS**
Independence/Autonomy
Social Competency
Sense of Purpose

OPTIONS

Personalize the "People Hunt" by using statements that you know apply to students.

Use the strategy to review academic content by writing appropriate questions (for example, Astronomy Hunt: A person who can explain the solar eclipse.)

PEOPLE HUNT WORKSHEET I

FIND:

1. A person who does not own a TV

   His or her name is_____

2. A person whose birthday is within a month of yours

   His or her name is_____

3. A person who can cross his or her eyes

   His or her name is_____

4. A person who traveled over 2,000 miles last summer

   His or her name is_____

5. A person who lives in a house where no one smokes

   His or her name is_____

6. A person who owns a horse

   His or her name is_____

7. A person who is new to this school

   His or her name is_____

8. A person who likes brussels sprouts

   His or her name is_____

9. A person who is an artist

   His or her name is_____

10. A person who has more than six brothers and sisters

    His or her name is_____

This page may be duplicated for classroom use.

PEOPLE HUNT WORKSHEET II

FIND:

1. A person who can speak two languages

   His or her name is_____

2. A person who has been to a concert

   His or her name is_____

3. A person who has two different colored eyes

   His or her name is_____

4. A person with a part-time job

   His or her name is_____

5. A person whose birthday is the same month as yours

   His or her name is_____

6. A person who can roll his or her tongue

   His or her name is_____

7. A person who has been ice skating this past year

   His or her name is_____

8. A person not born in this country

   His or her name is_____

9. A person who has more than four animals in his or her home

   His or her name is_____

10. A person who woke up with a smile this morning

    His or her name is_____

This page may be duplicated for classroom use.

PEOPLE HUNT WORKSHEET III

FIND:

1. A person not born in California (New York, Texas, etc.)

   His or her name is_____

2. A person who stayed home last summer

   His or her name is_____

3. A person whose birthday is one month before yours

   His or her name is_____

4. A person who is the oldest child in his or her family

   His or her name is_____

5. A person who can touch his or her nose with his or her tongue

   His or her name is_____

6. A person who likes to invent things

   His or her name is_____

7. A person who jogs for exercise

   His or her name is_____

8. A person who has four dogs in his or her home

   His or her name is_____

9. A person who has been horseback riding in the past three months

   His or her name is_____

10. A person who has planted a tree

    His or her name is_____

People Puzzles

Objectives

1. To build inclusion
2. To form or assign membership in tribes

Instructions

1. Before using the strategy, prepare one puzzle for each group or tribe. Cut each puzzle so that the number of pieces matches the number of people in each group or tribe.
2. To build random groups, put all the pieces of all the puzzles in a box and have each person take a piece. To assign tribes put the name of one person on each piece of puzzle, and pass out pieces to each person identified on the pieces.
3. Before having the students form their tribes, have a discussion about what possible put-downs could occur and how to avoid them.
4. Ask the students to circulate and find the puzzle pieces that match the ones they are carrying. Tell them they are not to talk while doing this. Tell them they may talk when their group's puzzle has been completed.
5. Once all of the puzzles have been completed, you may choose to have each tribe make up a story relating to the picture its puzzle has formed. Have each tribe select one member to be a storyteller and tell the tribe's story to the community.

Suggested Reflection Questions

CONTENT (COGNITIVE LEARNING)
▶ What made this task difficult/easy?
▶ Was this a fun way to find students who would be in your tribe?

COLLABORATIVE (SOCIAL LEARNING)
▶ How did you help students whose puzzle pieces didn't fit yours?
▶ What did you talk about when your puzzle was completed?
▶ How did you help each other during this activity?

PERSONAL LEARNING
▶ How did you feel when you first started this activity? At the end?
▶ How were you able to help your tribe?
▶ What did you discover about yourself from participating in this activity?

Appreciation

Invite statements of appreciation:
▶ "I liked it when..."
▶ "I'm a lot like you when..."
▶ "I admire you for..."

▶ **TIME**   20 minutes

▶ **GROUPING** tribes

▶ **MATERIALS** picture, puzzles

▶ **DEVELOPMENTAL TASKS**
Social Competency
Problem Solving

OPTIONS

Create puzzle sets, each containing related historical events, mathematical or scientific concepts. Have students circulate to find the related concepts, and then review with each other.

Use postcards to create puzzles.

Perception and Transmission of Information

▶ **TIME**   40 minutes

▶ **GROUPING** community

▶ **MATERIALS** copies of young girl/old woman drawing

▶ **DEVELOPMENTAL TASKS**
   Independence/Autonomy
   Social Competency

OPTIONS

Use prior to history curricula concerning warfare, debates, constitutional rights, or different political views.

Explore social topics, such as the viewpoint of parents versus teenagers.

Objectives

1. To promote inclusion and influence
2. To promote an understanding of different points of view
3. To demonstrate how perceptual limitations can affect communications

Instructions

1. Have the community meet in tribes.
2. After an inclusion activity, hand out copies of the young girl/old woman drawing to each tribe. Instruct the tribe members to glance at the drawings briefly, without discussion. Then collect all copies immediately.
3. Ask people to share what they saw in the drawing. Emphasize the concept that people perceive differently; ask questions such as, "Would you talk to this person on the bus?" or, "Does this person remind you of someone you may have met or know?"
4. Give copies of the drawing to each tribe member and have the tribes continue the discussion.
5. Assist students who have difficulty identifying both aspects of the drawing.
6. Have the tribe members expand their discussions to other areas in which their points of view might be limited by their perception of information.

Suggested Reflection Questions

CONTENT (COGNITIVE LEARNING)

▶ Why do some of you see a young girl while others see an old woman? Is there a correct way to see the picture?
▶ Why is this an important activity to do?

COLLABORATIVE (SOCIAL LEARNING)

▶ Why do conflicts arise between individuals who perceive information differently?
▶ How can you resolve conflicts based on different perceptions?
▶ How did community members show their appreciation of different perceptions during this activity?

PERSONAL LEARNING

▶ What did you feel towards the students who saw the drawing the same way you did/differently than you did?
▶ How did you feel when you "discovered" the other aspect of the drawing?
▶ Did you discover any hidden gifts or talents in yourself that you were not aware of?

Appreciation

Invite statements of appreciation:
▶ "I am a lot like you when..."
▶ "I felt good when you said..."

This page may be duplicated for classroom use.

Personal Contract

▶ TIME 15 minutes

▶ GROUPING tribes

▶ MATERIALS 5 x 8-inch
index cards, pencils

▶ DEVELOPMENTAL TASKS
Independence/Autonomy
Sense of Purpose

OPTIONS

Teach life skills using
real contracts.

Have students study
historical contracts.

Compare and contrast
social contracts and
laws.

Objectives

1. To reflect upon personal situations
2. To commit to new attitudes, behaviors or achievements
3. To experience support from peers
4. To build influence

Instructions

1. Have the community meet in tribes. Ask each tribe member to identify a personal behavior, attitude or achievement they would like to accomplish.
2. Explain how writing a "personal contract" makes change easier. Explain that a contract is a commitment that is specific, believable, and attainable in a certain period of time.
3. Give students time to consider, then have each write a personal contract as follows:

   "I, (name), will (describe specific commitment or action) by (specific date)."
   Signed:_____
   Witnessed:_____
   Witnessed:_____

4. Have each student ask two tribe members to sign as witnesses and be supportive of the change to be made.
5. Suggest each student ask tribe members to check on progress of the contract's completion.
6. Keep contracts in tribe envelopes for periodic review.

Suggested Reflection Questions

CONTENT (COGNITIVE LEARNING)
▶ For what personal behavior, attitude, or achievement did you write a contract?
▶ Why is developing a personal contract difficult?
▶ How can a personal contract help you make the change you want to make?

COLLABORATIVE (SOCIAL LEARNING)
▶ What role did the witnesses play in this contract?
▶ What support did you get from your tribe members?

PERSONAL LEARNING
▶ How does having a contract make you feel?
▶ How did you feel as a witness?
▶ How will this help you change?
▶ What personal strengths will help you complete your contract?

Appreciation

Invite statements of appreciation:
▶ "I appreciated..."
▶ "I like my contract because..."

Personal Journal

Objectives

1. To allow time and privacy for reflecting on personal learning
2. To provide a method for noting personal goals, commitments, hopes, and growth
3. To facilitate sharing of personal observations
4. To build inclusion

Instructions

1. Plan regular time throughout the week for students to write about personal learning, school experiences, and discovered interests and gifts. Tell the class that personal journals are a way to reflect on their own progress, hopes and goals, and that no one has access to another's journal without permission.
2. Urge the students to periodically review and compare their recent entries with former ones, and to congratulate themselves for signs of growth or learning. Suggest that they write "I Learned" statements.
3. Have tribe members share things from their personal journals when they choose to do so.

Suggested Reflection Questions

CONTENT (COGNITIVE LEARNING)

- ▶ What sort of information do you imagine most of you are writing in your journals?
- ▶ Why is keeping a personal journal a helpful thing to do?
- ▶ How can keeping a journal show you your personal growth?

COLLABORATIVE (SOCIAL LEARNING

- ▶ What communication skills were helpful when your tribe members shared from their personal journals?
- ▶ How does your tribe show support for each other?

PERSONAL LEARNING

- ▶ How does it feel to have a personal data bank?
- ▶ What are you learning about yourself through your journal?
- ▶ What special gifts or qualities do you appreciate about yourself?
- ▶ In what special ways do you notice yourself changing or growing?

Appreciation

Invite statements of appreciation:

- ▶ "I appreciate your need for privacy because..."
- ▶ "I liked it when you..."
- ▶ "I value who you are because..."

▶ **TIME**   ongoing

▶ **GROUPING** tribes, individuals

▶ **MATERIALS** notebooks*

▶ **DEVELOPMENTAL TASKS**
Independence/Autonomy
Sense of Purpose

OPTIONS

Have students write a journal for a historical event or person or a literary character.

Keep a personal journal as a reflection for a discovery learning experience.

Problem Solving through Appreciative Inquiry

► **TIME** varies

► **GROUPING** community or tribes

► **MATERIALS** none

► **DEVELOPMENTAL TASKS**
Social Competency
Sense of Purpose
Problem Solving

OPTIONS

Use appreciative inquiry as an active learning curriculum strategy by having students design role-plays using history or literature content to show how characters might have handled a situation in a different way to solve a people problem. Initiate thinking on the task by having students brainstorm or pose "what if..." questions.

Student Government: Use to resolve student issues.

Objectives

1. To improve group effectiveness and pride by looking for what the group is doing well and what the group values rather than identifying a problem to correct
2. To empower and give groups a sense of competency and pride
3. To encourage positive approaches to innovation and creativity

Instructions

1. Ask community groups or tribes to discuss and report back their conclusions on the question: "What do people usually do to solve a problem when a group of people (a team or organization) is not working well together?" Ask for a report back in 5 minutes.
2. Acknowledge their reported solutions (such as, people analyze what is wrong, blame others, make new rules, or somehow fix the problem). Continue by saying that a very positive way for groups to improve is to look at what they are doing well (or what is working well) instead of what is wrong. "Let's try this different way of problem solving."
3. Give the tribes 5–10 minutes to discuss one of the following questions:
   • Describe a time when you felt your group performed really well. What were people doing?
   • Describe a time when you felt proud to be a member of your tribe. What was happening?
   • What do people in your group do that you value and that contributes to success?
4. You may want to have the tribes list their responses before reporting to the class community.
5. Group members can also summarize their learning from the strategy and/or possible use of the approach to problem solving by writing in their journals.

Suggested Reflection Questions

CONTENT (COGNITIVE LEARNING)
► Why is it helpful to look at the positive side of a situation or problem?
► How could appreciative inquiry be used to study or research a topic in history or literature? What would you anticipate learning?

COLLABORATIVE (SOCIAL LEARNING)
► How did this approach help your tribe or the community?
► What do you intend to do differently together?
► What hopes do you have for your group now?

PERSONAL LEARNING
► What did you learn about yourself?
► What creative or positive contributions are you making to your tribe?
► How can appreciative inquiry be helpful to you in other groups?

Appreciation

Invite statements of appreciation:

- ▶ "I felt (feeling) when you..."
- ▶ "It's so helpful when you..."
- ▶ "I appreciate how you..."
- ▶ "I admire you for the way you..."

Productive Learning Groups

▶ **TIME**   40 minutes

▶ **GROUPING**   tribes, pairs

▶ **MATERIALS**   paper, pencils

▶ **DEVELOPMENTAL TASKS**
   Social Competency
   Problem Solving

OPTIONS

Use the strategy to "front load" expectations for group (tribe) work, substitute teacher days, field trip ideas, even classroom arrangements.

This strategy can also be used when the teacher is asked the inevitable question, "What do I do if I'm all done with all my work?" The student can design a productive _____!

Objectives

1. To involve students in defining class agreements
2. To alter the climate from negative to positive
3. To transfer responsibility to students
4. To experience influence

Instructions

1. Draw a large circle on the board and label it "Productive Learning Groups."
2. Ask the students to think about the following question: How would people act and interact in a productive learning group?
3. Have students divide up into pairs.
4. Ask the partners to discuss and make a list of what productive groups would be like. After ten minutes have them share their ideas with their tribe.
5. Have the tribes save the lists. Ask everyone to think about the question until the next day.
6. On the following day, use the strategy "One, Two, Three" or "Group Problem-Solving" to have the community select one to three ideas that they consider most important for their learning groups or classroom.
7. Post the ideas in a prominent place.
8. Ask, "How many of you want to make these agreements that the whole community respects for the next (week, month or year)?" Invite students to stand and say, "That's me!"
9. Ask, "Who will help to remind others to respect our group agreements?"

Suggested Reflection Questions

CONTENT (COGNITIVE LEARNING)
- What is a productive learning group like?
- What would have to change to make our groups or classroom productive?

COLLABORATIVE (SOCIAL LEARNING)
- What social skills would be needed in your productive group?
- How can these rules apply to other areas of life?
- How did working together in pairs help during this activity?
- What did you, as a group, do well together to make this activity successful?

PERSONAL LEARNING
- What personal skills did you use during this activity?
- What usually works best for you when you tackle a problem?

Appreciation
Invite statements of appreciation:
- "It felt good when..."
- "One thing I liked about what you said was..."

Put Down the Put-Downs

Objectives

1. To build community inclusion
2. To list put-downs and the feelings they cause
3. To share the personal experience of receiving a put-down
4. To practice brainstorming

Instructions

1. Have students meet in tribes.
2. Lead a brief discussion about put-downs (hurtful names and behaviors).
3. After reviewing the rules for brainstorming, have each tribe select a recorder.
4. Ask the tribes to brainstorm put-downs that people use in the class or school.
5. Then have each tribe make a list of the feelings they have when they receive a put-down. Give each student time to share a time when a put-down really was hurtful.
6. Ask the tribes to brainstorm: "What could we do to help each other put-down the put-downs?"
7. Have each tribe present their list to the class, and ask reflection questions.

Suggested Reflection Questions

CONTENT (COGNITIVE LEARNING)

- What were some of the "feeling words" you shared?
- What were some of your solutions for dealing with people who use put-downs?

COLLABORATIVE (SOCIAL LEARNING)

- Why do put-downs hurt your feelings?
- What are some important social skills to use when you brainstorm?
- How did your tribe members help each other to brainstorm or problem-solve during this activity?

PERSONAL LEARNING

- How did you feel when you remembered getting put-down?
- How do you feel when you put-down another person?
- How did you help your tribe reach a solution?
- What personal qualities can you use to carry out the solution?

Appreciation

Invite statements of appreciation:
- "Thanks for..."
- "One thing I liked about what you said was..."

▶ **TIME** 40 minutes

▶ **GROUPING** tribes

▶ **MATERIALS** paper, pencils

▶ **DEVELOPMENTAL TASKS**
Independence/Autonomy
Social Competency
Sense of Purpose
Problem Solving

OPTIONS

Have the community select two or three ideas for ending put-downs. Use sticker voting (Group Problem-Solving).

Approach the cause and effect of put-downs from a historical perspective.

Identify statements and discuss how they may or may not be put-downs. Encourage students to research how and why certain terms are derogatory. Watch a sit-com and have students tally put-downs; then discuss.

Put Yourself on the Line

TIME 15 minutes

GROUPING community, tribes

MATERIALS none

DEVELOPMENTAL TASKS
Independence/Autonomy
Sense of Purpose

OPTIONS

Use current events, social or historical issues.

Have students, in tribes, select a representative to put on the line and speak for the group.

Follow with Fold the Line and Paraphrase Passport.

Objectives

1. To practice taking a stand among peers
2. To build appreciation for different opinions
3. To use a structure to promote critical thinking on curriculum topics and issues
4. To experience influence

Instructions

1. Ask the community to stand up.
2. Describe an imaginary line down the center of the room. Say the imaginary line represents a "continuum." Identify positions at either end of the line as "strongly agree" and "strongly disagree." State that the middle position is for those who have no opinion, choose to pass, are non-risk-takers, or are "moderates."
3. Tell the students to move to places on the line that express their feelings or opinions when you call out statements. Examples:
   • Graffiti is a form of art.
   • One should never climb dangerous mountains.
   • Always do what your friends do so you won't be left out.
   • Select lesson topics or current events; or have students suggest topics.
4. When the students take their place on the line have the ones near each other discuss why they are there. Pick one representative from each area of the line to report to the community.
5. Have the tribes meet to share feelings on a particularly controversial topic.

Suggested Reflection Questions

CONTENT (COGNITIVE LEARNING)
• What did you learn?
• What did you see happen?
• Why is making your opinion public sometimes important?
• Why is recognizing individual opinions important?

COLLABORATIVE (SOCIAL LEARNING)
• Why is it important not to put down other people's opinions?
• Why might you not want to "take a stand" on a topic?
• What did the community do to help you feel comfortable about taking a stand?

PERSONAL LEARNING
• How did you feel about publicly taking a stand?
• Why might you have been tempted to change your position?
• What personal strengths kept you from changing your position?
• How are you a unique individual in this community?

Appreciation

Invite statements of appreciation:
• "I appreciated it when..."
• "One thing I like about this group is..."

Reason to Roam

Objectives

1. To promote inclusion and influence.
2. To experience the fun and creative power of brainstorming as a decision-making or problem solving technique.
3. To involve the whole class with curriculum related material.

Instructions

1. Ask each tribe or group of 4–6 to appoint two "roamers" (individuals that will visit each group when directed).
2. All members of the tribe/group should jot down ideas on a piece of paper that are generated by the group on a given topic.
3. Instruct the tribes/groups on the "DOVE" rules that they need to follow in order to "brainstorm." D: defer judgement, O: off beat, original, V: vast number, E: expand, elaborate
4. Explain that each group will have five minutes to call out and write down as many ideas possible on a given subject.
5. Stop the brainstorming after five minutes.
6. The facilitator should establish a direction for the "roamers" to move.
7. The two "roamers" from each group should move to another group sharing the ideas that were generated from their initial group, as well as, add any new ideas shared on their paper for three minutes.
8. The facillitator calls time after three minutes. The "roamers" follow this process until they have visited each group. The "roamers" return to their original tribe.
9. The facillitator gives five minutes to the tribe to compare papers adding any new information gained during the strategy.
10. Lively music can be used as a cue when it is time to move to a new group.

► **TIME** 30 minutes

► **GROUPING** tribes or groups of 4–6

► **MATERIALS** paper and pencils

► **DEVELOPMENTAL TASKS**
Independence/Autonomy
Sense of Purpose
Problem Solving

OPTIONS

Student Council: Develop a school policy for cell phones or electronic devices.

Suggested Reflection Questions

CONTENT (COGNITIVE LEARNING)

► Why is brainstorming fun?
► How do the "DOVE" rules help you to brainstorm?

COLLABORATIVE (SOCIAL LEARNING)

► What was the value of the roamers?
► What did you notice each time the "roamers" arrived in a group?
► What social skills were necessary for the success of this strategy?

PERSONAL LEARNING

► How did you contribute to this activity?
► What did you notice about the roamers role?
► What did you notice about those members of the group that remained in their tribe?

Adapted with permission from Kagan Publishing. Kagan, Spencer, Cooperative Learning.
©1994, Kagan Publishing, San Clemente, CA. 1-800-933-2667, www.kaganonline.com.

Appreciation

Invite statements of appreciation:

- ▶ " I liked it when..."
- ▶ " It felt good when..."
- ▶ " Your ideas helped me to..."

Reasons and Alternatives

Objectives

1. To explore motives and alternatives concerning the use of cigarettes, alcohol, or drugs
2. To develop peer support for non-use of alcohol and other drugs
3. To build inclusion and influence in tribes

Instructions

1. Have the community meet in tribes. Ask each tribe to appoint a recorder. Pass out two large sheets of paper and a marker to each tribe.
2. Tell the students that they will be brainstorming; review the rules of brainstorming.
3. Ask the tribes to brainstorm for five minutes on the subject: "Why do people smoke, drink alcohol, or use drugs?" Ask each recorder to jot down all ideas as quickly as they are called out.
4. After five minutes, stop the brainstorming and have the recorders take new sheets of paper. Ask the tribes now to brainstorm about another subject: "What are some alternatives to using cigarettes, alcohol, or other drugs?"
5. Stop the brainstorming after five minutes. Have the recorders report back to the tribe or community.
6. Ask the students to write in their personal journals what they intend to do about using chemical substances and how they would like to live their lives. Have them share their commitments with their tribe members.
7. Next ask the tribes to discuss what they are willing to do to help friends say "no" to the use of cigarettes, alcohol, or other drugs. Have each tribe make a list and report back to the community.

Suggested Reflection Questions

CONTENT (COGNITIVE LEARNING)

▶ What did you learn about substance abuse?
▶ How can this knowledge change your behavior?

COLLABORATIVE (SOCIAL LEARNING)

▶ Why is brainstorming a good structure for this lesson?
▶ What skills did your tribe use during the brainstorming process?
▶ What would your tribe like to do more of the next time you use a brainstorming strategy?

PERSONAL LEARNING

▶ How do you feel about your tribe members?
▶ What did you learn about yourself from this activity?
▶ What personal strengths will help you to live the commitment you have made?

Appreciation

Invite statements of appreciation:
▶ "It helped me when..."
▶ "I appreciated..."

▶ **TIME**   45–60 min.

▶ **GROUPING** tribes

▶ **MATERIALS** large paper, markers

▶ **DEVELOPMENTAL TASKS**
Independence/Autonomy
Sense of Purpose
Problem Solving

OPTIONS

Use a social, historical, or literature-based issue or dilemma.

Explore a scientific hypothesis.

This strategy can also be used as a pre-writing exercise.

Guidance: Why do people drop out of high school?

Why do people choose to join the military? How could friends support this?

Reflecting Feelings

TIME 40 minutes

GROUPING tribes

MATERIALS "Feeling Statements" worksheets

DEVELOPMENTAL TASKS
Independence/Autonomy
Social Competency
Sense of Purpose

OPTIONS

Create more challenging statements that relate to social, historical or current event issues. Discussion around various responses can be very valuable.

Use as a pre-writing exercise.

Use with Paraphrase Passport.

Objectives

1. To build community inclusion
2. To teach and practice listening skills
3. To share ideas and feelings about a given topic

Instructions

1. Discuss with the community how a person's feelings can be identified by the tone of his or her voice (harsh, friendly, concerned), body language (leaning forward, withdrawn), or words.
2. Ask the students to form triads and decide which triad members will be A, B, or C. Ask for a show of hands of all A's, all B's, and all C's to avoid confusion.
3. Explain that the triad members will play the following roles in each round (post a chart, if necessary):

	A	B	C
Round 1	Speaker	Feeling Reflector	Observer
Round 2	Feeling Reflector	Observer	Speaker
Round 3	Observer	Speaker	Feeling Reflector

4. Distribute a set of three feeling statements to each triad, and have each member draw one slip.
5. First, have the speaker tell the reflector who is speaking the statement, and then they are to role-play their statements with much feeling. The "reflectors" will rephrase the feeling back to the speaker. Example:
   Speaker: "A father is speaking to his son. He says, 'I am delighted that we can go fishing together on Saturday.'"
   Reflector: "You feel excited and very happy that we will be able to fish together all day on Saturday."
6. The Observer then tells the Speaker and Reflector what he or she heard and saw.
7. Rotate the roles so that everyone has a turn in each of the three roles.

Suggested Reflection Questions

CONTENT (COGNITIVE LEARNING)
▶ What did you learn about reflecting feelings?

COLLABORATIVE (SOCIAL LEARNING)
▶ Why is listening such an important skill?
▶ Why is the observer's role important?

PERSONAL LEARNING
▶ What strengths or skills did you use to play the different roles?
▶ How are you going to use this information tomorrow?

Appreciation

Invite statements of appreciation:
▶ "Thanks for..."
▶ "I liked it when..."

FEELING STATEMENTS

Friend: Just because I don't wear name brand clothes, the other kids treat me like I don't exist!

Friend:

- -

Student: I don't get this assignment. I don't see how this is going to help me.

Teacher:

- -

Mom: Your room is a mess! This is driving me crazy!

Son/Daughter:

_____

FEELING STATEMENTS

Friend: My mother won't let me talk on the phone for more than five minutes. She's even making me pay part of the phone bills.

Friend:

- -

Student: I never say anything in class because it doesn't come out right.

Friend:

- -

Friend: My mother finally gave in to letting me go overseas for the band trip.

Friend:

_____

FEELING STATEMENTS

Student: You're pretty cool. You take time to listen to what I have to say.

Teacher:

- -

Friend: My parents always complain about what I don't do, but they never notice when I do something right!

Friend:

- -

Friend: I wanted to go to the movies with all of you Friday night, but my parents just told me I'm grounded.

Friend:

- -

This page may be duplicated for classroom use.

Reporting Information through Multiple Intelligences

▶ TIME   varies

▶ GROUPING tribes

▶ MATERIALS content-related subject material

▶ DEVELOPMENTAL TASKS
   Independence/Autonomy
   Problem Solving

OPTIONS

Have students make a poster (possibly using a computer graphic program) that "snapshots" how all intelligences might be represented in a learning demonstration. Students can challenge one another by switching roles (intelligences) and/or switching snapshot posters to use as plans for presenting.

Give each tribe a different topic concept to present only through the multiple intelligences.

Objectives

1. To practice constructive thinking skills
2. To practice collaborative team skills
3. To transfer responsibility to students
4. To promote retention of content-related material

Instructions

Note: Students should already be familiar with the "brainstorming" strategy.

1. Review the characteristics of each of the nine multiple intelligences (see chapter 10).
2. Tell the students that as a tribe they will have time during the next several weeks to demonstrate each of the intelligences by presenting content-related material to the community in different ways. Give an example from a topic they have been learning or have already researched.
3. Have the tribes choose a recorder and list the nine multiple intelligences.
4. Give the tribes time to brainstorm how they plan to present the content-related material to the community through the use of the nine multiple intelligences.
5. Review the plans that the tribes have made.
6. Tell the students that they will have _____ (hours, days, or weeks) to prepare for their class presentation.
7. Prior to the presentations, prepare a peer evaluation sheet that lists the multiple intelligences. Have students evaluate how effective each presentation was at conveying the content-related material through the nine multiple intelligences.

Suggested Reflection Questions

CONTENT (COGNITIVE LEARNING)
▶ What did you learn from this activity?
▶ Which multiple intelligence was the easiest to prepare for? The hardest?

COLLABORATIVE (SOCIAL LEARNING)
▶ What did you do to make sure that everyone had a role?
▶ What collaborative skills were demonstrated?

PERSONAL LEARNING
▶ What did you notice about yourself during the preparation? The presentation?
▶ Through which multiple intelligence(s) do you prefer to learn new material?

Appreciation

Invite oral or written statements of appreciation:
▶ "You really helped out with..."
▶ "You are really good at..."

Roles People Play

1. To promote an awareness of helpful group roles
2. To learn how the accomplishment of group tasks depends upon helpful behaviors
3. To learn collaborative skills

▶ **TIME**   20 minutes

▶ **GROUPING**   community, tribes

▶ **MATERIALS** handout on roles

▶ **DEVELOPMENTAL TASKS**
  Independence/Autonomy
  Social Competency
  Sense of Purpose
  Problem Solving

Instructions

1. Discuss the objectives and ask students to review the Tribes agreements.
2. Distribute the handout on "Roles That People Play In Groups."
3. Ask the students to study the cartoon and decide which role (or roles) they usually play when working with others in their tribe.
4. Ask the students to write answers to the questions on the bottom of the handout. Allow five to ten minutes time.
5. Have them share their responses with a partner.
6. Ask the students to share with their tribe a helpful new role that he or she will try for the day (or week).

OPTION #1: A ROLE PLAY
- Have each tribe plan and present a brief role-play in which one person is playing an unhelpful role.
- Ask the class to guess which role is being demonstrated.

OPTION #2: FOR ADULT AND/OR MULTICULTURAL GROUPS
- Delete the "What People Say" right hand column on the role description handout before distributing it to the tribes.
- Have the groups brainstorm and list all the things that people of their own peer group culture may say.
- Then proceed with steps three to six in the instructions above, or use role-play option #1.

Suggested Reflection Questions

CONTENT (COGNITIVE LEARNING)
▶ What happens in a group when even one person is acting in an unhelpful role?

COLLABORATIVE (SOCIAL LEARNING)
▶ What helpful roles do people play in your tribe?
▶ How do those roles make working together easier?
▶ Are people in your tribe able to play different roles? How is that helpful?

PERSONAL LEARNING
▶ What feelings did you have during this strategy?
▶ What did you learn about yourself?
▶ What helpful role(s) do you often use in groups?

Appreciation

Invite statements of appreciation:
▶ "I appreciated it when..."
▶ "Thank you for..."

OPTIONS

Choose roles that apply to historical or social situations.

Try a "headband" approach, where the role is worn as a headband; the person wearing it has no knowledge of what role it is, and has to figure out the role, based on the behavior and statements of others.

DESCRIPTIONS OF HELPFUL ROLES	WHAT PEOPLE SAY
Encourager: Tells group positive things and keeps energy going well.	Right on! Good job! Yes! Let's do it. Keep going. Brilliant!
Organizer: Helps group stay on task and time; encourages management of materials and resources.	File the papers. We have one bottle of glue. First we should...
Peace Keeper: Helps members to solve problems, make decisions, express feelings and understand each other.	Time out. Let's talk about this! You both have a good point.
Idea Person: Gives and seeks helpful ideas. Initiates action and clarifies.	What if we looked at it this way? Another idea would be to... What ideas do you have? Let's brainstorm more ideas.
Helper: Is supportive and friendly, willing to listen and help others.	We need to hear from everyone. I'll help you. Let's work on it together.

UNHELPFUL ROLE DESCRIPTIONS	WHAT PEOPLE SAY
Joker: Claims attention by interrupting, goofing off, distracting and trying to be funny.	There's a spider on your head. At lunch I'm going to... Look at this! Want some gum?
Boss: Takes charge. Knows it all. Tells people what and how to do things. Usually doesn't listen well.	Do it my way! That's not right. The best way is to...
Sitter: Doesn't participate. Sits on the side. Always claims the right to pass. Will not help others. Can seem judgmental.	I pass. Don't count me in.
Put-Downer: Ridicules others and their ideas.	That's stupid. You're so dumb. We tried that once. How can you be so oblivious?
Talker: Goes on and on talking. Ignores others also wanting time. Controls by not pausing between sentences.	Blah, blah, blah. And then he said to me... I also know that... Stop interrupting me.

ROLES PEOPLE PLAY IN GROUPS

Encourager • Joker • Organizer • Boss • Peace Keeper • Talker • Idea Person • Sitter • Helper • Put-Downer

Questions

Why do you think that it's the easiest role for you to play?

What other role or roles would you like to play to help your group?

Which role do you usually play in a group?

How willing are you to try out a new helpful role today?

Self-Esteem Cards

▶ **TIME**   15 minutes

▶ **GROUPING** tribes

▶ **MATERIALS** 3 x 5-inch cards

▶ **DEVELOPMENTAL TASKS**
  Independence/Autonomy
  Social Competency
  Sense of Purpose

OPTIONS

Use to enable students to reflect on what they have learned about a topic.

Students can also suggest "test questions," or write "I learned" or appreciation statements regarding an assignment.

Objectives

1. To build self-esteem
2. To reinforce the concept of appreciation
3. To foster positive feelings among tribe members
4. To build inclusion

Instructions

Note: This strategy should not be used until tribe members know one another fairly well.

1. Have the community meet in tribes; pass out cards.
2. Instruct each tribe member to write his or her first name in an upper corner of the card.
3. Tell the tribe members to place all their cards in a center pile. Have each tribe member draw a card (not divulging whose card he or she has), and write a thoughtful, warm statement on the card about the student whose name is on the card.
4. Have the students return all of the cards to the central pile when done writing and repeat the process of drawing and writing four or five additional times. If anyone draws his own card, begin the drawing again or have the students exchange cards.
5. After the final writing, return all cards and draw again. This time have each tribe member read the remarks on the card to the student whose name is on the card, delivering the tribe's message as warmly and sincerely as possible while the rest of the tribe listens.

Suggested Reflection Questions

CONTENT (COGNITIVE LEARNING)
▶ What did you learn by doing this activity?
▶ How did you choose the statements you wrote for your tribe members?

COLLABORATIVE (SOCIAL LEARNING)
▶ How does making thoughtful, warm statements to each other bring your tribe closer together?
▶ Why is it important to receive positive statements from others?

PERSONAL LEARNING
▶ How did you feel while your card was being read to you?
▶ How did you contribute to your tribe during this activity?
▶ What unique qualities does your tribe appreciate about you?
▶ How do you feel about your tribe now?

Appreciation

Invite statements of appreciation:
  ▶ "I felt good when..."
  ▶ "Thank you for..."

Shred the Put-Downs

Objectives
1. To promote awareness and sensitize the students to the hurt of put-downs
2. To involve the students in eliminating put-downs
3. To create a positive community climate and inclusion

Instructions
1. Give each student a slip of paper.
2. Have each student write a hurtful put-down remark or behavior he or she never wants to hear or see again.
3. Have each tribe put their slips in a community box and ask three to four students to take turns reading the slips to the class.
4. Invite several students to share how they felt when put down by another person in the school.
5. Bring a small shredder to class and shred the put-downs together or visit the school office and have a shredding ceremony around the shredder. Students can "rip" slips if shredder is not available.
6. Invite statements of good-bye to the put-downs.
7. Ask the students what they could do to help each other keep the painful statements dead.

Suggested Reflection Questions

CONTENT (COGNITIVE LEARNING)
▶ What did you do?
▶ Why is it important to shred the put-downs?
▶ What can the community do to prevent put-downs?

COLLABORATIVE (SOCIAL LEARNING)
▶ What can your tribe do to prevent put-downs?
▶ What did the community or your tribe do to make this activity successful?

PERSONAL LEARNING
▶ How did it feel to shred the put-downs?
▶ What personal strengths will help you to keep those put-downs away? What can you do?

Appreciation
Invite statements of appreciation:
▶ "I appreciated..."
▶ "It was great when..."

▶ **TIME**   35 minutes

▶ **GROUPING**   community, tribes

▶ **MATERIALS** 2-inch paper slips, pencils

▶ **DEVELOPMENTAL TASKS**
  Independence/Autonomy
  Social Competency
  Sense of Purpose
  Problem Solving

OPTIONS
Use the strategy as a reflective process (such as, "Think about what not to do on the next report or project").

Singing the Blues

Objectives

1. To promote commonality and inclusion
2. To introduce sharing of concerns in a non-threatening, enjoyable way
3. To channel community energy

Instructions

1. Ask the community if they know what "the blues" are. State that in this activity, having "the blues" means feeling badly about something.
2. Ask if anyone has the blues and why.
3. Sing or strum a melody that is simple and fun. Example:
   > A student says his dog was hurt. Words could be "I've got the blues, I've got the blues, I've got the my-dog-was-hurt-blues."
4. Ask everyone to join in singing.
5. Share one of your own blues first. Lead the singing on it.
6. Invite the students to tell their blues and lead the singing.
7. Discourage the students from making fun of another's blues. Help them to understand it's a put-down to do so.

OPTIONS

Have students create songs, raps or poems about historical, social, literary or school events.

Suggested Reflection Questions

CONTENT (COGNITIVE LEARNING)
▶ What did you learn about "the blues" today?
▶ How were your "blues" similar?

COLLABORATIVE (SOCIAL LEARNING)
▶ How did the singing make it easier to share?
▶ How did sharing each other's "blues" in this way affect the community in a positive way?

PERSONAL LEARNING
▶ Do you feel different after "singing the blues" than you did before?
▶ How would it feel to sing about "good times?"
▶ What skills did you use to help each other with this activity?
▶ What special strengths did you discover about yourself?

Appreciation

Invite statements of appreciation:
▶ "I enjoyed singing because..."
▶ "I feel like you do when..."

Slip Game

Objectives

1. To build inclusion
2. To promote personal sharing

Instructions

1. Prepare a bag for each tribe containing slips of paper with questions on them. Make sure each bag contains the same number of question slips as the number of tribe members, plus a few extra. Examples:
   - "When are you really happy?"
   - "What is the most special positive quality about you?"
   - "When have you felt very proud?"
   - See more sample questions on next page.
2. Instruct the community to meet in tribes. Review the agreements. Pass out bags.
3. Everyone has the "right to pass" if they do not like the question that they draw and may select an alternative one from those that remain in the bag. They must put the original slip back after taking an alternative one. Ask tribe members to each draw a slip with their eyes closed; tell them about the right to pass and the option for drawing alternative questions.
4. Have tribe members take turns reading and answering their questions.

Suggested Reflection Questions

CONTENT (COGNITIVE LEARNING)
▶ What's one thing someone shared that you found interesting?

COLLABORATIVE (SOCIAL LEARNING)
▶ Why is the "right to pass" such an important agreement for this activity?
▶ How did having the opportunity to choose another question slip help you and your tribe be successful?
▶ How did your tribe help each other feel more comfortable about sharing as the activity progressed?

PERSONAL LEARNING
▶ Why could it be difficult/easy for you to share?
▶ How did you feel when you were answering the question you drew?
▶ What did you learn about yourself? What unique qualities are you proud of?
▶ How did you help your tribe in a special way?

Appreciation

Invite statements of appreciation:
▶ "I'm a lot like you when..."
▶ "I admired you for..."

▶ **TIME** varies

▶ **GROUPING** community, tribes

▶ **MATERIALS** question slips, paper bags

▶ **DEVELOPMENTAL TASKS**
  Independence/Autonomy
  Social Competency
  Sense of Purpose

OPTIONS

Use the strategy for discussion of lesson topics.

Have tribes develop questions and exchange with other tribes to answer.

Use as a whole class to review for a test.

SLIP GAME: Sample Questions

What makes you angry?

What makes you happy?

What makes you sad?

What do you do for fun?

Do you have any pets?

What is your favorite food?

What is your favorite place?

What is your favorite animal?

What is your favorite sport?

What is your favorite song?

What is your favorite TV program?

What do you and your friends do for fun?

If you could have one wish, what would it be?

What famous person would you like to be?

In what period of time, past or future, would you choose to live in?

What foreign country would you like to visit?

What would you like to be really good at?

What is your favorite story?

What is one food you don't like?

What do you do when you feel lonely?

What would you do with one million dollars?

Would you rather be rich, famous or happy?

What would you do if you were the president?

What would you do to improve school?

What qualities do you look for in a friend?

Who is the best person in the world?

What do you do when you get really angry?

Snowball I-Messages

Objectives
1. To create community inclusion and energize the class
2. To give individuals practice in writing I-Messages

Instructions
Note: Use the strategy "Teaching I-Messages" prior to using this one.
1. Ask each student to bring one piece of paper, a pencil and something firm to write on and sit in a community circle.
2. Review the elements of an "I-Message" and the difference between an "I-Message" and a "You-Message."
3. Give examples of an "I-Message" and a "You-Message" and ask the students to think of an example of each.
4. Ask several students to model an "I-Message" and then a "You-Message."
5. Ask each student to draw two lines that divide the paper into four squares, and to write a "You-Message" in one square.
6. After the students have done so, tell them you will give them two commands: "crumple" and "toss." Explain that when you say "crumple," they will crumple their papers into "snowballs," and when you say "toss," they will toss the "snowballs" into the center of the circle.
7. Then have the students pick up a "snowball," read the "You-Message," and change it into an "I-Message." Have the students write the "I-Message" in another square.
8. Repeat the process one more time.
9. Have each student take a snowball back to his or her tribe, and have the tribes critique the messages.

Suggested Reflection Questions

CONTENT (COGNITIVE LEARNING)
▶ Why is it important to know the difference between a "You-Message" and an "I-Message?"
▶ What kinds of messages do you get/give in "You-Messages?"

COLLABORATIVE (SOCIAL LEARNING)
▶ How can you use "I-Messages" in your life with others?
▶ How can you encourage the community or your tribe to use "I-Messages" with each other?

PERSONAL LEARNING
▶ How did it feel to change a "You-Message" into an "I-Message?"
▶ What communication or "people" skills do you feel particularly comfortable with?
▶ What "people" skills or personal strengths do others recognize in you?

Appreciation
Invite statements of appreciation:
▶ "I liked..."
▶ "I enjoyed it when..."

▶ **TIME**   45 minutes

▶ **GROUPING** community, tribes

▶ **MATERIALS** paper, pencils

▶ **DEVELOPMENTAL TASKS**
Independence/Autonomy
Social Competency

OPTIONS

Use examples from history or social situations; have students write "I Messages" and discuss possible responses.

Use for reviewing content. After each toss, share responses with neighbor and critique.

Something Good

TIME varies

GROUPING community

MATERIALS none

DEVELOPMENTAL TASKS
Social Competency
Sense of Purpose

Objectives
1. To build inclusion
2. To encourage sharing of positive feelings

Instructions
1. Have the community sit in a large circle.
2. Ask each student to share one positive experience that happened during the previous week or recent past. Say that there will be no discussion until all have shared.

Suggested Reflection Questions

CONTENT (COGNITIVE LEARNING)
▶ Were there any similarities about the "good things" you shared?
▶ When was the last time you told someone about a positive experience?

COLLABORATIVE (SOCIAL LEARNING)
▶ How can you tell that others are using good listening skills?
▶ Did you share more freely as the activity progressed? Why?
▶ How did this activity help the community?

PERSONAL LEARNING
▶ How did you feel while sharing with the community?
▶ What communication or "people skills" did you use during this activity?
▶ What did you learn about yourself?

Appreciation
Invite statements of appreciation:
▶ "I liked it when..."
▶ "I'm like you when..."
▶ "I felt good when..."

OPTIONS

Invite statements about the day's lesson, project or content standard.

Have students role play historical or social situations in terms of "something good."

Social Studies/ Language Arts: Find "something good" from current events to share.

For visual effect, pass around a stress ball with the earth design and state "something good in my/the world..."

Something I Cherish

Objectives
1. To increase communication skills
2. To build inclusion

Instructions
1. Ask the community to meet in tribes.
2. Ask each tribe member to take a turn sharing "one thing that I cherish," explaining why it is so special or why she or he wants others to know, etc.
3. To draw the tribes back into the community, have each tribe member share with the community one item that another member of his or her tribe cherishes. Make sure each tribe member speaks of and is spoken about by another member of his or her tribe.

▶ TIME   20 minutes

▶ GROUPING   community, tribes

▶ MATERIALS none

▶ DEVELOPMENTAL TASKS
Independence/Autonomy
Social Competency
Sense of Purpose

Suggested Reflection Questions

CONTENT (COGNITIVE LEARNING)
▶ What types of things do your tribe members cherish?
▶ Why is it important to share what you cherish with each other?

COLLABORATIVE (SOCIAL LEARNING)
▶ How could you tell that your tribe members were listening when others shared?
▶ How can this type of sharing help families, friendships, your tribe, this community?
▶ How did people show that they valued your contribution?

PERSONAL LEARNING
▶ How did you feel about sharing something you cherished?
▶ How were you able to help your tribe or the community during this activity?
▶ What did you discover about yourself?

Appreciation
Invite statements of appreciation:
▶ "I liked it when..."
▶ "I felt good when..."
▶ "I was interested when..."

OPTIONS
Use to role play curriculum content.

Invite students to create statements about their own learning, such as "I cherish my ability to read because..."

Use as a pre-writing exercise.

Social Studies: Share things that are cherished in different cultures.

Space Pioneers

TIME 35 minutes

GROUPING tribes

MATERIALS pencils, paper

DEVELOPMENTAL TASKS
Independence/Autonomy
Problem Solving

OPTIONS

Have the students…

Agree on a name for the new planet; or

Share one personal possession each would take on the trip; or

Brainstorm and agree on what supplies and equipment they would need.

Create a separate scenario with…

Advisors to design a model city; or

Advisors to work on a national policy for children.

Objectives

1. To give practice in assessing different qualities and opinions
2. To encourage sharing
3. To encourage understanding and acceptance of others' perspectives
4. To provide an opportunity to look at evolving styles of communication and leader-behavior within the group
5. To encourage influence

Instructions

Note: Use the strategy "Consensus Building" prior to having the class community do this strategy.

1. Read the "Space Pioneers" scenario (on next page) while students are seated in tribes.
2. Write the list of "Advisors" (or a similar list of your own selection) on the board for all to see.
3. Ask each participant to identify the five advisors they would want to help settle the newly discovered planet.
4. Discuss the difference between a group of people making a decision by consensus in contrast to voting.
5. Announce that the tribes have fifteen minutes to reach a consensus on which five advisors to take into space.
6. Ask the tribes to appoint a recorder to take notes.
7. After fifteen minutes have the recorders report the final consensus lists to the community.

Suggested Reflection Questions

CONTENT (COGNITIVE LEARNING)
▶ What do you see as the main purpose of Space Pioneers?
▶ Why would you want to, or not want to, go on this trip?

COLLABORATIVE (SOCIAL LEARNING)
▶ What did you have to do to reach consensus on who you would take?
▶ What was most effective about how your group came to an agreement?
▶ How did different group members provide leadership for this activity?

PERSONAL LEARNING
▶ How did you feel about your tribe's choice?
▶ What did you contribute to help your group make the selection?
▶ What unique strengths or skills did you discover about yourself?

Appreciation

Invite statements of appreciation:

- ▶ "I liked it when..."
- ▶ "I admired you for saying..."
- ▶ "I'm much like you when..."

Space Pioneers

A new planet has been discovered in our solar system. This planet resembles Earth in every way, except that there are no human beings living there. Our government wants the students of this class to be the first pioneers to settle on the newly discovered planet. They want you to select five adult advisors who you think would be valuable on the new planet. Select from the following list of ten people:

1. Zelda Learner, age 45, high school teacher
2. Oroville Oates, age 41, farmer
3. Clara Kettle, age 34, cook
4. Dr. Margarita Flowers, age 27, botanist
5. Woodrow Hammer, age 56, carpenter
6. Flo Nightengale, age 37, registered nurse
7. Irma Intel, age 32, engineer
8. Melvin Melody, age 24, musician
9. Reverend Adam Goodfellow, age 51, minister
10. Tiger Forest, age 24, golf pro

Spider Web

▶ **TIME**   varies depending on group size

▶ **GROUPING**   community

▶ **MATERIALS**   ball of colored yarn

▶ **DEVELOPMENTAL TASKS**
Independence/Autonomy
Social Competency
Sense of Purpose

OPTIONS

Make a statement of appreciation to someone in the circle; continue until each student has received a statement.

Toss the yarn up and into the center, see where it goes, and then give that person a statement of appreciation. Paraphrase what the previous person said before giving a statement of appreciation. Use "I learned..." statements.

Focus on giving information or descriptors of a historical event or figure, any science concept, or re-telling a literary piece in sequence.

Objectives

1. To build inclusion and a sense of community
2. To practice attentive listening

Instructions

1. Ask the community to sit in one large circle.
2. Explain that during this activity each student will have an opportunity to share his or her name and something special about himself or herself. Give the students a minute to think of something special.
3. Have one student begin the activity by stating his or her name and something about himself or herself. Example:
   "My name is Sue, and I am wonderful at organizing things."
4. Then, have the student hold onto the end of the yarn and roll the yarn ball to someone across from him or her in the circle. Have the students continue this process until everyone has either shared or passed and a "spider web" pattern has been created.
5. It is fun to "play" with the web before rolling it up. Have everyone pick up the web, stand, and hold it up overhead. Have them hold it waist high and shake it.
6. If time permits, have the students reroll the web one by one in reverse order.

Suggested Reflection Questions

CONTENT (COGNITIVE LEARNING)
▶ How can you symbolically interpret this "spider web?" Note symbolism, design, community involvement, etc.
▶ Why is this a good community-building activity?

COLLABORATIVE (SOCIAL LEARNING)
▶ What did you learn about each other as a result of this activity?
▶ How does "Spider Web" bring you closer together as a community?

PERSONAL LEARNING
▶ What did you learn about yourself as a result of this activity?
▶ How do you feel after participating in this activity?

Appreciation

Invite statements of appreciation:
▶ "I liked it when you said..."
▶ "I admire you for..."

Student-Developed Lesson Plans

Objectives

1. To promote tribal influence
2. To have students develop their own lesson plans

Instructions

1. Have tribes meet for two or three minutes and create their own inclusion.
2. Give each tribe a copy of the "Tribes Learning Experience" form found in the Resources section.
3. Discuss the elements that make up the plan:
   - an inclusion activity to awaken interest or connect to previous experiences
   - assessment
   - an academic learning goal
   - a social learning goal
   - a tribal strategy or cooperative learning structure (or a sequence of the same)
   - instructions
   - reflection questions
   - time for statements of appreciation.
4. Have each tribe plan a twenty-minute lesson on a theme or academic topic for younger students or the community.
5. When finished, the lessons can be presented or taught to the class by the tribes.

Suggested Reflection Questions

CONTENT (COGNITIVE LEARNING)

- What was the most difficult thing about this strategy?
- What did you learn by doing this strategy?

COLLABORATIVE (SOCIAL LEARNING)

- What did your tribe do to work well together?
- What does your tribe want to do more of to work together even better next time?

PERSONAL LEARNING

- How do you feel about developing lesson plans now?
- What did you do to help your tribe be successful?
- What strengths or skills did you discover about yourself?

Appreciation

Invite statements of appreciation:
- "I liked it when..."
- "I appreciated..."

- **TIME** 90 minutes
- **GROUPING** tribes
- **MATERIALS** copies of "Tribes Lesson Plan"
- **DEVELOPMENTAL TASKS** Independence/Autonomy Problem Solving

OPTIONS

Use this strategy as an alternative to homework assignments for various units of study. Students may choose to develop and teach a lesson.

Study Buddies

Objectives

1. To build interdependence
2. To practice study materials before a test
3. To experience influence

Instructions

1. Have the students choose some identical study material to be reviewed such as vocabulary words, or other subject-related material. (Examples: elements in Periodic table, game rules and scoring for tennis, Chinese dynasties, etc.).
2. Ask the students to get into pairs. (You may use strategies such as birthday line-up, fold-the-line, random buddies or numbered slips to form pairs.)
3. Ask the students to decide on a study strategy they will use. (Strategies might include quizzing each other, explaining concepts, reviewing difficult words, etc.)
4. Have the students use the strategy they have chosen to review the study material.

OPTIONS

Use the strategy for planning tasks, as well as review.

"Study buddies" can effectively organize and plan for an activity or project or approach to learning just as well as review or "study" after instruction.

This might also be effective for those students who have difficulty completing homework—assign a "Study Buddy"!

Suggested Reflection Questions

CONTENT (COGNITIVE LEARNING)
▶ What did you learn today?
▶ Why is studying together helpful?

COLLABORATIVE (SOCIAL LEARNING)
▶ How did you help each other make this strategy successful?
▶ What special qualities did you discover about your partner?

PERSONAL LEARNING
▶ How do you feel studying with another person?
▶ How do you usually prefer to study?
▶ What special strengths or skills did you use to make this activity successful?

Appreciation

Invite statements of appreciation:
▶ "I liked studying with you because..."
▶ "Thanks for helping me."

Suggestion Circle

Objectives

1. To encourage attentive listening
2. To experience group support for a concern
3. To assist a peer, colleague, or friend to resolve a problem
4. To experience individual problem-solving in the influence stage

Instructions

1. Have the community form a circle.
2. Review the agreements. Choose a recorder who will write down the suggestions made by the community.
3. Ask for a volunteer to share a concern or problem that he or she is experiencing and for which he or she would like some suggestions for resolving.
4. Tell the community that they are to listen without judgment or comment while the problem is being shared, but they may ask for additional information, if necessary, when the student has finished sharing.
5. Invite the students to make a suggestion, one at a time, to the person who shared. Encourage them not to repeat what someone else has already suggested.
6. Have the recorder give the list of possible solutions to the person who shared the problem.

Suggested Reflection Questions

CONTENT (COGNITIVE LEARNING)
- ▶ Why did we do this strategy?
- ▶ What types of suggestions were offered?

COLLABORATIVE (SOCIAL LEARNING)
- ▶ Why is it important to get ideas for solving problems from others?
- ▶ Which social skills did you, as a community, use during this strategy?
- ▶ Where else could this strategy be used?

PERSONAL LEARNING
- ▶ How did you feel to give suggestions?
- ▶ How could this type of a process help you?
- ▶ How did you contribute in a special way?

Appreciation

Invite statements of appreciation:
- ▶ "Thanks for..."
- ▶ "What made a difference for me was..."

- ▶ **TIME** 30 minutes
- ▶ **GROUPING** community
- ▶ **MATERIALS** none
- ▶ **DEVELOPMENTAL TASKS**
  Independence/Autonomy
  Social Competency
  Sense of Purpose
  Problem Solving

OPTIONS

An excellent strategy to use for classroom, social or school issues. This will ultimately save time as well as teach and model a valuable life skill.

Use mid-way through the completion of a project (e.g., a science or history project) for feedback.

Taking a Closer Look

▶ TIME   30 minutes

▶ GROUPING   tribes, pairs

▶ MATERIALS   question slips

▶ DEVELOPMENTAL TASKS
  Independence/Autonomy
  Social Competency
  Sense of Purpose

Objectives

1. To explore individual attitudes about the use of alcohol or other drugs
2. To practice attentive listening
3. To build peer support and influence

Instructions

1. Have the community divide up into pairs, and have each partner decide whether he or she will be an "A" or a "B." Pass out prepared question slips (see following page), or generate your own questions appropriate for the culture and age level of your students.
2. Suggest that the partners move to a comfortable place where they can hear each other well. Explain that partner A will begin by answering the questions while B listens, and that at the end of five minutes, the partners will switch roles.
3. Review the agreements, particularly attentive listening.
4. Give the signal to switch after five minutes, and call the partners back to the community circle after the additional five minutes.
5. Have the community discuss and reflect on the experience.

Suggested Reflection Questions

CONTENT (COGNITIVE LEARNING)

▶ What kind of messages did you get about using substances?
▶ How did this activity stretch your own thinking about drugs?

COLLABORATIVE (SOCIAL LEARNING)

▶ Why did we work in pairs rather than as a community?
▶ How did you and your partner help each other during this activity?

PERSONAL LEARNING

▶ Did you make any new decisions as a result of this experience? What were they?
▶ What did you discover about yourself from this activity?
▶ What is one thing that you felt proud of as you participated in this activity?

Appreciation

Invite statements of appreciation:
▶ "I really appreciated it when..."
▶ "(Name), you are special because..."
▶ "Thank you, (name), for..."

OPTIONS

Modify the questions to role play a social dilemma, historical event, or even the writing process (for example, How will you begin your essay?).

QUESTION SLIP
TAKING A CLOSER LOOK

1. What kinds of messages did you get about cigarettes, alcohol, or drugs when you were younger (right or wrong to use/okay for men, but not for women/beer and wine don't hurt you)?

2. Where did these messages come from (school/family/media/church/friends)?

3. What was the first decision you ever made about choosing to use or not use cigarettes, alcohol or drugs? How old were you? What happened? What process did you use to make a decision?

4. Describe what your life would be like if you did not use any of these substances. Option: What might it be like if you did use? Ask people to think about over-the-counter or prescription drugs they may use. Coffee?

5. What have you learned about chemical substances that you would want your brother, sister or child to know?

6. Would you feel comfortable with your child using cigarettes, drugs, or alcohol? What would you do if you were a parent to influence your child?

This page may be duplicated for classroom use.

Teaching Agreements

▶ **TIME** two class periods

▶ **GROUPING** tribes

▶ **MATERIALS** large paper, felt pens, poster paint

▶ **DEVELOPMENTAL TASKS**
Independence/Autonomy
Social Competency
Sense of Purpose
Problem Solving

OPTIONS

Use the strategy with any content topic. For example, have tribes choose math concepts to teach to the class while applying the concepts to real-life problems.

Look for current or historical events that clearly depict one of the agreements. Share with the class.

Look for quotations that depict each of the agreements and post on walls. Groups could put quotes into a powerpoint slide show.

Objectives

1. To have each tribe create a lesson to help teach an agreement to the community
2. To transfer responsibility to tribes for lesson development
3. To experience influence

Instructions

1. Review the agreements of attentive listening, right to pass, no put-downs, and mutual respect (and any others you've created for your class).
2. Explain to the students that you are looking for new and creative ways to teach these agreements and would like their help.
3. Have each tribe choose (or assign) one of the agreements. Explain that each tribe will create a lesson to teach that agreement to the community. Explain that they can use butcher paper, felt pens, and paint (or other art media or graphic programs you have available) to make any posters or signs needed to teach the lesson. Emphasize that you want them to be creative. Let them know they will have the rest of the period and one other period to create their lessons and share them with the community.
4. When the tribes are finished, have them present their lessons to the community.

Suggested Reflection Questions

CONTENT (COGNITIVE LEARNING)
▶ What did you learn about creating a lesson?
▶ Which agreement do you think is the most important? Why?

COLLABORATIVE (SOCIAL LEARNING)
▶ What social skills did your tribe need to be successful at this strategy?
▶ What allowed your tribe to be creative and innovative?

PERSONAL LEARNING
▶ How did you feel when your tribe presented its lesson?
▶ What did you contribute to help your tribe be successful?
▶ In what ways are you a creative person?
▶ What special skills did you discover about yourself?

Appreciation

Invite statements of appreciation:
▶ "You helped a lot when..."
▶ "I liked..."

Teaching I-Messages

Objectives

1. To give tribes practice in brainstorming and to introduce words to express feelings
2. To show the link between "feeling words" and "I-Messages"
3. To practice giving "I-Messages"

Instructions

Note: Teach this strategy before using "Snowball I-Messages."

1. Ask the community to sit in tribes, and have each tribe select a recorder. Explain that they will be brainstorming (see "Brainstorming" strategy).
2. Discuss various "feeling words" (happiness, anger, upset, love). Ask the tribes to brainstorm and write down as many "feeling words" as they can in five minutes.
3. After five minutes, ask the tribes to take turns calling out the "feeling words" they wrote down. Have a student record the words on the board. Lead a discussion on why sharing feelings is important for clear communication.
4. Ask, "Why is it important to have a way to let people know how their behavior affects us?" Explain that "I-Messages" are a way to share feelings but not blame.
5. Use the formats in chapter 9 to write examples of "I-Messages" and "You-Messages" on the board. Explain the difference between the two types of messages, and ask the class to contrast the impact they each have.
6. Have each tribe member write four "I-Messages" using the feeling words they listed earlier. Each person should write to a friend, a relative, a classmate and a teacher. Allow ten minutes work time.
7. Have the tribes review the "I-Messages" written by their tribe members. Have them help each other change statements that are "You-Messages" to "I-Messages."
8. Ask the students to practice using "I-Messages" during the next few days, and to report back to their tribe on what happened.

Suggested Reflection Questions

CONTENT (COGNITIVE LEARNING)
▶ Why is it important to use "I-Messages?"

COLLABORATIVE (SOCIAL LEARNING)
▶ How can "I-Messages" help you to lessen conflict with friends?
▶ How did your tribe support each other while learning to use "I-Messages?"

PERSONAL LEARNING
▶ How does it feel to receive a "You-Message?"/an "I-Message?"
▶ What did you discover about yourself?

Appreciation

Invite statements of appreciation:
▶ "It helped me when..."
▶ "I liked it when..."

▶ **TIME**   50 minutes

▶ **GROUPING** tribes

▶ **MATERIALS** large paper, felt pens

▶ **DEVELOPMENTAL TASKS**
Independence/Autonomy
Social Competency
Sense of Purpose

OPTIONS

Use current events or characters from literature as the "recipients" of the "I-messages."

Teaching Listening

▶ TIME   30 minutes

▶ GROUPING   tribes

▶ MATERIALS   none

▶ DEVELOPMENTAL TASKS
     Independence/Autonomy
     Social Competency

OPTIONS

This strategy can be used to review, discuss or assess any academic topic. It may also be extended into a written reflective practice exercise.

Objectives

1. To practice components of attentive listening:
   Attending, Paraphrasing, Reflecting Feelings
2. To share ideas and feelings about any given topic
3. To build inclusion

Instructions

1. Discuss and demonstrate attentive listening skills (refer to chapter 8). Write components on the board.
2. Ask the students to form triads, and designate each triad member as an A, B, or C. Ask for a show of hands of all A's, all B's and all C's to avoid confusion.
3. Explain that each person will have an opportunity to play each role; in round 1, A will observe, B will be speaker, and C will be listener. Post this chart:

	A	B	C
Round 1	Observer	Speaker	Listener
Round 2	Speaker	Listener	Observer
Round 3	Listener	Observer	Speaker

4. Give the speakers a topic of your choice to speak on for two to five minutes. Example: Should students be allowed to vote?
5. Ask the listeners to practice one or two components of attentive listening.
6. Ask the observers to pay attention to the interaction and after two to five minutes give feedback to the listeners. Ask them to include what they saw the listener doing both verbally and nonverbally, and their observations of how the speakers responded.
7. Have the triads repeat the process until all three members have had an opportunity to be observers, speakers, and listeners.

Suggested Reflection Questions

CONTENT (COGNITIVE LEARNING)
▶ Why was it important to have an observer?
▶ How can you be a good listener, speaker, or observer?

COLLABORATIVE (SOCIAL LEARNING)
▶ How can you tell if someone is being a good listener?
▶ How did your tribe use listening skills to make this activity successful?

PERSONAL LEARNING
▶ How did it feel to be listened to in that way?
▶ How well did you attend, paraphrase, and reflect feelings?
▶ What special skills did you bring to your group?

Appreciation

Invite statements of appreciation:
     ▶ "I felt good when..."
     ▶ "I liked it when..."

Teaching Paraphrasing/Reflecting Feelings

Objectives

1. To build community inclusion
2. To teach and practice the listening skills of paraphrasing and reflecting feelings
3. To share ideas and feelings about a given topic

Instructions

1. Have the students form pairs and decide who is partner #1 and who is #2.
2. Have the partners sit "knees to knees" and "eyes to eyes."
3. Demonstrate how to paraphrase a statement. Example:
   Heidi says, "Sometimes I think I'd like to be an airline pilot."
   Paraphrase response: "Now and then you wonder about becoming a pilot."
4. Ask the #1 partners to speak briefly on the topic: "A time when I listened carefully." Partners #2 are to listen and then paraphrase the statement they heard. After three minutes have the partners switch roles.
5. Ask the community, "What is the importance of paraphrasing?"
6. Demonstrate how to reflect feelings along with paraphrasing. Example:
   Heidi says, "Becoming an airline pilot would be exciting because there still are not many women pilots."
   Paraphrase: "You feel excited whenever you imagine being one of the few women pilots."
7. Ask the #2 partners to speak briefly on the topic: "A time that I found my work a challenge." Partners #1 are to listen and then paraphrase the key statement and feelings. After three minutes have the partners switch roles.
8. Have the partners share what each felt during the activity.

Suggested Reflection Questions

CONTENT (COGNITIVE LEARNING)
▶ What listening skills did you use during this strategy?
▶ How does good listening help to build community?

COLLABORATIVE (SOCIAL LEARNING)
▶ How does reflecting feelings help you communicate better?
▶ In what ways did you and your partner help each other during this activity?

PERSONAL LEARNING
▶ How would you feel if someone listened to you like this?
▶ How can you use these skills in your everyday life?
▶ How did you help your partner during this activity?

Appreciation

Invite statements of appreciation:
▶ "I could tell you were listening when..."
▶ "I appreciated your..."

▶ **TIME** 30 minutes
▶ **GROUPING** pairs
▶ **MATERIALS** none
▶ **DEVELOPMENTAL TASKS**
   Independence/Autonomy
   Social Competency
   Sense of Purpose

OPTIONS

Using any academic topic, develop (or have students develop) discussion questions designed for application, synthesis, and evaluation. For example, discuss the long-term implications of a national event.

That's Me—That's Us!

▶ **TIME** 40 minutes

▶ **GROUPING** community, tribes

▶ **MATERIALS** none

▶ **DEVELOPMENTAL TASKS**
Independence/Autonomy
Sense of Purpose

OPTIONS

Use teacher or student designed questions for review or assessment. Ask one of the students who responded "That's me!" to answer or explain. Invite students to ask for help from another person who is standing.

Objectives

1. To build community inclusion
2. To help the students identify personal or community skills, interests, or achievements

Instructions

1. Tell the students that you will call out a series of questions, and those who identify or agree are to jump up and say, "That's me!"
2. Start with a few simple topics that are appropriate to the students' grade level and interest. Examples:
   - How many people have moved in the last two years?
   - How many people have a younger sibling?
   - How many people like broccoli?
3. Use this strategy to learn how the tribes are working together. Ask the tribes to stand and say, "That's us!" Examples:
   - Which tribes had no put-downs today?
   - In which tribe did everyone participate on the task?
   - Which tribe figured out why the rain forest in the Amazon is threatened?

Suggested Reflection Questions

CONTENT (COGNITIVE LEARNING)
▶ What did you find out about your tribe members/community members?
▶ What's one more question you might add?

COLLABORATIVE (SOCIAL LEARNING)
▶ Why was listening important?
▶ How could you tell that your entire tribe would stand up?
▶ What did the community or your tribe members do to make this activity fun for each other?

PERSONAL LEARNING
▶ How did you feel about jumping up?
▶ What did you discover about yourself?

Appreciation

Invite statements of appreciation:
▶ "It helped me when..."
▶ "Thanks for..."

The Ideal Classroom

Objectives
1. To involve students in defining class agreements.
2. To foster a positive climate for learning.
3. To transfer responsibility to students.

Instructions
1. Write "The Ideal Classroom" on the board. Ask students, "How would people act and interact in an ideal classroom?"
2. Have students individually list their responses on an index card.
3. Have students partner with someone sitting near them, and talk about their lists.
4. Have students return to whole group. Ask for volunteers to help record responses on charts posted on the board and numbered one through five. The chart papers will only have numbers written at the top. [NOTE: In your mind, know that one = attentive listening; two = mutual respect; three = appreciation/no put downs; four = participation/right to pass; five = other.]
5. Ask the class to share responses to "How would people act and interact in an ideal classroom?" As students share responses, ask students who are assigned to particular charts to write the response on the appropriate chart.
6. After ideas are generated, ask the group to identify which number the response refers to. Label the charts. [NOTE: If ideas for certain charts have not been generated, then give input to stimulate student ideas.] Amazingly, students will contribute ideas that are aligned to the Tribes agreements.
7. Let students know that these will be the class agreements. The teacher may want to follow up with the double T-chart to further reinforce agreements at another time, or have students create agreement posters to put up on the walls.

Suggested Reflection Questions
CONTENT (COGNITIVE LEARNING)
▶ What is the ideal classroom?
▶ What kind of thinking did we do to come up with the classroom agreements?

COLLABORATIVE (SOCIAL LEARNING)
▶ What social skills would be needed in the ideal classroom?
▶ How can these rules apply to other areas of life?
▶ How did working together help the class?

PERSONAL LEARNING
▶ What personal skills did you use during this activity?
▶ How will you contribute to making this the ideal classroom?

Appreciation
Invite statements of appreciation:
▶ "It felt good when..."
▶ "One thing I liked about what you said was..."

▶ **TIME** 30 minutes

▶ **GROUPING** tribes

▶ **MATERIALS** none

▶ **DEVELOPMENTAL TASKS**
Independence/Autonomy
Social Competency
Sense of Purpose
Problem Solving

OPTIONS

Use this concept attainment strategy for content area discussion.

Use strategy to catalogue concepts related to a subject area (i.e., history, environment, literature, science).

The Week in Perspective

- ▶ **TIME** 10–15 minutes
- ▶ **GROUPING** tribes, pairs
- ▶ **MATERIALS** none
- ▶ **DEVELOPMENTAL TASKS**
  Independence/Autonomy
  Social Competency
  Sense of Purpose

OPTIONS

Use the strategy for current events, having students role play the interviewer and interviewee. Make it more challenging by asking students to employ various questioning skills, such as open vs. closed questions; content, collaborative and personal questions (review types of questions as described in this book).

Imagine yourself in a different period (past or future). Write and share probable responses to the questions.

Objectives

1. To give each student an opportunity to reflect on recent experiences
2. To increase communication skills and sharing
3. To build inclusion and influence

Instructions

1. Ask the community to form triads or pairs.
2. Tell the students that they will take turns interviewing each other. Ask them to decide who will be the first person to be interviewed, the second, and the third (if using triads).
3. Urge the students to listen attentively to the person being interviewed and not discuss anything he or she is saying.
4. Provide the students with questions to ask. Examples:
   - "What new and good thing happened to you this past week?"
   - "What was hard about your week?"
   - "Is there something you meant to do this week but put off?"
   - "What one thing did you do that you enjoyed?"

Suggested Reflection Questions

CONTENT (COGNITIVE LEARNING)
- ▶ What did you learn by doing this activity?
- ▶ Why is answering questions about your week easy/difficult?

COLLABORATIVE (SOCIAL LEARNING)
- ▶ What makes interviewing a challenging skill to master?
- ▶ Why are being the interviewer and the interviewee both important skills?
- ▶ How did your group help each other during this activity?
- ▶ How do you feel as a community now?

PERSONAL LEARNING
- ▶ How did you feel while you were being interviewed?
- ▶ What did you learn about yourself during this activity?
- ▶ How did you contribute to your group in a special way?
- ▶ What special "people skills" did you use during this activity?

Appreciation

Invite statements of appreciation:
- ▶ "I liked it when you said..."
- ▶ "I appreciate you for..."

Third-Party Mediation

Objectives
1. To provide a process for conflict resolution and a mutually agreeable solution
2. To model that a third-party-mediator does not make judgments or take sides
3. To develop trust and acceptance of individual differences
4. To build inclusion yet allow influence (a sense of value)

Instructions
Note: This method can be used with groups as well as individuals.

1. Call together two students who are in conflict and tell them that it is likely a mutually agreeable solution can be worked out. Ask if they would like that to happen. Make it clear that you will not take sides or set yourself up as a judge.
2. Ask each student, one at a time, to describe the conflict; say the other is not to interrupt. Encourage each student to focus on what is going on now rather than list past grievances. If they try to interrupt each other or are not listening, ask each to summarize the other's position.
3. Ask each student in turn to state how the situation makes him or her feel. Encourage use of "I-Messages." Reflect back their feelings. Have each person rephrase the other's feelings.
4. Have both students state what they would like as an outcome to the conflict. As mediator, encourage both to modify their "ideal states," look at alternatives, and decide what they would be willing to give up and work toward.
5. Have both students acknowledge what changes they each are willing to make.
6. Have the students create a list of the steps each agrees to take. Have them make an appointment to check back with the mediator.

▶ **TIME** varies

▶ **GROUPING** community, tribes

▶ **MATERIALS** none

▶ **DEVELOPMENTAL TASKS**
Independence/Autonomy
Sense of Purpose
Problem Solving

OPTIONS

Use this strategy to role play social or historical situations.

Suggested Reflection Questions

CONTENT (COGNITIVE LEARNING)
▶ What steps did the mediator use to help the two students resolve their conflict?
▶ Why is having a third-party mediator helpful in some conflicts?

COLLABORATIVE (SOCIAL LEARNING)
▶ What social skills did you and the community use as you observed the conflict?
▶ How did this activity help the community in a special way?

PERSONAL LEARNING
▶ Volunteers: What did you feel as we worked through your conflict? What personal strengths or special skills did you use to help resolve the conflict?
▶ Observers: What were you feeling for the students in conflict? How did you help the two students and the community as a whole while you observed this activity?
▶ How can this help you in the future? At home?

Appreciation
Invite statements of appreciation:
▶ "It was helpful when you..."
▶ "I appreciated..."

Three for Me!

▶ **TIME**   20 minutes

▶ **GROUPING** community

▶ **MATERIALS** none

▶ **DEVELOPMENTAL TASKS**
  Independence/Autonomy
  Sense of Purpose
  Problem Solving

OPTIONS

Use this strategy
in small groups or
tribes before a group
project. Encourage
the groups to draft a
written plan.

Objectives

1. To help the students verbalize their needs to be successful in class.
2. To increase awareness of the importance of stating your needs.
3. To build inclusion and community during the first week of class.

Instructions

1. Have the community sit in a large circle.
2. Review the Tribes agreements.
3. Ask the students to think about three things they need to be successful in the class. Example: "I need to review the material in a study group before a test, I learn best when I have visuals, and I need a quiet classroom when the teacher lectures."
4. Have everyone respond in turn. Allow time at the end for those who passed to respond if they desire.

Suggested Reflection Questions

CONTENT (COGNITIVE LEARNING)
▶ What similarities did you notice?
▶ What is the value of hearing this information?
▶ How can you use the information that was shared?

COLLABORATIVE (SOCIAL LEARNING)
▶ In what ways did the community listen to what you shared?
▶ How does sharing this information help our class or community?

PERSONAL LEARNING
▶ What new things did you notice about yourself during this activity?
▶ What did you feel when you listened to other students' needs to be successful in the class?

Appreciation

Invite statements of appreciation:
  ▶ "Thanks, (name), for..."
  ▶ "I appreciated your sharing..."

Thumbs Up, Thumbs Down

Objectives

1. To encourage active decision-making
2. To encourage the expression of opinions
3. To accept individual differences
4. To encourage influence

Instructions

1. Have the community sit in a circle.
2. Demonstrate three different ways the students can vote or express their opinions on an issue:
   - thumbs up—agree
   - thumbs down—disagree
   - thumbs sideways—no opinion or pass
3. Then, in rapid-fire sequence, ask controversial questions appropriate to the age level and interests of the community and have students vote. Examples:
   - "How do you feel about eating at fast food restaurants?"
   - "Playing soccer? Football? Skateboards?"
   - "People helping each other in tribe learning groups?"

Suggested Reflection Questions

CONTENT (COGNITIVE LEARNING)

- ▶ What other issues could you vote on?
- ▶ How did this type of voting differ from other voting you've done?
- ▶ Why is discovering different ways to vote important?

COLLABORATIVE (SOCIAL LEARNING)

- ▶ How is this type of voting helpful to our community?
- ▶ How did community members show their acceptance of different votes?

PERSONAL LEARNING

- ▶ How did you feel about making your opinions known in public like this?
- ▶ Why might you have been tempted to change your vote as you looked around?
- ▶ What special strengths kept you from changing your vote?
- ▶ How are you a unique individual in this community?

Appreciation

Invite statements of appreciation:
- ▶ "I felt good when..."
- ▶ "One thing I like about this group is..."

▶ **TIME** 5–10 minutes

▶ **GROUPING** community

▶ **MATERIALS** none

▶ **DEVELOPMENTAL TASKS**
Independence/Autonomy
Sense of Purpose

OPTIONS

This activity can be related to lesson topics by having the students vote on decisions made by characters in books or history, or by having the students express their opinions on lessons or activities.

This strategy can also easily be used as a quick check for understanding before, during, or after a learning event. Add a challenge by inviting students to volunteer questions.

Tower Building

▶ TIME   20–30 minutes

▶ GROUPING tribes, subgroups

▶ MATERIALS 8½ x 11-inch paper, masking tape

▶ DEVELOPMENTAL TASKS
Independence/Autonomy
Problem Solving

OPTIONS

Give the tribe five minutes to plan their towers before they start building. Then stop the action and let the tribes talk for thirty seconds. Have them continue nonverbally for the last five minutes.

Use index cards, folded either lengthwise or in half.

"Handicap" the students: someone cannot see, someone is only one handed, only one person can speak, one person must sit in one place and not move, etc.

Require the towers to be connected by roads, bridges, or some other fashion.

Objectives

1. To promote an awareness of influence issues
2. To explore nonverbal communication
3. To build tribe cohesiveness

Instructions

1. Have the community meet in tribes. Pass out fifteen to twenty pieces of paper and one roll of masking tape to each tribe.
2. Tell the tribes that they are to nonverbally construct a tower or castle using only the given supplies, and that they will have ten minutes to complete the task.
3. At the end of ten minutes, stop the action.
4. Have all the tribes view each other's buildings.
5. Ask tribe members to return to their tribes for discussion and reflection.

Suggested Reflection Questions

CONTENT (COGNITIVE LEARNING)
▶ What was the purpose of this activity beyond building a tower?
▶ Why might nonverbal communication be as important as verbal communication?

COLLABORATIVE (SOCIAL LEARNING)
▶ What social skills did you, as a group, need to successfully build your tower?
▶ How did leadership in your group develop while you were building your tower?
▶ How did your group make sure that all members got to participate?

PERSONAL LEARNING
▶ What did you learn about yourself?
▶ Is this your usual style of working with others?
▶ What special strengths did you use while working with others in your group?
▶ How would you change the way you work in a group?

Appreciation

Invite statements of appreciation:
▶ "I appreciated it when..."
▶ "I thought that (name) was very..."
▶ "Our tribe is..."

Tribal Peer Coaching

Objectives

1. To help slower learners understand or learn subject matter
2. To provide peer support for learning
3. To structure a cooperative learning experience
4. To build inclusion and encourage kindness
5. To experience influence

▶ **TIME**   varies

▶ **GROUPING**   tribes, triads, pairs

▶ **MATERIALS** vary

▶ **DEVELOPMENTAL TASKS**
   Independence/Autonomy
   Social Competency
   Sense of Purpose

Instructions

1. Have the community meet in tribes. Ask tribe members to share which members are very sure that they understand the concept or material from a lesson topic or unit.
2. Ask if those tribe members would be willing to be "coaches" for a short time to the other tribe members who may not be quite as sure.
3. Have tribe members form pairs or triads, with one coach in each subgroup.
4. Tell the coaches that their goal is to have their students be able to repeat back or explain to them the information or concept being learned. Suggest some ways that the coaches can be helpful.
5. Tell the students how much time will be allowed, and remind them of their attentive listening skills.
6. When time is up, ask those who were "students" to explain to their whole tribes what they learned from their coaches.

Suggested Reflection Questions

CONTENT (COGNITIVE LEARNING)

▶ What did you learn about coaching/being coached?
▶ Why is peer coaching a powerful way to help you learn?

COLLABORATIVE (SOCIAL LEARNING)

▶ What social skills does a peer coach need?
▶ What recommendations do you have for a peer coach?
▶ In what ways did your tribe or group work together well to make this activity successful?

PERSONAL LEARNING

▶ How did you feel as a coach/being coached?
▶ How did you help others during this activity?
▶ What special strengths or skills did you discover about yourself?

Appreciation

Invite statements of appreciation:

▶ "I appreciated it when..."
▶ "(Name), you really helped me when..."
▶ "Thank you, (name), I think you are..."

OPTIONS

Use this strategy for the development of student projects.

Use to help students edit their writing, review for assessment, or create portfolios.

Tribe Mimes/Role-Play

OPTIONS

Have the tribes define problem situations, write them on cards, and exchange them with other tribes to act out.

Objectives

1. To build self-esteem
2. To promote inclusion and influence
3. To act out or role-play dilemmas or problem situations

Instructions

Note: This strategy can be used very effectively with lesson topics.

1. Have the students meet in their tribes. Ask if anyone knows what a "mime" is or how circus clowns communicate with an audience. Explain that "mime" means acting out a message or image without speaking any words.
2. Give each tribe a written message or image to act out. Examples:
   - harnessing a horse
   - baking a cake
   - fixing a bicycle tire
   - washing a window
3. Have each tribe decide how to portray the message without speaking.
4. Have each tribe present its mime to the class, and have the other students guess what is being portrayed.
5. Then explain "role play" which means adding speech to what is being acted out. Give the tribes prepared cards that contain problem situations that may be confronting students. Example: Terry and Aaron are approached by two friends who ask them to hold a package they just got. Act out how Terry and Aaron could handle the situation so that they feel proud of themselves.
6. Give the tribes time to plan how to role-play the problem cards, and invite them to present their role-plays.
7. Be sure to follow all presentations with reflection questions.

Suggested Reflection Questions

CONTENT (COGNITIVE LEARNING)
▶ What did you learn from the mime presentations?
▶ Why is acting out a situation using mime a good way to learn?

COLLABORATIVE (SOCIAL LEARNING)
▶ What social skills did people in your tribe need to do mime?
▶ How did leadership in your tribe develop during this activity?

PERSONAL LEARNING
▶ How did you feel while you were acting your part? Observing others?
▶ What strengths or skills did you use while you were acting your part?
▶ How did you help your tribe in a special way?

Appreciation

Invite statements of appreciation:
▶ "I really liked it when..."
▶ "I enjoyed most seeing..."

Tribe Portrait

Objectives

1. To develop self-awareness
2. To develop awareness of spatial relationships
3. To develop cooperative skills
4. To practice observation skills
5. To build inclusion and influence

Instructions

1. Explain to the community that each tribe will draw a tribe self-portrait and that the portrait will include individual drawings of each tribe member.
2. Ask the community to meet in tribes, get their materials, and find a space to work.
3. Discuss possible put-downs that could occur and how to avoid them.
4. Each tribe member asks one other member to do a sketch of him or her.
5. "Artists" draw their subjects using pencils.
6. After completing portraits, have the artists check with subjects for additions or corrections.
7. After corrections and additions have been made, have the artists use marking pens on portrait.
8. When the portraits of all the tribe members are finished, the tribe decides how to present their portraits to the rest of the class.

Note: This project can best be done over a period of two to five days. Also, the teacher may move from tribe to tribe giving some instruction. Excellent opportunity to bring in outside art resource person to work with small groups.

Suggested Reflection Questions

CONTENT (COGNITIVE LEARNING)
- ▶ Why did you draw a tribal portrait?
- ▶ Why was it easy/difficult to draw a tribal portrait?

COLLABORATIVE (SOCIAL LEARNING)
- ▶ How did this task require you to work together?
- ▶ How well did you work together?
- ▶ How did you make sure that every member of your tribe participated?

PERSONAL LEARNING
- ▶ How did you feel when your portrait was being done?
- ▶ How did you feel when you saw your portrait?
- ▶ How did you help your tribe during this activity?
- ▶ What talents or gifts did you discover in yourself?

Appreciation

Invite statements of appreciation:
- ▶ "I like what you drew because..."
- ▶ "When I look at our tribal portrait I feel..."

▶ **TIME**   varies (see note)

▶ **GROUPING** tribes

▶ **MATERIALS** paper, felt pens, pencils, erasers

▶ **DEVELOPMENTAL TASKS**
Independence/Autonomy
Sense of Purpose

OPTIONS

Have tribes create portraits illustrating what they learned about a topic.

Tribes Team Together

► TIME   20–40 minutes

► GROUPING   tribes

► MATERIALS paper, pencil, poster paper

► DEVELOPMENTAL TASKS
   Independence/Autonomy
   Social Competency
   Sense of Purpose

OPTIONS

Have students tell as much as they can about a specific subject, such as the Civil War, Shakespeare, or even geometric shapes.

Objectives

1. To build inclusion and community in tribes or small groups
2. To review material learned (curriculum specific)
3. To develop critical thinking

Instructions

1. Have students meet in tribes or small groups of 4–5.
2. Ask students to share as much information as they can about themselves in two minutes (i.e., interests, hobbies, birth date, brother's name, etc.).
3. Have one student from each tribe leave the room.
4. Have each tribe, in turn, answer a question about the person that is missing (or about the subject-related material). Examples:
   - Has (person missing) ever broken a bone?
   - What is (missing person)'s favorite flavor of ice cream?
5. Have the tribe members from outside return to the room. (*Note:* It is very helpful to have the returning students line up at the back of the room with all of the other students in tribes facing forward, so there is no "helping.")
6. Ask the set of four questions again, to those students who have just returned to the room. Score points for matched answers.
7. Repeat steps 3-7 until all group members have had a chance to be the person who leaves the room.

Suggested Reflection Questions

CONTENT (COGNITIVE LEARNING)
► What did you learn by doing this activity?
► What questions were the hardest/the easiest? Why?
► Why did we do this activity in tribes instead of just pairs?

COLLABORATIVE (SOCIAL LEARNING)
► How did you make sure that everyone participated?
► How did your tribe cope with questions that were difficult to answer?
► How did your tribe members help each other?
► How do you feel as a tribe now?

PERSONAL LEARNING
► Which role did you like best? Why?
► How did you help your tribe in a special way?

Appreciation

Invite statements of appreciation:
► "You were really good at..."
► "That was fun when you..."

Two for Tuesday

Objectives

1. To build inclusion and community
2. To increase awareness of the importance of stating appreciations

Instructions

1. Have the community sit in a large circle.
2. Review the tribes agreements.
3. Ask the students to think of two statements of appreciation or two positive comments about themselves or others.
4. Have everyone respond in turn. Allow time at the end for those who passed to respond if they desire.

Suggested Reflection Questions

CONTENT (COGNITIVE LEARNING)

▶ What are some thoughts that people shared?
▶ Were there any similarities in things that people shared?

COLLABORATIVE (SOCIAL LEARNING)

▶ How did the community members show that they were listening to each other?
▶ How does sharing positive thoughts help communities?

PERSONAL LEARNING

▶ How did you feel about sharing with the community today?
▶ How did you contribute to the community in a special way?
▶ What do you appreciate about yourself today?

Appreciation

Invite statements of appreciation:
▶ "I appreciated it when..."
▶ "Thank you, (name), for..."

▶ **TIME**   20 minutes

▶ **GROUPING** community

▶ **MATERIALS** none

▶ **DEVELOPMENTAL TASKS**
Independence/Autonomy
Social Competency
Sense of Purpose

OPTIONS

Instead of two compliments, students can share two goals (general or daily goals), two things to do for homework, two healthy foods to eat, etc. Think "prevention, health, self-improvement."

Urgent!

▶ **TIME** varies

▶ **GROUPING** community, tribes

▶ **MATERIALS** none

▶ **DEVELOPMENTAL TASKS**
   Independence/Autonomy
   Social Competency
   Sense of Purpose

OPTIONS

Students can write statements addressed to characters in literature.

Use as a prewriting exercise for persuasive writing; follow the "I urge..." statements with opinions and facts.

Objectives

1. To build inclusion and influence
2. To provide students an opportunity to think of significant other persons in their lives
3. To encourage communicating with a special person
4. To promote caring and acceptance for the concerns of others

Instructions

1. Have the community sit in a circle. Review the agreements.
2. Invite each student who cares to participate to send a verbal message to a person in his or her life with whom he or she feels an urgent need to communicate. Messages can involve suggestions for change in a person's life, reaffirmation of caring and friendship, or messages to well known people (i.e., a President, character from literature, scientist, historical figure, etc.).
3. Explain that the format for a message is: "Dear (name), I urge you to…" Have each student end his or her message by saying: "Your (adjective) friend, (name)." Model a message yourself.
4. There is no follow-up discussion after this activity. All messages are sent in an atmosphere of total acceptance.

Appreciation

Invite statements of appreciation:
   ▶ "I liked it when..."
   ▶ "I felt good when..."
   ▶ "I appreciated it when..."

What We Need from Each Other

Objectives

1. To promote inclusion and mutual respect for a substitute teacher, student teacher, or volunteer
2. To identify needs and expectations
3. To promote transfer of responsibility for practicing collaborative skills

Instructions

1. Prepare the following chart with examples prior to the community circle:

What does (substitute's name) need from you?	*What do you need from (substitute's name)?*
Respect	Energizer break
Attentive Listening	Slow down

2. Prior to the arrival of the substitute, student teacher or volunteer, invite the community to respond to the questions on the chart. Record their responses in the appropriate columns. (*Note:* When student teachers or volunteers are in the classroom with the teacher, prepare the chart together as a community.)
3. Leave instructions for the substitute to review the chart with the students, and to initiate a discussion about what the community needs from each other for the day. Have the substitute encourage the community to add information to the chart.
4. Encourage the substitute to make a verbal statement of what she has heard that the students need for the day. Have the substitute ask the students to turn to a neighbor and make a verbal statement about what the community has agreed on.
5. Suggest that the substitute leave the chart up for the day so students can remind themselves and each other of the agreements.

Suggested Reflection Questions

CONTENT (COGNITIVE LEARNING)

- Why is it important to take the time to fill out this chart?
- What will the outcome for the community be after taking the time to do this?

COLLABORATIVE (SOCIAL LEARNING)

- Why is it important for the class to follow agreements when a new person joins our community?
- How will this chart help the community to follow the agreements?

PERSONAL LEARNING

- In what way did you help the community during this activity?
- What strengths and skills will you use to help the community follow through with what you have agreed upon?

Appreciation

Invite statements of appreciation:

- "I liked your suggestion..."
- "Thank you for including..."
- "You are really good at noticing..."

▶ **TIME** 20 minutes

▶ **GROUPING** community

▶ **MATERIALS** easel, large paper, markers

▶ **DEVELOPMENTAL TASKS**
Social Competency
Sense of Purpose
Problem Solving

OPTIONS

Use the strategy when you are having some difficult moments with your own students.

This is an excellent classroom management strategy to use and model, especially for new teachers.

Another option is to have the students use the strategy in a new group, before beginning to work on a task together.

What's in Your Wallet

▶ TIME   30 minutes

▶ GROUPING   tribes

▶ MATERIALS   personal items

▶ DEVELOPMENTAL TASKS
Independence/Autonomy
Sense of Purpose

OPTIONS

Use the strategy to discuss what people from different periods of history might carry with them.

Use as a pre-writing exercise.

Objectives

1. To create tribal inclusion
2. To give the students an opportunity to share something of themselves

Instructions

1. Remind the students of the agreements.
2. Ask each student to select something from his or her desk, wallet, purse, or backpack that is special and symbolic of him or her.
3. Ask the students to meet in their tribes to share their special items.

Suggested Reflection Questions

CONTENT (COGNITIVE LEARNING)
▶ What was the value of this strategy?
▶ What did you learn?

COLLABORATIVE (SOCIAL LEARNING)
▶ How could you tell when your tribe members were listening to each other?
▶ What would you, as a tribe, like to do more of to help each other listen even better?

PERSONAL LEARNING
▶ Was it hard for you to select something special to share? Why?
▶ How did you feel after sharing your special object?
▶ How does your special object relate to your special gifts or talents?

Appreciation

Invite statements of appreciation:
▶ "I liked it when..."
▶ "I appreciated you, (name), for..."

What's on Your Mind?

Objectives

1. To promote group support for a concern
2. To assist a peer, colleague or friend to resolve a problem
3. To promote influence

Instructions

1. Have the community members sit in a large circle.
2. Review the tribes agreements.
3. Ask the students to share, "What's currently on your mind?"
4. Have everyone respond in turn to the question. Allow time at the end for those who passed to respond if they desire.
5. List any concerns that require further exploration on a chart.
6. Take time to explore concerns listed on the chart. (Use the "Suggestion Circle" or "Client-Consultants" strategies to explore concerns, if needed.)

▶ **TIME** 20–30 min.

▶ **GROUPING** community

▶ **MATERIALS** none

▶ **DEVELOPMENTAL TASKS**
Independence/Autonomy
Social Competency
Sense of Purpose
Problem Solving

Suggested Reflection Questions

CONTENT (COGNITIVE LEARNING)

▶ What kinds of things were shared?
▶ What similarities did you notice?
▶ Why is it important to share?

COLLABORATIVE (SOCIAL LEARNING)

▶ How did the community members help each other?
▶ How can we continue to help others in our community?

PERSONAL LEARNING

▶ How does it feel to share what's on your mind?
▶ What personal strengths or skills did you use to help make this activity successful?
▶ What communication skills or "people" skills do you feel most comfortable using?

Appreciation

Invite statements of appreciation:
▶ "I liked it when..."
▶ "Thank you for..."
▶ "You were really helpful when..."

OPTIONS

Stop in the middle of the story you are reading, or in the middle of the history topic you are exploring, and ask, "What's on _____'s mind at the moment?"

You can also use this strategy as a "Think-pair-share" during a learning experience—especially good during Math class...

What's the Tint of Your Glasses?

▶ **TIME**   45 minutes

▶ **GROUPING** tribes

▶ **MATERIALS** poster paper, colored pencils/pens for each tribe

▶ **DEVELOPMENTAL TASKS**
Independence/Autonomy
Sense of Purpose

OPTIONS

Use the strategy to study a historical perspective.

Have students paraphrase responses before adding their own, as described in the strategy "Paraphrase Passport."

Explore points of view on a social issue, e.g., Should high school students have curfews?

Look at a situation from points of view from different generations or cultures.

Objectives

1. To build understanding that our different backgrounds give us different perspectives
2. To show that seeing things differently is okay.
3. To experience how different viewpoints help us to see the whole picture
4. To promote multicultural awareness, acceptance and understanding
5. To experience influence

Instructions

1. Have the community meet in tribes.
2. Have each student draw a pair of eyeglasses on a sheet of paper.
3. Ask each student to draw small designs or symbols on his or her glasses in response to the questions you will read. Examples:
   - What is your country of birth?
   - How many sisters and brothers do you have?
   - What language do your parents speak other than or in addition to English?
   - Have you ever lived on a farm or ranch? In a big city?
4. Have the tribe members compare glasses. Ask, "Do any look the same?"
5. Discuss how different experiences give people different perspectives and opinions. Example:
   - How a city person versus a country person might look at pigs in a pen (pigs are dirty/pigs are great).
6. Ask each tribe to make a list of three other examples.
7. Have each tribe report their list to the community. Ask, "What can happen when people believe everyone sees things the same way?" Discuss perceptions, assumptions, conflict, or respect for differences.

Suggested Reflection Questions

CONTENT (COGNITIVE LEARNING)
▶ What did you learn about how different people see the same thing?

COLLABORATIVE (SOCIAL LEARNING)
▶ In what ways did your tribe work together well during this activity?
▶ How did your tribe show support for each other's differences?

PERSONAL LEARNING
▶ How did you feel when someone had a different point of view?
▶ How can you help others see your point of view?
▶ What personal strengths did you use to communicate your point of view?

Appreciation
Invite statements of appreciation:
▶ "Thanks, (name), for..."
▶ "I appreciate your..."

When I Really Want to Learn Something!

Objectives
1. To promote an awareness of helpful learning strategies
2. To build inclusion and community.

Instructions
1. Use topic: "When I really want to learn something, here's how I do it."
2. Limit statements to one sentence per person.
3. Record all responses on chart paper.

Suggested Reflection Questions

CONTENT (COGNITIVE LEARNING)
▶ What similarities did you hear?
▶ What is one thing you learned in the community?

COLLABORATIVE (SOCIAL LEARNING)
▶ How can the information shared help our learning community?

PERSONAL LEARNING
▶ What did you discover about yourself?
▶ How will you use this information?

Appreciation
Invite statements of appreciation:
▶ "I appreciated..."
▶ "Thank you for..."

▶ **TIME** 20 minutes

▶ **GROUPING** community circle

▶ **MATERIALS** chart paper, pens

▶ **DEVELOPMENTAL TASKS**
Independence/Autonomy
Problem Solving

OPTIONS
Review chart and/or add to it before a new content unit or project.

Where Do I Stand?

▶ **TIME** 15–40 minutes

▶ **GROUPING** community, tribes

▶ **MATERIALS** animal signs, string, tape

▶ **DEVELOPMENTAL TASKS**
Independence/Autonomy
Social Competency

OPTIONS

Use four different metaphors that apply to a theme or topic. Have students move to the metaphor most meaningful to them.

Objectives

1. To encourage sharing
2. To encourage respect for individual differences
3. To experience inclusion and influence

Instructions

1. On large cards, print four animal names: lion, deer, fox, dove. (*Note:* Alternate signs could include: mountain, river, ocean, meadow; piano, trumpet, drum, flute; have students suggest signs.)
2. Post the animal signs near four areas of the classroom.
3. Ask each student to stand near the sign for the animal that they are most like when in their tribe. Encourage people to talk among themselves while they are deciding where to stand.
4. When all the students have chosen animals and have taken their places under the signs, ask them to share why they placed themselves where they did.
5. Continue the activity by repeating steps 3 and 4 with other situations. Examples:
   • How are you with your friends?
   • How are you with your family?
   • How are you by yourself?
   • How are you in a social situation with people you don't know?
6. Ask the students to meet in tribes and talk about their choices—why they stood where they did.
7. Have all write in their Personal Journals what they learned.

Suggested Reflection Questions

CONTENT (COGNITIVE LEARNING)
▶ What are the qualities of a lion/fox/dove/deer?
▶ What did you learn about other students in the community/about yourself?

COLLABORATIVE (SOCIAL LEARNING)
▶ Why would you find it difficult to take a stand?
▶ How is taking a stand an important skill for all of us?
▶ How did the community or tribe help you feel comfortable taking a stand?

PERSONAL LEARNING
▶ How did you feel when you took your stand?
▶ How did you feel sharing your reasons with the community?
▶ What did you learn about yourself?
▶ In what special ways did you contribute to the group?

Appreciation

Invite statements of appreciation:
▶ "I was interested when..."
▶ "I appreciated it when you said..."

Wishful Thinking

Objectives

1. To provide the opportunity to express a wish
2. To build inclusion

Instructions

1. Have the students sit or stand in a community circle or in tribes. Instruct them that no discussion is allowed during this activity.
2. Ask each student in turn to make a brief statement beginning with, "I wish…" related to personal life, feelings about politics, school, the community, etc.
3. If possible, take turns around the circle more than once.

Suggested Reflection Questions

CONTENT (COGNITIVE LEARNING)

▶ How easy/difficult was it for you to think of wishes to share?
▶ Why are wishes important?
▶ What wishes do you have in common?

COLLABORATIVE (SOCIAL LEARNING)

▶ How did your tribe members show that they were listening to each other's wishes?
▶ How did tribe members help each other share?

PERSONAL LEARNING

▶ How did you feel while you were sharing your wish/listening to others share?
▶ What skills did you use while participating in this activity?
▶ What did you learn about yourself?

Appreciation

Invite statements of appreciation:
▶ "I liked it when…"
▶ "I felt good when…"
▶ "I admired your honesty when…"

▶ **TIME** varies
▶ **GROUPING** tribes, community
▶ **MATERIALS** none
▶ **DEVELOPMENTAL TASKS**
  Independence/Autonomy
  Social Competency

OPTIONS

Use the strategy to share concerns about current events, school issues or content related topics. The strategy can be expanded for problem solving and/ or decision making.

Energizers

BUMPETY-BUMP-BUMP

Form a circle standing up, with a chosen "it" in the center. The "it" walks up to you and stands in front of you and says one of the following:

"Center, bumpety-bump-bump"

"Self, bumpety-bump-bump"

"Right, bumpety-bump-bump"

"Left, bumpety-bump-bump"

You must say his or her name, your name, or the person's name to the right or left of you before "it" completes saying "bumpety-bump-bump;" otherwise you become "it."

CHANGES

Have students get in pairs (or do in a full group by having five volunteers come and stand in the front of the room). Instructions are to look at your partner (or class volunteers) and notice and remember as much as you can about his or her appearance. Partners turn back to back (volunteers leave the room) and change three noticeable things about their appearance. Students must guess what changes have been made. This energizer is easy to repeat, because as time goes on, the changes can be more subtle, specific, even scientific (i.e., change three things involving color, quantity, your torso, etc.).

CLAP-SLAP

Get a rhythm going: two claps, two slaps on lap. Go around the circle filling the blanks to the following chant: My name is (Karen), I come from (Kuwait) and I sell (Kleenex). The first sound must match the beginning sound in your name.

DO AFTER ME

Sit in a large circle. One person begins by entering the circle and making a gesture, sound, or movement (the more ridiculous, the more fun), and then points to someone else in the circle to succeed him. This person makes the same gesture, sound, or movement as the preceding person made, and then adds her own performance. She then chooses the next person, and this person need only repeat the preceding action and add one before choosing someone new. The game is over when everyone has had a chance in the circle.

ELECTRICITY

Have everyone sit down in one large circle. Hold hands. One person starts a squeeze on one side and the next person quietly passes it on around the circle. Variation: send an "ooh" or an "aah" the other way.

FORK AND SPOON

This is a hilariously confusing exercise in communication. Have everyone seated in a circle. The leader has a fork in the right hand and a spoon in the left hand. The leader turns to the person on the right and, holding up the fork, says, "This is a fork." The person being spoken to says, "A what?" The leader repeats, "A fork," and hands the fork over. The person with the fork says, "Oh, a fork!" Now, the person with the fork turns to the person on his/her right and says, "This is a fork." The person being spoken to says, "A what?" The person with the fork turns to the leader and asks, "A what?" The leader says, "A fork." Then the person turns to his/her right and says, "A fork," and hands over the fork to the next person. That person says, "Oh, a fork," turns to the person on the right and begins again with, "This is a fork." When the person replies, "A What?" each person must go back up the line, one at a time, asking, "A what?" until the leader tells them, "A fork." Then, "Oh, a fork," is said down the line until it reaches the person holding and then handing over the fork, beginning again with, "This is a fork." Now that the fork is flowing smoothly to the right, start the process to the left with the spoon! The leader must now be alert for responding in both directions to the "A what?" questions, saying "A fork" to the right and "A spoon" to the left. Watch the fun when both the fork and the spoon reach the same person at once, usually midway around the circle.

HAGOO

Divide into two teams and form two lines. Have people stand shoulder to shoulder facing a person on the other team. Stand a yard apart. One person from each team will volunteer to walk past each person in the row of the opposite team. The people on the team try to make the volunteer from the other team smile as he/she walks by. No touching is allowed. If the volunteer cracks up he/she must join the opposite team. If he/she makes it to the end straight faced, he/she goes back in the row with his/her original team.

I LIKE MY NEIGHBORS

Have all members seated on chairs in a circle, with one person standing in the middle as "it." The person in the middle makes a statement such as, "I like my neighbors, especially those who are wearing running shoes (wearing glasses, are over fifteen, have a birthday in September, etc.)." All those people who are wearing running shoes must jump up from their seats and scramble to find a chair; the person in the middle also scrambles for an empty chair. The one person left standing becomes the new "it."

Extension: Two or more people seated away from each other may make eye contact and nonverbally "plot" to change places. When they make the dash to each others' seats, the "leader" may try to beat them to it.

LINEUP

Have students line up in order of birth date, height, number of family members, number of the bus they ride to school, alphabetical order of middle name, etc. Have them do this without talking. This is a good energizer for getting your group focused, settled, and silent. The lineup is also a handy way to get your class into random cooperative groups.

NAME WAVE

All stand in a circle. One person says his/her name and at the same time makes a motion or gesture. (Example: "Beth," as she waves her hand.) The person to the right says, "Beth," and waves her hand as Beth did. The name and motion spread around the circle in a "wave." When the circle is complete, the next person says his/her name and a different motion and that "waves" around the circle. Continue until all names are said and activated.

PEN PALS

Give each participant a 3 x 5 index card and tell them to write a little known fact about themselves on the card, something they won't mind the group eventually knowing. State that they are not to write their name on the card. Collect all cards, shuffle and redistribute. If someone gets his/her own card back, it is exchanged for another. When everyone has an unfamiliar card, have all stand and circulate, asking one another questions about the information on the card. For example, "Did you barrel race horses as a child?" When the person answering the description is found, he/she signs the card and puts it on a designated wall space. When you are finished, the community has an instant bulletin board of people and their accomplishments. This is a good full group inclusion energizer—good for parents on back-to-school night, too!

PEOPLE PATTERNS

Discuss types of patterns (A B A B, A B C A B C, A B B A B B). Have the members of a tribe or small group establish themselves in a pattern and stand in front of the class in that order. For example, an A B A B pattern might be "stripes on shirt, no stripes on shirt" or "earrings, no earrings." The people pattern should tell the audience what type of pattern they are demonstrating (A B A B, etc.). Members of the class must try to guess who can go next in the pattern; they may not guess the pattern until they have named a person to stand next in the people pattern. The person to correctly identify the pattern will join his or her tribe or small group to establish the next pattern. Pattern criteria should be clearly visible to all.

RAIN

Have everyone sit in a circle, facing the center. Ask all to close their eyes, pausing for a moment or two to become quiet while each person gets ready to hear the sound the person on the right will be making. Keep eyes closed as the rainstorm begins with the leader rubbing her palms together, back and forth. The person to the left joins her, and then the person to her left, and so on, around the circle. When the leader hears the drizzle sound being made by the person on the right, she starts snapping her fingers. When the snapping action has been picked up by everyone around the circle, the leader switches to hand clapping, then to thigh slapping, and finally to foot stomping. After foot stomping, the leader reverses the order of sounds, introducing thigh slapping, hand clapping, finger snapping and finally palm rubbing. For the last round, the leader stops rubbing her palms and takes the hand of the person on her left. Each person follows suit around the circle until there is silence once again.

SHUFFLE YOUR BUNS

Have all participants seated in a circle with chairs pushed in tight. (All chairs should be of equal height.) The leader stands and moves to the center of the circle, leaving one empty chair. Model the directions by saying, "Shuffle to the right." Only the person with the empty chair to his or her right may "shuffle their buns" into the chair to the right. As each person moves, he/she vacates his/her chair for the next person to "shuffle their buns." This begins to move around the circle quite rapidly. Now the leader may say, "Shuffle to the left." At this command, the person that just completed a shuffle to the right must reverse and "shuffle their buns" into the empty chair to the left. The procession then follows; each time a chair is vacated, someone is shuffling into it. It must be understood that one cannot "shuffle their buns" unless s/he is moving into an empty/vacated seat. Once the group has mastered shuffling their buns, the leader speeds up the process by reversing commands frequently enough so as to confuse the action. The object now is for the leader to shuffle his or her buns into an empty seat. Having interrupted the flow, the person now in the middle giving the "shuffle" commands is the person who failed to shuffle fast enough and lost his or her seat to the leader. To really get things rolling, give each person in the group a one-time-only opportunity to automatically reverse the shuffle by slapping the empty chair next to them instead of shuffling into it. This "confusion" allows the person in the middle a better opportunity to find a seat, and keeps anyone from having to be the middle person for too long.

SNOWBALL

Each student places his/her name on a piece of paper and wads it up. Students line up, half on either side of the room. At a signal they begin a snowball fight. At the end, each gets a snowball, learns new information about the person whose snowball they found, and shares it with the class.

THREE BALL PASS

This is a mini "group juggle." Using something that is easy to catch, establish a pattern around the room as follows: leader says someone's name and tosses him/her the ball; s/he chooses another person, says that person's name, and tosses him/her the ball; continue in this manner until each person has caught and tossed the ball once. The ball will end the pattern in the hands of the leader. Repeat the pattern until it can be done quickly. Begin again, and after several people have caught and tossed the ball, throw in the second ball, using the same pattern sequence; then throw in the third ball. This is a great energizer for learning names. After the group has mastered "Three Ball Pass," have them reverse the pattern! For a real challenge, have your group try it silently (after the pattern is established). Koosh balls work well.

TWO TRUTHS AND A LIE

This energizer is great for building inclusion and re-entry after a school vacation. Have each person write down three things about themselves, what they did over vacation, etc. Of these three statements, two must be true and one must be a lie. Suggest that the lie should not be very obvious; it can even be a small detail. The rest of the class (or small group) must guess which one is the lie.

ZAP

Have all participants stand in a circle. The leader has everyone "create some energy" by rubbing their hands together quickly, back and forth. Next the leader has everyone take a deep breath in, hold for two to three seconds, and breathe out. Do two more deep breaths, while continuously rubbing hands. Now the leader instructs (while all are still rubbing hands) that on the count of three, everyone will make a sweeping point with their right arm to the center of the circle and yell, "Zzzzzzaaaappp!" This energizer really creates some energy, while at the same time allowing for the expenditure of energy. Try zapping a person (only if they want to be zapped), or even social issues such as classroom put-downs.

ZOOM, ZOOM, BRAKE!

Have everyone stand in a community circle, facing in, shoulder to shoulder. Introduce the sound "zoom" and say that the sound goes zooming around the circle whenever you say it. When you say it, look to your right. That person immediately says, "zoom," while looking to his or her right and this continues quickly around the circle. After going around the circle once, say that the car was only in first gear. Shift up into second and then third gear, the "zoom" going faster each time with more power. Now introduce the "brake" by demonstrating a screeching noise along with a hand signal of pulling back the brake. Have everyone try it with his or her own screeching brake sound. Now the group is ready to play. The rules are that you only get to brake once. When someone "brakes," the zoom reverses direction and goes the opposite way around the circle. Eventually everyone will get a chance to "brake" or the facilitator can call an end to the noise.

*R*esources

Resources

THE HISTORY OF TRIBES AND TRIBES TLC®

The initial version of the Tribes process began to evolve in the early seventies, a time when concerned educators and parents began groping for ways to motivate children's learning, to manage behavior problems, and to stem the tide upon which many good teachers were leaving the profession. National surveys were alerting the general public and industry leaders that the majority of high school students did not have the knowledge or skills to do well in the world of work and social complexities that they would face in life. Twenty years ago? Or is it today?

Jeanne Gibbs had observed that children's achievement and behavior in school seemed to be influenced by the quality of the classroom and school environment. Being a student at heart, Jeanne began exploring studies on school climate, human development, and the dynamics of organizational systems. In 1973 she was asked to consult with the Contra Costa County Department of Education towards the prevention of substance abuse related problems. There was little research at that time on prevention other than studies which confirmed that informational curricula alone did not deter problems. The author reasoned that since environment influences human behavior, building positive environments within schools and families not only would be preventive, but could be significant in promoting academic learning and social development.

The concept made enough sense to some other visionaries at the California Department of Education who in 1974 funded a grant that would enable elementary school teachers to pilot a group development process that Jeanne had been using for many years within community settings. As the teachers began to experience the caring environment within their own work groups, they began to use the term, "tribe." Repeatedly they said, "We feel like a family... we feel like a tribe."

In 1976, Jeanne published the first instructional manual, titled *TRIBES: A Human Development Process for Educational Systems,* and then in 1978, Jeanne published the first of many copyrighted *Tribes books, titled TRIBES: A Process for Peer Involvement* (CenterSource Publications).

From 1975 through 1985 numerous applications of the group development process were made through a non-profit corporation which Jeanne founded. The "people process" proved to be valuable in alcohol recovery centers, juvenile facilities, daycare centers, and recreational programs. California schools began to request training when they learned that the Tribes group process decreased behavior problems, increased self-esteem, improved cooperation and achievement, and improved teachers' energy and morale.

Based on the extensive research of the cooperative learning field, the book, *Tribes, A Process for Social Development and Cooperative Learning,* was published in 1987. The demand for training accelerated throughout the country, and in 1991 quality materials incorporating new research, concepts and methods were designed by the author and her colleagues. The more comprehensive version of the Tribes process became known as "Tribes TLC®" and resulted in the writing and publication of *Tribes, A New*

Way of Learning and Being Together (1994), which has been expanded and revised several times.[1] The most recent edition is titled *Reaching All by Creating Tribes Learning Communities* (2006).[2]

In 1994, the Research Triangle Institute, under a U.S. Department of Education contract, identified Tribes TLC® as an exemplary program to teach social skills to Kindergarten to 12th grade students.[3] The Council of the Great City Schools cited Tribes as a model to prevent violence.[4]

In 2001, the author researched and wrote a middle level book, titled *Discovering Gifts in Middle School: Learning in a Caring Culture Called Tribes,* which emphasizes the need for schools to become responsive to the contextual basis of adolescent development in order to attain both greater achievement and success for students as well as a new spirit, energy and the discovery of gifts throughout the whole school community.[5]

In 2003, the Collaborative for Academic, Social and Emotional Learning (CASEL) identified Tribes TLC an evidenced-based "SELect Program."[6] In 2005, the Office of Juvenile Justice Delinquency Prevention (OJJDP) identified Tribes Learning Communities as an evidence-based Promising Program in their Model Programs Guide.[7] In 2006, CSAP's WesternCAPT (Center for Substance Abuse Prevention's Center for the Application of Prevention Technologies) recognized Tribes Learning Communities as a Promising Practice that addresses both protective and risk factors for the prevention of substance abuse.

In 2005, CenterSource Systems published an important new book, titled *What Is It About Tribes? The Research-Based Components of the Developmental Process of Tribes Learning Communities.* This important book by Bonnie Benard of WestEd, is an in-depth response to questions that educators have been asking for many years: "What is it about the process of 'Tribes' that makes it work so well in so many schools, cultures and countries?" The author brings hundreds of research studies and literature references into enlightening coherence to discover how and why the student-centered active-learning process transforms people, classrooms, and schools.[8]

Application of the Tribes process continues to grow with the advent of Jeanne's new book, *Engaging All by Creating High School Learning Communities,* that is based on current and evolving best practices for the secondary level. As now defined, the primary mission of Tribes TLC® is "to assure the healthy development of every child in the school community so that each has the knowledge, skills and resiliency to be successful in our rapidly changing world." Indeed, this can happen when schools engage all teachers, administrators, students and families in working together as a learning community dedicated to caring and support, active participation, and positive expectations for all.

References—See Notes section of this book for references.

A FACT SHEET ON TRIBES TLC®

THERE ARE CERTIFIED TRIBES TLC® TRAINERS SERVING:

All U.S. States and Canada, as well as Australia, New Zealand, the United Kingdom, the Dominican Republic, Mexico, Ecuador, Colombia, Venezuela, the Northern Marianas, and the United Arab Emirates.

DEMOGRAPHICS OF TRAINERS

Certified Tribes TLC Trainers include individuals of almost all races and ethnic groups. Over one fourth of the 1300 trainers are bilingual or multilingual. Approximately one third are administrators (Assistant Superintendents, Principals, Coordinators, State Department Officials and Program Managers). There are also Psychologists, Private Consultants, Deacons, University Instructors and, of course, public and private school classroom teachers, including National Board Certified teachers. The Certified Tribes Trainers have degrees ranging from Bachelors to PhDs. Ages of the trainers range from age 22 to 76. There are trainers living in 42 U.S. states, as well as many other countries.

THE TRIBES PROCESS CAN BE FOUND IN:

- ▶ Public Schools
- ▶ Private Schools
- ▶ Parochial Schools
- ▶ Native American, First Nation, Aboriginal Schools and schools serving other Indigenous populations
- ▶ International Schools
- ▶ University Programs
- ▶ State Departments of Education
- ▶ After School Programs
- ▶ Recreation Programs
- ▶ Family Resource Centers
- ▶ Church groups
- ▶ Drug and Alcohol Treatment Centers
- ▶ Regional Educational Centers

FUNDING

Funding sources for training in the Tribes process come from Federal, State and local resources as well as Foundations. Call CenterSource for more information.

TRIBES TLC IS RECOGNIZED AS A MODEL OR PROMISING PROGRAM BY:

- ▶ Collaborative for Academic, Social and Emotional Learning
- ▶ Office of Juvenile Justice Delinquency Prevention
- ▶ Center for Substance Abuse Prevention's Western CAPT
- ▶ Helping America's Youth

THE ORIGIN OF "REFLECTION," THE PELICAN

In one way or another, the talkative pelican that flies throughout the pages of this book insisted on becoming a notable character in all of the Tribes books and materials. This occurred, despite author Jeanne Gibbs more or less ignoring the swooping pelican tribes that flew around her houseboat while she lived in Sausalito, California. The big birds would land and perch for long times on the pilings alongside her boat, seemingly to observe the kayaks, sailboats, cruisers and other activity going by.

An important occasion took place one day when ten 4th and a 5th grade students from a Tribes school, a 4th grade teacher, and a parent came to visit. The occasion arose because the teacher of the 5th graders was not using Tribes learning groups, as had been the practice of all of the other teachers the students had been with since 1st grade. They wanted to talk about writing a letter to the 5th grade teacher—a letter that would urge her to have them learning in Tribes.

Lunching on the deck of the houseboat was exciting enough, but the hot dogs, chips and lemonade were quickly forgotten when a friendly pelican landed on top of the boat. People became quiet and spellbound as they observed the big bird—and as she observed them. After a time she flew off.

Mindful of the students' letter writing plan, after lunch and a lot of discussion about pelicans, Jeanne said, "Let's close our eyes for a few minutes. Now imagine that your school has a glass roof and ceilings so that our pelican could look down and see whatever was happening in your two classrooms. What would she see? What are the students doing? What is the teacher doing? Think about it silently."

Three or four minutes later, everyone wanted to talk at once. "In our 4th grade class the pelican would see our desks together in small groups. People would be talking and working together." "Yeah, helping each other figure stuff out." "Some people are sitting on the carpet, designing a building." "They're sharing materials—they're laughing." "And one tribe is planning how to act out the story they read." "People are moving around the classroom to get things and ideas from other tribes." "The teacher is walking around. She's not just asking them a bunch of questions." "No, people are asking for her ideas."

The parent then asked, "And what would the pelican be seeing in the 5th grade classroom?" "Oh, everyone is sitting alone in straight rows." "The new teacher is talking lots, writing stuff on the board and asking lots of questions." "Not many kids are putting up their hands to answer." "Some even have their heads down on their desks." "And two guys are poking each other." "The teacher is passing those fat workbooks down the rows." "The kids look real bored."

The writing club's conclusion was that the next time they met they would write what the pelican may have seen and what they hoped the 5th grade teacher would consider doing.

Some days later the 5th grade students and parent delivered the letter to the teacher and a copy to the Principal. It took awhile, but the teacher took their message to heart. She participated in a Tribes TLC training, enjoyed learning from other teachers, and gradually transformed the classroom into a student-centered Tribes Learning Community.

After reflecting on her experience with the students, Jeanne rather spontaneously named the pelican "Reflection" and began to emphasize the importance of having students reflect on current situations, events and their own learning. The literature is replete with studies on the impact that timely reflection (reflective practice) has on academic learning, behavior, self-responsibility and social competency. Reflective practice is an essential practice to accomplish whole school reform, systems change, productive professional learning communities and authentic assessment.

There are many, many pelicans in the Tribes books, articles and materials. Reflection, the pelican, is a meta-cognitive symbol to remind all of us to introduce and make *reflective practice* an on-going norm in all school systems. If somehow you missed the invitation from Jeanne on page 112 of this book here it is again….

> *Invite the pelican that soars over the Tribes Trail to be your constant companion. Her name is Reflection. She will tell you, rather immodestly, that she makes the Tribes process work well anywhere. At times, you will want to ignore her calls: "timeout," "stop the action, teacher," "time to reflect," or "what's happening now?" Reflection knows that if you watch from the bird's eye view, classroom management goes more smoothly. Reflection is a wise bird who can describe just what she saw or heard while people worked together. You will find her questions on the pages of every Tribes strategy. Reflection clears up confusion and helps everyone soar to greater heights.*

THE IMPACT OF GROUP PROCESSING

Tribes has always emphasized the importance of using reflection or process questions after each group strategy or learning experience. The motto shared among Tribes teachers has been, "The activity alone is not enough!" Throughout the years, CenterSource Systems trainers have been helping teachers define three types of reflection questions (1) about the content of a lesson; (2) about the collaborative social skills used by students; and (3) about the personal learning that a lesson had for the students. Reflection questions were emphasized as a way to develop metacognition (learning about our learning) and responsibility among students to improve their learning groups. Empirical studies confirm that the time spent with students on "group processing" leads to the greater retention of subject matter and academic achievement.

The study "The Impact of Group Processing on Achievement in Cooperative Learning Groups" by Stuart Yager, Roger Johnson, David Johnson, and Bill Snider describes three learning conditions assessed in three classes composed of 84 3rd graders. An intensive five-week unit on transportation was taught in all three classrooms but in different processes.

Classroom A used the conventional individualistic learning method whereby students study alone and fill daily worksheets. Classrooms B and C used cooperative learning groups (four students to a group) with students working together and each group completing the worksheets together. In addition, classroom C spent 5 minutes processing their work as a group and setting goals for improvement. A 50-item factual knowledge multiple choice test on the subject was given to all children prior to the unit and three weeks after the unit. A 25-item test was given after twelve instructional days and another 25-item test as soon as the unit was completed.

The graph was constructed from the research data. The first bar graph for each class shows achievement and the second bar graph indicates retention of knowledge after three weeks. Pretest scores for all students had averaged about 50%. In classroom A, using the individualistic approach, marginal gains moved from 50 to 65% in achievement, with retention dropping to 58% three weeks after the unit was completed. In classroom B, using cooperative learning groups and no processing, gains moved from 50 to 78%, with 73% retention. Results in classroom C, using cooperative learning groups with processing are impressive, with higher achievement (87%) and no loss in the retention of knowledge after three weeks.

Other studies by the same researchers show comparably dramatic results from the contribution of group processing to learning and individual achievement. Interested readers can learn more by visiting the website of the Cooperative Learning Center at the University of Minnesota (www.co-operation.org), where Drs. David and Roger Johnson continue to document their work and where the following studies can be accessed: Stuart Yager, Roger Johnson and David Johnson, "Oral Discussion, Group-to-Individual Transfer, and Achievement in Cooperative Learning Groups," *Journal of Educational Psychology*, 77:60-66, 1985. Stuart Yager, Roger Johnson, David Johnson, and Bill Snider, "The Impact of Group Processing Achievement in Cooperative Learning Groups," *The Journal of Social Psychology*, 126:389-397, 1986.

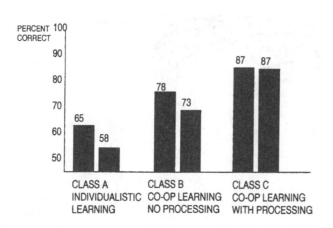

INTERACTIONS IN PERSONALIZED LEARNING

Personal Needs	Relationships	School Practices

Developmental Needs, Talents, and Aspirations

Voice
The need to express personal perspective
→ **RECOGNITION** ←
Equity
Democratic processes for deliberation

Belonging
The need to create individual and group identities
→ **ACCEPTANCE** ←
Community
Shared commitment to all students

Choice
The need to examine options and choose a path
→ **TRUST** ←
Opportunity
Range of options for individual development

Freedom
The need to take risks and assess effects
→ **RESPECT** ←
Responsibility
Experimentation with adult roles

Imagination
The need to create a projected views of self
→ **PURPOSE** ←
Challenge
Tasks that mirror adult roles

Success
The need to demonstrate mastery
→ **CONFIRMATION** ←
Expectations
Clear standards for performance

Flexible Options for Engaged Learning

Personal Learning: Using information from the school experience to direct ones' own life and to improve the life of the community

GRAPHIC ORGANIZER
REACHING ALL WITH A CIRCULAR CURRICULUM—EXAMPLE

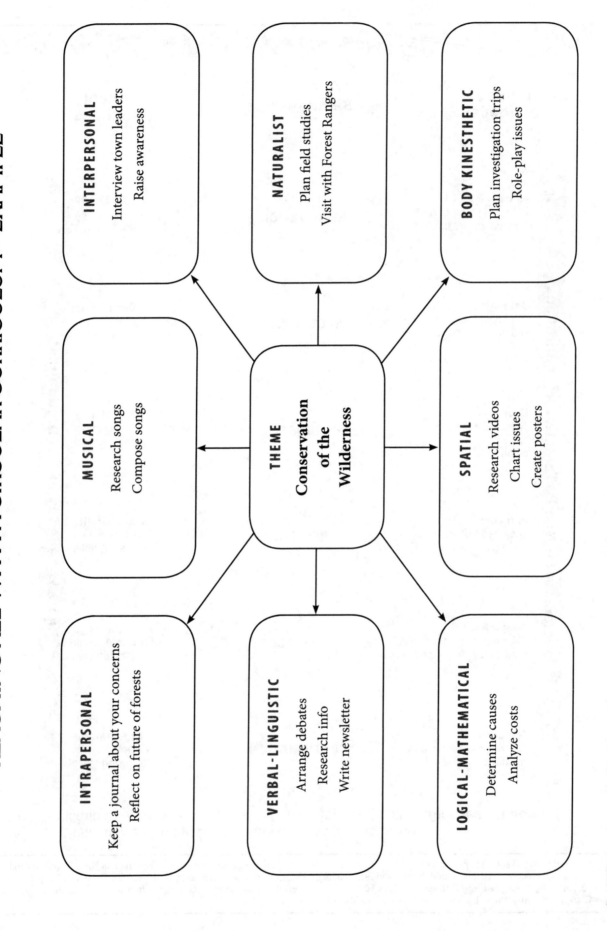

INTERPERSONAL
Interview town leaders
Raise awareness

NATURALIST
Plan field studies
Visit with Forest Rangers

BODY KINESTHETIC
Plan investigation trips
Role-play issues

MUSICAL
Research songs
Compose songs

THEME
Conservation
of the
Wilderness

SPATIAL
Research videos
Chart issues
Create posters

INTRAPERSONAL
Keep a journal about your concerns
Reflect on future of forests

VERBAL-LINGUISTIC
Arrange debates
Research info
Write newsletter

LOGICAL-MATHEMATICAL
Determine causes
Analyze costs

GRAPHIC ORGANIZER
REACHING ALL WITH A CIRCULAR CURRICULUM

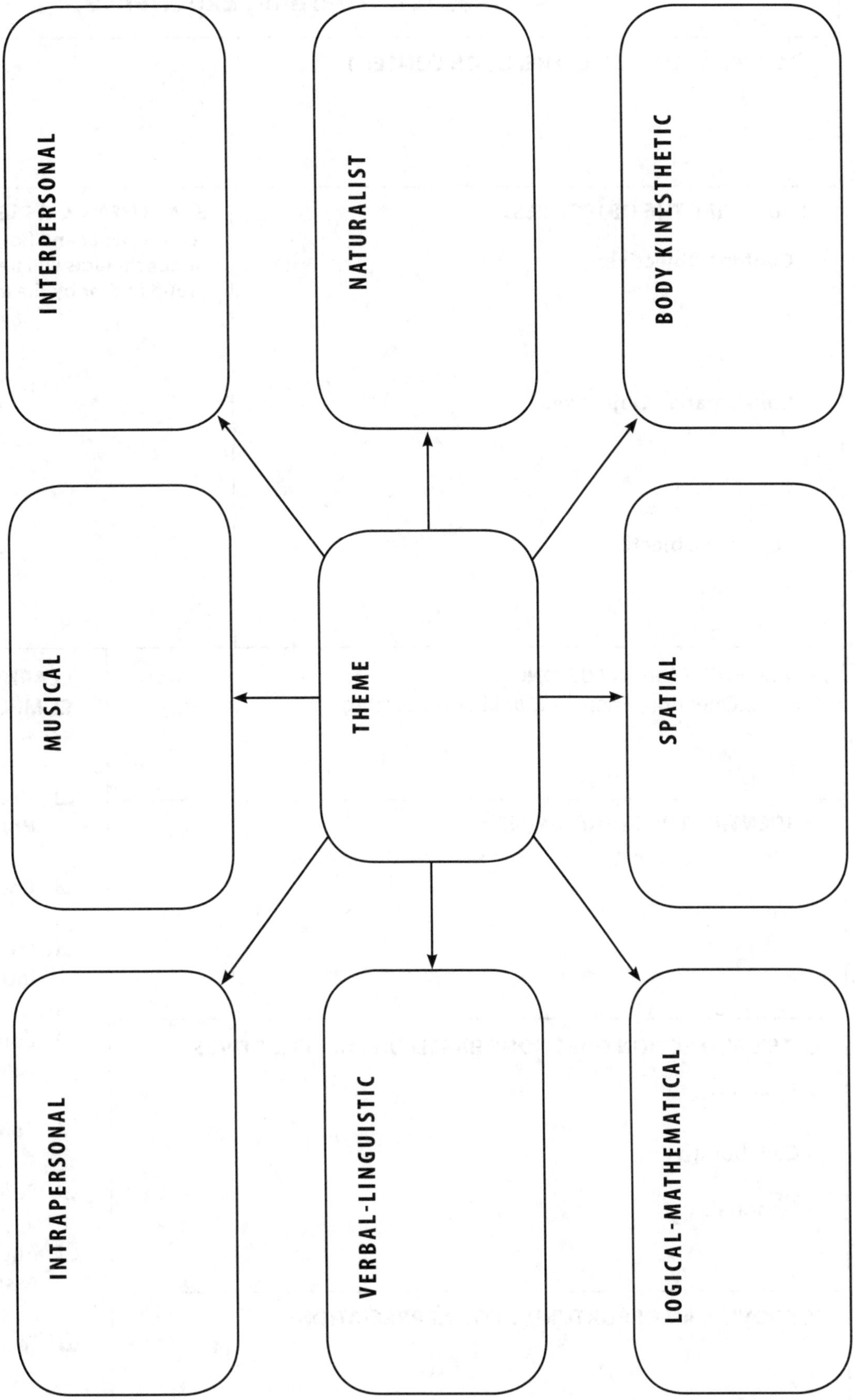

```
          INTERPERSONAL

MUSICAL          THEME          NATURALIST

          SPATIAL

INTRAPERSONAL   VERBAL-LINGUISTIC   BODY KINESTHETIC

                LOGICAL-MATHEMATICAL
```

INTERPERSONAL

NATURALIST

BODY KINESTHETIC

MUSICAL

THEME

SPATIAL

INTRAPERSONAL

VERBAL-LINGUISTIC

LOGICAL-MATHEMATICAL

This page may be duplicated for classroom use.

A Tribes TLC® Learning Experience

1. CURRICULUM TOPIC, THEME, OR CONTENT:

2. IDENTIFY THE OBJECTIVES:

Content Objective:

Collaborative Objective:

Personal Objective:

3. AUTHENTIC ASSESSMENT: Determine what and how the objectives or benchmarks will be achieved by the group and/or by the individual students.

4. PROVIDE FOR INCLUSION:
A You Question, Energizer, or Linking Strategy

5. IDENTIFY THE STRATEGY(IES):

6. ASK REFLECTION QUESTIONS BASED ON THE OBJECTIVES:

Content:

Collaborative:

Personal:

7. PROVIDE AN OPPORTUNITY FOR APPRECIATION:

LEARNING COMPONENTS:
(check)

❑ Group Development Process

❑ Cognitive Theory

❑ Multiple Intelligences

❑ Cooperative Learning

❑ Constructivism

❑ Reflective Practice

❑ Authentic Assessment

❑ Technology

This form may be duplicated for classroom use.

FORM A: STUDENT ASSESSMENT

OUR GROUP'S WORK TOGETHER

Group or Tribe Name _____ Date _____

Using the numbers 1 (poorly), 2 (okay), and 3 (great!), rate how well your group did the following:

RATING   SOCIAL SKILL OR GROUP INTERACTION

_____   1. We listened to each other.

_____   2. We checked our understanding of the task.

_____   3. We shared ideas and information.

_____   4. We encouraged and helped each other.

_____   5. We stayed on the task and used our time well.

_____   6. Other:

Total Score: _____

This form may be duplicated for classroom use.

FORM A: STUDENT ASSESSMENT

OUR GROUP'S WORK TOGETHER

Group or Tribe Name _____ Date _____

Using the numbers 1 (poorly), 2 (okay), and 3 (great!), rate how well your group did the following:

RATING   SOCIAL SKILL OR GROUP INTERACTION

_____   1. We listened to each other.

_____   2. We checked our understanding of the task.

_____   3. We shared ideas and information.

_____   4. We encouraged and helped each other.

_____   5. We stayed on the task and used our time well.

_____   6. Other:

Total Score: _____

This form may be duplicated for classroom use.

FORM B: STUDENT ASSESSMENT

PARTICIPATION IN MY GROUP   Date _____

Name _____   Tribe _____

	NEVER	SOMETIMES	MOSTLY	ALWAYS
1. I listened to people in my group.				
2. I helped other people.				
3. I contributed ideas and information.				
4. I helped to clarify and summarize ideas and information.				
5. I encouraged others.				
6. I participated in making decisions.				
7. I expressed appreciation to others.				
8. I helped us to reflect on what we learned.				

NOTES

FORM C: STUDENT ASSESSMENT

MY CONSTRUCTIVE THINKING SKILLS　　　　Date _____

Name _____　　　Tribe _____

INSTRUCTIONS:

Read the descriptions of constructive thinking skills below and estimate how well you do each skill. You can use a different colored pencil or pen each week to evaluate your own progress in using these skills.

	NEVER	SOMETIMES	MOSTLY	ALWAYS
1. I am able to **access information** (using the library, computer, articles, interviewing, and working with others).				
2. I can **organize information** (using graphics, charts, note cards, computer data entry).				
3. I am able to **compare and summarize** facts and ideas.				
4. I can **plan and use** what I learn to solve problems and be creative.				
5. I am able to **reflect and evaluate** how well something is working and make improvements.				

OTHER COMMENTS

Helping Parents Learn About Learning Communities

TIME REQUIRED: 60 minutes

FACILITATORS: Two parent leader-volunteers who have participated in Tribes training—or two Tribes-trained teachers or educators from the school.

MATERIALS: Tribes agreements posted on wall, 3 x 5-inch cards, pencils, large pieces of paper, felt pens

Note: This strategy can be used as a special session during Back-to-School night or on other occasions to inform parents about the commitment that the school has made to create learning communities.

OBJECTIVES

1. To develop participation and mutual support among parents.
2. To provide parents with a satisfying initial experience of the Tribes process.
3. To motivate parents to continue meeting throughout the year as a learning community.
4. To provide information on the goals of Tribes, its process, and collaborative agreements.
5. To help parents learn how to foster resiliency in their children.

INSTRUCTIONS

8 min.	1. As parents arrive, the teacher and parent facilitators (PFs) invite the parents to sit in small groups of prearranged chairs or desks (four to seven in a group).
	2. The teacher welcomes all, gives an overview of the hour, and tells why the Tribes process is being used within the school to build learning communities. He or she introduces the PFs and briefly describes their role.
4 min.	3. The PFs share their names, students' names, and their commitment to having parents become a supportive learning community.
	4. The PFs then describe the Tribes agreements and ask the parents to honor them during their time together. They demonstrate the Tribes hand signal as a way to call attention.
5 min.	5. The parent facilitators discuss the importance of the Tribes agreements and attentive listening, and they demonstrate the skills.
1 min.	6. After asking each group to select a timekeeper, the PFs each ask the parents to share their name and one great quality about their student. Ask the timekeepers in each group to monitor the sharing time.
5 min.	7. The PFs ask the parents to think about, then share with one other person in the group, two things they hope for their child during the year. As one parent shares, the other notes down in one to three words the parent's hopes on a card. When the time is up, the PFs collect the cards.
5 min.	8. The teacher responds to some of the hopes listed, tying them to classroom or school-wide goals for the year.
5 min.	9. The PFs ask the following reflection questions: • How many people enjoyed being able to talk with other parents tonight? • How many would like to get together this way again?
5 min.	10. The PFs demonstrate and invite statements of appreciation in tribes.
5 min.	11. They invite everyone to close in a community circle, sharing, "I learned" statements.

This material may be duplicated for classroom use.

TRIBES PROFESSIONAL DEVELOPMENT

BRING YOUR SCHOOL TO LIFE WITH TRIBES TLC® PROFESSIONAL DEVELOPMENT

Tribes is a community building process—a culture and active learning pedagogy best learned by experiencing it. You can make the process come alive for your district or school by scheduling training for your teachers, administration and support staff.

CenterSource Systems has a network of licensed trainers who conduct professional development training in many countries throughout the world. Schedule an overview presentation and classroom demonstration at your school where the key concepts of Tribes are explained and demonstrated through typical training strategies and our videos. Give your administration, school board and staff the information they need to consider whole school training. Schools and districts committed to the full implementation of Tribes TLC® can arrange training and support to teams and faculties through the following staff development opportunities:

ENGAGING ALL BY CREATING HIGH SCHOOL LEARNING COMMUNITIES

The purpose of this 24-hour experiential training is to provide the research-based concepts, experience, and strategies that are essential for engaging all by creating high school learning communities. Among the topics to be considered will be: critical indicators of the very different needs of 21st century youth, voices of students themselves, and a consensus of recommendations from the literature and studies, including the National Association of Secondary School Principals (NASSP). Participants will explore the most promising strategy for sustained, substantive school improvement—that of building the capacity of school personnel—"the insiders"—to function as a collegial learning community, in which teachers collaboratively learn together, tailor curricula to ways in which students of today's world best can learn, support each other in implementation, and reflect together continuously on their own enhanced learning—as well as that of their students. Participants will understand why and how the research-based developmental process of Tribes Learning Communities, when implemented well, can transform the culture, structures and pedagogy of the whole high school system—particularly one committed to preparing today's students for an entirely different era—the Era of Learning.

TRIBES TLC®—Building Community for Learning (Tribes "Basic" Training)

The purpose of this 24-hour experiential training is to prepare teachers, administrators and support staff personnel at the K–8 or elementary level to develop a caring school and classroom environment, and to reach and teach students through an active learning approach that promotes student development, motivation and academic achievement.

> What Tribes can bring to a class is dynamite—what it can bring to a total staff is spectacular!
>
> —LESLIE MCPEAK, PRINCIPAL
> MODESTO CITY SCHOOLS

DISCOVERING GIFTS IN MIDDLE SCHOOL

The purpose of this 24-hour experiential training is to provide a research-based approach for middle level school educators to focus their schools on the critical developmental learning needs of young adolescents. The training illuminates how to transform the cultures of middle schools into caring learning communities that support the full range of students' growth and development as well as establishing academic excellence.

ARTISTRY FOR LEARNING

The purpose of this 24-hour experiential advanced-level training is to increase the capacity of teachers and administrators within Tribes Learning Community Schools to intensify quality implementation of the research-based developmental process of Tribes—thereby to assure that all students, no matter their diversity and ability, achieve higher social, emotional and academic learning.

COLLABORATION: THE ART FORM OF LEADERSHIP—
Leading for Results in a Tribes Learning Community

The purpose of this 12-hour experiential training is to bring together school leaders and leadership teams who have already been trained in the process of Tribes TLC® so that they can explore and complete authentic leadership tasks and gain a new exciting view of their roles in reculturing the school community. The Tribes collegial team learning experiences will create a professional learning community environment that will support and sustain increased student learning and achievement.

IMPLEMENTING AFTER-SCHOOL TRIBES

The purpose of this 12-hour experiential training is to prepare after-school educators, youth workers, and community members to develop a caring learning center environment and to reach and teach children and youth through an active learning approach that promotes human development, resiliency, and social-emotional competence. Using multiple intelligences, brain compatible learning and cooperative methods, the community learning center climate and staff awareness will begin to reflect the message of life-long learning, personal development, and social responsibility as the keys to success in the 21st century.

TRAINING-OF-DISTRICT TRAINERS

CenterSource Systems has designed a capacity building model for professional development so that your district or school can have your own Certified Tribes TLC® Trainers providing on-going training, coaching and support to teachers, administrators, resource personnel and parent community groups. The CenterSource Systems 40-hour Training-of-District Trainers provides in-depth skills, knowledge, experience and quality training materials to your own qualified personnel. A variety of training modules enable them to facilitate the Basic Tribes Course, support faculty groups, initiate parent community groups and conduct classroom demonstrations.

SUMMER INSTITUTE FOR DISTRICT TRAINERS

The purpose of the Tribes TLC® Summer Institute is to advance the professional capacity of the Tribes Learning Community international network of trainers to lead and accelerate academic, social and emotional learning for all students in their schools and to develop the leadership capacity to sustain and intensify the implementation of Tribes through the development of professional learning communities in their schools and districts.

Follow-up coaching and support at your school site is available throughout the year so that your staff can fully implement the process of Tribes and intensify its use throughout the whole school community.

Tribes TLC has been recognized by—
    CASEL as a SELECT Program
    CSAP's Western CAPT, Promising Program
    OJJDP, Promising Program
    Helping America's Youth, Level 3 Program

FOR ADDITIONAL INFORMATION, CALL OR WRITE:

CenterSource Systems, LLC
7975 Cameron Drive, Bldg 500
Windsor, California 95492

Phone: 800-810-1701 or 707-838-1061
FAX: 707-838-1062
Email: tribes@tribes.com
Website: www.tribes.com

TRIBES LEARNING COMMUNITIES®
A MODEL AND PROMISING PROGRAM

CASEL SELect PROGRAM

After an extensive program and evaluation review, Tribes was chosen by the Collaborative for Academic, Social and Emotional Learning (CASEL) as one of 22 SELect Programs. CASEL summarizes the conceptual framework, criteria, and program review results in their publication, *Safe and Sound: An Education Leader's Guide to Evidence-Based Social and Emotional Learning (SEL) Programs.* (www.casel.org)

Tribes TLC® earned recognition as a CASEL SELect Program by demonstrating the following essential requirements:

▶ provides outstanding coverage in five essential SEL areas

▶ has well-designed evaluation demonstrating effectiveness

▶ offers high-quality professional development.

OJJDP Model Programs Guide

Tribes TLC® has been included in the OJJDP (Office of Juvenile Justice Delinquency Prevention) *Model Programs Guide.* OJJDP, an office of the U.S. Department of Justice, created the Model Programs Guide to assist educational practitioners and communities in "implementing evidence-based prevention and intervention programs that can make a difference in the lives of children and communities." (www.dsgonline.com)

The Guide's ratings are derived from four dimensions of program effectiveness:

▶ conceptual framework of the program

▶ program fidelity

▶ evaluation design

▶ empirical evidence demonstrating the prevention or reduction of problem behaviors, the reduction of risk factors, and the enhancement of protective factors.

Tribes is recognized as an OJJDP prevention program in the categories of:

▶ academic skills enhancement

▶ afterschool and recreation

▶ classroom curricula

▶ conflict resolution and interpersonal skills

▶ leadership and youth development.

CSAP'S WESTERN CAPT

Tribes TLC® is recognized as a promising practice by the Center for Substance Abuse Prevention's Western CAPT (Centers for the Application of Prevention Technologies). Promising practices are programs and strategies that have quantitative data showing positive outcomes in preventing or delaying substance abuse over a period of time. Tribes Learning Communities is listed as a comprehensive practice that addresses both risk and protective factors in the areas of family, school, individual, peer, and community.

CSAP's WesternCAPT has identified guiding principles as recommendations on how to create effective prevention programs and to gauge the program's potential effectiveness. The guiding principles can also be used to design innovative programs and strategies that are appropriate to the community's needs.

Visit http://captus.samhsa.gov/western/western.cfm

HELPING AMERICA'S YOUTH

Tribes Learning Communities is recognized in the evidence-based *Community Guide to Helping America's Youth* (HAY). The Guide represents a collaborative effort of nine federal departments, including the U.S. Department of Education, Department of Justice, Department of Health and Human Services, Department of Housing and Urban Development, Office of National Drug Control Policy, and National and Community Service. (www.helpingamericasyouth.gov)

Tribes is recognized as a program that displays "a strong theoretical base and has been demonstrated to prevent delinquency and other child and youthful problems or reduce risk factors and enhance protective factors for them." The rating is based on evaluation studies and identifies the concepts of risk and protective factors as frameworks for effective programs.

FUNDING SOURCES FOR TRIBES IMPLEMENTATION

Tribes TLC® has been implemented using a variety of grant and foundation funding sources with a focus on enhancing academic achievement, professional development, mentor teaching, beginning teacher training, developing leadership, safe and drug free schools, comprehensive school reform, alcohol, tobacco and other drug abuse prevention, violence and bullying prevention, conflict resolution and mediation, character education, service learning, small learning communities, alternative education, charter schools, youth development, delinquency prevention, community development, technology in education, English language acquisition, diversity, multi-cultural education, health, wellness and physical education.

Contact CenterSource for additional information and supporting documentation.

EVALUATION OF TRIBES LEARNING COMMUNITIES

Evaluation of Tribes Learning Community Schools has shown that:

▶ *Tribes TLC has a positive impact on classroom environment*

▶ *teachers spend less time managing student behavior*

▶ *students are less likely to be referred for disciplinary problems*

▶ *the Tribes process helps teachers address academic standards*

▶ *students in well-implemented classrooms score significantly higher on standardized tests than students from comparison groups*

▶ *teachers report increased staff collegiality and planning.*

WestEd conducted a 2-year evaluation of Tribes TLC that involved administering surveys in 13 schools and collecting standardized test results for 40 Tribes schools and 80 control schools. The evaluators found that:

▶ the Tribes TLC process was fully implemented

▶ Tribes was seen as a vehicle for facilitating continuous school improvement

▶ there was evidence of improved student inclusion, collaboration, respect for multi-cultural populations, sense of value, resiliency, and student engagement

▶ students and staff enjoyed safe and supportive classroom and school environments

▶ teachers and principals reported declines in student referrals and suspensions

▶ there was evidence of better classroom management and increased teacher collaboration and planning

▶ three-quarters of teachers reported that the Tribes process helped them to address academic standards and helped students master standards

▶ 2nd and 5th grade reading and math scores increased more in high-growth Tribes schools than in comparison schools.

The **School District of Beloit** in Wisconsin conducted a 3-year evaluation of the Tribes process that included more than 3,000 elementary and middle school students. Dr. Derick Kiger presented the study at the 2001 American Education Research Association Annual Meeting and earned the First Place Instructional Program Evaluation Award.

Evaluators found that:

▶ 4th graders from Tribes classrooms where the program was well-implemented scored significantly higher on the CTBS than students from less well-implemented Tribes classrooms

▶ sixty percent of the teachers reported that they spent less time managing student behavior because of the Tribes process.

In **Tulsa, Oklahoma,** Dr. Judith Holt used a randomized design to conduct an evaluation of the impact of Tribes on discipline referrals at a middle school. The study found that:

▶ students based in Tribes classrooms were significantly less likely (27%) than non-Tribes students (73%) to be referred to the principal's or counselor's office for disciplinary problems of all types, including disruptive behavior, refusal to work or follow directions, and fighting.

The **Central Oahu School District** in the State of Hawaii conducted a study of 17 elementary schools that implemented the process of Tribes. The evaluators found that:

▶ mutual respect was the most common practice for students and faculty.

Fifty-five classroom teachers and their students in **Spring Branch ISD** in Texas participated in a Tribes evaluation survey, which found that in Tribes classrooms:

▶ teachers spent less time managing student behavior

▶ teachers had more time for creative teaching

▶ students saw new learning as "fun"

▶ mutual respect was evidenced through behaviors

▶ group behaviors changed even at bus stops as students began accepting more responsibility for their behavior.

MATERIALS FOR THE TRIBES LEARNING COMMUNITY

Engaging All by Creating High School Learning Communities
by Jeanne Gibbs
Item 115 $39.95
This comprehensive and dynamic 544 page book provides the research-based pedagogy, concepts and strategies that are essential for engaging all by creating high school learning communities. The book includes critical indicators of the needs of 21st century youth and recommendations from the literature, including the National Association of Secondary School Principals (NASSP). Readers will explore the *most promising strategy* for substantive school improvement—that of building the capacity of school personnel to function as a *collegial learning community*. Readers will understand *why* and *how* to transform the culture, structures and pedagogy of the whole high school system to prepare today's students for the Era of Learning. 2008.

Reaching All by Creating Tribes Learning Communities
by Jeanne Gibbs
Item 100 $32.95
This 30th anniversary edition shows teachers how to reach students by developing a caring environment as the foundation for growth and learning. Material details how to teach essential collaborative skills, design interactive learning experiences, work with multiple learning styles, foster the development of resiliency, and support school community change. 2006.

Discovering Gifts in Middle School: Learning in a Caring Culture Called Tribes
by Jeanne Gibbs
Item 140 $32.95
This comprehensive book supports middle level schools to make adolescent developmental growth and learning the over-riding focus of the whole school community. The author presents a lively synthesis of a wealth of research studies and effective practices. The major emphasis on middle level schools becoming responsive to the contextual basis of adolescent development leads not only to greater achievement and success for students but a new spirit, energy and the discovery of gifts throughout the whole school community. 2001.

What Is It About Tribes? The Research-Based Components of the Developmental Process of Tribes Learning Communities
by Bonnie Benard
Item 110 $19.95
This enlightening book, by Bonnie Benard of WestEd, is an in-depth response to questions that educators have been asking for many years: "What is it about the process of 'Tribes' that makes it work so well in so many schools, cultures and countries? What is it that helps all kinds of students love learning?" The reader will discover why and how implementing the core components of the process of Tribes transforms people, classrooms and schools—not because the approach is a curriculum to be taught or a program to be replicated—but because it is an on-going student-centered active-learning process that everyone in a school lives daily and owns. The book will also prove to be invaluable in the writing of grants, and designing parent, community and district programs. 2005.

Guiding Your School Community
by Jeanne Gibbs
Item 130 $14.95
In this 110-page book written with school Administrators in mind, you will learn why and how the positive Tribes culture will develop community throughout an entire educational system. You will gain an understanding of how to initiate, support and sustain the Tribes process over time. 1999.

Four Tribes TLC Videos on DVD

Item 150 $39.95

All of our most popular videos are contained on this one DVD.

1. Tribes, Learning for the 21st Century
2. Creating Futures of Promise
3. Tribes, A New Way of Learning

plus a FREE bonus video produced by the School District of Beloit, Wisconsin.
(You can also view the Beloit video on the Tribes home page.)

Energizer Box

Item 162 $21.95

This colorful desktop card file contains 101 tried and true energizers that are a great way to revitalize students throughout the day.

Middle School Journal Teacher Manual

Item 142 $15.00

The teacher manual accompanies the Middle School Student Journal (Item 143). The manual provides important concepts, tips, and instruction for the teacher to successfully use the student journals as an active and reflective learning resource in the classroom. The journal is based on social emotional learning and the Tribes TLC® process. Teachers will have greater success if they have already participated in a 24-hour Tribes TLC® training.

Middle School Student Journal

Item 143 $6.00

The student journal is based on social emotional learning and the Tribes TLC® process. The pages have been carefully constructed to help middle school students explore the special ways they learn, how they relate to others, their interests, skills, and gifts, as well as setting goals for the future. The journal was designed to be used at least twice a week and to support what teachers learned in a 24-hour Tribes TLC® training.

Tribes Buttons and Magnets

(2 1/4 inches)

Item 165E   English (50 Buttons) $20.00
Item 165H   Hawaiian (50 Buttons) $20.00
Item 165S   Spanish (50 Buttons) $20.00
Item 166   (25 Magnets) $20.00

Assorted Tribes buttons in English, Spanish or Hawaiian. We also put the agreements on a flexi-magnet for your kids to take home for the fridge. Great for the whole school, parent nights, Tribes Celebration days, and just for fun.

The Tribes Assessment Kit: Reflecting on the Tribes TLC® Process

Item 400 $75.00

The Tribes Assessment Kit will help your school strengthen its implementation of the process and assess outcomes. The Kit includes four assessment instruments and directions for use in classrooms and throughout the school.

MAIL, FAX, OR PHONE IN YOUR ORDER TODAY! OR ORDER ONLINE AT: WWW.TRIBES.COM

CenterSource Systems, LLC, 7975 Cameron Drive, #500, Windsor, CA 95492

Phone: 800-810-1701   707-838-1061   Fax: 707-838-1062

TRIBES TLC® MATERIALS ORDER FORM

ITEM NO.	DESCRIPTION	PRICE	QTY.	COST
100	*Reaching All by Creating Tribes Learning Communities* by Jeanne Gibbs	$32.95		
110	*What Is It About Tribes?* by Bonnie Benard	$19.95		
115	*Engaging All by Creating High School Learning Communities* by Jeanne Gibbs	$39.95		
120	*Tribus, una nueva forma de aprender y convivir juntos* by Jeanne Gibbs	$32.95		
130	*Guiding Your School Community* by Jeanne Gibbs (Tribes Administrators book)	$14.95		
140	*Discovering Gifts in Middle School* by Jeanne Gibbs	$32.95		
142	*Middle School Journal Teacher Manual*	$15.00		
143	*Middle School Student Journal*	$ 6.00		
145	*Cooperative Learning* by Spencer Kagan	$35.00		
147	*Silly Sports & Goofy Games* by Spencer Kagan	$25.00		
150	*DVD—All four Tribes Videos on one DVD*	$39.95		
151	*Video: Tribes, A New Way of Learning and Being Together*—VHS Tape	$22.95		
153	*Teaching Peace* (audio tape) by Red Grammer	$10.00		
154	*Teaching Peace* (CD) by Red Grammer	$15.00		
155	*Teaching Peace Song Book & Teacher's Guide* by Kathy Grammer	$15.00		
161	*Video: Creating Futures of Promise* (15 minute video on Resiliency)—VHS Tape	$22.95		
162	*Energizer Box* (desktop card file with 101 Energizers)	$21.95		
165	*Tribes Buttons Assorted* (2¼ inches) Bag of 50 ❑ English ❑ Spanish ❑ Hawaiian	$20.00		
166	*Magnets* (Bag of 25) Agreements with Teddy Bear ❑ English ❑ Spanish	$20.00		
170	*Video: Tribes—Learning for the 21st Century*—VHS Tape	$22.95		
173	*Tribes Postcards* (Pack of 50) ❑ English ❑ Spanish	$10.00		
175	*Tribes Book Bag* (15" L x 13" H)	$14.95		
182	*Denim Shirt with Pelican Logo* ❑ Medium ❑ Large ❑ X-Large	$28.50		
184	*Lapel Pin*—1¼ inch cloisonné with Pelican Logo	$ 5.00		
185	*Poster—Tribes Agreements* (19" x 25")	$ 7.95		
186	*Poster—Tribes Trail* (19" x 25")	$ 7.95		
400	*Tribes TLC® Assessment Kit*	$75.00		

METHOD OF PAYMENT

Check enclosed for $_____

❑ MasterCard ❑ VISA ❑ Am. Express

#_____

Exp. Date: MM/YY _____ /_____

Purchase Order # _____

Please attach purchase order to this form

SHIPPING RATES:	CONTINENTAL USA	HI, AK & CANADA
Order under $25.00	= $6	= $10
$25.00–$74.99	= $8	= $14
$75.00–$124.99	= $10	= $18
$125.00–$349.99	= 10%	= 15%
$350 or more	= 8%	= 14%

All shipping is via UPS ground or USPS Priority Mail
Call for international or rush shipping rates.

* California residents: include sales tax for your county

SUBTOTAL	
SHIPPING	
SALES TAX*	
TOTAL	

SOLD TO: NAME _____

ORGANIZATION _____

ADDRESS _____

CITY/STATE/ZIP _____

DAY PHONE _____

SHIP TO: NAME _____

ORGANIZATION _____

ADDRESS _____

CITY/STATE/ZIP _____

DAY PHONE _____

PHONE: 800 810 1701 OR 707 838 1061 FAX: 707 838 1062 WWW.TRIBES.COM
CENTERSOURCE SYSTEMS, LLC 7975 CAMERON DRIVE, SUITE 500 WINDSOR, CA 95492

*A*ppendix

Appendix

Notes

THE TIME IS NOW

1. Words are from the song, *Teaching Peace,* written and sung by Red Grammar on the audio tape *Teaching Peace.* Recorded by The Children's Group, Toronto, Canada. The tape is available from CenterSource Systems. www.tribes.com

2. Thornburgh, N. (2006, April). Drop out nation. *Time Magazine,* 167(16), p. 30. The article cites a 2001 study by Jay Greene, Manhattan Institute, that led Greene and other researchers to estimate the national graduation rate at 64–71 percent. The rate has remained fairly stable since 1970 despite the vigorous educational reform movement.

3. Bridgeland, J., Dilulio, Jr., J, & Morison, K. B. *The silent epidemic: Perspectives on high school dropout students.* A report by Civic Enterprises in association with Peter D. Hart Associates for the Bill and Melinda Gates Foundation.

4. Peterson, Kevin. (2005). *High schools failing the next generation.* Achieve Surveys. www.stateline.org

5. Erickson, F. & Shultz, J. (1992). Students' experience of the curriculum. In: Jackson, P. (Ed.). *Handbook of research on curriculum.* New York, NY: Macmillan, pp. 465–487.

6. Vail, Kathleen. (November 2004). *Remaking high school.* American School Board Journal, pp. 15–19.

7. Peterson, Kevin. (2005).

8. Statement made by Tom Vander Ark, Director of Education for the Bill and Melinda Gates Foundation, as quoted in Kathleen Vail's article, Remaking school. *American School Board Journal,* November 2004.

9. Botstein, Leon. (1997). *Education and the promise of American culture.* New York, NY: Doubleday. Botstein, at the age of 23, became the youngest college President in American history upon his appointment as President of Bard College in 1975. The book is an exploration of the promise of American culture, education and democracy—and how schools can be restructured to reflect the realities of modern childhood.

10. The statement is from the Foreword written by respected educator, Ted Sizer, Chairman Emeritus, Coalition of Essential Schools, for the publication, *Breaking ranks II: Strategies for high school reform.* (2004). National Association of Secondary School Principals (NASSP), p. xi.

11. Schmoker, Michael. (2004, April). *Tipping point: From feckless reform to substantive instructional improvement.* Phi Delta Kappan International.

12. Pope, Denise Clark. (2001). *Doing school: How we are creating a generation of stressed out, materialistic, and miseducated students.* New Haven, CT: Yale University Press, pp. 149, 175.

13. Fullan, Michael. (2007). *The NEW meaning of educational change.* (Fourth Edition). New York, NY: Teachers College Press, Columbia University.

14. Black, Susan. (2004, May). Reform at the top: Improving high schools calls for comprehensive change, not piecemeal tinkering. *American School Board Journal,* p. 36–38.

15. Senge, Peter, et. al. (2002). *Schools that learn.* New York, NY: Doubleday.

16. Covey, Stephen. (1996). Three roles of the leader in the new paradigm. In: Hasselbein, F., Goldsmith, M. & Beckland, R. (Eds.). *The leader of the future.* San Francisco, CA: Jossey–Bass, p. 149.

17. Schmoker, Michael. (April, 2004).

18. Little, Judith. (1990, Summer). The persistence of privacy: Autonomy and initiative in teachers' professional relations. *Teachers College Record,* pp. 526–27.

19. Barth, Roland S. (2001). *Learning by heart.* San Francisco, CA: Jossey–Bass, p. xiv.

CHAPTER 1: LISTEN TO THE VOICES

1. Pope, Denise Clark. (2001). *Doing school: How we are creating a generation of stressed out, materialistic, and miseducated students.* New Haven, CT: Yale University Press, p. viii.

2. *Breaking ranks II: Strategies for high school reform.* (2004). National Association of Secondary School Principals, p. xv.

3. Sarason, Seymour. (1990). *The predictable failure of school reform.* San Francisco, CA: Jossey–Bass.

4. Statement from educator, Larry Cuban on the back cover endorsement of Denise Clark Pope's book, *Doing school.* (2001).

5. Catherine Pinot's statement is from the article, Students' voices chime in to improve schools, by John Gehring. *Education Week,* May12, 2004.

6. Cushman, Kathleen. (2003). *Fires in the bathroom: Advice for teachers from high school students.* The New Press, p. 4.

7. A short publication, *A guide to facilitating action research for youth,* is available from Mathew Goldwasser, Ph.D. at Research for Action in Philadelphia.

8. Erickson, F. & Shultz, J. (1992). Students' experience of the curriculum. In: Jackson, P. (Ed.). *Handbook of research on curriculum.* New York, NY: Macmillan, p. 481.

9. Reported by Pedro Noguera in his article, Beyond size: The challenge of high school reform. *Ed Leadership.* (2002, February). pp. 60–63.

10. Gewertz, Catherine. (2004, November 3). Student–designed poll shows teenagers feel lack of adult interest. *Education Week.* The initiative to empower students and cultivate them as allies in bettering their schools was organized by What Kids Can Do, Inc., a Providence, R.I. based non–profit that promotes youth development and is financed by the Met Life Foundation.

11. *Students as allies in improving their schools: Key findings from student and teacher surveys.* (October 2004). www.whatkidscando.org

12. The summation was drawn from focus groups and the books and articles listed in the above references.

13. Eckert, Penelope. (1989). *Jocks and burnouts: Social categories and identity in the high school.* New York, NY: Teachers College Press, Columbia University.

14. Ancess, J. & Darling–Hammond, Linda. (2003). *Beating the odds: High schools as communities of commitment and student learning outcomes.* New York, NY: Teachers College Press, Columbia University.

15. Bronfenbrenner, Urie. (1979). *The ecology of human development: Experiments by nature and design.* Cambridge, MA: Harvard University Press.

CHAPTER 2: LEARNING WHO THEY ARE

1. Myles Horton developed the Highlander education program and the Citizenship Schools to educate activists to catalyze social change with his "two-eye" theory of teaching described as " keeping one eye on where people are and one eye on where they can be." Horton, Myles, with Judith Kohl & Herbert Kohl. (1990). *The long haul: An autobiography.* New York, NY: Doubleday, p. 131.

2. Stoddard, Lynn. (1992). *Redesigning education: A guide for developing human greatness.* (1992). Tucson, AZ: Zepher Press.

3. Dewey, John. (1916). *Democracy and education.* New York, NY: Free Press.

4. The Collaborative for Academic, Social and Emotional Learning (CASEL) is dedicated to the development of children and youth's social–emotional competencies and the capacity of schools, parents and communities to support that development. Based on a comprehensive review of Tribes Learning Communities (TribesTLC®), CASEL recognized Tribes as one of 22 evidence–based SELect Programs. www.casel.org. Another valuable resource for information and practices on social-emotional and character development, can be found at www.teachSECD.com. Dr. Maurice Elias, a founding member of CASEL, is a Professor of Psychology at Rutgers University and Director of the Rutgers Social-Emotional Learning Lab and the Developing Safe and Civil School (DSACS) Initiative.

5. Keith Larick is the Superintendent of the Tracy Unified School District in the Bay Area of California. His statement opens the 15–minute video tape, *Learning for the 21st Century.* It is available from CenterSource Systems.

6. Littky, Dennis, with Grabelle, Samantha. (2004). *The BIG picture: Education is everybody's business.* Alexandria, VA: Association for Supervision and Curriculum Development (ASCD).

7. Gardner. Howard. (1990). *Art education and human development.* Santa Monica, CA: The Getty Center for Education in the Arts.

8. Rogoff, B. (2004). *The cultural nature of human development.* New York, NY: Oxford University Press, p. 156.

9. Bronfenbrenner, Urie. (1979). *The ecology of human development: Experiments by nature and design.* Cambridge, MA: Harvard University Press, p. 9.

10. Armstrong, Thomas. (2006). *The best schools: How human development research should inform educational practice.* Alexandria, VA: Association for Supervision and Curriculum Development (ASCD), p. 23.

11. Armstrong, Thomas. (2006). p. 36.

12. Armstrong, Thomas. (2006). p. 39.

13. Benard, Bonnie. (2005). *What is it about Tribes? The research-based components of Tribes Learning Communities.* Research Contract: West Ed, Oakland, CA. Publisher: CenterSource Systems, Windsor, CA. p. 11.

14. Statement made by Gene Carter, Executive Director, Association for Supervision and Curriculum Development, on February 1, 2006, in response to President George W. Bush's State of the Union speech.

15. Collaborative for Academic, Social and Emotional Learning (CASEL). www.casel.org

16. Comer, J.P., Haynes, N.M., Joyner, E.T. & Ben–Avie, M. (1999). *Child by child: The Comer process for change in education.* New York, NY: Teachers College Press, Columbia University.

17. Comer, J.P. (2001, April 23). *Schools that develop children.* The American Prospect, 12(7).

18. Solomon, D., Battistich, V. & Watson, M. (1993, March). *A longitudinal investigation of the effects of a school intervention program on children's social development.* Paper presented at the biennial meeting of the Society for Research in Child Development, San Ramon, CA.

19. American Psychological Association's Board of Educational Affairs, Learner–Centered Principles Work Group. (1997, November). *Learner-centered psychological principles: A framework for school reform and redesign.*

20. *Time Magazine: Science.* (2004, May 20). What makes teens tick? pp. 56–65.

21. Sylwester, Robert. (1995). *A celebration of neurons: An educator's guide to the human brain.* Alexandria, VA: Association for Supervision and Curriculum Development (ASCD), p. 77.

22. *Teenage brain: A work in progress. A brief overview of research into brain development during adolescence.* National Institute of Mental Health. (2001). http:www.nimh.nih.gov/publicat/teenbrain.cfm

23. The developmental profiles were summarized from many sources including:

    Elkind, David. (1999, Feb. 24). The social determination of childhood and adolescence. *Education Week.*

    Erickson, Erik. H. (1996). *Identity, youth and crisis.* New York, NY: W.W. Norton.

    Piaget, Jean. (1950). *The psychology of intelligence.* New York, NY: Harcourt Brace.

    Pipher, Mary. (1995). *Reviving Ophelia: Saving the lives of adolescent girls.* New York, NY: Ballantine Books.

    Thompson, Michael. (2004). *The pressured child: Helping your child find success in school and life.* New York, NY: Ballantine Books, pp. 62–66.

24. Michael Thompson, author of *The Pressured Child,* regards the two sets of necessary skills as "academic development." p. 6.

25. Erickson, Erik. (1963). *Childhood and society.* New York, NY: W.W. Norton, p. 306.

26. Botstein, Leon. (1997). *Jefferson's children: Education and the promise of American culture.* (1997). New York, NY: Doubleday, p. 85.

27. Naisbett, John. (1999). *High tech, high touch: Technology and our search for meaning.* New York, NY: Broadway Books.

28. Barnhart, Carol. News article in *The Enquirer.* We can't afford to waste resources of the gifted. Quoting, Marylou Kelly Streznuski. (2004). *Gifted Grownups.* Retrieval 2/18/08. http://news.enquirer.com/apps/pbcs.dll/article

29. Renzulli, J.S. What Makes Giftedness? Re-examining a definition. *Phi Delta Kappan,* 60, pp. 180–181.

30. Webb, J.T., et al. (2004). *Misdiagnosis and dual diagnosis of gifted children.* Supporting Emotional Needs of the Gifted (SENG). Retrieval 2/18/2008. www.sengifted.org

31. A nation deceived: How schools hold back America's brightest students. Nicolas Colangelo, et. al. *The Templeton national report on acceleration.* Retrieval 2/12/08. http://www.nationdeceived.org/index.html

32. *Competencies needed by teachers of gifted and talented students.* National Association for Gifted Children. Position Statements: Retrieval 2/18/08. www.nagc.org/index.aspx?id=574&an

33. Cohen, Jonathan. (Ed.). (1999). *Educating hearts and minds: Social and emotional learning and the passage into adolescence.* New York, NY: Teachers College Press, Columbia University, p. 3.

Johnathan Cohen, Ph.D., is Director of the Center for Social and Emotional Education and Adjunct Associate Professor in Psychology at Teachers College, Columbia University.

34. The Collaborative for Academic, Social and Emotional Learning (CASEL) is based at the University of Illinois, Chicago. It provides international leadership to advance the science, principles and practices of school–based social and emotional learning. A wealth of research, articles and materials are available at www.casel.org. Respected educator Dr. Maurice Elias, a founding member of CASEL, is a Professor of Psychology at Rutgers University and Director of the Rutgers Social-Emotional Learning Lab and the Developing Safe and Civil School (DSACS) Initiative. www.teach-SECD.com In addition to other publications, Dr. Elias has written a concise and valuable document on the implementation of SEL internationally. Elias, Maurice. (1999). Academic and social-emotional learning. *Educational Practices Series,* 11. UNESCO with the International Academy of Education and the International Bureau of Education. http://www.ibe.unesco.org.

35. Goleman, Daniel. (1995). *Emotional intelligence.* New York, NY: Bantam Books.

36. Cohen, Jonathan. (1999). p. 7.

CHAPTER 3: TIMES ARE A'CHANGING

1. The well–known statement by Margaret Mead is quoted in many publications. It was a privilege to hear her daughter Mary Catherine Bateson discuss the implications of it at the *In Praise of Education* conference, Bellevue, WA, June 18,1999.

2. Toffler, Alvin. (1980). *Third wave.* New York, NY: William Morrow Company.

3. Handel, Michael J. (2005). *Worker skills and job requirements: Is there a mismatch?* Washington, DC: Economic Policy Institute.

4. Colteryahn, Karen & Davis, Patty (2004, January). Eight trends you need to know now. *TD Magazine.* Alexandria, VA: American Society for Training and Development (ASTD), pp. 28–36.

   Davis, Patty, Naughton, Jennifer, & Rothwell, William. (2004, April). New roles and new competencies for the profession. *TD Magazine.* Alexandria, VA: American Society for Training and Development (ASTD), pp. 26–36.

   Rothwell, William & Wellins, Rich. (2004, May). Mapping your future: Putting new competencies to work for you. *TD Magazine,* Alexandria, VA: American Society for Training and Development (ASTD), pp. 94–101.

   Yeager, Neil & Hough, Lee. (1998). *Power interviews: Job–winning tactics from Fortune 500 recruiters.* New York, NY: John Wiley & Sons, Inc.

5. Cited by Harold Hodgekinson of the Institute for Educational Leadership, at the Northwest Regional Educational Laboratory Education for Work Conference, *Guess Who's Coming To Work.* Portland, Oregon, 1990.

6. James, Jennifer. (2005, April). *The human face of technological change.* Keynote at the ASCD Annual Conference, Orlando, FL.

7. Cohen, Stephen. (July 2004). Performance improvement through relationship building. *TD Magazine,* Alexandria, VA: American Society for Training and Development (ASTD), pp. 41–47.

8. Yeager, Neil & Hough, Lee. (1998).

9. Marshall, Ray & Tucker, Marc. (1992). *Thinking for a living: Education and the wealth of nations.* New York, NY: Basic Books.

10. Secretary's Commission on Achieving Necessary Skills. (1999). *SCANS Report for America 2000: What work requires of schools.* U.S. Department of Labor.

11. Huitt, W. (1999, October). *The SCANS report revisited.* Paper delivered at the Fifth Annual Gulf South Business and Vocational Education Conference, Valdosta State University, Valdosta, GA, April 18, 1997. Retrieved 10/20/05. http://chiron.valdosta.edu/whuitt/col/student/scanspap.html

12. SCANS. (1999).

13. Costa, Arthur L. & Kallick, Bena. (Eds). (2000). *Discovering and exploring habits of mind.* Alexandria, VA: Association for Supervision and Curriculum Development (ASCD), p. 7.

14. The brief summary on resiliency research and concepts contained in this chapter are based on Bonnie Benard's twenty years of outstanding work and her fine book, *Resiliency: What we have learned.* (2004). San Francisco, CA: WestEd. This reference may be found on page 43. We urge readers to secure copies of the book for their professional libraries and teacher study groups. The Appendix contains more than 500 suggestions for initiating caring and support, high expectations, and participation/contribution within schools, families and community, and is invaluable for program planning. The book is available from CenterSource Systems at www.tribes.com/catalog or 800–810–1701.

15. Benard. (2004). p. 7.

16. Werner, Emily & Smith, Ruth. (1989). *Vulnerable but invincible: A longitudinal study of resilient children and youth.* New York, NY: Adams, Bannister and Cox.

17. Benard. (2004). p. 107.

18. Bronfenbrenner, Urie. (1979). *The ecology of human development: Experiments by nature and design.* Cambridge, MA: Harvard University Press.

CHAPTER 4: ASSURING FUTURES OF PROMISE

1. Benard, Bonnie. (1991). *Fostering resiliency in kids: Protective factors in the family, school, and community.* Portland, OR: Northwest Regional Educational Laboratory.

2. Benard. (1991).

3. Resnick, M., Bearman, P., Blum, R., Bauman, K., Harris, K., Jones, J., Tabor, J., Beuring, T., Sieving, R., Shew, M., Ireland, M., Bearinger, L. & Udry, J. (1997). Protecting adolescents from harm: Findings from the national longitudinal study on adolescent health. *Journal of the American Medical Association,* 278, pp. 823–832.

4. Werner, E. & Smith, R. (1992). *Overcoming the odds: High–risk children from birth to adulthood.* New York, NY: Cornell University Press.

5. Noddings, N. (1988, December). Schools face crisis in caring. *Education Week,* p. 32.

6. Meier, D. (1995). *The power of their ideas: Lessons for America from a small school in Harlem.* Boston, MA: Beacon Press.

7. Hattie, J., Marsh, H., Neill, J., & Richards, G. (1997). Adventure education and outward bound: Out–of–class experiences that make a lasting difference. *Review of Educational Research,* 67, pp. 43–87.

8. Muller, W. (1996). *How, then, shall we live? Four simple questions that reveal the beauty and meaning of our lives.* New York, NY: Bantam Books.

9. Kessler, R. (2000). *The soul of education: Helping students find connection, compassion, and character at school.* Alexandria, VA: Association for Supervision and Curriculum Development (ASCD).

10. Catterall, J. (1997). Involvement in the arts and success in secondary school. *Americans for the Arts Monographs, 1*(9).

11. Melchior, A. (1996–1998). *National evaluation of Learn and Serve America: Interim and final evaluation.* National Corporation for Community Service.

12. Sergiovanni, T. (1994). *Building community in schools.* San Francisco, CA: Jossey–Bass.

CHAPTER 5: WEAVING ESSENTIAL PRINCIPLES TO RECREATE THE SYSTEM

1. Ted Sizer, author of the Foreword to *Breaking ranks II: Strategies for leading high school reform.* (2004). NASSP. He is Chairman Emeritus of the Coalition of Better Schools and Professor Emeritus of Brown University. The quote is from p. xi.

2. *Breaking Ranks: Changing an American Institution.* (1996). National Association of Secondary School Principals (NASSP) with support from the Carnegie Foundation for the Advancement of Teaching, p. 4.

3. According to a recent report by Harvard University's Civil Rights Project, the Urban Institute, Advocates for Children of New York, and the Civil Society Institute.

4. Statement by Tom Vander Ark, Executive Directory of the Melissa and Bill Gates Foundation multimillion dollar education initiative.

5. Mathews, Jay. (2005, May 16). How to build a better high school. *Newsweek Magazine,* p. 54.

6. *Breaking ranks II: Strategies for leading high school reform.* (2004). NASSP, pp. xvi, 5.

7. *Newsweek Magazine.* (2005, May 16). p. 54.

8. Schmoker, Michael. (April 2004). *From feckless reform to substantive instructional improvement.* Bloomington, IN: Phi Beta Kappan International.

   Barth, Roland. (1990). *Improving schools from within: Teachers, parents and principals make the difference.* Jossey–Bass. And *Learning by heart.* (2001).

9. The history of the Tribes Learning Community process, listing of countries, types of schools, courses, evaluations etcetera is contained in the Appendix of this book.

10. Comer, James. (1999). *Child by child: The Comer process for change in education.* New York, NY: Teachers College Press, Columbia University.

11. Comer, James. (1997, March). Maintaining a focus on child development. *Phi Delta Kappan.*

    Sizer, Ted. (1984, 1997). *Horace's challenge: The dilemma of the American high school.* New York, NY: Houghton Mifflin.

    Meier, D. (1995). *The power of their ideas: Lessons for America from a small school in Harlem.* Boston, MA: Beacon Press.

    Dewey, John. (1956). *The child and the curriculum and the child and society.* Chicago, IL: University of Chicago Press.

12. Johnson, David, Johnson, Roger & Smith, Karl. (1995). Cooperative learning and individual student achievement. In: *Secondary schools and cooperative learning: Theories, models and strategies.* New York, NY: Garland Publishing.

    Fosnot, Catherine. (1996). Constructivism: A psychological theory of learning. In: *Constructivism: Theory, perspectives and practice.* New York, NY: Teachers College Press, Columbia University.

    Elias, M.J., Wang, M.C., Weissberg, R.P., Zins, J.E. & Walberg, H.J. (2002). The other side of the report card: Student success depends on more than test scores. *American School Board Journal,* 189(11), pp. 28–30.

    Gay, Geneva. (2000). *Culturally responsive teaching: Theory, research and practice.* New York, NY: Teachers College Press, Columbia University.

13. Fullan, Michael. (2001). *Leading in a culture of change.* San Francisco, CA: Jossey–Bass.

14. Werner, Emily & Smith, Ruth. (1989). *Vulnerable but invincible: A longitudinal study of resilient children and youth.* New York, NY: Adams, Bannister and Cox.

    Bruner, Jerome. (1996). *The culture of education.* Cambridge, MA: Harvard University Press.

    Meier, D. (1995).

    Fullan, Michael. (1994). *Turning systemic thinking on its head.* U.S. Department of Education.

    Gay, Geneva. (2000).

15. Benard, Bonnie. (1991). *Fostering resiliency in kids: Protective factors in families, schools and community.* Portland, OR: Western Regional Center for Drug Free Schools and Communities, Northwest Regional Educational Laboratory.

16. Bruner, Jerome. (1996).

    Fosnot, Catherine. (1996). Constructivism: A psychological theory of learning. In: *Constructivism: Theory, perspectives and practice.* New York, NY: Teachers College Press, Columbia University.

17. Darling–Hammond, Linda. (1993, March). Reforming the school reform agenda. *Phi Delta Kappan,* pp. 74–76.

18. Fosnot, Catherine. (1996).

19. Johnson, David & Johnson, Roger. (1989). *Cooperation and competition: Theory and research.* Edina, MN: Interaction Book Company.

20. Caine, Geoffrey & Caine, Renate. (1991). *Making connections: Teaching and the human brain.* Alexandria, VA: Association for Supervision and Curriculum Development (ASCD).

    Johnson, David, Johnson, Roger & Smith, Karl. (1995).

    Jensen, Eric. (1988). *Teaching with the brain in mind.* Alexandria, VA: Association for Supervision and Curriculum Development (ASCD).

    Gardner, Howard. (1999). *Intelligence reframed: Multiple intelligences for the 21st century.* New York, NY: Basic Books.

21. *Breaking ranks II.* (2004). National Association of Secondary School Principals (NASSP), p. 5.

22. Fullan, Michael. (2007). *The NEW meaning of educational change* (Fourth edition). New York, NY: Teachers College Press, Columbia University.

23. Barth, Roland S. (2001). *Learning by heart.* San Francisco, CA: Jossey–Bass, p. 39.

24. Elias, M.J., Wang, M.C., Weissberg, R.P., Zins, J.E. & Walberg, H.J. (2002). The other side of the report card: Student success depends on more than test scores. *American School Board Journal,* 189(11), pp. 28–30.

    Readers can find a wealth of research information on the connection and impact of social and emotional learning to academic achievement at the Collaborative for Academic, Social and Emotional Learning (CASEL) website. www.casel.org

25. Noddings, Nel. (1995, January). A morally defensible mission for schools of the 21st century. *Phi Delta Kappan,* p. 366.

CHAPTER 6: CREATING THE PERSONALIZED CARING CULTURE

1. Goodlad, John. (1997). *In praise of education.* New York, NY: Teachers College Press, Columbia University, p. 103.

2. Sizer, Ted. (2004). Foreword, *Breaking ranks II.* NASSP, p. xi.

3. *Breaking ranks II.* (2004). p. 5.

4. *Breaking ranks II.* (2004). p. xvii.

5. Barth, Roland S. (2001). *Learning by heart.* San Francisco, CA: Jossey–Bass, p. 7.

6. Harrison, R. & Stokes, H. (1992). *Diagnosing organizational culture.* San Diego, CA: Pfeiffer & Company.

7. Bruner, J.S. (1996). *The culture of education.* Cambridge, MA: Harvard University Press, p. 98.

8. Barth, Roland. (2001). p. 8.

9. Barth (2001). p. 9.

10. Barth (2001). p. 9.

11. Bruner, J.S. (1996). p. 99.

12. Benard, Bonnie. (2004). *Resiliency: What we have learned.* San Francisco, CA: West Ed, p. 70.

13. Benard. (2004). p. 46.

14. Benard. (2004). pp. 71–73.

15. Benard. (2004). p. 45.

16. Benard. (2004). p. 73.

17. Benard. (2004). p. 77.

18. Benard. (2004). pp. 81–85.

19. Wheelock, Anne. (1998). *Safe to be smart: Building a culture for standards–based reform in the middle grades.* Columbus, OH: National Middle School Association.

20. Pipher, Mary. (1995). *Reviving Ophelia: Saving the lives of adolescent girls.* New York, NY: Ballantine Books, p. 44.

21. Cohen, Judy, et. al. (1996). *Girls in the middle: Working to succeed in school.* Washington, DC: American Association of University Women Educational Foundation, pp. 14–15.

22. Pipher. (1995). p. 290.

23. The quote is from James Hillman's book, *The soul's code,* cited by Ron Taffel in *Nurturing good children now.* (1999). New York, NY: Golden Books, p. 1.

24. Kagan, Spencer. (1994). *Cooperative learning.* San Clemente, CA: Kagan Publishing, pp. 2, 7.

25. Gay, Geneva. (2000). *Culturally responsive teaching: Theory, research and practice.* New York, NY: Teachers College Press, Columbia University.

26. Brandt, Ron. (Ed.). (2000). *Education in a new era.* Alexandria, VA: Association for Supervision and Curriculum Development (ASCD), p. 34.

27. Gay. (2000). p. 29.

28. Christensen, Linda. (2000). *Reading, writing and rising up: Teaching about social justice and the power of the written word.* Milwaukee, WI: Rethinking Schools, p. 103.

29. Sarason, Seymour. (1972). *The culture of settings and the future societies.* San Francisco, CA: Jossey–Bass.

30. Goodlad, John. (1997). *In praise of education.* New York, NY: Teachers College Press, Columbia University, p. 24.

CHAPTER 7: ESTABLISHING COMMUNITY FOR ALL

1. Meier, Deborah. (1992–1993). Reinventing teaching. *Teachers College Record,* 4, pp. 594–609.

2. Senge, Peter, et. al. (2002). *Schools that learn.* New York, NY: Doubleday.

3. *Breaking ranks II: Strategies for leading high school reform.* (2004). NASSP, p. 5.

4. Sergiovanni, Thomas. (1996). *Leadership for the schoolhouse.* San Francisco, CA: Jossey–Bass, p. 97.

5. Johnson, David W. & Johnson, Roger T. (1989). *Cooperation and competition: Theory and research.* Edina, MN: Interaction Book Company, pp. 169–179.

   Pedersen, J. & Digby, A. (Eds.). (1995). Cooperative learning and nonacademic outcomes of schooling, In: *Secondary schools and cooperative learning: Theories, models and strategies.* New York, NY: Garland Publishing, pp. 81–150.

6. Kohn, Alfie. (1996). *Beyond discipline: From compliance to community.* Alexandria, VA: Association for Supervision and Curriculum Development (ASCD), p. 101.

7. Sergiovanni, Thomas. (1994). *Building community in schools.* San Francisco, CA: Jossey–Bass, p. 4.

8. Lickona, Thomas. (1991). *Education for character: How our schools can teach respect and responsibility.* New York, NY: Bantam Books, p. 95.

9. Sergoivanni, Thomas. (1994).

10. Sergiovanni, Thomas. (1999). The story of community. In: J. Retallick, B. Cocklin & K. Coombe. (Eds.). *Learning communities in action: Issues, strategies and contexts.* New York, NY: Routledge, pp. 16–17.

11. Benard, Bonnie. (2005). *What is it about Tribes? The research–based components of Tribes Learning Communities.* Research Contract: West Ed, Oakland, CA. Publisher: CenterSource Systems, p. 85.

12. Caine, Geoffrey & Renate. (1991). *Making connections: Teaching and the human brain.* Alexandria, VA: Association for Supervision and Curriculum Development (ASCD).

13. Johnson, David W. & Johnson, Roger T. (1989).

14. Wheelock, Anne. (1998). *Safe to be smart: Building a culture for standards–based reform in the middle grades.* Columbus, OH: National Middle School Association.

15. Jensen, Eric. (1998). *Teaching with the brain in mind.* Alexandria, VA: Association for Supervision and Curriculum Development (ASCD).

16. See comments of Laura Horton, Fort–Francis River Board of Education, Ontario, and Anne Wilson, Ojibwe First Nation elder of Manitou Rapids, Ontario. In: Gibbs, J. (2006). *Reaching all by creating Tribes Learning Communities.* Windsor, CA: CenterSource Systems, pp. 66, 81.

17. Gibbs, J. (2006). p. 72.

18. Sarason, Seymour. (1990). *The predictable failure of school reform.* San Francisco: Jossey–Bass.

19. Kohn, Alfie. (1996). pp. 76–77.

20. Early group learning research (and common sense) led to the practice in Tribes of using long–term membership groups rather than rotating people in and out of random task groups. Since then many other cooperative learning research studies and practioneers advocate the practice. The early research first justifying the practice was done by:

Lott, Albert & Lott, Bernice. (1966, April). Group cohesiveness and individual learning. *Journal of Educational Psychology,* 57, pp. 61–72.

Fox, Robert, Luszki, Margaret & Schmuck, Richard. (1966). *Social relations in the classroom: Diagnosing learning environments.* Chicago, IL: SRA, Inc.

21. McKnight, John. (1992, July–August). Are social service agencies the enemy of the people? *Utne Reader,* pp. 89–90.

22. Starhawk. (1997). *Dreaming the dark.* New York, NY: Beacon Press, p. 92.

CHAPTER 8: STRUCTURING AND PERSONALIZING THE COMMUNITY OF LEARNERS

1. Barth, Roland, S. (1990). *Improving schools from within.* San Francisco, CA: Jossey–Bass, p. 43.

2. *Breaking ranks II: Strategies for leading high school reform.* (2004). Reston, VA: National Association of Secondary School Principals (NASSP), p. 17.

3. Clarke, J. (2003). *Changing systems to personalize learning: Introduction to the personalization workshops.* Providence, RI: Education Alliance at Brown University.

4. Clarke, J. & Frazer, E. (2003). Making learning personal: Educational practices that work. In: DiMartino, J., Clarke, J. & Wold, D. (Eds.). *Personalized learning: Preparing high school students to create their futures.* Lanham, MD: Rowman and Littlefield. and in: *Breaking ranks II.* (2004), p. 71. Reprinted with permission.

5. *Breaking ranks II.* (2004). p. 67.

6. Boyer, E. (1995). *The basic school: A community of learners.* Princeton, NJ: Carnegie Foundation for the Advancement of Teaching, pp. 17–18.

7. Schmoker, Michael. (2004, February). Tipping point: From feckless reform to substantive instructional improvement. *Phi Beta Kappan,* 85(6).

8. Lezotte, L. W. (2002). *Assembly required: A continuous school improvement system.* Okemons, MI: Effective Schools Products, Ltd.

9. Elmore, Richard F. (2005). *School reform from the inside out: Policy, practice and performance.* Cambridge, MA: Harvard Education Press, p. 3.

10. McLaughlin, Milbrey W. & Talbert, Joan E. (2006). *Building school-based teacher learning communities: Professional strategies to improve student achievement.* New York, NY: Teachers College Press, p. 56.

11. *Breaking ranks II.* (2004). p. 32.

12. The Effective Schools movement began in 1966 with the publication of the Coleman Report and led to research on "why some schools make a difference" and defining seven Correlates of Effective Schools. The latter led to The Core Beliefs of the Effective Schools Process as cited in DuFour, R., Eaker, R., and DuFour, Rebecca. (2005). *On common ground: The power of professional learning communities.* Bloomington, IN: Solution Tree, pp. 184–185.

13. Bybee, Roger. (1997). *Constructivism and the 5 E's: The biological science curriculum study.* Miami, FL: Museum of Science.

14. Hertz–Lazarowitz, Rachel & Shachar, H. (1990). Changes in teachers' verbal behavior in cooperative classrooms. *Cooperative Learning,* 11(2), pp. 13–14.

15. Reich, Robert. (1991). *The work of nations.* New York, NY: Alfred A. Knopf.

16. *Breaking ranks II.* (2004). pp. 10–12.

17. *Breaking ranks II.* (2004). p. 10.

18. Benard, B. (2004). *Resiliency: What we have learned.* San Francisco, CA: WestEd, pp. 44–48.

19. Anderson, V. (1997, February). High schools told: Get goin' on freshmen. *Catalyst.* Received on 11/27/05 from http://www.catalyst–chicago.org/arch/02–97/027main.htm

20. In the province of Ontario, the Ministry of Education's Double Cohort Study of 2002 concluded that 25% of students drop out prior to completing their diploma requirements.

   More specifically, the Toronto District School Board concluded in its Grade 9 Cohort Study of 2000–2004 that 38% of their students who dropped out completed only five of their eight courses of study in their first year of high school. Conversely, 33% and an additional 21% of students who dropped out completed 6 or 7 courses respectively.

21. Zins, J., Weissberg, R., Wang, M. & Walberg, H. (Eds.). (2004). *Building academic success on social and emotional learning: What does the research say?* New York, NY: Teachers College Press, Columbia University, p. 3.

22. The respected coach is Arnold Martinez of Moanalua High School, Honolulu, Hawaii.

23. Benard, B. (2005). *What is it about Tribes? The research–based components of the developmental process of Tribes Learning Communities.* Windsor, CA: CenterSource Systems, p. 181.

24. Benard, B. (2005). p. 181

25. Elden Seta, Music Director for 17 years at the Moanalua High School, Honolulu, Hawaii, and recipient of a national Milken Award in 2004.

26. Benard, B. (2005). pp. 182–187.

27. Nakkula, M. (2004). Identity and possibility: Adolescent development and the potential of schools. In: *Adolescents at school: Perspectives on youth identity and education.* Michael Sadowski (Ed.). Cambridge, MA: Harvard Education Press, p. 13.

CHAPTER 9: LEARNING IN COLLEGIAL LEARNING COMMUNITIES

1. Little, Judith Warren. (1981). *School success and staff development in urban desegregated schools. A summary of recently completed research.* Boulder, CO: Center for Action Research.

2. Csikszentmihaly, Mihaly. (2000, April 19). Education for the 21st century. *Education Week.*

3. Kohn, Alfie. (1996). *Beyond discipline: From compliance to community.* Alexandria, VA: Association for Supervision and Curriculum Development (ASCD).

4. The statement by Margaret Mead was shared by her daughter, Mary Catherine Bateson, at the conference, *In Praise of Education,* Bellevue Washington, June 18, 1999.

5. McLaughlin, Milbrey W. & Talbert, Joan E. (2006). *Building school-based teacher learning communities.* New York, NY: Teachers College Press, pp. 1–2. Milbrey McLaughlin is the David Jacks Professor of Education and Public Policy at Stanford University, Co–director of the Center for Research on the Context of Teaching, and Executive Director of the John W. Gardner Center for Youth and Their Communities. Joan Talbert is Senior Research Scholar and Co–Director of the Center for Research on the Context of Teaching, Stanford University School of Education.

6. McNulty, Ray. (2004). New era ushers in deeper understanding of learning. *Education Updates,* 46(2), ASCD.

7. Elmore, Richard F. (2005). *School reform from the inside out: Policy, practice and performance.* Cambridge, MA: Harvard University Press, p. 14.

8. Elmore, Richard F. (2005). p. 15.

9. *Breaking ranks II.* (2004). p. xvi.

10. *Breaking ranks: Changing an American institution.* (1996). National Association of Secondary School Principals, p. 6.

11. Schmoker, Michael. (2006). *Results now: How we can achieve unprecedented improvements in teaching and learning.* Alexandria, VA: Association for Supervision and Curriculum Development (ASCD), pp. 45–46.

12. Newmann, F. & Wehlage, G. (1995). *Successful school restructuring: A report to the public and educators.* Madison, WI: Center on Organization and Restructuring School, pp. 30, 32.

13. American Institutes of Research. (1999). *An educator's guide to school-wide reform.* Arlington, VA: Educational Research Service.

14. Lee, Valerie & Smith, J. (1995). Effects of high school restructuring and size on gains in achievement and engagement for early secondary school students. *American Journal of Education, 70,* pp. 128–150.

15. Rutter, M., Maughan, B., Mortimore, P., Ouston, J. & Smith, A. (1979). *Fifteen thousand hours: Secondary schools and their effects on children.* Cambridge, MA: Harvard University Press.

16. Fullan, Michael. (1999). *Change forces: The sequel.* Philadelphia, PA: The Falmer Press, p. 31.

17. Rowan, B. (1990). Commitment and control: Alternative strategies for the organizational design of schools. *Review of Educational Research, 6,* pp. 353–389.

18. Lieberman, Ann. (1995). *The work of restructuring schools: Building from the ground up.* New York, NY: Teachers College Press, Columbia University, p. 593.

19. Newmann, F. & Wehlage, G. (1995). pp. 30–32.

20. Elmore, Richard F. (2005). p. 207.

21. Elmore, Richard F. (2005). p. 123.

22. McLaughlin, Milbrey W. & Talbert, Joan E. (2006). pp. 1–2.

23. Cochran-Smith, M. & Lytle, S. (1999). Relationships of knowledge and practice: Teacher learning in communities. *Review of Research in Education, 24(2),* pp. 249–305.

24. Barth, Roland S. (1990). *Improving schools from within.* San Francisco, CA: Jossey-Bass, p. 15.

25. Barth, Roland S. (1990). p. 16.

26. Johnson, David, Johnson, Roger, & Smith, Karl. (1995). Cooperative learning and individual student achievement. In J. Pedersen & A. Digby. (Eds.). *Secondary schools and cooperative learning: Theories, models and strategies.* New York, NY: Garland Publishing, p. 69.

27. McLaughlin, Milbrey W. & Talbert, Joan E. (2006). p. 7.

28. Little, Judith Warren. (1993). Teachers' professional development in a climate of education reform. *Educational Evaluation and Policy Analysis, 15(2),* pp. 129–152.

29. Moanalua High School Professional Development Program. Honolulu, Hawaii. www.mohs.k12.hi.us

30. Delpit, Lisa. (1996). *City kids, city teachers: Reports from the front row. The politics of reaching literate discourse.* Ayres, W. & Ford, P. (Eds.). New York, NY: The New Press, p. 208.

CHAPTER 10: LEARNING HOW 21ST CENTURY YOUTH LEARN

1. Barth, Roland. (2005). *Learning by heart.* San Francisco, CA: Jossey-Bass, p. 16.

2. Barth, Roland. (2005). p. 18.

3. Stern, D. & Huber, G.L. (1997). *Active learning for students and teachers: Reports from eight countries.* Frankfurt am Main, Germany: Peter Lang, p. 13.

4. Stern, D. & Huber, G.L. (1997). p. 13.

5. Benard, B. (2005). *What is it about Tribes? The research-based components of the developmental process of Tribes Learning Communities.* Windsor, CA: CenterSource Systems, p. 151.

6. National Research Council/National Academy of Sciences Reports. (2003). *How people learn* and *Engaging schools: Fostering high school students' motivation to learn.* Washington, DC: The National Academies.

7. Halperin, S. & Partee, G. (1997). *Some things do make a difference for youth: A compendium of evaluations of youth programs and practices.* Washington, DC: American Youth Policy Forum.

8. Tanner, B., Bottoms, G., Feagin, C. & Bearman, A. (2001). *Instructional strategies: How teachers teach matters.* Atlanta, GA: Southern Region Educational Board.

9. Valliant, G.E. (1977). *Adaptation to life.* Boston, MA: Little, Brown and Company.

10. Cohen, Jonathan. (Ed.). (1999). *Educating hearts and minds: Social and emotional learning and the passage into adolescence.* New York, NY: Teachers College Press, Columbia University, p. 3.

11. Naisbett, John. (1999). *High tech, high touch: Technology and our search for meaning.* New York, NY: Broadway Books.

12. Goleman, Daniel. (1995). *Emotional intelligence.* New York, NY: Bantam Books.

13. Cohen. (1999). p. 7.

14. Benard, Bonnie. (2004). *Resiliency: What we have learned.* San Francisco, CA: West Ed, p. 44.

15. *Breaking ranks II: Strategies for leading high school reform.* (2004). NASSP, p. 17.

16. Wolfe, Patricia. (2001). *Brain matters: Translating research into classroom practice.* Alexandria, VA: ASCD, p. 3.

17. Wolfe, Patricia. (2001). p. 1.

18. Pert, Candace. (1997). *Molecules of emotion: The science behind mind-body medicine.* New York, NY: Simon and Schuster.

   Jensen, Eric. (1998). *Teaching with the brain in mind.* Alexandria, VA: Association for Supervision and Curriculum Development (ASCD).

   Caine, Goeffrey & Caine, Renata. (1991). *Making connections: Teaching and the human brain.* Alexandria, VA: Association for Supervision and Curriculum Development (ASCD).

19. The nine principles for student-centered active learning are based on:

   McCombs, Barbara L. *Twelve learner-centered psychological principles.* Midwest Center Educational Laboratory. www.mcrel.org

   Learner-centered principles: A framework for school redesign and reform. American Psychological Association.

   Duffy, Thomas & Jonassen, David. (Eds.). (1992). *Constructivism and the technology of instruction.* Hillsdale, NJ: Lawrence Erlbaum Associates.

20. Stigler, James & Hiebert, James. (1997). *The teaching gap.* Study funded by the U.S. Department of Education. Los Angeles, CA: Free Press.

21. Anderson, Keisha-Gaye. (2000, Jan–Feb). U.S. fails math. *Psychology Today.*

22. Gardner, Howard. (1993). *Frames of mind: Theory of multiple intelligences.* New York, NY: Basic Books.

23. Stoddard, Lynn. (1992). *Redesigning education: A guide for developing human greatness.* Tucson, AZ: Zephyr Press.

24. Botstein, Leon. (1997). *Jefferson's children: Education and the promise of American culture.* New York, NY: Doubleday, p. 111.

25. Lazear, David. (1989). *Seven ways of teaching: The artistry of teaching with multiple intelligences.* Palatine, IL: Skylight Publishing, p. 9.

26. Johnson, David W., Johnson, Roger T. & Smith, Karl. (1995). Cooperative learning and individual student achievement In: *Secondary schools and cooperative learning: Theories, models and strategies.* (Eds.) Pedersen, Jon & Digby, Annette. New York, NY: Garland Publishing.

27. Johnson, David W., Johnson, Roger T. & Smith, Karl. (1995). p. 4.

28. Johnson, David W., Johnson, Roger T. & Holubec, Edythe Johnson. (1994). *New circles of learning: Cooperation in the classroom and school.* Alexandria, VA: ASCD, p. 15.

29. Johnson, et. al. (1994). p. 16.

30. Johnson, et. al. (1994). p. 23.

31. Johnson, et. al. (1994). p. 24.

32. Johnson, et. al. (1994). p. 2.

33. Johnson, David & Johnson, Robert. (1995). Non-academic outcomes in schooling. In: *Secondary schools and cooperative learning: Theories, models and strategies.* (Eds.) Pedersen, Jon & Digby, Annette. New York, NY: Garland Publishing.

34. The chart is a synthesis from two documents:

    Brooks, M. and Brooks, J. (1999). *The case for constructivist classrooms.* Alexandria, VA: Association for Supervision and Curriculum Development (ASCD), p. 7.

    Gibbs, Jeanne. (2006). *Reaching all by creating Tribes Learning Communities.* Windsor, CA: CenterSource Systems, p. 7.

35. Fosnot, Catherine Twomey. (1996). *Constructivism: Theory, perspectives and practice.* New York, NY: Teachers College Press, Columbia University.

CHAPTER 11: LEARNING THROUGH DISCOVERY AND TECHNOLOGY

1. Adler, Mortimer. (1982). *The padideia proposal: An educational manifesto.* New York, NY: Macmillan, p. 50.

2. Marlowe, Bruce & Page, Marilyn. (1998). *Creating and sustaining the constructivist classroom.* Thousand Oaks, CA: Corwin Press, p. 27.

3. Darling-Hammond, Linda. (1997). *The right to learn: A blueprint for creating schools that work.* San Francisco, CA: Jossey-Bass, p. 96.

4. Fosnot, Catherine Twomey. (1996). Constructivism: A psychological theory of learning. In: Catherine Fosnot (Ed.). *Constructivism: Theory, perspectives and practice.* New York, NY: Teachers College Press, Columbia University.

5. Oseas, Andrea & Wood, Julie M. (2003). Multiple literacies: New skills for a new millennium. In: David T. Gordon. (Ed.). *Better teaching and learning in the digital classroom.* Cambridge, MA: Harvard Education Press, pp. 15–16.

6. Oseas, Andrea & Wood, Julie M. (2003). p. 17.

7. A dozen leading progressive scholars, including those named, have recently organized the Forum for Education and Democracy (www.forumforeducation.org). The initial mission is to make significant changes in the U.S. Elementary and Secondary Education Act, also known as the No Child Left Behind Act, and are initiating a national call to action to "truly leave no child behind."

8. Merrill, David. (1992). Constructivism and instructional design. In: Duffy, T. & Jonassen. D. (Eds.). *Constructivism and the technology of instruction.* Hillsdale, NJ: Erlbaum Associates, pp. 102–103.

9. Windschitl, Mark. (1999, June). The challenges of sustaining a constructivist classroom culture. *Phi Delta Kappan,* p. 754.

10. Oseas, Andrea & Wood, Julie M. (2003). p. 15.

11. Yager, S., Johnson, D. & Johnson, R. (1985). Oral discussion, group-to-individual transfer, and achievement in cooperative learning groups. *Journal of Educational Psychology, 77,* pp. 60–66.

12. Yager, S., Johnson, D., Johnson, R. & Snyder, Bill. (1986). The impact of group processing and achievement in cooperative learning groups. *The Journal of Social Psychology, 126,* pp. 389–397.

13. Gardner, Howard. (2000). *The disciplined mind: Beyond facts and standardized tests: The K–12 education that every child deserves.* New York, NY: Penguin Putnam, pp. 19–20.

14. Anderson, Lorin W. & Drathwohl, David R., et. al. (2000). *A taxonomy for learning, teaching, and assessing: A revision of Bloom's taxonomy of educational objectives.* New York, NY: Longman, pp. 67–68.

15. Barth, Roland. (1990). *Improving schools from within.* San Francisco, CA: Jossey-Bass.

16. Schoen, Donald. (1987). *Education for the reflective practitioner.* (Revised Edition). San Francisco, CA: Jossey-Bass.

17. Gardner, Howard. (2000). p. 80.

18. Madaus, G., West, Mary M., Harmon, M., Lomax, R. & Viator, K. (1992). *The influence of testing on teaching math and science in grades 4–12: Executive summary.* Boston, MA: Center for the Study of Testing, Evaluation and Educational Policy, p. 2.

19. Leonard Atkins is the Boston president of the National Association for the Advancement of Colored People. He made the statement after 80% of Black and 85% of Latino 10th graders failed the Massachusetts Comprehensive Assessment System (MCAS) math test in May 2000 compared to 45% of White students. Cited in *Failing our kids: Why the testing craze won't fix our schools.* Milwaukee, WI: Rethinking Schools, Ltd, p. 126.

20. New compact to adopt the whole child. (2007, March). *Education Update.* Association of Supervision and Curriculum Development (ASCD), 49(3).

21. Paris, Scott & Ayres, Linda. (1999). *Becoming reflective students and teachers with portfolios and authentic assessment.* Washington, DC: American Psychological Association, pp. 7–8.

22. Paris, S. & Ayres, L. (1999). p. 28.

23. Paris, S. & Ayres, L. (1999). p. 54.

24. Stiggins, R., Arter, J., Chappuis, J. & Chappuis, S. (2004). *Classroom assessment for student learning.* Portland, OR: Assessment Training Institute, Inc.

25. Davies, A. (2007). *Making classroom assessment work.* (2nd Edition). Merville, BC, Canada: Connections Publishing.

26. Davies, A. & Busick, K. (2007) *What's working in high schools?* Merville, BC, Canada: Connections Publishing.

27. O'Connor, K. (2002). *How to grade for learning: Linking grades to standards.* Glenview, IL: LessonLab.

28. Paris, S. & Ayres, L. (1999). p. 58.

29. Prensky, Marc. (Dec 2005/Jan 2006). Listen to the natives. *Education Leadership,* p. 9.

30. Gordon, David. (2003). *Better teaching and learning in the digital classroom.* Cambridge, MA: Harvard Education Press, pp. 4–5.

31. David Thornburg is recognized as one of the top ten most influential people in educational technology and learning in the past two decades. In addition to his work at the state and local level, he is also involved at the Federal level in helping to shape telecommunications and education policy for the benefit of all learners. In his capacity as Senior Fellow of the Congressional Institute for the Future, David shares his perspectives with policy makers throughout the country.

32. *Breaking ranks II.* (2004). p. 183.

33. Wiske, Stone. (2003). A new culture for teaching in the 21st century. In: David T. Gordon. (Ed.). *The digital classroom: How technology is changing the way we learn.* Cambridge, MA: Harvard University Press, p. 73.

34. Ross, Heather & Daniel, Ben. (2005). *Technology and community enhanced learning: Tribes in the classroom.* Paper presented at the Proceedings of the 3rd Annual International Conference on Education, Honolulu, Hawaii, pp. 3720–3726. The researchers at the Education and Communication Technology, Department of Curriculum Studies, University of Saskatchewan, Saskatoon, Canada are conducting an on-going empirical research study to understand how trained Tribes TLC teachers work to integrate technologies into their classrooms.

35. Gardner, Howard. (2003). Can technology exploit our many ways of knowing? In: David T. Gordon. (Ed.). *The digital classroom: How technology is changing the way we learn.* Cambridge, MA: Harvard University Press, p. 33.

36. Ian Jukes is the Director of the InfoSavvy Group, an international consulting group that provides leadership and program development in the areas of assessment and evaluation, strategic alignment, curriculum design and publication, professional development, hardware and software acquisition as well as conference keynotes and workshop presentations.

37. Moersch, Christopher. (2002). *Beyond hardware: Using existing technology to promote higher-level thinking.* Eugene, OR: International Society for Technology in Education, pp. 47–49.

38. *New teachers and technology in education.* (1999). Market Data Retrieval. www.schooldata.com

39. Statement by David Blake of the National Education Association (NEA) as quoted in Gordon, David T. (2003). *The digital classroom.* p. 86.

40. Making connections: The MeneMac online learning community. (2005). *Educational Perspectives, 38,* p. 2.

41. Riel, Margaret. (1999). *Technology in shared minds made visible.* Keynote address to the National Educational Computer Conference.

42. Toch, Thomas. (2003). *High schools on a human scale: How small schools can transform American education.* Boston, MA: Beacon, pp. 73–74.

43. Rennebohm Franz, K. & Gragert, E. In: Gordon, David T. (Ed.). (2003). *Better teaching and learning in the digital classroom.* Cambridge, MA: Harvard University Press. pp. 149–159.

44. Gordon, David. (2003). *Better teaching and learning in the digital classroom.* Cambridge, MA: Harvard University Press, pp. 149–159.

45. Sophie from Ireland. Retrieved 5/16/06 from http://www.kidink.org/English/voice/index.html

CHAPTER 12: INITIATING THE ACTIVE LEARNING PROCESS

1. Campbell, Joseph. (1970). *The masks of God: Creative mythology.* New York, NY: Viking Press, p. 52.

2. Burke, Pat Guild. (1997). Do the learning theories overlap? *Educational Leadership.* ASCD.

3. Valliant, G.E. (1977). *Adaptation to life.* Boston, MA: Little, Brown and Company.

4. Bybee, Roger. (1997). *Constructivism and the 5 E's: The biological science curriculum study.* Miami, Fl: Museum of Science.

5. Yager, S., Johnson, D., Johnson, R. & Snyder, B. (1986). The impact of group processing and achievement in cooperative learning groups. *The Journal of Social Psychology, 26,* pp. 389–397.

6. *SCANS report for America 2000: What work requires of schools.* (1999). Secretary's Commission on Achieving Necessary Skills, U.S. Department of Labor.

7. The statement by Julia Lewis is from Robert Coles' 1998 article, In school. *Boston Globe Magazine,* p. 15.

CHAPTER 13: BUILDING SMALL LEARNING GROUPS

1. Benard, B. (2005). *What is it about Tribes? The research-based components of the developmental process of Tribes Learning Communities.* Windsor, CA: CenterSource Systems, p. 56.

2. Costa, A. & Kallick, B. (2000). *Discovering and exploring habits of mind.* Alexandria, VA: ASCD.

3. Kohn, Alfie. (1996). *Beyond discipline: From compliance to community.* Alexandria, VA: Association for Supervision and Curriculum Development (ASCD), pp. 76–77.

4. Frankl, Viktor. (2000). *Man's ultimate search for meaning.* New York, NY: Perseus Book Group.

CHAPTER 14: DESIGNING COOPERATIVE LEARNING EXPERIENCES

1. Benard, B. (2005). *What is it about Tribes? The research-based components of the developmental process of Tribes Learning Communities.* Windsor, CA: CenterSource Systems, p. 199.

2. Wallis, Claudia & Steptoe, Sonia. (2006, December 18). How to build a student for the 21st century. *Time Magazine,* 168(25), pp. 50–56.

3. Johnson, David W. & Johnson, Roger, T. (1989). *Cooperation and competition: Theory and research.* Edina, MN: Interaction Book Company.

4. Johnson. (1989).

5. Brady, Marion. (1989). *What's worth teaching? Selecting, organizing and integrating knowledge.* New York, NY: New York State University Press.

6. Littky, Dennis. (2004). *The BIG picture: Education is everyone's business.* Alexandria, VA: Association for Supervision and Curriculum Development (ASCD), p. 47.

7. Johnson, David W. & Johnson, Roger, T. (1989). *Cooperation and competition: Theory and research.* Edina, MN: Interaction Book Company, p. 25.

8. *SCANS report for America 2000: What work requires of schools.* Secretary's Commission on Achieving Necessary Skills. Washington, DC: U.S. Department of Labor, 1991–1998.

9. Kagan, Spencer. (1999). *Cooperative learning.* San Clemente, CA: Kagan Publishing.

10. Sarason, Seymour. (1990). *The predictable failure of school reform.* San Francisco, CA: Jossey–Bass.

11. Gardner, Howard. (1999). *Intelligence reframed: Multiple intelligences for the 21st Century.* New York, NY: Basic Books.

12. For additional information about Thomas Armstrong's work regarding multiple intelligences and human development, we recommend his new book, *Best schools: How human development research should inform education practices.* (2006). Alexandria, VA: Association for Supervision and Curriculum Development (ASCD).

13. Tomlinson, Carol Ann. (2003). *Fulfilling the promise of the differentiated classroom: Strategies and tools for responsive teaching.* Alexandria, VA: Association for Supervision and Curriculum Development, pp. 2–3. Dr. Tomlinson is a professor of Educational Leadership, Foundations and Policy at the University of Virginia.

14. Tomlinson. (2003).

15. The statement was made by Carol Ann Tomlinson in a Special Feature Session wth Jay McTighe, *Understanding by design and differentiated instruction: What's the connection and why should we care?* at the Association for Supervision and Curriculum Development conference, April 1–3, 2006, Chicago, Illinois.

16. *Breaking ranks II: Strategies for leading high school reform.* (2004). Reston, VA: National Association of Secondary School Principals. See recommendations #21 and 22, on p. 18.

17. Yager, S., Johnson, D. & Johnson, R. (1985). Oral discussion, group–to–individual transfer, and achievement in cooperative learning groups. *Journal of Educational Psychology, 77,* pp. 60–66.

Yager, S., Johnson, D., and Johnson, R. & Snyder, B. (1986). The impact of group processing and achievement in cooperative learning groups. *The Journal of Social Psychology, 126,* pp. 389–397.

18. Appreciative Inquiry is now being used in the organizational development field. It emerged in the mid–seventies when David Cooperrider and his associates at Case Western Reserve University felt a need to challenge the traditional problem–based approach being used throughout corporations. Sue Annis Hammond's 1996 book, *Appreciative Inquiry,* provides a brief overview of the process. Plano, TX: The Thin Book Company.

CHAPTER 15: DESIGNING DISCOVERY LEARNING EXPERIENCES

1. Rainer Maria Rilke was a Czechloslavakian poet (1875–1926), who as an existentialist advocated reflecting on the moments of truth as perceived by the heart.

2. *A call to action: Transforming high school for all youth.* (2005). Washington, DC: National High School Alliance & the Carnegie Foundation of New York. http://www.hsalliance.org

3. Dykstra, Dewey. (1996). Teaching introductory physics to college students. In: Fosnot, Catherine (Ed.). *Constructivism: Theory, perspectives and practice.* New York, NY: Teachers College Press, p. 202.

4. Windchitl, Mark. (1999, June). The challenge of sustaining a constructivist classroom culture. *Phi Delta Kappan,* p. 545.

5. The concepts of Russian cognitive theorist, Lev Vygotsky, as they pertain to social learning are discussed well by Gordon Wells in his 1996 paper, *Dialogic inquiry in education: Building on the legacy of Vygotsky.* Toronto, Canada: Ontario Institute for Studies in Education, University of Toronto.

6. Bybee, Roger. *Constructivism and the five e's: The biological science curriculum study.* Miami, FL: Miami Museum of Science.

7. The National Center for Improving Science Education and the National Science Resource Center of the Smithsonian Institution studies consistently indicate that inquiry–based science programs are highly effective at improving the learning and teaching of science. A wealth of studies on investigation and inquiry substantiate the same for all curricula subjects. See: Marlowe, Bruce & Page, Marilyn. (1998). *Creating and sustaining the constructivist classroom.* Thousand Oaks, CA: Corwin Press, pp. 20–25.

8. Ohanian, Susan. There's only one true technique for good discipline. In: *Who's in charge? A teacher speaks her mind.* (1994). Montclair, NJ: Boynton/Cook.

9. Postman, Neil & Weingartner, Charles. (1969). *Teaching as a subversive activity.* New York, NY: Dell Publishing.

10. It is important for the teacher-guide not to seek polished action plans (to be graded) but at this point collaborative ideas and the interest and commitment of group members to work on the learning task. The teacher-guide is always in control by approving or not, suggesting and helping to define resources or activities that support the discovery.

11. Asp, Elliott. (2000). Assessment in education: Where have we been? Where are we headed? In: Brandt, Ron. (Ed.). *Education in a new era.* Alexandria, VA: ASCD, pp. 124–125.

12. The material "In a Discovery Learning Classroom" is adapted from a list contained in *Classroom Compass,* Southwest Educational Development Laboratory, 1999, v. 1, no. 2. The laboratory attributes the suggestions to an adaptation made from Brooks, M. & Brooks, J. (1993). In: *Search for understanding: The case for constructivist classrooms.* Alexandria, VA: ASCD.

13. Gewertz, Catherine. (2007, June). *Soft skills in big demand.* Statement by Bob Perlman, New Technology Foundation. *Education Week.* Downloaded from http://www.edweek.org/ew/articles/2007/06/12/12/40 soft.h26.html, p. 3.

14. The statement was made by Walt Haney of the Center for the Study of Testing, Evaluation and Education Policy, Boston College. In: Wheelock, Anne. (2000). *Safe to be smart: Building a culture for standards–based reform in the middle grades.* Alexandria, VA: ASCD, p. 164.

15. Haney, Walt. (2000). In: Wheelock. (2000).

16. The Tribes assessment kit is available from CenterSource Systems. See order form in the Resources Section or phone 1–800–810–1701.

17. Nancy Atwell's poignant confession is from her 1987 book, *In the middle: Writing, reading and learning with adolescents.* Upper Montclair, NJ: Boynton/Cook, p. 127.

18. Postman, Neil & Weingartner, Charles. (1969). *Teaching as a subversive activity.* New York, NY: Dell, p. 3.

CHAPTER 16: EMBRACING THE FUTURE

1. Houston, Paul. (1998, May). *The School Administrator,* 5(55).

2. Gardner, Howard. (2000). *The disciplined mind: Beyond facts and standardized tests: The K–12 education that every child deserves.* New York, NY: Penguin Putnam, p. 232.

3. The whole child. (2007, March 5). *SmartBrief Special Report.* Association for Supervision and Curriculum Development (ASCD).

4. Prensky, Marc. (2006). *Don't bother me, mom. I'm learning.* St. Paul, MN: Paragon House, pp. 30–31.

5. Prensky, Marc. (2006). p. 30.

6. Steck, Goeffrey. (2006, May 30). With a common touch. *Leadership* (Ed.). Fairfield, NJ: The Economic Press, Inc., p. 8.

7. Anderson, Mark. In: Prensky. (2006). p. 139.

8. Stewart, Vivien. (2007, April). Becoming citizens of the world. *Educational Leadership,* p. 14.

9. Gardner, Howard. (2007). *Five minds for the future.* Boston, MA: Harvard Business School Press.

10. The phrase "Get Me Some Poets for Managers" is attributed to Sidney Harman, multimillionare CEO of a stero components company, who says he doesn't find it all that valuable to hire MBAs, but seeks "systems thinkers which poets are, to contemplate the world in which we live, interpret and understand that the world turns." In: Pink, Daniel H. (2005). p. 143.

11. Pink, Daniel H. (2005). *A whole new mind. Why right–brainers will rule the future.* New York, NY: The Penquin Group.

12. Martin, Roger. In: Pink. (2005). p. 78.

13. Pink, D. (2005). p. 50.

14. Pink. D. (2005). pp. 65–67.

15. Pink. D. (2005). p. 67.

16. Ornstein, Robert. (1997). *The right mind: Making sense of the hemi-spheres.* Harcourt Brace, p. 2.

17. *A call to action: Transforming high school for all youth.* (2005). Washington, DC: National High School Alliance & the Carnegie Foundation of New York, p. 6. http://www.hsalliance.org

18. Sergiovanni, Thomas J. (1999). *Rethinking leadership: A collection of articles.* Arlington Heights, IL: Skylight Training and Publishing, pp. 97–99.

19. Sergiovanni, T. (1999). p. 87.

20. Barth, Roland S. (2001, February). Teacher Leader, *Phi Delta Kappan,* p. 444.

    Note: One study reports areas of participation that principals use to transfer leadership to teachers:

    choosing textbooks and instructional materials
    shaping the curriculum
    setting standards for student behavior
    deciding whether students are tracked into special classes
    designing staff development and in–service programs
    setting promotion and retention policies
    deciding school budgets
    selecting new teachers, and
    selecting new administration.

21. Schein, E. (1985). *Organization cultures and leadership: A dynamic view.* San Francisco, CA: Jossey–Bass.

22. De Pree, Max. (2001, February). Teacher leader. *Phi Delta Kappan,* p. 434.

23. Barth, Roland S. (1997, March 5). The leader as learner. *Education Week.*

24. National Staff Development Council. (2000) *Learning to lead, leading to learn: Improving school quality through principal professional development.* Oxford, OH: NSDC.

25. Fullan, Michael. (2007). *The NEW meaning of change* (4th edition). New York, NY: Teachers College Press, Columbia University, p. 55.

26. Darling–Hammond, Linda. (2000). *Studies of excellence in teacher education: Preparation in undergraduate years.* Washington, DC: American Association of Colleges for Teacher Education, pp. 14–15.

27. Kessler, R. (2000). *The soul of education: Helping students find connection, compassion and character at school.* Alexandria, VA: ASCD.

28. Palmer, Parker. (1998). *The courage to teach: Exploring the inner landscape of a teacher's life.* San Francisco, CA: Jossey–Bass.

29. Fullan, Michael. (2007). p. 11.

30. Fullan, Michael. (2007). p. 11.

31. Barth, Roland. (1990). *Improving schools from within.* San Francisco, CA: Jossey–Bass.

32. Hall, G. & Hord, S. (2001). *Implementation of change patterns, principles and potholes.* Needham Heights, MA: Allyn & Bacon.

    The authors thank Lorraine Katherine Holt for sharing her Masters report, *Tribes: A journey in a grade one classroom,* as submitted for the degree of Master of Education, Ontario Institute for Studies in Education, University of Toronto, 2005. The report led to our discovery of the work of Hall and Hord on implementation patterns.

33. Fullan, Michael. (2007). p. 54.

34. The whole child. (2007, March 5). *SmartBrief Special Report.* Association of Supervision and Curriculum Development.

35. Littky, Dennis. (2004). *The BIG picture: Education is everyone's business.* Alexandria, VA: Association for Supervision and Curriculum Development (ASCD), p. 200.

36. Maya Angelou is a respected former poet laureate of the United States, and Reynolds Professor at Wake Forest University in Winston–Salem, North Carolina. Her writings are filled with wisdom, love of humanity and songs of life.

THE HISTORY OF TRIBES AND TRIBES TLC®

1. Gibbs, J. (2001). *Tribes: A new way of learning and being together.* Windsor, CA: CenterSource Systems.

2. Gibbs, J. (2006). *Reaching all by creating Tribes Learning Communities.* Windsor, CA: CenterSource Systems.

3. Alberg, J., Eller, S. & Petry, C. (1994). *A resource guide for social skills instruction.* Longmount, CO: Center for Research in Education, Research Triangle Institute, Sopers Publishers.

4. Newkumet, M. & Casserly, M. (1994). *Urban school safety: Strategies of the great city schools.* Washington, DC: Council of the Great City Schools.

5. Gibbs, J. (2001). *Discovering gifts in middle school: Learning in a caring culture called Tribes.* Windsor, CA: CenterSource Systems.

6. Collaborative for Academic, Social and Emotional Learning (CASEL). (2003). *Safe and sound: An education leader's guide to evidence-based social and emotional learning programs.* Chicago, IL: CASEL, University of Illinois, Chicago. www.casel.org

7. Office of Juvenile Justice Delinquency Prevention (OJJDP). (2005). *Model programs guide.* Washington, DC: OJJDP, Department of Justice. www.ojjdp.ncjrs.gov

8. Benard, B. (2005). *What is it about Tribes? The research-based components of the developmental process of Tribes Learning Communities.* Windsor, CA: CenterSource Systems. www.tribes.com

Bibliography

Adler, Mortimer. (1982). *The padideia proposal: An educational manifesto.* New York, NY: Macmillan.

Alberg, J., Eller, S., & Petry, C. (1994). *A resource guide for social skills instruction.* Longmount, CO: Center for Research in Education, Research Triangle Institute, Sopers Publishers.

American Institutes of Research. (1999). *An educator's guide to school-wide reform.* Arlington, VA: Educational Research Service.

American Psychological Association. *Learner-Centered Principles: A Framework for School Redesign and Reform.* American Psychological Association.

Ancess, J. & Darling-Hammond, L. (2003). *Beating the odds: High schools as communities of commitment and student learning outcomes.* New York, NY: Teachers College Press.

Anderson, Keisha-Gaye. (2000, Jan-Feb). U.S. fails math. *Psychology Today.*

Anderson, Lorin W. & Drathwohl, David R., et.al. (2000). *A taxonomy for learning, teaching, and assessing: A revision of Bloom's taxonomy of educational objectives.* New York, NY: Longman.

Anderson, V. (1997, February). High schools told: Get goin' on freshmen. *Catalyst.* Received on 11/27/05. http://www.catalyst-chicago.org/arch/02-97/027main.htm

Armstrong, Thomas. (1999). *7 kinds of smart: Identifying and developing your multiple intelligences.* New York, NY: Penguin Putnam.

Armstrong, Thomas. (2006). *The best schools: How human development research should inform educational practice.* Alexandria, VA: Association for Supervision and Curriculum Development (ASCD).

Asp, Elliott. (2000). Assessment in education: Where have we been? Where are we headed? In: Brandt, Ron (Ed.). *Education in a new era.* Alexandria, VA: Association for Supervision and Curriculum Development (ASCD).

Association for Supervision and Curriculum Development (ASCD). (2007, March 5). The whole child. *SmartBrief Special Report.* Association for Supervision and Curriculum Development (ASCD).

Association for Supervision and Curriculum Development (ASCD). New compact to adopt the whole child. (2007, March). *Education Update,* Association for Supervision and Curriculum Development (ASCD), 49(3).

Atkins, Leonard. *Failing our kids: Why the testing craze won't fix our schools.* Milwaukee, WI: Rethinking Schools Ltd.

Atwell, Nancy. (1987). *In the middle: Writing, reading and learning with adolescents.* Upper Montclair, NJ: Boynton/Cook.

Barnhart, Carol. We can't afford to waste resources of the gifted. *The Enquirer.* Quoting Marylou Kelly Streznuski. (2004). *Gifted Grownups.* Retrieval 2/18/08. http://news.enquirer.com/apps/pbcs.dll/article

Barth, Roland S. (1990). *Improving schools from within: Teachers, parents and principals make the difference.* San Francisco, CA: Jossey-Bass.

Barth, Roland S. (1997, March). The leader as learner. *Education Week.*

Barth, Roland S. (2001). *Learning by heart.* San Francisco, CA: Jossey-Bass.

Barth, Roland S. (2001, February). Teacher Leader. *Phi Delta Kappan.*

Benard, Bonnie. (1991). *Fostering resiliency in kids: Protective factors in families, schools and community.* Portland, OR: Western Regional Center for Drug Free Schools and Communities, Northwest Regional Educational Laboratory.

Benard, Bonnie. (2004). *Resiliency: What we have learned.* San Francisco, CA: WestEd.

Benard, Bonnie. (2005). *What is it about Tribes? The research-based components of the developmental process of Tribes Learning Communities.* Windsor, CA: CenterSource Systems. www.tribes.com

Black, Susan. (2004, May). Reform at the top: Improving high schools calls for comprehensive change, not piecemeal tinkering. *American School Board Journal.*

Botstein, Leon. (1997). *Education and the promise of American culture.* New York, NY: Doubleday.

Boyer, E. (1995). *The basic school: A community of learners.* Princeton, NJ: Carnegie Foundation for the Advancement of Teaching.

Brady, Marion. (1989). *What's worth teaching? Selecting, organizing and integrating knowledge.* New York, NY: New York State University Press.

Brandt, Ron. (Ed.). (2000). *Education in a new era.* Alexandria, VA: Association for Supervision and Curriculum Development.

Breaking ranks II: Strategies for leading high school reform. (2004). Reston, VA: National Association of Secondary School Principals.

Breaking ranks: Changing an American institution. (1996). Reston, VA: National Association of Secondary School Principals.

Bridgeland, J., Dilulio, Jr., J, & Morison, K. B. *The silent epidemic: Perspectives on high school dropout students.* A report by Civic Enterprises in association with Peter D. Hart Associates for the Bill and Melinda Gates Foundation.

Bronfenbrenner, Urie. (1979). *The ecology of human development: Experiments by nature and design.* Cambridge, MA: Harvard University Press.

Brooks, J.G., & Brooks, M.G. (1999). *In search of understanding: The case for constructivist classrooms.* Alexandria, VA: Association for Supervision and Curriculum Development.

Bruner, Jerome S. (1996). *The culture of education.* Cambridge, MA: Harvard University Press.

Burke, Pat Guild. (1997). Do the learning theories overlap? *Educational Leadership.* Association for Supervision and Curriculum Development.

Bybee, Roger. (1997). *Constructivism and the 5 E's: The biological science curriculum study.* Miami, Fl: Museum of Science.

Caine, Geoffrey & Caine, Renate. (1991). *Making connections: Teaching and the human brain.* Alexandria, VA: Association for Supervision and Curriculum Development (ASCD).

Campbell, Joseph. (1970). *The masks of God: Creative mythology.* New York, NY: Viking Press.

Catterall, J. (1997). Involvement in the arts and success in secondary school. *Americans for the Arts Monographs,* 1(9).

Christensen, Linda. (2000). *Reading, writing and rising up: Teaching about social justice and the power of the written word.* Milwaukee, WI: Rethinking Schools.

Clarke, John & Frazer, Edorah. (2003). Making learning personal: Educational practices that work. In: DiMartino, J., Clarke, J., & Wold, D. (Eds.). *Personalized learning: Preparing high school students to create their futures.* Lanham, MD: Rowman & Littlefield. And in: *Breaking ranks II.* (2004). National Association of Secondary School Principals.

Clarke, John. (2003). *Changing systems to personalize learning: Introduction to the personalization workshops.* Providence, RI: Education Alliance at Brown University.

Clinchy, Evans. (2007). *Rescuing the public schools: What it will take to leave no child behind.* New York, NY: Teachers College Press, Columbia University.

Cochran-Smith, M. & Lytle, S. (1999). Relationships of knowledge and practice: Teacher learning in communities. *Review of Research in Education,* 24(2).

Cohen, Jonathan. (Ed.). (1999). *Educating hearts and minds: Social and emotional learning and the passage into adolescence.* New York, NY: Teachers College Press, Columbia University.

Cohen, Judy, et. al. (1996). *Girls in the middle: Working to succeed in school.* Washington, DC: American Association of University Women Educational Foundation.

Cohen, Stephen. (2004, July). Performance improvement through relationship building. *TD Magazine.* Alexandria, VA: American Society for Training and Development (ASTD).

Colangelo, Nicolas, et.al. *A nation deceived: How schools hold back America's brightest students.* The Templeton National Report on Acceleration. Retrieval 2/12/08. http://www.nationdeceived.org/index.html

Coles, Robert. (1998). In School. *Boston Globe Magazine.*

Collaborative for Academic, Social and Emotional Learning (CASEL). (2003). *Safe and sound: An education leader's guide to evidence-based social and emotional learning programs.* Chicago, IL: Collaborative for Academic, Social and Emotional Learning CASEL, University of Illinois, Chicago. www.casel.org

Colteryahn, Karen & Davis, Patty (2004, January). *Eight trends you need to know now.*

Comer, J.P. (2001, April 23). Schools that develop children. *The American Prospect,* 12(7).

Comer, J.P., Haynes, N.M., Joyner, E.T. & Ben-Avie, M. (1999). *Child by child: The Comer process for change in education.* New York, NY: Teachers College Press, Columbia University.

Comer, James. (1997, March). Maintaining a focus on child development. *Phi Delta Kappan.*

Comer, James. (1999). *Child by child: The Comer process for change in education.* New York, NY: Teachers College Press.

Costa, Arthur & Kallick, Bena. (2000). *Discovering and exploring habits of mind.* Alexandria, VA: Association for Supervision and Curriculum Development (ASCD).

Costa, Arthur & Kallick, Bena. (2000). *Habits of mind: A developmental series.* Alexandria, VA: Association for Supervision and Curriculum Development (ASCD).

Covey, Stephen. (1996). Three roles of the leader in the new paradigm. In: Hasselbein, F., Goldsmith, M., & Beckland, R. (Eds.). *The leader of the future.* San Francisco, CA: Jossey-Bass.

Csikszentmihaly, Mihaly. (2000, April 19). Education for the 21st century. *Education Week.*

Cushman, Kathleen. (2003). *Fires in the bathroom: Advice for teachers from high school students.* The New Press.

Darling-Hammond, Linda. (1993, March). Reforming the school reform agenda. *Phi Delta Kappan.*

Darling-Hammond, Linda. (1997). *The right to learn: A blueprint for creating schools that work.* San Francisco, CA: Jossey-Bass.

Darling-Hammond, Linda. (2000). *Studies of excellence in teacher education: Preparation in undergraduate years.* Washington, DC: American Association of Colleges for Teacher Education.

Davies, A. & Busick, K. (Eds.) (2007). *Classroom assessment: What's working in high schools?* Courtenay, BC, Canada: Connections Publishing.

Davies, Anne. (2007). *Making classroom assessment work.* (2nd Edition). Courtenay, BC, Canada: Connections Publishing.

Davis, Patty, Naughton, Jennifer, & Rothwell, William. (2004, April). New roles and new competencies for the profession. *TD Magazine.* Alexandria, VA: American Society for Training and Development (ASTD).

De Pree, Max. (2001, February). Teacher leader. *Phi Delta Kappan.*

Delpit, Lisa. (1996). City kids, city teachers: Reports from the front row. In: *The politics of reaching literate discourse.* Ayres, W. and Ford, P. (Eds.). New York, NY: The New Press.

Dewey, John. (1916). *Democracy and education.* New York, NY: Free Press.

Dewey, John. (1956). *The child and the curriculum and the child and society.* Chicago, IL: University of Chicago Press.

Duffy, Thomas & Jonassen, David (Eds.). (1992). *Constructivism and the technology of instruction.* Hillsdale, NJ: Lawrence Erlbaum Associates.

DuFour, R., Eaker, R., and DuFour, Rebecca. (2005). *On common ground: The power of professional learning communities.* Bloomington, IN: Solution Tree.

Dykstra, Dewey. (1996). Teaching introductory physics to college students. In: Fosnot, Catherine (Ed.). *Constructivism: Theory, perspectives and practice.* New York, NY: Teachers College Press, Columbia University.

Eckert, Penelope. (1989). *Jocks and burnouts: Social categories and identity in the high school.* New York, NY: Teachers College Press, Columbia University.

Elias, Maurice & Arnold, Harriett. (Eds.). (2006). *The educator's guide to emotional intelligence and academic achievement: Social and emotional learning in the classroom.* Thousand Oaks, CA: Corwin Press.

Elias, Maurice. (1999). Academic and social-emotional learning. *Educational Practices Series,* 11. UNESCO with the International Academy of Education and the International Bureau of Education. http://www.ibe.unesco.org

Elias, Maurice. (Ed.). (1997). *Promoting social and emotional learning: Guidelines for educators.* Association for Supervision and Curriculum Development (ASCD).

Elias, M.J., Wang, M.C., Weissberg, R.P., Zins, J.E. & Walberg, H.J. (2002). The other side of the report card: Student success depends on more than test scores. *American School Board Journal,* 189 (11).

Elkind, David. (1999, Feb. 24). The social determination of childhood and adolescence, *Education Week.*

Elmore, Richard F. (2005). *School reform from the inside out: Policy, practice and performance.* Cambridge, MA: Harvard University Press.

Erickson, Erik. (1963). *Childhood and society.* New York, NY: W.W. Norton.

Erickson, Erik. (1996). *Identity, youth and crisis.* New York, NY: W.W. Norton.

Erickson, F. and Shultz, J. (1992). Students' experience of the curriculum. In Jackson, P. (Ed.). *Handbook of Research on Curriculum.* New York, NY: Macmillan.

Fosnot, Catherine. (Ed.). (1996). *Constructivism: Theory, perspectives and practice.* New York, NY: Teachers College Press.

Fox, Robert, Luszki, Margaret & Schmuck, Richard. (1966). *Social relations in the classroom: Diagnosing learning environments.* Chicago, IL: SRA, Inc.

Frankl, Viktor. (2000). *Man's ultimate search for meaning.* New York, NY: Perseus Book Group.

Fullan, Michael. (1994). *Turning systemic thinking on its head.* U.S. Department of Education.

Fullan, Michael. (1999). *Change forces: The sequel.* Philadelphia, PA: The Falmer Press.

Fullan, Michael. (2001). *Leading in a culture of change.* San Francisco, CA: Jossey-Bass.

Fullan, Michael. (2007). *The NEW meaning of educational change.* (4th edition). New York, NY: Teachers College Press, Columbia University.

Gardner, Howard. (1990). *Art education and human development.* Santa Monica, CA: The Getty Center for Education in the Arts.

Gardner, Howard. (1993). *Frames of mind: Theory of multiple intelligences.* New York, NY: Basic Books.

Gardner, Howard. (1999). *Intelligence reframed: Multiple intelligences for the 21st century.* New York, NY: Basic Books.

Gardner, Howard. (2000). *The disciplined mind: Beyond facts and standardized tests: The K–12 education that every child deserves.* New York, NY: Penguin Putnam.

Gardner, Howard. (2003). Can technology exploit our many ways of knowing? In: David T. Gordon (Ed.). *The digital classroom: How technology is changing the way we learn.* Cambridge, MA: Harvard Education Press.

Gardner, Howard. (2007). *Five minds for the future.* Boston, MA: Harvard Business School Press.

Gay, Geneva. (2000). *Culturally responsive teaching: Theory, research and practice.* New York, NY: Teachers College Press, Columbia University.

Gehring, John. (2004, May) Students' voices chime in to improve schools. *Education Week.*

Gewertz, Catherine. (2004, November 3). Student-designed poll shows teenagers feel lack of adult interest. *Education Week.*

Gewertz, Catherine. (2007, June). Soft skills in big demand. Statement by Bob Perlman. New Technology Foundation.

Education Week. Downloaded from http://www.edweek.org/ew/articles/2007/06/12/12/40 soft.h26.html

Gibbs, Jeanne. (2001). *Discovering gifts in middle school: Learning in a caring culture called Tribes.* Windsor, CA: CenterSource Systems.

Gibbs, Jeanne. (2001). *Tribes: A new way of learning and being together.* Windsor, CA: CenterSource Systems.

Gibbs, Jeanne. (2006). *Reaching all by creating Tribes Learning Communities.* Windsor, CA: CenterSource Systems.

Goleman, Daniel. (1995). *Emotional intelligence.* New York, NY: Bantam Books.

Goodlad, John. (1997). *In praise of education.* New York, NY: Teachers College Press, Columbia University.

Gordon, David. (2003). *Better teaching and learning in the digital classroom.* Cambridge, MA: Harvard Education Press.

Hall, G. & Hord, S. (2001). *Implementation of change patterns, principles and potholes.* Needham Heights, MA: Allyn & Bacon.

Halperin, S, & Partee, G. (1997). *Some things do make a difference for youth: A compendium of evaluations of youth programs and practices.* Washington, DC: American Youth Policy Forum.

Hammond, Sue Annis. (1996). *Appreciative inquiry.* Plano, TX: The Thin Book Company.

Handel, Michael J. (2005). *Worker skills and job requirements: Is there a mismatch?* Washington, DC: Economic Policy Institute.

Harrison, R. & Stokes, H. (1992). *Diagnosing organizational culture.* San Diego, CA: Pfeiffer & Company.

Hattie, J., Marsh, H., Neill, J., & Richards, G. (1997). Adventure education and outward bound: Out-of-class experiences that make a lasting difference. *Review of Educational Research, 67.*

Hertz-Lazarowitz, Rachel & Shachar, H. (1990). Changes in teachers' verbal behavior in cooperative classrooms. *Cooperative Learning, 11(2).*

Holt, Lorraine Katherine. (2005). *Tribes: A journey in a grade one classroom (Master's thesis).* Toronto, Canada: Ontario Institute for Studies in Education, University of Toronto.

Horton, Myles, with Kohl, Judith & Kohl, Herbert. (1990) *The long haul: An autobiography.* New York, NY: Doubleday.

Houston, Paul. (1998, May). *The school administrator, 5(55).*

Huitt, W. (1999, October). *The SCANS Report Revisited.* Paper delivered at the Fifth Annual Gulf South Business and Vocational Education Conference, Valdosta State University, Valdosta, GA, April 18, 1997. Retrieved 10/20/05. http://chiron.valdosta.edu/whuitt/col/student/scanspap.html

James, Jennifer. (2005, April). *The human face of technological change.* Keynote at the ASCD Annual Conference, Orlando, FL.

Jensen, Eric. (1988). *Teaching with the brain in mind.* Alexandria, VA: Association for Supervision and Curriculum Development (ASCD).

Johnson, David & Johnson, Robert. (1995). Non-academic outcomes in schooling. In: *Secondary schools and cooperative learning: Theories, models and strategies.* Pedersen, Jon, and Digby, Annette (Eds.). New York, NY: Garland Publishing.

Johnson, David W. & Johnson, Roger T. (1989). *Cooperation and competition: Theory and research.* Edina, MN: Interaction Book Company.

Johnson, David W., Johnson, Roger T. & Smith, Karl. (1995). Cooperative learning and individual student achievement. In: *Secondary schools: Theories, models and strategies.* Pedersen, Jon, & Digby, Annette (Eds.). New York, NY: Garland Publishing.

Johnson, David W., Johnson, Roger, T. and Holubec, Edythe Johnson. (1994). *New circles of learning: Cooperation in the classroom and school.* Alexandria, VA: Association for Supervision and Curriculum Development (ASCD).

Kagan, Spencer. (1994). *Cooperative learning.* San Clemente, CA: Kagan Publishing.

Kessler, R. (2000). *The soul of education: Helping students find connection, compassion, and character at school.* Alexandria, VA: Association for Supervision and Curriculum Development (ASCD).

Kohn, Alfie. (1996). *Beyond discipline: From compliance to community.* Alexandria, VA: Association for Supervision and Curriculum Development (ASCD).

Lazear, David. (1989). *Seven ways of teaching: The artistry of teaching with multiple intelligences.* Palatine, IL: Skylight Publishing.

Learner-Centered Principles Work Group, Board of Educational Affairs, American Psychological Association. (1997, November). *Learner-centered psychological principles: A framework for school reform and redesign.* American Psychological Association.

Lee, Valerie & Smith, J. (1995). Effects of high school restructuring and size on gains in achievement and engagement for early secondary school students. *American Journal of Education, 70.*

Lee, Valerie E. & Ready, Douglas D. (2007). *Schools within schools: Possibilities and pitfalls of high school reform.* New York, NY: Teachers College, Columbia University Lesson Lab, Pearson Education Inc.

Lezotte, L. W. (2002). *Assembly required: A continuous school improvement system.* Okemons, MI: Effective Schools Products, Ltd.

Lickona, Thomas. (1991). *Education for character: How our schools can teach respect and responsibility.* New York, NY: Bantam Books.

Lieberman, Ann. (1995). *The work of restructuring schools: Building from the ground up.* New York, NY: Teachers College Press.

Littky, Dennis, with Grabelle, Samantha. (2004). *The BIG picture: Education is everybody's business.* Alexandria, VA: Association for Supervision and Curriculum Development (ASCD).

Little, Judith Warren. (1981). *School success and staff development in urban desegregated schools: A summary of recently completed research.* Boulder, CO: Center for Action Research.

Little, Judith Warren. (1993). Teachers' professional development in a climate of education reform. *Educational Evaluation and Policy Analysis*, 15(2).

Little, Judith Warren. (1990, Summer). The persistence of privacy: Autonomy and initiative in teachers' professional relations. *Teachers College Record*.

Lott, Albert & Lott, Bernice. (1966, April). Group cohesiveness and individual learning. *Journal of Educational Psychology*, 57.

Madaus, G., West, Mary M., Harmon, M., Lomax, R. & Viator, K. (1992). *The influence of testing on teaching math and science in grades 4–12: Executive summary*. Boston, MA: Center for the Study of Testing, Evaluation and Educational Policy.

Market Data Retrieval. (1999). *New Teachers and Technology in Education*. Market Data Retrieval. www.schooldata.com

Marlowe, Bruce & Page, Marilyn. (1998). *Creating and sustaining the constructivist classroom*. Thousand Oaks, CA: Corwin Press.

Marshall, Ray & Tucker, Marc. (1992). *Thinking for a living: Education and the wealth of nations*. New York, NY: Basic Books.

Mathews, Jay. (2005, May 16). How to build a better high school. *Newsweek Magazine*.

McCombs, Barbara L. *Twelve Learner-Centered Psychological Principles*. Midwest Center Educational Laboratory. www.mcrel.org

McKnight, John. (1992, July–August). Are social service agencies the enemy of the people? *Utne Reader*.

McLaughlin, Milbrey W. & Talbert, Joan E. (2006). *Building school-based teacher learning communities: Professional strategies to improve student achievement*. New York, NY: Teachers College Press, Columbia University.

McNulty, Ray. (2004). New era ushers in deeper understanding of learning. *Education Updates*, Association for Supervision and Curriculum Development (ASCD), 46(2).

Meier, D. (1995). *The power of their ideas: Lessons for America from a small school in Harlem*. Boston, MA: Beacon Press.

Meier, Deborah. (1992-1993). Reinventing teaching. *Teachers College Record*, 4.

Melchior, A. (1996-1998). *National evaluation of Learn and Serve America: Interim and final evaluation*. National Corporation for Community Service.

Merrill, David. (1992). Constructivism and instructional design. In: Duffy, T. & Jonassen, D. (Eds.). *Constructivism and the technology of instruction*. Hillsdale, NJ: Erlbaum Associates.

Moersch, Christopher. (2002). *Beyond hardware: Using existing technology to promote higher-level thinking*. Eugene, OR: International Society for Technology in Education.

Muller, W. (1996). *How, then, shall we live? Four simple questions that reveal the beauty and meaning of our lives*. New York, NY: Bantam Books.

Naisbett, John. (1999). *High tech, high touch: Technology and our search for meaning*. New York, NY: Broadway Books.

Nakkula, M. (2004). Identity and possibility: Adolescent development and the potential of schools. In: *Adolescents at school: Perspectives on youth identity and education*. Michael Sadowski (Ed.). Cambridge, MA: Harvard Education Press.

National Association for Gifted Children. *Thirty-two competencies needed by teachers of gifted and talented students*. National Association for Gifted Children. Position Statements. Retrieval 2/18/08. www.nagc.org/index.aspx?id=574&an

National High School Alliance. (2005). *A call to action: Transforming high school for all youth*. Washington, DC: National High School Alliance & the Carnegie Foundation of New York. http://www.hsalliance.org

National Institute of Mental Health. (2001). *Teenage brain: A work in progress. A brief overview of research into brain development during adolescence*. National Institute of Mental Health. http:www.nimh.nih.gov/publicat/teenbrain.cfm

National Research Council/National Academy of Sciences. (2003). *How people learn* and *Engaging schools: Fostering high school students' motivation to learn*. Washington, DC: The National Academies.

National Staff Development Council. (2000). *Learning to lead, leading to learn: Improving school quality through principal professional development*. Oxford, OH: National Staff Development Council (NSDC).

Newkumet, M. & Casserly, M. (1994). *Urban school safety: Strategies of the great city schools*. Washington, DC: Council of the Great City Schools.

Newmann, F. & Wehlage, G. (1995). *Successful school restructuring: A report to the public and educators*. Madison, WI: Center on Organization and Restructuring School.

Noddings, Nel. (1988, December). Schools face crisis in caring. *Education Week*.

Noddings, Nel. (1995, January). A morally defensible mission for schools of the 21st century. *Phi Delta Kappan*.

Noguera, Pedro. (2002, February). Beyond size: The challenge of high school reform. *Ed Leadership*.

O'Connor, Ken. (2002). *How to grade for learning: Linking grades to standards*. Glenview, IL: Lesson Lab, Pearson Education, Inc.

Office of Juvenile Justice Delinquency Prevention (OJJDP). (2005). *Model programs guide*. Washington, DC: OJJDP, Department of Justice. www.ojjdp.ncjrs.gov

Ohanian, Susan. There's only one true technique for good discipline. In: *Who's in charge? A teacher speaks her mind*. (1994). Montclair, NJ: Boynton/Cook.

Ornstein, Robert. (1997). *The right mind: Making sense of the hemispheres*. Harcourt Brace.

Oseas, Andrea & Wood, Julie M. (2003). Multiple literacies: New skills for a new millennium. In: Gordon, David T. (Ed.). *Better teaching and learning in the digital classroom*. Cambridge, MA: Harvard Education Press.

Palmer, Parker. (1998). *The courage to teach: Exploring the inner landscape of a teacher's life.* San Francisco, CA: Jossey-Bass.

Paris, Scott & Ayres, Linda. (1999). *Becoming reflective students and teachers with portfolios and authentic assessment.* Washington, DC: American Psychological Association.

Pedersen, J. & Digby, A. (Eds.). (1995). Cooperative learning and nonacademic outcomes of schooling. In: *Secondary schools and cooperative learning: Theories, models and strategies.* New York, NY: Garland Publishing.

Pert, Candace. (1997). *Molecules of emotion: The science behind mind-body medicine.* New York, NY: Simon and Schuster.

Peterson, Kevin. (2005). *High schools failing the next generation.* Achieve Surveys. www.stateline.org

Pflaum, William D. (2004). *The technology fix: The promise and reality of computers in our schools.* Alexandria, VA: Association for Supervision and Curriculum Development (ASCD).

Piaget, Jean. (1950). *The psychology of intelligence.* New York, NY: Harcourt Brace.

Pink, Daniel H. (2005). *A whole new mind: Why right-brainers will rule the future.* New York, NY: The Penguin Group.

Pipher, Mary. (1995). *Reviving Ophelia: Saving the lives of adolescent girls.* New York, NY: Ballantine Books.

Pope, Denise Clark. (2001). *Doing school: How we are creating a generation of stressed out, materialistic, and miseducated students.* New Haven, CT: Yale University Press.

Postman, Neil & Weingartner, Charles. (1969). *Teaching as a subversive activity.* New York, NY: Dell Publishing.

Prensky, Marc. (2006). *Don't bother me mom. I'm learning.* St. Paul, MN: Paragon House.

Prensky, Marc. (Dec 2005/Jan 2006). Listen to the natives. *Educational Leadership.*

Reich, Robert. (1991). *The work of nations.* New York, NY: Alfred A. Knopf.

Rennebohm Franz, K. & Gragert, E. In: Gordon, David T. (Ed.). (2003). *Better teaching and learning in the digital classroom.* Cambridge, MA: Harvard Education Press.

Renzulli, J.S. What makes giftedness? Re-examining a definition. *Phi Delta Kappan,* 60.

Resnick, M., Bearman, P., Blum, R., Bauman, K., Harris, K., Jones, J., Tabor, J., Beuring, T., Sieving, R., Shew, M., Ireland, M., Bearinger, L. & Udry, J. (1997). Protecting adolescents from harm: Findings from the national longitudinal study on adolescent health. *Journal of the American Medical Association,* 278.

Riel, Margaret. (1999). *Technology in shared minds made visible.* Keynote address to the National Educational Computer Conference.

Rogoff, B. (2004). *The cultural nature of human development.* New York, NY: Oxford University Press.

Ross, Heather & Daniel, Ben. (2005). *Technology and community-enhanced learning: Tribes in the classroom.* Paper presented at the 3rd Annual International Conference on Education, Honolulu, Hawaii. Education and Communication Technology, Department of Curriculum Studies, University of Saskatchewan, Saskatoon, Canada.

Rothwell, William & Wellins, Rich. (2004, May). Mapping your future: Putting new competencies to work for you. *TD Magazine,* Alexandria, VA: American Society for Training and Development (ASTD).

Rowan, B. (1990). Commitment and control: Alternative strategies for the organizational design of schools. *Review of Educational Research,* 6.

Rutter, M., Maughan, B., Mortimore, P., Ouston, J. & Smith, A. (1979). *Fifteen thousand hours: Secondary schools and their effects on children.* Cambridge, MA: Harvard University Press.

Sarason, Seymour. (1972). *The culture of settings and the future societies.* San Francisco, CA: Jossey-Bass.

Sarason, Seymour. (1990). *The predictable failure of school reform.* San Francisco, CA: Jossey-Bass.

Schein, E. (1985). *Organization cultures and leadership: A dynamic view.* San Francisco, CA: Jossey-Bass.

Schmoker, Michael. (2004, April). *Tipping point: From feckless reform to substantive instructional improvement.* Bloomington, IN: Phi Delta Kappan International.

Schmoker, Michael. (2006). *Results now: How we can achieve unprecedented improvements in teaching and learning.* Alexandria, VA: Association for Supervision and Curriculum Development (ASCD).

Schoen, Donald. (1987). *Education: The reflective practitioner.* (Revised edition). San Francisco, CA: Jossey-Bass.

Secretary's Commission on Achieving Necessary Skills. (1999). *SCANS report for America 2000: What work requires of schools.* Washington, DC: Secretary's Commission on Achieving Necessary Skills, U.S. Department of Labor.

Senge, Peter, et. al. (2002). *Schools that learn.* New York, NY: Doubleday.

Sergiovanni, T. (1994). *Building community in schools.* San Francisco, CA: Jossey-Bass.

Sergiovanni, Thomas J. (1999). *Rethinking leadership: A collection of articles.* Arlington Heights, IL: Skylight Training and Publishing.

Sergiovanni, Thomas. (1996). *Leadership for the schoolhouse.* San Francisco, CA: Jossey-Bass.

Sergiovanni, Thomas. (1999). The story of community. In: Retallick, J., Cocklin, B. & Coombe, K. (Eds.). *Learning communities in action: Issues, strategies and contexts.* New York, NY: Routledge.

Sizer, Ted. (1984, 1997). *Horace's challenge: The dilemma of the American high school.* New York, NY: Houghton Mifflin.

Sizer, Ted. (2004). Foreword. *Breaking Ranks II.* National Association of Secondary School Principals (NASSP).

Solomon, D., Battistich, V. & Watson, M. (1993, March). *A longitudinal investigation of the effects of a school intervention program on children's social development.* Paper presented at the biennial meeting of the Society for Research in Child Development, San Ramon, CA.

Southwest Educational Development Laboratory. (1999). *Classroom Compass,* 1(2), Southwest Educational Development Laboratory.

Starhawk. (1997). *Dreaming the dark.* New York, NY: Beacon Press.

Steck, Goeffrey. (2006, May 30). With a common touch. *Leadership.* (Ed.). Fairfield, NJ: The Economic Press, Inc.

Stern, D. & Huber, G.L. (Eds.). (1997). *Active learning for students and teachers: Reports from eight countries.* Frankfurt am Main, Germany: Peter Lang.

Stewart, Vivien. (2007, April). Becoming citizens of the world. *Educational Leadership.*

Stiggins, Richard., Arter, Judith., Chappuis, Jan & Chappuis, Stephpen. (2004). *Classroom assessment for student learning: Doing it right, using it well.* Portland, OR: Assessment Training Institute.

Stigler, James & Hiebert, James. (1997). *The teaching gap.* Study funded by the U.S. Department of Education. Los Angeles, CA: Free Press.

Stoddard, Lynn. (1992). *Redesigning education: A guide for developing human greatness.* Tucson, AZ: Zephyr Press.

Sueoka, Lynne. (2005). Making connections: The MeneMac online learning community. *Educational Perspectives,* 38.

Sylwester, Robert (1995). *A celebration of neurons: An educator's guide to the human brain.* Alexandria, VA: Association for Supervision and Curriculum Development (ASCD).

Taffel, Ron. (1999). *Nurturing good children now.* New York, NY: Golden Books.

Tanner, B., Bottoms, G., Feagin, C. & Bearman, A. (2001). *Instructional strategies: How teachers teach matters.* Atlanta, GA: Southern Region Educational Board.

Thompson, Michael. (2004). *The pressured child: Helping your child find success in school and life.* New York, NY: Ballantine Books.

Thornburgh, N. (2006, April). Drop out nation. *Time Magazine,* 167(16).

Time Magazine: Science. (2004, May 20). What makes teens tick?

Toch, Thomas. (2003). *High schools on a human scale: How small schools can transform American education.* Boston, MA: Beacon.

Toffler, Alvin. (1980). *Third wave.* New York, NY: William Morrow Company.

Tomlinson, Carol Ann & Demirsky Allan, Susan. (2000). *Leadership for differentiating schools and classrooms.* Alexandria, VA: Association for Supervision and Curriculum Development (ASCD).

Tomlinson, Carol Ann & Demirsky Allan, Susan. (2003). *Fulfilling the promise of the differentiated classroom: Strategies and tools for responsive teaching.* Alexandria, VA: Association for Supervision and Curriculum Development (ASCD).

Tomlinson, Carol Ann & McTighe, Jay. (2006). *Integrating differentiated instruction and understanding by design.* Alexandria,

VA: Association for Supervision and Curriculum Development (ASCD).

Tomlinson, Carol Ann. (1999). *The differentiated classroom: Responding to the needs of all learners.* Alexandria, VA: Association for Supervision and Curriculum Development (ASCD).

Vail, Kathleen. (2004, November). Remaking high school. *American School Board Journal.*

Valliant, G.E. (1977). *Adaptation to life.* Boston, MA: Little, Brown and Company.

Wallis, Claudia & Steptoe, Sonia. (2006, December 18). How to build a student for the 21st century. *Time Magazine,* 168(25).

Webb, J.T., et al. (2004). *Misdiagnosis and dual diagnosis of gifted children.* Supporting Emotional Needs of the Gifted (SENG). Retrieval 2/18/2008. www.sengifted.org

Wells, Gordon. (1996). *Dialogic inquiry in education: Building on the legacy of Vygotsky.* Toronto, Canada: Ontario Institute for Studies in Education, University of Toronto.

Werner, E. & Smith, R. (1992). *Overcoming the odds: High-risk children from birth to adulthood.* New York, NY: Cornell University Press.

Werner, Emily & Smith, Ruth. (1989). *Vulnerable but invincible: A longitudinal study of resilient children and youth.* New York, NY: Adams, Bannister and Cox.

Wheelock, Anne. (1998). *Safe to be smart: Building a culture for standards-based reform in the middle grades.* Columbus, OH: National Middle School Association.

Windchitl, Mark. (1999, June). The challenge of sustaining a constructivist classroom culture. *Phi Delta Kappan.*

Wiske, Stone. (2003). A new culture for teaching in the 21st century. In: Gordon, David T. (Ed.). *The digital classroom: How technology is changing the way we learn.* Cambridge, MA: Harvard Education Press.

Wolfe, Patricia. (2001). *Brain matters: Translating research into classroom practice.* Alexandria, VA: Association for Supervision and Curriculum Development (ASCD).

Yager, S., Johnson, D. & Johnson, R. (1985). Oral discussion, group-to-individual transfer, and achievement in cooperative learning groups. *Journal of Educational Psychology.*

Yager, S., Johnson, D. Johnson, R. & Snyder, B. (1986). The impact of group processing and achievement in cooperative learning groups. *The Journal of Social Psychology,* 126.

Yeager, Neil & Hough, Lee. (1998). *Power interviews: Job-winning tactics from Fortune 500 recruiters.* New York, NY: John Wiley & Sons, Inc.

Zins, J., Weissberg, R., Wang, M. & Walberg, H. (Eds.). (2004). *Building academic success on social and emotional learning: What does the research say?* New York, NY: Teachers College Press, Columbia University.

Index

TERI USHIJIMA, ED.D.

Dr. Teri Ushijima is the Complex Area Superintendent of the Central Oahu District Southside Schools of the State of Hawaii Department of Education. Her wealth of experience as an elementary school teacher, school counselor, high school vice–principal, certified Tribes trainer and experiences in designing and promoting professional development underlies the sound principles and practices Teri provides as a highly respected school leader and author. Teri earned her Ed.D. from the University of Southern California in Educational Leadership and Administration. Teri also holds a M.Ed. in Reading and Children's Literature, a MLIS Degree for School Library Science, and her B.Ed. in Education.

Teri was the recipient of the prestigious National Milken Foundation Award in 2006 representing the State of Hawaii. In addition to all of her administrative work, she has been the President of the Hawaii affiliate of the Association for Supervision and Curriculum Development (ASCD) where she has served on the Leadership Council and Nomination Committee. Jeanne Gibbs is quick to add that this book never would have happened had it not been for the time, effort and brilliance that Teri Ushijima provided as the co–author of this book.

JEANNE GIBBS

Jeanne Gibbs graduated from Northwestern University with a degree in chemistry and worked in the field until she became more interested in the chemistry of people and systems that affect our lives. Her professional work for the last thirty years has been focused on synthesizing a comprehensive range of literature and studies into an applicable educational process that promotes human development and learning. The process known simply as "Tribes" or "Tribes Learning Communities," creates a caring motivational culture, collaborative learning communities and active learning instruction that corresponds to the unique ways in which today's 21st century students best can learn... and succeed in school and life.

Jeanne supervised implementations of the community learning process throughout hundreds of schools and youth–serving agencies for many years while managing a non–profit corporation which she had founded. Ever–growing requests from schools, districts and universities throughout the United States, Canada, Australia and other countries led her to establish CenterSource Systems in 1995 as "the home of Tribes."

Jeanne has retired many times, none of which last long due to her passionate purpose. It is no surprise that people across many countries know Jeanne for her warm and generous spirit... and ability to build community wherever she goes.